28   32

Nikolaief

R.Ingoul

Dnieper R.

Kerson

Odessa   *Oichakof*   *Liman*   MER
Kinbourn

Ovidiopol   *Perekop*   D'AZOF
Ikermann

C R I   46

C. Tarkhan   *Eupatoria*   É   E
Salghir R.

Karasoubazar

G. de Kalamita   *Simferopol*   *Theodosie*

Bakhtchisaray

Sébastopol   *Balaklava*   44

B^ches du Danube

Black Sea

E R   N   O   I   R   E

Sinope   42

Canal de Constantinople (Bosphore)

Ereki   *Voiava*

Scutari   *Uba Tchai*

R A   *Tchai*   O   *Kiankary*

Boly

Atlas

Ismil   *Kirmes sou*

Sakaria R.

Brousse   *Soghut*   **Angora**   40

28   30   32

Paris, Imp. F rhard.

A
CULINARY
CAMPAIGN

THE AUTHOR,
from a photograph by Bingham (Paris).

A
CULINARY
CAMPAIGN
BY
ALEXIS SOYER

WITH INTRODUCTIONS BY

MICHAEL BARTHORP

&

ELIZABETH RAY

SOUTHOVER PRESS
1995

This edition first published by
SOUTHOVER PRESS
2 Cockshut Road, Lewes, East Sussex BN7 1JH
Copyright © Introduction Michael Barthorp
© Introduction Elizabeth Ray
A catalogue record for this book is available from the British Library
ISBN 1-870962-11-7
Typeset in Garamond 10/11 by Saxon Graphics Ltd, Derby
Printed in England on wood-free paper by
Villiers Publications Ltd, 19 Sylvan Avenue, Finchley, London N3 2LE
for Southover Press

CONTENTS

EDITOR'S NOTE

The Victorians had a passion for the hyphen. I have removed quite a number of them to make it easier for the modern reader. For the same reason I have dispensed with some of Soyer's superfluous commas. But I have kept as much as practically possible of his idiosyncratic spelling, which helps to give the flavour of his work. All the footnotes are his, except where I think a further explanation is useful; these footnotes have my initials.

Only two sections have been left out. The first is a chapter on food for the needy, nearly all of which was published in 1847 in Soyer's *Poor Man's Regenerator*. The other, omitted to save space, is a series of letters from army officers praising the field stove, of which there are plenty of examples in the text.

Otherwise nothing has been changed. All the original engravings by Dalziel are here, though not necessarily in their original order.

I am indebted to Elizabeth Ray for her detective work on printer's errors in the edition of 1857, and to Michael Barthorp and Elizabeth Ray for their help in finding maps.

A. B.

ILLUSTRATIONS NOT IN THE ORIGINAL TEXT

End papers from *Histoire de la Guerre du Crimée* Camille Rousset, 1877. Detailed map of the Crimea from *The War in the Crimea,* General Sir Edward Hamley, 1896. The Barrack Hospital, Scutari, from *The Life of Florence Nightingale,* Sarah Tooley, 1910.

INTRODUCTION I

The background

In early 1854 a British army under Lord Raglan left England to confront the first European power it had faced for forty years — Imperial Russia. It would do so in alliance with its old enemy, the French, in support of Turkey, which guarded the only outlet from Russia's Black Sea into the Mediterranean. Russia, the old ally of the Napoleonic War, had become aggressive and expansionist, but looking towards Asia rather than Europe. Neither France nor Britain could contemplate with equanimity any Russian naval or military presence in the Eastern Mediterranean. France had its North African Empire and interests in the Levant as well as its ambitious new Emperor, Napoleon III, who was keen to make his mark. Britain feared that any such presence would threaten one of its routes to its great possessions in India, a country upon which it was believed Russian eyes were covetously fixed, and to which Russian threats had already been perceived out of the Caucasus via Persia and Afghanistan some dozen years earlier. Turkey therefore, already at war with Russia in the Balkans, had to be supported.

By the time Raglan's army was concentrated in the Near East, the Turks had halted the Russian advance on the Danube. Thus there seemed nothing for it to do except swelter and contract disease in its pestilential camps in Bulgaria. However, having gone to so much trouble, the British Government, together with the French, then appreciated a new and worthwhile task: the capture and destruction of Sebastopol, on the southern tip of the Crimean Peninsula, home of the Russian Black Sea Fleet, the very force which one day might emerge in the Eastern Mediterranean, if it were not stopped.

So to the Crimea the Allied armies sailed. Having landed successfully on 14 September 1854, they defeated a Russian army at the Battle of the Alma six days later, pondered the advisibility of an immediate assault upon Sebastopol, decided against it, and marched round the city to lay siege to it from the other side. They established their camps and siege-works on the uplands to its east, with the French on the left, the British on the right based on the small harbour of Balaclava.

On 25 October a Russian force from the Crimean interior attempted to cut off the British infantry divisions on the upland from their base at Balaclava, in the battle chiefly famous to posterity for the gallantry and near-destruction of Lord Cardigan's Light Cavalry Brigade. A fortnight later a much larger Russian force, from the interior and from Sebastopol, launched its first major attack upon the British position on the upland. In this, the great Battle of Inkerman, every Russian assault was held and thrown back, not by the tactical skill of Lord Raglan and his commanders, but by the quick thinking and leadership of the ordinary regimental officers and the valour, endurance and skill-at-arms of their men, infantrymen and gunners, hence the name by which it afterwards became known — "the Soldiers' Battle".

After Inkerman the British army faced two tasks: the prosecution of the siege, and surviving the terrible Russian winter on the upland for which it was totally unprepared. A modern army is a balanced force of fighting Arms — armour, guns, infantry and engineers – backed up by logistic Services – medical, supplies, catering, transport, ordnance; without such Services the Arms cannot function effectively in the area of operations. The Crimean army had cavalry, guns, infantry and sappers, all better trained and more effective than posterity has usually given them credit for, as they proved at Inkerman, but it was woefully short of logistic backing.

For example, a man wounded at Inkerman, or in the trenches before Sebastopol, would, if he was lucky, be carried by his comrades or the regimental bandsmen, on one of the only ten stretchers allotted to an infantry battalion, to the regimental surgeons, who would perform such first aid as they could, before despatching him, if he had survived, to the staff surgeons. Their work suffered from a shortage of medical supplies and a total lack of trained orderlies and nurses. For an operation the nearest soldiers would be called in to hold the wretched patient down. If he needed further treatment or convalescence, he would be sent down to Balaclava, there to await shipment to the base hospitals at Constantinople. But the means of getting him to the ship were almost entirely 'ad hoc': in a blanket carried by four men, on the back of a cavalry horse, the back of an infantryman, whatever was available. There was no properly organised system. An hurriedly assembled ambulance corps had been cobbled together but, since it was manned by elderly and often drunken pensioners, it was useless. Many wounded therefore died during the painful journey to the harbour, or on board ship, where they lay packed together. If and when they reached Constantinople, there awaited them the dreadful conditions of the base hospitals: overcrowded, vermin-ridden, revoltingly unhygienic, insufficient and overworked doctors, inadequate medicaments, hopeless nursing, everything quite fearful.

The men who were spared this fate, up on the bare, wind-swept, rain-soaked, snow-driven upland in that first Crimean winter, found that the shortcomings of the medical facilities were paralleled by their pathetic living conditions. Their threadbare, leaking tents were liable to be blown away by gales. Their uniforms were ragged and worn thin through having received no replacement clothing since the landing, and with no outer garments save for greatcoats made of cheap, shoddy grey baize, often wet through; at night only one equally shoddy blanket to keep out the cold and damp. The barren, stony ground yielded only a few twigs and roots to kindle a fire to warm themselves by and to cook their meagre rations of salt beef and biscuit. They received no fruit nor vegetables, while to wash the food down or to produce a warming drink after long hours in the trenches, they were expected to brew coffee from raw green beans, always assuming they could find the wherewithal to make a fire to roast them on. The brave, patient, enduring men, who had bested the Russians in every encounter, who had stood loyally by their regimental officers – they, too, suffering the same conditions – bore it all the heroic fortitude, but they deserved better from the nation that had sent them to fight, and from their higher command which required such sacrifices from them yet so often seemed oblivious of their suffering.

No military force, however well-found, well-equipped and well-trained, will survive for long if its higher direction is incompetent or negligent. It must have forceful, energetic, experienced commanders who know their work and what needs to be done, together with properly trained, hard-working staffs to implement their decisions, transmit their orders to the fighting troops, and ensure those troops are fit to fight. Lord Raglan was a brave, kindly, thoroughly decent man, but he was over 66, in indifferent health, had never before commanded in the field, and spent most of his service life in an office in Whitehall in the shadow of the Duke of Wellington. Wellington, in the Peninsular War, had always taken great pains to ensure his army was properly provided for, so much so that one officer found it "incomprehensible" that a man like Raglan, who had served so long under the Duke, "should have allowed his army to waste away from want of method and arrangement"[1].

Most of Raglan's senior divisional commanders were in their sixties, or near to them. A few had experienced some active service in India or Africa since their youthful days in the Napoleonic War; some had never heard a shot fired in anger. As for their staffs, most were quite inexperienced and untrained for the work, often owing their positions to interest or influential connections with their commanders. During the first dreadful winter, while the regimental officers and their men suffered appalling privations, it was said that Raglan's staff had "good beds, good fires and good dinners"[2], and were seldom seen near the camps, the trenches and what passed for the field hospitals.

The British Army of the mid-19th century was not really a properly constituted army at all but rather a collection of regiments. Their activities were supervised, to a greater or lesser degree, by whatever senior officer in whose area they happened to be stationed at any given time, at home or abroad, the whole overseen by the Commander-in-Chief at the Horse Guards in Whitehall. Within each regiment there was, in peacetime, a great gulf fixed between officers and soldiers. The former were the sons of the gentry and the upper classes, yet most of them having a paternal care for their men, while the latter were the sons of the impoverished and unemployed, but usually finding in the regiment a new family and a better life than they had left behind; between the two, as the all-important link, stood the non-commissioned-officers, the sergeants and corporals. Since every regiment considered itself better than any other, and providing it had a good commanding officer, officers and men would pull together to maintain their regiment's reputation and efficiency. In time of war officers and men would be drawn closer together through shared dangers and discomforts; Crimean officers' letters and diaries are full of admiration and affection for their men whom they had barely known in peacetime. Thus, by the standards existing at the time, the regiments individually worked well on the whole, as they demonstrated in the Crimean battles. But although a battle like Inkerman could be won by regiments acting more or less independently, a campaign as a whole could not be conducted conclusively in that way.

The collection of regiments that sailed to the East in 1854 were grouped into brigades and divisions under their appointed commanders — but only when they arrived there. They were strangers to each other, none had practised or trained together before, and little thought had been given, either by their commanders or the authorities at home, as to how they were to function, to live and to survive. Doubtless it was fondly believed that British bayonets would carry all before them, as indeed the men behind those bayonets usually did. Nevertheless Russia was a mighty military power and what if the work could not be completed before

Russia's other great weapon – its savage winter – descended? The French army in the Crimea had come prepared for such an eventuality, but no one in Whitehall, nor in Raglan's headquarters, seems to have thought it worthy of much consideration. Consequently there ensued the terrible sufferings of that first winter and the tragic waste of men who had given their all without complaint, while the people of England and their rulers slumbered peacefully in their warm beds.

That those at home became alerted to their soldiers' plight was due to officers writing home of the conditions and, perhaps most of all, to the reports in *The Times* of its great war-correspondent, W. H. Russell. As a result of this one civilian's efforts to alleviate that plight, two others went out to add their contribution. One was Florence Nightingale. The other was the author of this book, Alexis Soyer. The first was to minister to the soldiers' health, the second to their stomachs upon which, as the first Napoleon maintained, an army marches to victory.

The Crimean army survived to march and fight again, to take Sebastopol, and, as is not always remembered, to win the war, thereby denying the Black Sea and the Dardenelles to Russia for a further fifteen years. There can be no doubt that the regaining of its strength was due in part to the better feeding arrangements instituted by Alexis Soyer, which included the stove that bore his name – an article of cooking equipment which was to remain in the service of the British Army well into the lifetime of many who will read this reprinting of his Crimean memoirs.

MICHAEL BARTHORP

[1] Lt-Gen. Sir Charles Ash Windham, *Crimean Diary and Letters* ed. Maj. Hugh Pearce. Kegan Paul (1897).
[2] Ibid.

INTRODUCTION II

Campaign Food

Alexis Soyer was inventive, imaginative and a very good organiser. He also had great charm, which he used to good effect to get his own way; he was warm-hearted, flamboyant and enthusiastic. All these characteristics he needed, and used, during his time in the Crimea. He already knew several of the senior army officers, such as Lord Raglan, from his time at the Reform Club, and this helped him in his dealings and demands when he reached the scene of the war.

When Soyer made his impulsive offer to the Government to go out to the Crimea, he produced a working model of the stove with which he is so closely associated. From his account in the Culinary Campaign it reads as if this were thought of almost overnight, but he had, for many years, occupied himself with kitchen arrangements and gadgets of all kinds. When he went to Ireland in the 1840s he created an extremely efficient soup kitchen and, in his "Shilling Cookery" published in 1854, he describes "Soyer's Kitchen for the Army", which was a horsedrawn boiler with an oven in the top part, capable of providing for one thousand men and "would cook whilst on the march, if on an even road". He also produced a Baking Stewing Pan, which could be hung over a fire or placed on a hob, and would steam or boil, with a padlock securing the lid so no one could open it before the contents were cooked.

He had, therefore, been working on some kind of army cooking apparatus for some time, which received its final touches with the incentive of the Crimea War, as his stove seems to be a combination of the two devices of a steam boiler with a removable container on top.

The stoves were not ready by the time of his departure from London, but he had enough to occupy him with the improvements necessary at the hospital in Scutari, where he found only one of the kitchens adequate for his use, and little or no organisation there. There were no trained cooks among the soldiers and, although the rations themselves were, on the whole, adequate, except for the lack of vegetables, the way in which they were used was a wasteful disaster. One of his inventions, produced apparently after he arrived, was the Scutari teapot, with a removable filter for the tea, enabling less tea to be used to better effect than the previous method of putting a heap of tea in a cloth and dunking it into a boiler that had previously been used for soup.

Soyer had taken a team of helpers to Scutari with him, using them to teach his methods to selected soldiers who could then act as cooks, and he carefully wrote down his recipes so that there could be no excuse for not following them. He continued this method in the Crimea itself, where he went after he had got the hospital kitchens in some sort of order. A few years later, after Soyer's death, the War Office published "Instructions to Military Hospital Cooks", incorporating his recipes and methods.

The English soldier had an allowance of one pound of meat and a similar amount of bread per day which, with the rest of the rations of coffee, salt, sugar, water and so on, each man had to carry and cook himself, first finding fuel for a fire in order to do so. The French had a smaller meat ration, but a bigger one of bread, and they made better use of both by forming into messes of twelve, with one of that number acting as cook for the day, taking it in turns to do so. This enabled more time and care to be given to the preparation and cooking of the food, particularly the salt meat, which formed a large part of the diet, as it had to be soaked for some hours to make it palatable. One soldier on his own didn't have time to do this properly, so often the meat was undercooked. No vegetables were included in the ration allowance and scurvy was common. "For six weeks lime juice, at that time so necessary, remained unissued, because neither the medical nor the Commissariat officer would make up their mind to ask the commander of the army if it were to be regarded as a medical comfort or an article of Commissariat issue."[1] A typical instance of the confusion and lack of planning that existed in the army at that time.

Meat was available in cans, though not always of very good quality, although milk in cans kept well. A firm in Paris, Chollet, was producing pressed, dried vegetables which, when reconstituted, made an acceptable substitute for the fresh, so portable preserved food was to be had, and Soyer sent off for a consignment of these Chollet-cakes, marking them into three-day allowances. It was possible to send such orders very speedily thanks to the newly invented electric telegraph which played such a significant part in the conduct of the war. For the first time people at home were aware, through dispatches and newspaper reports, of the conditions of the troops, and were appalled.

Hard biscuit was much used in the rations, but men with scorbutic gums couldn't eat it, and soft bread was needed. Again the French managed things better and baked very good bread which the English soldiers bought whenever they could. Soyer produced a 'bread-biscuit' which would keep for a long time and, although biscuity in texture, was very palatable when dunked in soup or tea. Grain was readily obtainable but there were no mills to grind it. However, things improved and two ships were adapted to become mill and bakery. Anchored in the harbour they were soon able to supply good bread on the spot. The butchers, either from ignorance or laziness, divided meat into "five quarters", the fifth being the head, feet and messy bits of the animals, which were discarded and buried. When Soyer opened his first field kitchen on the arrival of his stoves, he "arranged with the butcher for a supply of four ox-heads and six ox-feet, out of the number he daily buried" and continued to do this, making a valuable addition to the rations, and at no extra cost.

The stoves proved so valuable that the army has used them ever since, still called the Soyer stove. They were in use during the Gulf War, though fired by bottled gas or even petrol, instead of coal or wood. Rather like over-sized dustbins, with a chimney to take away any smoke, Florence Nightingale wrote of them "Soyer's stoves will boil, stew, bake and steam, in short, do everything but grill, ensuring that variety in cooking which is proved essential to health", and went on to comment "Did we but know its extreme importance . . . we should have paid a little more attention to Cooking in the case of Armies".[2]

Soyer did pay attention and, apart from the stoves, left his mark in many ways: organising kitchens, teaching soldiers to be cooks, leaving written instructions for recipes, bringing common sense to the rations, abolishing waste and cooking in bulk so that many were fed at one time instead of each soldier having to cook for himself. All this contributed to the welfare of the army, and many lessons were learnt.

ELIZABETH RAY

[1] Furse, G.A. *Provisioning of Armies in the Field.* 1899
[2] Nightingale, Florence. *Notes on matters affecting health, efficiency and hospital administration of the British Army.* 1858

Further sources
Bushby, H.J. *A Month in the Camp before Sebastopol.* 1855
Cole, Howard. *The Story of the Army Catering Corps and its predecessors.* 1984
Heath, Sir Leopold. *Letters from the Black Sea.* 1897

To the

RIGHT HONOURABLE LORD PANMURE, K. T.

My Lord,

Grateful, indeed, do I feel for the unlimited confidence reposed in me by your Lordship during my late Mission in the East, and especially so for your kind condescension in permitting me to dedicate to your Lordship this work, which at once puts the final seal to your Lordship's appreciation of my humble services.
With the most profound respect,
I have the honour to remain,
My Lord,
Your Lordship's most humble and dutiful Servant,
ALEXIS SOYER.

PREFACE

THE Author of this work begs to inform his readers that his principal object in producing his "Culinary Campaign" is to perpetuate the successful efforts made by him to improve the dieting of the Hospitals of the British army in the East, as well as the soldiers' rations in the Camp before Sebastopol.

The literary portion the Author has dished up to the best of his ability; and if any of his readers do not relish its historical contents, he trusts that the many new and valuable receipts, applicable to the Army, Navy, Military and Civil Institutions, and the public in general, will make up in succulence for any literary deficiencies that may be found in its pages.

At the same time, the Author takes this opportunity of publicly returning his most grateful thanks to the late authorities at the seat of war for their universal courtesy, friendship, and great assistance, without which success would have been an impossibility.

A CULINARY CAMPAIGN

By A. SOYER.

ILLUSTRATED BY H. G. HINE.

ORIGINAL INTRODUCTION

A SUPPER AT THE "ALBION" AND ITS CONSEQUENCES

"HURRAH! hurrah! bravo! bravo!" For a few minutes rounds of applause and shouts of laughter from the juveniles were heard and loudly re-echoed throughout the vast cupola of Old Drury, sending home the delighted spectators, in fits of sneezing and coughing, through a variegated atmosphere. Sir Henry W——, turning to me, exclaimed, "Hallo, Mr. Soyer, the pantomime is over early this evening!" and looking at his watch, continued, "Why, it is only half-past eleven o'clock."

"Yes, Sir Henry; but quite late enough for children, who after this time begin to mingle gaping with laughter."

"True enough," replied Sir Henry; "it is painful to see those dear cherubs kept at the theatre till midnight, or even later. Have you been long here?"

"No," I replied, "only a few minutes; just time enough to witness the grand finale, and to hear the screaming and laughter of the children, which to me is always very amusing."

"Very true, very true; I am of your opinion, and never tire of children's mirth."

In a few minutes the theatre was nearly emptied of spectators, but still full of smoke. Considering myself that evening as free as a butterfly on a spring morning, though unable, like that light-hearted insect, to flit from flower to flower, I was trying to escape, with the swiftness of an eel, down the gigantic and crowded staircase, hoping to get off unobserved, as I had to start early in the morning for the country, when suddenly a friendly hand pressed me forcibly by the arm. The owner of the same cried, "Stop! Stop! my friend; I have been hunting all over the theatre for you." I at once recognised an old Devonshire acquaintance, whom I was indeed much pleased to see, having received a most kind reception from him at my last visit to that delightful county—so justly named the garden of England.

"Well, my dear sir," said he, "myself and several acquaintances of yours are here for a few days, and have ordered a supper this evening at the 'Albion.' We heard you were at Drury Lane, and I have come to ask you to join us."

"I must say it is very kind of you, Mr. Turner; but you must excuse me, as I am going as far as St. James's Street, by appointment; besides, I leave for the country early tomorrow morning. But I shall be happy to spend tomorrow evening with you and your friends; therefore, I beg you will apologise for me."

"Tomorrow very likely we shall be off again; we only came for a couple of days, to breathe the London air, and then return."

"I beg your pardon—you mean London fog, not air."

"Why, yes, fog should be the word; but for all that, I love London in any season; so no excuse—I shall not leave you; you must join us, or your friend the squire will be greatly disappointed. He came from the Great Western Hotel this evening on purpose to see you."

Finding it almost impossible to get out of it, and my friend having promised we should break up early, I accepted, saying, "You must allow me to go as far as the 'Wellington,' as I have an appointment there; I will be back in about half-an-hour."

My incredulous country friend would not grant permission till I had assured him that I would faithfully keep my promise, and return.

This dialogue took place in the entrance of the vestibule, where a number of ladies and children were waiting—some for their carriages and broughams, others for those public inconveniences called cabs. This bevy of beauty and group of children, the pride of young England, seemed to interest my provincial friend so much, that I had some trouble to get him out. It was then nearly twelve o'clock. The front steps were also crowded; the weather was chilly and damp; a thick yellowish fog, properly mixed with a good portion of soot, formed a shower of black pearls, which, gracefully descending through the murky air, alighted, without asking permission, upon the rosy cheeks of unveiled fair dames, spotting their visages, if not *à la* Pompadour or *à la* Watteau, at least *à la* Hogarth. A few steps lower we entered a dense crowd—a most unpicturesque miscellany of individuals, unclassically called the London mob. "Mind your pockets," said I to my country friend.

"By Jove, it's too late," said he, feeling in his pocket—"my handkerchief is gone!"

"Is that all?" I inquired.

"Well, let me see," he observed, feeling again: "yes, thank God! my watch and purse are quite safe."

"Ah," I continued, laughing, "the old adage which prompts us to thank God for all things is quite correct; for you are actually thanking Him for the loss of your handkerchief."

"Not at all, I was thanking Him for the safety of my watch and purse." After a hearty laugh we parted, he going to the Albion, and I to the Wellington.

On my arrival there, I found that my friend had been and was gone. My intelligent cabby soon brought me back through the dense atmosphere to that far-famed temple of Comus, at which crowds of celebrities meet nightly—some to restore themselves internally, others to sharpen their wits at that tantalising abode of good cheer. Upon entering, I inquired of a waiter, a stranger to me, if he could inform me where my six friends intended to sup.

"Yes, sir, directly." Speaking down the trumpet: "Below! a Welsh rarebit and fresh toast—two kidneys underdone—scalloped oyster—a chop—two taters! Look sharp below!" To the barmaid: "Two stouts, miss—one pale—four brandies hot, two without—one whisky—three gin—pint sherry—bottle of port!"

"What an intelligent waiter!" thought I, "to have so good a memory." Having waited till he had given his orders, I again said, "Pray, my fine fellow, in which room are my friends going to sup? They have a private room, no doubt?"

"Yes, sir, a private room for two."

"No, not for two—for six."

"Oh! I don't mean that, sir: I want a rump-steak for two," said he; "stewed tripe for one—three grogs—bottle pale Bass." And off he went to the coffee-room.

"Plague upon the fellow!" said I to myself.

As the barmaid could not give me any information upon the subject, and I perceived through a half-opened door on the right-hand side of the bar a table laid for six, I went in, making sure it was for my friends, and that they had not yet arrived. Indeed, I had myself returned from my appointment much sooner than I had expected. I sat down, and was reading the evening paper, when a waiter came in. "After you with the paper, sir."

"I have done; you may take it."

"There's the *Times*, sir, if you have not seen it."

"No, I have not; let me have a look at it." After reading one of the leaders, my attention was drawn to a long article written by the Crimean correspondent of that journal. When I had read it carefully a second time, a few minutes' reflection on my part enabled me to collect my ideas, and established in my mind a certain assurance that I could, if allowed by Government, render service in the cooking of the food, the administration of the same, as well as the distribution of the provisions. These were matters in which I could detect, through the description of that eye-witness, the writer of the above-mentioned article, some change was much needed. I therefore wrote the following letter to the *Times*, it being then nearly one o'clock in the morning:—

THE HOSPITAL KITCHENS AT SCUTARI.

To the Editor of the Times

Sir,—After carefully perusing the letter of your correspondent, dated Scutari, in your impression of Wednesday last, I perceive that, although the kitchen under the superintendence of Miss Nightingale affords so much relief, the system of management at the large one in the Barrack Hospital is far from being perfect. I propose offering my services gratuitously, and proceeding direct to Scutari, at my own personal expense, to regulate that important department, if the Government will honour me with their confidence, and grant me the full power of acting according to my knowledge and experience in such matters.
I have the honour to remain, Sir,

Your obedient servant,

Feb. 2, 1855.   A. Soyer.

After despatching this letter, I again inquired about my friends and my anticipated supper, which for some time had escaped my memory. "Did you ring, sir?"

"No, I did not, sir, but the bell has;" recognising my stupid waiter.

"Oh, sir! are you here?"

"Of course I am; don't you see me?"

"Well, sir, your friends have had supper; they inquired everywhere for you; I told them you could not wait, as you had two ladies to see home as far as Brompton."

"You foolish fellow! I never spoke to you about ladies, Brompton, or any such thing; I merely asked you where my friends were to sup; to which you replied, 'Rump-steak for two, tripe for one, two taters, pat of butter, one pale Bass, and three kidneys for a gentleman, under-done.'"

"No more you did, sir. It was number three who told me to say so; not you, sir; you're quite right, sir!"

"I am sure I am right; but as for you, your head is quite wrong!"

"Well, I assure you, sir, we have so much to do at times, we hardly know what we are about."

"I don't think you do," said I, sharply.

"But I tell you what, sir, they are there still, and you had better go to them."

"No, it is too late now; give them this note from me when they go out; and here is sixpence for yourself, for through your mistake you have after all rendered me a service. I did not wish to come here this evening, as I have an early engagement for tomorrow, so I will have a bit of supper and go home."

"Well, do, sir; I thank you, and am very glad I have given you satisfaction at last."

"Send Little Ben here; he knows what I like for supper."

"Hallo, Mr. Soyer, everybody in the coffee-room has been inquiring after you this evening," said Little Ben upon entering.

"I know; but that foolish waiter who was here just now made such a mull of everything, that he quite upset our party; I could not get any answer from him, so I made sure this table was laid out for us, and here I stuck."

"No, sir, your friends supped in the coffee-room, and are still there, if you like to have your supper near them."

"No, no; give me what you like here."

"What shall it be, sir?—oysters, broiled kidneys, chops, steaks, stewed tripe, broiled bones?"

"Have you nothing else?"

"Yes, sir, grilled fowl and scalloped oysters; only they will take some time preparing."

"Well, give me scalloped oysters, and my favourite Welsh rarebit, made in my style—you know; a pint of port wine, and fresh toast for the rarebit."

"Yes, sir; the cook knows—I'll tell him it is for you."

"But how is it you never vary your supper bill of fare? It is very scanty of choice for such a large tavern as this. I do not mean to complain, but give a little change now and then, by introducing a few new dishes."

"Ah! you're right, sir; it would please the customers, and be much better for us waiters, to have something new to offer; but, bless you, sir! I have been many years in this place, and it was always the same; and no doubt will remain so for as long again, unless a gentleman like you takes it in hand—they would then attend to it; but, of course, you have something else to do."

"So I have; yet I don't see why, in my next book upon cookery, I should not devote a few pages to the London suppers. I intend doing so, and, when published, I shall be happy to present you with a copy."

"That will be first-rate, sir; I thank you, and won't I recommend the new dishes *à la* Soyer, as some of our customers call them!"

"Well, my man, upon second thoughts, as you seem so anxious about it, and I am not going to join my friends, give me a pen and ink, and while supper is preparing, I will write a few practical receipts, which can be easily introduced without interfering with your duty or the kitchen; they will, no doubt, prove agreeable to your customers, who are in general a class of *bon vivants*, fond of good things as well as of variety in the bill of fare."

"Here is the pen, paper, and ink, sir."

"Thank you; come again in about twenty minutes, and they shall be ready; or, if you are not in a hurry, stay."

"No, sir, I am not; our supper business is over."

"Well, now listen: first, I do not intend to criticise your bill of fare, which is as much varied, if not more so, than that offered at other large taverns, and it is quite as well executed. Now, respecting kidneys—you consume a large quantity of them?"

"So we do, sir."

"Then I will give you a receipt or two for dressing them:—

No. 1.—Take two kidneys, split them lengthways as close to the sinew as possible without parting them; remove the thin skin, lay them flat upon the table, and season rather highly with salt and pepper; then run them crossways upon a wooden, metal, or silver skewer, forcing the sinew upwards; this will prevent their curling up again while cooking. Next dip them in some well-beaten eggs, to which you have added about a tablespoonful of dissolved butter; or rub them over with a paste-brush, which will do it more equally; roll them in fine bread-crumbs, and slightly beat them on both sides with the flat of your knife to cause the crumbs to stick to the kidneys. Put them upon the gridiron, over a sharp fire, at a proper distance; they will require from five to eight minutes doing, according to size.

For the uninitiated, the following plan is the best to ascertain when they are properly done. Press with the prongs of a fork or the point of the knife upon the thick part of the kidney; if done through, it will feel firm and elastic to the touch. When the kidneys are done, slip them off the skewer on to a hot dish, and place in each a piece of butter, à la maître d'hôtel, about the size of a small walnut; send to table, and by the time it reaches the guest, the butter will be half-melted; quite so when the kidney is cut by the customer, who, by turning the pieces and blending the butter with the gravy, will make a rich sauce, and partake of a delicious as well as a wholesome dish.

"Partaking of overdone kidneys at night is the forerunner of the nightmare."

"You're right, sir; that it is," said Little Ben; "for at times we have some left, and keep them warm for supper; and they get as tough as pieces of leather, when after eating three or four—and I am always very tired at night—I never can sleep. Now I think of it, the tough kidneys must be the cause; and if I do sleep, Mr. Soyer, I have such awful dreams that I feel more fatigued when I rise than when I go to bed."

"Of course," I replied, "I am well aware of that; they cannot digest; therefore, you see the importance of having them properly done."

"Very much so indeed; I quite understand it now, and perceive that if they cannot at all times be done to perfection, underdone is much preferable to overdone. I perfectly understand you, sir; but you see we require such a quantity."

"Well, I have only given you the receipt for two. I will now, if you like, give you the receipt for a hundred."

"Do, sir; that will suit us better."

"I suppose they are most in request for supper?"

"Indeed they are, sir."

"Then, in the course of the day, the cook should prepare a hundred precisely as the first—viz., ready for cooking. They should be put upon skewers, two, three, or four in a row; so that, when called for, he has only to remove them from the larder to the gridiron. About two pounds of butter à la maître d'hôtel should be prepared and kept in a cool place to be ready when required. By following this plan, you could easily cook several hundred during the evening, if called for. Should any remain unsold, they will keep till the next day, and will only require rolling in the crumbs again previous to broiling."

"I see, sir; it will save a great deal of time by having them prepared beforehand."

"But suppose you had none prepared beforehand, a dozen can soon be got ready by an active cook. The addition of the dissolved butter to the eggs keeps the kidneys fresh and moist, and inserting them upon the skewer retains them flat, and they are cooked more regularly in half the time, while without the skewer they curl up, and are frequently underdone on one side and cooked too much on the other."

"I plainly understand what you mean."

"These details upon the same subject are perhaps tedious to you."

"Not at all, sir; I see the importance of them."

"Well, the other receipts will come quite plain and easy to you. To tell the truth, I have had those overdone kidneys upon my conscience for some time. Mind, I do not intend to erase the plain broiled kidneys from the supper bill of fare, for I am very fond of them when properly cooked."

"They are very good; and many gentlemen will not have them any other way."

"Well, I do not blame them, for they are both agreeable and nutritious that way; but here is another appetizing receipt, which we will call à la Roberto Diavolo."

No. 2.—Put two plain kidneys upon a skewer, and with a pastebrush butter them over. Set them upon the gridiron as near the fire as possible, for they cannot be done too fast; turn them every minute, and when half done season with salt, pepper, and a small spoonful of cayenne; chop some gherkins and a little green chillies, if handy; or, instead of either, a tablespoonful of chopped piccalilli with the liquor. Put these on a hot plate, with a teaspoonful of lemon-juice and a pat of butter. Take up the kidneys, and slip them burning hot from the skewer to the plate; turn them round four or five times in the mixture, and serve immediately. A small piece of glaze added to the butter will prove a great addition. Three, four, or five minutes will do them, according to the size.

Kidneys à la brochette, Paris fashion

The Parisian *gourmet* would not eat a kidney if it was not served upon the silver skewer; the only merit of which is, that they keep hot longer and look better than when the skewer is omitted; as they often shrink, especially if the sinew has not been properly divided in the splitting of them.

"As, no doubt, you have something to do, you had better leave me; I will write a few more receipts. Bring me my supper in a quarter of an hour, and they will be ready."

"Very well, sir; I will give a look round and order your supper."

To the minute Little Ben walked in with the scalloped oysters, which I must admit looked remarkably tempting. He handed me my supper, but upon reflection I did not hand him the receipts, only a list of their names, intending to put them into the cookery-book I had promised him, knowing well enough that it was not in his power to bring them out. He thanked me for my lecture on cookery, as he called it, and the following bill of fare. I paid my bill, and left.

New Bill of Fare for Tavern Suppers

Rump-steak and fried potatoes; ditto with shalot, pimento, and anchovy butter. Relishing-steak, fillet of beef à la Parisienne; ditto à la Chateaubriand.

Mutton chops à la bouchère; ditto semi-provençale; ditto Marseilles fashion; ditto with relishing sauce.

Plain cutlets with fried potatoes, à la maître d'hôtel, à la Sultana, semi-provençale.

Lamb chops à la boulangère, à l'Américaine, à la printanière.

Pork chops with pimento butter, à la Tartare; ditto camp fashion.

Veal cutlets en papillote; with maître d'hôtel butter; with relishing butter; with fried potatoes.

Kidneys on toast, semi-curried; ditto with sherry or port; ditto with champagne. For kidneys à la maître d'hôtel, à la brochette, and à la Roberto Diavolo, see Receipts, page 6.

Stewed and curried tripe; ditto Lyonnaise fashion.

Lobsters au gratin in the shell; scalloped ditto; curried on toast; lobster cutlets; new salad, Tartar fashion; plain salad with anchovies; crabs au gratin in the shell; crab salad with eggs.

Grilled chicken and Sultana sauce; à la Roberto Diavolo, with relishing sauce; new broiled devil, Mayonnaise sauce; chicken, American fashion.

Stewed oysters on toast; ditto American fashion, au gratin; fried oysters.

Omelettes with fine herbs, mushrooms, sprue grass, ham, and parmesan; poached eggs with cream; ditto with maître d'hôtel sauce; semi-curried, with ham or bacon.

Buttered eggs with mushrooms, sprue grass, ham with shalots, parsley, and chervil.

Mirrored eggs with tongue, ham, or bacon; curried eggs; ditto with onion sauce and tomato sauce.

Rarebit à la Soyer with sherry or champagne.

Fried potatoes in slices; ditto with maître d'hôtel butter; ditto with Cayenne pepper.

Cold asparagus salad, while in season; new potato salad, German fashion; ditto, French and haricot beans.*

For receipts in Bill of Fare, see Addenda.

A Hansom cab was waiting at the door, so I jumped in.

"Beg your pardon, sir, I am engaged," said cabby; "but if you're not going far, I think I shall have plenty of time to take you."

"Do so, my man; I live close by, in Bloomsbury Street, Bedford Square. Here's a shilling for you—go ahead, cabby."

Pst! pst! and off we were. In a few minutes, thanks to the evaporation of the thick fog and its having left only a feeble skeleton of its former substance, I found myself at my street door, and was trying for some time to open it with the wrong key, all the while thinking to myself what an extraordinary and uncomfortable evening I had passed to return so late. Perceiving my mistake, I changed the key; opening and shutting the door violently, I rushed upstairs with the intention of booking that evening in my daily tablet as one of the most tedious and uncomfortable I had spent throughout the series of cheerful years granted to me by a Supreme Power. The fire was out, the supper divided between my two friends the Angola cats, the servants in bed, the gas turned off, and the lucifers, I believe, gone to their Mephistophelian domain.

---

* He also approved of my observation, that I was well aware that people could not expect to find those dishes on the bill of fare every day, but only one or two nightly. To ensure success, I would advise the proprietors of all extensive supper-houses to adopt the plan I so successfully introduced at the Reform Club many years since, which was to make a small bill of fare of eight or ten dishes which were ready, and cross out such as run short during the evening, recommending only those which remained. This saved time, words, and confusion; besides giving an opportunity of introducing one or two novelties daily, which would pay well if properly attended to. It would also gratify the consumer, who should not be kept waiting for his supper till fresh provisions were sent for and cooked, as at that hour many persons would content themselves with a less variety of dishes rather than wait.

I

BY RAIL AND COACH TO VIRGINIA WATER

A MOST curious dream haunted my mind throughout the night, one of those indescribable phantasmagorian illusions which set all the vibrations of the heart at work without moving the frame, or in imagination only, quite depriving our senses for the time of the true sense of existence. Scarcely had the first gleam of Aurora peeped through my curtains, than a double knock was heard at the street door, apprising me that the time for rising had come, and forthwith brought back my wandering senses to the realities of human life: a minute after, a friend popped into my dressing-room, exclaiming, "Hallo! so you are going to the seat of the war, I hear."

"The seat of the war! who told you so?"

"Why, the *Times*, to be sure; I have just read your letter, which, at all events, is very likely to carry you as far as Constantinople."

"You don't say so! What! is my letter in the *Times* today?"

"Of course it is," he replied.

"I sent it so late last night, I did not suppose it could appear till tomorrow, if at all."

"They would not have inserted it, arriving so late, I assure you, had they not thought it of great importance, and that you were likely to improve the hospital diets. No doubt you will soon set them to rights. I read the article, and must say I was much pleased when I saw your letter, and that is what brought me here so early: but mind, it is a long journey, and rather a dangerous one."

"Well, my dear friend, if Government honour me with their confidence, I shall be happy to start immediately, and rough it for a short time—say a couple of months, which will be about the time required."

"My opinion is, that you will soon hear from the authorities."

"I say again, they are perfectly welcome to my humble services."

"Are you going out this morning?"

"Yes, I am; excuse my shaving."

"Oh, by all means; which way are you going?"

"Anywhere but to a wintry place."

"Where's that—Gravesend or Margate?"

"Oh dear, no—Virginia Water."

"To stay?"

"No; only to settle a few important matters there, prior to my departure for Paris."

"You were there the best part of last summer."

"So I was; who told you that?"

"Don't you recollect the party you gave there, when Messrs. R—— and ladies were present, with myself, my wife, and two daughters? We never enjoyed such a day in our lives; it really was a splendid affair altogether; and what an excellent dinner you gave us in the open air, in the long avenue of beech trees facing the lake! I shall not forget it as long as I live—I may say we, for my young ones often talk about it. There were about twenty-four guests— you recollect, of course?"

"Certainly I do now, and what a lovely day it was!"

"Never saw a finer," said my friend; "the ladies walked round the lake without their bonnets, and with nothing but their parasols to screen them from the sun. But I tell you who was most amusing amongst the party—that old Yorkshire farmer."

"Ha, ha! old Lawrence—he is a squire now, if you please, and has retired. He was very kind to me on the occasion of the grand agricultural dinner at Exeter; the ox I roasted whole upon that occasion came from his farm; it was roasted by gas, and in the castle yard."

"Ah, I recollect seeing an engraving of it in the *Illustrated London News*; I can't help laughing when I think of the old man, for at every fresh dish of which he partook—and he tasted a good many—he exclaimed—'Well! hang me, if I know what stuff I am eating, but it's precious good!'"

"I know he is very eccentric; he stayed with me nearly a week, and really made me laugh heartily with his genuine repartee. He is a good and a charitable man, I assure you. I taught his housekeeper how to make cheap soup while I was at his residence, and ever since the old gentleman has given it four times a week to the poor round his small estate, during the winter season."

"I know the soup you mean. I cut the receipt from the paper in the year '47, at the time of the famine in Ireland, when you were sent there by Government."

"Exactly."

"We tried it ourselves; and my wife's mother has ever since given it throughout the winter to about twelve or fifteen poor people. The old lady was at first obliged to make it herself, her cook saying that no soup could be made with such a small quantity of meat. She would not even attempt to make it."

"I believe you; but those people are not aware that in Scotland, where the strongest people in the British dominions are to be found, and especially in the Highlands, they live principally upon oatmeal porridge and vegetables, partaking of a very small portion of animal food;—and did you ever see a finer carnation cheek, or purer blood, than that which flows through the frame of a Scotch lassie, or in the veins of the descendants of the Bruce?"

"No, never; not even on the Continent. But, to return to the receipts: I would advise you to publish them. They would be eagerly purchased, and would render greater service. You must be aware that a slip from a newspaper is often lost."

"Very true; and I intend to give a series of new receipts on food for the poor, still more simplified."

"With reference to our conversation about old Lawrence: no doubt he is a good fellow, and a genuine rough diamond into the bargain."

"Yes," said I, "and you may add, of the finest water. By the bye, didn't he go to bed rather top-heavy?"

"Ah, that he did, and fancied himself at home blowing up his old woman, as he calls her, for having let the cat into the dairy, and being unable to find his gun to shoot her. What most astonished the old boy, he told me on the coach next morning on our way to London, was having no headache and feeling as hungry as a hunter—as I did myself. He made sure, after such a mixture of dishes, wines, liquors, and spirits of all kinds, that he should be ill and unable to eat anything for a couple of days. Quite the contrary, however: when at Staines, we made a hearty breakfast at the hotel; and for my part, I never felt better in my life."

"And do you know," I replied, "I should have been surprised if my dinner had produced the contrary effect; rest assured, that a dinner well conceived and properly executed, coupled with well-selected beverages, is more than half digested. As Hippocrates says, very justly, 'What pleases the palate nourishes;' and we may add, greatly helps to accelerate the digestion when properly cooked. The palate alone can relish the charm of degustation, and only feels satiated when the stomach, being the working organ, refuses to deal with improper food, never failing to acquaint you physically of its ill treatment, both as regards ill-cooked food or bad beverages. Now, to illustrate this argument more forcibly, I would wager that I could give a first-class indigestion to the greatest *gourmet*, even while using the most *recherché* provisions, without his being able to detect any fault in the preparation of the dishes of which he had partaken; and this simply by improperly classifying the condiments used in the preparation; thus deceiving the cleverest doctors and the finest palate by a mere counterbalance of unctuous seasoning, which no doubt caused the celebrated Leibnitz* to say, in his treatise upon the chemistry of food, now translated into English, and to which I have already referred in my *Shilling Cookery Book*, 'That among all the arts known to man, there is none of which enjoys a juster appreciation, and the products of which are more universally admired, than that which is concerned in the preparation of our food. Led by an instinct which has almost reached the dignity of conscious knowledge, as the unerring guide, and by the sense of taste, which protects the health, the experienced cook, with respect to the choice, admixture, and preparation of food, has made acquisitions surpassing all that chemical and physiological science have done in regard to the doctrine or theory of nutrition'."

"Well, no doubt if the celebrated Leibnitz, who is considered one of the greatest authorities of the age, says so, you cannot be wrong, having had so much practice in the culinary art."

"I also maintain that with the simplest and cheapest of all aliments, when in good condition, I have turned out a most wholesome and palatable food, quite worthy of the most refined palate, or of that of the initiated epicure. For instance, if only first-class provisions could be converted into succulent dishes, the gastronomic bill of fare of this sublunary world would indeed be so limited that more than two-thirds of its inhabitants would be classified as martyrs to the Mageric art—or, more plainly speaking, martyrs to the science of cookery—a too often neglected art, though of daily requirement; for, believe me, the everlasting pleasures of the table, which favour all ages, are not only the basis of

* Soyer means Liebig, Baron Justus von, German Chemist. 1803—1873—AB.

good health when properly managed, but also the soul of sociability, not merely in high circles, but in every class of society, no matter how humble, the stomach of each individual having been nursed according to rank and wealth. Those most to be pitied are the real epicures of limited means, or the wealthy man without appetite or of bad digestion. The proverb is quite correct, 'What the eye does not see the heart cannot grieve;' and appetite being the best of sauce, will cause the coarsest food to be digested with delight by a robust stomach. By the same rule, what is more relished by our noble epicure than a dry sandwich or a coarse crust of bread and cheese at a farmhouse after a hard day's sport?"

"Upon my word, you are perfectly right; appetite is really the best of sauce, for I often make a good and hearty supper upon baked potatoes, a little salt, and butter."

"Now, my friend, I am ready to start; come with me—it is a fine frosty morning, and will do you good—come on."

"I wish I could, but my City business is very heavy this morning, so I must decline; besides, we have a railway meeting called for three o'clock at the London Tavern."

"Master, here's a Hansom coming this way; shall I call it?"

"Yes, Annette, that's a good girl." I shook hands with my friend, and jumped into the cab—"I say, coachman, look sharp and drive to the Windsor railway station; I fear I shall miss the special train."

"No, you will not," said my friend, looking at his watch, "you have full twenty minutes; goodbye, a pleasant journey."

"Well, adieu! I shall see you some evening at Jullien's or Drury Lane Theatre."

"Very probably."

"Stay a minute, cabby;"—to the servant—"Annette, put any letters which may come on my desk; if anybody calls, say I shall be here tomorrow or next day at the latest."

"Very well, sir, I will do so."

On my arrival at the station, I merely had time to take my ticket and run to the train, which was just on the move. In a few seconds we were flying over rows of houses like vampires, leaving the then desolate Royal property, Vauxhall tumble-down theatre, with its skeleton firework frame, on the left. We passed through Chiswick, Barnes, Mortlake, Kew, with its toyish pagoda, leaving to the left Richmond, with its picturesque banks, cheerful villas, heroine of the hill, and its exquisite maids of honour;* at the same time crossing the Thames, cheerfully smiling beneath us in its serpentine bed. Its limpid currents flowed merrily downwards to the mighty ocean through green bushes, aquatic plants, and the alabaster-coloured plumage of hundreds of swans. In twenty-five minutes we arrived at Staines station. I descended and immediately ascended again, but on the top of the Virginia Water coach, which generally waits for the special train. "Very frosty this morning, coachman."

"Hallo, Mr. Soyer! is that you? We have not seen you God knows how long. I suppose you have left us for good now?"

* Small cakes said to have originated with the Maids of Honour of Elizabeth I. Soyer gives the recipe in *The Modern Housewife*, 1848—AB

"No, not quite; but your flat and unpicturesque country looks so dull and unsociable at this time of year."

"Then you prefer town just now?" said he.

"I certainly do; there is always something to be seen there, and to keep one alive, morning, noon, and night."

"Very true, Mr. Soyer; we are very dull here in winter." The top of the coach was loaded with passengers. "Well, boy, what are you about below?"

"All right, coachman," cried the parcel-boy. "Pst! pst! Go it, my Britons!"

We were now at full trot, the north wind in our faces, and a kind of heavy sleet, which in a few minutes changed the colour of our noses to a deep crimson, very much like the unfashionable colour of beetroot, freezing our whiskers and moustaches like sugar-candy, but by no means quite so sweet-tasted. By way of a joke, I said to the coachman, "This is the good old English way of travelling, is it not?"

"That it is, sir; and I'm very glad to see you know how to appreciate it. Talk about your railways, it's perfect nonsense compared with a good four-in-hand coach, sir." As he said this, he whipped his horses. "Pst! go ahead, my true blue! I recollect the good old time when we took from fourteen to fifteen hours from London to Dover, changing horses and drinking your glass of grog at almost every inn on the road—in fact, enjoying ourselves all night, especially when the widow was out."

"What widow?" said I.

"The moon, to be sure!"

"That is a bright idea of yours. I was not aware the pale queen of night was a widow."

"Lord bless you, sir, she must be a widow, for she always comes out alone, and keeps very late hours; a maid or a married woman can't do that, you know," said he, laughing heartily.

"If your remark is not correct, it is at all events very original."

"But to come back to coach-travelling—then you really knew if you were travelling or stopping at home; while now they pack you up under lock and key, in strong wooden boxes, such as we keep our horses in at the stable; and at the head of them they have a kind of long iron saveloy, full of nothing, which runs away with the lot like mad, belching and swearing all the way, taking sights at us poor coachmen just so," putting his hand to his nose, "when we go by, as though we were a set of ragamuffins. Call that a gentlemanly way of travelling, sir! They make fun of all the passengers who are a little behind time, saying the like of this: 'Don't you wish you may get it?' If you drop anything by accident, the deuce a bit will they stop to pick it up; and you are no sooner in than they turn you out, and pocket your money without blushing, the same as though they had dragged you about from morning till night, as we used to do in the good old time. That was indeed money honestly earned, sir!"

"There certainly is a great deal of truth in your argument," said I, laughing at his devotion to his old business.

"Is it not brimful of truth, sir?"

"Of course it is!" I was by this time about half frozen.

"Ah, sir, you're a gentleman, and know life as well as I do. Depend upon it, sir, coach-travelling is the best after all—no danger of being smashed to pieces or of breaking your limbs. Not the slightest accident ever can happen. Hallo!" said he, stopping the horses short, "what the deuce is the matter with that horse? Look out, Bob!"

"Yes, sir; the old trace is broke again."

"The deuce it is! Well, we must mend it."

"You can't—it's broke in a fresh place, and we have no rope here." The coachman getting down, unceremoniously threw the reins to me. "Hold them fast, sir."

"Well, well, my lad, you must run back and fetch another." The snow was then falling heavily, and we had not got more than a mile on the road. In about forty minutes the boy returned, perspiring terribly, though covered with snow.

"I've not been long, coachman, have I?"

"Not been long, my lad—why, my cargo is nearly frozen to death!"

"You're right, coachman," said an old gentleman. "And I promise you I will never travel by your coach again. This is the second time this month."

"Well, sir, we are not travelling now—we are at a stand-still, and no mistake."

"You may joke, but I don't like it."

"No more do I," said coachman; "so we are of the same opinion." At this we all laughed, except the old gentleman.

In a short time all was right again. The coachman had resumed his important position as well as the reins, which I abdicated to my great satisfaction, and we were on the move. "Very slippery, governor; my horses can scarcely keep their feet. Thank God, we are not in a hurry; we can do the journey much more comfortably."

"Excuse me," said I, "if I do not hold exactly the same opinion as I did just now about the railway."

"My dear sir, are you in a hurry?" he asked.

"Yes, I am, and very cold besides."

"What a pity you did not say so before! I should have made my stud fly, and beat to atoms that fussy stuff they call steam."

"That's a good man; show off a bit."

"Pst! pst! pst! Look out for a full charge, Cossack; fly away, Cannon-ball. Pst! pst! that's it, lads." We were now nearly at a gallop.

"Coachman," said I, "I see that your horses have martial names, if they have not a very martial appearance. Pray, who gave them such warlike titles?"

"The boys in the stable, sir. Everybody dreams of war now, sir; the very air we breathe smells of powder. Don't you think so, sir?"

"No, I think it smells of cheese."

"By the bye, there's a basket of cheese for that foreign gentleman who lives at Virginia Water. Jump up, boy, and move that basket of cheese from here."

We arrived at Wimbledon Common, and stopped to take up parcels and boxes, during which time the coachman pointed out to the old country gentleman with whom he had the argument, the window of the room where Cournet, the French officer of Marines, and the opponent of Barthélemy, who had just been hanged, died after the Windsor duel. He was saying that since Barthélemy had been hanged the house was no longer haunted, and that the pool of blood, which never could be washed out, had suddenly disappeared.

"Marvellous!" exclaimed the old gentleman; "I never heard anything like that in my life."

"No more did I," said our witty coachman, winking at me. The boy now called over the various parcels, and Cossack went off as fast as a cannon-ball. We made a few more stoppages at Englefield Green, to deliver several scolding letters and parcels from mistresses to their servants having charge of the summer abodes of wealthy merchants who reside in London during the winter. At one house, during the unloading of two or three boxes and a child's cradle, a tidy-looking girl, who was waiting till they were taken in, had opened her letter, over which she appeared very sulky. The coachman, perceiving this, said, smiling—"Any answer, Sally?"

"No!" said Sally. "Oh, yes; tell the old lady that I will not live with her any longer;" and the girl cried.

"What's the matter?" said the coachman.

"She's an old plague! there's my Harry of the 46th has not been here these four months, and she writes to say she hears that he comes every day."

"Of course not—how could he? he's been gone to the war with his regiment ever since last September."

Sally, crying still louder, and wiping her eyes with her apron, exclaimed, "Perhaps the poor fellow is killed by this time, and don't care a fig about me."

"Well, well, lass, never mind that; soldiers are used to it."

"Do you think I shall ever see him again, Mr. Coachman?"

"No doubt, my lass, but you must wait a little longer; and when he does come back, if he has distinguished, instead of extinguished, himself, he will have the Crimean medal, and perhaps be made a colonel—captain—general—marshal—or even a corporal; who knows? in these war times, every brave man has a chance."

"Thank you, Mr. Coachman, you make me very happy—I shan't cry any more."

"But, Sally, am I to tell your mistress what you said?"

"Oh, dear, no! because I should lose my place; they are not such bad people after all, and master is so very kind to me."

"I shall say nothing about it."

"Pray, say nothing."

"Pst, pst! now, my true blues, full speed for Virginia Water." In twenty minutes we were before the very picturesque inn called the "Wheatsheaf;" every living soul came out to welcome us, thinking some accident had happened. There was the landlord, landlady, thin and bulky barmaids, house and kitchen maid, cook, pot and post boy, and a number of customers.

"What has happened that you are so late today?" said the landlord to the coachman.

"Nothing particular, governor; only a trace broke, and we had to fetch another: besides, the roads are very slippery." To the barmaid—"Give us a light, girl, and a go of keep-me-warm."

"Don't believe him, sir," exclaimed an old lady, who, upon the sudden stoppage when the trace broke, had a quarrel with the coachman. In opening the window violently, she broke it in twenty pieces; popping her head, half of which was covered with snow, out of the window—"He is a perfect brute," said she; "he tried to upset us, and then would not move for above an hour at least—see the state I am in; is it not a great shame, a woman like me?"

"Well, madam," said the landlord, "why don't you shut the window?"

"What's the use of pulling it up?—it's broken in a thousand pieces, all through that nasty fellow!"

"I can assure you, madam, he bears a very good character with the gentry about here."

The coachman, lighting his short pipe, and coming near them, said, "Don't take notice of the old lady, she means no harm."

"Don't I, though! I say again, before everybody, you are a brute and a villain!"

"Go it, marm, go it," said he, getting up. "It's nothing new to me—my wife tells me that every day, which is partly the cause we have no family." The favourite horse language of the coachman was again heard—"Fly away to the assault like a set of Zouaves!" and in a few minutes nothing but a small black spot, resembling a fly crossing a sheet of paper, was seen running up the snow-covered hill which leads to the small village of Virginia Water.

I speedily joined the worthy and well-known landlord of the "Wheatsheaf"—Mr. Jennings, and his cheerful wife and barmaid; all of whom gave me a hearty country welcome, shaking my hands and arms in every direction *ad libitum*, in anticipation, no doubt, of my remembering them for a few days at all events. At the close of this gymnastic exercise, I requested them to give me some breakfast, in the small pavilion near the garden; also some pens, ink, and paper. My request was at once attended to.

"Do you intend to stay with us a few days, Mr. Soyer?" asked the landlord.

"No; I shall try and get back this evening, if possible—but tomorrow morning, at the latest. I only came to close a few pending accounts of my last summer's stay at your lovely Virginia Water, and am going to Paris for the Exhibition, having been offered the superintendence of a large establishment."

"But I hear that the Exhibition is postponed till next year."

"So it is; but this is to be quite a new building, and erected close to the Exhibition, if we can get permission granted."

"Good morning, sir; I shall see you before you leave. I am only going to the farm."

"Yes, you will."

I was sitting down to my breakfast, when, to my annoyance, as I had much business to transact, some one knocked at the door, and, without waiting for the reply, came in. It was the landlord, with a face full of anxiety and astonishment, his glasses raised to his forehead, a newspaper in his hand, and looking as serious as if he had just been married, or had lost one of his favourite pups. "I say, master," said he, "do you mean it?"

"Mean what, man?"

"But now, really! do you mean it?"

"I'm puzzled to know to what you allude. Is it about my trip to Paris?"

"Paris! no, that has nothing to do with the letter of yours I have just read in the *Times* of this day."—"Oh! now I understand you, and can easily account for your long face and evident astonishment."

"Now you understand me, don't you?"

"Of course I do."

"Well, allow me to tell you frankly that you are very foolish; you are not a military man, and have made the offer, it is true, very likely in a moment of enthusiasm; but plead any excuse you can to get out of it if you are sent for; remain where you are—'Good folks are scarce,' says the proverb."

"Thanks to the proverb first, and you afterwards," said I.

"And if you do go, it is a hundred to one against your returning."

"Many thanks for your frank advice; but I am determined to go, and if Government send for me, I wish to be ready at a day's notice; so sure I am that I can render some services to my fellow-creatures by so doing."

"I have no doubt you can—but you may catch the fever, or God knows what besides! Why, they are dying by fifties and sixties a day in the hospital at Scutari; look, here is the latest account, the names of the poor fellows defunct, and number of their regiments. There is no mistake in that."

"I am aware of all that; but mind you, my firm belief is, that no fruit falls from the tree to the ground till it is perfectly ripe; and I also believe that we are never gathered from this frivolous world till we are really wanted in the other."

"Such being your determination, it is no use talking any more about it; I only hope your health will not fail you, and that you will return and keep us alive as you did last year. I can assure you, your joyful dinner party, or 'feet shampeter,' as Mary the barmaid called it, and you used to say in French, was the talk of the country round. It is only three days ago that Colonel Cholmondely was inquiring after you, and asking whether you had left the neighbourhood."

"Ah, really! how is the Colonel?"

"He looks remarkably well, I assure you, and will be very glad to see you."

"When you see the Colonel, pray present my most sincere compliments."

"So I will."

"I'm off, but hope to see you this evening; goodbye, in case I do not." The days being short, and my business more complicated than I had anticipated, prevented my visiting my favourite summer spot, the *Paradis Champêtre* of England.*

I slept that evening at the Wheatsheaf; I had given orders to be called the next morning at day-break, and was crossing the avenue of lime trees leading to

---

* This spot is little known to the English in general, and to many who have travelled over the world; but as no such delightful place exists anywhere but in England, how can it possibly interest an Englishman? First of all, it is too close for the wealthy, and too far for the people, being six miles by coach from either Windsor or Staines. During the five months I spent there last summer, the greatest number of visitors I counted daily was about twenty or thirty round the lake, which is seven and a half miles in circumference. I should also observe that Louis Napoleon, being a man of great taste, has imitated it in the Bois de Bologne as nearly as possible; and by going there, every Englishman will have an idea of that which he possesses at home, without troubling himself, while in London, to go as far as Virginia Water.

the lake, in anticipation of witnessing, as I was wont of a summer's morning, its interminable sheet of silvery waters and green moss velvet banks, sprinkled with myriads of daisies—or stars of the fields—intermixed with golden cups, covered with pearly dew, bordered also by mountainous trees forming a formidable forest; the glittering Chinese fishing temple, Corinthian ruin, the flag floating on the castle tower, "Royal George" frigate and barks, the swans, and the music of thousands of birds with their notes of freedom so wild and full of nature. Alas! all my illusions were dispelled, as I could scarcely see a yard before me; a thick veil, caused by a severe white frost, seemed to monopolise and wrap in its virgin folds the beauty of this lovely spot. Though greatly disappointed, I was returning to the humble country inn with my soul filled by sublime reminiscences of that charming spot, worthy of the enchanted gardens of Armida, when a deformed and awkward-looking lout of a stableman, peeping from a clump of evergreens, thus accosted me:—"Will you take a red herring for breakfast, sir?"

I leave my readers to imagine the effect produced upon my then exalted imagination. Pushing him violently from me, "Away with you! unsociable and ill-timed Quasimodo!" I said. Having thus unceremoniously repulsed my evil genius, and being by that electric shock entirely deprived of my appetite, I ordered a post-chaise in lieu of breakfast, and in a short time was at the turnpike-gate adjoining the inn, waiting for change to pay the toll. It was then about ten minutes to eight o'clock.

In three-quarters of an hour the post-chaise took me to the railway station, and an hour after I was ascending my homely staircase, when the servant apprised me that many persons had called; some had left their cards, and a mounted groom had brought a letter, saying he would call at noon for an answer. Amongst the various letters I found upon my desk, I recognised one in the handwriting of the Duchess of Sutherland. It was as follows:—

The Duchess of Sutherland will be much pleased to see Monsieur Soyer at Stafford House at two o'clock this day; or ten tomorrow morning, if more convenient to Monsieur Soyer.
7th February, 1856.

I had scarcely read this letter, when a double knock was heard at the street door. It was the footman from Stafford House, sent for an answer. I at once informed him I was going to wait upon her Grace; but as he was there, he might say that, at two o'clock precisely, I would do myself the honour of attending at Stafford House. Concluding, naturally enough, that the summons had reference to my letter, I immediately began to reflect how I should explain the plan I intended to adopt, in case my services were required. In the first place, I had decided that the most important question of all would be the entire freedom of my actions when I arrived at Scutari. This, of course, could not be granted, unless the Government, impressed with the importance of the subject, thought proper to do so. The active part would easily develop itself to my free and experienced mind.

II

A SUMMONS TO STAFFORD HOUSE

AT ten minutes to two I entered the superb portico of Stafford House, and was shown to the ground-floor library by the Duke's piper, young Mackenzie. "Her Grace will be with you presently," said he. "Walk in, sir, and I will apprise the Duchess of your arrival; who, I am aware, is anxious to see you."

I thanked him for his politeness, and he left me alone. I had scarcely time to cast a glance of admiration upon one of the *chefs-d'œuvre* of Landseer, representing the juvenile Stafford family, when her Grace entered, followed by the Duke and Duchess of Argyle, the Marquis and Marchioness of Stafford, the Marquis of Kildare, Lord and Lady Blantyre, her brother, and the children—about eighteen in number—Lady Grosvenor, and others. The Duchess of Sutherland introduced me to the noble circle, and requested all to be seated, which request was at once complied with; and her Grace addressed me in these terms:—"Monsieur Soyer, we have read with deep interest your letter which has appeared in the *Times*, and I cannot but express my admiration of your noble devotion when any good can be effected, or the position of the suffering be relieved or ameliorated by your assistance. The results of your interference would be very important—and especially at the present time—in our hospitals at Scutari, and in the Crimea, where, in consequence of such unexpected calamities, all is in the greatest confusion. I shall also observe to you, that I am well aware this offer is not your *premier coup d'essai*, or first trial. But I should advise you to consider the matter well, in case the Government accept your services. Judging from the tenor of the letters I receive daily from various departments at Scutari, I can perceive great difficulties, of which you are perhaps not aware."

"Your Grace," I replied, "is extremely kind to initiate me into the true position of the case; and first of all, I beg to observe that, were there no great difficulties to surmount, I should not have offered my services. But will you permit me to set forth, in a few words, the plan I propose adopting if Government should honour me with their confidence?"

"Pray do," exclaimed several of the circle, especially the Duke of Argyle, close to whom I was seated. Looking at his watch, and addressing me, the Duke continued, "Pray, Mr. Soyer, give me a slight conception of your project, as I have only a few minutes to stay. The Council of the Ministry, of which I am a member, meet in about an hour, and I must be there. I should be very glad to submit your plans to them; it might greatly tend to their adoption."

"Very true; your Grace shall judge if they are practicable or not. First of all, I should beg the entire confidence of the Government relative to my actions concerning the culinary department of the hospitals—that is, that they should grant me the power of obtaining the necessary articles of food already in the hospitals, and other things which might require to be purchased by either the commissariat or purveyor's department, without the slightest delay, as the want of such power would tend to certain failure—which I wish to avoid; while the possession of their confidence will ensure success. I will then pledge my word to do everything in my power, and with the greatest economy, and, if possible, with the same quantity of provisions as at present allowed by Government, or even less, which would be a source of high gratification to me; and I sincerely hope to be able to do so after the inquiries I made this morning, previous to attending your Grace's appointment; for I perceive, in many instances, that too much is given of one thing, and not enough of another. Having, therefore, the power to vary the ingredients and quantity, as well as to change inferior provisions for better, when possible, will greatly assist me in my undertaking."

"I have no doubt," said her Grace, "that what you request will be granted without the least hesitation."

"My plan would also be, never to act without the sanction of the doctor-in-chief respecting the diets I mean to introduce; and I would not interfere in the slightest degree with any former department, or displace a man from his duty except for incapacity, insubordination, or bad conduct; for believe me, if I am sent to Scutari, I go with the intention of doing all the good I can, and simplifying my difficult undertaking in such a manner as to ensure success. I should also claim the power of being able to condemn inferior provisions, and to substitute better, always without deviating from any army contract which has been, or may be, made by the Government, as I do not mean to hold myself responsible for the purchase of any provisions or stores, but merely to give my approval or disapproval of them. Upon my arrival at Scutari, I propose at once to take two hundred patients, and diet them for a week or more, according to the doctor's approbation, and then gradually increase the number, till I have the whole under my direction, if approved of by the chief medical officer. Such is the plan I propose adopting, and I shall beg your Grace to give me your opinion upon it."

"The way you intend carrying out your plan seems very practicable."

"Well," said the Duke, addressing the Duchess of Sutherland, "you must excuse me leaving now, as I have but a short time to get to Downing Street. Mr. Soyer, I shall have much pleasure in submitting your plan to the Ministerial Council, and will report progress."

After the Duke's departure, a general conversation was opened upon the subject, and having exchanged a few words with Lord and Lady Blantyre and the Duchess of Sutherland, who kindly promised to acquaint me with the result, I withdrew, and left Stafford House. No sooner home, having obtained the correct ration-scale of provisions from Dr. Andrews's office, than I formed a very fair idea of what I could do for the best.

The next morning, February 11th, about ten o'clock, I received the following communication from her Grace:

The Duchess of Sutherland has just seen his Grace the Duke of Argyle, who has spoken to Lord Panmure upon the subject of Mr. Soyer's offer. She thinks Lord Panmure is willing to forward the humane and practical views of Mr. Soyer, and will see Mr. Soyer at the War Office tomorrow.

The Duchess wishes to have the pleasure of seeing Monsieur Soyer after his visit to Lord Panmure.

Upon receipt of this letter I immediately went, as desired, to the War Department to see Lord Panmure's private secretary, Mr. Ramsay, and inquire when and where I could see his lordship. The hearty reception I met with from that gentleman was a most favourable augury, and encouraged me to persist in the very precarious undertaking in which I was about to engage, although many friends and near relations strongly tried to prevent me from pursuing it, placing constantly before my eyes the most sinister pictures, which, I am proud to say, never for a moment altered my mind. Having but one object in view, I was determined to see only the best side of the medal, and chance the rest.

Mr. Ramsay having arranged my interview with Lord Panmure for the next morning, I then retired, thanking him much for his very kind and courteous reception. I went home to test a few samples of diets and aliments I had prepared from the soldiers' rations; placing the whole of them in small vases, well packed, I sent them to Stafford House, there to remain till my arrival. In about an hour I had a second interview with the Duchess of Sutherland and a number of her noble family. After speaking of my visit to the War Office, and my appointment with his lordship for the morning,

"Lord Blantyre," the Duchess said, "has some business at the War Department today, and I shall trouble his lordship to remit another letter from me on the subject to Lord Panmure, who has, at the present time, so much to do that it is likely your interview might be postponed for another day."

"I can assure your Grace that the extreme interest you take in my behalf appears to me a good omen, assuring me of success, in case I should be sent to the seat of war. I would also observe that, being well aware of the value of Lord Panmure's time, in a few minutes I shall be able to unfold my plan, and he will no doubt at once perceive whether it is practicable or not, and will give me a decided answer; therefore, to lose time, on either side, would be impolitic. But, before I leave, will your Grace honour me by inspecting a few samples of hospital diets which I have prepared as a test, from the rations as at present given to the soldiers? They will form part of my new system, if approved by the medical officers."

"Have you some here, Mr. Soyer?"

"Yes, your Grace, I have; one of the footmen has taken charge of them till required."

The order having been given, a footman entered with the samples on a plateau, with spoons &c., which were tasted by the select and noble party, who at once pronounced them very palatable, and to which I remarked, that through the nature of the ingredients they could not fail to be nutritious and light.

"It is to be regretted," I said, "that the cooks in many hospitals are not allowed to put the seasoning in the savoury diets, which restriction will invariably produce very unsatisfactory results. I will here repeat the saying of Hippocrates:—'What pleases the palate nourishes.' If this great man has said so, it is a pity that some of his modern disciples have altered or deviated from such an ancient and just maxim, for I will vouch that a diet properly seasoned is far more generous and invigorating to the patient than the unpalatable food prepared without anything of the sort; at the same time many maladies will require various degrees of seasoning, as too much in some cases would prove equally if not more injurious than the want of it in others. This point must be left to the doctor's discretion. I am also aware that in some hospitals salt and pepper are allowed, and, I may say, too abundantly; and each patient is permitted to season his food, not according to his taste, but his judgment: this is another evil, as he is or may be at the time entirely deprived of either taste or judgment. These remarks will be the first I shall submit to the notice of the principal doctor, and I am morally certain he will agree with me as soon as they are properly explained."

"A most important observation," said the Duchess; "for, even when in the enjoyment of good health, what is more disagreeable than an insipid dish?"

"I have always, madame, maintained that the cook must season for guests or patients, and not these for the cook."

"In fact," said I to the Marquis of Stafford, who had tasted several of the samples, "does not your lordship opine that salt and pepper should be almost excluded from the ward, and that the cook should be as responsible for seasoning the food as the apothecary is for making up the doctor's prescription correctly?"

"Certainly; but can you persuade them to do so?"

"Very easily; by my system of diet, every recipe will be printed, framed, and hung up in the kitchen, so that any person, even a soldier (provided he can read), will be capable of executing them well, as each receipt will be comprised in a few lines."

"Ah! that will, indeed, be most valuable, and readily applied in every hospital."

During this conversation, the Duchess of Sutherland and the Marquis of Stafford had tasted another kind of food which I had made for the camp. It was prepared from peas-meal, in which I had introduced a due proportion of salt and pepper,—called "Symon's ground baked peas-meal,"—and by pouring a pint of boiling water upon a good tablespoonful of it, made a most excellent and thick purée of peas quite hot. I one day, as a trial, ate nothing but that and a biscuit, and did not feel the least inclined for anything else. I do not mean to imply that such fare would do for a continuance, but when nothing else could be obtained, it certainly would be a great comfort for the troops to get a hot meal, made in a few minutes, and without trouble. All present tasted this, and expressed themselves very favourably about it. Having also left some samples of coffee, I was retiring, when the Duchess of Sutherland kindly reminded me that she should be happy to see me the morning after my interview with the Minister-at-War. Of course I should not have failed in presenting myself, even without this kind invitation.

III

OFF TO THE WAR

At nine o'clock next morning I was at the War Office by appointment. Lord Panmure arrived at half-past, and by the kindness of Mr. Ramsay, who had mentioned my arrival, I was immediately introduced and most cordially received. After a few words on my part, as I had not had the pleasure of seeing Lord Panmure since I left the Reform Club, he inquired what I proposed doing in respect to the cooking department of Scutari Hospital. Stating briefly that which I had previously explained in detail to the Duke of Argyle when at Stafford House, and with which Lord Panmure seemed to be perfectly acquainted, he said to me,—

"You must, after you have done there, go to the Crimea, and cheer up those brave fellows in the camp;—see what you can do! Your joyful countenance will do them good, Soyer; try to teach them to make the best of their rations!"

I then observed that, first of all, I must try and succeed in the hospitals; secondly, that, if the troops in the Crimea had the same small tin camp-kettle I had seen in the camp at Chobham, it would be impossible for me to improve their style of cooking, as they were much too small, and burnt too much fuel, more especially in the open air.

"Well," said Lord Panmure, "can you substitute anything more applicable for the camp, and which can be easily carried with the regiments while on [the] march?"

"I will set my head to work and try, and if any plan which I consider practicable strikes me, I will have a model of it made, and submit the same for your lordship's approval."

"Well, do."

"With reference to the hospital at Scutari, I believe that is a permanent building, situated near a large metropolis, full of resources, and I have nothing to risk going there and setting to work immediately. I shall start in the full conviction of being able to do some good, if your lordship honours me with your full confidence and grants me the power of acting according to my own judgment in a profession which I have successfully practised for upwards of twenty years."

"Very good, Soyer! I shall give orders to that effect, and furnish you with letters of introduction to every department."

"Now, I hope you will do me the honour of accepting my services as I offered them, through the medium of the public press; such acceptance on the part of your lordship will, I can assure you, much facilitate the progress of my undertaking."

"I understand your meaning, Mr. Soyer; but I must make some arrangement for your expenses."

"Those, of course, I shall accept, or I should be giving offence to your lordship as well as the Government; more especially as I am, after visiting Scutari, to proceed to the Crimea."

"Well, tell me when you can start,—the mail leaves at noon tomorrow."

"I should be most happy to leave tomorrow, but previous to my departure for so long and unexpected a journey, I have some important private affairs to settle; it will therefore be impossible."

"Ah, truly! then I leave it to you, Soyer; but the sooner you go the better."

"Your lordship may depend upon my anxiety and promptitude; not a day, or even a minute shall be lost."

"Fare you well, Soyer; come and see me before your departure."

"Of course I will; but, begging your pardon, to whom shall I address myself for any further information I may require?"

"To myself, and no one else," was Lord Panmure's reply.

"I should be sorry to interrupt you in the incessant business you have from morning till night."

"My secretary, Mr. Ramsay, will always be here; but do not hesitate, if you require it, to see me."

"I certainly will not."

After a few words with Mr. Ramsay upon the subject of my interview, and what was decided upon, I immediately went to inform the Duchess of Sutherland of the result of my visit, at which her Grace expressed her gratification, and requested me to call again prior to my departure for the East, stating that she would give me some important letters of introduction to persons at Scutari, which would be most useful to me. After promising to do this, I retired. My intention was then to pay a visit to the Duke of Cambridge, who at that time took great interest in the subject, he having lately visited the hospital at Scutari, and made important observations upon the system of cooking carried on there.

As I was on my way to St. James's Palace, I met his Highness, accompanied by the Honourable James Macdonald, leaving the house; and having paid my respects, he inquired if I was going to Scutari, to which I replied in the affirmative. In a few words I gave him the result of my interview with Lord Panmure, and also spoke of the warm interest the Duchess of Sutherland took in the subject.

"Yes, I am aware of it," said he. "I had the pleasure of seeing her Grace yesterday." I then made a few inquiries respecting the state of the hospitals there, which his highness very kindly described to me.

The Duke remarked—"Your friend Comte will be able to give you all the information you may require, as he was with me at Scutari, and saw all the kitchen department in detail."

"Many thanks, your highness; I shall do myself the pleasure of paying him an early visit."

Five minutes after I was with my friend Comte, the Duke of Cambridge's *chef de cuisine*, who kindly initiated me into all the doings, both in the camp and in the hospitals on the Bosphorus. This information was of great service to me.*

Upon leaving my friend I hastily returned home, intending to draw out the plan of a model for a portable camp or field stove, which could also be applied to the use

* I have since learned that this gentleman during the campaign did so much good, and was so earnest in his endeavours to relieve the sufferings of the wounded at the battle of Inkermann, the allied as well as the Russian troops, that I intend to devote a page of this work to him, and also mention the names of the generals and others who spoke in such high terms of his exertions.

of the hospitals. Having heard that no regular kitchens had been established there, I was anxious to have a simple apparatus to take out with me of which I understood the working, and which might be put in action immediately on my arrival. In a very short time I hit upon an idea which I thought could be easily carried out, and would answer perfectly. Losing no time, I jumped into a cab and immediately drove to the eminent gas engineers and stove makers, Messrs. Smith and Phillips, of Snow Hill. On submitting my plan to those scientific gentlemen, they pronounced it practicable, and promised me a model, one inch to the foot, to be ready in a day or two.

Although the snow was falling heavily, I paid an early visit to Lord Shaftesbury, to whom I had the honour of being permitted to dedicate my last work—the "Cookery for the People."

His lordship gave me a most cordial reception, and was much pleased to hear of my intention of going to the East. Lord Shaftesbury made several useful observations respecting the importance of my mission. I bade him adieu. His lordship kindly wished me all the success I could desire, and said that he should be happy to hear of my proceedings, of which I promised to inform him a short time after my arrival.

As I had a letter of introduction from Mr. Ramsay to Dr. Andrews, I proceeded to that gentleman's office, where I found several medical gentlemen waiting, with some of whom I had the pleasure of being acquainted. Others were engaged testing samples of preserved milk in glasses; and having asked me to test some, I selected one which they all agreed was the best: I believe it turned out to be Gamble's preserved* milk, in tins. My letter of introduction having been given to the doctor, I had an immediate interview.

After listening to my few inquiries, he kindly wrote me a letter of introduction to Dr. Cumming, the superintendent at Scutari, and all the hospitals on the Bosphorus, promising me his support, and requesting that I might have all I required in my department upon application to the purveyor. He then put me in communication with a gentleman in charge of the stores, who would give me all the information respecting the kitchen utensils then in use in the hospitals. Having taken notes of everything, I retired perfectly satisfied with the important information I had gathered in so short a time.

I was well aware of the multiplicity of business daily transacted by the doctor, and the difficulty of obtaining a private interview with him, even on business, as one of the assistant porters told me when I called early one morning, that I might call till doomsday, and not be able to see him. This, of course, I took for granted, as no doubt the doctor would upon this solemn occasion be more engaged than ever. I must, however, observe that he at first took me for a merchant who had been for several years trying to persuade the English faculty to sanction or adopt the use of leeches to the same extent as is done in France. Not much flattered by the comparison, I wished him better manners for the future.

"I beg your pardon, sir; but not being on the military list, I did not know you. Why didn't you tell me you was Monseer Soyewere, then I should have knowed you? Of course, everybody knows you in England, Ireland, Wales, and Scotland."

"Well, never mind; but did I not give you my card?"

"Of course you did; but I could not make out the name of So-ye-were from five

* Evaporated milk—AB

such letters as that," said he, showing my card to some one present. "Soyer! surely that never can be So-ye-were!"

"You spell and write admirably. Thank you for the wrinkle. I shall have my card altered."

I told the cabman to drive me to the residence of Mr. Stafford, M.P., at whose chambers I had the day before left a letter of introduction from the Duchess of Sutherland. I had the pleasure of a very interesting interview with that gentleman, who had then just returned from Scutari. Having given me the necessary details of what was most required, and about the number of assistants I should take with me to ensure immediate success, he promised to furnish me with several letters of introduction, if I would send or call for them before my departure.

"I shall, certainly," said I, "much prefer calling, were it only to have the advantage of a little more of your valuable information upon any subject which may strike you after my departure; and I thank you for your kind and valuable suggestions."

"When do you think of starting?"

"In a couple of days at the latest."

"Very well; the letters shall be ready without fail, and two or three small parcels, which you will be kind enough to deliver for me—one especially for Miss Nightingale, rather fragile, and which I cannot send by post."

"I shall be most happy; jusqu'au plaisir de vous revoir."

I devoted the rest of that day to my private affairs, packing, and paying farewell visits. The next morning, at half-past nine, Messrs. Smith and Phillips, according to promise, brought me a most beautiful small model of the field stove, which they warranted first-rate, and to be capable of working in or out of doors, and in all weathers. I immediately proceeded to the War Office, to show the model, and explain the principle to Lord Panmure. In the waiting-room I had the honour of meeting the Duke of Cambridge, which gave me an excellent opportunity of explaining its merits. The Duke appeared to approve of it, and particularly noticed the great economy of fuel consequent upon the construction and smallness of the furnace. The Duke made some important remarks, and gave me a few hints upon the cooking regulations both in the hospitals and in the camps. These I took note of, and after explaining my plan of transport, I was quite delighted at having had such an opportunity of conversing with the Duke on a subject in which I was aware he felt particular interest. Mr. Ramsay, the secretary, having sent for me, I quitted the Duke; and, before leaving, I informed him that I had seen my friend Comte, and that he had given me all the assistance in his power, and had also told me that his highness had presented the hospital with a very nice *petite batterie de cuisine*, which, no doubt, I should find very useful upon my arrival.

"Adieu, Monsieur Soyer, I wish you well, and hope you will succeed."

On reaching Mr. Ramsay's office, that gentleman kindly informed me that if I wished to see Lord Panmure I had better wait till he went to take his luncheon. I then stated that my object was to show his lordship the model of a stove I had invented for the use both of the hospitals and the army.

"Walk into the next room; Lord Panmure will be there in a few minutes, and you will have plenty of time to show it without interfering with his business."

I had not waited ten minutes before Lord Panmure came in alone.

"Ah, Mr. Soyer, what have you there?"

"The model of a stove I wish to submit to your lordship. It is one which will, I believe, suit admirably for cooking both in and out of doors."

After closely examining it, and listening to the details I had previously given to the Duke of Cambridge, Lord Panmure approved of it, and requested me to have another made, which he might keep by him for inspection.

He then inquired how many cooks I should take with me.

"Only a few from Paris," I replied, "as I wish to make a trial before engaging many people; besides, I hope to be able, in a very short time, to instruct the soldiers, who, being under discipline, might prove as useful as any cooks."

Lord Panmure seemed pleased at my anxiety to instruct the soldiers; and, as he very justly remarked—"We want them to learn how to cook their rations to the best advantage, and that your instructions should remain for ever among them. Well, I have settled all you wished me to do; and my secretary, Mr. Ramsay, will remit you all the letters you require. When do you think of starting?"

"By the next mail."

"Well!" said his lordship, shaking me heartily by the hand, "Goodbye, if I do not see you again before your departure."

"It would only be troubling you; I therefore beg to take this opportunity of thanking your lordship for the kind reception and encouragement I have received, and, still more, for the confidence with which you have honoured me. I assure you that it will cause me to be most careful and economical, and it will be my pride to improve the diet without increasing the expense to Government. This may not be effected at first; but when the system is once introduced, and fairly established, I will answer for both a great amelioration as well as a saving."

"I am confident, Soyer, that you will do your best."

"Your lordship may depend upon me for that, were it only for my own sake."

"Well, write as soon as you arrive, and let us know how you get on."

Upon leaving, I met Mr. Ramsay, and related to him *verbatim* what had passed between Lord Panmure and myself. I then showed him the model, which he understood perfectly well, and gave me the engineer, Mr. Brunel's, address. I called upon that gentleman, and had the pleasure of an interview. He at once gave his full and entire approval of the principle, saying, "You really come at a most propitious time; Dr. Mayne and myself are actually busily engaged discussing a plan for establishing kitchens in the Smyrna hospital. Yours will answer very well, and assist us materially, as it is always a tedious department to construct in order to be effective, and work properly. No doubt they will be applicable to every public institution; besides, what a small quantity of fuel they must consume."

"Very little, indeed; and with this simple regulator you may manage the ebullition to a nicety, even in the open air. I shall also beg to remark, that they will be made of a beautiful metal, that will never require tinning; and the whole, though light in weight, will be extremely strong, and will last several years without needing repairs, or, at least, very trifling ones, that will not interfere with their use for a single day. They will take up but little room, and may be easily kept clean. No bricks are required, no chimney to be swept, and they can be as easily removed as any piece of furniture in your room."

"You are perfectly right; and I give you my candid opinion, they are the very stoves required for the purpose. I should like Dr. Mayne to see it; if you can, call as you go to the War Office, and show him the model. I can then speak with him upon the subject."

"With the greatest of pleasure."

As Dr. Mayne had not arrived when I called, I went and fetched a passport for myself, and one for my secretary. Upon my return, the doctor had examined the model, and seemed much pleased, saying—"It will answer very well." I left the address of the manufacturers with him, and then retired. They were immediately adopted both at Smyrna, and later at Rankioi.

A gentleman present, who seemed to have taken a great deal of interest in our descriptive conversation, followed me to the door, and, in a low voice, asked if I had taken out a patent.

"No, I have not; but I shall put my name and label upon them."

"Well, if you were to take out a patent, you would make a fortune."

"You may be right; but upon such an occasion I should fancy myself wrong. I will therefore give it, *pro bono publico*. I am well aware that by making it more complete I could take out either registration or patent, but I would not do that for the world; as it would be immediately reported that I expected to be repaid for my services by the profits of the patent of the stove, and upon these grounds I decline any such proceeding."

As it was then about three o'clock, I went, by appointment, to Sir Benjamin Hawes's office to bid that gentleman adieu, and to receive his final orders, showing him at the same time the model, which he seemed to appreciate thoroughly. He gave me the best advice, and promised me his powerful support throughout my culinary campaign. In return, I engaged to communicate all my movements, and retired.

At noon, next day, I again called at Stafford House, "not by appointment." On being informed of my visit, the Duchess at once favoured me with an audience. "I am come," said I, "to announce my departure. I wish, ere I leave tomorrow, to thank your Grace, and to show you the model of my new stove which I mean to introduce into the hospital kitchens."

"Ah!" exclaimed her Grace, "I must go and fetch the Duke. He will be highly pleased with it, and he wished very much to see you before your departure."

The Duke soon entered the great hall, with a large party, to whom I explained the principle, as I had before done to the Duke of Cambridge. I also stated that the day previous I had had the honour of showing it to Lord Panmure, and Mr. Brunel, the celebrated engineer, all of whom were much pleased with its efficacy, simplicity, and economy; more especially Mr. Brunel, who so highly appreciated the principle of its construction, that he at once adopted it, and applied it to the hospital kitchens at Smyrna and Rankioi, which he was there about to fit up.

The Duke made many remarks respecting the simplicity of its construction and the immense economy of fuel, "the transport of which," I observed, "was so extremely difficult and costly." I also remarked that one stove might be placed in a tent or hut containing fifty or sixty men; and they could cook there without the smallest inconvenience or difficulty, while it would throw out sufficient heat, "being in use nearly all day, viz., for breakfast, dinner, and tea," to warm the hut in winter, while in summer it might be turned out of doors.

Having been complimented by all present, I was about to retire, when the

Duchess observed that she had written several letters of introduction for me. "Among the number," said her Grace, "you will find one for Miss Nightingale."

I returned my sincere thanks to all present, and in particular to the Duke and Duchess. I assured them that the kindness and great encouragement I had received from them would be for ever engraved in my memory. The Duke remarked that he was very glad to see me in such high spirits. I acknowledged this with a bow.

"But, Mr. Soyer, suppose you should be taken ill?" said the Duchess.

"Well, your Grace—*cela est à la volonté de Dieu*—at present I am happy to say I have not any fears on that head, and am quite resigned to whatever Providence may dictate. Once more I beg to reiterate my feelings of gratitude, and bid your Grace and your illustrious family adieu."

As it was nearly one o'clock, I called upon Mr. Ramsay, who had all my letters ready. He did me the honour to introduce me to General Vivian, of the Turkish Contingent, and his brother, Captain Ramsay, the general's aide-de-camp. Anticipating the pleasure of meeting those gentlemen in the East, I departed with the best wishes of all.

Mr. Ramsay gave me a letter for the Honourable Mrs. Herbert, to whom I was anxious to pay a visit, well aware of the important information I could gather from that benevolent lady, who was in constant communication with the hospitals in the East, and also with Miss Nightingale. I was very kindly received; but, instead of giving me an encouraging prospect of success, that lady very candidly informed me that the number of letters she daily received were most unsatisfactory, and that she did not think it possible for me to restore order in the cooking department at the great barrack hospital. "The difficulties you will encounter," said she, "are incalculable."

"So I anticipate," was my reply; "but I must observe, that I love difficulties, in order to surmount them. And with the power so graciously conferred upon me by Lord Panmure, I cannot fail to do some good, if my health does not fail me."

"I hope," said Mrs. Herbert, "you will succeed, and shall be happy to hear of an amelioration. When do you think of going?"

"Tomorrow." Bidding her adieu, and thanking her for her kind reception, I retired.

On reaching home, I found the promised letters from Mr. Stafford, all my luggage packed, and was on the point of starting, when I learned that the gentleman who was going with me as secretary, and had his passport ready, declined to accompany me. His relations and friends had persuaded him not to go, the fever being so bad there, and so many deaths occurring daily. I was thus placed in an awkward position, and was, moreover, pestered at home by intrusive visitors, and no end of ridiculous letters. I thought of starting alone; but, upon reflection, I decided upon passing the evening at the Adelaide Hotel, at London Bridge, and in the morning looking out for another party; thus, to my great annoyance, losing another day. To start alone without a first-class companion for so long a journey was a sad affair. I must observe that I had previously engaged two young men, at high wages, as cooks, one of whom declined going to Scutari, but did not mind the Crimea; the other fell ill. Thus, my prospects on the eve of my departure were anything but favourable.

Next morning, while driving along Piccadilly, I met a friend, who, in congratulating me upon my proposed journey, and wishing me success in my undertaking, said, "So Mr. L—— is going with you as secretary, is he not?"

"No, he is not! he has left me in the lurch at the last minute; and, my dear fellow, I can tell you what, there is a chance for you—it is only for two or three months—you will be well paid, and all expenses defrayed."

"It is very kind of you to make me the offer," he replied; "but I cannot leave my business at a minute's notice. How long could you give me to prepare?"

"Oh! I am off this evening by the mail."

"I have no clothes ready for travelling."

"Never mind that; you can get all you require in Paris, where I shall remain two days upon business."

"Indeed! then in two hours I will give you a decided answer."

At the expiration of that time my friend made his appearance. We drew up an agreement, got his passport, and started the same evening; but not on the sly, as I had anticipated. Having forgotten to warn T. G. not to mention the fact of our intended journey, he had called upon several of his friends, with some of whom I was acquainted, and to my surprise, when I reached the station, I found about twenty assembled to bid us farewell. If I mention this circumstance, it is only to have an opportunity of publicly thanking those gentlemen for their hearty farewell, and three cheers—the echo of which still vibrates in my heart, and was through the whole of my culinary campaign a high source of gratification to my feelings. That night we slept at the Pavilion Hotel, Folkestone.

IV

DELIGHTS OF TRAVEL

THE Boulogne steamer was to start at half-past seven in the morning; the weather was anything but favourable, as rain was falling in torrents, and a thick fog coming on. T. G. and myself were ready to start, when a sad adventure occurred—my pocket-book, containing the best part of my cash and my official letters, was not to be found.* As I recollected having put it safely in the side pocket of my great coat before leaving the Adelaide Hotel, I feared that during the journey (owing to the fatigues of the day I had slept some time in the train) it might have been abstracted from my pocket.

After hunting in vain all about the room, I informed Mr. Giovanni and Mr. Brydes, the landlord of the hotel, of my loss, and those gentlemen immediately instituted inquiries. The news was soon known all through the hotel, and the crier was ordered to go round the town. I also dispatched T. G. to London Bridge house, where I had been surrounded by a number of friends. While making a last search in the room, by accident I shook the heavy wooden frame of the bed, from which everything had been removed—bedding, beds, and all, but without success—to my astonishment and delight, I heard something fall. It was my lost pocket-book. I had thrown my great coat over me in the night (the weather being cold), and the book had worked its way out, and got between the frame of the bedstead and the wall. Upon this discovery I immediately telegraphed for T. G. to return, in these words: "Stop a gentleman of colour—it's all right."

On the arrival of the train at Tonbridge, the cry of "Stop the gentleman of colour" was loudly shouted along the station. "All right, all right," cried T. G.; "here I am." He immediately jumped into the special down train, and arrived time enough to save the steamer.

The *quid pro quo* of passengers as well as railway employés was, that the thief had been captured, and it served him right. I heard afterwards this was the exclamation of many at the time.

T. G.'s devotion was certainly not repaid, but, when explained at the hotel, the incident caused great mirth. This was our first tribulation, which, though unpleasant, had the merit of being the first germ of excitement.

The same morning, in a rough sea and heavy rain, we sailed for Boulogne-sur-Mer. The steamer was very much crowded with Crimean passengers, and almost everyone paid the usual nautical debt to Neptune, looking more or less uninteresting. The beauty of the female part of the passengers had faded, and nothing but pale, livid faces remained, in place of the blooming, peachlike countenances. A very thick fog came on, and the speed of the steamer was of course checked.

* I had bought a cash-belt, but upon trying it, on the point of our departure, I found it too short. This circumstance caused me to place everything in my pocket-book.

We progressed slowly through the opaque atmosphere and heavy rain. After we had made all the signals required, the steam-whistle was heard, and we found ourselves going ahead towards the round tower on the right hand side of the port, the sight of which seemed to astonish the crew of the vessel, and more so one of the passengers, an old gentleman, who exclaimed, "We are in the same position as the *Amphitrite*, which was wrecked in 1833, when above two hundred souls perished. A fisherman named Pierre Hénin distinguished himself so greatly on that occasion, that he was decorated by both countries—France and England."

I observed, that the sea must have been about three times as rough at that time, and it was to be hoped, in case of danger, we should meet with several Pierre Hénins. However, by backing for about twenty minutes, and the fog clearing off by degrees, we arrived safely, but too late for the train. The jetty was rather crowded for that time of the year. Our delay and the fog had rendered our passage interesting—rather more so than pleasant. My intention was to take the first train, when, on reaching the jetty, who should I perceive but my friend M. Léon, the Emperor's first valet-de-chambre, one of the persons that have been longest employed about his Majesty's person, having been with him above sixteen years. He is much esteemed by his imperial master, none but himself approaching his person while in his private apartment. It is M. Léon who sleeps before door of his illustrious master's chamber while travelling, as the Mamelouk Roustan did before that of Napoleon the First. "Hollo!" he exclaimed, "are you here, my dear friend?"

"Yes, I am. What brings you here at this season?—And where is his Majesty?" said I.

"You may depend upon it," he replied, "that if the Emperor were not here, I should not be at Boulogne; but we have only come for a few days. The Emperor is going to attend a review tomorrow. I hear you are going to the Crimea."

"Yes, I am."

"So we saw by the newspapers, and the Emperor was much pleased to hear it, and expressed his satisfaction by no doubt thinking it was an excellent idea for you to be sent over there. When do you start?"

"Almost directly," I replied.

"Stay here tonight. I will tell the Emperor you are here. Come and sup with me this evening."

"Thank you, I will." We then parted; I sending some of my attendants on to Paris. The implacable douaniers then commenced their perilous sport; and although, thanks to a friend of mine, I had an official passport from the French Embassy, signed by Count Walewski, two of my boxes containing my Shilling Cookery Books were confiscated till the next morning, but eventually allowed to pass free of duty, but not of trouble, and would have been the cause of my losing a day for nothing, had it not been that we were too late for the train. At ten minutes to seven o'clock, through a very heavy rain and a brisk gale, we arrived at the "Grand Hôtel du Pavillon," which had just been finished, and was inhabited for the first time. This hotel is situated about five hundred yards from the Etablissement des Bains, at the foot of the bank, on the right hand side of that establishment. Any person who has visited Boulogne must be acquainted with the spot. It is rather remarkable that soon after the arrival of the Emperor—in fact, he only just had time to dress after his journey—an avalanche of earth fell from the top of the bank, shaking the very foundations of the hotel. At the back of the house the earth reached higher than the second floor, breaking the windows. Some of the *débris* actually fell into the Emperor's dressing-room, only a few minutes after he had left it. The slip of earth was supposed to have been caused by the melting of the snow, which had lain there for some time, as well as the rain, which had been pouring down, night and day, for a week.

My friend was just sitting down to supper, when I joined them, it being then eight o'clock, *heure militaire*, punctuality being the motto in every department in the imperial household. Having introduced my secretary, T. G., the conversation turned upon the avalanche, then upon the *grand repas de corps*, as it is called in France, or military banquet, given that evening to the generals and officers of the Camp de Boulogne. But the most important part of the conversation was upon the contemplated departure of Napoleon for the East. He was to travel from Paris to Marseilles incog., with but very few of his suite. "Everything," said M. Léon, "is packed and ready, and we may start at an hour's notice. Your friend Benoit has already sent his *batterie de cuisine*, and a quantity of preserved provisions." (M. Benoit is the Emperor's *chef de cuisine*.)*

Whilst we were conversing, a footman entered, in a state of anxiety and excitement, and exclaimed—"There is not a single cigar, and the Emperor has asked for some."

"Very well," said the maître d'hôtel, "go and buy some." In about half an hour he returned with a square box, three parts full of various kinds of cigars, which he had no doubt purchased at all the nearest grocers' shops, clearing out their stock of *French* Havana cigars.

"Couldn't you get better ones than these?" said the maître d'hôtel.

"No doubt I could, but not near."

"Then, take them up." He despatched another servant to the Rue de l'Ecu for a box of good ones, which arrived too late. Owing to a most unexpected circumstance, the company only had the opportunity of partaking of a few of them, for they scarcely had time to light cigars, when a telegraphic dispatch arrived. My friend M. Léon told one of the attendants to go and see if his Majesty had left the banqueting-room, and if he was in his cabinet. While this was passing, I took the dispatch in my hand, and by way of a joke, said to him, "As France and England are now allied, and have the same policy, I have here an official English Government letter, which, if you like, I will exchange for your dispatch."

"It might be done," said he, laughing; "but, upon consideration, the Emperor would very likely prefer his own." The servant returned, and informed him that the Emperor was still at table. The dispatch remained about ten minutes longer near M. Léon, when they came and apprised him that Napoleon was in his cabinet. M. Léon went up with the dispatch, and in a few minutes returned, saying to me, "Do you know what the contents of the letter you wished to exchange for yours were?"

"Certainly not," I replied.

"The contents are, that the Emperor Nicholas is dead." Everyone was thunderstruck by the unexpected announcement, and we could hardly believe it. "If you

---

* That his Majesty was going early in March to the Crimea I can assert as a positive fact. Having met with many unbelievers on this subject in the Crimea is the cause of my relating this anecdote; and no doubt nothing but the following unexpected news could have prevented his majesty from following out his determination.

come up quickly, you will hear the Emperor himself announce it to the company in the banqueting-room."

We obeyed, but only arrived in time to hear the last words—"a cessé de vivre." Special orders were then given that no demonstration should be made, and a low and mournful conversational sound was alone heard amongst those assembled. A few minutes after leaving the imperial palace, a friend and myself were quietly taking our coffee at a celebrated establishment, and in conversation said loud enough to be heard by our neighbours, that certainly the death of the Emperor Nicholas was very likely to change the state of affairs, as the present Emperor, Alexander was, so we had always heard, rather a pacificator. Before we could finish the remark, an elderly gentleman, who was sitting near us, exclaimed, "What do you say? What do you say, sir?—the Emperor Nicholas dead?"

"Yes, sir, he is dead."

"Go to——, sir; that's another Crimean shave, like the taking of Sebastopol."

"Sir," I replied, "I can vouch for this not being a shave, and that his Majesty, the Emperor Nicholas the First of Russia, expired yesterday; and what is more, I will lay you a wager of it."

In a few minutes some jumped upon the chairs and benches, others upon the billiard-table, looking at me, no doubt anxious to see whether I was intoxicated or mad. One gentleman raising his voice, said, "I'll bet anything this report is not true."

"Done for a dozen of champagne."

"I take you, and we will drink your health at your own expense."

We scarcely had time to deposit our money with the lady who presided at the bar of the establishment when mine was again in my pocket. A number of officers who had returned from the banquet entered, and affirmed the truth of what I had stated. Nevertheless, no one could believe it; so I proposed returning my money to the stakeholder till the next morning, and turning the champagne into an early *déjeuner à la fourchette*.

At the custom-house the following morning I was detained, and reached twenty-five minutes behind the time appointed by my friend, and perhaps thereby lost the chance of a short interview with the Emperor, which made me bless the douaniers who were so long at their breakfast, and longer still in clearing my luggage. I found my friend M. Léon smoking his short pipe at the hotel door, with his hands in his *pantalon à la cosaque*, a type *de troupier* well worthy of the past and present empire; so I made sure his Majesty was off.

"Oh, here you are at last—a fine fellow truly, and very punctual indeed! Why, his Majesty has been gone this half-hour. I intimated you were still here, and he would probably have seen you; but mind, if you don't look sharp, we shall be at Constantinople before you. You are sure to see his Majesty there, for the first thing he will do will be to visit all the hospitals, both French and English."

"I am very glad to hear you say so, for the loss is on my side; but what can you do when you are in the hands of the authorities; if you recollect, the last time I was here, I fared worse, for I was locked up more than two hours for coming without a passport, fancying myself a true Briton, as they are allowed to land without any."

"Then you really expect to go?" I again asked.

"Nothing can be more certain, when I tell you that everything is ready for our departure. I much regret missing so excellent an opportunity. When do you leave?"

"This afternoon; our places are taken by telegraph at Marseilles through the War Office; and I shall only remain in Paris twenty-four hours, instead of two days, as I had anticipated."

Having related the scene at the café the previous evening, and invited him to the déjeuner, he declined attending it, on the ground that some unexpected news from Russia might cause his Majesty to return to Paris immediately.

"Do you mean to say," I exclaimed, "that you had not heard of the Emperor Nicholas being indisposed previous to the arrival of the dispatch which announced his death?"

"Oh, yes; we did hear last evening. This was the third dispatch we received yesterday, but we never dreamed of his dying till that one came."

"Well, many thanks for your kindness, my dear friend; and I hope to see you at Scutari soon. I shall pay you a visit there."

"Do," said he; "I understand we shall have one of the Sultan's palaces on the Bosphorus. Adieu!"

After the déjeuner, and a protracted journey to the Boulogne Camp, my friend and myself took the last train and arrived early in the morning at Paris. My first visit was to the military hospital of the Val de Grace, the Invalides, the Hôtel Dieu, &c. I was politely shown over each establishment by the authorities on duty, and took notes of all the ingredients used for the preparation of the daily diets of both officers and soldiers.

We started the same evening for Lyons, stayed a few hours there, and visited the military hospital at that place, and took the steamer to Avignon. On board we found the Smyrna ladies, about thirty in number, under the orders of Mrs. M. Cooke; there were also many doctors. I had seen them the day previous at the Hôtel des Princes, Rue Richelieu, but had not the slightest knowledge of who or what they were. As the ladies were all dressed in grey, I took them for Quakeresses upon a pilgrimage.

KITCHEN AT AJACCIO OF NAPOLEON THE FIRST.

V

COMFORT ON SHORE AND PENANCE AT SEA

ON arriving at Marseilles, I made inquiries at the station as to what provisions could be obtained for the army, if required. I bade my friends adieu, in hopes of having the pleasure of seeing them on board the next day, and in particular Mr. and Mrs. Cooke, who really took their duty to heart, and had a most difficult task to perform. After viewing all the *magasins* of Marseilles and its warehouses, I perceived that my countrymen, in the way of national business, were very little boys, who could hardly walk, when compared with English commercial men and the houses of Crosse and Blackwell, Fortnum and Mason, Hogarth, Gamble, &c. Having done my duty, so far as the victualling department was concerned, I found that with such a stock of provisions any Government might keep its army in a state of perfect *starvation*—should the French Government depend upon them—though at the same time the quantity and quality might have served very well for a dainty picnic of a couple of thousand epicures, the price also being so high.

Passing by the Bureau des Messageries Impériales, I called in to see about our places for the next day. I found an old friend, of fifteen years' standing at least, at the head of that department. "Ho! pardieu," said he, "I thought it was you, having seen several paragraphs respecting your departure for the Crimea. I was afraid at one time you would have gone by sea. I have two first cabin berths for you tomorrow; but as you are a very gallant man, you will not mind sleeping upon deck from here to Smyrna."

"Sleeping upon deck! what do you mean? My places have been taken this week past."

"I know that—I have two first-cabin berths for you. How many cooks and attendants have you got with you?"

"We are about eight in number."

"Oh, I can manage them then; although I assure you we are cramped everywhere."

"What do you mean by my sleeping upon deck?"

"Why, because if you don't, some of those ladies who are going to Smyrna must. Four of them must sleep upon deck, as all the places are taken; and I am sure you are too gallant to allow them to sleep in the open air while you remain snug in your cabin. Tell me, are you obliged to start with them?"

"Certainly not."

"Then, wait for the next boat; it will not make forty-eight hours' difference, and you will be very comfortable. You will go by Messina and Athens, and be there nearly as soon. Moreover, you will be rendering a great service to those ladies; besides, we should pack five or six persons in your cabin."

"Very well, transfer our places."

"The next vessel is quite new, and it will be her first voyage. She is most handsomely fitted up, and you will meet with capital company on board. All the first cabins are taken by English and French officers; you are sure to know some of them."

"Very well; at what time shall we be here?"

"Be ready the day after tomorrow, about three p.m., at the Hôtel d'Orient, where you are staying. I will send some men with a few cabs. Mind you have all your luggage ready."

"I will. Many thanks for your kindness."

The next day, after visiting several public institutions, I was very desirous to taste an excellent dish called the bouillabaisse, which is exclusively a Marseillaise dish, as turtle-soup and roast beef and plum-pudding are essentially English. I therefore invited a few friends to that far-famed place, the "Reserve." Among my guests, I had the pleasure of numbering a most eminent, amiable, and gallant gentleman, Captain Taunton, who, a few weeks previous, I heard, had the temerity to run his ship, the *Fury*, so close to the port of Sebastopol, that a round shot passed through her beam.

The Captain, my friend M. Giraldo, and myself, formed the trio of degustators of the Grand Provençale dish called the bouillabaisse, as well as another celebrated one called the olio. The first one I, with veneration and justice, recognised as worthy of being immortalized in the archives of cookery. The olio, like many of its companions, so admired by the Marseillais, is only to be appreciated by the inhabitants of that city, who must have sprung from a bed of garlic, instead of that more genteel and more sweetly-perfumed one, the parsley-bed—so well known to the juveniles, who are made to believe they were found ruralizing amidst that delicate aromatic plant.

The bouillabaisse pertains to Marseilles, as the whitebait to Greenwich and Blackwall. Even at Marseilles it is only at a few houses that you can get it in perfection, among which the celebrated "Restaurant de la Reserve" ranks as A1, and next, the "Grand Hôtel des Colonies."

After all, the "Reserve" is the principal place. This beautiful and picturesque restaurant, with its pavilion and slim turrets, is gracefully situated on the top of the high rock at the entrance of the old seaport. When required, the proprietor procures the particular fish alive, at the threshold of his door, and shell-fish required for the composition of this dainty dish.* In less than an hour—during which time we had partaken of a few small oysters, and some shell-fish peculiar to Marseilles— the bouillabaisse was upon the table, smoking hot, and perfuming the room with its aroma.

Although the bouillabaisse can be made with any kind of firm fish, in all countries, and at all seasons of the year, I should be deceiving my readers were I to say that it could be made in the same perfection as at Marseilles; nevertheless, it can be made good if the receipt is closely followed. The choice of fish for the purpose in England, although not as suitable as those of the Marseillaise coast, being of a different nature, will still produce an excellent, dainty dish.

Though this *petit déjeuner* was very *recherché*, the bouillabaisse threw all the accessory dishes into the shade. The landlord, who favoured us with his company

---

* A magnificent palace, dedicated to the Empress Eugénie, designed by the Emperor, is now in course of erection near the spot.

at dessert, informed me he made it himself; and at my request, favoured me with the receipt, and the names of the fish composing it.

I returned my best thanks for the condescension and trouble on his part in so doing.

"Ah, Monsieur Soyer," said he, "you may thank your name for that. I have often seen you mentioned in our papers, and should have been sorry if you had left our seaport without tasting our national dish in perfection." He observed, in handing it to me, "You are, of course, aware that this dish cannot be made except at a seaport."

"I am well aware of that fact," I answered, "and that this semi-soup and stew ought, by right, to be made at a seaport; nevertheless, the finest seaport I have ever seen in England, and I might say in the world, for fish, is London; therefore, my dear sir, give me the receipt, and I shall, no doubt, fish out the fish from a good quarter."

Original Receipt for the Bouillabaisse a la Marseillaise.

Before entering upon details, I will specify the different kinds of fish most applicable. They are of two classes: one acting as a mucilaginous agent, the other merely imparting the flavour; also an essential point. The first class comprises—whitings, loups or lupins, red mullets, soles, and turbots. The second—gurnets, boudroies or boudreuils, lobsters or crayfish, sea toads or rascasses, galinettes, limbers, lazagnes or lucrèces. These latter are plentiful in the Mediterranean seas.

As a general rule, this ragoût should be cooked in a stewpan, rather broad than deep, and of thin metal, in order to [assist] the ebullition proceeding quickly. Those in tin or thin iron are the most appropriate, as the concoction must be done in a few minutes, and with such rapidity that the liquor must be reduced to the necessary point by the time the fish is cooked. It should also be sent to table and eaten at once, as the shortest delay will cause the quality to deteriorate. The principal fish must be cut in pieces or slices sufficiently sized to serve each guest, the others being merely accessories.

Receipt.—Slice up two large onions, place them in a stewpan as before mentioned, wide but not deep, and of thin metal, add a few spoonfuls of olive oil, and fry the onions of a pale brown colour. Next, place the pieces of fish in the pan, cover them with warm water, but no more than the depth of the contents; add salt, "in moderation," half a bay leaf, the flesh of half a lemon, without pips or rind, two tomatoes cut in dice after extracting the seeds, a small tumbler of light white wine, a few peppercorns, and four cloves of garlic. Set on a fierce stove and boil for twelve minutes; by this time the liquor should be reduced to a third of its original quantity. Add a small portion of saffron, a tablespoonful of chopped parsley, allow it to boil a few seconds longer, taste, and correct the seasoning, if required, and remove from the fire.

During this process you should have prepared two dozen of slices of light French bread or penny roll, about half an inch in thickness, which place in a tureen or dish, pour over them some of the liquor from the ragoût, let it soak a minute or so, and again pour over in order to soak the top as well as the bottom of the layers of bread. Dish up separately the best pieces of fish with the remaining liquor, and serve.

The variation called Bourride, differs in this only, viz., the addition of seven or eight yolks of eggs to a good portion of the liquor, which is stirred quickly over the fire till of the consistence of a custard cream, and then poured upon the slices of bread, with the addition of a tablespoonful of eau d'ail, or aioli.

The eau d'ail or aioli is prepared by crushing several cloves of garlic, and saturating them with water; adding the requisite quantity to the bourride.

My reason for printing this receipt, although partly impracticable in England, is, that it is the original as given to me by the worthy host of the "Reserve," as so successfully made by him.

But as many of the fish required are not to be obtained in England, and the quantity of garlic used would be objectionable to an English palate, I beg to refer my readers to the Addenda for a Bouillabaisse à l'Anglaise, which possesses two great qualities:—firstly, to suit the palate of the *gourmet*; secondly, that of being very strengthening. The broth is very generous and wholesome for the invalid,—for the authenticity of which assertion I appeal to the faculty.

Giraldo now informed us it was past three o'clock, and that we must be on board by half-past six at latest. So shortly after, much to our regret, we left our worthy landlord and his sanctum of good cheer, and at half-past four left the Hôtel d'Orient to go on board the steamer, accompanied by the gallant Captain Taunton, Mr. Giraldo, and a few other friends.

Upon arriving at the docks, a most painful sight fell under our notice; it was indeed a spectacle calculated to pain the soul of the greatest philosopher. The quays round the harbour were thickly lined with sick and wounded. There were about seven or eight hundred, who had just been landed from two French steamers, one from Constantinople, the other from the Crimea. Some were placed upon straw, others upon bedding, until they could be removed to the hospital, according to the nature of their cases. Their appearance, I regret to say, was more than indescribable. All the afflictions so common to the fate of war seemed to have met and fallen at once upon those brave fellows, who, a few months previous, were the pride of their country. Many of them, to their sorrow, had not enjoyed a chance of facing the enemy; while those who were wounded looked joyful compared with those who were the victims of epidemics—typhus fever, diarrhœa, dysentery, cholera, or frost-bites. I conversed with several; not one complained, but merely regretted the friends who had died on the passage and those sick left behind, and bewailed that they had done so little for their country in the campaign. M. Giraldo, who had superintended the disembarkation, informed me that such scenes were of daily occurrence at Marseilles; adding, this must be very encouraging for you. Saying also in irony, "lend soldiers to the Turks—how well they thrive under the banner of Mahomet! Well, well, my dear sir, after all, this is nothing more than the fortune of war: 'à la guerre comme à la guerre'."

This was the first disastrous sight I witnessed in this great war, and though anything but encouraging, merely grated upon my sensibility, without in the least affecting my mind. I must say T. G. showed much firmness upon this solemn occasion, which firmness rather failed him afterwards.

At five we were on the deck of the *Simois*, the name of our vessel. It was her first trip, she having only arrived a few days previous from Liverpool. All on board was in great confusion; a part of the vessel had just taken fire, and the sailors were engaged putting it out, and cutting away the burning portions; however, it was soon extinguished. We then learnt that upon coming into dock she had met with serious damage, which they had scarcely had time to repair, and the painters were still on board busily employed varnishing the first cabin. I was next told that about four hundred troops, who were expected, had not arrived, and that we should start without them. A lady, who was standing by, exclaimed, "Oh, thank God for that! I cannot bear soldiers."

"I thought," I said, "it was a very bad job instead of a good one, as the vessel would be crank, through not being sufficiently loaded, and would in consequence roll very much."

The weather being reported very rough outside, we were in suspense as to whether we should leave that night or not. On a sudden the screw slowly commenced its revolutions, and propelled us, not without difficulty, from the narrow port to the wide ocean—passing amongst huge rocks, on the very summit of which the furious waves were breaking. The evening was fast advancing, and the vessel was already rolling very heavily. We soon made the rock of Monte Cristo, immortalized by Dumas. A yellowish sunset, piercing the heavy rain, faintly lighted the crest of this arid and uninhabitable spot. Shortly after, all was darkness, and many retired. Two or three remained till about ten o'clock, when the steward cheerfully informed us, that the weather was about the same as when the *Semillante* was lost ten days before, and not a soul escaped. Nearly five hundred troops, besides passengers and crew, were drowned.

"Was she bound eastward?" inquired a passenger.

"Yes, sir, she was; we are steering the same course, but there is another passage. I hope we shall get through before night tomorrow, and if the sea holds as rough as it is now, no doubt we shall take the other."

We all turned into our berths, laughing at his mournful tale. Before going, I said: "Believe me, steward, we are safer than ever, for you seldom hear of two accidents alike."

"Very true, sir; but this boat seems unlucky. I can't tell you all the mishaps we have had in her since I have been on board, and that is only one month." She was then rolling at a tremendous rate. At each plunge, a fearful noise was heard. Upon inquiry, some one on board informed me that he believed they had projectiles for ballast, and these were rolling and shifting at each plunge the steamer made. Such a cargo, though quite in harmony with the martial trip, was anything but pleasing. Everything rolled and tumbled about fearfully during the whole of the night. At length day broke, with a glowing sun and a heavy sea running mountains high; so much so, that it was dangerous to attempt the passage. Such must have been the case, as the mail-boats are not allowed to stop except in cases of extreme danger. Our careful commander gave orders to bring up in the Bay of Ajaccio. After sixteen hours' flirtation on the wild ocean, we entered this calm and peaceable port, much to the relief of all. We then collected round the table; and while partaking of a light lunch, we had time to become acquainted with each other. Among our *compagnons de voyage* were General Cannon, Captain Arbuckle, Colonel St. George, of the Artillery, Captain Ponsonby, Major Turner, Captain Gordon,—Murrogh, Esq.,—Ball, Esq., the Queen's Messenger, and three or four French officers, among whom was Captain Boucher, aide-de-camp to General Canrobert, and afterwards to General Bosquet. After some remarks upon our unfavourable start, we all blessed our stars for the shelter we were then enjoying in the peaceable harbour, so picturesquely surrounded by its beautiful *petite ville*, the cradle of the first Napoleon—Ajaccio—so well situated in that savage and energetic island of poetically ferocious heroism, habits, and eternal vendettas, so interesting to all since the revival of that illustrious dynasty in the person of Napoleon the Third.

All of course were anxious to visit this celebrated spot; and on inquiring of the commander, he told us he should sail the next morning early if the weather was more favourable. We formed ourselves into parties of five or six, and as it was only three o'clock, we had plenty of time before us: our greatest anxiety was to visit the house in which the great Napoleon was born. Our party arrived first, as we had a very clever guide, who promised if possible to introduce us to La Signora Grossetti, saying we should have a great treat, as the old lady, who was then eighty-three years of age, had been all her life in the Buonaparte family in Corsica. We luckily met the old lady just coming out, and upon being introduced, she immediately returned to do us the honours of the house. She has been housekeeper there for above thirty years. After visiting the apartments which are always on view—viz., the drawing-room, dining-room, concert and ball room, library, and the small bedroom in which that almost fabulous hero was born, I asked the old gentlewoman, as a special favour, to show me the kitchen. No one was ever more astonished than she appeared to be at my request. "Why, surely there is nothing to be seen there but ruins, and I don't even know where the key is."

All this redoubled my interest. We went upstairs, and found in an old drawer three rusty keys, which we brought down; one of them opened the door, which, on being pushed rather forcibly, fell from its hinges. We then descended, and opened the shutters, which likewise tumbled from their fastenings. After visiting the various departments which constitute a gentleman's kitchen, I wrote upon the stove the following letter to the public press, which, through the mismanagement of my servant, who threw it into the post without paying the postage, never reached its destination:—

Twenty Minutes in the Kitchen of the House of the Emperor Napoleon the First.

MR. EDITOR,—It is an incontestable truism that "It is an ill wind that blows nobody good;" but in this case it will be found the reverse. Owing to most terribly rough weather, in fourteen hours from our departure from Marseilles, *en route* to Constantinople, we are brought up here by our prudent Captain, sheltering us in the bosom of the harbour of Ajaccio, the birthplace of the alliance now existing between the two great nations of France and England. Such reminiscences of the first of the great Napoleon's family caused the shore to be invaded in a few minutes by the numerous passengers, particularly the distinguished military men of both nations. Many visited the Hôtel de Ville, full of objects of interest, reminding one of the late empire; others, the Letitia House; and some inquired, with great coolness, if it were possible to see either of the Corsican Brothers now in existence. In a very few minutes my curiosity was gratified by a cursory examination of the above-mentioned interesting subjects; and by a great deal of courtesy and perseverance, I obtained from La Signora Grossetti (who had been in the late Emperor's family from her infancy) the rusted key of the kitchen door of that interesting and now deserted domicile—such a request having never before been made by the numerous travellers who daily visit it.

And it is, Mr. Editor, while writing upon the stove in this celebrated kitchen—which first alimented the brain of that great hero—that I beg to address you the following few lines at random, as the weather bids fair and our departure is immediate. On my left hand is a well-constructed charcoal stove, containing six nine-inch square cooking-places, covered with glazed red tiles (a piece of which I have procured, and intend placing in my kitchen at Scutari); an oval one, about eighteen inches long by about six inches wide, on which the most delicious fish, game, meat, and poultry, were no doubt submitted to the highest perfection of the culinary art. At the spot at which I am now writing, the roasting by wood fire, and the broiling by red ashes, were carried on, as I perceive, by the remains of the hearth.

There is also the old Jack, with the pulley that supported the rope and weights. On my right is an old semi-circular oven, partly in ruins, with an old-fashioned wrought-iron door, in which no doubt the cakes and choice pastry were prepared to gratify the imperial infant's palate. Larders, confectionery, and all the requisite appointments of a kitchen are not wanting; which, though in a most dilapidated state, still left an appearance of grandeur which none but a family of distinction could afford—very different from what has been often reported and believed by the vulgar—viz., that this great man had his origin in the bosom of an indigent family.

With the highest consideration, believe me, Mr. Editor, yours very faithfully,

A. SOYER.

March 13, 1855.

The old lady seemed much pleased with the very extraordinary interest I took in the place, and proposed to show us her private apartment at the top of the house, which she assured us was full of reminiscences of the Emperor's childhood. His wooden armchair and desk, inkstand, and a few boy's toys—such as a small gun, soldiers, shako, &c.—are carefully preserved by the old and faithful servant of her illustrious master. Though of great age, she was very animated, and made all sorts of inquiries about the war, and if we had seen the present Emperor; having satisfied her curiosity, we retired, highly pleased with our visit to Ajaccio.

We were much indebted to La Signora Grossetti, who had really shown us things that no former traveller could boast of having seen. I could not part with the old dame without saluting her on both cheeks, which she very kindly returned, it being the custom of the country, as she said. This scene terminated, much to the surprise and enjoyment of my *compagnons de voyage*—Captain Gordon and Mr. Munro of the Ordnance, with several French officers—our interview with that kind and extraordinary lady.

I had taken (as I mentioned in my letter) a piece of tile from the charcoal stove, and a rough wooden meat-hook which I found in the larder, dating, as the Signora told me, from that epoch. Our time being short, and the night rapidly approaching, we re-embarked, and related, to the great delight of all, our amorous adventure with the nurse of the first Napoleon. All regretted not having been of our party. We spent a very charming evening on board, each one relating what he had seen. The Town Hall, I must observe, is very interesting, being filled with relics of the Buonaparte family, with full-length portraits of the father and mother of the Emperor. I was also much pleased at seeing one of the best statuettes of the late *arbiter elegantiarum*, the celebrated Count D'Orsay, given by him to the present Emperor for the town of Ajaccio. It is the well-known statuette of Napoleon the First on horseback; and in a frame beside it is the original letter of presentation written by the Count himself, which I can vouch for, "having many of his letters in my possession." The style is so charming, that I regret not having had time to take a copy.

Next morning, with a fresh breeze, bright sun, and a clear sky, we left this immortal and delightful spot, where avenues of orange trees, loaded with ripe fruit, ornament both sides of the streets; and at the same time, "by the bizarrerie of nature," the chain of mountains which surround this romantic spot are always covered with snow. In ten minutes we were again launched upon the wide ocean. Though the sea was not so rough, the waves dashed about furiously, and made the vessel roll even more than the day before. This is always the case after a gale. We were all much amused at the *restaurateur* of the steamer, who kept cursing everybody, because all his glass and crockery were smashed to pieces; and all because, as he declared, the vessel had started before she had been properly fitted up. The Captain, in trying to soothe him, drove him raving mad, and he commenced throwing overboard all the plates, dishes, and glass on which he could lay his hands. At length he caught hold of a leg of mutton, and was about to serve it in the same manner. I happened to be near him, and not quite approving of casting good victuals overboard while at sea, I took upon myself to object to this part of his proceedings. I was the more induced to do this because I had promised my illustrious *compagnons de voyage* to look after the cook and his cooking, with which he really took much pains, and gave us great satisfaction. The infuriated Marseillais poured a volley of the most foul language in his Provençal dialect, while he and I were holding the doomed leg of mutton. He then asked me who I was?

"A passenger," I replied; "and one who has a most decided objection to your feeding the fish—with legs of mutton," I continued, boldly. He then gave it up; and, in acknowledging he was in the wrong, exclaimed, at the top of his voice, "I wish you no harm, but I should be highly pleased if you and all in the steamer were at the bottom of the sea."

"Wherefore?"

"You ask me wherefore! Because I shall lose above a thousand francs."

"The directors will make that up," I said.

"Not a sou," said he.

The comical part of this scene was enhanced by the continual rolling of the ship.

This incident kept us alive till we reached Messina. The following letter, addressed to the *Illustrated London News*, will explain my subsequent proceedings:—

ACROPOLIS, ATHENS, *March 18.*

Having left Marseilles, on the 12th inst., for Constantinople, in the prosecution of my mission to the Hospital at Scutari, owing to a sudden and unexpected change from a beautifully calm to a rough and stormy sea, M. Favre, the captain of our vessel (the *Simois*), was compelled to seek shelter in the peaceable harbour of Ajaccio, in Corsica, the birthplace of the immortal Emperor Napoleon I. Since our departure from that celebrated port, a favourable breeze succeeding a most tempestuous gale, soon brought us alongside the Levrazzi Rocks, on which the French frigate *Semillante* was wrecked a few weeks ago, and all her passengers and crew lost. At night we were gratified with the sight of a slight eruption of the Stromboli Mountain, which rises immediately from the ocean to the height of several thousand feet. Next morning we arrived at Messina, the spring garden of Sicily, where, in the open air, orange and lemon trees were in full blossom, and covered with delicious fruit. Lilies, roses, and violets perfume the air; whilst peas, beans, artichokes, and asparagus are gathered at the foot of the lofty mountains covered with snow. Although Messina is well known to travellers, yet they are not so well acquainted with the productions of its early spring. After a few hours' ramble in this interesting city, our party embarked, and rapidly passed on our left the small but pretty town of Reggio, and on our right the mighty Mount Etna, covered with deep snow. In less than forty-seven hours the *Simois* brought us before the Piraeus, the voyage never before having been accomplished under fifty.

The *Simois* is an English vessel, built at Liverpool by Mr. Layward, and recently purchased by the Messageries Impériales, and this is her first voyage in this sea. From the unexpected quickness of our passage, we were allowed to remain at this port four hours, and availed ourselves of the opportunity of visiting Athens. At the present time, in the ancient Parthenon, I am cooking, with my new camp-stove, on a fallen capital of the stupendous ruins, a *petit déjeûner à la fourchette*, with Greek and Sicilian wines, for my distinguished fellow-travellers; amongst whom are General Cannon (Behram Pacha); Colonel St. George, of the Woolwich Artillery; Captain Gordon; Captains Turner and Ponsonby; G. Munro, Esq.; W. S. Ball, Esq., Q.F.M.S.; Captain Arbuckle; Captain Boucher, Aide-de-camp of General Canrobert; and Signor Pitaki, the Governor of the Acropolis.

We shall speedily re-embark for Constantinople.   A. SOYER.

COOKING ON THE MAGIC STOVE IN THE ACROPOLIS AT ATHENS

VI

THE LAND OF THE MOSLEM

ON leaving the Piraeus the weather was fine, and the sea as smooth as a lake. All our party were themselves again—jovial, happy, and talkative at meals; reading, writing, games at cards, draughts, dominoes, &c., filling up the time. We were like one happy and united family. I paid my daily visit to the *restaurateur* and his *chef*, with whom I was soon on good terms. Towards evening, we collected on the upper deck, where many French sous-officiers from the second-class cabin joined us, and sang most admirably, from the simple ballad to the gay gaudriole, the high operatic solo, and comic or classic choruses.

Next morning, we passed the straits and town of the Dardanelles, where the Allied flags were gaily floating from the houses of the respective Consulates. We made but a short stay in its cheerful and animated bay to deliver the mail. The rapid current, with the numbers of Greeks, in their gay costumes and slim caiques, trying to sell the passengers all sorts of things, and so do them out of a few piastres, rendered our short stay at that place highly amusing. Our next and last stay, before reaching Constantinople was Gallipoli, where everyone of our party landed, and remained on shore about an hour. General Cannon had an excellent idea; he sent some oysters on board, which made a good addition to our bill of fare. The Gallipoli oysters are small and ill-formed, but very sweet. The same cannot be said of the town and its inhabitants—both extremely dirty. Indeed, this first Oriental seaport contrasts most outrageously with the grand paraphernalia of the "Arabian Nights." The evening before our arrival, to our sorrow, we learnt from the Captain that, owing to the favourable winds we had experienced during the last sixty hours, if nothing happened, we should enter the Bosphorus before daybreak. Thus all chance of the view of the grand panorama of Constantine, so highly praised by travellers, and especially by poets, which we had so long anticipated, was entirely lost. What can be more charming and refreshing, after a long sea-passage, where life has long been suspended in space between heaven and the mighty deep, than the gradual development of a cheerful panorama, a view of which we had been some time anticipating?

The first quarter of the moon, forming the crescent—the favourite emblem of the Moslem—was seen now and then peeping through the murky clouds, which, in their swift career, cast a dewy shadow upon the ocean. This did not, however, prevent our philharmonic party from mustering upon deck in greater numbers than on previous occasions, probably because it was the last. We kept it up till eleven o'clock, and then retired perfectly delighted with our voyage, having already forgotten our unfavourable departure, and regretting nothing but our too-early arrival in the Bosphorus. The night was calm, and, on going on deck at daybreak, I heard, to my great satisfaction, that we had proceeded very slowly all night, there having been a thick fog, which was slowly disappearing—"a thing," said the Captain, "seldom seen in the sea of Marmora." I returned to my cabin, and only lay down that I might be ready when Constantinople came in sight, as the Captain had promised to send and let me know.

About eight in the morning everyone was on deck, and the crew busily engaged getting up the luggage, as our arrival was fixed for nine o'clock. We then commenced inquiring about the hotels. All fixed upon Messerie's hotel, called "L'Hôtel d'Angleterre," as being the best. By this time, we were slowly approaching the mouth of the Bosphorus. The weather was anything but favourable—rain kept falling—everything on deck was wet, and the air very chilly. General Cannon said to me, "I am very sorry, Mr. Soyer, for your sake, and that of Captain Ponsonby and Colonel St. George, that we shall not see the famed view of Constantinople to advantage. I have already witnessed it, this being my third voyage. However, as the weather is very changeable here, it may be a fine day after all." The great Oriental City was then opening to view, but, owing to the thick atmosphere, appeared nothing but a confused mass. Twenty minutes later we were entering the Bosphorus, the grandeur and magnificence of which, though often described, I cannot pass without a few remarks.

My mind was quite overpowered when I learnt that the monster building before us was the Scutari Hospital—a town in itself—and I reflected that it was full of sick and wounded; that each patient would require from three to four articles of diet daily, making a total of several thousand per diem to be provided in some shape or other; and that I had undertaken to reform and introduce a better organization in the cooking department, where all was confusion, in so strange a country. I must confess that, for an hour or so, I was quite at a loss to think how I should commence operations. I did not know one official there. I had not the least idea how I should be received; and, after all, I might probably catch the fever, or some other complaint at the time raging within its walls. Suddenly I recollected the plan I had explained to the Duchess of Sutherland and her noble circle, which was to be tried upon a hundred patients. This had entirely escaped my memory; and in a few minutes my puzzled brain was as clear as a bell, and I felt confident of success. "If I succeed with a hundred," said I, "in a very short time I can manage a thousand, providing I meet with proper support."

I afterwards learnt from the doctor on board, that the large red brick building on the right, about half a mile from the Barrack Hospital, was called the General Hospital, in which there were at least five or six hundred patients. My resolution as to how I should act was then fixed; nothing appeared difficult to me; and, instead of fearing the undertaking, I was most anxious to begin. Having been advised to call at Pera, to announce my arrival, and pay my duty to Lord Stratford de Redcliffe, before going to Scutari, I ordered my people to go on shore as soon as possible; for, during my reverie upon hospital duties, our good vessel had anchored.

There was only room at Messerie's Hotel for General Cannon and his aide-de-camp. He had bespoken his apartments. Two young gentlemen apprised us of the fact, and recommended their hotel, as we could not get accommodation at the "Hôtel d'Angleterre." As I had a letter of introduction to Mr. Messerie, I directed my friend T. G. to call there and make inquiries; and if he found that we could not be received, to go to the "Hôtel des Ambassadeurs," that establishment being the next in standing. As I promised to remain on board till he returned, I was left almost alone. There was only a lady and her maid. The former was going by a transport ship the same evening, to join her husband at Balaklava; she therefore had no time to go on shore. Colonel St. George, Captains Ponsonby and Gordon, Mr. Ball, and General Canrobert's aides-de-camp, and others, had all left.

By this time the weather had assumed a most brilliant aspect—the morose and monotonous-looking clouds, which before monopolised the region in the immediate vicinity of the famed city of Mahomet, had been chased away by a strong breeze; the sun shed his golden rays in gorgeous streams from the purple vault of heaven, and the utmost depths of the lucid waters of the Bosphorus reflected his splendours. The entrance of the Corne d'Or—so called, no doubt, because it takes the shape of a horn of plenty—is in truth a Golden Horn, from the facilities it affords for maritime and commercial intercourse, as well as navigation, penetrating, as it does, into the very bosom of the imperial city. Constantinople, like London, has no quays; and on every side this immense metropolis plunges its feet, or banks, into the Bosphorus, from which it rises, offering to the view the most magnificent spectacle beneath the canopy of heaven. This is particularly the case from the Seraglio Point, where the real city of Istamboul is seated. The soil rises from the level of the water, presenting a vast amphitheatre of myriads of houses, mosques, minarets, and monuments of all descriptions, intermixed with forests of sombre cypress trees.

A dragoman whom I engaged, and who spoke very good English, gave me a description of the surrounding scenery. Nothing can be more ravishing than the living panorama of the Bosphorus, covered with caiques and their caidjees, darting about on all sides like water-flies. The elegance of those frail barks, and the cleanliness of the light and cheerful costume of their owners, so well develops the Oriental style, that it cannot fail in forcibly striking every stranger. Numerous large sailing vessels, steamboats, Greek and Turkish barques, and even men-of-war (many being then stationed in the Golden Horn), made me forget for some time my mobile panorama, to dwell upon the nautical one, which, so new to me, unexpectedly attracted my attention, when my dragoman informed me that it was near eleven o'clock, and that my men had returned for the luggage.

"Very well," said I; "but pray explain to me the various places by which we are now surrounded."

"Certainly, sir, with great pleasure. I know every spot, palace, and monument. On entering the Bosphorus this morning, you passed before the Castle of the Seven Towers, where the ambassadors were formerly imprisoned. Those islands to the left are the Isles des Princes. All the Europeans go and spend their Sundays there. In summer many reside there, and come to business in the morning, returning at night."

"Those hills yonder, I suppose, are very pretty?"

"Oh, very much so indeed. Almost facing them is the Asiatic shore: that pretty place to the left is called Kadikoi—a very pretty summer residence, inhabited by rich merchants, particularly Greeks and Armenians. It is full of beautiful houses and gardens, and is much celebrated for its fine fruits. A little further this way is the General Hospital—that red brick building."

"That I am aware of. And the other is the great Barrack Hospital, with its hundreds of windows and four square towers. They are full of English sick and wounded—that I of course knew."

"Next to it is a splendid mosque called the Sultan's mosque. It is frequented by his Majesty when he resides at his summer kiosque of Hyder Pacha. That forest of cypress trees is the grand Champ des Morts, or the favourite Turkish cemetery. It extends several miles. Several generations are buried there."

"Well, what follows?"

"This beautiful and picturesque spot, sir, is called Scutari. It is full of kiosques and Turkish families, pachas, &c. It contains about a hundred thousand inhabitants, almost all Turks, and extends beyond the front of the Sultan's new palace of Dolma Bachi. You can see it from here. It is not quite finished, and is constructed chiefly of white marble. Lower down is a palace inhabited by the Sultan. It is lighted by gas—quite a new thing in Constantinople. That large building above, on the heights, is the grand hospital of Pera, now used by the French; and all the neighbourhood as far as the pointed tower is called Pera, the Christian quarter, where are the foreign embassies and foreign merchants' residences. The large yellowish building with the colonnade you see facing us so boldly is the Russian Embassy. They are about to convert it into a hospital for the sick French officers. The beautiful mosque and large square you see at the bottom is called Tophané. It contains a large cannon-foundry; and in the centre of the square is the kiosque belonging to the Sultan's brother. His Majesty frequently visits this place when he attends his favourite mosque.

"This large tower is called the Galata Tower, and from the top the fire-signal is made; and I can assure you that in the winter its guardians have something to do, as there is a fire every day or night. Lower down, towards the bridge, is called Galata, where all mercantile and commercial, as well as naval, business is transacted. Every rich merchant of Pera has a counting-house there. The building at the bottom is the Custom House, or, as it should be called, the confusion house; for if unfortunately you get goods in, 'tis a hundred to one if you ever get them out again. The rough bridge you see yonder has only existed these last twenty years. Before that was built, people were obliged to cross from Stamboul to the European shore in caiques; and now, when three or four large vessels have to pass through the bridge, it remains open for several hours, keeping passengers waiting for that time. Two more light bridges lower down cross the Golden Horn, and the navigation terminates about two miles above the last bridge. In caiques you can go as far as the sweet waters of Europe, which are about five miles further up."

"Thank you," said I; "pray be less prolix in your descriptions."

"Well, now, sir, as we are come to Stamboul, or the real city of Constantinople, allow me to explain to you the names of some of those beautiful mosques with which you see this vast city is crowded. The first and most important is the Mosque of Sultan Bajazid, very remarkable for the number of its volatile inhabitants, consisting of several thousands of beautiful tame pigeons. That high tower behind it is called the Seraskier's Tower, and also serves the purpose of a signal-tower in case of fire, the same as that of Pera. Then follow the mosques of Sultan Selim, Mahomet, Sedya Tamissi, Solimaniek, Bayazid, Osmanliek, Sultan Achmet, Irene, and the great Saint Sophia, which I would in particular advise you to visit."

"Of course I shall do that, you may be certain."

"On the prominent part of this side of Saint Sophia the ceremony of the Bairam is celebrated, at the close of the great feast of the Ramadan. All the nobility of the

Empire are in duty bound to appear in new and most gaudy costumes at this magnificent Oriental pageant, which this year will take place at the end of June, at about three o'clock in the morning."

"What a singular hour for so great a ceremony!" I remarked.

"Oh, that cannot be helped," he replied, "as it is regulated by the revolution of the moon. An old Turk, with whom I am well acquainted, told me that he recollected its having happened at twelve o'clock in the day, and in the middle of winter."

"A strange custom," said I.

"Well, sir, if you feel interested in Turkish habits and religion, you should inquire about the six weeks of Ramadan, when they starve all day, and get intoxicated to madness at night."

"Thank you for your information; but pray continue your description."

"I will. Near the very spot where this festival takes place is the Sultan Mahmoud's palace, the top of which you can see through those high trees."

"Pray, what are those rows of small domes, like well-corked bottles?"

"They are the kitchen chimneys."

"What, all of them?"

"Yes, sir; I have often been there, and know well enough that, although the Sultan no longer inhabits it, two or three hundred men-cooks remain in the kitchens."

"For what purpose, my friend, if no one lives there?"

"Oh, somebody does. I believe there is a college for some of the favourite sons of high Turkish families. Here," he continued, "look at this uneven row of houses with lattices. Do you know what they are?"

"No; pray what are they?"

"Why, Sultan Mahmoud's harem; and it is most probably still inhabited by a few of his old favourites and their suites, which are very numerous."

"Well, upon my word, those species of chalets put me very much in mind of chicken-cages."

The English officer's wife, to whom I have before referred, and with whom I had some conversation during the passage, came upon deck while my dragoman was describing the surrounding scenery, and listened with vivid interest, taking notes of the most interesting passages. The dragoman, turning quickly round—"Madam," said he, "you see that colossal spout shooting out at a sharp incline towards the water. That is the spot from whence, if any of the Turkish ladies prove disobedient or faithless to their imperial lord and master, they are stiched up in a sack alive, accompanied by a starving cat and a venomous serpent, and shot into that mighty watery grave, the Bosphorus."

"Monsieur Soyer, do you think that is true?"

"I believe such things have been done, madam, for it was pointed out to me the first thing this morning as having been used for that purpose. I recollect some years since reading the same tale either in a French or English work; I believe it was French. At all events, European manners and customs are progressing throughout the world, and have even reached Turkey. I hear from everyone that the Sultan is a most amiable and humane man. I would therefore recommend you to reserve your look of horror and indignation for more modern calamities. You may be certain, if such things have happened, they will never happen again, for, thank Heaven, we live in a civilized era."

"We should, perhaps, doubt such reports."

"You are quite right, madam."

"There is another curious tale related of the Leander Tower," said the lady.

"There is; but my dragoman tells me the proper name for it is *La Tour de la Jeune Fille*, as they say in French, or the Maiden's Tower."

"I was here when a French tutor came to Constantinople," said my dragoman, "and the first thing he asked me was—'Where is the Maiden's Tower?' as the English call it. At all events, madam, the story runs thus:—A great beauty, the daughter of some pacha, had her fortune told by a celebrated gipsy, who apprised her that she would never marry, as she was fated to die young. The girl, terrified at the prediction, ran, and in tears related to her father the fatal destiny said to be in reserve for her. He immediately sent for the old witch, and she repeated the fatal prophecy, adding, moreover, that the young girl would die from the bite of a serpent or some such venomous reptile. The pacha having repeatedly asked the old woman if that was the only kind of speedy death with which his daughter was menaced, and having received a reply in the affirmative, parted upon very friendly terms with the hag, who was possessed, as he said, by an evil spirit. He then caused this tower to be built for his daughter's residence, and for several years she lived in this picturesque place, without being visited by anyone but her father, who continually supplied her with provisions of the most delicate kind, and nosegays of the finest flowers. It happened one day, that, on taking up one of the bouquets in order to inhale the perfume, a small insect stung her on the lip, and in a few hours she expired in great agony, before any succour could be obtained, as there was no communication with the land, nor any antidote in readiness. So awful an event, in so secluded a spot, had never been contemplated. The pacha's intention had been to keep his daughter there till she was of age to be married, and thus break the spell of the old sorceress. The legend was thus related to me by an Armenian gentleman who has lived here nearly all his lifetime."

"Well, I admit that I have not only heard the story before, but I recollect the incident of the death of the young girl, from the bite of a reptile very well; and I also heard that the name of the Tower of Leander is applied to it; but it has not the least relation to the legend of the two lovers celebrated by Lord Byron, who also swam from Sestos to Abydos."

As my people had returned, and were waiting for me, I bade my fair *compagnon de voyage* adieu, expressing a hope to have the pleasure of meeting her in Balaklava. Our two caidjees rapidly flew away with us from the side of the *Simois*, and soon landed us at the Tophané tumbledown stairs. We are now on shore; but what a contrast!—the fairy scene has disappeared, and we appear to be in the midst of a penny show. The Tophané landing place is nothing but a heap of rotten planks, parts of which have given way, and the holes are rather dangerous, as one might easily slip and break a leg. The very clean and picturesque caidjees were waiting amidst heaps of manure and the carcase of a dead horse, which had been thrown into the Bosphorus and had drifted on shore. A number of ill-looking, half-famished dogs were feeding upon that heap of corruption. On inquiring of the son of the proprietor of the hotel, who accompanied me, he coolly told me that it had only been there a day or two, and would probably remain for months—particularly the skeleton—when the dogs had devoured all the flesh. The odour arising from the carcass, and the filth daily cast into the water, was very unwholesome, and quite unbearable; and very glad was I to quit the great landing-place of Tophané—so called, no doubt, from the extraordinary amount of daily traffic between the shipping above and the Asiatic shore. About seventy or eighty caiques are always waiting there, as it is the principal landing point at Constantinople.

Following my guide, we passed through a number of dirty narrow streets, full of a black liquid mud, very ill paved—if they could be called paved at all—amidst which numerous leperous and villanous-looking dogs were snarling and fighting. Donkeys loaded with tiles, stones, and long logs of wood filled up the filthy road; besides gangs of powerful and noisy Turkish hamals or porters, carrying enormous loads upon long poles. The enchanting mirage of the panoramic Constantinople vanished rapidly from before my disenchanted eyes; this ephemeral Paradise of Mahomet changing at once into an almost insupportable purgatory. I could not imagine how such a mass of ruins and of miserable wooden houses could, from so short a distance, take such a brilliant aspect or create such ravishing sensations, as the first view of Constantinople had raised in my mind from the deck of the *Simois*. I now envied the fate of our fair fellow-traveller who so much regretted that she could not disembark—were it only for a few hours. Those few hours, nay, the first, would have sufficed to break the spell. Reader, though this is an exact description of our entrance into Constantinople, I reasoned thus—It is an immense metropolis, and no doubt something great exists within its walls. I must wait patiently and try to find it out.

Reproaching my dragoman for bringing me through such a vile part of the city, he quietly replied, in English, "There is no other road, sir; it has rained very much lately, which is the cause of so much mud." I now perceived, that as far as the names of pavements go, the difference between Constantinople and London was not so great,—the former being *muck-muddy-mised*, and the latter *macadamised*.

At this moment we were turning the corner of the Grand Mosque of Sultan Soliman; and a pacha, in all his obesity, mounted upon an Arabian horse, and followed by his suite, six in number, rode full gallop through a pond of liquid slush, splashing everyone from head to foot on either side of the narrow street. An English soldier at once sent him his military blessing; and the Turk, spurring his horse, exclaimed, "Not Bono Johnny; Not Bono Johnny;" that being the name given to the English by the Turks. After passing through several similar streets, consisting of ruinous wooden shanties and shops of the lowest order, viz., "chibouque* tube and pipe-bowl makers," the interior of which were dirty and mean, with scarcely any kind of stock, we arrived at a fountain, in front of which was a semi-perpendicular and narrow street. My guide informed me that my hotel was at the end of this street. "It is," he continued, "the Hôtel d'Angleterre, called by the English—Messerie's Hotel."

"Thank God for that," said I. In about twenty minutes we arrived at the said hotel. As I had sent my letter to Mr. Messerie, he soon appeared, and very cordially shook me by the hand, and politely expressed his regret at not being able to accommodate me. He recommended the Hôtel des Ambassadeurs. On my saying that I was going there, he made me promise to call upon him the next morning, the distance from his house being but a few paces.

* Long-stemmed Turkish tobacco pipe—AB

When I arrived, I at once retired to my apartment, quite worn out with fatigue. Having taken some refreshment, I made up my mind not to dine at the table d'hôte. I learnt that Colonel St. George, Captain Ponsonby, &c., had gone to the Hôtel de l'Europe, and I therefore felt free for that evening. About five o'clock, Mons. Pantaleone Veracleo, a young Greek, the son of the hotel-keeper, came and informed me that the table d'hôte would be ready at six. Thanking him for his attention, I proceeded to ask several questions about Constantinople, and also the distance from the hotel to the British Embassy?

"Not five minutes' walk, sir," said he; "you can see it from the top of the hotel. Our house is the highest in Pera!"

We mounted to the terrace, and my conductor pointed it out to me. From this terrace I again beheld a similar panorama to that which I had witnessed on board the *Simois*, and by which I had been so much charmed. In order to enjoy it fully, I expressed my desire to remain a short time alone. Having directed my attention to the different points of view, Mr. Veracleo left me.

THE BARRACK HOSPITAL AT SCUTARI.

VII

A BIRD'S-EYE VIEW OF CONSTANTINOPLE
FROM PERA

THE rays of the sun on that showery March day assumed, towards five p.m., in the regions of the West, a most brilliant aspect. The vaporous edges of the humid clouds seemed gilded with vermilion and silver tints. The floods of light, like living fire, fell upon the rich masses of the domes of various mosques, and hundreds of pointed and slender minarets. While gazing in loneliness and contemplation, from the terrace of the Hôtel des Ambassadeurs, at this charming spot in the East, to which the beautiful mirage of an Oriental sunset lent an indescribable charm, a shrieking voice was heard from the lower terrace, saying, "Il signor, la table d'outre est servi! et il se refroidit fortement! La soupe il étoit tout à fait déménagée of the tureen!" Looking over the railing, I perceived the interpreter of the hotel, who was unfortunately the possessor of several tongues, addressing himself to me. He, no doubt, meant to imply that the table d'hôte had been served, and the soup already removed from the table. This *olla podrida* of languages having produced no effect upon my mind, half an hour after, the son of the hotel-keeper made his appearance, who, though speaking French like certain horned beasts in Spain, clearly gave me to understand that I was too late for dinner. Taking advantage of his unexpected visit, I inquired, looking towards the arsenal, "What part of the metropolis is that opening near us?"

"Le Petit Champ des Morts, or the Small Field of the Dead,—so-called, though nearly two miles in circumference, which is now so full that no further interments are allowed within its area,"—he replied.

By the aid of an opera-glass, I plainly distinguished beneath us a large pile of irregular stones, encircled by a railing. I, at first sight, took this for the ruins of a kind of hippodrome which might have succumbed to an earthquake, each stone having lost its perpendicular, as though purposely to mock its fellow, and not making the slightest attempt to perpetuate the grandeur of their solemn mission. Horses, mules, and donkeys, were seen dragging loads of large planks to and fro, six or eight on either side. The ends of the planks kept cutting rather deep zig-zags into the soft ground, and were continually catching against tombstones. The whole formed a kind of gigantic American bagatelle board, where, when the ball is violently thrown to the top, it descends by degrees, catching the points in every direction in its way down. Next to it music was heard. Boys were romping, some playing with marbles, or five para pieces, making use of the stones for their point of departure. Lemonade, cakes, raki, and variegated bonbons, oranges, lemons, &c., were briskly purchased by the promenaders, who, amongst this *cohue-bohue* of industry, were seen gaily crossing and recrossing the green paths. Some reclined against the gravestones, forming, as it were, an armchair. Amongst them, however, were but few Mussulmans, some turning Dervishes and Howlers, Greeks, Armenians, French, Perotes, Smyrniotes, and here and there gazing with astonishing disapprobation, some of the children of Albion. All excepting the latter might be seen gaily fluttering from tombstone to tombstone, like busy bees from flower to flower, in a perfumed pasture in summer. Here and there clumps of cypress trees looked like the mournful guardians of this desecrated spot. Some of the marble stones are still vividly stained with the blood of the haughty and rebellious Janissaries, whose crumbling bodies lay beneath. Such is the pious veneration of the Oriental population for the remains of their ancestors in the Petit Champ des Morts at Pera.

The principal buildings which grace this foreign quarter are the English, French, Austrian, Russian, Sardinian, and Prussian embassies. The former, called the Palais d'Angleterre, now the residence of Lord Stratford de Redcliffe, interested me most, as I was in duty bound to pay my humble respects to his lordship and her ladyship the next morning. It brought to my mind from a distance the celebrated building of the Reform Club, which gave Barry his high reputation as an architect, and where your humble servant passed above two lustres of his culinary career.

While the new moon was faintly shining through transparent clouds, the hundred minarets of Stamboul and its vicinity had been illuminated for a festival, and their fiery collarettes à la Vandyke proudly carried those rings of diamonds high towards the heavenly sphere. Eight o'clock was striking at the Catholic church of Saint Mary. All was darkness and silence. Hastily retiring to my bedroom, perfectly satisfied with having fed my mind, although I had probably neglected internal restoration, I soon fell into a most profound slumber, in which I saw nothing but churchyards, clumps of cypress trees, mosques, and illuminated minarets, till I awoke at daybreak.

My wandering mind having fluttered all night about the Oriental metropolis, I was not in the slightest degree surprised to find myself in the morning in the land which had given birth to the *Arabian Nights*. The sound of a cracked bell was heard from the bottom of the staircase, inviting each traveller to his morning meal. There was a goodly number present, and we sat down about thirty-five. The majority were military men, of various ranks, mostly French and English. Some expressed their regret at my absence the previous evening, fancying—so much for imagination—the dinner would have been more choice had the landlord been personally acquainted with me. At all events, the breakfast-table was well supplied, and I made a hearty meal, amidst the buzzing of various languages.

As it was nearly eleven o'clock by the time I had finished, I started for the Embassy, and after about twenty minutes of most laborious gymnastic exercise over the ill-paved Rue (Ruelle it should be called) de Pera, I entered the small wooden gate at the grand entrance of the Palais d'Angleterre, which is majestically located in a fine open space of ground, encircled by a large terrace, with parterres of shrubs and high trees, from which spot a most favourable view of the rich mass of building around is obtained. Modest grandeur, boldness, and simplicity of execution, seem to have been the architect's sole ambition. I shall probably, in another chapter, describe the beauty and comfort of its interior. The porter having taken my card, I was immediately shown into the library. A few moments spent in this sanctuary of belles lettres afforded me a fair opportunity of closely examining a very excellent and well-executed painting, the style of which assured me that it was a good portrait of his Sublime Majesty, the present Sultan, Abdul Medjid. Ten minutes had scarcely elapsed, when Lady Stratford entered, and addressed me in French, with a smile of welcome difficult to forget. "Well, Monsieur Soyer, we heard of your departure from England for the East."

"No doubt you did, my lady."

"And I sincerely hope that you will succeed in your laudable undertaking. I have no doubt your suggestions will prove highly beneficial, and be well received by the authorities at the various hospitals, which, in your department, are much in want of some kind of regulation. I also hope that the Minister-at-War has invested you with power to act according to your own judgment."

"I am happy to inform your ladyship," said I, "that her Majesty's Government has not only granted me the power required to superintend and, if possible, improve the diet at the Hospital, but have also honoured me with their full confidence as regards ordering anything extra which may be required, so long as it tends to the comfort of the sick."

"Well, I am very happy to hear that such is the case," replied her ladyship; "for without such power your services would not have been so effective."

"I can assure your ladyship that I would not have undertaken this task if such powers had not been granted to me by Lord Panmure. I was well aware of the numerous difficulties I should meet with, which are almost unavoidable in every kind of administration. But so highly do I appreciate the honour conferred upon me, that, far from taking advantage of the unlimited confidence reposed in me, it will be my pride to try and make all my contemplated improvements with the present governmental allowance; and I have no doubt that in time, by judicious organization and good management, as well as by using everything to the best advantage, I shall economize, instead of increasing the expense to the nation. Having heard that your ladyship has, from the commencement of this serious war, devoted the best part of your time to the various hospitals, in watching over the sick and wounded, I shall esteem it a great favour if you will direct me how to act, in order to insure prompt success, and what articles of diet are most required for the patients."

"It will afford me great pleasure, Monsieur Soyer, to give you the principal information; but Signor Roco Vido, my head manager and cook, will furnish the details, as he daily prepares large quantities of comforts,—such as beef-tea, mutton and chicken broth, calfs'-foot jelly, &c., &c.,—and distributes them himself at the Barrack and General Hospitals, also at Hyder Pacha, where the officers are."

"Indeed, my lady. Such information from Signor Roco would be invaluable to me."

"Very well; I will send for him."

"I beg your ladyship's pardon, but I always understood that the hospitals were on the other side the Bosphorus."

"Yes, Monsieur Soyer, the great military ones are; but as at the beginning of the campaign, after the battle of the Alma, none of them had extra diet kitchens, we prepare food here and send it over."

"I understand that the Bosphorus is sometimes so rough that no one can cross it."

"Such is the case; but we have a good-sized caique, and I can assure you that, although it is so very dangerous, it has never missed going one day; and since the battle of Inkermann, it often goes to Kululee, where we have opened another hospital, nearly three miles from this. Before you see Signor Roco, if you will follow me, I will inquire whether Lord Stratford is disengaged, as I have no doubt he will be pleased to see you."

"I am your ladyship's most humble servant," was my reply.

After walking over the best part of the grand square gallery, and crossing before the magnificent marble hall and gigantic staircase, we ascended to a loftier story. A gentle tap at the door gained us admittance to the santuary of high diplomacy. A plain screen was all the furniture to be seen. A few words from her ladyship soon brought me in communication with his Excellency, who, though much engaged (being surrounded by mountains of official papers), received me in a most cheerful and friendly manner. After I had said a few words relative to the mission entrusted to me by the British Government, and her ladyship had briefly narrated our former conversation, Lord Stratford kindly expressed the pleasure it would give him to hear of my success in that important department. "A good diet," said Lady Stratford, "being of paramount importance to everyone in a state of debility. Monsieur Soyer," continued her ladyship, "also wishes to see Roco, to learn from him, as he has now had several months' practice making various aliments for the patients, what kinds are most in request by the doctors."

"No doubt," Lord Redcliffe replied, "Roco will be happy to give you all the information you may require upon the subject. He is a very good man, and exerts himself to the utmost for the hospitals."

Lord Stratford again expressed his good wishes and promises of kind support, whereupon her ladyship and your humble servant retired. The ambassadress then ordered the footman in waiting to conduct me to Signor Roco's apartment, expressing her desire to meet me with him the next day at the Kululee and Scutari hospitals. I promised to attend at those places on the following morning, and took my leave.

A walk through the gallery and corridor of that noble mansion brought us to Signor Roco Vido's door. An indication on the outside apprised me that my cicerone was a child of *la belle Italie*, which at first caused me some fear lest this should create impediments and delay in our business transactions, as I only understood the language of the Italian opera. A few words from the footman soon brought me in amicable contact with the major domo of the Palais d'Angleterre, who spoke excellent English, and, like his illustrious master, was surrounded by archives, but only of culinary and household affairs. The contents of these, though not so important to the world, were nearly as substantial, more especially the bill of fare, which in itself is capable of influencing any diplomatic subject. A good one gratifies the stomach and soothes the brain, which is necessarily influenced by the quality, succulence, and scientific preparation of the aliments imparted to the first organ.

Such was the important office entrusted to the guidance of Signor Roco Vido. And who can say, after all, that the late destructive war was not partly, or even entirely, caused by a dinner? Did not the French revolution of '48 emanate from a banquet? and upon this occasion, 1854, six years after, a most unaccountable gastronomic event occurred. Lord Stratford de Redcliffe, on his return to Constantinople as plenipotentiary, had for the first time invited his Excellency

Prince Menschikoff to a grand diplomatic dinner, where all the representatives of the then united Courts were to assemble. The day was fixed for the 21st of March, 1854, and the invitations were cordially accepted, most especially by the representative of the Czar; he being, no doubt, anxious to read upon the brow of the diplomatist the political feeling of his nation. That very day, towards noon, the Sultan's mother died. In the morning she had written a letter to his Excellency, expressive of her full confidence that he would study the future welfare of her son in his relations with the British Government. On account of this mournful event, and with a most profound feeling of respect and veneration for the Imperial mourner, the dinner was postponed for a week; and while the dark veil was laid over the banqueting table, and the black seal was set upon the *batterie de cuisine* and numerous *bouches à feu de l'Ambassade britannique*, his Excellency Prince Menschikoff was on board a Russian man-of-war anchored at the mouth of the Black Sea, waiting with all the dignity and defiance imaginable for the determination of peace or war. The diplomatic banquet never took place! the war did!

I consider a postponed diplomatic dinner to be an universal calamity, especially when only a few hours' notice of the postponement is given; and I cannot but quote the *Gastronomic Regenerator**, page 342, published in the year 1842, in which I say—

"Rien ne dispose mieux l'esprit humain à des transactions amicales qu'un dîner bien conçu et artistement préparé. Lisez l'histoire, et vous y trouverez que, dans tous les temps et chez tous les peuples, le bien qui s'est fait, et quelquefois le mal, fut toujours précédé ou suivi d'un copieux dîner."

Translation.—"Nothing can prepare the human mind for amicable intercourse better than a well-conceived and artistically-prepared dinner. Read history, and you will ascertain that at all periods, and amongst all nations, the benefits, and sometimes the evils, they experienced, were either preceded or followed by a good dinner."

---

* The Gastronomic Regenerator by Alexis Soyer—AB

VIII

FIRST VIEW OF THE SCENE OF ACTION

THE same day, I despatched one of my men to the Barrack Hospital at Scutari, to inform Lord William Paulet—at that period Brigadier-General of the British Army—of my arrival at Constantinople, and to inquire at what hour his lordship would favour me with an interview. Upon my return from the Palais d'Angleterre, I found that my man Julien had arrived from Scutari, much pleased with his lordship's reception, but terribly frightened by his passage *en caïque* across the Bosphorus, which that day was so rough that all his clothes were wet through. "The caidjee would not take me there and back for less than five shillings," said he.

"Well, never mind that, so long as you have seen his lordship and are safe upon *terra firma*."

"I must tell you, sir, that upon announcing your arrival, his lordship seemed very much pleased, and observed, 'So Monsieur Soyer has arrived! Where is he?' 'At Pera, my lord, at the Hôtel des Ambassadeurs.' 'I had the pleasure of knowing M. Soyer,' said his lordship, 'when he came to Ireland in the year of the famine. Tell him I shall be happy to see him any time tomorrow between the hours of nine and four.' 'Thank you, my lord. I shall not fail to acquaint M. Soyer of the kind reception you have given me on his behalf.'"

Highly gratified at the kind reception I had received from Lord and Lady Stratford de Redcliffe, and fixing my visit to Lord William Paulet for nine or ten the next morning, I then visited General Cannon at Messerie's Hotel, to inform him of the progress I was making, and to tell him that all appeared encouraging. I felt it my duty to do this, as he and all the officers on board the *Simois* expressed considerable interest in my undertaking. As General Cannon was out, I had the pleasure of seeing his aide-de-camp, Captain Harbuckle, who promised to inform the General of the subject of my visit. On inquiring for Mr. Messerie, I found him busily engaged in the entrance-hall. He took me to his private room, and we had a long conversation. He very kindly gave me much valuable information respecting the products of the country, which, he stated, differed much from those found in the English markets in quality, though little in price, as all kinds of provisions had risen to double, and in some cases triple, what they were before the commencement of the war.

"That," I answered, "could not fail to be the case, considering the immense influx of troops daily arriving at Constantinople."

"Any information or assistance you may require, Monsieur, I shall, as a *confrère*, be happy to give you, and will also endeavour to render myself useful as well as agreeable."

I promised to pay him a visit now and then when I came to Pera, and we parted. It would be difficult for anyone to imagine the immense number of persons who daily went in and out of this large hotel. The spacious hall was crowded with baggage. In fact, there is but one hotel in Pera, or we might say in Constantinople, and that is the one.

I next called at the "Hôtel de l'Europe," to see Captain Ponsonby and Colonel St. George. I found they had just before left, with the intention of dining at the table d'hôte at the "Hôtel des Ambassadeurs." Upon my arrival there, I found a number of my fellow-travellers, all come, as they said, in expectation of finding a better dinner than at their hotel, in consequence of my being there. We certainly had a very tolerable dinner, which stamped for a time the reputation of the hotel for having one of the best tables d'hôte in Constantinople. The room was very spacious and lofty, the table well laid out, ornamented with numerous fine bouquets of flowers, and lighted with wax lights. We sat down about forty, principally military men.

Over glasses of Greek champagne and Bordeaux wine, several laughable anecdotes relating to our voyage were told. Expressions of admiration at the view of the Moslem city from the Bosphorus—of disappointment at the disenchantment experienced on landing—were freely uttered. In fact, we all seemed to enter upon our campaign with most flourishing prospects; but we could not help remarking, and feeling at heart, the want of ladies at our board. Not one adorned our festival. This gave us a sad *prestige* of the deprivation of female society we should be condemned to in the Crimea. Such was to be our fate throughout the campaign. At the time, none seemed to feel the loss of those they loved or had loved so dearly. No; all were for war! war! and glory at any risk. Bloodshed, epidemics, destruction, loss of life, &c., were matters of little moment. The very air we breathed seemed to smell of powder. All these horrors had steeled men's hearts, and in so doing, seemed to have banished all rational feeling for home. Men seldom thought of their wives and families, or at least never spoke of them; and if a young and tender-hearted warrior did think of his anticipated fair companion or *fiancée*, he dared not talk of her—everyone would have laughed at him.

In spite of this, one member of the fair sisterhood, and the ornament of her sex, was not forgotten; and when the health of Victoria, Queen of England, was proposed by a French Colonel, the shouts and hurrahs it elicited did not cease for many minutes. Why such enthusiasm? Believe me, it was not in honour of her Majesty's sex. No! it was an acknowledgment of the martial glory of the country; for, a few minutes after, the same sentiment was expressed for the Emperor of France; and again, for the union and alliance of the three nations. This proceeding, instead of opening the heart to feelings of love, and of calling forth the last sentiment of the kind which might have lingered there, aroused a sterner inspiration. Such are what I call the calamities, if not the horrors, of war; where all is destruction, and humanity is rendered inhuman. This was the prevailing feeling of about forty well-bred and brave military men—fifteen of whom were French, and the remainder Englishmen—sitting at the table d'hôte of the "Hôtel des Ambassadeurs," at Pera, on the 20th of March, 1854. Of that company, nearly a third, a few months after, had sacrificed their lives for the glory of their country.

The next morning, at half-past eight, I went with my dragoman to the horrid Tophané landing-place. There I was surrounded by at least twenty caidjees, who added to the disagreeables of this spot an evil of which I was not aware at my first visit. Just fancy twenty Turks screaming out their to me unknown language, and performing, at the same time, a peculiar pantomime with their fists so close to your visage, you might almost fancy they were telling you that, if you dared to take any other caique than theirs, they would punch your head for you, or throw you into the Bosphorus. In such a scene of noise and confusion, it is almost, if not altogether, impossible for one to make up one's mind whether one requires one caique or several. The mistake occurs in this, that they offer you a caique with one, two, or three caidjees.

As the Bosphorus was very rough, my man hired a craft with three pair of oars—the two and three-oared boats being the only ones that went out that day—the small caiques with one pair of oars seldom venturing out in such weather. We soon stepped into the boat; and, to my delight, we had no sooner set foot in the one we had selected, than, as if by a magic spell, every tongue was silent. About two minutes after, just as we were pushing off, two English officers made their appearance, and experienced more trouble than I had done, as I had with me a man who spoke their language. We got afloat quickly enough, and the short spiteful waves constantly dashed in our faces, and rocked us about in all directions. To my astonishment, the rowers took quite a different direction to the Barrack Hospital, which appeared to me close at hand. On making a remark to this effect to my dragoman, he told me the current was so strong that they were obliged to fetch up a long way to avoid being dashed against the Seraglio Point, or the chains and hawsers of the vessels at anchor. "Oh, thank you," said I, "let them go as many miles round as they please, especially as I have till four o'clock to see his lordship."

After a long pull we came close to the Tour de la Jeune Fille, and I told my man Auguste to inquire respecting the truth of the tale narrated in a previous chapter. The only reply he could get from the three caidjees respecting this wonderful story was, that they knew of no young maiden who dwelt there; but that, on the contrary, an old Armenian woman, in summer time, sold bad coffee and worse tobacco. A few weeks afterwards the *café* was opened, and, instead of *la jeune fille*, there was an obesity of about sixty years old—*coiffée à la grecque*—fresh flowers ornamenting the remains of what, no doubt, was once a fine head of hair.

The current here is so strong and rapid, that the waves inundate the best part of the tower. Auguste told me this place was at all times the most dangerous, and that in bad weather a single-oared caique could not cross near it. A few minutes after, under shelter of the high Scutari banks and out of the current, we were, comparatively speaking, in smooth water. But our poor caidjees were in a violent perspiration, though the weather was rather cold, and paused to take breath. It took us above an hour to cross, though you could see the hospital close at hand at starting. At last we arrived at the landing-place, which, thanks to the English, was far better than the Tophané one.

The hospital being on an elevated spot, and not more than a thousand yards distant, appeared three times as large as it did from the deck of the *Simois*; and here again, at sight of such a gigantic establishment, my courage failed me, and for the second time I regretted having undertaken such a difficult task. I immediately went to the grand hospital entrance, the residence of Lord W. Paulet, thanking my stars that I had the honour of being known to him. I was shown the general's quarters, and sent in my card. I was desired to follow, and had no sooner entered, than his lordship came to meet me, and shook hands cordially.

"Monsieur Soyer," said he, "we have not had the pleasure of meeting since 1847, when I saw you in Dublin,—the year of the famine in Ireland."

These words recalled the scene to my mind.

"I was at the Royal Barracks, with the Duke of Cambridge, when you opened your kitchen in the Barrack Square—in fact, before our window. The Duke and myself paid you a visit the day the Lord-Lieutenant opened it. You had nearly a thousand visitors that morning, and fed between four and five thousand poor people in the course of the day. The samples of food prepared by you were excellent, though made at such a moderate price, I assure you," his lordship continued, speaking to some gentlemen present, one of whom knew me while at the Reform Club.

"Indeed, my lord, you give me much pleasure by recalling reminiscences of my success at that period; and I accept the same as a good omen for my present undertaking, especially when taken in connexion with your valuable support."

"Monsieur Soyer, you may depend upon my support; but I tell you beforehand, you will have no end of difficulties."

"Well, my lord, with your support, a good will, and perseverance, I have no doubt of doing some good." I then presented Lord Panmure's letter respecting my mission. While his lordship was reading it, I was asked by several officers present, "What are you sent out for?" Lord William Paulet, overhearing them, replied, "To set us to rights in our kitchen department, to be sure. This letter from the Minister-at-War shall be closely attended to, Monsieur Soyer, and I will this day give orders to that effect."

From this I understood that Lord Panmure had given instructions for everything I might require.

"Well," said his lordship, "how many cooks have you brought with you?"

"Four, my lord."

"Only four! I thought you would want many more than that. However, let me know what you require. You are staying at Pera?"

"Yes; but I intend coming over tomorrow, to make a beginning."

"I must get you a house in town; we are so full here, we have no room to spare."

"I'm not sorry for that—it will be a change of air—though I shall require a small room in the hospital."

"We'll see about that—but tell me, of how many does your staff consist?"

"About seven or eight."

"I'll try and get you a house to yourself."

"Many thanks, my lord. I assure you that the kind reception accorded to me will never be forgotten by your humble servant. In order that no time may be lost—and I am aware that your lordship's is highly valuable—will you kindly instruct some one to show me Dr. Cumming's apartment, as I have a letter of introduction to that gentleman from Dr. Andrew Smith; and I am anxious to confer with the Doctor upon the subject of the new diets, and submit them for his special approval."

His lordship then directed Dr. Rutherford to show me to Dr. Cumming's office, which we reached through a long corridor lined with beds on either side, and occupied by sick and wounded. The apartment was full of persons waiting to see the doctor. On sending in my card I was immediately admitted, and very politely received. Dr. Cumming was, of course, full of business. He read the letter from Dr. A. Smith, and then said, "Monsieur Soyer, you may depend upon it that I will do all in my power to assist you."

I then stated my plan of commencing with a hundred patients, of which he highly approved. "The next thing," I observed, "will be to find a suitable place for a kitchen."

"I think," said he, "the General Hospital will be the best to begin at, as it has always been used as an hospital. You will find everything more appropriate there." I expressed a great desire to commence with the Barrack Hospital, to which Dr. Cumming immediately consented.

"Dr. Rutherford, you will perhaps be kind enough to show Mr. Soyer over the hospital, and assist him in selecting a suitable spot to commence operations." Doctor Cumming again repeated his promise of giving me every support, and said, "You know my office, and I shall at all times be glad to see you upon matters of business."

"You may depend upon it, Doctor, that I shall only trouble you with indispensable matters, and such with which it is most important you should be acquainted."

We then parted. The Doctor and myself walked round the whole of the corridors, both sides of which were filled with patients. The numerous wards round the barracks, each of which held about thirty patients, were also full. These melancholy sights have been so often depicted in letters in the public press, that it would only be re-opening an old wound were I to dilate upon them. There is a wide difference between seeing the thing upon the spot, in all its painful and wretched truth, and in merely reading a well-written description. This fact all who have witnessed such spectacles have felt, without being able or willing to describe. I must say that, in spite of the *sang froid* and energy I possess, the sight of such calamities made a most extraordinary impression upon me, and produced an effect which lasted for several days afterwards. At length I found a place on one of the large staircases, in which I could make an excellent model kitchen, and of this discovery I at once informed Dr. Cumming. The afternoon was drawing to a close, and being obliged to return to Pera, I was compelled to leave without seeing Miss Nightingale, for whom I had brought several letters—one in particular, from the Duchess of Sutherland.

In the evening I went to the British Embassy to have a little conversation with Signor Roco Vido, respecting the Kululee hospital, and obtained from him a list of the various sorts of diets he had been supplying. He then informed me that our visit to Kululee with her ladyship was deferred for a day or two on account of so many visitors staying at the Embassy on their way to the Crimea. This news I received with much pleasure, being anxious to commence operations at the Barrack Hospital. As it was near Lord Stratford's dinner-hour, he requested me to sit down, and gave me the book containing the account of all that he had supplied from the beginning of the war. This I took for my guide.

The list of articles supplied by Signor Roco Vido to the different hospitals is so various that it would fill several pages, and would not be interesting or useful. They consisted principally of beef-tea, chicken and mutton broth, calfs'-foot jelly, arrowroot, semolina, &c. &c. The supply commenced four days after the battle of the Alma, on which occasion several wounded Russians were taken prisoners and brought to the Barrack Hospital. They were about twenty in number, among whom was General Chekanoff, who died seven days after from his wounds. He had received three bayonet thrusts, and two balls had passed through his body: his age was sixty-five. He lies in the Cemetery near the General Hospital at Scutari. A small piece of rotten plank marks the resting-place of this brave defender of his country's cause, from which in a short time the inscription will probably be erased.* Signor Marco Vido, brother of Roco Vido, who afterwards acted as Miss Nightingale's interpreter, informed me that at that time the barracks which were afterwards turned into an hospital were entirely destitute of beds, sheets, blankets, chairs, tables, cooking utensils, or food of any description, the whole of which were supplied by Lady de Redcliffe; the General Hospital was then used by the Turkish army. This was the origin of the largest and most unique hospital in the world. Signor Marco Vido did not quit the general's side till he had expired. The latter expressed his sincere thanks to him, and also to her ladyship, for the extreme kindness shown to him.

Signor Roco re-entered, as I was about to leave, having just written a few words of thanks. He said, "I have told my lady you are here. She will be glad to see you before dinner, if you wish it."

"No, my dear sir, I do not wish to disturb her ladyship; but pray tell her that I am entirely at her orders respecting the Kululee or Hyder Pacha Hospitals."

"By the bye, I am going early tomorrow to Hyder Pacha,—perhaps you would like to come with me?" said he.

"I shall be most happy, if you go before twelve o'clock," I replied, "as at that hour I have several appointments at the Barrack Hospital."

"We will start at eight o'clock, if you like."

* This remark may probably come to the notice of his friends, and lead to a monument being erected to his memory, which, no doubt, he well deserves.

IX

COMMENCEMENT OF THE CULINARY CAMPAIGN

THE next morning we started as agreed upon. On arriving at Scutari, I met a soldier who informed me that a house in Cambridge Street was being prepared for my reception. "It is not two minutes' walk from here," said he; "will you go and see it?"

"Thank you, not this morning; my friend is in a great hurry. When will it be ready?"

"Tomorrow, or next day, at the latest."

"That will do very well. Where can I find you if I want to see you?"

"At the Engineers' office; my name is Corporal Hardy."

"I thank you."

On our way to Hyder Pacha, we met Mr. Bracebridge, talking to Dr. MacHree,* the head doctor at that hospital; both of which gentlemen I very much wished to see. Upon being introduced to Mr. Bracebridge, I recognised him as an old acquaintance of my friend, the late Baronet Sir George Chetwynd, of Greedon Hall, Staffordshire, whom he frequently visited. He informed me that Miss Nightingale had heard of my arrival, and that she would be much pleased to see me.

"I was going to pay my respects," said I, "to Mademoiselle this afternoon after post-time."

"Oh, that will do very well," he replied: "she will have great pleasure in seeing you."

As the Doctor was on his way to headquarters, and Mr. Bracebridge was going in another direction, we continued our journey, which, though short, was very fatiguing, the roads being very bad in consequence of a continuance of heavy rain. At last we arrived at the hospital, which, although the smallest, is certainly the most elegant. It was one of the Sultan's kiosques, and was divided into three departments— one for the officers, and two for the men. About three hundred and forty men and twenty officers were there at the time, as I was told; the latter complained very much about their cooking, the inferiority of which was unavoidable, as there was only a very small kitchen, badly built, which smoked all day, and was without ventilation. It was there that the Duke of Cambridge and staff remained during his indisposition; but I must observe that the Duke had a first-rate culinary artist, who went through the campaign with him. The Duke was only attended by a few gentlemen, and consequently it had not at the time of my visit twenty occupants. Nothing could be done properly for them, till I had built a rough wooden kitchen, and placed a civilian cook under the orders of the doctor and purveyor who had the regulation of the diets. This hospital, though very pretty, was never considered healthy, it being surrounded by gardens and marshy meadows.

---

* Possibly a printer's error and Soyer means Dr. MacIlray who was in charge of surgical operations in Scutari—AB

After inspecting the mess-kitchen, we retired, and thence went to the General Hospital. The doctor-in-chief not being there, we were shown round by a staff-doctor. I found the kitchen very dark, and badly built, for such a number of patients; but the distribution of food and the regulation of the same were on a much better footing than at the Barrack Hospital. On noticing this to the head cook, he gave the credit to Dr. O'Flaherty. Upon being introduced to that gentleman, I recognised him as one of my visitors in Dublin, at the same time as Brigadier-General Lord W. Paulet. I promised to have the kitchen altered as soon as it could possibly be done, and started for the Barrack Hospital to visit Miss Nightingale. As Signor Roco had settled his business, he left me and returned to Pera; consequently, I entered the great Barrack Hospital alone. The entrance was crowded with officers of rank and medical gentlemen. The High Street, facing the General's quarters, was literally crammed with soldiers, more or less conscious of the state of warlike affairs. Most of them kept vandyking from the gin palace to their quarters, their red jackets forming a strange contrast to the quiet dress and solemn air of the Moslem soldiers upon duty.

After shaking hands with some officers and doctors whom I had the pleasure of knowing in England, I inquired of a sentry for Miss Nightingale's apartment, which he at once pointed out to me. On my entering the ante-room, a Sœur de Charité, whom I addressed, informed me that somebody was with that lady. She added, "I am aware that Miss Nightingale wishes to see you, so I will let her know that you are here." I hoped to have a few minutes to myself in order to take an observation of this sanctuary of benevolence; but my project was defeated by my being immediately admitted; and this compels me to trace this picture from memory.

Upon entering the room, I was saluted by a lady, and not doubting that this was our heroine, "Madam," said I, "allow me to present my humble respects. I presume I have the honour of addressing Miss Nightingale."

"Yes, sir. Monsieur Soyer, I believe?"

"The same, Madam."

"Pray take a seat. I hear you had a rough voyage out."

"Very much so, especially from Marseilles to Ajaccio."

"So I heard, Monsieur Soyer."

"I have brought several parcels and letters for you; among the latter, one from the Duchess of Sutherland."

After having perused this epistle, Miss Nightingale remarked: "I believe her Grace is right; you will no doubt be able to render great service in the kitchen department."

"For which I shall need the goodwill and assistance of all the heads of this monster establishment; and I must beg, above all things, that you who have already done so much for the sick and the wounded, will be kind enough to give me the benefit of your valuable experience."

"I will, Monsieur Soyer; but first of all, I should advise you to see Lord William Paulet, Dr. Cumming, and the Purveyor-in-Chief, Mr. Milton."

"Many thanks for your kind advice. I had the pleasure of seeing Lord William yesterday, as well as Dr. Cumming. To Mr. Milton I shall pay my respects upon leaving you."

"You had better do so; for the principal part of your business you will have to transact with those gentlemen."

"A very excellent remark, which I shall not fail to attend to."

"Another gentleman you must see in the purveyor's department is Mr. Tucker. You will then be able to commence operations."

"Very true: I shall not think of commencing before I am well acquainted with everyone in each department that has reference to the cooking. I shall submit every sample of diets, with a statement of the quantity and kind of ingredients of which they are composed, for the approval and opinion of the medical authorities; as I shall have to deal with patients, and not with epicures."

"Perfectly right," said Miss Nightingale.

"That no time may be lost, I should very much like this afternoon to visit the kitchens now in use, inspect the stores, and procure a statement of the daily rations allowed to each patient, if I can have one of the inspectors to go round with me."

"Certainly you can; I will send for somebody who will be happy to accompany you."

"Perhaps you would favour us with your company, as I should be most happy to attend to any suggestion you might like to make."

"I will go with you with great pleasure; but here comes Doctor Macgregor, the under-superintendent, who will be our guide. He told me that he had met you before."

"Yes; we met yesterday at Lord William Paulet's."

"Doctor," said Miss Nightingale, "Monsieur Soyer wishes you to accompany him round the various kitchens and store-rooms."

"I will do that with the greatest pleasure; but he had better be introduced to Mr. Milton and to Mr. Tucker. Mr. Milton is out, but Mr. Tucker will do instead."

Our visitorial pilgrimage then commenced. We first visited Miss Nightingale's dietary kitchen, in which I immediately recognised the whole of the little camp *batterie de cuisine* which my friend Comte told me that the Duke of Cambridge had presented to the hospital. Justice was indeed done to it, for every separate article of which it was composed was in use. Miss Nightingale had a civilian cook as well as an assistant. Everything appeared in as good order as could be expected, considering what there was to be done. I noticed the very bad quality of the charcoal, which smoked terribly, and was nothing but dust. Of course, this interfered materially with the expedition of the cooking, which is a subject of vital importance in an hospital, where punctuality is as essential as quality. Addressing the Doctor, I said, "Suppose you have fifty or a hundred patients under your direction—according to the disease you vary the diet, and according to the state of the patient you vary the hour of his meal."

"Of course we do."

"Then, this defect, simple as it may appear, should be reported and immediately remedied."

"The only excuse I can find for the rations and diets not being ready at the time required is entirely owing to the bad quality of the charcoal, which, as regards time, would deceive the best of cooks, and is quite sufficient to upset the best of culinary arrangements. However, I will take note of the various things which strike me as being out of order or bad, and this will give me a good chance of effecting an immediate improvement."

"You are perfectly right," said Miss Nightingale. "I assure you that Dumont, my cook, is always complaining of the charcoal, which, as you see, is so full of dust that it will not burn; and some days he cannot manage to cook at all with it."

"Well, I will endeavour to remedy this great evil."

"Doctor," said Miss Nightingale, "you had better tell Monsieur Soyer to whom he is to apply in this matter."

"Oh, Mr. Milton or Mr. Tucker will be able to give him the necessary information. We will now visit another."

About half-way down the long corridor, we found another extra-diet kitchen, managed by soldiers; but it was far from being in good order—on the contrary, all was in the greatest confusion. The kitchen was full of smoke, and everything was boiling too fast. In consequence of the bad quality of the charcoal, a wall of bricks had been raised round each stove, and thus wood and charcoal were used *ad libitum*, burning the rice pudding, and over-doing everything. In fact, everything had the disagreeable flavour of being burnt. As I did not wish to alarm them, I merely remarked that the fire was too fierce; and, on the following morning; I took one of my men with me to teach them how to manage better.

We then visited several other kitchens, all of which were, more or less, in the same state. To this there was, however, a single exception, to which I must do justice by observing, that, though not quite perfect as a model—being short of cooking utensils—still it was clean, and everything we tasted was far superior in flavour. Nothing was burnt, except a slight catch in the rice pudding; but this was a mere trifle, compared with the way the viands were spoilt in the other places. The beef-tea, chicken-broth, &c., were nicely done, although they all wanted seasoning. At my first visit to the various diet kitchens, I tasted the soups made for the patients, which I found quite free from the slightest suspicion of seasoning, and consequently tasteless. I then asked to have a couple of basins filled with this. To one I added the requisite seasoning, and requested Doctor Cumming to taste of both. The Doctor complied with my request, and could scarcely believe it possible that such an improvement could be effected by so trifling an addition. He then expressed his approval and decided that in future the cook should season the soup, instead of leaving the same to the irregular tastes of the patients.

"Well," said Doctor Macgregor, "this is by the doctor's order, you may be sure."

"I have not the pleasure of knowing that gentleman, yet, though I admire his kitchen very much, and must admit that he keeps it in good order, I shall certainly tell him when I see him that I do not agree with his method of not seasoning the broths, &c., while in course of preparation. It is very true they ought not to be too highly seasoned; but it is the province of the cook, as I before said, to season for the patient, and not the patient for the cook. Instead of giving so much salt in the ward, I would allow each patient but little or none at all; because in all cookery it is the combination of good and wholesome ingredients properly blended which constitutes the best of broths or diets; and this rule holds good for the bill of fare of all nations."

"This seems logical enough;" said the Doctor; "nor do I approve of the quantity of salt and pepper given in the wards."

"But, Doctor, there is another evil; some people are more partial to salt than others, and, only a few minutes ago, I saw a patient begging his neighbour to give him a portion of his share."

"I am aware they do that, Monsieur Soyer."

"Be kind enough to favour me with the name of the doctor."

"His name is Dr. Taylor; he will be glad to see you, Monsieur Soyer," said Miss Nightingale, smiling. "I can assure you he is a great cook, and manages his own kitchen. He comes down here two or three times every day. He is attending a board this morning, or he would certainly have been here."

"If that is the case, we shall have no difficulty in understanding each other. I will do myself the pleasure of calling upon him."

"You will be sure to find him in his office at nine o'clock tomorrow," said Dr. Macgregor. We then crossed the yard to the general kitchen, as Miss Nightingale called it. Upon entering it, I found, to my surprise, a superb kitchen, built, I believe, by the Turks, and fitted up with twenty copper boilers, to make the tea, as the men's dinners had just been served.

"This is a magnificent kitchen," I observed to Miss Nightingale. "I was not aware there was anything of the kind here."

"So it is, Monsieur Soyer; but see how badly everything is managed."

"Well, this can be remedied."

On going to the top of the marble steps, about eight in number, I perceived that every boiler was made of yellow copper, and screwed to its marble bed. I immediately inquired about the tinning, as I perceived the boilers were much in want of this. Copper is, as I have before remarked, the worst metal which could possibly be employed for hospital uses. I took notes of all, and having inquired of the men how they cooked the patients' dinners, I told them to go on as usual, and that I would be with them at seven the next morning, to put them in the right way. As it was getting late, I was about taking my departure, when Miss Nightingale informed me that there was a similar kitchen on the other side of the yard, and advised me to go and see it.

"Like this one do you say, Mademoiselle?"

"Yes, exactly like it."

"You astonish me. Of course I will go directly. I shall, however, be sorry to trouble you to come so far."

"Oh, no trouble at all, Monsieur Soyer. I am much interested in any improvement or amelioration which may be introduced in so important a department."

We did, indeed, find just such another kitchen as the last, partitioned off in the centre. "This one," said I, will be large enough for all that we require."

"You don't say so," observed Dr. Macgregor.

"Quite large enough, I can assure you; the only inconvenience is its great distance from the building. However, I shall try and manage somehow. This kitchen is cleaner than the other, and the head man appears more intelligent; still there is a great deal to be done, in order to set the whole to rights."

"I was certain you would say so," Miss Nightingale observed.

"Oh, but I am far from despairing. Indeed, I feel confident that I shall succeed. All I require is, that they will go on just as if I had not arrived. I shall come tomorrow at seven o'clock, and watch their proceedings, without removing anyone from his post, and have no doubt I shall be able to introduce a much better system."

After we had examined this kitchen, Miss Nightingale prepared to leave us. I promised to call upon her the following day, to go round the wards, and see the dinners served.

As the lady was leaving, I said, "I have an appointment with Lord W. Paulet at eleven, and one with Dr. Cumming at half-past—therefore I will afterwards do myself the honour of fetching you, Mademoiselle."

"That will be the best plan; and probably his lordship will come with us."

With this the lady withdrew. Dr. Macgregor and myself next went to the purveyor's department, to see Mr. Tucker, whom I found to be an old London friend of mine, of ten years' standing. "You are about the last person, friend Soyer," said Mr. Tucker, "whom I should have expected to see here."

"I am indeed in luck, as I hear you are the gentleman from whom I shall probably require the most assistance."

"Anything you may require, M. Soyer, I have orders to let you have; and you may rest assured that Mr. Milton and myself will assist you to the utmost of our power. There is another person here who knows you—Mr. Bailey, the storekeeper."

"These are indeed good tidings. Tomorrow, Mr. Tucker, I shall be here early, to see how they manage the cooking. Perhaps you will be kind enough to allow some of your men to show me the various store-rooms and the fresh provisions."

"I will make that all right, you may depend upon it."

As my house was not quite ready I crossed over to Pera, and in the evening went to the English Embassy, to settle some business with Signor Roco Vido, and to ascertain whether Lady Stratford had fixed the day for our visit to the hospital at Kululee. This was to be my last night in Pera, as my house at Scutari was to be ready the following day.

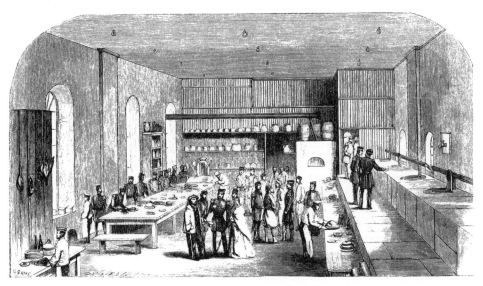

THE BARRACK HOSPITAL KITCHEN, SCUTARI.

X

A TOUR ROUND THE KITCHEN

At half-past six the next morning I was in the kitchen. The soldiers were at that hour making the coffee and tea for breakfast. I went with the serjeant on duty to inspect the quality of the meat, the quantity allowed, and the place of distribution. I found the meat of a very inferior quality, the method of distribution too complicated. When the weight of the quantity allowed was explained to me I found it correct. I was at first much puzzled at finding that some patients upon full diet received three quarters of a pound, some half a pound, and some a quarter of a pound of meat, accordingly as they were placed upon full, half, or quarter diet allowance—a system unavoidable in a hospital, but which would deceive the best cook. On some days, in providing for a hundred patients, this would make a difference of from ten to twenty pounds of meat, according to the number of half or quarter diets. Yet the same quantity of soup would nevertheless be required.

I made a note of this, and next perceived that every mess took their meat separately. Some messes numbered fifteen, twenty, or even thirty. The meat was spitted upon a rough piece of wood about two feet long, and then tied as tight as possible with a strong cord. Although this was a very bad method, I did not choose to interfere, as it was important for me to show them the evil effects of their system, and ensure a reform by pointing out a better. We then went to the store-rooms, and looked over what the contractor called the mixed vegetables, though they were principally of one kind, and half of these unfit for use. After having seen the rations weighed, I sent orders to the cooks not to commence operations until I arrived. We examined all kinds of preserved meats, soups, sweetmeats, &c. I next went to see the poultry, which I found of very inferior quality, consisting principally of old fowls, badly plucked and drawn. The gizzards, heads, and feet, which make such good broth, were thrown away. Mr. Bailey, whom I had not yet seen, then entered. When I had explained what we had already done, and the plan it would be most advisable to adopt for the future, he promised to bring the contractor, that we might talk the matter over. I examined the bread, which was very good indeed.

Mr. Bailey accompanied me to the various kitchens, where I had ordered the men to proceed as usual, and the same in the extra-diet kitchen. During our progress I had the pleasure of meeting and being introduced to most of the medical gentlemen as they were visiting the patients in the corridors and wards. Having been informed that Mr. Milton, the purveyor-in-chief, had arrived, I called at his office, but unfortunately he had just gone to some store-room—no one could tell which. I left my compliments, and a message to say that I should call again. I went to see Dr. Cumming, and report progress, and engaged to let him taste some of my cooking the following day. My next visit was to Lord W. Paulet, whom I found surrounded by military gentlemen of all ranks. He called me in, and, in a most good-natured manner, introduced me to his visitors, saying, "Now M. Soyer is come, I fear he will feed the sick soldiers so well, that they will be sorry to recover and leave the hospital."

"Should such prove to be the case, it will be the best of all bad complaints."

Some of the company inquired whether I was going to the Crimea.

"I must first make my *début* here," was my reply, "and then we shall see."

"Monsieur Soyer, what can I do for you?"

"Your lordship can do what I require in two minutes. Will you be kind enough to send me a carpenter or two, and a bricklayer, to do some little matters I wish to have attended to?"

"Certainly; I will drop a line to Captain Gordon, the chief engineer, to that effect. His office is over the way—you had better go and see him."

"Captain Gordon," said a soldier, who brought some letters, "is gone to Pera."

"I am happy to be able to inform your lordship that I am progressing very fast, and that everyone is very obliging to me."

"I am glad to hear that, Monsieur Soyer."

"I suppose you could not spare time about one o'clock, to go round and see the meals served out?"

"I will try; but I fear I shall hardly have leisure. See what I have to do," he continued, pointing to a pile of letters which the soldier had just brought in; "as Doctor Macgregor is going round with you, he will give me an account of everything."

It was then noon, and about dinner-time. So I returned to the kitchen, where all was in the greatest confusion. Such a noise I never heard before. They were waiting for their soup and meat, and using coarse language, without making the least progress in the distribution. The market at old Billingsgate, during the first morning sale, was nothing compared to this military row. Each man had two tin cans for the soup. They kept running about and knocking against each other, in most admirable disorder. Such confusion, thought I, is enough to kill a dozen patients daily. As a natural consequence, several must go without anything; as, owing to the confusion, some of the orderly waiters get more and others less than their allowance. Any attempt to alter this at the time, would have been as wise as endeavouring to stop the current of the Bosphorus. As I did not wish to lose the chance of seeing the rations served out in the wards, I went for Dr. Macgregor, and we called for Mr. Milton—but the latter had not returned. I then fetched Miss Nightingale, and we went through the wards. The process of serving out the rations, though not quite such a noisy scene as that I had before witnessed, was far from being perfect. In the first place, the patients were allowed to eat the meat before the soup. As I was confident that this could not be by the doctor's order, I asked the reason. The reply was, "we have only one plate." (What they called a plate, was a round and deep tin dish, which held a pound of meat and a pint of soup.) I therefore recommended them to cut the meat as usual into small pieces, and pour the pint of boiling soup over it. This method had the advantage of keeping the meat hot.

"It will enable the patients," I said, "to eat both the soup and meat warm, instead of cold—the daily practice, in consequence of the slow process of carving."

"Very true," said Dr. Macgregor. "Nay, more, the soup will comfort and dispose the stomach for the better digestion of the meat and potatoes. When the men are very hungry, they will often swallow their food without properly masticating it, and the meat is also probably tough."

We then tasted both the soup and meat. The former was thin and without seasoning; the latter, mutton, tough and tasteless. The potatoes were watery. All these defects I promised to rectify the next day. We proceeded to a ward where they complained bitterly that the meat was never done; in fact, it was quite raw, and then of course the cook was blamed.

"Now," said I to Miss Nightingale, "I will wager anything that we shall find some parts very well done, and some, no doubt, too much done, though it is all cooked in the same caldron."

"How do you account for that, Monsieur Soyer? is it owing to the bad quality of the meat?"

"Not at all; that may come from the same sheep, and yet vary."

At another mess, the meat was well done, a small piece at the end only being over-cooked.

"I will explain this to you, madam," said I. "I remarked this morning that the man tied all the joints together very tight, after having put them upon a 'skewer,' as he calls it, almost as large as a wooden leg. The consequence is, that when the meat is thrown into boiling water, it is not properly done; the meat swells, and it is impossible for the heat or the water even to get at it."

"Ah, I noticed that several of the men did exactly as you say this morning," said Miss Nightingale. "The parts which are well done were placed loose upon the stick; and this explains the mystery—but I shall alter that tomorrow."

Having afterwards inspected several extra-diet kitchens, and tasted various things, I perceived what I could accomplish, both as regarded convalescents and extra diets. Miss Nightingale having again offered to render any assistance in her power, left us, as she had a great deal to attend to. I retraced my steps to Dr. Cumming's, and stated my opinion of the present system of cooking; and explained what I proposed doing, of all of which he approved highly. I then returned to the kitchen, and sent a requisition for six rations of everything allowed for making the soup. I proceeded thus:—

To eight pints of water I put four pounds of meat, a quarter of a pound of barley, a little salt and pepper, and the allowance of vegetables, and in about an hour I produced a very good soup—some of which I sent to several doctors. They tasted and praised it highly, as being very nourishing and palatable. I then carried some to Dr. Cumming, who approved of its composition; but expressed his opinion that it would probably be too expensive. I then informed him I had made it with the ration allowance, taking the meat at half-diet scale. He was much pleased with the meat, which he pronounced highly palatable, and thought that the seasoning should be put in with the other ingredients. I explained that I could still improve it by the simple addition of a small quantity of sugar and flour.

"The purveyor will not, I am certain, refuse that," said he.

"Oh, I am aware of that; but I wish to manage it without increasing the expense. I must accomplish that, if possible." Miss Nightingale and Dr. Macgregor, to both of whom I sent some, praised it even more than the others had done, particularly the meat, which they stated to be of a very excellent flavour, and they had the opportunity of tasting the former. Mr. Milton came in, and though I had not had the pleasure of seeing that gentleman, from the description I had heard of him, and his pleasing manner, I knew I was not mistaken in saying—"Mr. Milton, allow me to have the honour of tendering my best compliments and thanks for your prompt visit."

"No person could be more welcome here than you are, Monsieur Soyer. I only regret I was not in my office when you called. I should have been happy to have accompanied you round the wards. Your very just remarks have been repeated to me and the plan you mean to adopt explained, but I fear you will meet with so many difficulties that you will get tired before you have achieved much good."

"Not at all," I replied; "you will see a great change by tomorrow, which must be attributed chiefly to the politeness and cordial assistance I have met with from the members of every department—especially your own—which to me is the most important."

"I have given orders that everything you may require is to be placed at your disposal, if in store; and any alteration or suggestion which is likely to be beneficial will be immediately attended to. You have only to ask for anything you need in the way of cooking utensils, and it shall, if possible, be procured."

"My great object and delight will be to effect a change with the daily allowance."

"That would certainly be as well; but I fancy it cannot be done. The provisions here are of a quality very inferior to what we get in London."

"You are quite right, if they are all like those I saw this morning. Favour me by tasting these two soups. Julien! please to give Mr. Milton two small basins of soup—one of mine, and one of that made at the hospital." On tasting mine first he pronounced it very good and palatable, and of an excellent flavour. The other, although made with exactly the same materials, he could hardly swallow. It had no seasoning, had a blackish appearance, and was quite tasteless.

"There is no comparison," said Mr. Milton.

"All the soup will in future be like the sample I have made, and I can greatly improve it by the addition of a few pounds of brown sugar and a little flour extra."

"Monsieur Soyer, I beg you will not regard such trivial expenses, at any rate for the present; what is required you shall have."

"I see the fresh vegetables are very bad—as you have a quantity of preserved ones, I shall mix them."

"In future we must try and get better meat, poultry, and eggs; and, above all, charcoal. I am aware you have justly complained of them. Have you seen our bread?"

"Yes, I have, and very good it is too."

"That is really all we can manage to my satisfaction. As regards the meat and poultry, I will send you the contractor; but the charcoal is in the commissariat department. I shall write an official letter respecting it. I see," he continued, looking at some, "it is all dust, and seems quite wet."

"Pray send off a letter; and if you will give me the name of the gentleman who is at the head of that department, I shall be happy to make his acquaintance; and beg of him not to allow any delay, as I consider this the most important matter of all."

I repeated the reason for saying this which I have before mentioned.

After listening attentively to my remarks, Mr. Milton said,—

"You may well call it the most important, and the sooner it is altered the better."

We parted. I then told the soldier-cooks to have the boilers thoroughly cleaned, and everything in from the stores by eight o'clock the next morning, as I intended making the soup myself. I left Julien, my head man, with them to superintend matters.

Having called upon Doctor Taylor, I had a long conversation with him upon cookery. In the course of this he said,—

"On finding that the cooking was so badly done, I took upon myself, not only to superintend the men, but also to cook and teach them; and I must say I found them very willing. How could I expect them to know anything about it? they had never been taught to do it."

"True, Doctor; and, as soon as they begin to know a little about it, they are recalled to their regiments, and replaced by newcomers as ignorant as they were themselves at first."

"Exactly; and I tell you what, Monsieur Soyer, though we may be very good doctors, and possess a thorough knowledge of medical science, we still need the aid of culinary science; for the one without the other will produce but very unsatisfactory results. Since I have turned my attention to it, I am more and more fortified in the opinion which I have expressed before several medical boards, that a doctor, to be well qualified, should have some knowledge of the art of cookery, and this he ought to acquire in the first stage of his medical education."

"Indeed, Doctor, it is not with the view of elevating my profession, to which I have now devoted my attention for more than twenty-seven years, that I say I am persuaded that this science has been too lightly treated. In corroboration of your just remark, I have, as you will find, already stated in my various works upon cookery, that to make a good cook it is of paramount importance that a man should possess some chemical as well as medical knowledge."

"I agree with you, Monsieur Soyer," said he.

"As soon as my kitchen is ready, Doctor, I hope you will favour me with a visit."

"With much pleasure. Let me know when it is finished."

To my great regret, I was obliged to see about returning to Pera, some delay having taken place in the completion of my house. On reaching the landing-place not a caique was to be had, the weather was so bad they could not cross. A friend offered me shelter for that night at a small restaurant kept by a Greek called Demetri. There were seventeen of us lying on straw sofas, with the privilege of covering ourselves with our greatcoats, if fortunate enough to possess one. Rooms were at a premium in Scutari. It was also necessary for anybody who wished to have the benefit of his greatcoat to keep awake all night; for no sooner did you begin to doze that some of your sleeping partners, who happened to be wide awake, endeavoured to appropriate the coveted garment to their use; and the weather being very chilly, this proved anything but pleasant. Unfortunately, after passing an uncomfortable night, I did not feel much refreshed, and was almost unfit to undertake the difficult task I had before me. However, I was up at six, and in the kitchen by seven. None of my orders had been attended to. My own people were not there as they ought to have been; and the men told me they could not get the rations till ten o'clock, that being the usual time for issuing them.

"Really," said I; "and pray who told you so?"

"The serjeant and some of the orderlies," was the reply.

"We shall see all about that; come with me."

The truth is, I did find it very difficult to get anything; but, in less than half-an-hour after I had been to the purveyor's headquarters my new regiment began to manœuvre admirably under my command. By eight o'clock everything was ready for the cooking, except my cooks, who had been sleeping in a store-room upon some straw, and had a regular fray with the allied rats. These animals, it appears, had come to welcome them to Scutari.

Upon inspecting the boilers, my first fear was realized—there was nothing but copper—all the tinning had worn away. And very difficult was it to ascertain this fact, these immense and deep caldrons being securely screwed to the marble basement, and extremely difficult, not only to remove, but also to tin when removed. I consider it most advisable that all large establishments should have their cooking apparatus made of malleable iron, which is extremely clean, is much cheaper, and does not require tinning: the lid may be made of copper for appearance' sake, but not so the boiler. The kitchen battery of the wealthy alone should be copper, as they can afford to employ professional persons for the preparation of their diet, who never would attempt using them when coppery. (For my important visit to the Consumptive Hospital at Brompton, see Addenda.)

That day I was obliged to use them. Having put the proper quantity of water into each copper, with the meat, barley, vegetables, and salt and pepper, we lighted the fires; and after allowing the ingredients to simmer for two hours and a half, an excellent soup was made; I only adding a little sugar and flour to finish it.

The receipt for this excellent soup, so highly approved of and immediately adopted by the medical men, will be found in my Hospital Diets, with a scale of proportions from ten to a hundred.

The meat was so poor that there was no fat to skim off the soup. It was therefore served out at once, as described in the receipt. Several doctors went round with me, and asked the men how they liked it. They were all highly delighted with it, and praised it very much. I also took care that the rations of meat should not be tied together on the skewer.

The orderlies were now ordered not to tie their rations of meat so tight. Upon inspection I found that they had a most curious method of marking their different lots. Some used a piece of red cloth cut from an old jacket; others half a dozen old buttons tied together; old knives, forks, scissors, &c., but one in particular had hit upon an idea which could not fail to meet with our entire approval. The discovery of this brilliant idea was greeted with shouts of laughter from Miss Nightingale, the doctors, and myself. It consisted in tying a pair of old snuffers to the lot.

All this rubbish was daily boiled with the meat, but probably required more cooking. On telling the man with the snuffers that it was a very dirty trick to put such things in the soup, the reply was—"How can it be dirty, sir? sure they have been boiling this last month."

When all the dinners had been served out, I perceived a large copper half full of rich broth with about three inches of fat upon it. I inquired what they did with this?

"Throw it away, sir."

"Throw it away?" we all exclaimed.

"Yes, sir; it's the water in which the fresh beef has been cooked."

"Do you call that water? I call it strong broth. Why don't you make soup of it?"

"We orderlies don't like soup, sir."

"Then you really do throw it away?"

"Yes, sir; it is good for nothing."

I took a ladle and removed a large basinful of beautiful fat, which, when cold, was better for cooking purposes than the rank butter procured from Constantinople at from ten to fifteen piastres per pound. The next day I showed the men how to make a most delicious soup with what they had before so foolishly thrown away. This method they were henceforward very glad to adopt. Not less than seventy pounds of beef had been daily boiled in this manner, and without salt. It would hardly be credited, but for its truth I can appeal to Miss Nightingale and others who were present.

Nothing was needed but a sharp look-out after the cooks in order tó ensure complete success. The day after I had the coppers tinned. The next thing was to have a charcoal stove built, an oven, a store-room, and a larder partitioned off; and a kitchen dresser and chopping-block made. Through the kindness of the Chief Engineer, Captain Gordon, these things were accomplished in a few days, and at a trifling expense. If not a very magnificent, it was, as will be seen, a very spacious and handy kitchen.

In a few days I made experiments in small quantities upon all the various extra diets, such as chicken, mutton, and veal broth, the cooking of fowls, beef and mutton tea, &c. I did not forget the beverages, such as rice water, lemonades, arrowroot, panada ditto, barley water, sago jelly, &c.; rice pudding, sago, bread, vermicelli and macaroni ditto. The receipts will be found in the Addenda, under the head of "Hospital Diets."

A gentleman, Mr. Black, who was a first-class interpreter, was then introduced to me by the Purveyor-in-Chief, and appointed to assist me in any way I might require his aid. He was highly recommended by Miss Nightingale, and a number of first-class doctors, as well as by Lord William Paulet. It is with gratitude that I acknowledge the great assistance I received from that gentleman during his stay with me, and the energy he displayed in procuring everything I required. He spoke French fluently, also the Turkish, Greek, and Armenian languages. This rendered him invaluable to me, as I was obliged to employ people speaking those different languages in my numerous kitchens. And what was more remarkable still, he was the husband of the celebrated Maid of Athens, whose company I had the pleasure of enjoying several times; and although this interesting personage is now in her tenth lustre, some remains of the great Byron seem still engraved on the physiognomy of the once celebrated Greek beauty; and she informed me that when Lord Byron wrote his poem on her, she was but ten years of age, he at the time residing opposite the house of her parents at Athens.

XI

FIRST OPERATIONS

IN a short time, and without much trouble, I initiated the soldier-cooks into my method, and taught the serjeant to see it properly executed. I shall here describe the process fully, as it will be generally useful for hospitals or public institutions. In the first place I drew up two receipts—the one by weight and the other by measure, the former for beef and the latter for mutton soups. Mutton was the principal meat used for patients in a state of convalescence. These receipts I had carefully copied and hung up in the kitchen, at the same time supplying the cooks with weights and scales. I also taught them how to stew the meat well, and to manage the fires so as to prevent over-boiling or burning, as well as to economize the fuel. It was no longer a matter of much difficulty. Every soldier had become a cook; and if in case of any of them being removed to their regiments, one of the initiated, under the direction of the above-mentioned serjeant, who was not changed, soon made a new recruit capable of cooking for any number. So simple was this plan, that it was as easy to cook for thousands as it had before been for hundreds, and to do it to perfection.*

Although this was as perfect as possible, a great difficulty still remained, as the number varied daily, some days increasing, others decreasing; and as the whole was cooked by messes, the same caldron was required to cook for two hundred and fifty persons one day, and perhaps for one hundred and seventy the next. This caused great confusion and delay, as well as continual quarrelling among the cooks and orderlies, the latter complaining of not getting their full share; and if this happened, it was a matter of vital importance to the patient, who was thus deprived of the proper quantity of sustenance ordered by the medical man. In fact, it led to many very serious results. I therefore settled that all the caldrons should be filled every day; and as each boiler would cook for one hundred and fifty, in one only was it necessary that the quantity should vary. As it was most probable that this one would vary daily, I made a supplementary scale for it, from five diets to one hundred, leaving only a few pounds to be guessed. If any mistake occurred, it could be of no material consequence. I also had tinned iron skewers made, with numbers to each, to prevent the meat being mixed in the boilers, as expedition, cleanliness, and proportion should be the motto of all such establishments. This plan was followed to the last.

* I earnestly recommend the adoption of this plan in every public institution, civil or military. For example, put in the caldron, which we will suppose holds fifty gallons, so much water, so many pounds of meat, vegetables, salt, pepper, and sugar; add the barley, light the fire; stir now and then with a long wooden spaddle to prevent the barley sticking at the bottom of the caldron; when boiling, reduce the fire. Simmer gently two and a half hours, if mutton is used; if beef, three hours. Never skim it, only take the fat off, if any, which use for other purposes, or instead of butter (see Hospital receipt in Addenda). If two or more boilers are required, the quantities given in the scale only need increasing.

As all the boilers had been well tinned, I showed the men how to make tea on a large scale. Their plan was to tie the tea in a piece of cloth, and throw it into the boiling water. In a few minutes the cloth had shrunk so much, that the aroma of the tea, instead of being diffused, was retained in the centre, the inside of the bag being scarcely soaked. This I proposed to remedy by having fine nets made for the purpose. Miss Nightingale immediately had this done, and they were a great improvement. This, after all, was not quite satisfactory, as the tea had to be made in the same boilers as the soup and meat. The coppers were fixtures, and of such large dimensions, that it was almost impossible to clean them properly. I therefore invented my Scutari Teapot, with its valuable and economical improvement upon the old system, the model of which is given at the end of the book. (See Addenda.)

DESCRIPTION OF TEAPOT

I had a large kettle made, holding eight quarts, and put a coffee filter to it. I then placed the rations of tea for about twenty men in the filter, poured in the boiling water, and, to my astonishment, made about one-fourth more tea, perfectly clear, and without the least sediment. Four of these kettles made enough tea for all the hospital, and this at once induced me to order some upon a smaller scale for the various wards, where at night it is often of the greatest importance that tea should be prepared quickly, in large quantities. I cannot too strongly recommend it to large families, institutions, and other establishments, for its economy of time, and a saving of at least twenty-five per cent. upon the quantity of tea required. I tried it in Miss Nightingale's room at Scutari, before several persons; and the Reverend Mr. Blackwood, the chaplain, persuaded me to bring it out for the benefit of the poorer classes, as much for its cleanliness as its economy. This, reader, I claim more as a happy thought than an invention; but I always had an idea that tea should be suspended in the water, instead of being allowed to fall to the bottom, as is generally the case. Coffee may be made in these vessels, as the construction is the same as that of a coffee-pot.

By this time my kiosque, or, as it was afterwards named, Soyer House, was ready. It was situated in Cambridge Street, near the Scutari Grand Champ des Morts. Thanks to this, my daily trip across the Bosphorus was at an end, and as the March winds had a great influence upon its current, I preferred *terra firma* to rolling about in its whimsical stream of daily pearls, evening diamonds, and shoals of immense porpoises, which towards sunset commence to accompany you with their nautical summersaults. These at first terrified the uninitiated, who could not help fearing the sudden appearance of an unexpected passenger on board the caique.

The time having been fixed by Lady Stratford de Redcliffe for our visit to Kululee, in company with a doctor from that hospital I rode over there. It is about five miles from Scutari, along the edge of the Bosphorus; and from an ancient Jewish cemetery on the top of one of the hills the beauty of the panorama is such as to defy description. My opinion is, that such another view does not exist in any other spot under the canopy of heaven. Under its inspiration I entirely forgot the annoyance I had endured in that labyrinth of ruin and filth. From this spot the metropolis of Constantine, backed by a sky of fire, presented so sublime and picturesque an appearance, that in an enchanted dream alone could one hope to realize the effect of the mirage. It embraced the city and the whole length of the

Bosphorus, down to the entrance of the Black Sea. Leaving this beautiful landscape, we passed through several dull though very pretty villages, and shortly after arrived at the hospital and barrack of Kululee. It is surrounded by kiosques and country seats. The country appears very rich and fertile, but owing to the indolence of the inhabitants, "which may be adopted as a proverb," produces little. Although Nature has done so much for the Moslem race, she seems also to have deprived them of the faculty of exertion, and consequently of doing anything for themselves.

Shortly after our arrival we saw, through the golden rays of a dazzling sunlight, several caiques gaily dancing on the turbulent waves of the Bosphorus. They darted swiftly towards us; the caidjees wore white jackets with flowing sleeves. In a few minutes Lady Stratford landed, attended by several of her fair companions. "Have you been over the hospital, Monsieur Soyer?" said Lady Stratford, on landing.

"No, I have not, my lady."

"I am glad of that, as I wish to explain everything to you respecting the various kitchen departments myself. You must know, Monsieur Soyer, that we have three separate hospitals here. Although they are under the direction of one doctor, they form three distinct establishments. We will now visit the Barrack Hospital, as we are so close to it, and then the other two."

Several remarks were made upon the delightful situation of Kululee. Lady Stratford in the meantime sent Signor Roco to apprise Dr. Humfries of our arrival. We commenced visiting the store-rooms, provisions, kitchens, larders, &c. I found in the extra-diet kitchen several very good and well-prepared diets; and amongst these some very nice calfs'-foot jelly, and excellent rice pudding made by the Sisters of Mercy. I took notes of what was required in kitchen utensils—alterations and improvements in that department; and as one of Captain Gordon's best men was with me, our business proceeded very rapidly.

Lady Stratford proposed that we should next visit the principal kitchen. "I think from its appearance, Monsieur Soyer, that it is in a very bad state." Such proved to be the case. It was in perfect darkness, full of smoke, and the stoves, as large as those at Scutari, required considerable alterations, the furnaces being inside, instead of out, as at Scutari. The brickwork was quite burnt out, and all the smoke came in the kitchen, blinding the men, who could not support the extra fatigue caused by this nuisance, even preferring their dangerous duty in the trenches to this kind of culinary inquisition, as it might very justly have been called. They were in consequence changed every week, or even oftener. The result of this was bad cookery and the consumption of about 170 per cent. more wood than was necessary. The men actually piled small trees, cut into lengths of five or six feet, upon the fires; and when the soup boiled too fast they threw pailsful of water upon the burning wood, thus filling the place with dust and steam. As the boilers were screwed down in the same manner as those at Scutari Barrack Hospital, they had never been tinned since first used. I at once had the furnaces put in order, and the skylight over them repaired. I gave them my receipts, and sent one of my men over for a few days to teach them how to make the soup. I also promised Lady Stratford, who took so much interest in the success of that hospital, to call as often as I could; and, after the opening of my kitchens at Scutari, to spend a few days there, and superintend the cooking myself.

We then went to the General Hospital, on the top of the hill, which contained three hundred patients. Having had the honour of being introduced to the Sisters of Mercy, I took notes of all that was wanted there, and we lastly proceeded to the Riding School Hospital, appropriated to the convalescents. There I had the pleasure of being introduced to Miss Stanley, who had the superintendence of the Sisters. This establishment had neither kitchen nor cooking utensils. However, by the aid of the engineer who accompanied us, everything was soon settled.

Yet, after all, I ordered nothing that was not indispensable; and I must remark that, with all the power with which I was invested by the War Department, coupled with the willing assistance of Captain Gordon, I found it a difficult matter to get a plank, or even a nail, fixed in any of the hospitals. At the same time, I may add, with pride and gratitude, that throughout the Crimean campagn I was most highly favoured by every department; for if anything I required was procurable, I had it.

Lady Stratford and visitors having expressed their satisfaction at the success of our visit, I was on the point of retiring with Signor Roco Vido, when Lady Stratford asked what day the kitchen at Scutari would be opened. "On Monday next," was my reply. "I presume we shall be honoured with your ladyship's presence, and that of your suite."—"I shall not fail to attend, Monsieur Soyer," were her ladyship's words.

The Sisters having thanked me, we retired. We returned in a beautiful Oriental moonlight by the same road—the panorama of the morning being now tinted by the reflection of the soft rays of the moon.

Just as I had set everybody to work in the various hospitals, and my Scutari kitchen was nearly finished, an entirely new plan suggested itself to my mind. It was as follows:—Instead of commencing with a hundred patients at a time, as I had at first intended, I changed my mind, and preferred making a grand opening, resolving to invite all the heads of the medical department in the various hospitals, as well as some of the most eminent among the French and Turkish medical staff. This, I was aware, was a bold experiment; for had I failed—and many unforeseen events might have caused such a result—my reputation would have suffered. I was, therefore, well aware that risking the labour of twenty years against an uncertainty; as all those I was about to invite would come to watch my proceedings with the eyes of Argus, and would judge of my plans accordingly. At all events, my sample trials had already given great satisfaction to two eminent doctors. In pursuance of this plan, I went to Lord William Paulet, explained it, and begged him to send, or cause to be sent, invitations to all the principal officers to honour me with their presence upon the occasion, which his lordship kindly promised to do. I also apprised the doctor-in-chief, who promised to attend himself, and invite the principal medical gentlemen to do the same.

The opening day was fixed for the following Monday—it was then Tuesday—leaving me till Thursday to finish my preparations. On the Friday morning, after having inspected several kitchens, and gone through a number of wards, I was suddenly taken ill. I seemed to have forgotten everything, and experienced at the same time a sensation of brain fever. There were, however, none of its symptoms. Although I was quite conscious of what I had to do, I was entirely incapable of doing it, or of ordering anything or directing anyone. In fact, I began to fear that all my former endeavours would prove useless, and the opening of my kitchen be a marked failure. The day appointed by Lord Paulet could not easily be changed, and such a course would have caused the success of my project to be doubted. Though I had a couple of assistants, neither of them could carry it out for me, as they did not know my plans. This sudden indisposition I only mentioned to my people and to Doctor Macgregor, who told me to keep quiet, and gave me some soothing medicine. It was Sunday afternoon before my head was clear, and, after a good night's rest, I felt myself again, and quite able to open my kitchen on the day appointed.

The doctor attributed this mental disorder to the effect produced by the immense number of sick and wounded I was in the habit of seeing daily, and the numerous dead bodies passing before the windows to be buried. I had also witnessed several cases of autopsy and some operations. "This," he said, "with the constant worry of business, has unnerved you to that extent, that had you unfortunately taken the fever, you would perhaps never have recovered your senses." However, thanks to a kind Providence, I was able to open my kitchen at the appointed time. It met with perfect success, and the entire approbation of all medical gentlemen and visitors present. They all expressed themselves highly gratified, and declared that the various samples of diets I then submitted for their opinion were much preferable to those produced under the old system, besides having the merit of being concocted with the same ration allowance.

The plan I adopted was this:—my samples of diets and extra diets being prepared, I arranged the basins containing the different diets on the table, and in juxta-position I placed those prepared by the soldiers, affixing a number to each, to enable the people present to make a comparison. All was ready by eleven o'clock, and one being the time appointed for the arrival of the visitors, I fetched Doctor Cumming, and requested him to taste the several samples, and give me his candid opinion; observing that everything was made from the usual allowance, and cost about the same, or even less, when made in large quantities.

No. 1, was beef-tea. Tasting my sample first, Doctor Cumming pronounced it good; the other, without taste or flavour. No. 1 was adopted.

Then followed chicken-broth, mutton-broth, beef-soup, rice-water, barley-water, arrowroot-water, ditto with wine, sago with port, calfs'-foot jelly, &c. Everything was found superior, and so highly commended by the doctor-in-chief, I no longer had any doubt of success, nor of the general approval of all the faculty. I promised to lay the recipes for my new diets before the doctor the next day, and he retired.*

About half-past twelve, the kitchen was crowded to excess with military and medical men. Lord William Paulet entered, followed by his staff, and accompanied by Mr. Milton, Mr. and Mrs. Bracebridge, &c. They were much pleased with the cleanly appearance of the kitchen, and equally surprised at the alteration which it had undergone in so short a time. I then showed his lordship round, carefully pointing out to him the simple but useful alterations I had effected; and requested him to taste the various samples, compare the one with the other, and give his candid opinion thereupon. Having done this, Lord W. Paulet expressed his high satisfaction, and to confirm it, while in the kitchen, wrote the following letter:—

* If I dwell so minutely upon these apparently frivolous details, it is only because I wish to show that I did not introduce anything until it had first met with the approval of the medical gentlemen.

Lord William Paulet to Monsieur Soyer

It is with great pleasure that I state I have carefully viewed and tasted the new diets introduced by Monsieur Soyer in the hospitals this day; and had I not seen and tasted them, I could not have believed that such an amelioration could have been produced from the same materials as allowed by Government.   W. Paulet.

Above a hundred officials from the various hospitals were present, and many of the Sisters of Mercy. Not one person had anything to say in disapproval; but, on the contrary, praised everything. This was sufficient to stamp it with success. The only thing I regretted was, that—owing to the rough state of the Bosphorus that day—Lady Stratford de Redcliffe, as well as a number of military men and medical officers from the French and Turkish hospitals, were not present. However, they visited my kitchen some days after, and having inspected everything, added their testimonials of approbation to those I had already received. They were particularly struck with the cleanliness and order in a place where so much was done daily.

The day after the opening, I proposed to Doctors Cumming and Macgregor, the superintendent, to take one wing of the hospital, which contained one-fourth of the patients, and supply these with all which they might require. This I did with the greatest ease, and without the least confusion, much to the satisfaction of the patients. I continued to do this for three days, and then took half of the hospital in hand. As I wished fully to impress the patients with the superiority of my newly-adopted diets, I then took the other half in hand, and put the first back to the old *régime*, for a day or two, as I was not quite prepared to undertake the whole at once. The patients immediately became dissatisfied, so I was obliged to go with Dr. Macgregor to them and explain the reason of the sudden change, which was only momentary, three cheers from my numerous guests closing my laconic, though effective, speech.

XII

THE SCUTARI MISSION ACCOMPLISHED

A FEW days afterwards, I closed all the extra-diet kitchens, with the exception of the one under the direction of Miss Nightingale, and another under the direction of Dr. Taylor, having discharged about twenty soldier-cooks, who consumed daily ten times more fuel than was required; this at the same time much deteriorated the quality of the extra-diets, which required the greatest attention as regarded the regulation of the heat. We prepared everything in the one large kitchen—viz., breakfast, dinner, tea, extra-diets, the cooking for the orderlies, &c., included. Having got all under my own eye, I placed two civilian cooks in charge of the extra-diets, with six soldiers to assist them, who might at the same time be instructed, instead of the twelve before required—thus simplifying the whole process.

The only difficulty that remained was, how to send the dinners hot to the various wards, on account of the distance being so great. Miss Nightingale submitted a very excellent plan, which was adopted with success. It is very similar to that in use in the French hospitals, with this difference, that we introduced double cases in which to carry boiling water, thus keeping the contents of the several divisions hot much longer. Two of these cases were sufficient for each ward, and after they had been in use for a week, no establishment could be in better order. Had there been room in the hospital we could have accommodated as many more patients with the greatest ease, the receipts being regulated by weight and measure, from an ounce for certain articles, to seven or eight cwt. for others. I must also observe, in thanking Mr. Milton, the purveyor, that he rendered me the full amount of assistance he had promised, and without such powerful aid, as well as that of Mr. Tucker, it would have been impossible for me to have made so much progress in so short a period.

In the first place, the provisions were improved—the old fowls got unexpectedly younger, and the fuel was better. I was thus perfectly satisfied, and so was everybody else—medical officers as well as patients. As soon as the alterations at the General Hospital were completed, which made a very good kitchen, being clean, light, and commodious, instead of being ill-adapted for the purpose, as I at first found it, I paid a second visit to Doctor Lawson, the chief medical officer of this hospital. I then tried some experiments before him and numerous other doctors similar to those I had previously made at the Barrack Hospital, and with the same success; and I must say, as far as the extra-diet went, in justice to Doctor O'Flaherty, the under-superintendent, with a great deal less trouble than I experienced at the Barrack Hospital; Doctor O'Flaherty having carefully watched over and disposed of that very important department. I next went to Kululee, then in charge of the new lady manager, Miss Hutton, who had replaced Miss Stanley. I received the following letter from that lady, and at once placed myself at her disposal.

KULULEE HOSPITAL, *April*, 14th, 1855.

MONSIEUR,—I hear that you are on the point of leaving Scutari. When may we hope that you will come to Kululee? A few days of your instruction and superintendence might effect more good than I can express.

I am, yours, &c.,

EMILY HUTTON.

The day after the receipt of this I went to Kululee, where I had the pleasure of seeing Miss Hutton for the first time, and met with a most gracious reception from that lady and her assistants. We next visited the General Hospital upon the heights, where I was introduced to the matron and the Irish Sisters of Charity. These ladies were very anxious to obtain some utensils and have a new extra-diet kitchen built. Captain Gordon's assistant made a small sketch of the place, and undertook to have it done at once, being aware of its necessity. I left quite satisfied that it would be immediately put in execution.

It only remained for me to give a list of the utensils required to the purveyor-in-chief; and shortly after, in company with that gentleman, I paid another visit to the hospital, where, thanks to his attention, they had a most effective kitchen. I regretted that the large kitchen for the convalescent belonged to the Turkish authorities, as it could not be altered to my liking. Nothing could be altered without an order from the Turkish officials, and to obtain this, would have taken as long a time as the duration of the war. Upon leaving the General Hospital, we visited the Barrack Hospital, where we found every department perfect—the orders given upon our former visit with Lady Stratford de Redcliffe having been carried out to the letter. I was now introduced to Doctor Humphrey, who had been appointed in lieu of another medical gentleman. He accompanied us round the hospital, and kindly offered me a bed for the night, which I accepted—having to cook for the patients the next morning, as well as to instruct some soldier-cooks who were at the convalescent hospital, called the Riding School. The next day I was in full action, and received visits from every doctor and Sister of Charity, who all approved of the diets, as well as my new teapot, in which I made in the space of ten minutes, out of the ration tea, enough strong tea for about thirty persons; thus effecting a saving of at least ten per cent. At the desire of Miss Hutton, I afterwards sent a civilian cook to the Barrack Hospital, to carry out the system, and to set the various kitchen departments in order. But I must observe in full justice to that lady, who had succeeded Miss Stanley, that since my last visit to these hospitals, every department under her care was so much improved that hardly anything was required to perfect them. Although the hospitals were full of patients, the lady assistants who attended this duty appeared to devote their utmost energies to the benevolent and humane cause for which they had left their native homes.

Thence I went to the Palace Hospital, Hyder Pacha, and having had a new kitchen built for the use of the officers, placed a good civilian cook in it, and with the assent and assistance of Doctors Cumming and M'Elray,* the doctor-in-chief, composed a bill of fare for their mess. Having arranged everything in the various hospitals to my satisfaction, I was honoured by several visits from Lady Stratford de Redcliffe, who expressed her own and Lord Stratford's approbation of my

*This is certainly Dr MacIlray—AB

management, and both afterwards took a most lively interest in the success of my proceedings. I then was requested by Lord Panmure to proceed to the Crimea for the same purpose, and also to try and improve the system of camp cookery for the soldiers. I therefore informed Lord William Paulet of my anticipated departure for the seat of war, showing him, at the same time, my small model field stove. Having explained its principle, he expressed his approval of its simplicity. I said, "I expect ten of those stoves, which, upon arrival, I wish to have forwarded to the Crimea. I have managed to make use of the Turkish coppers at the hospital, which answer perfectly well, and of the existence of which I was not aware before leaving England. They are the same as those adopted in the hospital at Smyrna, and, although too large for camp use, would do very well for my trial before the Crimean authorities. If these stoves are approved of, those for the army on march or in camp can be made thus—viz., two for a company, both of which can be carried on the back of one mule, with sufficient wood inside for two days. When on march, they will cook either under cover or in the open air, and in all weathers, and the quantity of fuel required will be a mere trifle compared with the present consumption. Thus you perceive, my lord, that two small ones will cook for a full company of a hundred or a hundred and twenty men, though I am aware a company seldom exceeds a hundred in number. This will not matter much; and it is better to have them too large than too small. We can also have smaller ones for picket and outpost duty."

"You are right, Monsieur Soyer; and I must say your plan appears very sensible and well conceived. I heartily wish you the same success in the Crimea that you have met with here."

"In order to prevent any inconvenience from my departure from the hospital, I will put all in good trim, and leave the whole under the superintendence of a corporal who is now well acquainted with my system; and I shall request several doctors to send occasionally for soup, broth, pudding, &c., unknown to the cook, to see if any alteration takes place after my departure; and perhaps your lordship would oblige me by doing the same. This will make them attentive to the proportions required and the proper management of the cooking."

"I assure you I often send for a basin of the soldiers' soup for my lunch, it is so very good."

"I do not think you will find any difference after my departure, although many persons say that it is all very well so long as I am here, but that as soon as my back is turned it will be as bad as ever. Colonel Dennis, in particular, will not be persuaded; I will vouch for the contrary, as my receipts are all done by weight and measure, and that causes much less trouble. Before I came they had never done working, and all for want of a proper system of management. Doctor Cumming and myself have talked over the subject, and we have no fear of the result. The only thing required is for the serjeant in charge to see all properly attended to in the morning."

"I shall be happy to give you a letter to Lord Raglan, with whom I suppose you are acquainted."

"I am; but it is above twelve years since I had the pleasure of seeing his lordship, and that was at the Reform Club; therefore a letter from your lordship, in addition to one from the Minister-at-War, cannot fail to be very acceptable."

"It shall be ready for you tomorrow morning. By the way, I hope you do not intend to go before the new purveyor-in-chief comes. It is most important that you should see him."

"Indeed! I was not aware that we were to have a new purveyor-in-chief. I very much regret it—but is Mr. Milton going?"

"Of course he is: he only came out here till another could be appointed. He cannot remain, as he holds a very important appointment at the War Office, and his presence is required in London. I should advise you to see him, and mention about your stoves. He will forward them to Balaklava for you."

"I will do so, my lord. I much regret taking up so much of your valuable time."

"Do not mention that, Monsieur Soyer. This is business, and to my mind of great importance."

"A fresh tribulation!" thought I; "a new purveyor-in-chief, who, in my absence, may upset everything I have done!" I went immediately to Miss Nightingale, to inquire whether she had heard of this change. I met Mr. Bracebridge there, and he told me that he had known it for some time. He informed me that Miss Nightingale and himself were going to the Crimea, and proposed that we should all start together. I, of course, was much pleased at the news, as I knew that Miss Nightingale would be of great assistance to me in the hospitals in the Crimea. I then promised Mr. Bracebridge to be ready on the day fixed for our departure. Mr. Bracebridge said, "Miss Nightingale is engaged at present. Do you wish to see her?"

"No; I am going to Mr. Milton, to speak about the stoves I mentioned the other day, and to inquire when the new purveyor-in-chief is coming."

"Oh, I can tell you that—he will be here tomorrow without fail."

"That will do nicely. We shall just have time to become acquainted, and settle everything before my departure to the seat of war."

I found Mr. Milton preparing for his departure.

"Well, Monsieur Soyer, have you any message for London?" said he, with a jovial face and a smile.

"It is with great regret that I have just heard of your intended departure, and the arrival of a new purveyor-in-chief."

"I assure you that I have had quite enough of Scutari and its bother, and much prefer the London fog to the bright sun of the East and its accessory annoyances. The fact is, I was only here *pro tem.*, till someone could be permanently appointed, but I did not expect to be recalled so early. Yesterday I received my *feuille de route*, as you call it in French, from the War Office. I hope to have the pleasure of introducing you to Mr. Robertson, my successor, tomorrow, and the day after I shall probably be off."

"I shall start a few days after you, but not exactly in the same direction."

"Where are you going, Monsieur Soyer?"

"Why, are you not aware that Miss Nightingale, Mr. Bracebridge, and myself are going on Saturday next to the Crimea?"

"Oh, that's right! Someone was saying you would not go to the camp."

"What could make them say so? Not fear on my part—for of that I never dream; besides, our lives are more in danger here in the hospital than in the open air. The observation I made to the Minister-at-War, respecting the camp, was this,—that unless I could invent a cooking apparatus for the army to supersede the tin kettles I had seen at Chobham, it would be useless to attempt to teach the men to cook. An officer who happened to be present observed, 'You're right, Monsieur Soyer; they appear very unfit for a heavy company.—I have remarked that myself.' By the bye, have you seen the French canteens—*marmites*, as they call them? They are very superior, and much larger than ours, besides being made of better metal. One soldier is, however, required to cook for every sixteen men with them, and they present the same difficulty with respect to open-air cooking.* This is especially the case on a long march—while those stoves, the model of which I had submitted to the War Office, were quite free from any such inconvenience."

"They will be ordered," said Mr. Milton, "as soon as they are approved of by the Crimean authorities."

"I am glad to hear you say so; but my greatest anxiety now, Mr. Milton, is to see the new purveyor-in-chief, and have a fair understanding with him, so that during my absence he may not undo what you and I have so successfully commenced."

"You may depend upon it that I shall advise him for the best on that subject," said Mr. Milton.

The evening was spent cheefully at Doctor Macgregor's. The American clock upon the doctor's chimney-piece deceived his guests, if not the doctor, who was at once good-natured, amiable, and uncommonly fond of anecdote, and, like a true Scotchman, professed an immense deal of veneration of, and attachment to, his whisky toddy. "The day," he used to say, "is for manual labour, the evening for comfort and sociality; but, alas! in my case, night and day are the same—I may be called at any hour; therefore, the longer you favour me with your company, my friends, the better I shall like it, you may depend."

We now perceived that the clock was under the powerful influence of the doctor's "treatment;" nevertheless, common sense induced us all to rise and leave, and after a hearty shaking of hands, and no end of good wishes, we parted. On arriving at the second door, which opened upon one of the grand avenues of sick and wounded, we retired in a silent and mournful procession—except the groans of the sufferers, nothing was heard but the friction of our boots upon the stone floor, already worn into a kind of groove between the rows of beds upon which lay the sick and wounded, caused by the constant passing and repassing of the doctors, Sisters of Mercy, orderlies, and other officials in attendance upon the patients.

---

* I believe I am correct in stating that, in the French army, one soldier has to cook for a squad of sixteen men, while in camp, and that he has charge of two canteen kettles. I always saw five or six men cooking for a company in each kitchen; there were ten kitchens to a regiment of ten companies. This the soldiers told me themselves.

I make this remark to corroborate what I afterwards said in Paris before several French officers who contradicted me, but who, I believe, were not in the Crimean war. They stated that they only had two cooks to one company while campaigning. Upon making inquiries of a corporal who had charge of that department in his regiment while in the Crimea, he assured me that it was one man to each kettle, and not one to two—afterwards divided into two messes, forming a squad of nine or ten men, which would be equal to one hundred men to a regiment of one thousand in strength, instead of eight, as I at first calculated, or about ten squads to a company. While in barracks, comparatively speaking, it only requires a few men per regiment.

As we turned the angle of the long corridor to the right, we perceived, at a great distance, a faint light flying from bed to bed, like a will-o'-the-wisp flickering in a meadow on a summer's eve, which at last rested upon one spot; or as a bee sporting from flower to flower, till it at length lights upon a delicious floral banquet, which the insect determines not to leave till it has extracted the last drop of honey from the devoted pistil.

But, alas! as we approached, we perceived our mistake. A group in the shape of a *silhouette* unfolded its outline in light shade. As we came nearer and nearer, the picture burst upon us. A dying soldier was half reclining upon his bed. Life, you could observe, was fast bidding him adieu; Death, that implacable deity, was anxiously waiting for his soul to convey it to its eternal destination.

But stop! near him was a guardian angel, sitting at the foot of his bed, and most devotedly engaged pencilling down his last wishes to be despatched to his homely friends or relations. A watch and a few more trinkets were consigned to the care of the writer; a lighted lamp was held by another person, and threw a painful yellowish *coloris* over that mournful picture, which a Rembrandt alone could have traced, but which everybody, as long as the world lasts, would have understood, felt, and admired. It was then near two o'clock in the morning.

Approaching, I made inquiries of Miss Nightingale as to the complaint of her patient, when she replied in French, that the poor fellow was given up by the doctors, and was not likely to get through the night; "so I have been engaged noting down his last wishes, in order to forward them to his relatives."

The next morning, Miss Nightingale, Mr. Bracebridge, and myself had a long conversation respecting our plan of operations in the coming campaign. Having settled everything to our satisfaction, I once more went round the hospitals; and, upon reaching home, I heard that Mr. Robertson had arrived. He had been represented to me, by some person or other, as a very old and infirm man, wearing green spectacles. At the time I heard this, I was in the company of a very illustrious personage, who was visiting my kitchen, and he also listened to the serjeant giving this description, and very justly observed, that for such a fatiguing situation a young man was required. "Now," he continued, pointing from the kitchen door to the building, "observe the tremendous distance it is from one end of the building to the other. A purveyor should go round once a day, independent of the business of his office. I tell you what—I have found out this much myself, that the head, when properly screwed on, lasts much longer than the legs; and when both are required at the same time, there is an additional strain."

While we were discussing this important subject, in walked Mr. Milton, accompanied by an old gentleman, as described by the serjeant, and a third person. To my surprise, Mr. Robertson was not the reverend old man. He happened to be one of Mr. Robertson's friends, instead of himself.* Instead of being an old man, I found him the very person wanted—about thirty years of age—full of vigour and intelligence. In a short time I was perfectly acquainted with his qualifications for the

---

* If I have here related this anecdote, it is with the intention of showing the effect produced by the report upon all engaged in the hospitals, who felt that a gentleman of that age, though very capable, might, with his antique notions, upset what was then going on so well.

office to which he had been appointed—requiring, as I said before, so much bodily exercise. The few days I had to remain at Scutari enabled us to come to a perfect understanding.

"Monsieur Soyer," said Mr. Milton, "I now leave you in very good hands. I have explained everything to Mr. Robertson respecting your department, and I am certain he will be kind enough to attend to it in your absence. I am off for England tomorrow; therefore, fare you well; take care of yourself in the Crimea. I have also spoken to Mr. Robertson about your stoves; he will forward them to the Crimea as soon as they arrive."

"I wish you a pleasant journey, Mr. Milton. I hope to have the pleasure of seeing you in London."

Mr. Robertson accompanied me round the various stores, and after passing all in review, and noting what would be required in future, we parted. I felt fully convinced that my former efforts would not be destroyed, as I had at first feared. The next day we went to the General and the Palace Hospitals and Kululee, and made similar arrangements. I now felt almost free of the hospitals, though my intention was to run down from the Crimea now and then to have a look at them, as the least mismanagement would create confusion. I then requested Lord W. Paulet to devote a few hours, before my departure, to visiting the other hospitals, and he very kindly fixed upon that afternoon. Mr. Robertson, Lord W. Paulet, the Hon. Captain Bourke, his lordship's aide-de-camp, and myself rode over to the various hospitals, and I pointed out the improvements I had made, all of which Lord W. Paulet considered very effective and judicious, and promised that they should be followed up, referring me at the same time to Mr. Robertson. "That gentleman," he said, "is now major domo in the purveyor's department."

I told Lord W. Paulet that Mr. Robertson and myself had already settled everything, and we rode back to the Barrack Hospital. Lord W. Paulet very kindly invited me to dine with him, and I much regretted that time did not allow of my accepting the invitation, as we had to leave the next morning, and I wished to see Miss Nightingale and Mr. Bracebridge; but I promised to return and spend a part of the evening with him, which I did, and very merrily too. I must say that, in all the transaction connected with my mission to the Crimea, to no gentleman am I more indebted than to Lord W. Paulet, whose gracious reception, continued kindness, and the extreme confidence he placed in me, gave me such extraordinary encouragement that it greatly tended to my success: a failure might have been the result, had he treated me otherwise. Lord W. Paulet gave me the promised letters, and signed the following paper:—

SCUTARI BARRACK HOSPITAL, CONSTANTINOPLE.

May 1st, 1855.

To BRIGADIER-GENERAL LORD WM. PAULET.—Important regulations to insure for the future a good, clean, wholesome, and nutritious class of food, and delicate beverages, to be daily produced for the comfort of the sick and wounded in all the hospitals of the East, as well as for the standing army, which will prove economical both in a saving of time, and also in a pecuniary sense. Monsieur Soyer most respectfully solicits the assistance of Brigadier-General Lord Wm. Paulet in granting the following requisites, which Monsieur Soyer considers indispensable to carry out the objects of the important mission conferred on him by the Government of her Britannic Majesty Queen Victoria the First, and of which his lordship has already given proofs of his high approval and satisfaction, as well as his assistance in facilitating the introduction of a completely new system of diet, which has met with the approval of Doctor Cumming, the chief medical officer, and every medical gentleman connected with his staff in the various English hospitals at Constantinople.

First requisite.—That for every important hospital, a professed man-cook shall be engaged, with a civilian assistant, instead of military, as is now the case, and the principal to be under military rules and regulations.

Second.—That all military men now engaged cooking in the hospitals and barrack kitchens shall be immediately instructed in the art of camp cooking. As they are already acquainted with the plain mode of cooking, it will only require a few lessons from Monsieur Soyer, under his new and simple style, to become thoroughly conversant with this branch of culinary operations, highly essential at the present crisis, and about which the Right Honourable Lord Panmure, her Majesty's Minister-at-War, expressed the greatest anxiety personally to Monsieur Soyer, on his mission to Scutari, with a view to disseminating the system throughout the army. Monsieur Soyer feels assured that if present in the camp for a few weeks he will be enabled to carry out this important object, at the same time introducing wholesome and nutritious food made out of the usual allowances of provisions supplied to the army, so soon as his field or bivouac stove shall be adopted by the Crimean authorities.

A. SOYER.

Approved. W. PAULET, B.-General, Commanding Troops. *Scutari, May 1st,* 1855.

I then returned my thanks and bade his lordship adieu. Thus terminated my Scutari duties, which were afterwards carried on to my entire satisfaction under the direction of Mr. Robertson, and supported by Lord W. Paulet; later by General Storks, now Sir Henry, who succeeded his lordship.

Shortly after the opening of my kitchen, I received a visit from General Vivian and his aide-de-camp, Captain Ramsey. During his visit Miss Nightingale entered the kitchen. I then introduced the General to her, and we had a very animated and interesting conversation relating to hospital treatment, &c. The General expressed his high gratification at being introduced to Miss Nightingale, and I then had the honour of showing him through the hospital, not omitting the other kitchens, where the cooking was still carried on upon the old system, as I had not had, in that short space of time, an opportunity to remedy it. The General and Captain Ramsey expressed their high approval and satisfaction of the great improvement I had already made in the culinary department of that monster establishment. I may, perhaps, be pardoned for being vain enough to quote the gallant General's remark prior to his leaving my kitchen, which remark encouraged me so much in the prosecution of my labours. It was thus:—

"Monsieur Soyer, Miss Nightingale's name and your own will be for ever associated in the archives of this memorable war."

XIII

DEPARTURE FOR THE CRIMEA

THE 2nd of May was the day on which we set sail for the Crimea. It was indeed a lovely day—the air was redolent with perfume and freshness; not a ripple seemed to ruffle the surface of the mighty Bosphorus, whose ever-foaming current appeared to have buried itself deep in the bed of that turbulent stream. A few caiques were seen here and there swiftly gliding over its calm surface, occasionally disturbed by the dipping of the seagulls. The Bosphorus gulls have a peculiar chalky colour, differing from that of the ocean bird, which circumstance, no doubt, caused Lord Byron, in his beautiful poem, to call them the ghosts of the Houris, launched to eternity in the depths of that solemn flood of romance, poetical love, and tragic reminiscence. While skimming its surface they darted now and then with the rapidity of lightning down upon a rash little denizen of the deep who had ventured too near the surface of the limpid element to bask in the warmth of the generous rays of that friend of the whole world, the sun. All was peace, love, and repose. A vaporous golden tint seemed to envelope the world-famed city of Constantinople—its mosques, forests of minarets, Golden Horn, and European and Asiatic shores, with the Oriental atmosphere so peculiar to the Bosphorus. Nature seemed to be in its most sublime humour; heaven, earth, and ocean had that day agreed to be in love with humanity.

On a sudden, the report of cannon is heard, and the roar of this fatal messenger of war is echoed and re-echoed from every part of the city. Caiques of large dimensions, gorgeously decorated with gilding and rich silken hangings, manned by numerous oarsmen, leave the marble staircase of the Dolma Batchi Palace. Numbers of smaller caiques follow in the wake of this nautical procession, which directs its course towards the Moslem city of Stamboul. As the flotilla passed close to us, we perceived that it contained the Sultan and his suite, proceeding to the Mosque of Sultan Mahomet—it being Friday, and the Turkish Sunday. His Sublime Majesty is always saluted with about fifty guns at his departure, and the same number on his return from that ceremony.

This startling shock awoke me from a kind of lethargy, and made me recollect that I had embarked in a caique at Tophané, and that I was then afloat. Of a sudden we were hailed several times from a large ship close at hand, with the words "Chabouk! Chabouk! Balabak!" which means, "make haste, boatman." At the same time, the hissing of a steamer, just getting under way, was heard. In a trice we were alongside, and a minute after I was upon the deck of the *Robert Lowe*. A few words of remonstrance were addressed to me by the captain. "Indeed, Monsieur Soyer, we were going without you! You are full half an hour behind time. Mr. Bracebridge and Miss Nightingale have inquired several times after you."

"Well, captain, I assure you they told me at Major Macdonald's office that you would not start till noon."

"That was our intention; but having shipped all the troops, I wished to leave earlier, as we must make our time for entering the harbour of Balaklava, which is now so full that if we were to miss our turn we might be kept outside for a day or two, and that would not be at all pleasant, especially if we happen to have rough weather. Here is Mr. Bracebridge; he is, no doubt, looking for you."

The screw was by this time propelling us slowly out of the Golden Horn.

"Good morning, Monsieur Soyer; have you all your people on board?" said Mr. Bracebridge.

"Yes, I have."

"I have only seen your secretary."

"Oh, I am sure they are here; I sent them on board this morning before nine o'clock, previous to going to Pera. Pray how is Miss Nightingale?"

"She will be on deck directly. By the bye, is Mademoiselle a good sailor?"

"Tolerably good; with this weather no one need fear being ill at sea," said I, "though I hear the Black Sea is so very changeable, and that a tremendous hurricane often comes up suddenly even in the middle of summer. At all events, we have a good start."

We were then passing between lower Scutari and the Sultan's palace, and facing us was the Sound of the Bosphorus, presenting a most delightful view of the European and the Asiatic shores. When I observed to Mr. Bracebridge that it was a pity Miss Nightingale was not on deck, he answered, "You're right; I will go and fetch her."

A few minutes afterwards that lady made her appearance.

"What a delightful day! and did you ever see a finer panorama?"

"Never, Monsieur Soyer."

"What a glorious mine of subjects for a Claude Lorraine, mademoiselle! It is much to be regretted that he never visited these Moslem shores."

The vessel was now going at full speed.

"We are near Kululee," said Mr. Bracebridge.

"Yes, we are," said I; "and there is our friend the Bey on the palace steps. Look at him, Miss; he is in his grand costume. I wonder what is going on there today?"

"Today," replied Mr. Bracebridge, "is Friday, the Turkish Sunday. Did you not hear the cannon just now, when the Sultan went to the Mosque?"

"Oh, yes, I not only heard it, but also saw the procession, and very nearly lost the boat."

"I was told you were rather behind."

"So much so, that you were upon the move."

Miss Nightingale observed that although the Kululee hospitals were so well situated, it was reported by medical men that they were very unhealthy, more especially the lower one.

"So I hear, Mademoiselle; but my opinion is, that it is owing to defective drainage. They were making fresh ventilators in the wards of the lower one yesterday, which will be a very great improvement. Miss Stanley is gone?"

"Yes," said Miss Nightingale; "she has been very unwell for some time."

We then passed before the Godfrey Tower, proudly standing on its rocky shore, at the base of which myriads of tombstones stagger about in pompous disorder, under the shady wings of multitudes of dark cypress trees, the solemn guardians of this land of repose. Then we came to the Sweet Waters of Asia, where thousands of

Turks and Turkish ladies resort on their days of festival. We next passed Therapia, where all the foreign ambassadors reside in summer; and I exchanged a few words with Miss Nightingale respecting the Naval Hospital there. Buyukderé, the Brighton of Constantinople, came next; and the large marble palace on our right, built, but never finished, by Ibrahim Pacha, and that of the Sultan Valide, the Giant's Mountain. Ten minutes after, we entered the Euxine or Black Sea, full sail, with a fair wind and fine weather.

The Oriental coast had partly disappeared, and everyone was anxious to inspect his fellow-passengers, and find out whether he had any friends on board. The vessel was crammed with military men and Government officials, besides about six hundred troops. Having the pleasure of knowing many of the officers, a general conversation relating to the war soon commenced. Miss Nightingale had retired, with several of her Sisters, to their apartment, and very few persons were aware of the fact of her being on board, and they were all very anxious to see her; but evening came on, and we were not again favoured with her presence that day. The next day being Sunday, Miss Nightingale and myself, accompanied by the captain, went round the lower deck to visit the soldiers, who were busily employed making their pudding. Having questioned them upon their method of cooking, and visited the cookhouse, I at once perceived what facilities were offered to me for making an immense amelioration in the present system of naval cookery, especially in the method of cooking salt meat, &c. (See naval recipes in Addenda.) I took the opportunity of giving them a few hints. Miss Nightingale heard that there were some invalids on board, and she asked to see them. One poor fellow, who had been suffering from an attack of fever since our departure, refused to take his medicine. Miss Nightingale asked the reason of his objection. He replied, "Because I took some once, and it made me sick; and I haven't liked physic ever since."

We could not help laughing at his simple remark. Miss Nightingale said, "But if I give it you myself, you will take it, won't you?"

The soldier, looking very hard at her, replied, "Well, sure enough, ma'am, it will make me sick just the same." For all that he took the medicine, and seemed to feel very grateful. None but an eye-witness or a disinterested observer can judge of the effect produced by a female's attention to the sick soldier. Far from home, he seems to hear the voice of her who nursed him in childhood—a mother or sister. He will listen to and receive advice, finding sudden relief from the cheering accents of a woman's lips, while he would scarcely take the slightest notice of the kindest orderly's attentions. The man was not aware that it was Miss Nightingale. A woman's friendly voice had spoken to his heart, and he felt more composed.

The sun darted his rays almost perpendicularly upon the deck of the beautiful ship, the *Robert Lowe*, which glided rather than floated over that inconstant ocean—the whimsical Mother Black Sea, called in French "La Mère Noire," who safely bore her children upon her tranquil bosom in the morning, and at night rocked the cradle with such furious love, that she changed the smile of comfort to sickness and tears in the evening. The sails were furled, and the awning was now stretched amidships. About twelve o'clock all the soldiers, under command of Major Campbell, about six hundred in number, met upon deck, and divine service was read by the Major himself. Miss Nightingale, Mr. Bracebridge, myself, and all the officers on board, were present. Nothing recurs more vividly to my recollection than the impression made upon my mind by that religious ceremony, performed so solemnly, between heaven and the ocean. It appeared as though all were impressed with the sacred mission they were called upon to fulfil, and that every brave fellow present was saying his last prayer, and preparing himself in case of emergency, should it be his fate to succumb on the field of battle in the defence of his country, to appear with a free and pure conscience before his Creator, in whose hands alone are the issues of life and death. Many of those poor fellows afterwards paid that tribute to their country. Such are the chances of war. This ceremony, though not performed by a clergyman, had such an effect upon my mind, that I shall never forget it.

The remainder of the afternoon was passed on deck, and as it was a day of rest and delightful weather, we were favoured with the company of the ladies, including that of Miss Nightingale.

Although I had frequently conversed with Miss Nightingale upon business transactions, this was the first and best opportunity I had of appreciating her amiable character and interesting powers of conversation. For more than an hour I talked with her, upon the deck of the good ship *Robert Lowe*. The subject was her duty, not of what she had already done, but of what she was about to do. She gave me good advice as to the best way for me to proceed in my new undertaking. "Monsieur Soyer," she said, "you will find everything very different in the Crimea to what it was at Scutari, though you had there a great many difficulties, the distance from supplies being so much greater." We then arranged that as soon as we were a little organized, our first visit should be to the General Hospital and the Sanatorium, next to the General Camp Hospital before Balaklava. The first thing Miss Nightingale did after our arrival was to write to the commander-in-chief, Lord Raglan, announcing it. I remarked that I had an official letter to his lordship from the War Department.

"I am aware of that, Monsieur Soyer, and that you and Mr. Bracebridge should go to headquarters together the day we arrive; but it is important his lordship should be immediately acquainted by letter of our arrival."

"Well, Mademoiselle," said I, "you have been in the military service longer than I have, and I am not surprised at your being better acquainted with the rules of war than myself." Miss Nightingale smiled kindly at the remark.

Having had the honour and the opportunity of seeing Miss Nightingale almost daily for above a year, my readers will no doubt be pleased, and feel interested, by my giving a short description of this estimable lady, whose fame in this war has been almost universal.

She is rather high in stature, fair in complexion, and slim in person; her hair is brown, and is worn quite plain; her physiognomy is most pleasing; her eyes, of a bluish tint, speak volumes, and are always sparkling with intelligence; her mouth is small and well formed, while her lips act in unison, and make known the impression of her heart—one seems the reflex of the other. Her visage, as regards expression, is very remarkable, and one can almost anticipate by her countenance what she is about to say: alternately, with matters of the most grave import, a gentle smile passes radiantly over her countenance, thus proving her evenness of temper; at other times, when wit or a pleasantry prevails, the heroine is lost in the happy, good-natured smile which pervades her face, and you recognise only the charming woman. Her dress is generally of greyish or black tint; she wears a simple white cap, and often a rough apron. In a word, her whole appearance is religiously simple and unsophisticated. In conversation no member of the fair sex can be more amiable and gentle than Miss Nightingale. Removed from her arduous and cavalier-like duties, which require the nerve of a Hercules,—and she possesses it when required,—she is Rachel on the stage in both tragedy and comedy.

During the voyage Miss Nightingale conversed with the captain, Major Campbell, and one or two more gentlemen on board. Dinner-time arrived—four bells apprized us of the fact—the deck was soon cleared, and the table surrounded. The *pièces de résistance* were attacked on all sides. The last decent piece of roast beef we were to see or partake of for some time was that day before us. Miss Nightingale and the Sisters of Mercy dined in their cabin. The conversation was so very lively, that one might have fancied that we were going on a pleasure excursion instead of the solemn pilgrimage from whence so many were never to return. All bore testimony to the good fare provided by the captain, and exquisite pale sherry flowed in the glasses, in honour first of her Majesty, then Miss Nightingale, next the ladies, and last, not least, the army and navy. Some good old port, with a fine crust, properly decanted without shaking, was then introduced, with the inseparable and justly-famed Stilton cheese and fresh plain salad.

This sudden change of countenance in the happy homely groups, who only a few minutes before were as grave as grave—in fact, morally and properly grave, exchanging peaceably word for word while upon deck—cannot be attributed to the walk down, nor to the temperature of the room, nor even the charming architectural paintings upon glass which adorned the chief cabin of the *Robert Lowe*, nor the laying out of the table, "which was perfect." No, not at all. It was the dinner— yes, the dinner!—which made me heartily second the opinion of my illustrious compatriot, Brillat Savarin, when he justly remarks in one of his immortal aphorisms, that if there is one hour spent more pleasantly than another in the course of the day, that one is the first hour at the dinner table. Though he intends his remark for epicures, it can easily be applied to all classes of society, according to the difference of time each man can afford from his occupations or peculiar habits. But out of this reunion of hilarity I will here give an anecdote which will probably amuse, if not interest, the reader.

P. M. AND THE LOOKING-GLASS.

On the eve of my departure from Scutari I fell in with a travelling gentleman named Peter Morrison, a personage of no small importance in his own estimation, who was very desirous of accompanying me through my Crimean campaign, and of making himself useful to me should his services be required. Remuneration was to him a secondary consideration. According to himself, "moving accidents by flood and field, and peril in the imminent deadly breach" excited his martial ardour, and these had no terrors for him—while he was far removed from their sphere of action. He afterwards gave us to understand that he was courting a wealthy lady, who, being decidedly of opinion that

None but the brave deserve the fair,

had declared that none should wed her who had not both "fought and bled for his country." P. M., as I shall designate this redoubtable hero, needed some such stimulus to risk his life in his country's cause, as the sequel will show; for he preferred, with due regard to his complexion, albeit none of the fairest, the shelter of the *bays* used in my kitchen to any laurels he might reap on the field of Mars, as, when in front of the enemy, his courage, like that of Bob Acres, "oozed out at his fingers' ends." But to our anecdote.

During a gale a few weeks before we went on board, a looking-glass had been broken in the cabin, the steward, as the ship made a heavy lurch, having sent his head through it while carrying a dish to the table. Probably the glass was not set flat in the frame, as his head had made a perfect star of a hundred jets. The circular hole looked just as if a shot had passed through it. Three small boards were fixed across to keep it together.

Whilst at dinner, P. M., who was sitting next me, inquired how the glass had been broken.

"Upon my word," said I, "I do not know; but one of the mates says it was done by a round shot. (*This the mate had said in joke.*) The captain, who was very jocular, perceiving P. M. was rather uneasy at the information, merely replied, "Ah, and I had a very narrow escape on the occasion. I was sitting at the head of the table at the time, nearly opposite the spot."

P. M. exclaimed, in great trepidation, "What do you say, captain?—it was a cannon-ball which broke the glass?"

"I did not say so," replied the captain, "but such, unfortunately, is the case."

"Well," said P. M., "I do not like the job I have undertaken. You don't mean to say our lives will be endangered at Balaklava?"

"Oh dear, no; not in the least, except they fire upon us."

"I tell you what it is, I shall not stand it; for I bargained for nothing of the kind."

"At any rate," said I, looking at the captain, who was laughing in his sleeve, "if you are killed by a shot or shell, or die by illness, all your former bargains will be of no avail, and off you must go."

"Had I been aware of that, I certainly should never have left Scutari."

The next morning we heard that some of the men, having raised a kind of mutiny or fight on board, had been imprisoned. Being anxious to see a prison on board a ship, I proceeded with Major Campbell to visit them. The prison was upon deck, in the open air, and instead of being in chains, the prisoners were made fast with ropes to the deck. Two of them seemed in great trouble, having entirely lost their senses the night before. They were trying to recollect and inform the commander how the quarrel began, when another, who imagined he had completely recovered, stated the fact thus: "General, if you will allow me, I will tell you the truth, the whole truth, and nothing but the truth; and instead of kissing the good book, which I have not got by me, but which I had when I paid my last visit to his Majesty the Lord Mayor of London, let me kiss your glove instead."

"We want no nonsense here; so look sharp, and tell us what it was all about."

"Yes, Colonel, I will, as far as I know. You see, Jarvis, who is a relation of Martin's wife, called her ugly names, and said she wasn't proper. Upon that we fought—Joe fought—I fought—till we couldn't fight any longer, and being dark we found it very troublesome, as we didn't know whom we might be hitting. I do not know who said she wasn't proper—I don't know the wench—she might be proper, after all, for what I know—that's all."

"Corporal," said the Major, "don't let those men land till I see you."

By this time the Russian coast was in view. Breakfast was just over, and everybody was on deck—the weather being beautiful. Miss Nightingale, Mr. Bracebridge, and myself, with telescopes, were looking at the convent and the monastery, still inhabited by Russian monks. The first reports of the cannon of Sebastopol were here faintly heard—the wind being favourable, as the captain informed us. On the right hand, on a lofty high peaked mountain, the Russian picket was plainly seen mounting guard. An hour after we were in the Bay of Balaklava, in view of the Genoese Tower, planted on a high rock, at the elevation of about two hundred feet above the level of the sea, at the spur of a range of mountains extending along the shore. A few topmasts are all that can be seen on entering the gorge; and no one can imagine, though so near, that such a harbour is in existence as the one we were approaching. The signal having been given by hoisting the flag on the top of the Genoese Tower, we entered the far-famed, and now universally known, grand, though small, Harbour of Balaklava, the entrance to which seems impracticable. We then slowly threaded our way through that forest of masts and huge vessels piled and packed so close together in the little harbour. The principal vessels at that time lying there were,—the *Himalaya, Jura, Etna, Leander, Star of the South, London, Baraguay d'Hilliers, &c.* It is impossible to describe the animation of the scene better than by comparing it to the emigration of a large colony of ants from their habitation to a new quarter. Many people were aware that Miss Nightingale was coming that day in the *Robert Lowe*, and the decks of all the large vessels at anchor were crowded with curious spectators, in expectation of seeing that lady, of whose devotion to the sick and wounded they had heard so much.

COSSACK BAY.

We had no sooner entered the harbour than, to P. M.'s horror, he saw painted on the rock in large letters—"Cossack Bay." At this moment, five or six ill-looking Bashi Bazouks, and as many Turks, with their large turbans, yathagans, kresses, daggers, firelocks, &c., were descending the mountain to the rock upon which the fatal name was written, and immediately caused P. M. to inquire if they were enemies. I replied that I thought they were, being upon Cossack Bay.

"I say, Monsieur Soyer," said P. M., "this is beyond a joke; for if those ugly fellows choose to fire upon us, they can do so as easy as possible."

"No doubt they can," said I.

"I shall not give them a chance," cried P. M., and off he bolted.

The *Robert Lowe* had anchored, and was moored in her new berth on the right-hand side of the harbour, nearly opposite the commandant's house. Although the operation of getting in had taken nearly two hours, so interesting was the sight that no one had thought of making preparations to leave the vessel, which is generally the first thing thought of. Miss Nightingale pointed out to me the hospital called the "Sanatorium," situated on the top of the hill, near the Genoese heights and fortifications. Turning round, she next pointed to a row of white buildings, which constituted the General Hospital, which she said she should like to visit that day if time allowed. Mr. Bracebridge came and informed us that the captain would be happy for us to stay on board as long as he remained in harbour, which might be a few days—or till we found a ship to suit us. As it was impossible to procure either a house, hut, or even a tent, in Balaklava, we of course accepted the offer. The day was drawing to a close, and, as we were rather fatigued, we postponed our visit to the hospital till the next morning.

MISS. NIGHTINGALE AND THE DYING SOLDIER.

XIV

COMMENCEMENT OF MY CAMPAIGN IN
THE CRIMEA

No sooner was it known that Miss Nightingale had arrived, than hosts of visitors poured in from all directions, amongst whom were Commissary Filder, Mr. Henderson, Chief Doctor at the Balaklava Hospital, the Clergyman, Doctor Sutherland, Mr. Anderson, &c., &c., which caused her to hold a kind of floating drawing-room. Mr. Bracebridge was also busily engaged, so I did not see him again till dinner-time. I despatched the four soldier-cooks I had instructed and brought with me to the Sanatorium, as the troops were landing, and they were required on shore. Having settled my future plan of operations with my secretary, and closed our post for the next day, I was quite at liberty to accompany Miss Nightingale in the morning on her visit to the various hospitals, as we had previously decided.

The same evening, about nine, a terrible cannonade was heard from the besieged city, which produced more effect upon us than upon the initiated. The report of the fusillade was also plainly heard. This proved to be a sortie, which it appeared often happened, and produced no effect upon the inhabitants. Such, however, was not the case with P. M., though I tried to persuade him that there was no danger, "except," said I, "in case the enemy should prove victorious, and retake Balaklava, which might happen through some *ruse de guerre* unknown to the allied army." "Well," said P. M., "but I did not bargain for that, and I assure you I very much regret having come at all. Oh, give me London and Red Lion Square before any of your seats of war, for I see no fun in glory."

"Now we are in for it," I said, "we must go bravely through it. Screw your courage to the sticking point, and Wigham Ward for ever!"

The next morning, at seven, everybody was up and busily engaged, when Mr. Bracebridge came and told me that Miss Nightingale had been up, writing since daybreak, and would be ready immediately after breakfast. About eight o'clock, in poured a second series of visitors. Among the earliest arrivals were Sir J. Macneil and Captain Tulloch; the former gentleman I had the pleasure of knowing at the Reform Club a few years back. We then had a short conversation touching the soldiers' food, and cooking in general. Colonel Harding, Admiral Boxer, Commissary Filder, &c., came next. Miss Nightingale had given notice that she must be at the hospital by half-past ten, and was then upon deck ready to start. I took the opportunity of impressing upon her the necessity of leaving the ship at once, or the day would pass without our doing anything. We embarked in a small boat and went on shore, followed by young Thomas, the drummer-boy, whom I must introduce to my readers as a little wonder; and, although he had not taken time to grow to manhood, he did not like to be called a boy. Although but twelve years old, he always called himself Miss Nightingale's and Mr. Bracebridge's man. He was a regular *enfant de troupe*, full of activity, wit, intelligence, and glee. He had quitted his instruments and sticks, as he called them, to devote his civil and military career to Miss Nightingale, that lady having claimed his services. To her he was as devoted as an aide-de-camp to his general. Before the enemy could have approached his adored mistress, the drummer-boy would have been cut to pieces. This he told me himself at a later period, when a report was in circulation that the Russians were likely to attack Balaklava by the Kamara side. Miss Nightingale's hut, being the nearest that way on the Genoese heights, would certainly have been attacked first.

Though the weather was fine overhead, there was about ten inches of mud in the unpaved and uneven streets of Balaklava, which caused us to be half-an-hour going a distance that might, under ordinary circumstances, have been accomplished in ten minutes. On our arrival at the General Hospital, we were received by Miss Weare, the matron of the hospital, "under Miss Nightingale." Miss Nightingale requested me to try and find Doctor Henderson, who unluckily, as we thought through a mistake, was waiting for us at the Sanatorium on the Genoese heights. In his absence, Miss Weare and the medical superintendent showed us over the wards, which were crammed full of sick and wounded. We then visited the general kitchen, which, though rather short of cooking utensils and accommodation, was kept tolerably clean. A civilian cook was engaged making rather good soup, but it had boiled too fast. At all events, it was a satisfaction to me to find someone willing to improve, as he observed. Promising to send him my receipts and have his kitchen comfortably arranged, and to supply him with a few tin utensils, we left him.

We next went to the extra-diet kitchen, which was anything but a comfortable one, though Mrs. Davis, who made the extra-diets, managed pretty well, by dint of perseverance and a deal of trouble. She was compelled to use preserved soups, which are not wholesome for delicate or weak stomachs, and are, moreover, generally served up too strong, as scarcely anyone who uses them will take the trouble to read the instructions pasted upon each case, and add the proper quantity of water required. These are at all times better adapted for persons in health than for the sick, always excepting the essence of beef (see Hospital Diets), which, when properly seasoned according to my receipt, is really very good. I made a list of what apparatus and kitchen utensils were required, and then we left Mrs. Davis, much pleased with Miss Nightingale's kind remarks, my approbation of her services, and, above all, very proud of having, two days before, been visited and highly complimented by Lady Stratford de Redcliffe and the other ladies. Lord Stratford and family had passed us at sea the day before, on their return to Constantinople, on board the *Caradoc*; a circumstance I much regretted, as I had anticipated the pleasure of accompanying Lord and Lady de Redcliffe to the various camp and hospital kitchens. We then left the General Hospital, and ascended to the Sanatorium by a narrow and almost perpendicular road cut out of the rock; in consequence of the ups and downs, it took us full three-quarters of an hour to accomplish the distance, and very uncomfortably too, the roads being so dirty. The view during the ascent is transcendantly beautiful and refreshing—the sight of the harbour beneath filled with ships, the chain of rocky mountains, distant view of the Guards' camp, the village of Kadikoi, its Greek church, the Zouave camp, and the traffic of thousands below, busily running to and fro, formed a naval and military tableau which well repaid us for our trouble. On reaching the verge of the hill facing the grand tower, which proudly bore the British flagstaff, Miss Nightingale and myself made an involuntary halt to admire this splendid view.

"Did you ever see anything more picturesque than this, Mademoiselle? And were it not for the everlasting report of the cannon, could you not believe you were in the Land of Promise, redolent with the green bloom of nature, which almost covers those rocky mountains? Turn your eyes on that side towards the busy harbour—can you not imagine you are looking at Landseer's celebrated pictures on one side of Peace and the other side of War?"

Miss Nightingale replied, "I had heard Balaklava was a very pretty place, but I did not expect to find anything so beautiful."

"I believe, Mademoiselle, that gentleman coming down from the Sanatorium is Dr. Henderson? I recollect having seen him inquiring after you last evening."

"So it is, Monsieur Soyer; I suppose he has waited so long for us, that he is coming back to the General Hospital."

"Thomas," said I to the boy, "run and tell that gentleman Miss Nightingale is coming, or he may take another road, and miss us." A few minutes after, we met the doctor, who very much regretted not having met us at the General Hospital, according to promise. Several important cases sent from the trenches (among which was the amputation of an arm) had delayed him.

"I suppose, doctor, you use chloroform in all cases of amputation?"

"Yes, we do, Monsieur Soyer, and with very great success, not having lost a single patient since its application."

By this time we had arrived at the hospital, which is composed of immense rows of huts, erected on the crest of the lofty mountain facing the sea, commanding a beautiful view of the bay. Miss Nightingale observed that no doubt the site was a healthy one, but that it would be very hot in summer and equally cold in winter.

"Well," said the doctor, "we thought of that ourselves; but really Balaklava is so mountainous that for the life of us we could not pitch upon any other spot. However, the least breeze from the sea will be felt in summer, and in winter we must contrive to screen it somehow. Should we have another storm like that of the 14th of last November, we should be blown away."

One of the men, hearing the storm mentioned, told me that he had witnessed it from beginning to end. I then asked him a few particulars, and he related the circumstance as follows, while Dr. Henderson and Miss Nightingale were walking among the ruins, talking over business matters.

"Would you believe it, sir—the furious waves seemed to fly right over the tower, and the shipping in the bay was almost invisible for a long time. In fact, we thought that all the vessels were lost; from the mass of water blown into the air, we took it to be the level of the sea or the beginning of a second deluge." Pointing with his hand towards the bay, "That is the spot where the *Prince* was lost, and further on you see the place where the *Retribution* was at anchor, with the Duke of Cambridge on board. The storm lasted above ten hours. We were quite wet in the tower, and could not get out. Had we done so, we should probably have been blown down the hill or into the sea. In the ravine above sixty large poplar trees were torn up by the roots by one gust of wind."

"How was it, in the first place, that you came to be there?"

"Why, you see, sir, we were stationed there to manage the signals for ships to enter the harbour, and I happened to be on duty at the time."

"It must have been a fearful sight," said I.

"Sight, sir!—there was nothing to be seen for many hours; and it was only towards night that it cleared up a little, and then we could see the masts of the shipping in the harbour, rolling about like a forest under the influence of the shock of an earthquake. The next day, I was put on fatigue duty, to bury the corpses washed on shore from the wreck of the *Prince*, and a dreadful job it was, I assure you, sir."

"Where were they buried?"

"Over the way, on the edge of Leander Bay. You may see the spot from this," pointing it out. "There are above twenty there, to my knowledge; but some were never found." Thanking him for his information, I invited him to come and see me when my kitchens were open, and get a basin of good soup whenever he pleased. I then rejoined the doctor and Miss Nightingale, who were returning to the hospital.

We visited the various wards, each of which contained about thirty patients. Miss Nightingale had a kind word for all, and many a conversation with those who had been severely wounded. Having seen five or six of the wards, I begged Miss Nightingale to excuse my accompanying her through the others; as I wished, in order to lose no time, to go and visit the kitchens, and set my men to work, which plan she much approved of, saying that when she had seen the hospitals, she should like to visit the kitchens also. As I was going out, I met Mr. Bracebridge on horseback, coming to meet us. We went to the kitchens, which we found were built of mud, exposed to the open air, unroofed, and burning much fuel. I immediately fixed upon a spot to build a kitchen, and sketched a plan, which I submitted to the doctor and Miss Nightingale, who had then joined us. We also visited those mud mounts called cookhouses, looked over the provision stores, and departed. Miss Nightingale, Dr. Henderson, and myself, returned together by the same road, Miss Nightingale intending to visit an officer patient who was at the doctor's house. Mr. Bracebridge being on horseback, was compelled to take another road. On reaching the doctor's house, Miss Nightingale was introduced to the patient, who was suffering from a very severe attack of typhus fever. I stayed in the front room, making my sketch for the new hospital kitchens. At length Miss Nightingale retired, after giving words of consolation to the patient, and promising the doctor to send a nurse who would set him to rights.

As we were returning to the vessel, I could not help remarking that Miss Nightingale seemed much fatigued; upon which she replied, "I do feel rather tired, those roads are so bad." I inquired about the patient she had visited.

"The poor young man," said she, "is very ill. I very much fear for his life." She then stated what a bad attack of fever it was. Upon this I remarked that it was very imprudent of her to remain so long near him.

"Oh, Monsieur Soyer, I am used to that."

"Very true, Mademoiselle, but then it is in large airy wards, and not in small rooms, like the one you have just left."

"I must say that I have been very fortunate through my Scutari campaign, and I hope to be as fortunate in the Crimea."

"I hope so too, but would recommend you to be careful of your health, as I am sure the army cannot spare you."

By this time we were near the *Robert Lowe*—a boat was ready to take us on board, and Mr. Bracebridge was anxiously waiting our arrival, to inform Miss Nightingale that Lord Raglan had been on board, and also to the General Hospital, in order to see her, and was very much disappointed at not having had that pleasure. It was arranged that we should visit the camp next day, and that I should go and deliver my official letter, and present my humble duty to Lord Raglan. Miss Nightingale decided upon taking that opportunity of returning his lordship's visit. Doctor Sutherland and Mr. Anderson, of the Sanitary Commission, who happened to be on board, arranged about the horses, and the time of our departure the next morning.

At nine, we were all on shore and mounted. There were about eight of us ready to escort our heroine to the seat of war. Miss Nightingale was attired simply in a genteel amazone, or riding-habit, and had quite a martial air. She was mounted upon a very pretty mare, of a golden colour, which, by its gambols and caracoling, seemed proud to carry its noble charge. The weather was very fine. Our cavalcade produced an extraordinary effect upon the motley crowd of all nations assembled at Balaklava, who were astonished at seeing a lady so well escorted. It was not so, however, with those who knew who knew who the lady was.

On the road to headquarters, we met several officers whom I had the pleasure of knowing in England. All made inquiries respecting the lady in our party. As I knew that Miss Nightingale wished to preserve her incognito as much as possible, and especially in the camp, I referred them to Mr. Bracebridge. At that time the number of the fair sex in the Crimea numbered four, always excepting the Sisters of Mercy, who were never seen out.

It took us about half-an-hour to go from the Col of Balaklava to Kadikoi (about a mile distant), having to fight our way through a dense crowd of Greeks, Armenians, Jews, Maltese, &c.—hundreds of mules, horses, donkeys, artillery waggons, cannon, shot and shell, oxen and horses kicking each other, waggons upset in deep mud-holes, infantry and cavalry passing and repassing. The road was execrable, and not nearly wide enough for the immense amount of traffic. Amidst this Babel of tongues and deafening noise, we were obliged to speak at the top of our voices in order to make ourselves heard. Our horses, by way of enjoying the fun, kept prancing and kicking in all directions, particularly our fair lady's palfrey, which could not be kept quiet. Many females would have felt very nervous in such a position; but Miss Nightingale appeared to rise above such weakness, and even, on the contrary, to take considerable interest in this her first introduction to the turmoils of war. We at length emerged from the crowd, without having sustained much damage. One of our cavaliers had part of his mackintosh carried away by a log of wood that projected from the back of a mule, and P. M. lost a strap, which nearly unseated him. His mule kept kicking and prancing about, which, one is constrained to confess, is not over pleasant, especially in a crowd—and such a crowd. As we were at last out of danger, we could not help laughing at the misfortunes of our friends. Such was our debut on the soil of the seat of war.

Our first visit was to the hospital at Kadikoi, in a small Greek church at the end of the village. Upon our arrival, we were informed that the doctor was not in, so we promised to call again. We then galloped to the top of a high hill on the left, on which we could not help making a halt, as we were quite struck by the grandeur and novelty of the scene. We could plainly distinguish everything for five miles around us. The camps, with their myriads of white tents, appeared like large beds of mushrooms growing at random. The sound of trumpets, the beating of drums, the roar of cannon from Sebastopol, made a fearful noise, whilst military manœuvres, and sentries placed in every direction, gave a most martial aspect to the landscape, backed by the bold and rugged range of mountains by which Balaklava is surrounded.

Having gazed for some time, highly delighted with the scene, so novel to us, we proceeded on our journey. As Miss Nightingale wished to see one of the small regimental hospitals, Doctor Sutherland recommended us to visit that of the 11th Hussars. We were received by the doctor, who very kindly showed us over. Miss Nightingale and myself inspected the kitchen, which, though far from being comfortable or convenient, was, at all events, very ingeniously contrived. Having made my notes, we called at two other regiments, and afterwards proceeded direct to headquarters. Mr. Bracebridge and myself at once rode to Lord Raglan's house, the front of which was crowded with staff officers and gentlemen on horseback. On asking whether his lordship was within, we were answered in the negative, and were informed that he would probably not return before dinner-time. I then inquired for Colonel Steele, his lordship's secretary, for whom I also had a letter. That gentleman received us cordially, and having read Lord Panmure's letter, promised to give me his utmost support. Mr. Bracebridge stated he had come to thank Lord Raglan in Miss Nightingale's name, for his kind visit of the day before. I next inquired when I could see Lord Raglan. Colonel Steele replied, "When you like, Monsieur Soyer, but for a day or two he will be very much engaged, as he is preparing for the reception of the Sardinian army, which is shortly expected. Lord Raglan is aware of your arrival, and I will give orders for anything you may require in order to enable you to commence operations."

"As I have a great deal to do at the Balaklava Hospital, I shall commence operations there, and will call in a few days to see the commander-in-chief."

"Come whenever you like, Monsieur Soyer; Lord Raglan will be glad to see you. He has often spoken of you at the dinner table."

"Really! I am glad to hear that. I had the honour of knowing his lordship many years ago."

"So he was saying."

After having conversed with several officers whom I knew, I was about to retire, when Colonel Steele said that he would write a note that afternoon to the Chief Engineer, ordering him to send me some carpenters, and give me all the assistance I might require. I thanked the colonel, and retired.

Mr. Bracebridge had in the meantime joined Miss Nightingale, and informed her that, owing to Lord Raglan's absence, he had not mentioned her intended visit, but merely mentioned his own. Dr. Sutherland then inquired if Doctor Hall was at home, and on being told he was not, we started direct to the General Hospital before Sebastopol, in anticipation of meeting him there. He had, however, been and left. The chief doctor was also absent on duty, as no previous appointment had been made. We were shown round by the superintendent. The hospital was quite full, having at the time about four hundred sick and wounded. The place was in consequence rather crowded, but, nevertheless, well ventilated, and everything seemed in good order. Dr. Sutherland made several remarks upon an improved system of ventilation. I went to see the kitchen, which I did not find in a better state than the one at the Sanatorium.

A short time after, Mr. Bracebridge came and informed me that Miss Nightingale wished to speak with me. Having passed a close review, I was about returning to our party, when I met Miss Nightingale coming towards this gipsy cooking encampment, in which there was considerably too much to do for so important an establishment. We promised to call next day, or the one following, to see Doctors Taylor and Mouatt, and retired through a long row of huts. Some of the men had found out that it was "the good lady of Scutari," as they called her; for Miss Nightingale was then but little known by name, it being her first visit to the Crimea. I heard afterwards, that some of them had been patients at the Scutari Hospital, and had experienced the full benefit of that benevolent lady's kind care and attention. A great number were waiting at the doors—sick and convalescent— and gave her three hearty cheers as we passed, followed by three times three. Miss Nightingale seemed much affected by so unexpected a reception, and, being on horseback, could only bow gracefully to them by way of returning thanks. Her horse being very restless, in consequence of the shouts of such a number of men, Mr. Anderson dismounted, and taking Miss Nightingale's nag by the bridle, led it gently along.

We then proceeded through the English and French camps, which, for miles, surrounded the doomed Sebastopol. The scene, though more extensive, was not nearly so picturesque as when beheld from the top of the hill at Balaklava. The afternoon was then drawing on, and Dr. Sutherland advised us to go home, as it was a very difficult matter for one to find the way in the dark through the camp; but Mr. Anderson proposed to have a peep at Sebastopol. It was four o'clock, and they were firing sharply on both sides. Miss Nightingale, to whom the offer was made, immediately accepted it; so we formed a column, and, for the first time, fearlessly faced the enemy, and prepared to go under fire. P. M. turned round to me, saying quietly, but with great trepidation—

"I say, Monsieur Soyer, of course you would not take Miss Nightingale where there will be any danger."

We soon after reached the flag-staff at the head of the Woronzoff Road, and the sentry informed us we must dismount, as we were in danger, at the same time pointing to the marks of a number of cannon balls and splinters of shell, which, he said, they sent whenever they saw a group of people, especially on horseback. He added that they would send a shot or a shell in a moment. Fortunately, P. M. did not hear this, or we should have lost his agreeable company. I mentioned this to Miss Nightingale and to Mr. Bracebridge, who both laughed heartily.

We then dismounted. The sentry begged of us to go into a kind of redoubt, built of stone, where there was a telescope. "There," said he, "you will be in safety, and have a good view of the town."

This was true enough; the day being clear, and the sun pouring its rays on the city, we could plainly discern the large buildings, Greek temple, church, club-house, hospital, barracks, the harbour of Sebastopol, and the fortifications—viz., the Malakoff, Redan, Quarantine, Fort Constantine, and the Flagstaff batteries—and could see every shot sent by the allied armies as well as by the enemy. The bursting of shells could easily be distinguished. We were about to retire, when Mr. Anderson proposed going a couple of hundred yards further—to the Three-Mortar Battery. Miss Nightingale immediately seconded the proposal, but the sentry strongly objected, saying it was too dangerous; that only a few days before those mortars had poured a very heavy fire into the city, and that the Russians kept a good look-out upon them.

"Oh, never mind," said Mr. Anderson; "I was there two days ago, and they have no powder to waste upon a few individuals."

Although I was very anxious to get so far, and to go with them, I could not help observing to Miss Nightingale that there was a picket in the Woronzoff Road, to indicate the limits, and it was very imprudent of her to run such a risk for no purpose. I further remarked that, should any accident happen to her, no one would pity, but, on the contrary, blame her—that all the good she had done would fall into oblivion, and she would scarcely be regretted.

The sentry then repeated his caution, saying, "Madam, even where you stand you are in great danger; some of the shot reach more than half a mile beyond this." Mr. Bracebridge, though of my opinion, did not say much to dissuade her. The sentry then said, "Well, madam, if you do not fear risking your life, I cannot prevent your going; but remember that, if anything happens, I have witnesses to prove that it was not through my neglect in not informing you of the danger you incur by going to the Three-Mortar Battery."

"My good young man," replied Miss Nightingale, in French, "more dead and wounded have passed through my hands than I hope you will ever see in the battle-field during the whole of your military career; believe me, I have no fear of death." She then started with Mr. Anderson, who was very impatient at so much time being lost. Mr. Bracebridge and myself followed. P.M. was still in the redoubt, ensconced behind a gabion, looking through the telescope, when I suddenly called him. He came running out, as I had taken him by surprise, and he exclaimed, "I say, where the deuce are you all going!"

"Oh, not far—only to the second trench."

"But, my dear sir, there is a great deal of danger." Taking him by the arm, Mr. Bracebridge and myself commenced talking upon indifferent topics, and so got him to advance. As he saw Miss Nightingale before us, he managed to raise courage enough to keep from running away, while the cannonading and bursting of shells was heard plainer, and could be seen much better. He again said, "Why should we go to the trenches? This is very rash to risk one's life for nothing; it is what I call giving a chance away."

To comfort him, I called Mr. Bracebridge and Miss Nightingale. "P.M.," said I, "seems to fancy there is some danger in the trenches, and I wish to impress upon his mind that there is much less danger there than where we are", when a shell came whistling over our heads, and Mr. Anderson hearing it cried out, "A shell! a shell!" upon which P.M. immediately caught me by the shoulders with both hands, and placed himself in a crouching position behind me, which made us all laugh heartily at his expense, as the shell was not directed anywhere near us. I have frequently laughed since with Miss Nightingale at his idea that if the shell had struck me, he would have been any safer than if he had stood by himself.

At all events, we arrived in the Three-Mortar Battery without accident. It contained three large mortars, and instead of being two hundred yards, as

Mr. Anderson had called the distance, was full half a mile from the Flagstaff, going towards Sebastopol, and quite exposed to fire, had they thought it worth while to play upon us. We had, however, an excellent view of the besieged city, such as very few amateurs can boast of having obtained. Before leaving the battery I begged Miss Nightingale, as a favour, to give me her hand, which she did. I then requested her to ascend the stone rampart next the wooden gun carriage, and lastly, to sit upon the centre mortar, to which requests she very gracefully and kindly acceded. I then boldly exclaimed, "Gentlemen, behold this amiable lady sitting fearlessly upon that terrible instrument of war! behold the heroic daughter of England—the soldier's friend!" All present shouted, "Bravo! bravo! hurrah! hurrah! Long live the daughter of England!"

As the cannonade increased instead of diminishing, this gave a kind of martial note of approval to our solemn and enthusiastic ceremony.

We then left the spot, again to risk our noble selves, as I observed to our friend P.M.

"Oh," said he, "I shall run."

Upon this I observed, "You may do as you like; but you will thereby incur more danger, as they will take you for a deserter."

"Oh, that's true again; well, but you may say what you like about bravery—let me tell you, Monsieur Soyer, that I did not bargain for being brave, and I think the sooner we get out of this the better. Only listen to the roaring of the cannon."

We all laughed heartily at his fears and wry faces. Such were never before seen in the Crimea. At last we regained the redoubt, quite safe and sound, which the French corporal on duty attributed to their not thinking it worth while to fire upon us, and partly to the presence of a lady. He remarked that ladies often came to this spot to get a view, and that he had never known the enemy to fire while they were present.

"Well," I replied, "we certainly cannot extol their gallantry too highly. But can they distinguish persons at this distance from their camp?"

"Of course they can, from their advanced batteries. Persons coming this way can be seen plainly five minutes before they reach this spot, unless they come by the Woronzoff Road."

The sun was by this time fast sinking in the vast ocean in front of Sebastopol, giving us to understand that night was about to spread its gloomy wings over the camp, and that in less than two hours it would envelop us in its mysterious darkness, as well as the besieged and their assailants. Alas! how many of those brave fellows who saw that sun set never beheld it rise again. Such was the subject of our conversation while remounting our horses, with hearts full of emotion, and of the awful grandeur of this great war, which, instead of comprising four or five battles, might well be called a single one, or the hundred battle war, lasting nearly fifteen months without intermission, excepting only the few hours when the flag of truce was hoisted, in order that the last religious rites to the mortal remains of the noble departed might be performed. Oh war! war! where is thy fair side? Thou art only a paraphernalia of destruction and misery!

We started at a sharp trot, and were hardly half way to Balaklava when the dusk of evening was settled over the noisy camps, through which we were then passing at full gallop. Mr. Anderson, knowing the road, as he thought, endeavoured to cross the camp by a short cut, when we were overtaken by night, and lost our way. What with the regiments sounding their bugles and the drums beating the retreat, it would have puzzled the coolest head and annoyed the best field-horses. Finding ourselves in one of the Zouave camps, we inquired of the men in which direction Balaklava lay. A group of about ten collected round us, and very politely pointed out the road. It was in a straight line, and not so much out of the way.

"But," said they, "you cannot cut across the camp, as this is the first day we hold the ground, and you are certain to be arrested by the sentries, and clapped in the violon* for the night." They also informed us that it was imprudent to gallop through the camp, for if the colonel was about, or it was reported to him, he would be sure to stop us.

Another exclaimed, in French, "Don't be afraid, friends; the colonel is not very severe in cases in which ladies are concerned. The officers are now devouring their popotes** and taking their evening grog. There is no danger, captain; make the best of your way, as it is getting late, and there are a set of scamps prowling about who would think nothing of waylaying you for the sake of a five-franc piece."

Miss Nightingale, Mr. Bracebridge, and Mr. Anderson were riding slowly in front; P. M. was anxious to know what the Zouaves said, so I translated it as above, for the edification of my brave companion. We then started at a smart pace, but could not come up with our *avant garde*. We made another halt near a group who were sitting on the grass close to their tent, playing some game with a set of mutton bones, and drinking coffee. Others were singing their favourite African song, the "Beau Zouave d'Afrique—Vlan—sont toujours en avant—Vlan—Vlan— Rataplan—plan—plan." Upon inquiring if they had seen two gentlemen and a lady on horseback, they replied, "Yes," and pointed out the road they had taken.

On asking them how they liked camp life, their answer was, "Oh, very much in Algeria, but not at all here; the weather is so bad, and that trench business is such dull work. We should prefer a battle once or twice a week in the open field to being shot at like so many rabbits in the trenches."

Upon asking what they were drinking, they said, "Coffee; would you like to taste it?" "With great pleasure," said I. Upon which they gave me some. It was not bad, but required a little more sugar. "Well," they said, "we sometimes buy some, as we are only allowed about enough for breakfast." I requested their acceptance of a few shillings to drink *la goutte*, which one of them immediately refused, saying, "No, no, Bourgeois; we did not ask you to taste our coffee wishing to make you pay for it."

"I know that, my dear fellow; this is to drink our health."

"We will do that, then, and no mistake."

"Good evening, my men, and thank you," said I. P. M. then started off at a gallop. I immediately stopped him, pretending that if we were seen we were sure to be locked up all night, our lady fair not being with us, the colonel would not joke.

"Well," said he, fiercely, "it would only be for one night, I suppose."

"Yes, one at least."

"I should prefer being locked up all night in the guardhouse to venturing in the dark among so many brigands as the Zouaves say there are roaming about. There we should be in safety; while here we may be shot at any moment."

* The cells—AB
** Meal, or can be officer's mess—AB

As we were descending a deep ravine, we heard a female voice, and then the voices of gentlemen. I had no doubt but that these proceeded from Miss Nightingale and party, who were going slowly down the rocky side of the ravine. Leaping from our horses, we went faster on foot; and in about ten minutes succeeded, thanks to the light of the stars, in catching them. When within hail, I called out, "Who goes there?" The reply assured me they were our fair lady and her two cavaliers. On our joining them they said they almost felt afraid that we had been made prisoners; and Mr. Anderson said he had already given us up. Miss Nightingale and Mr. Bracebridge were of the same opinion, and they laughed heartily at P. M.'s description of our dreadful adventure, as he called it. We were then at the other side of the ravine, and close to a road which Mr. Anderson recognised as the one leading from Balaklava to headquarters.

At last, we were in a fair way of reaching home that night, which P. M. had long despaired of. The conversation became very animated; and I much amused Miss Nightingale and party with my recital of what the Zouave had said respecting his colonel. I also related the coffee business—Miss Nightingale made particular inquiries as to its quality. Having replied to her questions, and being a little ahead, I arrived first at the top of a high hill, and immediately caught sight of the hundreds of lights in the little low shops at Kadikoi. We were all right at last; but the road being steep and very greasy, Miss Nightingale's pony slipped fearfully, which induced Mr. Anderson, who was nearest to her, to dismount and lead it down the hill as far as the village. We then passed through Kadikoi, which presented a different scene to that of the morning, but still animated, from the groups of Turkish and Greek labourers returning to their quarters, and a quantity of drunken men rolling about. We reached the watering-place at the end of the harbour at last. Miss Nightingale's pony, which was again led by Mr. Anderson—this spot being, night and day, full of horses—suddenly turned round to get to the trough, very nearly throwing Miss Nightingale off, and probably would have done so, had it not been held by Mr. Anderson, who received a tremendous knock in the face from the brute's head. This accident made him bleed profusely, and gave him a pair of black eyes. Of this we were not aware until we arrived at the hospital, and could scarcely believe it when we did.

Miss Nightingale and a doctor attended him immediately; and upon inquiring when it happened, he coolly replied, "About ten minutes ago, while we were watering the horses."

"But," said Miss Nightingale, "you never mentioned it."

"Of course not," he replied; "why should I? it would only have made you nervous; and I knew that nothing could be done till we arrived here." After his wound had been dressed, he declared that the shock was so violent at the time, he actually thought his head had been split open.

We regretted that, after having gone through such an adventurous day without accident, a casualty should have happened just at our return. Our valiant friend, P. M., quietly vowed never to go camp-ranging again, especially on a mule who was always bolting before or lagging behind, but never kept parallel with our steeds. Indeed, we called the animal Clockwork, as, when wound up, he would go fast enough, but when run out, nothing but rewinding would move him.

A few days after, by the merest chance, I found a leaf from our friend P. M.'s diary, of which, no doubt, a copy had been sent to his fair Dulcinea. It read as follows:—

Balaklava, Thursday.—Got up at five o'clock. Off for the day, accompanying M. Soyer and other friends. My mule very restive. Accident the first—broke a strap. Weather very hot, water scarce, wine and beer more so. Ride up a ravine—nearly spilt. Quarrel with a Bashi Bazouk. Gallop away from my friends. Splendid view of headquarters. Visit the sick and wounded at General Hospital: Miss Nightingale present—troops greet her with cheers. First glance of Sebastopol, peeping through the gabions. Dangerous visit to the Three-Gun Battery. A shell! a shell! Barely have time to lie flat upon the grass. One of our party wounded by a splinter. Dangerous travelling at night. Take coffee with the Zouaves. Arrive home safely, but very hungry, after our perilous expedition.

We left Mr. Anderson, the horses were taken from us, and we went on board the *Robert Lowe*. The captain was in great anxiety about us, thinking that something had occurred to Miss Nightingale, who, indeed, appeared much fatigued with her glorious excursion. She made no remark on the subject; but, on the contrary, requested me to accompany her early the next morning to both hospitals. This I promised to do with great pleasure; and so ended that lady's first visit to the camp hospitals in the Crimea.

Seven bells was striking—all was silent and at rest in the harbour—nothing was heard save the noise of the bells from the different ships, the booming of the cannon at Sebastopol, with now and then the sharp rattle of musketry, and the gloomy voice of the sentinel's challenge—"Who goes there?"

"A friend."

"Pass, friend. All's well."

XV

THE ENGLISH AND TURKISH
COMMANDERS-IN-CHIEF

THE next morning was wet, chilly, and uncomfortable; and I heard with sorrow that Miss Nightingale was rather indisposed. It did not, indeed, surprise me, considering the fatigue she had undergone the previous day—more especially as she had taken no refreshment the whole of the time. I made sure that she would postpone her visit to the hospitals. Numbers of visitors poured in as usual; amongst them was Admiral Boxer, Chief Admiral of the Port of Balaklava. Mr. Bracebridge was upon deck, and directly he saw the admiral waiting, he went and spoke to him. "Good morning, admiral," said Mr. Bracebridge, and then did me the honour of introducing me.

"Oh! so you are the Monsieur Soyer I have often heard of; and I made sure you were a much older man than you appear to be."

"Did you, indeed, admiral?"

"Yes, that I did. I bought one of your large cookery books about fifteen years ago, and in your portrait you are represented as a man of about forty years of age."

"I must have grown ten years younger since then; as I am only forty-five now, admiral."

"I wish you had put that receipt for growing younger into your book. I should have tried it long ago, and have been satisfied with five years, knowing as much as I do."

"Well done, admiral," said a friend of his. "If Monsieur Soyer could give such receipts as that, everybody would like to take a leaf out of his book."

"At all events, Monsieur Soyer, you are welcome to Balaklava, and when you like to come and see me upon business—mind, I don't invite you for anything else at present, as all here is business, business, from morning till night, and sometimes all night."

"I assure you, Monsieur Soyer," said his nephew, "the admiral is always out first and on his rounds; and I, who seldom leave, often find him writing when everyone else is fast asleep."

"Well, well, business must be attended to," said Admiral Boxer. "At all events, recollect that I give you the *entrée* of the admiral's ship."

"Many thanks, admiral. You may rest assured I will not trouble you often, and then only upon special business."

"Monsieur Soyer, several officers from Scutari have spoken very highly of your services there; and I sincerely trust you will be as successful here.—By the bye, I must be off." Looking at his watch. "Oh, I have ten minutes yet; but could I not see Miss Nightingale?"

"Certainly, admiral. Some gentlemen are with her now—Doctor Henderson and your Balaklava chaplain."

"Oh, never mind, if the lady is engaged; but I believe you came on board the same ship, and wish to remain together. I must look out for another vessel for you, as the *Robert Lowe* will be off in a day or two."

"In that case, admiral, pray see Mr. Bracebridge about it. He is there talking to Thomas, his servant. I will fetch him."

"Pray, Mr. Bracebridge," said the admiral, "give my compliments to Miss Nightingale, and tell her from me that I am sorry to disturb her, but the *Robert Lowe* will sail in a day or two; however, I am going my rounds, and will try and get her quarters upon one of the best vessels in the harbour, and let you know, Mr. Bracebridge. Goodbye! goodbye!"

In a second he was in his boat, holding the helm, and talking to every one he met. His boat was seen in every part of the harbour, and often in the bay, even in rather rough weather. From daybreak till sunset, he might be seen rowing about like a hunted pirate—very active, quick, and expeditious—though very sailor-like—rather rough and straightforward—by report generally liked. Such I found Admiral Boxer.

The weather having cleared up a little, and as I made sure that Miss Nightingale would not go out as it was so very dirty on shore, I prepared to visit the hospitals alone, in order to see how the workmen were going on; intending to ride thence to headquarters. I purposed getting there about one or two o'clock, his lordship's lunch-time—the most likely hour to obtain an interview. On my way to Mr. Bracebridge's cabin, to inform him of my design, and ask him at the same time to go with me—he having expressed a wish that we should go together—Thomas, Miss Nightingale's page, came and inquired if I was ready to go with her to the hospitals.

"Pray, my lad, tell Miss Nightingale that I was going alone; but that, if she is well enough to go, I shall be very happy to accompany her." Before I had time, however, to finish the sentence, Miss Nightingale had ascended the cabin stairs, and, I must say, looked very well.

"Good morning, mademoiselle; how are you after your long journey of yesterday? I heard you were rather indisposed."

"I did feel unwell this morning, but am much better now. I am extremely sorry about Mr. Anderson, who, I am afraid, will be very much disfigured by last night's accident."

"I hope it will not prove very serious."

"It may not; but it will be very disagreeable, as he is obliged to see so many people."

"No matter; all wounds are honourable in time of war, excepting, perhaps, a pair of black eyes."

"But what has become of your brave *compagnon de voyage*, P. M.? Has he recovered from the effects of his fright?"

"All I know is, that he was not at breakfast this morning, and he told everybody last evening that he would not, for any amount of money, again accompany you, mademoiselle, or even her Majesty, through such danger as he incurred yesterday." Everyone who knew him laughed at his bravery, particularly Miss Nightingale, who, turning to Mr. Bracebridge, said—"Monsieur Soyer and myself are going to the General Hospital, and thence to the Sanatorium, where I wish you to be kind enough to meet us."

"About what time?" inquired Mr. Bracebridge.

"Two o'clock, as at that hour Mr. Anderson and Dr. Sutherland will be there about the ventilation."

We then started. The roads were very muddy. I observed to Miss Nightingale that she ought to have had boots made on purpose for such rough walking, to which she assented, saying, "I will do so, Monsieur Soyer."

As we were passing, I left my card at Colonel Hardinge's, the commandant of Balaklava. I had the pleasure of meeting many officers there with whom I was acquainted; they all gave me pressing invitations to visit them in camp, and others to dine with them. As I had no time to stay, I promised to call upon everyone, and rejoined Miss Nightingale. On arriving at the hospital I found the workmen in full activity. Miss Nightingale remained there about two hours. We went next to the Sanatorium, and, in going up the hill, called upon the sick officer who was in Dr. Henderson's hut. The nurse said that he was a little better, but far from being well. He was delirious at times.

"You had better go back to the hospital this evening, Mrs.——, and tell Miss Weare to appoint another nurse to attend in your stead."

"Thank you, madam, I will do so; and am rather glad of it, as I feel very tired."

We then proceeded to the Genoese Heights, where I had the pleasure of meeting Captain King, the chief engineer, whom I found very ready to assist me in every way.

"You are aware," said he, "that we are not in London; and I cannot build a kitchen in the Crimea such as you had at the Reform Club."

"I should be very sorry if you could, as in that case you would have to get somebody to manage it, for I assure you I should not like to begin my gastronomic career again; and I must say I feel every bit as proud in having to cook for the soldiers, if not more so, than ever I did in cooking for the greatest epicures or the first lords of England."

"Then," said Captain King, "we shall work well together."

"I have no doubt of it, captain, as I only require a few workmen, such as carpenters and bricklayers; some planks, nails, and a few bricks and a little mortar. If my new field stoves were finished I should not trouble you at all, as they will cook in the open air, and do not require any fixing."

"If you do not need anything more elaborate than your kitchen here, we shall be able to give you satisfaction. Have you seen the plan I have drawn out for you?"

"Yes, I have—it will do very well."

I then went to look after our party. Miss Nightingale, Dr. Sutherland, the hospital surveyor, and several other doctors, were all together, and they had nearly finished their rounds. They informed me that they were going to see a small naval hospital, situated nearly at the top of the high mountain to the left of the Sanatorium.

The boy Thomas came, and said Miss Nightingale was going home immediately, inquiring, at the same time, for Mr. Bracebridge.

"He has been here," I said, "these two hours; and I saw him ride with Captain King towards the heights, as if he was going to the naval hospital."

"Very well, sir, I will tell Dr. Sutherland."

We were then all going towards the new kitchen. I showed my plan to Miss Nightingale and Dr. Sutherland, who both admired its simplicity and expedition as regards cooking. I observed that this one, when completed, would serve as a model for any others which might be required in the camp.

"Where are the utensils?" asked the hospital purveyor; "we have nothing in store."

"I assure you you are mistaken," said I, "because it was only yesterday that I saw them in Mr. Fitzgerald's store-room."

"I declare," said he, "that for days and days I have been asking for kitchen utensils, and the only things I could get were some spoons, a frying-pan, and large forks."

"Oh," said I, "very likely; but they only arrived with us, and were ordered, at my suggestion, by Mr. Robertson, the purveyor-in-chief at Scutari."

"I beg your pardon; that's all right; but I can assure you that if you had depended upon the Balaklava or Kadikoi tinkers, they would have made you pay as much as five or six shillings for an article worth one in London."

Miss Nightingale and party were by this time half way to Balaklava, but we soon caught them. The weather was bad, the road worse, and rain kept falling. In fact, the mud was so deep in front of the ship, that we were obliged to form a kind of bridge across the road for the lady to get to the boat to go on board. Dr. Sutherland, the captain of the *Diamond*, and the doctor of the Naval Brigade, then made an appointment to go and visit the new hospital building for the sick sailors on the Leander Bay side, facing the Genoese Tower. After this we parted— to meet early the next morning. Upon our return, a message was delivered from the admiral, to the effect that there were two ships at our disposal, and requesting Mr. Bracebridge to go and see them, and choose the one he liked best without delay, as probably the *Robert Lowe* would leave the harbour for Constantinople.

Mr. Bracebridge attended to the order immediately, and having inspected both, selected the *London*, as she was likely to remain the longest. The captain informed us that it had at one time been called the *Great London*, and that it was launched in the beginning of the reign of George the Third. The inhabitants of London used to go and view it as a curiosity; but when it sailed from the Thames the crowd was immense. It was built by Mr. Green.

This being probably our last day on board the *Robert Lowe*, we invited a few friends to dine with us, and, despite the bad weather, we passed a very pleasant and sociable evening, enlivened by the sound of merry glees and national songs. Our hearts and souls were fluttering either in France or England, according to the style of harmony. As Miss Nightingale's state cabin was at a good distance from the saloon, she could not be in the slightest way disturbed by the double harmony which reigned among us. The conversation was turned chiefly upon the arrival of the Sardinian army, and of the destruction by fire of one of their vessels, called the *Capitole*. She was filled with troops, but I believe none were lost. This made a sad pendant to the French vessel, the *Semillante*, wrecked some time before.

The next morning, some large vessels were reported in sight, supposed to be the Sardinian fleet, though, from their great distance and the contrary winds, they were not expected in till late in the afternoon. This led to the departure of the *Robert Lowe* that day, and earlier than the captain had expected. We all left her early, and

Miss Nightingale installed her nurses in the Sanatorium at the Genoese Heights, near the Tower, a sketch of which appeared in the *Illustrated London News*, of the latter end of May, 1855, where we accompanied her with a numerous escort.

As it seemed probable that Miss Nightingale would be engaged the whole of the day classing her ladies in their various departments, we postponed our visit to the Leander Bay naval hospital till the morrow. It was also necessary for us to take up our quarters on board the *London*. The morning had been gloomy, and about one o'clock it began to rain. I thought this would be a good opportunity for obtaining an audience with Lord Raglan at headquarters. Having mentioned the matter to Mr. Bracebridge, he approved it, and proposed accompanying me. We dressed to face the weather. I rode the mule, and off we went through the rain and deep mud.

In going, we took the longest way and the worst road, and were nearly two hours on our journey instead of three-quarters of an hour, which is about the time required, and even less in fine weather. We had almost reached the general's house, when we perceived, at a short distance, a kind of squadron of cavalry coming towards Balaklava. Mr. Bracebridge exclaimed, "If I am not mistaken, Lord Raglan and his staff are going out."

We perceived that some of them wore their rough weather coats. We immediately galloped towards them, and found that it really was Lord Raglan and his staff, with about thirty mounted officers, amongst whom were some attached to the French and Turkish army.

Our first intention was to retire, but seeing Colonel Steele, I rode up to him, told him I had called, and requested him to fix an hour for an audience. Colonel Steele replied, "You could not have come at a better time. Come with me; I will introduce you to his lordship; he will be delighted to see you; he has been inquiring daily after you and Miss Nightingale."

While this conversation was going on, we had got quite close to Lord Raglan. Colonel Steele addressed him, "I beg pardon, my lord; Monsieur Soyer is here." Lord Raglan turned suddenly round, and, before I had time to salute him, said, "Ah, Monsieur Soyer, how are you? I am indeed very glad to see you." I assured his lordship I felt highly flattered at his kind reception.

"You are welcome to the seat of war, Monsieur Soyer. It is many years since we had the pleasure of seeing each other."

"It must be about ten years, my Lord."

"More than that; let me see—it cannot be less than fourteen, I am sure. I recollect going with some friends of mine, to visit you in your interesting kitchen at the Reform Club. You remember?

"So well, that I recollect your lordship saying you never had a good dinner excepting when they gave you the *pot-au-feu* made after my receipt, and that I was one of your great benefactors."

"Perfectly right, Monsieur Soyer. You have been one not only to me, but the public at large, in making all your receipts known. Since we met, you have worked very hard, and, although I did not see you, I watched your progress and industry."

"I am still quite ready to render myself useful, and willing to work harder than ever, under your direction."

"Well, well, you may depend upon it I shall do all in my power to render your services available." Turning to an officer on his left, Lord Raglan said, "Will you allow me to introduce Monsieur Soyer?" Then addressing himself to me, Lord Raglan said, "Monsieur Soyer—His Excellency Omer Pacha."

"I bowed to the distinguished Turkish commander, who said in French, "Ah, Monsieur Soyer, I have frequently heard Beyram Pacha speak of you; only yesterday he mentioned your name. He is acquainted with you?"

"Yes, your excellency; I had the honour of sailing from Marseilles to Constantinople in company with the general."

"He told me you were about to open a large hotel at Eupatoria."

"No, no, your excellency; Monsieur Soyer is come to show our soldiers how to make the best of their rations, which I consider very kind of him; and no doubt they will improve under his tuition. They will not change their old style of cooking for anyone else. Myself, several colonels, and even generals, have taken a deal of interest and trouble in trying to teach them a better way of cooking. They adopt our plan while we are present, but when once our backs are turned, they go on in their old way."

"Very true, very true," said Omer Pacha. "It is just the same with my men. Show them anything better than their pilaff, they will not adopt it for the world."

"You have done wonders, Monsieur Soyer, in the hospitals at Scutari, as I perceive from the report and the letter addressed to me by Lord William Paulet."

"I am very happy to have succeeded so well; and hope the system will in time be followed out by every hospital, as it is less trouble than the old one, not more expensive, and has been highly approved by all the medical authorities."

"Oh," said Lord Raglan, "if it has been approved of by the faculty, there is no doubt of its being adopted at home."

"I have great numbers of testimonials from the heads of the medical departments." By this time we had arrived near Kadikoi, which then consisted of only a few wooden huts. The rain never ceased, and we went at a foot-pace all the way, which gave us an opportunity of conversing. I had the honour of riding on Lord Raglan's right side, and Omer Pacha was on his left. No sooner did we come within view of the plain of Balaklava, than his lordship pointed out the spot where the battle was fought, and asked me if I could see a small church at a distance.

"Perfectly well," was my answer.

"From this spot, on a fine day, you can see the enemy quite distinctly," said Lord Raglan; "and on that large mound which appears so close to us, you can easily see their sentries."

"So I can, my lord. Is that a Russian picket?"

"Yes, it is."

I thanked Lord Raglan for the information; saying, "As I have no particular fancy to have the honour of being made a prisoner of war, I shall take care not to go too near our friends the enemies." His lordship turned round and made some remark to Omer Pacha, who laughed heartily; but I did not distinctly hear what he said— the road was rugged, and Lord Raglan wore a mackintosh with a hood over his head—it was, however, to the effect that the Russians could not secure a more useful prisoner than myself, especially for——(the name escaped me), who is a great epicure.

We were by that time near the Col of Balaklava. Lord Raglan asked me if I had seen the Sardinians land. I replied that, although I knew they were expected, I was not aware of their arrival.

"Oh yes, General della Marmora has arrived, and I am going to receive him."

A large crowd had by this time gathered round the general and his staff. When near the harbour, I took leave of his lordship, who kindly invited me to call at head-quarters, whenever I liked, and told me that Colonel Steele would give me all the information and assistance I might require to carry out my views. I followed the brilliant *cortège*, being anxious to witness the reception of the Sardinian general, which was most cordial and effective, especially when the band struck up "God save the Queen;" such an animated and enthusiastic *tableau* never met my eyes. The sketch was worthy [of] the pencil of the great Horace Vernet.*

Mr. Bracebridge, who had been introduced to Lord Raglan at the same time as myself, but who drew back and conversed with Colonel Steele, left us at the small bridge leading from the Col into Balaklava, and went direct to the town side, while we turned to the left hand, where the Sardinian fleet was anchored. The arrival of the Sardinians had created quite a stir in Balaklava. Towards dusk, they might be seen in all directions. Their dress, manner, language, &c., all formed a marked contrast to the usual daily routine. The fraternization between them and the English took place immediately; they were like brothers who, not having met for many years, were at last united in order to defend the same cause and brave the same dangers. All was joy, heroism, and thirst for glory. The incessant roar of the cannon of Sebastopol had for the first time re-echoed on board the English and Sardinian men-of-war, producing a double impression upon the feelings of both armies. The evening closed with the vibration in the ear of "God save the Queen," "Partant pour la Syrie," and the grand Sardinian national air, which was performed by their band.

---

* French genre and battle painter, 1789—1863.—AB

XVI

A NEW ENEMY

A QUARTER to eleven had struck when I made my first appearance on board the *London*. All had turned in and were asleep, and the lights were out in the chief cabin. The night watch showed me my berth, which I could feel, but not see; so I crept into it half undressed, the best way I could, and in a few minutes, from the fatigues of the day, I fell into a deep slumber. This lasted for several hours; and I was at last aroused by several persevering rats, who tried, at the risk of their lives, to pull a piece of Sardinian biscuit out of my greatcoat pocket. This I had obtained on board the *Carlo Alberto* as a sample.

The presence of such unwelcome visitors made me spring quickly out of my slice of a bed, which is very judiciously called cabin-berth; and, as I found it too small for one, I had a great objection to extra lodgers. I therefore stood upon the offensive and the defensive, which caused my assailants to flee in the greatest confusion, and with such celerity that I was unable to make any of them prisoners. Relying upon the effects of their defeat, fatigue enticed me to try another dose of sleep, when all at once, with the perseverance of Zouaves, the rats returned to the assault, and running over my face, made me capitulate immediately, and leave them in possession of my nautical bedchamber. I spent the remainder of the night uncomfortably enough upon the narrow cabin benches, falling now and then on the floor by way of variation. The light at last began to peep through the cabin windows, and I could look after my garments, which I at once rescued from the teeth of my enemies, the Zouave rats. Not a morsel of the biscuit was left; they had gnawed two large holes in a new greatcoat, no doubt to save the buttons, which they had not swallowed, but very nearly nibbled off. When I was dressed, I rushed upon deck, and began to breathe freely. The sun shone, and the morning gave promise of a fine day. At eight we had breakfast, and I related my night's sport to the captain, Mr. Bracebridge, and others. Everyone laughed heartily at my tribulation, which was poor consolation for such a victim as I had been.

On inquiring about Miss Nightingale, I learnt from Mr. Bracebridge that she had come on board late in the evening. I remarked that it was very imprudent of her remaining so late out in such bad weather; and I told Mr. Bracebridge that he ought to prevent it, as she was sure to be taken ill. "So I told her," Mr. Bracebridge replied, "but she says it will not be for long—only till the sisters are installed; then she will be able to come home sooner. You were highly honoured yesterday, Monsieur Soyer; how you seemed to amuse Lord Raglan and Omer Pacha!"

"Yes, indeed, his lordship is very lively and jocular."

Having explained all that took place, I asked him where he went after leaving us.

"As I did not see Miss Nightingale return from the Genoese heights, I went in search of her. By the bye, are you going with us?"

"Going where?"

"Why, to Leander Bay, to visit the sailors' new hospital."

"Of course I am," I replied. "The present Admiral (Lushington), Captain Hamilton, Doctors Smart and Sutherland will accompany Miss Nightingale."

The Doctor of the *Diamond* called for us in his boat, and beneath a glowing sun, on a fine spring day, we crossed the busy harbour. The Sardinian man-of-war was the greatest attraction. The band played a fine march and some original melodies, which enlivened our short trip. All the shipping had hoisted their flags, and other vessels were seen in the offing, conveying the remainder of the Sardinian army.

While we were crossing, Miss Nightingale inquired about my doings of the previous day, which I carefully related to her, dwelling particularly upon the kind reception I had received from Lord Raglan and Omer Pacha, and the willingness of the former to assist me in my undertaking.

"I am very glad to hear it," said Miss Nightingale; "but, for all that, you will have innumerable difficulties to contend with. Not a man is at work at your kitchen. They say they have no more planks, and all do just as they please. The engineering department is over-burdened with work. For my part, I can get nothing done, nor can the purveyor-in-chief. I don't blame anyone; but if delays of this kind occur for such trifles, what will it be for so important an affair as your general and extra-diet kitchens?"

"You are right, and I thank you for the hint. Upon our return, I will go and see Captain King."

We had then arrived in Leander Bay. I pointed out the spot at which the poor victims of the wreck of the *Prince* were buried—the sight of which made a singular impression upon every member of the party, especially when I told them the number which lay there. There was scarcely any earth over them; and the workmen told us the stench from the bodies was so dreadful, they were often compelled to leave their work in consequence. Another said we did not perceive it because the wind was in another direction. Mr. Bracebridge took note of this, in order to mention the matter to Dr. Sutherland, who knew nothing of it at the time. On reaching the green mountain, at the top of which is situated the new Naval Hospital, we were greeted by the sight of a complete garden of wild flowers, vines, and aromatic plants. This repaid us for the dismal scene below. Several French soldiers were picking the flowers, and gathering salad and wild sorrel.

At the hospital we met Dr. Sutherland and Mr. Anderson, who had not recovered from the effect of his accident, and still had a pair of black eyes. The Commander had been waiting some time for us, and was on the point of retiring, when our arrival induced him to change his intention. We visited the hospital, which, though a small one, was delightfully situated. The huts were built on a new principle, with a new style of ventilation. The kitchen had then only just been commenced. I gave the sailor cook, a Maltese, who seemed very intelligent, a few hints, and promised to send the doctor a plan, and to give him my hospital receipts. The latter I had been expecting for some time from Constantinople; but they had been lost, and I was obliged to have them reprinted. The plan, however, I sent. It was adopted, and, upon my second visit, everything was going on very satisfactorily.

We then separated into groups, and enjoyed a delightful ramble over the rocks and mountains, herborising for a couple of hours. When we again reunited, we all had enormous bouquets of flowers, collected in honour of our fair lady, who could not help laughing at the appearance of her beaux and their bouquets. Only one was accepted, and the fortunate candidate was our worthy friend the invalid, Mr. Anderson. We carried our botanical harvest home, and descended the hill full of health and spirits. Even the cannon of Sebastopol was silent, at least to our ears, the wind being the wrong way for the report to reach us. In a few minutes we were once more afloat, and were about conducting Miss Nightingale on board, when she said that she wished to go to the General Hospital; so Captain Hamilton landed us as near to it as possible. We then separated—Dr. Smart and Mr. Anderson inviting me to go and see them often, as they had much to inform me of relating to the food of the army.

Dr. Smart accompanied Miss Nightingale to the hospital, and I went to find Captain King; but he had gone to the Sanatorium—at least so they told me at his office. I went up there, being anxious to have this kitchen completed, as it was really much wanted. The hospital was getting fuller every day, and I had a great desire to commence operations at the camp. The Captain was not there, nor could I find a single workman. To my great sorrow, I met Miss Nightingale coming down the hill, attended by a nurse or two, and the page-boy. She was walking through the mud in thin boots. The weather had entirely changed, and a heavy rain was falling. Upon meeting her, I could not refrain from expressing my fear that she would catch cold. She had been to ask the nurse at Dr. Henderson's how the officer patient was. Upon reaching the harbour, we took a Maltese boat, and arrived on board the *London* almost wet through.

A different cabin to the one I had occupied the night before was allotted to me. All the rat holes had been stopped, and by special favour I was allowed a night-lamp. I had the pleasure of seeing the rats run about, which afforded me the opportunity of hunting them at my ease. I then perceived that several escaped through the bull's-eye, which I immediately closed, and so captured three. I then commenced killing them with a stick, and in so doing made noise enough to arouse everybody. Some of the crew came to see what was the matter, while the Captain, who was half asleep, and rather deaf, told the mate to send for the police and turn the drunken man out.

Having explained to the first mate the cause of my nocturnal disturbance, he told me that they were sure to come in at the bull's-eye, if left open, that being the easiest way for them when in harbour. "And," said he, "they travel that way from one ship to another in bands of ten or twenty at a time." He then showed me how to close and fasten the bull's-eye, after which he retired to his berth. All at once, one of the brutes, which had remained concealed, in attempting to escape upset the lamp upon the floor and extinguished it, and thus compelled me for the second time to seek to repose upon the hard and unsophisticated cabin bench, when the Captain made his appearance rather in a state of *négligé*, holding a rushlight in one hand and a sword in the other, with a nightcap tied round with a red riband upon his head. In great anxiety, he inquired what the row was about.

"The row, Captain," said I, "is nothing. It's only the bull's-eye in my cabin, which being half open, the rats have got in again."

"What do you say, Monsieur Soyer?"

"Nothing," again I shouted.

"Call that nothing? I never had such a row in my ship before. Bless my soul," said he, "what a nuisance those rats are! They make quite as free in my cabin; but, being used to it, I do not care so much about them. The worst of it is that we can never keep a bit of cheese or a candle; they eat them up as fast as I buy them."

"It is certainly very provoking, Captain; but why not try and catch them?"

"Oh, bless you, we have tried everything—poison, traps, broken glass. We caught a few, but I would give the world to have them all caught."

"I can give you a receipt which will enable you to have them almost all caught in a few days."

"The deuce you could!" said he, coming and sitting opposite to me. "Tell me how it is done—I shall be so much obliged to you; but I must go and put something on first, I am so cold." As he said this, I perceived that the skylight over his head was open.

"Oh, never mind that; it won't take two minutes to tell you—listen to me."

"So I will," he said.

"The place where you keep your cheese would be the very spot to make the trial. The thing is quite easy. Have your cheese and candles removed."

"So I will; but I wish you would let me put a coat on—I am getting so very cold."

"Never mind about that; I shall not keep you a minute—listen to me."

"So I will."

"When the cabin is perfectly empty, have it cleaned and well scrubbed."

"That will be done."

"When it is dry, take half a pound of good Cheshire cheese, scrape it fine, and mix it with about two pounds of rough breadcrumbs."

"Yes, I will."

"Perhaps you think it is a pity to give them half a pound of good cheese."

"Not at all, because the vermin eat pounds of it daily."

"Mix both well together."

"Yes, I understand—and make them into balls."

"No, not at all—only spread the lot upon the floor, leave the door and window open, and go to bed. Of course they will come and eat."

"I should say they would," he observed.

"The next evening do the same, cutting the cheese a trifle larger. They will come again and eat it."

"What next?" said he.

"The third night, leave the doors and windows open; go to bed as usual, and put nothing at all in the cabin."

"What then?" he asked again, in a state of anxiety.

"Why, of course, when they come and find nothing to eat, and being in still greater numbers than the two previous nights, they will be all caught."

"How," said he, "will they be all caught?"

"Why, of course, finding nothing to eat, they will be all taken in."

"That be d——d! I have made a nice fool of myself, standing here half naked to listen to such rubbish as that."

Having said this, he ran into his cabin, and for a long while I heard him sneezing and muttering to himself. The word "fool" was all that I could catch; and soon after all was silent till daybreak.

On waking, I at first regretted having carried the joke so far, when all at once I heard the good captain burst out laughing and sneezing. The first visit I had in the morning, while shaving in my cabin, was from the captain. As it was then only six o'clock, I made sure he was coming to challenge me, and began to think of choosing my favourite weapons, which I had so successfully employed on a similar occasion in London, after a serious discussion with a red republican on the subject of monarchy.

One afternoon, at a French restaurant in the Haymarket, a rather animated discussion, *apropos* of the new republic of the year '48, took place between myself and a person whom I afterwards ascertained to be the duellist Cournet, an officer in the French navy, who has already been mentioned in the earlier pages of this work.

My entire disapproval of the conduct of the friends of liberty, as shown by their wanton destruction of everything, both useful and ornamental, even to the court breeches and white inexpressibles of the National Guard (which were exposed to dry at every window of the Palace of the Tuileries, thus giving to that noble building somewhat the appearance of Rag Fair), was so strongly expressed, that Cournet, "taking umbrage thereat," after calling me a monarchist and an enemy to liberty, insisted upon my meeting him the next morning, to give him the satisfaction due from one gentleman to another.

I replied to his challenge by desiring that the matter should be settled at once.

He answered, in a haughty tone, "Comme vous voudrez, monsieur. C'est à vous le choix des armes. Nous tirerons ce que vous voudrez!"

"Eh, bien," said I, "puisque c'est à moi le choix des armes, sortons à l'instant même, monsieur, et nous allons nous tirer les cheveux."

"As you please, sir. The choice of weapons is yours."

"In that case, I suppose we must pull triggers for it."

"Sir," replied he, "we will pull any mortal thing you please."

"Good," said I; "then we will at once proceed to pull each other's hair."

The roar of laughter which followed this sally somewhat calmed the ire of this rabid and irascible duellist, more especially when he was informed who I was, and that my province was to make people live well, and not die badly.

The Captain, however, entered with a smile on his countenance, and looked altogether pleased. He begged of me to say nothing about it, as the crew would laugh at him, and it was necessary on board ship to be very severe. Moreover, he declared that he wished to catch some of his brother captains, who, like him, were very much pestered with rats.

As I was extremely anxious to see Captain King respecting the slow progress of the kitchen, I started about seven o'clock, expecting to find him at home. After a long and disagreeable mountainous walk, I arrived too late. "But," said his man, "you will very likely meet him at his office about nine o'clock, or else at the Sanatorium or headquarters, or at Kadikoi, as he told me he was going to those places."

"I suppose I have a chance of finding him anywhere, except at Sebastopol," I replied.

More fortunate than on former occasions, I met the captain on horseback going to his office. We mounted the tumbledown rotten wooden staircase of this late palazzo, now converted into one of the principal and most important departments in the British army in the Crimea—viz., the office of the chief engineer. The large room which was dedicated to the captain would hold, at a pinch, seven or eight people of a very moderate size standing; the second about five; and the third none, being filled with plans, models, and drawings.

Such was the castle of a king in Balaklava; and I have seen from thirty to forty people waiting in the mud to have an interview with his Majesty, who, I must confess, received his loyal subjects with a most humorous and happy countenance, having always a smile for a friend and kind words for everybody. When we got in, I immediately locked the door, informing him that he, the king, was my prisoner for at least ten minutes, as that was all the time I should require. We went earnestly to business. I submitted my various plans, and requested him to have the Sanatorium kitchen finished. To this he agreed, promising to do all he could for me, at the same time observing they were short of materials and good workmen.

I then set the captain and king at liberty.

I next went to see Commissary Filder, being anxious to fix a time for inspecting the provisions in general use.

A MODERN BOTANICAL GARDEN—NATURE OUTDONE.

XVII

RECEPTION AT ENGLISH AND FRENCH
HEADQUARTERS

ON my return to our ship, I left my card at Colonel Hardinge's. He kindly invited me to breakfast; and I regretted that I could not accept the invitation, having promised Colonel Steele to be at headquarters at eleven o'clock. After a little business conversation respecting the arrival of the fuel, he gave me an estimate of the number of vessels required daily for that purpose alone, the number of men employed in loading and unloading the ships, the encumbrance it caused in the harbour, the room required for storing it, the number of mules for carrying it to the various camps, and the difficulty of distribution. "No one," said he, "can imagine the immense quantity of labour that is required for keeping up the supplies of fuel."

"I am going today," I remarked, "to see the commander-in-chief; and I intend to submit a small model of my camp kitchen for his inspection." In a few words I explained its principle, and stated the small quantity of fuel it would require. Colonel Hardinge remarked, "Why, you will save at least between three and four hundred per cent.; for it is not the cost of the coal or wood which is the principal item, but the labour, expense, and inconvenience of transport. All these will be greatly reduced."

"I am much obliged to you," I said, "for your very encouraging remarks."

"Any more information you may require I shall at all times be happy to afford; and as you have no horses yet, whenever you want a pony, let me know."

"I feel grateful, Colonel, for your kind reception."

Crowds of people were waiting for an audience, yet I managed to escape. Balaklava House was indeed a palace compared with the rest of the Tartaric habitations. On arriving on board the *London*, I heard with regret that Miss Nightingale was indisposed. Mr. Bracebridge did not think it was anything very serious. Mrs. Roberts, Miss Nightingale's head nurse, who always accompanied her and attended her during the voyage, informed me that Miss Nightingale was not going out, having much writing to do, it being post-day.

Mr. Bracebridge wished me to go with him to see Mr. Upton, the son of the architect who built the harbour and docks of Sebastopol. On my reminding him of my appointment at headquarters (which he had forgotten), Mr. Bracebridge proposed going the next morning, as he had a particular desire to see Mr. Upton and family. "I hear," said he, "Mr. Upton is a Warwickshire man. His father was born at the small village of Grendon, close to my place and that of your late friend, Sir George Chetwynd, of Grendon Hall."

"Really! I know the place very well; and tomorrow I shall be happy to accompany you, unless fresh orders from headquarters interfere with the arrangement."

"Your pony is ready, Monsieur Soyer," said the steward of the ship. I sent for Miss Nightingale's page, Thomas.

"Do you want me, Monsieur Soyer?" asked the boy.

"Yes, my lad, I do. Tell your mistress I am going to headquarters; give her my best compliments, and say I shall have the pleasure of seeing Lord Raglan; and ask her if I can take any message for her to him, or to anyone else in the camp."

The Captain, who was smoking on the upper deck, called out, "Who caught the rats?"

"You mean, who caught the captain," said I, "who could not smell a rat?"

The boy returned, and informed me that Miss Nightingale was very much obliged to me, and that she had written to Lord Raglan upon business that very morning.

I then started. The roads were still very heavy from the immense quantity of rain which had fallen, but the weather was fine overhead, and everybody seemed to be out. People, in fact, sprang up like mushrooms in a green field after a little rain and a few hours of August sunshine. I met numerous friends and acquaintances between Balaklava and Kadikoi. Many of these—military as well as medical gentlemen—I had seen at Scutari. Indeed, the excursion put me more in mind of riding in Hyde Park on a Sunday afternoon, than being in a distant country, and at the seat of war. For above a mile it was a constant nodding of heads and shaking of hands. As my time was short, I felt anxious to get on my journey as fast as possible. I did not know the way to headquarters, so I inquired of an officer which was the shortest road. He kindly informed me that he was going there, and knew the short cuts, but that he was in a great hurry, and if I could ride fast, he should be much pleased to show me the way. Of course I expressed my willingness to accommodate my pace to his, and away we went across country. After riding for twenty-five minutes, we arrived near the ever-celebrated farm which constituted the headquarters. Its appearance was by no means grand nor imposing, and put me very much in mind of Shakespeare's house at Stratford, or the humble cot of the poet Burns in Ayrshire.

My readers are too well acquainted with the locality and the non-architectural design of the house and its dependencies for me to attempt giving a description. The well-known spot was first taken as the English headquarters, and retaken by drawing, daguerreotyping, engraving, photographing, lithographing, &c.: in fact, it became, as well as the wooden French headquarters, so celebrated during the wartime, that the Tuileries, Windsor, and the marble palace of Dolma Batchi were actually cast into the shade, and a very deep shade too. Even cities were at a discount compared with Sebastopol. Yes, Sebastopol, pretty, picturesque Sebastopol, with its few thousand inhabitants, was in everybody's mouth and thoughts.

The courtyard at headquarters that morning presented a very lively scene. I found it, to my great disappointment, filled with officers' chargers, which were being slowly led about by the orderlies. There were some belonging to Sardinians, French, and Turks, besides English ones. This sight made me despair of seeing the General that morning, and I feared that I should lose another day. Time was then precious to me.

Upon inquiry, I was informed that the Sardinian General, Della Marmora, was returning a visit to Lord Raglan and to General Canrobert, and that they would all be off directly, as a grand review of their troops was to take place the following day. This afforded me an opportunity of paying my second visit to Dr. Hall, the chief superintendent. He was out, but I was told that he would be home by one or two o'clock. On retracing my steps to headquarters, I found, as I had been at first informed, everyone on the point of departure. The different uniforms formed an exquisite contrast in the military cavalcade. The courtyard was soon cleared, and I went in, and had the pleasure of seeing General Airey, Colonel Steele, &c. Colonel Steele said I was just in time to see Lord Raglan, and I was at once ushered in.

"What have you to show me, Monsieur Soyer?" said Lord Raglan, after a kind greeting.

"I wish to submit to your lordship's inspection the model of my field stove, and if you approve of it, the progress of my undertaking will be greatly accelerated."

"Very well; explain it at once."

"In the first place, here is a simple plan of the kitchen in course of erection at the Sanatorium Hospital." I pointed out the details, which his lordship seemed to understand at first sight.

"If that is all you require, surely you can have it done without much delay."

"That is all; but I require men as well."

"You shall have them—orders will be given to that effect."

"This one will serve as model for all the others: they will be upon a similar scale. For example, the General Hospital before Sebastopol does not require one on so extensive a scale, though the most important."

"Well, what you require must be done. By the bye, Monsieur Soyer, you are very fortunate in having had the honour of escorting Miss Nightingale to the seat of war."

"I am fully aware, my Lord, that it is a great honour."

"The lady mentioned you in her letter to me, as well as Mr. Bracebridge, whom I know very well. I went to Balaklava the other day to visit her."

"So I heard; but Miss Nightingale was at the Sanatorium whilst your lordship went to the General Hospital."

"They could not tell me where she was—therefore I did not go to the Sanatorium. I saw a poor lady who seems very ill. I told her she had better take care of herself, and have someone to nurse her, instead of nursing others. She spoke very good French, and a very lady-like person she is."

"I know whom your lordship means—the lady is Miss Weare."

"I almost forget the name, but I believe that was it."

Lord Raglan made many inquiries respecting Miss Nightingale, whose character he seemed to admire very much. We then returned to business matters. I expressed my desire to visit the hospital kitchens in the camp, in company with some of the authorities. To this Lord Raglan immediately acceded.

"No person could be better than Dr. Hall. Do you know him, Monsieur Soyer?"

"No, my Lord, I have not that pleasure; I called upon him twice, but unfortunately he was out."

"He lives close at hand, and I will send for him."

I told Lord Raglan that I had just left his hut, and that he was absent, but would be certain to be back by three or four o'clock.

"Very well; then you can settle that together."

As I perceived that numbers of persons were waiting to see his lordship, and that messages were continually being sent in, I said that I should be happy to wait, and would call again.

"No, no, not at all," said Lord Raglan; "if you were to wait, you might do so for a month. What is that you have under your arm? Is it a cooking apparatus?"

"Yes, this is the model of the field stove I have invented, and which I wish to submit for your lordship's opinion and approval, by command of Lord Panmure, who approved of it very highly. Mr. Brunel, the great engineer, did the same. They are now in use in various hospitals, particularly at Smyrna, and at Scutari, where they answer admirably. They can also be used in the field, as they will cook either in or out of doors. Those for out-of-door purposes only require to be made smaller and lighter than the hospital ones."

Having carefully explained the principle upon which it was constructed, Lord Raglan thought it would answer perfectly, and asked, "Do you wish to have them adopted immediately?"

"Not before you have seen them at work, my Lord."

"Ah, that will do better."

"I am expecting some of them shortly; in fact, they should have been here before."

"Well, you had better make inquiries about them, or they may be delayed somewhere, as this happens almost every day."

Several gentlemen were present when I explained the principle of the stove, in which Lord Raglan seemed much interested, showing the model and taking the trouble to explain its principle to them himself. Colonel Symonds said, "Monsieur Soyer, I will go and fetch his Excellency Omer Pacha; he is much interested in this kind of thing."

"Do, Colonel," said Lord Raglan. Then turning to me: "I am much pleased with what I have seen, and have no doubt those stoves will prove a great boon to the army; but mind, they must not be made too heavy, and they must be adapted for companies. Neither must you forget the smaller ones which I mentioned to you, for picket and outpost duty." Omer Pacha entered. "Now," said Lord Raglan, "form your own opinion of Soyer's field stove, and let me know what you think of it."

"Monsieur Soyer," said Omer Pacha, "what have you good to eat there?"

"Nothing at present, your Excellency; but by and by, when my plans are adopted, we shall be able to cook for and feed the army with ease."

"Ah, this is a matter of great importance. Pray explain your plans to me." When I had done this, Omer Pacha said, "It will first be necessary to have something to cook."

The truth of the observation I respectfully admitted, with a low bow, adding, "Your Excellency is right; but as the probability is that something to be cooked never yet entirely failed, and in expectation of better times coming, we confidently hope that the provisions for the army will shortly be on the increase instead of the decrease. This hope has induced me to invent this apparatus, of which, when its principle has been fully explained, I have no doubt you will, with Lord Raglan, approve."

"Monsieur Soyer, I have no doubt that, as regards cooking, you are a very clever man; but if you could manage to cook a dinner out of nothing, you would be more clever still."

"Not having tried the experiment, I really cannot say whether I could do so or not; but I will try, and then report progress to your Excellency."

A hearty laugh from all present terminated this *petite plaisanterie*. This brought to my mind the story of a very promising schoolboy, who, when asked by a learned man whether he could speak Latin, replied, "I cannot tell, sir."

"Why can't you tell, my boy?"

"Because I never tried, sir," was the answer.

"At all events," I continued, addressing Omer Pacha, "you will perceive that if I cannot make something out of nothing, I am able to do a great deal with a little, which in war-time is a very important matter."

"Very true; but pray show me the interior of this little model."

Having shown and explained the apparatus, Omer Pacha admitted its practicability, and, after giving me a few hints on the Turkish system of camp cookery, retired, followed by his staff, wishing me every success. Lord Raglan met Omer Pacha in the passage, and they exchanged a few words, which I could hear bore reference to the subject we had discussed. I was leaving, when Lord Raglan re-entered.

"So you are going, Monsieur Soyer?"

"Yes, my Lord. I fear my visit has been too long."

"No, not at all—this is rather a quiet day, and before you go I wish you would be kind enough to look at my kitchen."

"I shall be most happy to do so."

"Do you know my cook?—his name is Armand—he is not a *cordon bleu*, but he is a good man, and does his best with what he can get."

"The French proverb *à la guerre comme à la guerre* is very applicable to the circumstances—nay, rather too much so to permit one to hope to obtain a good dinner."

"Very true," said Lord Raglan; "and we are really so tired of those preserved meats."

"Indeed; but some of them are not bad."

"The great fault is, that the meat is always overdone. How do you account for that, Monsieur Soyer?"

"If it were not so, they would not keep. When I was sent for to Deptford to report upon Golding's preserved meats—which, no doubt, your lordship recollects——"

"I do, indeed; they were too bad to be forgotten."

"I assure your lordship the fault was more in the cooking than in the bad quality of the meat—some of which I found in a state of liquid putrefaction. No doubt, the meat was not of prime quality, and many improper things were introduced. Nevertheless, if the articles had been properly preserved, they would have been found as sweet when taken out as when they were put in. For example, the entrails of any animal might be enclosed in these tin cases in the state in which they came from the animal, and, if well preserved, upon opening them a couple of years after, they would be found pretty much in their original state, excepting being slightly discoloured by the cooking—but whole, and not in a liquid state, as those were. The meat was, therefore, either not cooked enough, or some atmospheric air had remained in it which caused putrefaction."

"Could not any other way of preserving be introduced?"

"Many experiments have been tried, but almost all proved unsuccessful. I, at one time, made several myself, the results of some of which I submitted to Captain Miles, Admiral Berkeley, Sir Charles Napier, &c., and they were found very good. They were then about a month old, but the time the government wished for the test was a twelvemonth. I was certain they would keep any length of time, but as I was then very much engaged at the Reform Club, and also writing my cookery-book, *The Modern Housewife*, I did not pursue it further. The principal improvement in my method was the omission of the liquids previously introduced, either broth or water. I only put the meat in well seasoned, and left it to cook slowly in its own gravy; and when opened, it turned out surrounded by a firm jelly, and cut solid."

"I should advise you to turn your immediate attention to that subject."

"I will, my Lord, as soon as time permits. I shall now go and see your kitchen, and pay a visit to your *chef de cuisine.*"

"Pray do, and see whether you can contrive to improve it. I believe it is a very bad one, for he is always complaining. When you return, lunch will be upon the table, and you can take some refreshment."

Thanking Lord Raglan for his extreme kindness, I took my leave. I was anxious to see Colonel Steele, to inform him of the result of my interview; but as he was out, I proceeded to the kitchen, which was some distance from the house, across the courtyard. The *chef* had gone to Kamiesch to market: I therefore postponed my visit, and returned to the dining-room to take some refreshment. Afterwards I went in search of Doctor Hall, whom at last I had the good fortune to find at home, if such a small place could be called a home. It was about ten feet square, and the height of a sentry-box, affording about enough room for four persons to stand up in, and only for two to sit down. This *petit châlet* was for all that nicely furnished, and the spot where most of the hospital business was transacted both for the East and the Crimea, it being the general headquarters for the various medical departments. Such was the habitation, office, and château of the present Sir John Hall.

At the door I was received by his major domo, a Frenchman named Louis, a very intelligent man, and one as well known in the camp from his extraordinary look, shrewdness, eccentricity, and style of riding, as the doctor himself. On alighting, Louis took my horse by the bridle, and walking to the entrance, introduced me to the doctor, who was very busy writing. He got up and requested me to enter, which I did.

"Pray be seated, Monsieur Soyer—I am very happy to see you. I heard of your arrival, and also of your former visits."

"Today, doctor, I have been more fortunate."

"You see, Monsieur Soyer, I have so many places to visit every day, particularly in the morning, that I am very seldom at home."

I could but smile at the word "home," which, as my readers will understand by my description, was but a humble one. Such was the general amount of luxury in the establishments in the Crimea.

"As I am aware, doctor, of the value of your time, do not let me disturb you in the least. A few minutes will settle our business. First of all, I have a letter of introduction from Dr. Cumming."

"Let me see it."

It contained only a few lines, and was to the following effect:—

To Dr. Hall, *Chief of the Medical Department, Crimea.*

Dear Sir,—Monsieur Soyer, who you are well aware has rendered us important service in the culinary department of our hospitals on the Bosphorus, prior to going to the Crimea begs of me to give him a letter of introduction to you. Hoping that his services may prove as successful in the Crimea as they have been here,

I remain, dear Sir, yours faithfully,
Dr. Cumming.

When Dr. Hall had read the letter, and expressed his satisfaction at the contents, I related the result of my interview with the commander-in-chief, and my desire to visit the camp hospitals with the doctor at his earliest convenience. Dr. Hall immediately fixed the next day for the purpose, and kindly offered to send a pony for me about eight the next morning.

After having exchanged the usual compliments, we parted. Before I left, the doctor called Louis and gave him the order for the pony. As it was only three o'clock, and I had a few hours to spare, I felt inclined to visit the French camp, in order to compare their system of cooking with that in use among the English, as well as to make some inquiries about their provisions.

The French headquarters did not bear the slightest resemblance to the English. The pile was entirely constructed of wood, and thus gave a wide scope to the architects to distinguish themselves in the modern science of joining and building, and to render as convenient and comfortable as possible this seat of important business transactions. It was in fact a well-built village, of which the general-in-chief was the lord; and, though not gaudy, still luxuriously comfortable, with every department distinct and well arranged. This was, to a certain extent, the case at the English headquarters, but a farm did not afford sufficient space and accommodation. At the commencement of the campaign, it was no uncommon thing for a general to rest from the fatigues of war in a small dilapidated room something like a good-sized English pigsty.

The French headquarters, like the English, were surrounded by the staff and principal business offices, which, though answering the same purpose, presented quite a different appearance. In the arrangement of the offices and the manners of the inhabitants, one could in fact distinguish France from England, and England from France.

The vicinity was well guarded—several regiments being encamped round that select group of habitations. It was only with a silver key one could open the doors of the field kitchens and *popotes*, which key was always to be found at the regimental canteen. A few bottles of wine, glasses of absinthe or vermouth, were enough to initiate me in less than two hours in all that I required to know relating to my mission.

After settling my account with three or four coquettish and cavalier-like *vivandières*, wishing them all the commercial prosperity imaginable, and shaking hands with several companies of the various regiments, including those of the Imperial Guard, who had just arrived, I cheerfully retired with the gratification of having conquered a portion of the *élite* of the French armies—of course, I only mean in pure friendship. Moreover, I gained most honourable titles, from lieutenant to captain, colonel, and now and then general. At all events, my passport through that important part of the French camp was signed by several hundreds of

those brave fellows, as well as by innumerable smiles from the fair and dark hero-
ines, the *cantinières* of the first French division. With a promise to return soon, I
retired, having experienced much gratification and enriched my budget of anecdote.

In this interesting visit to the French camp, headquarters, canteens, &c., and
becoming well acquainted with the officers' and soldiers' *popotes*—which name I
immediately added to my gastronomic bill of fare—the three hours I had to spare
nearly expired. The sun was rapidly descending to the level of the ocean in the
direction of Kamiesch.

Having paid my bill at the canteen, and shaken hands with nearly a whole regiment, I jumped on my pony and galloped all the way home, perfectly satisfied with
my day's work, which at the time I felt was one of the most interesting of my life.

XVIII

A UNIVERSAL CALAMITY

ALAS! how short are the moments in which real happiness favours us with its charms, and how quickly it deserts one in the midst of mirth and joy! On this eventful day, I was doomed to experience the truth of the saying that "sorrow treads upon the heels of joy;" for I had scarcely set my foot upon the deck of the *London*, when P. M. came and apprised me that Miss Nightingale was not expected to live. It appeared that after my departure she had a terrible attack of fever, and was obliged to be immediately removed to the hospital. On asking to which establishment this excellent lady had been taken, I was told the Sanatorium. P. M. continued, "Several doctors, Mr. and Mrs. Bracebridge, and myself, accompanied her there—I have only been back a few minutes."

"Why did you not take her to the General Hospital? It was much nearer."

"Don't you know that cholera is raging there?"

"There certainly are a few cases. Do you think I can do anything for her?"

"No, I am sure you cannot; she is not allowed to take anything, and the doctors have forbidden anyone to be admitted, except her private nurse, Mrs. Roberts."

It was then getting late—Mr. Bracebridge had not returned. The captain and P. M. gave me a full account of this lamentable event. It appeared that about noon Miss Weare had come on board to see Miss Nightingale upon business. She found that lady very poorly, but thinking it was a slight indisposition, took no notice of it, more especially as Miss Nightingale did not complain in the least. About two, by the orders of Mrs. Roberts, they were obliged to send in a great hurry for a doctor. Mrs. Roberts stated that her mistress had been suddenly taken dangerously ill— that she was in fact attacked by the worst form of Crimean fever. The first thing ordered by the doctor was her instant removal to the hospital on the heights.

"So," said the captain, who was relating this part of the sad history, "I set all my men to work. We got a stretcher from the hospital, and she was carried very carefully by my men and some soldiers sent by the governor."

"I followed through Balaklava," said P. M., "amidst a regular procession of soldiers, holding a white umbrella over her face. The crowd was so great, we could scarcely pass, and it took us nearly an hour to get up to the heights. I assure you, all Balaklava was in an uproar."

"What do the doctors say of the case?"

"That the lady is dangerously ill, and that no one must go near her, not even Mr. Bracebridge."

"What mournful tidings!" I said. "I should not be surprised if she caught the fever from the patient at Dr. Henderson's. I warned her of the danger of exposing herself so much several times."

"By the bye, where is Mr. Bracebridge?"

"I left him there."

"Does he intend to come back, or stay where he is?"

"I don't know, but I do not see what good he can do there."

"I hope we shall hear better news when he returns."

"Now, Mr. Soyer, tell us about your visit to headquarters. Did you see Lord Raglan?"

"Certainly I did."

"And how were you received?" asked the captain.

"Admirably," I replied.

"I hear his lordship is a most amiable and kind man."

"He is indeed, I assure you; and I cannot but express my gratitude for the reception he afforded me. I am certain he will be very sorry to hear of Miss Nightingale's serious and sudden illness, for he inquired very kindly after her this morning."

My companions made many more inquiries respecting the events of the day; but I had forgotten all, I was so absorbed by this unexpected blow. It seemed likely to upset all our plans. I spoke to the captain of the several visits Miss Nightingale had paid to the sick officer at Dr. Henderson's at the time he was so dangerously ill, remarking upon her neglect of herself by going all day without refreshment, and braving all weathers. We could not help noticing how singular it appeared, that after her hard labours at Scutari, and escaping both the cholera and fevers which raged there, she should be so suddenly taken ill at Balaklava. It was indeed very melancholy and remarkable. At last Mr. Bracebridge returned. He informed us that Miss Nightingale was a little better, but that such a violent case of fever required a certain time. "Mrs. Roberts," he continued, "is with her, and the boy to go for the doctor, in case he should be needed."

"Poor boy!" said the captain, "how he cried when he saw his mistress carried upon a stretcher by soldiers!"

"Yes," said Mr. Bracebridge, "he is a very affectionate lad."

After a few questions about my visit to Lord Raglan, being all very much fagged, we retired for the night. Upon that occasion, owing to excessive fatigue and the absence of rats, which had at length been successfully turned out of my cabin without making use of my receipt, I enjoyed a comfortable night's rest. The next morning, at eight precisely, Louis was at his post with the pony, of which I could not, however, make use, not knowing what alteration Miss Nightingale's illness might cause at both hospitals, where, no doubt, my presence would be required. I sent Dr. Hall a note, apologizing for not waiting upon him that day, and postponing our visit to the day following, if agreeable to him. Louis promised to send me an answer at five o'clock by the doctor's courier. No news had been received at the General Hospital from the Sanatorium; therefore Mr. Bracebridge and myself went up the first thing, instead of going to Mr. Upton, as we had previously arranged. On our arrival, the report was anything but favourable; and this seemed to paralyse all our energies. Indeed, for a few days no business of consequence was transacted. My kitchen at the Sanatorium alone progressed. I offered my services to Drs. Henderson and Hadley, in case I could be of use to Miss Nightingale. Dr. Henderson said, "I am the only cook she requires at present. We must wait nearly a week before I can leave her in your hands, even should her illness take a favourable turn." I then begged of him to give me his private opinion of her state.

"She is suffering, I assure you, Monsieur Soyer, from as bad an attack of fever as I have seen; but I should say the chances are in her favour, because she does not fret in the slightest degree, but is perfectly composed."

On calling at the General Hospital for Dr. Hall's reply, I found that he had fixed the same time the next day for our visit. We then returned on board the *London*. Many inquiries respecting Miss Nightingale had been made by almost all the authorities, amongst whom were Sir John Macneil, Captain Tulloch, Admiral Boxer, the Governor, Commissary Filder, and Dr. Sutherland. The latter went at once to see her. Finding she had all proper attention, he came in the evening, and requested us to leave her as quiet as possible. He told Mr. Bracebridge on no account to go near her, not even if sent for, as any excitement might be fatal. This request was of course punctually attended to.

The remainder of the Sardinian army had now arrived. The disembarkation kept the harbour in a constant bustle, morning, noon, and night. It was, in fact, a real maritime bivouac, and our vessel very much resembled the famed metropolis from which it takes its name. During the night a strong bridge was built over it, communicating with the shore on the one side, and one of the Sardinian ships, which had been towed alongside, on the other. This was made for the purpose of landing men and horses. At five in the morning I was up and on deck, as from the noise it was impossible to sleep. The first person on board was Admiral Boxer, as busy as could be, giving his orders. On seeing me, he inquired about Miss Nightingale.

"What a good job," said he, "they were able to remove her from here!"

"You are right, admiral. I perceive you are about to put the troops from one of the vessels on shore."

"From one, say you? I am landing the whole of the Sardinian army, and some of our own troops besides."

"At any rate, I think this is one of the greatest curiosities of the Crimean war."

"Why?" asked the admiral, talking to twenty others at the time.

"Why, admiral, pray who would have thought of seeing while in the Crimea a Sardinian army cross London Bridge?"

"Ha! ha! ha! true enough; that's not bad; singular things are seen and done in time of war. What do you think of their soldiers, Monsieur Soyer?"

"Fine fellows!"

"They are fine fellows. But I wish they spoke English—we should get on much quicker."

"I'll speak to them for you, if you like, admiral."

"Ah, to be sure, so you can."

I immediately set about acting as interpreter between the English admiral and the Sardinian captains. In his anxiety to get rid of them as quickly as possible, Admiral Boxer asked whether they had pretty much what they required; a question which brought about ten complainants on deck, who surrounded me. One had no hay, barley, or water for his horses. They all spoke at the same time, and made a hubbub which could only be feebly imitated at the Paris Stock Exchange.

"What's all this row about? This will never do," said the admiral. "Pray don't tell them who I am, or they will bother my life out."

"I have told them, and that's why they are making such a row. I asked them, as you wished me, whether they had everything they wanted."

"I said pretty much what they wanted."

"I know you did, admiral, and so I told them; but they say they don't know the meaning of that."

"Tell them they are fine fellows—fine fellows, and that there is a beautiful camp ready for them, where they will find everything they require, without any drawback. I will send lots of men to wait upon them directly; but they must get out of the harbour before night."

General della Marmora sent for the admiral; so he left me to settle the matter, which I did in a very few words.

"My dear fellows," said I to them, "your valuable services will be much better appreciated by your sovereign and general-in-chief if you put up with a little inconvenience for the present, and remain quiet, than if, on the contrary, you are too particular."

"Do you know, monsieur, that our horses have not had a drop of water today?"

"Colonel," said I, "I am not at all surprised at that; and more, you must put up with it."

"Why?" he asked.

"Simply because you can't get it, unless you like to do as I did yesterday—give them soda-water."

"Do you mean to say there is no water at all in this grand vessel?"

"None, except soda-water."

"Eh bien," said another, "give de soda-water alors."

"What, for the horses?"

"Oui, for the chevals!"

"Here, my man," said I to one of the crew, "tell the steward to bring a dozen of soda-water for the colonel's horse. Mind, colonel, it costs a shilling a bottle; but, as you are a good customer, and take a dozen, no doubt he will let you have it cheaper."

"I will not pay a sou for this bubbling water. I know what you mean. It fizzes like champagne, but it is not good to drink. The horses will never touch it. I thought it was spring-water that you called soda-water."

At all events, the soda-water was brought, to the great annoyance of the colonel, who thought he should have to pay for it; but I sent for some sherry and a few glasses, and we drank a bottle or two, instead of giving it to the horses, to the great gratification of the colonel, who, after partaking of it, said he liked it much better with sherry than brandy. About twenty banabaks soon after arrived with water in skins and leathern horse-buckets. The horses were properly watered; and thus ended the Sardinian revolt in the harbour of Balaklava, on the 14th of May, in the year 1855, beneath the ruins of the Genoese Tower and fortifications built by their ancestors.

The Sardinian troops and horses soon after crossed new London Bridge; by eight o'clock I was mounting my horse to go and meet Dr. Hall. The troops that had then landed were in full march towards their very picturesque camp at the top of the mountain; a band of music was playing at their head, and their artillery train and baggage-waggons followed. The weather was brilliant, and the heat of the sun intense. Louis was mounted upon a fine black horse, which the doctor had brought from Alexandria. Nobody but Louis could ride him, on account of his tricks. His appearance was worthy of the finest circus in the world for the performance of the high school of equitation. To this splendid animal Louis owed his reputation and popularity; and, as he lived at headquarters, all the staff knew him. It is hardly possible to describe his personal appearance. He was short in stature, with extraordinary large ears; his long moustaches, hair, and eyebrows were between the colour of a canary bird and that of the dun pony I was riding. His dress was of a similar colour, with the exception of his cap, which was, if possible, of an intenser yellow. This contrast of colours in an individual mounted upon such a splendid charger, caused him to be remarked by everyone throughout the camp.

Our ride seemed very short, for Louis, who is a very clever fellow, was full of anecdote, and related some that were really very amusing. He spoke several languages, frequently mingling one with another. He spoke his own language, the French, worse than any other, he had been so long away from his native land. He was present at the battles of Alma, Balaklava, Inkermann, and the Tchernaya, where his charger was wounded close to the Traktir Bridge, he, as usual during an action, keeping in close attendance on his brave master, more especially if danger was imminent; and no better fate had he at the battle of Inkermann, where he was seriously wounded in the leg, and the traces of both wounds are, I regret to say, still apparent. On the eve of my departure from the seat of war, I, out of veneration for this once splendid charger, purchased him of his owner, who would probably have been obliged to abandon his faithful steed to the tender mercies of the hungry inhabitants, who, doubtless, had they got him in their clutches, would have given him a dressing *à la Tartare*, or perhaps converted his body into those suspicious articles of food, sausages. On his voyage home, in charge of a careful groom, Neptune had no more respect for this four-legged hero than for the commonest quadruped; for not only was he pitched, bit, and tossed about in all directions, but worse still, when the ship *Clarendon* arrived off Cadiz, she struck on a sunken rock, and the most valueless animals were thrown overboard; but "Inkermann," with his usual luck, in spite of Mars and Neptune, escaped the plunge taken by his less fortunate companions, and is now in London, enjoying, as hitherto, his full feed, though in the profoundest retirement, having sold out of the army. Louis spoke very highly of his master, and never seemed to be pleased or displeased at anything—good news, bad, or indifferent, were all the same to him. If you said to him, "The weather is very bad," he would answer, "I have nothing to do with that, no more than if it were fine." On asking him, at our first interview, if he was a Frenchman, "Of course I am," he replied; "all my family were Frenchmen." I must say that, with all his eccentricity, he was very obliging; and I feel very grateful for the kind attentions he paid me, particularly during my serious illness, when he often visited me. Upon our arrival, the doctor's horse was at the door, and his master soon made his appearance.

"Good morning, Doctor! I fear we are behind time."

"I can always employ my time here," said he, looking at his watch; "you are only a few minutes late."

We then started. Louis asked whether he was to accompany us; to which the doctor answered, "No: I expect Dr. Henderson from Balaklava, to be on the way; tell him we are gone to the General Hospital."

During our ride, I told my companion about the Sardinian insurrection near our new London Bridge, which seemed to amuse him very much. He informed me that Miss Nightingale had passed a better night, but was far from being out of danger. The cannon of Sebastopol made a fearful noise.

"Have you seen Sebastopol yet, Monsieur Soyer?"

"Yes, I have, Doctor, and was rather close, too!" and I related our Nightingale campaign.

"Today you will have another view, quite as good, though not so dangerous."

We then began talking upon business, and I was speaking of my having visited the military and civil hospitals in France, when Dr. Henderson galloped after us, and a conversation ensued relative to the arrival of the armies, and the fact that many of the men had been attacked by fever, before their hospitals were ready. Dr. Hall decided upon a course of action, and we alighted at the General Hospital. The doctor, Mr. Mouatt, was unfortunately out, but was expected back shortly. Dr. Henderson left us, and I accompanied Dr. Hall round several huts. He visited all the worst cases, which were at that time very numerous. We then repaired to the kitchen, which, as I have before said, was far from being equal to the requirements of such an immense hospital. It was in the open air, and ill provided with things necessary for the establishment. Having pointed this out to Dr. Hall, he immediately agreed that one similar to that at the Sanatorium should be erected; but Dr. Mouatt was not present. The want of materials and of workmen was so great, that, previous to its erection, I was obliged to leave the Crimea and return to Scutari for a short time. My head man there had been taken ill, and his life was, as he thought, in great danger. Several times prior to my return he had threatened to run away, which would quite have upset all my former efforts.

I remained in the Crimea about ten days longer, and my reader will perceive that every minute of my time was occupied. I devoted some of it to the most important hospital of all—the one before Sebastopol; a plan for the improvement of which I immediately made and forwarded to the proper parties, so much was I impressed with the necessity of having a kitchen erected immediately. Fearing that I should be obliged to leave the Crimea for Scutari before it could be even commenced, the day after my visit I wrote two official letters, one to Lord Raglan, and the other to Dr. Hall. The general-in-chief and Dr. Hall had both visited the spot, and agreed with me that it was one of the most important hospitals in the East. It was situated under the very walls of Sebastopol, subject to a divided attack, or to a *sortie*, and might at any moment be suddenly encumbered with a large number of wounded, requiring a great quantity of nutritious articles, more particularly beverages, after any surgical operation. In reply I received the following communications:—

BEFORE SEBASTOPOL, 30*th May*, 1855.

SIR,—I am directed by Lord Raglan to acknowledge the receipt of your several communications of the 25th and 28th instants, and to express to you his lordship's thanks for the valuable information contained therein.

I have the honor to be, Sir,

Your obedient servant,

THOS. STEELE,

Mons. Soyer.

Lieut.-Col., Military Sec.

MY DEAR MR. SOYER,—I have this day received your letter of the 22nd June, and am much obliged to you for your thoughtful care of our wants in the all-important business of cooking for both sick and well. Our new hospital is nearly fit for the reception of patients; but you know how tedious the want of labour makes everything here. I was out at the Monastery yesterday, and was glad to see that they had commenced on the kitchen, and were going to fit it up after your excellent model at the Castle.

Very truly yours,

5th July, 1855. J. HALL.

I also had several interviews with Dr. Mouatt, who took my suggestion during my absence in hand, but never apparently succeeded in carrying it out, although the materials requisite were simply planks, nails, and bricks.

I merely advert to the foregoing in answer to some observations that were wafted about the camp to the effect that I never took much trouble about this particular hospital, while in reality it was the very first which attracted my attention, as the above letters will convince my readers.

Upon our return from the hospital to headquarters, I called at Colonel Steele's. Lord Raglan was just going out, and the first question he asked, even before I had time to pay my respects, was—"How is poor Miss Nightingale?"

"A little better today. Dr. Henderson, whom I have just seen, says she has passed a better night."

"Well, I hope she has; I shall pay her a visit as soon as possible—that is, when she is a little better. Was she ill at all at Scutari?"

"Not, my Lord, while I was there, and, I think, not before. It is rather remarkable that she should catch the Crimean fever just after her arrival."

I told Lord Raglan of her imprudence in visiting a patient at Dr. Henderson's, who had been attacked by the worst form of Crimean fever; also, of her remaining out so late, and not taking any refreshment.

"She appears," said Lord Raglan, "to have no fear."

"None whatever."

I recounted her visit to the Three-Gun battery, and the scene that took place upon the centre mortar. Lord Raglan remarked—"It should be called the Nightingale mortar."

He then jumped upon his horse, and I had but a few minutes to explain the result of my visit with Dr. Hall to the various hospitals. I mentioned that the most important thing was the immediate erection of a kitchen for the General Hospital, in case of a decided attack upon Sebastopol.

"Very true, Monsieur Soyer," said Lord Raglan.

I stated that I had addressed a letter to his lordship to that effect.

"Yes, I have seen it, and it shall be attended to."

Lord Raglan and his staff then started in the direction of the French headquarters, and I towards Balaklava, where I arrived about dusk. I left my pony at the General Hospital, and walked to the opposite side of the harbour, which I had in the morning left all in confusion, and, to my astonishment, found quiet and almost deserted. The only person I saw was Admiral Boxer, who came and thanked me for the assistance I had given him in the morning.

"Don't mention it, admiral," said I; "I shall at all times be happy to do everything in my power to render myself agreeable to you. Pray tell me, where are they all gone?"

"To their camp, to be sure."

"What—regiments, horses, and all?"

"Yes, the vessels alongside this morning have not only discharged their cargoes, but are, I believe, out of the harbour and anchored in the bay. We shall have two more in, which must be discharged tomorrow."

"This silence is almost inconceivable after so much noise and bustle."

"It is," said the admiral. "I don't understand those Sardinians, they speak so fast and loud; but they are fine fellows for all that, and no mistake."

The words were hardly out of his mouth, when two Sardinians attached to the commissariat came towards us, and inquired whether we understood French or Italian. I informed them that I spoke French.

"Then, pray, sir, can you tell us where to find ce diable d'amiral Anglais?"

"What do they say?" asked Admiral Boxer, addressing me.

"Nothing particular," I replied. "Gentlemen," said I, turning to the Sardinians, "what could the admiral do for you? It is very probable that I shall have the pleasure of seeing him this evening."

The one who had as yet scarcely spoken exclaimed—"A truce to the pleasure! I wish I could get hold of him, I would tell him my mind in a few words."

"Pray be calm, gentlemen."

All this time Admiral Boxer kept asking—"What do they say? They are speaking about me, I know they are. Tell them they are a fine set of fellows, and I will do anything for them, but they must be out by tomorrow night."

"Very well; but first let me inquire what the row is all about."

"Do so."

"Now, gentlemen, what is it you want? for here is a person who can do as much for you as the admiral himself, and perhaps more."

"Ah, pray ask him, then."

"But you have not yet told me what you require."

"Eh bien!" they said, both speaking at once, "pray, my friend, ask this gentleman to tell the English admiral to postpone the order for our landing tomorrow morning till the next day. It is impossible for us to land our men and horses so early. We have above four hundred horses on board; not half of which have been watered today, nor can they be, till we find some water. There is only a small pump to draw it from the hold of the vessel, and it takes hours to water a few horses."

Having explained this their chief trouble to the admiral, he said—"Tell them there will be plenty of water for them by four o'clock in the morning."

When I had done so, they inquired whether they could depend upon that gentleman's word. I assured them that they might.

"With respect to the other matters, we ought to see the admiral himself."

"Oh, don't trouble yourself; I will do the rest for you."

This was merely a request concerning themselves. I did not like to trouble the admiral about it, and I thought the best way to get rid of them was to show them his flag-ship, telling them they might go there if they liked, but that it was a hundred to one if they found him on board.

"No, no!" said one of them; "it is dinner-time, and the English like their dinner too well; he is sure to be at home, so we will go and see." Having their boat with them, they went across.

The admiral asked—"What do they want besides the water for their horses?"

"Oh, they were inquiring about the camp."

I then related all our conversation, at which the admiral laughed heartily, saying he could understand some of it, but they spoke so very fast.

"When they come on board tomorrow, they will be sure to recognise me."

"Oh no! having only seen you in the dark, they will not know you again; and I shall be there. Don't trouble yourself; they will be quiet enough when they get all they want, and they have a very fine camp."

"Have you seen it?"

"No, admiral, not yet."

"Then you ought to go and see it; they are building a large hospital there. Mind, they have reason to complain. I am aware they ought to have more time; but see what a fleet I have in such a small harbour, and every day there are more troops coming. Perhaps an expedition of our own troops will sail shortly, so I must be prepared for everything. That is what has kept me on this side of the harbour tonight; besides, I wished to see how they were going on with the new quay."

"You have done wonders, admiral, on this side of the harbour since my arrival."

"Remember, Monsieur Soyer, we cannot always do as we like. We are not in England." We parted for the night.

XIX

HAPS AND MISHAPS IN CAMP

ON reaching the *London*, I found Mr. Bracebridge dressed and waiting for me to go and dine on board the *Baraguay d'Hilliers*, with Sir John Macneil and Captain Tulloch. We had that evening a most interesting conversation on all kinds of army stores and provisions. Sir John, who took a vital interest in my mission, gave me several important hints, and I submitted my opinion of the salt as well as fresh meats—fresh and dried vegetables, and especially the bread, which at that period arrived daily from Constantinople, but which, in consequence of its being sometimes put on board ship before it had got quite cool, lost a great deal of its nutritive quality during the passage. Had it been made in the Crimea of the same materials, it would have been very good. I was informed that bakeries were to be established. I told Sir John that I had made a kind of bread-biscuit, somewhat like common bread, but baked in flat cakes about twelve times the size of an ordinary biscuit; it would keep for months, and then eat well, though rather dry; it would soak well in tea, coffee, or soup, and be very palatable; it was made of three parts flour and one of peameal, and was reported upon by the medical gentlemen as being very nutritious and wholesome. A few days later I had the pleasure of showing some to those gentlemen, and they both highly approved of it. I afterwards had some made on board the *Abundance*. I submitted it to them, and they pronounced it excellent.*

The evening we spent on board the *Baraguay d'Hilliers* will not be soon forgotten. After a short nautical and nocturnal trip upon the water, we arrived safely in our old *London*. On our way to the *Baraguay d'Hilliers*, Mr. Bracebridge informed me that Miss Nightingale was pronounced out of danger, and that the news had been telegraphed to London. The medical men were of the opinion that she should return to Scutari, and after a few days' rest proceed to England. Although out of danger, she would not be able to quit Balaklava for eight or ten days. The next morning, at seven o'clock, I was at the Sanatorium kitchen, which was finished. I set my soldier-cooks to work, and all went on admirably. It was then ten o'clock, so I called upon Dr. Hadley (the chief doctor at the Sanatorium, who had succeeded Dr. Henderson, and to both of these gentlemen I must return my sincere thanks for their assistance and kindness), and requested him to come and taste some extra-diets and soups I had prepared for the convalescents. Recollecting that I had not called upon Lord Raglan's *chef de cuisine*, I mentioned the circumstance to Dr. Hadley, stating how much I wished to do so, but that I had no horse. Dr. Hadley very kindly offered me his pony, a fine grey, smartly caparisoned, which

---

* I have such confidence in the nutritive qualities and the importance to the army and navy of these bread-biscuits, that I intend to recommend their adoption in both departments. For a campaign they are invaluable; and at sea they would make an excellent change, being as light as bread.

I at once accepted. When I had mounted, Dr. Hadley said—"Soyer, if you fall off, mind and get up again; for," said he, "joking apart, though the pony is very quiet, recollect the road to Balaklava is a queer one, therefore take care of yourself. We should not mind so much if we had done with you; but as we really require your services, for our own sakes take care of yourself."

"I will do so," said I, laughing, "were it only for the sake of your pony, which might get loose if I were to fall off, and you might not recover him again."

"Never mind the pony," said he: "you may lose him; but, whatever you do, don't lose the saddle. We had better have a bit of supper on your return this evening, off that Yorkshire ham—you can cook it on your bivouac stove."

"So we will, Doctor. I shall be back at six."

"Don't stay in the camp after dark; I can assure you it is a very dangerous place. Robberies and murders are of frequent occurrence, though we hear but little about them. We have no police, and no newspapers are published here, so we know nothing but what passes in our own circle."

"You are perfectly right, Doctor; though I am not afraid, as I never travel without a revolver; yet it is best to be upon the safe side."

Having fixed upon six o'clock for my return, and seven for supper, I started. There were about twenty convalescents outside the wards, enjoying the warmth of the sun's rays. They were all in high glee at hearing our dialogue, which seemed to revive them from a state of lethargy to the consciousness of life.

The ride from the top of the Genoese heights to Balaklava harbour, by a new road, through mud, over rocks, rivulets, &c., and mounted upon a strange nag, was anything but pleasant to my feelings as a horseman. At all events, after numerous slippery evolutions on the part of my new charger, I found myself safe at the bottom of the ravine; but here another difficulty presented itself. The quay of the harbour was encumbered with French and Sardinian waggons, mules, and horses. The French, who had a wine depot there for the troops, were strongly fortified with about a hundred pipes of wine, instead of gabions. So crowded was the road from the immense traffic and the unloading of shipping stores, that it took me nearly half-an-hour to ride a few hundred yards. This brought me as far as the Commissariat, where I had to call upon Commissary Filder. I found that he had just returned from headquarters. We had about ten minutes' conversation upon business. I related the result of my visit to the various provision stores—made remarks upon the same, and particularly upon the dry vegetables at that time issued to the troops. He then referred me to Under-Commissary Adams, to whom I promised a scale for a fresh composition of dry vegetables in cake, more suitable for the troops, in lieu of the finer and more expensive quality then issued in boxes. They were composed of one vegetable only, and were much too highly dried, having thus lost their aroma as well as their nutritious qualities. I therefore proposed that the firm of Messrs. Chollet, in Paris, should prepare a sample of cakes of dried vegetables, to be called coarse julienne, for the army. Each hundredweight of fresh vegetables was to consist of the following proportions:—

Twenty pounds of carrots, twenty pounds of turnips, ten of parsnips, fifteen of onions, twenty of cabbage, five of celery, and ten of leeks; with one pound of aromatic seasoning, composed of four ounces of thyme, four of winter savory, two of bayleaf, four of pepper, and an ounce of cloves; the whole to be pulverized and mixed with the vegetables.

Each cake was to serve for one hundred men, and to be marked in compartments of ten rations each, like chocolate cakes, instead of being marked upon the wrapper, which is always torn off when the vegetables are issued, and the soldiers cannot tell about quantity. This plan will obviate that evil; for I had seen in camp piles of this excellent vegetable rising pyramidically from the soldiers' canteen pan while cooking, in consequence of their having put in the best part of three days' rations instead of one. The dry rations are issued for three days at a time.

My proposition having met with the approval of the authorities, was at once forwarded to the War Office.

I also promised to submit to Commissary Filder's notice several plans for improvement in the distribution of the meat.

"Monsieur Soyer," said he, "anything you may propose or point out as an improvement will, so far as it is practicable, be carried out. Lose no time; the sooner you let us have it the better."

After this interview, I went to inspect the kitchen, where I saw Mr. Fitzgerald, the purveyor, to whom I also made my report. As this is the first time I have had the pleasure of introducing this gentleman to the notice of my readers, it would be an omission on my part were I not to return my grateful acknowledgments for the readiness with which he at all times assisted me to obtain what I required for the hospitals in the Crimea. It is true he was at first rather reluctant; this I attributed to his not having received the proper instructions from the authorities.

Having the best part of the day before me, I set off at a gallop towards headquarters, intending to keep the promise I had made Lord Raglan respecting his dilapidated culinary department, and also to make the acquaintance of M. Armand, his *chef de cuisine*. As I was not well acquainted with the road across the country, I made up my mind to follow the high one which passes close to headquarters. When about halfway, I perceived a group of officers standing by the road-side round a kind of tent much like a gipsy tent. I was riding towards it, when, to my astonishment, several voices called out—"Soyer! Soyer! come here—come this way!" I readily complied with the invitation, and found two or three gentlemen whom I had the pleasure of knowing. During our conversation, an old dame of a jovial appearance, but a few shades darker than the white lily, issued from the tent, bawling out, in order to make her voice heard above the noise, "Who is my new son?" to which one of the officers replied, "Monsieur Soyer, to be sure; don't you know him?"

"God bless me, my son, are you Monsieur Soyer of whom I heard so much in Jamaica? Well, to be sure! I have sold many and many a score of your Relish and other sauces—God knows how many."

"My dear lady," said I, "don't blame me for that; I assure you I am not at all offended with you for so doing, and shall allow you to sell as much more in the Crimea."

"So I would if I could only get them. Bless me, I had a gross about ten days ago, and they are all gone; nor can I get any more for another month perhaps. Come down, my son, and take a glass of champagne with my old friend, Sir John Campbell."

I immediately alighted, and Sir John came towards me and shook me heartily by the hand, saying, "Welcome to the seat of war, Monsieur Soyer!"

"Many thanks, general, for your kind wishes. I had the pleasure of leaving my card at Cathcart's Hill the other day."

"You did; and I was very sorry that I was out when you called; but mind, you must come and dine with me some day."

"Thank you, general, I shall do myself the honour."

"Now, Mrs. Seacole, give us another bottle of champagne."

"Mrs. Seacole," I exclaimed; "is that lady the celebrated Mrs. Seacole?"

"Of course," said the general.

She then came forth from her bivouac cellar, with two bottles in her hands, exclaiming, "I shall stand mine, and no mistake."

We all declared it would never do for a lady to stand treat in the Crimea.

"Lord bless you, Monsieur Soyer," said the lady, "don't you know me?"

"Yes, I do now, my dear madam."

"Well, all those fine fellows you see here are my Jamaica sons—are you not?" said she, opening the champagne, and addressing the general.

"We are, Mrs. Seacole, and a very good mother you have been to us."

"I have known you, general, for many years."

"Well, here's a health to all."

We emptied our glasses, and returned the compliment. The general then left, again expressing his desire to see me at Cathcart's Hill.

"Walk inside, walk inside, my sons; you will be better there—it is not so hot. Go in, Monsieur Soyer."

No sooner had we entered than the old lady expressed her desire to consult me about what she should do to make money in her new speculation, in which she had embarked a large capital, pointing to two iron houses in course of construction on the other side of the road. She told me that her intention was to have beds there for visitors, which I persuaded her not to do, saying, "all the visitors—and they are few in number—sleep on board the vessels in the harbour, and the officers under canvass in the camp. Lay in a good stock of hams, wines, spirits, ale and porter, sauces, pickles, and a few preserves and dry vegetables—in short, anything which will not spoil by keeping."

"Yes," said she, "I mean to have all that."

"In that case you will no doubt make money, as you are so well known to all the army."

"I assure you, the last time Lord Raglan passed here, he spoke to me for more than ten minutes, and promised to do all he could for me."

"That's right," we all said.

"I know Miss Nightingale too. She was very kind to me when I passed through Scutari, on my way here; she gave me lodging and everything I required, in the hospital."

"We passed this way a few days before Miss Nightingale was taken ill," said I.

"I know you did; and I am sure, if the lady had known I was here, she would have called to see me. Thank God, I hear she is quite out of danger."

"Yes, she is improving."

"When you see her, present my best respects, and tell the dear lady that I shall go and see her."

"I will, Mrs. Seacole. Goodbye."

"Goodbye, my son."

On getting up in a hurry to be off, I missed my horse, and found one of the officers' chargers, which had been left in charge of the same man to whom I had given mine, led by a Zouave. Upon inquiring of the Zouave where the man had gone, he informed me that he did not know, but that he had given him a shilling (which he showed me) to hold this animal for, as far as he could understand, about an hour, while he went on the grey in the direction of headquarters. I called Mrs. Seacole out, and told her what had happened. She stepped up to the Zouave, and he began talking so fast, that I shall not forget the expression he made as long as I live. His speech may be thus translated: "By the name of Jupiter! I have neither stolen nor sold your horse. Look at me! (showing his corporation.) If you like, captain, to lend me this quadruped, I will soon find the voyou (meaning a low rascal). There is my name and the number of my regiment. We are encamped near the French headquarters."

All this time Mrs. Seacole had been looking about, and every grey pony she saw far or near was mine—at least in her eyes. The two officers mounted their horses, and went one one way and the other another, but soon returned, having found nothing. Having sent in all directions without being able to obtain any trace of the pony, we concluded that the animal was lost. I take this opportunity of publicly thanking those two gentlemen for the vivid interest they took in trying to find the borrowed steed. I very much regret that I do not recollect their names. They will no doubt remember the circumstance if this little work falls into their hands.*

All our efforts to find the pony being useless, I made up my mind to walk back to Balaklava. Just as I was thanking Mrs. Seacole for her extraordinary exertions, Mr. Day, her partner, came in, and he advised me to go at once to the *Hue and Cry*, at headquarters.

"How am I to do this?" I asked.

"Take my pony. It is not twenty minutes' ride from hence; and you will stand a good chance of getting it back, especially if the man who held it was an Englishman. He is sure to be found in the English camp."

Thanking him for his kindness, I mounted, and started full gallop for headquarters. I made inquiries at the Post Office, where I had the pleasure of meeting Mr. Russell, who introduced me to Mr. Angel, the postmaster. I then inquired for the *Hue and Cry*, and related the circumstances under which I had lost my pony. All seemed highly amused. They laughed heartily at my expense, and I could not help joining in the merriment. Mr. Angel invited me to dine with him, having a few friends that evening to join his popote.

---

* The difficulty of recollecting the names and the rank of military men in the Crimea is great. This is particularly the case with me. The performance of my manifold duties compelled me to cross and re-cross hundreds of times from vessel to vessel, hospital to hospital, and camp to camp. I met and received attentions and aid from numbers, of whom it is impossible to retain more than a slight photographic sketch of their noble Saxon countenances. From the peculiarity of my costume, I was almost as well known to everyone in the camp as a *chien du régiment*.

I offer this explanation as an apology to anyone whom I may have inadvertently annoyed—if any such there be—in my account of my Crimean campaign, by not giving the proper rank or name.

"I am much obliged, my dear sir; but I am staying at Balaklava, and I suppose you dine late."

"About six o'clock," replied Mr. Angel. "You can sleep here. We have no bed, it's true; but I can lend you a blanket; and there is a small hut, which is empty, you can have all to yourself. Mr. Bracebridge slept there the night before last, when on a visit to Captain Boucher, a friend of his."

"Oh, as far as that goes, I shall be comfortable enough."

"Then you will dine with me?"

"I will," said I, "and am much obliged for your kind invitation."

I thought by accepting it, I should have an excellent opportunity of looking out for my pony in the morning if I did not happen to find it that night; I therefore went to the *Hue and Cry*, and gave the best description, to my knowledge, as I had not had the honour of his acquaintance long, and did not know of any private marks by which he might be recognised. They gave me but faint hopes of seeing it again, and by way of comforting me, showed me a long list of missing horses, mules, and ponies, enough to fill half a column of the *Times*.

"I don't care so much about the pony, as that can be replaced; but the saddle is a new one from London, and neither the animal nor the saddle belong to me."

"You may, perhaps," said one, "find the horse, but not the saddle, especially if it is gone to the French camp, for, believe me, the Zouaves are very fond of English saddles, as well as everything they can get hold of which does not require feeding; so they will probably keep the saddle and turn the horse loose. At all events, we will do what we can for you; but I advise you to look out for yourself."

It was then about four o'clock, and I had an hour's ride about the camp, but it was all in vain. Every inquiry proved fruitless; and I could not obtain the slightest clue to the lost pony. I could not help smiling when I recollected Dr. Hadley's last words, "You may lose the horse but don't lose the saddle." Hoping for better luck next day, I returned to headquarters, and begged Lord Raglan's groom to give Mr. Day's pony a night's lodging. Making sure Monsieur Armand would be in, I went to see him. He was rather busy, but he received me very politely, and showed me what he called his kitchen, though it had not the slightest claim to the title, as it was all but destitute of culinary utensils. The provisions were of inferior quality; but, as he told me, the best he could procure. I then offered my services if I could be of any use in getting stoves or a small oven erected.

"Ever since I have been here," he replied, "I have been asking for one or two charcoal stoves and a few shelves, but not a thing can I obtain for love or money."

"Upon my word you surprise me! How can that be in the house of the commander-in-chief? Truly, everyone has much to do."

"Such is the case."

"Never mind; I think I shall be able to get something done for you, as his lordship has spoken to me upon the subject."

"I shall be much obliged to you if you will," said he; and then pointed out the principal things he required, which were soon afterwards furnished.

As it was nearly six o'clock, I left him, and returned to the Post Office, where a sumptuous table was laid out. There was actually a tablecloth and real plates, knives, forks, and various kinds of glasses. In fact, for the Crimea, it was as the French say, *épatant*. We sat down six to dinner; and had some very strong preserved soup, a very nice tough fowl—the remainder of the bill of fare was made from the ration meat. We had very good wine; and, perhaps, never was a dinner better relished, or accompanied with more mirth and jokes. Russell the great was the hero, besides having an Angel for the host. Towards eight o'clock, the party amounted to about fifteen, as far as we could discern through the clouded atmosphere with which the room was filled. Everyone was smoking; some large chibouques, long and short pipes, a few cigars, but no cigarettes. The unexpected increase to our party, I must observe, was partly owing to our vocal abilities, several lively choruses having attracted Mr. Angel's illustrious neighbours, as the denizens of the woods were allured by the melody of Orpheus.

Our mirth at last became so boisterous that it not only brought around us men of all ranks, but attracted the attention of the commander-in-chief, who sent to inquire what the noise was about. This we considered a rather inharmonious inquiry, but found that, by decreasing the pitch of our vocal organs from allegro to piano, we should produce as much effect, with less noise, as his lordship wisely called it; though I heard the next day, that Lord Raglan, who was sitting at his door enjoying the fresh air with several gentlemen of his staff, enjoyed it, and gave orders that we should not be disturbed. Complaints poured in from the numerous tents which surrounded headquarters. It was then about ten o'clock, which is equivalent to twelve or one p.m. in London. The *mot d'ordre* from our chairman was, "Tell those who cannot sleep to join our bacchanalian party." So many took the hint, that no room could at length be obtained in the modern Crimean Temple of Momus.

At last the order took a more positive character, for the very Angel who was presiding, observed, and very justly, that they were all playing the devil with him, and still more so with his cellar, which being but meagrely stocked, could not long stand so severe an attack. He therefore begged all newcomers to go back to their quarters, and bring or send the liquid requisite to keep up the spirits of the guests till midnight—which was done. Everyone, like Cinderella, disappeared, by slipping quietly out at the most convenient opportunity.

XX

EXPEDITIONS ON HORSE AND ON FOOT

NEXT morning, I found myself wrapped up in a horse-cloth, with a pair of top-boots for a pillow. The unfeeling and ungrateful board to which I had entrusted my precious limbs had by the morning stamped his patron's seal upon my back. The following day we learnt that a terrible sortie had taken place in the night, and that there had been a severe loss of men on both sides. At an early hour the courtyard was thronged with officers; despatches were flying in every direction; the cannon was roaring as usual, but the fusillade had ceased. I then went to the stable for my pony, when I found the owner, Mr. Day, upon his back, just going home.

"Ah, Monsieur Soyer, I made sure that you had lost my pony as well as your own. I expected you back immediately, being in want of it."

"I was not aware of that, or I would have walked from your place sooner than have deprived you of it."

"Oh, never mind. Have you heard anything of your animal?"

"No! but I am going to look after him this morning. That is the reason why I slept at headquarters last night."

"I am going about the camp," said he, "and will inquire for you."

He then started, of course leaving me without a horse, and with dreadful pains in my back and legs, which I attributed to the softness of the bed with which I had been favoured; though I could not boast of a single feather, like that Tocrisse of a recruit, who took one out of his master's feather bed, laid it down on the boarded floor of his hut, and next morning told his companions that his master must be foolish to sleep upon a feather bed.

"Why?" asked they.

"Why, if one feather is so hard, what must the lot the captain sleeps upon be?"

The worst of my position was, how to get another horse, as it was impossible for me to walk all day about the camp, being so stiff and tired. I went to Lord Raglan's coachman, and inquired if he had one to spare. He replied—

"Monsieur Soyer, we can spare a pony for you, but you must ask permission of the master of the horse or Lord Raglan, as I have special orders not to lend one upon my own responsibility. I am sure his lordship will let you have it immediately."

At this moment I caught sight of Lord Raglan's valet, and I begged him to make the request; which he did, and came to tell me that his lordship desired I should have it by all means. Once more mounted, I made an early call upon the friends of the previous night, most of whom resided round headquarters. I had the pleasure of being introduced to General Estcourt, who took me to see the printing press where my receipts for the army were done—some of which have appeared in the public press. Afterwards I went with him to his quarters, which, though small, were very neatly arranged. The taste was not military, and I thought that I detected the work of a female hand, which I could not help remarking to the general.

"You are right, Monsieur," said he, smiling—"it has only lately been arranged by ladies. Mrs. Estcourt and my sister are here, and this is a little bit of their handy-work. They are staying on board ship at Balaklava, and come here every day. Before they arrived I had only this small room (showing me his bed made upon boards) where I sleep as well as ever I did in my life. The only thing which awakes me in the night is when the cannon ceases firing—I am so used to it."

"I believe that, general, and have no doubt you seldom miss hearing a report. In fact, you are the nearest of those at headquarters to Sebastopol."

I then inquired about the sortie of the previous night. The general said he did not know the result of it, and very kindly invited me to breakfast, which I declined, having to go round the French camp in search of my pony.

"I shall be happy," said General Estcourt, "to do anything I can for you; and if you call in the afternoon, my wife and her sister will be here, and I will introduce you to them."

Thanking him kindly, I retired, and proceeded round the French camp making inquiries; then to their headquarters, where I met Captain Boucher, General Canrobert's aide-de-camp, with whom I had the pleasure of travelling. He promised to introduce me to the general, who, he said, would be very glad to see me. Upon my telling him about my pony, he remarked—

"If he is in our camp you are sure to get him back, for we have put a stop to that kind of piracy by very severe punishment. They used to come and steal our horses from our very stables; but tell me what sort of a horse he is, and I will advertise him with the others, and we shall know in less than five or six hours if he is in our camp. The plan we have adopted cannot fail."

Having described the animal to the captain, I thanked him for his kindness.

Considering my French review terminated, I thought of returning at once to the English headquarters, having to see several of the authorities upon business. On my way I happened to pass by a nice French canteen. I inquired if I could get any breakfast? A rather stout vivandière, dressed in the uniform of the Imperial Guard, very politely said to me:

"What a stupid question to ask! Do you think we have not everything required for the purpose here? Perhaps, Captain of the Lord knows what regiment, you think we have come out merely to thread pearls, sing 'Partant pour la Syrie,' and dance the Fandango."

On my way I visited several regimental kitchens and tasted the soup. Some was better than at others. They had no vegetables excepting some vegetable marrow—more likely to spoil the soup than improve it. I made several important discoveries respecting the system of cooking pursued in the French camp, after visiting, with some of my new acquaintants, a row of twelve kitchens, which number, they informed me, was required for each regiment—being at the rate of one per company. One man was told off as cook for every squad or mess of sixteen. The buildings were composed of mud and stone, and covered an extent of about four hundred yards. I bade my brave companions farewell, and left them quite a happy man, having entirely forgotten horse and saddle, in making the discovery that in lieu of four hundred yards of space, a dozen buildings, and about eighty men for each regiment, an immense consumption of fuel, and smoke enough to blind three parts of the army—as the men were all cooks in turn—my system was simple, effective, and vastly superior to that even of the French, which had hitherto always been considered as preferable to the English. This was indeed the case, for all French soldiers understand a little cooking, and their canteen pan was far superior to that in use amongst the English troops, which I condemned at first sight in the camp at Chobham.

I returned to headquarters, intending to communicate my discovery to Lord Raglan; but learning that he was very busy, and would not be disengaged till evening, I went to Colonel Steele, who, in spite of the pressure of business, gave me an immediate audience, and promised to speak to Lord Raglan on the subject. Headquarters were that day, in a manner, taken by storm. They were literally besieged, and this gave me an opportunity of getting acquainted with several officers and other officials whom I had not the pleasure of knowing—or, at least, only by sight. Amongst these were Sir George Brown, Sir W. Codrington, Sir Colin Campbell, Lord Rokeby, Captain Whitmore, and Brevet-Major A. Macdonald.

Lord Raglan passed me in the passage, and said, "You wish to see me, Monsieur Soyer?"

Knowing his lordship was much occupied, I replied, "Colonel Steele will give you the particulars that I came to communicate."

"That will do; but have you found your horse?"

"No, my lord."

"I have been to visit Miss Nightingale. She is still very ill. Bad job, bad job, poor lady!" he continued, walking away towards Colonel Steele's office, with his hands full of papers.

After this I called upon Doctor Hall, with whom I had a few minutes' conversation upon business. Louis was somewhere about, busily engaged, and, as usual, unwilling to give a direct reply, no matter what question you put to him. He came to see me. I inquired if he knew anything about the sortie of the previous night, upon which he answered that the black horse he rode the day before had thrown him in the mud, and made him in such a mess. I replied in his style:

"The sun is very hot today."

Upon which he observed, "he never was there in his life."

I begged of him to tell me how he was tomorrow.

"Don't believe that," said he; "it is quite false."

An interesting young man indeed was Louis.

A very great curiosity then made its appearance, breaking the thread of our scientific conversation. What, reader, do you think it was? A carriage!—a thing unknown in the camp—or at least a bad imitation of one—drawn by two very obstinate mules, one pulling against the other, which seemed to amuse my intelligent friend Louis, who never liked to see anything going on smoothly. General Estcourt went out to meet it, and two ladies alighted. To this Louis thoroughly objected, saying—"Ladies, indeed! they are the two female Zouaves who performed in the *Anglaises pour Rire*, at the theatre in their camp. One," said he, "is Jean Hughet—the other Panaudet, aide-de-camp to the drum-major of a regiment of cavalry. The first plays Lady Painbeche in that tragedy—the other, Lady Don't-you-wish-you-may-get-it."

Very fertile indeed was the brain of Louis at composition of the higher school; and, like Marplot,* never wishing to see anything in its right light, he succeeded

* Marplot, or the Second Part of the Busy Body. A comedy by Susannah Centlivre, produced in 1710—AB

admirably. The sight of a carriage was something wonderful, but two ladies at once, and fashionably dressed, was too much good luck. I advanced towards them, and had the honour of being introduced by the general to Mrs. Estcourt and his sister. The general invited me to walk in, and I had the honour of taking a glass of wine with the fair—who might well be called fairies at the time—ladies being so scarce, in fact, all but invisible, in the Crimea.

After a short, but very interesting, conversation with the ladies, I retired, leaving some copies of my receipts with Mrs. Estcourt, who kindly undertook to look at the proofs before printing. Thence I proceeded to the General Camp Hospital, and there met Doctor Mouatt, who told me he was waiting for the bricks for his oven from the Ordnance Office at headquarters. I informed him that I had given in the plan for a kitchen, and endeavoured to convince him of the necessity of having it done at once.

"I am well aware of that, and it shall be attended to."

All inquiries respecting my pony were fruitless. At last, upon asking at a canteen, a soldier told me he had heard of one being found in some regiment, but could not tell me which one, though he thought it was somewhere about Cathcart's Hill.

On arriving at Cathcart's Hill, I met Sir John Campbell, who invited me to take some refreshment and a glass of Bordeaux. We descended to his rocky abode in front of Sebastopol, whence you could trace every shot or shell which passed, as well as view the whole city. On recounting my adventure of the lost pony, and of my being absent two days from Balaklava,

"We heard," said the aide-de-camp to Sir John, "that you had lost two ponies."

"No! no!" said I, "one at a time is quite enough, captain."

"I can assure you that is the joke at headquarters. I also heard of your concert à la Soyer."

"We spent a regular London evening," I replied.

"I wish I had been there," said the general; "we are getting very dull in our division. Before you go, Mons. Soyer, come and see my kitchen."

"I will, general."

Though very small, it was more deserving that title than the one at Lord Raglan's.

"Here," said Sir John, "is our ration meat; I am sure you cannot make a tempting dish out of these materials, especially from the salt meat, which requires so much soaking, it is so hard."

"Well, general, I will not say I can make a dish worthy of Lucullus out of this; but I will try to make something palatable and fit to eat."

"I can assure you, Monsieur Soyer, that if you succeed, it will be conferring a great boon upon the army; and you must give them the receipts."

I did as follows: I cut about two pounds of salt beef, and as much salt pork, in pieces of about a quarter of a pound in weight, placed them in a canteen pan with cold water, and set it on the fire. When lukewarm, I took the pan off, washed the meat well, and threw the water away. I then added three pints of fresh water, a quarter of a pound of onions sliced, two ounces of sugar, a teaspoonful of pepper, and two ounces of rice. I set it to stew and simmer gently for two hours. The general said:—

"You must come and dine with us about that time."

"I should certainly much like to taste it, general; but I must be at Balaklava before seven o'clock tonight. Tomorrow I am coming over to the General Hospital, and if you will be kind enough to order some to be saved for me, that I may taste it when I come, I shall esteem it a great favour."

"I will do so, Monsieur Soyer, but try and be here to dinner. We shall dine about five o'clock."

The stew by this time began to simmer, and upon tasting the broth, I found it already very palatable, without being too salt. I begged of the cook to let it simmer very gently, which he promised to do.

We prepared to separate. Before leaving, I said, "The soldiers will be able to do their rations the same way. I have recommended it to Commissary Filder, who has agreed to it, and consented that the salt rations should be issued the night before, thus giving the soldiers time to soak the meat well. In consequence of this, it will require less sugar; although it is rumoured that a quarter of an ounce is to be added to their daily rations. They will then have as much as they require; and when my new field stoves are issued, they will admit both of the soaking and the cooking of the meat; and various messes can be made, almost impracticable in the small tin canteens now in use."

I then told the general of my visit to the French kitchens, and what I had seen there. He agreed with me that they employed too many men, especially in time of war. It is true that the French soldiers understood cooking much better than our men did, but, nevertheless, their system admitted of great improvements. We were then standing in front of Sir John's cave facing Sebastopol. Of a sudden all the batteries ceased firing, and Sir John exclaimed, "Hallo! there is a flag of truce hoisted on the Russian side, and it is accepted. No doubt it is for leave to bury the dead. Now is the time to have a good peep at Sebastopol, Mons. Soyer; you have two hours for that purpose."

The generals, staff officers, and a number of military men who were present as lookers-on, started off; and I of course followed, making sure Sebastopol was not more than a mile and a half or two miles distant—which, *à vol d'oiseau*, it was not; but there were four or five deep ravines, which made the distance much longer. The few who started from the hill were joined by many on the road, and we soon formed a small cavalcade of amateurs. I understood, from several parties of whom I inquired, that we should have plenty of time to go and return before the recommencement of hostilities, and that there was not, therefore, the slightest danger. As it was on the French side the sortie had taken place, some went one way and some another; and only about six of us went towards the French trenches. Upon our arrival we experienced some difficulty in getting in, and it was full twenty minutes before they would admit us.

One of the gentlemen present—an English officer, unknown to me—wrote our names upon his card, and, by order of the commandant of a battery, we were allowed to enter. The sight is too painful to dwell upon, from the immense numbers of dead and wounded piled one upon the other. They were mostly young men, who had fallen so bravely in defence of their country in this glorious, though disastrous, combat. I could not help remarking, both in the French and Russian dead, that those who had been killed by gun-shots passing through the body lay as if they had fallen into a sweet slumber, with a smile upon their cold lips, and a happy and pleasing expression of countenance, very different to the fearful and contorted appearance generally presented, when from our comfortable homes we are summoned by that "strict serjeant—Death," in consequence of old age or illness. This induced me to say to my companions in the trenches, "It appears to me as if death had not time to convey them to his mournful shore, but that the genius of glory had unexpectedly stepped in, and taken possession of their souls, which were now happily ascending to heaven and a better world; while, on the contrary, those who have lost a limb or received serious wounds in the head, appear to have expired in the most painful torture."

The funeral service was going on rapidly and solemnly on all sides. The main attack had been against the French, and their newly-arrived Imperial Guard suffered considerable loss. The greater part of the time allowed for the armistice had now elapsed, and we therefore thought of retiring. None of us were, however, acquainted with the French trenches, and it took us a considerable time to find our way out. I must have taken a wrong turn, or at least the man to whom I had entrusted my pony had done so, although I had given him a franc, and promised him another on getting out all right, merely to see that no one untied the pony. As he was on duty at the time, and agreed to do this, I trusted him with it. My friends found their steeds where they had left them. Pondering upon my ill-luck, and fearing the pony, which belonged to Lord Raglan, was also lost, I felt much perplexed, so I scrambled up between the gabions,* and perceived, to my great joy, a man leading my pony about in the ravine. I met the person with whom I had left him, and he told me that his commanding-officer would not allow the pony to remain there any longer, as hostilities would begin again immediately, and being in sight of the enemy, they might think it belonged to a superior, and direct their fire that way; and having some other duties to perform, he gave my steed in charge of another man, and requested me to give the other man the franc I had promised him.

I ran off to the man, making sure I should reach him in two minutes, but it took me above twenty. Instead of going towards him, I got near the Russian side, and had it been dark instead of day, I have no doubt I should have been taken prisoner, from being unable in the short time left of the suspension of hostilities to retrace my steps. One of the sentries who had seen us came and advised me to be off as soon as possible, as the firing would begin again directly. Thanking him, I got my pony, and was no sooner mounted than the cannonade and fusillade thundered in every direction; and some missiles passed me much too close to be pleasant.

A regiment of French soldiers who had just been relieved from duty, and were on their way to their quarters, told me they were going to the Clocheton, a place of which I had heard, but did not know. I followed them, as the night was fast setting in and rain was falling. I passed it, with a jolly set of fellows, full of song, cognac, and rum; and, as I stood some drink, I was set down in their estimation as a gentleman. I afterwards slept upon some straw, on the floor of the canteen. My horse had a very good meal, and plenty of water, but was compelled to remain out all night, which annoyed me very much. It could not, however, be helped. We had a very noisy night, and several shots were heard hissing over our heads, as we were only a few hundred yards from the small house called the Clocheton, so celebrated and well known in the French camp. It was from that picturesque spot that Monsieur de Bazancourt wrote his popular history of the war.

* Wicker baskets filled with earth or stones used for fortifications—AB

XXI

MATTERS GRAVE AND GAY

AT six the next morning I started, and made it my business to visit the kitchens in the Turkish and Sardinian camps, on my way home. At eight I made my triumphal entry into Balaklava. My return seemed to be quite an event, as it had not only been reported that I had lost three horses, but also that I had lost myself. I found, when I got on board the *London*—which was still vomiting forth troops, horses, guns, and projectiles of all kinds, to feed the voracious appetite of mighty, grand, but very unsociable and terrible Mr. War, with whom I had lately had the unexpected honour of being on a little too familiar terms—that everyone had missed me for three days, and the last they had heard of me was that I had been seen going towards Sebastopol at the time the flag of truce was hoisted. No one had seen me return, and they concluded that poor Soyer had either been killed, wounded, or taken prisoner.

I was told that Mr. Bracebridge had been anxiously inquiring for me in every direction, and that p. m. had just gone in a great hurry to the telegraph office, to send word to headquarters. Seeing the affair was getting rather serious, I set off at full gallop to stop him, and found him in the office, writing the following lines:—

"Monsieur Soyer has been absent from Balaklava these last three days, and has not been heard of. An answer will oblige."

My unexpected arrival put him in good spirits. I convinced him that I was neither killed, wounded, nor taken prisoner, and having related my adventures, I inquired about business.

The first thing he told me was that Miss Nightingale was getting better. This I knew, having made inquiries on board. Then he informed me that Lord Raglan had visited her. This I also knew. Then that Thomas, my head man, had been all over the camp, hunting for me; that the hospital kitchens were all going on well. He next informed me that Dr. Hadley was morally in deep mourning, not so much on account of his pony, or even myself, but his saddle and bridle, which he said no money could replace, it having been made to order in London. I observed that I was worse off than he was, as from his kindness in lending me the pony, I had been so long away.

"But, P. M., will you be kind enough to jump on that pony, and go to him. Say I will see him in the afternoon, and of course that I shall be happy to pay for both pony and saddle."

"I will do so; but he told me yesterday that he didn't care a fig about the pony—it was the saddle he regretted."

"When did he first hear I had lost it?"

"Why, not four hours after you left. Mrs. Seacole sent all over the camp for it, and some officers who were present at the time brought the news, at which everyone laughed; but I assure you the case was getting very serious at last."

"Never mind—*à la guerre comme à la guerre*—we must expect something a little out of the way in campaigning."

"I tell you what, Monsieur Soyer, I began to think it was a great deal out of the way. You have only one life, like the rest of us, and you cannot be spared by us, not even to go to the Russians."

P. M. started on his mission to Dr. Hadley, and I returned to the *London*, and wrote the receipt for the composition of the preserved vegetables, which I had promised to Commissary Filder, and took it over myself. On my way I met about a score of friends, or at all events persons who knew me, and had heard the false report. I was informed that Admiral Boxer was much put out about my absence, and at not receiving any tidings about me.

To my great astonishment, I met my secretary on foot, and at once inquired what he had done with the pony, making sure that he had lost it, or that he had been thrown, and the animal had run away, as it was a very mettlesome little creature.

"It is nothing of the kind; it was worse. The brute is marked 'L. R., headquarters;' and before I reached Dr. Hadley's house, a policeman stopped me and took it away, saying it had been stolen from Monsieur Soyer; and there was a regular row at headquarters about it. The fellow wanted to take me up, though I told him I was your secretary. And mind you, had it not been for an officer—a friend of yours, who knew me—having dined with us on board the *Robert Lowe*, I really cannot tell how I should have managed."

"Where is the pony now?"

"God knows. Perhaps that fellow has stolen it."

"I hope not. Describe the man. Who was he?"

"A soldier, I believe; but let us go to the Commandant's, and inquire, for I think he took the pony to the stable-yard."

Upon making inquiries, we heard the animal had been sent direct to headquarters. Thus terminated the adventures connected with my first interview with the good and benevolent Mrs. Seacole, whom I have ever since christened La Mère Noire, although she has a fair daughter.

Before the evening was over I had visited the various hospitals, inspected a fresh arrival of provisions—particularly fresh vegetables, which were sent from Constantinople weekly, for the use of the hospitals and camp. These often arrived in a bad state, owing to the heat of the weather, which was intense. The difficulty of transport and distribution throughout the camps rendered the dry composition I had submitted to the Commissariat much preferable, more especially for issue to the troops in camp.

The great event during my unexpected and adventurous absence was the arrival of Lord Ward in his beautiful steamer, the *London*, filled with all kinds of provisions, to be gratuitously distributed among the soldiers, more as a luxury than a necessity. Provisions were not at this time so scarce as they had been—the soldiers were receiving ample rations. Facility and method in the cooking was what was most required.

THE 24TH OF MAY,—THE QUEEN'S BIRTHDAY IN THE HARBOUR OF BALAKLAVA.

At midday a royal salute was fired; shouts were heard in all directions, and about noon the band struck up "God save the Queen." The ships were gaily dressed out with their flags, and this put every sailor in good humour. They were regaled with plenty of roast beef and plum pudding, and abundance of rum. Tunes struck up in every direction—"Drops of brandy," "Barley bree," hornpipes, &c.; but the "Ratcatcher's Daughter" would have been most in harmony. I was then dining with Captain Shepherd and a party of about ten, on board his superb ship, the *Triton*. When dinner was over, we left the jovial board to smoke our cigars upon deck. We went to breathe the fresh air, and to watch the frolics of the joyous but rather tumultuous crew, who were performing their nautical steps between decks, to the shrieking sounds of a damaged fiddle and still more damaging fiddler. The tunes we listened to produced upon our ears the effect we anticipated, but the air we were breathing quite the contrary effect upon our noses. Captain Heath, the harbour-master, who was then living on board, also gave a dinner-party that day; and as his numerous guests appeared upon deck, there was quite an array of naval and military men.

I seldom smoke, and I remarked that the air we were so anxious to breathe was anything but wholesome or agreeable. Thereupon the commander of the *Diamond* observed that an unpleasant odour arose from the sea.

"It does not come from the water," I replied, "but from the shore."

"What can it be, Monsieur Soyer?" said he.

"Don't you know, captain—you who daily visit your naval hospital on the heights, that on that bank are the bodies of the poor unfortunate fellows lost in the *Prince*, and the sea has washed away the earth which covered them? Some of them are actually on a level with the ground."

"Impossible," said he; "I can't believe it."

"If you like," I replied, "I will convince you of the fact."

Some of those who overheard our conversation begged Captain Shepherd to let us have a boat, with which request the captain complied. It was a fine moonlight night when we started, and we soon reached the spot. The smell had disappeared; so he said I was mistaken.

"Not at all, captain," said I. "Pray thrust your oar through the soil we are standing upon."

It was covered with lime, and he did as I requested, and found that what I had stated was correct. We then returned on board, and mentioned the fact. All admitted that it was a dreadful thing, and might bring on cholera. Captains Heath and Shepherd observed that it was intended to throw a mound three feet deep over them, and that it was likely the heavy weather had washed away the gravel. The remains of some of these bodies were plainly visible, the most singular thing being their extraordinary state of preservation.

I noticed that the Board of Health were aware of this, and had taken sanitary measures by having great quantities of lime thrown over the remains. Captain Heath observed that the mound would very likely be completed the following day. I believe that such was the case, for a short time after I saw it was done.

This unpleasant discovery broke up our party sooner than was intended, but it did not disturb the mirth of the sailors; their fun lasted till daybreak. This corner of the harbour was seldom frequented, which no doubt was the reason that the exposure of the bodies had not been noticed sooner. In pointing out this fact to Colonel

Hardinge, he observed that under the water his power ceased. Admiral Boxer's nephew, who was there, remarked that above the level of the water he had no power; so that the tide, alternately washing over and receding from the bodies, led me to infer that neither the naval nor military authorities could remove the nuisance, as it must have been well known to many that the bodies from the wreck were deposited there.

The floating bakeries called the *Brusier* and the *Abundance* were now ready to commence baking, and were visited by all the authorities—Lord Raglan, Sir John Macneil, Colonel Tulloch, Commissary Filder, Dr. Sutherland, the Admiral and the Commandant, &c. The vessels were so crowded, that Captain Thompson, with whom I had the pleasure of being well acquainted, expressed his fears of never being able to make a fair beginning. Good bread was at that time, I must say, the most important thing wanted. Bakeries were in course of erection at Kadikoi, so that between the steamers and them about twenty-five or thirty thousand rations could be made, producing a supply of bread four days per week, and the other three biscuit. No one could then wish for better field rations.

While at the Sanatorium, making inquiry about Miss Nightingale, I heard from the purveyor that the doctor's advice was that she should go direct to England, when able to travel. My friend, Dr. Hadley, whom I was going to face boldly, and scold for causing me so much trouble with his saddle and bridle, had been waiting anxiously for my return. In despair, he had gone out in search of them. I therefore did not see, though I heard much about him.

Having met Mr. Parker, the clergyman, he informed me that he had been told that I had lost four horses in three days—viz., three myself, and my secretary one, and that none of them belonged to me. Upon this I replied, "Therein lies the merit of being trusted. Had they been my own it would have been nothing, as any fool can manage to lose his own horse, but it requires a good deal of skill and standing in society to lose four belonging to other persons, in so short a space of time."

My mishap afforded much amusement; and the standing jest in camp for some time was, "Who lost the four horses?" I was very anxious to know the actual state of Miss Nightingale's health, and went to her hut to inquire. I found Mrs. Roberts, who was quite astonished and very much delighted to see me.

"Thank God, Monsieur Soyer," she exclaimed, "you are here again. We have all been in such a way about you. Why, it was reported that you had been taken prisoner by the Russians. I must go and tell Miss Nightingale you are found again."

"Don't disturb her now. I understand Lord Raglan has been to see her."

"Yes, he has, and I made a serious mistake. It was about five o'clock in the afternoon when he came. Miss Nightingale was dozing, after a very restless night. We had a storm that day, and it was very wet."

"Pray go on, madam," said I, seeing she made a pause.

"Well, sir, I was in my room sewing, when two men on horseback, wrapped in large gutta-percha cloaks, and dripping wet, knocked at the door. I went out, and one inquired in which hut Miss Nightingale resided. He spoke so loud, that I said, 'Hist! hist! Don't make such a horrible noise as that, my man,' at the same time making a sign with both hands for him to be quiet. He then repeated his question, but not in so loud a tone. I told him this was the hut."

"'All right,' said he, jumping from his horse, and he was walking straight in, when

I pushed him back, asking him what he meant and whom he wanted.

"'Miss Nightingale,' said he.

"'And pray who are you?'

"'Oh, only a soldier,' was his reply; 'but I must see her—I have come a long way—my name is Raglan—she knows me very well.'

"Miss Nightingale overhearing him, called me in, saying, 'Oh! Mrs. Roberts, it is Lord Raglan. Pray tell him I have a very bad fever, and it will be dangerous for him to come near me.'

"'I have no fear of fever or anything else,' said Lord Raglan.

"And before I had time to turn round, in came his lordship. He took up a stool, sat down at the foot of the bed, and kindly asked Miss Nightingale how she was, expressing his sorrow at her illness, and thanking and praising her for the good she had done for the troops. He wished her a speedy recovery, and hoped that she might be able to continue her charitable and invaluable exertions, so highly appreciated by everyone, as well as by himself. He then bade Miss Nightingale goodbye, and went away. As he was going out, I wished to apologize.

"'No! no! not at all, my dear lady,' said Lord Raglan; 'you did very right; for I perceive that Miss Nightingale has not yet received my letter, in which I announced my intention of paying her a visit today—having previously inquired of the doctor if she could be seen.'"

"No doubt," I said, "his lordship quite enjoyed the fun."

"I think he did, for they were laughing so when they went away. However, it did my mistress no good. She became very nervous afterwards, and was worse for a day or two; but she is doing well now. I am sure his lordship would be very sorry if he knew that such was the case."

"That he would; for he did it out of pure respect and kindness."

"Exactly. I never heard a gentleman speak more kindly to anyone. But only fancy, sir, what fun for me to try to turn the commander-in-chief out of doors."

"How were you to tell who it was? And supposing you knew, even then you would have done right, as you had not received his lordship's letter, and had special orders from the doctor to let no one in, not even Mr. Bracebridge."

"Mr. Bracebridge came two or three times a day. The doctors recommend Miss Nightingale to go to London as soon as possible; but, Lord bless you, sir! she will not be in a fit state for removal for a fortnight or three weeks."

"I am sorry to hear that, because I should have liked to go back to Scutari with her. My field stoves have not arrived, and Julien, my head man at Scutari, has been ill; so I must look sharp after the hospitals on the Bosphorus, as my principal object in coming out was to set them to rights. In fact, I only offered my services for the Barrack Hospital, as I had not at that time heard of the others,—viz., Kululee, the General, and the Palace Hospitals."

"You must not rely upon what I say, Monsieur Soyer; for we might be off sooner."

"How are my kitchens going on?"

"Oh, very well indeed now, sir."

"I am sure to see Mr. Bracebridge on board today; and when Miss Nightingale is better, I will come daily and make some delicate broth, pudding, or jelly for her. Doctor Henderson tells me that as soon as he can put his illustrious patient under my care he will do so; then I shall require your assistance, as I consider you an excellent extra-diet cook."

The weather having set in fine, everything became more cheerful. Small dinner parties were given by the Guards and the Cavalry. Several gentlemen, at the head of whom was Colonel Carleton, clubbed together and engaged a man cook, who turned out a tolerable good dinner. He cooked almost *al fresco*. Those regiments stationed close to Balaklava fared the best, as they could procure provisions from the stewards of the vessels in harbour. Colonel Carleton, one of our modern epicures, whom I had the pleasure of dining with while encamped there, gave us an excellent dinner; and, for several reasons, never invited more than five guests to dine with him:—firstly, from his good sense as a *gourmet*; and, secondly, having no room for more. Dinner invitations poured in from all quarters, both from sea and land. For some time, it appeared as if the champagne corks were firing instead of the cannon at Sebastopol, as the wind was in the wrong direction, and the report of the guns was scarcely heard at Balaklava. It took me about an hour every morning to write apologies to invitations—so numerous were they, and my duties would not admit of my dining out every day. Moreover, the medical gentlemen then strongly recommended moderation and care in the use of food.

There was, however, one unexpected invitation I could not decline. One evening, as I was returning late from the camp, I met several of the heroes of Balaklava; amongst these Colonel Peel and Major Cook of the 11th Hussars, with whom I had the pleasure of being acquainted at Scutari. They would take no refusal, so I was compelled to accompany them to their mess-room and dine with them, which invite I was not long accepting, requiring at the time no end of restoratives for myself and charger, after a hard day's duty. It was indeed a splendid place for the Crimea—the camp being still in the infancy of luxury. A table was laid for sixteen guests, who had wisely opened a kind of club in a large hut. The rations were artistically turned to good account, and numerous little extras were procured from Balaklava, particularly fish. Two fine clout, or knotted turbots,* with the etceteras, gave an appearance of luxurious festivity; and though no one could boast of the elegance of the service, at all events there were a few plates, knives, and forks upon the table—at that time luxuries were not requisite. Good health—a ferocious appetite—lots of capital ale, porter, sherry, port, champagne—laughter, puns, and fun in abundance—witty anecdotes, and plenty of songs, good, bad, and indifferent, prevailed. The sixteen officers were joined by about twenty more after dinner. They sat down anywhere and everywhere, even out of doors. It was, in fact, the most martial festival I had seen during my visit to the Crimea, and quite cast in the shade our former semi-banquet at headquarters.

It was midnight ere this jovial party broke up; and a few minutes after I was on my way home. The sentry on duty at the Col of Balaklava was calling out, with the lungs of a Stentor, "Who goes there?" to a group bearing lighted torches coming towards him; and several voices, in a mournful tone, replied, "Friends."

---

* A peculiar kind of turbot found in the Black Sea, with scales, each scale something like the head of a large iron nail; and though, when the fish is thickly covered, it in a measure spoils its appearance, yet it does not in the slightest interfere with the quality, but, on the contrary, leaves a gelatinous succulence round it, entirely peculiar to this rough-outfitted denizen of the ocean.

"Pass, friends." A sudden change of scene and sensation soon took place! On approaching the group, and inquiring what was the matter, I perceived four Sardinian soldiers bearing a sick officer upon a stretcher. He was followed by several others. The Sardinians at that time suffered terribly from fever and cholera, and their daily loss of men was something fearful. They were admitted to the General Hospital, as there was not sufficient room in their own.

Following the group with solemn interest as far as the General Hospital, I learned that the precious burden they were carrying was one of the bravest officers of this small though perfect model of an army. It was a Major Crossetti, in the bloom of life, his age only six-and-thirty, who was suddenly attacked by cholera; and Miss Weare (the head lady under Miss Nightingale) begged of me to go and offer consolation, as well as to interpret and explain to the doctors what his servant required. He had then only just been attacked. In less than two hours, the fatal malady had increased to that extent that no hope was entertained of saving him, though every attention had been immediately afforded. Alas! all was of no avail.

The contraction and sudden change of one of the finest and noblest military faces I ever beheld, graced by a beard of an auburn tinge, to the hideous transformation caused by that awful disease, will never be effaced from my memory, and is far too piteous to be described. I remained with him more than three hours, but he died during the night; his poor servant, a Savoyard, who had been with him from his boyhood, wept bitterly. Miss Weare, though very unwell, remained at his side till he had expired. He kept asking, his moist hand clasped in mine, "Pensez-vous que je vais mourir?"—Do you think I am about to die?

"No, no! impossible, so young!" I ejaculated.

"I would not care if it were on the field of battle; but I have done nothing for my country in this war."

The words I addressed to him seemed to console him greatly. Miss Weare, however, informed me privately that the case had taken such a turn that nothing could save him.

A few days prior to my departure from the Crimea, my final reminiscence of this noble departed soldier was to see his name engraved on marble in letters of gold on the grand national Sardinian Monument so picturesquely situated on the summit of the high rock above the Sanatorium.

A few days after this, the *London* and its bridge was in more confusion than ever, and the landing of the Sardinian troops appeared a mere trifle compared with this unexpected movement. It was the departure of the fleet for Kertch, and the whole of the troops, horses, provisions, ammunition, &c., passed over our then almost uninhabitable *City of London*. I must say, the precision and celerity with which this fleet was embarked and despatched was admirable. The evening before, I had promised to go early and superintend the cooking of one of the regiments, when, to my great surprise, I found the colonel, his officers, and men upon deck just embarking. I was with them the afternoon before till three o'clock, and they then knew nothing about it. Admiral Boxer came and informed me that the *London* was to follow the expedition, and he was under the necessity of removing us, not much to our sorrow, for the everlasting thoroughfare made our nautical *London* very disagreeable; and it was with great delight that we left *town* for a quieter and better habitation, observing at the same time to the admiral, that I feared I was in disgrace both with the army and navy.

"Why so, Monsieur Soyer?"

"Because the Minister-at-War turned me out of London at a few days' notice, and you, admiral, do the same kind of thing in as many minutes. You are about transferring me, it seems, to the *Baraguay d'Hilliers*."

"Ah, and a fine ship she is, too, Monsieur Soyer."

Sir John Macneil and Colonel Tulloch had quitted the *Baraguay d'Hilliers*, a very fine vessel, and we had their apartment in the state cabin, so called because it was so large and commodious. The *Baraguay d'Hilliers* was moored next to the *Abundance*, and so close that we were able to walk from one ship to the other, which gave me the facility of watching the process and system of that important floating bakery, as well as the perfection of its mechanism. The first two samples of bread made were, one very white, and the other rather brown. Captain Johnson asked me which I liked best. I replied, "The brown, by all means, for the troops; and I am sure that Lord Raglan, Sir John McNeill, Dr. Hall, and other competent gentlemen, will express the same opinion."

"Monsieur Soyer, I must differ from you, for this is much finer and whiter."

"It is because it is so white that I object to it. The change from almost black Turkish bread to the very white will create a bad feeling amongst the troops, who will fancy they have been imposed upon. For my taste, give me the whitey-brown; there is less show and more nutriment in it: besides, it is better adapted for the purpose."

"Well," said Captain Johnson, "for my own eating, I prefer the white; though I must say the other is very good."

"Depend upon it, captain, the soldiers want food, not luxuries. I'll tell you what I will do for you: I am going to headquarters, and will take the samples to Lord Raglan and Dr. Hall."

"I shall be much obliged if you will," said he, "as we want to commence supplying tomorrow."

On reaching headquarters, I met Dr. Hall going to the general. I showed him the samples; we canvassed their respective merits for a few minutes, and the Doctor was of the same opinion as myself. I saw Lord Raglan in the camp; and he said, "The whitey-brown, by all means. I never wish to have better bread upon my table."

The good done by this bakery was incalculable. They baked from fifteen to sixteen thousand rations daily, with perfect ease. In justice to the system, I must say, it answered admirably. I carefully watched its progress, and though the quality of the bread often varied, which was entirely owing to the difference in the quality of the flour supplied—and this is unavoidable in so large a supply as is required for an army,—I can certify that the working of the flour in the bruiser, the process of manipulation, and the baking were carefully attended to. In the beginning, it is true, yeast could not be procured in sufficient quantities. At last, they discovered a way of making it themselves. It is due to their exertions to say, that the bakery at Kadikoi was not making as good bread as the *Abundance*. It is true, they did not possess the same facilities. We had made on board the *Abundance* several samples of bread-biscuit, which I had the honour of submitting to the Duke of Newcastle during his visit to Scutari. He tasted it both in its dry state, and also soaked in broth, three months after having been baked, and highly approved of it, considering it an excellent invention for the soldier's camp meal, as well as for the navy.

This is the same bread-biscuit mentioned by a correspondent in the following letter, addressed to the *Times*.

MISS NIGHTINGALE AND M. SOYER.
To the Editor of the Times.

SIR,—The sympathies of the British nation being at this moment directed to the army of the East, I feel that information as to the hospital department will interest many. Miss Nightingale returned to Scutari on the 4th inst., having left it on the 4th of the preceding month. Miss Nightingale, on her arrival at Balaklava, immediately began an active investigation of the state of the two hospitals there, as well as of the sailors' hospitals and the field hospitals in the camp, in which she had the invaluable assistance of the Sanitary Commissioners and M. Soyer, as well as the advice and the moral support of Sir John McNeill and Colonel Tulloch, commissioners, and of Dr. Hall and the medical staff. The affairs of the sisters and nurses were arranged, new huts built, kitchens erected and arranged, and a vigorous action in the whole department begun, with the full assent and aid of the medical officers, when Miss Nightingale was seized with the Crimean fever and carried up to the hut hospital on the Genoese heights.

She became convalescent after about twelve days, and was recommended to take a voyage to England; she, however, though in a state of extreme weakness and exhaustion, refused to entertain the idea of going beyond Scutari, trusting that she might be enabled the sooner to return to her advanced post at Balaklava. Lord Ward, with a generous perseverance in well-doing, forced Miss Nightingale to accept his steam-yacht the *London*, which was placed at her disposal on the 3rd inst., and in this vessel she happily and rapidly performed the voyage to Scutari. The Hon. W. Wellesley, Dr. Curgewan, Lord Ward's medical man, Mr. and Mrs. Bracebridge, M. Soyer, whose enterprise has been associated with that of Miss Nightingale at Balaklava, besides Mrs. Roberts, chief nurse, and servants, were on board. Miss Nightingale was visited while sick by Lord Raglan at the huts, and again on board the *London*, and was received on landing at Scutari by Lord W. Paulet, Commandant, Dr. Cumming, Inspector-General, and Dr. Macgregor, Deputy Inspector. The house of the chaplain is placed at her disposal by the Rev. Mr. Sabin, and she has been offered the use of the British Palace at Pera by Lord and Lady Stratford de Redcliffe. Miss Nightingale is extremely weak, but has no remains of fever, and no danger is apprehended.

The sanitarium, in huts on the Genoese heights at Balaklava, is now in full action, and will accommodate about six hundred, at the elevation of seven hundred feet above the sea. The wounded are doing well there, and the kitchen has been perfected by M. Soyer. One of the large huts is used as a chapel, and the whole staff of medical men, purveyors, chaplain, sisters, and nurses (Mrs. Shaw Stewart* superintendent), are well chosen and practically zealous. A second sanitarium, on St. George's Monastery heights, is ready for one hundred and fifty, and rapidly progressing. Good water is found in both situations.

In the General Hospital, above the head of the harbour, with its huts adjacent to the main building, about two hundred and fifty patients (chiefly sick) are attended (two huts being given up for cholera). The medical men are especially active there, the orderlies have been much improved in number and quality by recent regulation, the kitchen and chief cook have been recommended by M. Soyer, and the chief purveyor has shown anxiety to make ample provision of requisites, now happily to be found in abundance; but the situation is not a good one; the heat is great, and the crowds frequenting the purveyor's stores inconveniently near to the sick wards. The sisters and nurses (Miss Weare superintendent) are actively employed, and inhabit a hut adjacent to the main building.

* Sir Michael Shaw Stewart's sister.

The ship *Abundance*, lately arrived, has its bakery at work day and night, turning out excellent bread, which will take the place of the sour and mouldy article often sent from the contractors at Constantinople. M. Soyer has invented a most important kind of bread, which seems to unite the advantage of the loaf and the biscuit, and has found out a method of cooking salt rations which makes them most palatable and entirely removes the salt. His receipts have been highly approved, and will be printed by the authority of headquarters. The camp kitchens he has invented for field hospitals will soon be in activity, as those of the chief hospitals already are; but his suggestions and their application are of so practical and extensive a nature that they will require a second letter from,

Sir, your obedient servant,

C. H. B.

Scutari Barrack Hospital, June 7.

To the Editor of the Times.

SIR,—I shall do myself the pleasure of forwarding you by the next post a *résumé* of my culinary progress in the Crimea, adding to it the promised receipts, as well as some of those which I have already very successfully introduced into the camps, made out of the rations issued to the troops. I am also happy to inform you, that though so close to Sebastopol, I have not yet met with a single enemy; and were it not for the continual roaring of the cannon, the bursting of shells, and the heat of the sun, I could fancy myself in England's happy land. But instead of enemies, on the contrary, from headquarters to every camp and regiment, the officers and medical gentlemen have rendered me the utmost assistance, so ready are they to improve the cooking of the food for their brave companions in arms. The provisions allowed by Government I consider bountiful, and only require to be applied to the best advantage. With the highest consideration,

I have the honour to be, Sir,

Your most obedient servant,

A. SOYER.

Camp before Sebastopol, June 3.

XXII

PREPARATIONS FOR ANOTHER TRIP

MISS NIGHTINGALE was at this period gradually recovering, and the time for her departure drew near. That lady and Mr. Bracebridge had both expressed their wish for me to return to Scutari with them, which I was also very anxious to do. I wanted to give an important *coup d'œil* at the hospitals there, which were still very full. So I made the most of my remaining time; visited the French, Turkish, and Sardinian camps, and their hospitals, from each of which, I am proud to say, I gleaned some important and useful dietetic information. It was, however, better suited to the camp than to the permanent hospitals. What struck me most in the French and Sardinian treatments, which are based upon a similar system, was this— viz., that too much liquid of a weak nature was administered to the patients, and in too great quantities—especially as the climate had so great a tendency to produce diarrhœa, dysentery, and cholera.

I had remarked during my stay at Scutari, and when the hospital was filled with patients suffering from those diseases, that the succulent mutton and barley broth I had introduced was selected daily from the dietary by the English doctors, in preference to beef-tea, chicken-broth, &c.; as well as the receipts for plain boiled rice, savoury rice, slightly curried rice, rice-pulp, ground rice pudding, sago-jelly, sago-panada; and for beverages, strong rice-water, barley-water, and arrowroot-water, in preference to lemonade during the first stage of those diseases; and that numbers of these light though nutritious dishes were selected by the doctors when the disease was at its height.

Though I am aware that in different countries men have different constitutions, I also remarked that the Turkish system of diet closely resembled the English, as they used a great deal of rice, flour—stewed, broiled, and boiled meats, &c. &c. In giving this opinion *en passant,* it is only with the intention of submitting to the public, if not to the faculty, things which struck me forcibly during my visits to those important establishments, in which everybody has and ever will take a national interest. Nor can I bring these few remarks to a close without returning my grateful thanks to the authorities in these various establishments for their very courteous attention upon all occasions.

We remained about a fortnight longer in the Crimea, which time I spent in attending to my duties both in the camp and in the hospitals. One morning I had the pleasure of being introduced to Lord Ward, who was very anxious to see Miss Nightingale, as he had a number of letters as well as parcels for that lady. On my informing his lordship that Miss Nightingale was ill, and would not be able to see anyone for some time, I believe he forwarded them to her. As I was very desirous of seeing his vessel, he very kindly invited me to visit him on board; and we parted—I to meet Mr. Bracebridge, and to accompany him on our long-promised visit to Mr. Upton; and Lord Ward, to pay his first visit to headquarters and the camp.

In a short time we arrived at Mr. Upton's house, and were very kindly received. Mr. Upton is a very short, fair man, still young, and very pale. His daughters are two of the prettiest little girls I ever saw, aged respectively nine and eleven years. He seemed to have suffered much from his confinement, but spoke highly of the treatment he had received from the English while in captivity. His goods were exposed on view, and the sale was to take place a few days after. Having been set at liberty, he was about to return to his native place, near Atherstone in Warwickshire. Everything connected with that gentleman and his family, as well as what relates to his late father, is too well known to require to be repeated.

Six days had elapsed, and I had received no news of the lost pony. The endeavours to find his saddle were also fruitless; and the pony was quite a secondary consideration. This put me in mind of a most extraordinary case of absence of mind in a man who had been gambling, and unexpectedly found himself in great distress, having nothing left but his horse, which was starving for want of provender. On a sudden, a bright idea flashed across his mind. In order to save it, he went and sold the horse to buy some hay. Had the Doctor found the saddle, it was ten to one against his being able to purchase another pony, they were so scarce at the time.

On the seventh day, I happened to be riding triumphantly through the camp with my tall guardsman Thomas before me. He was carrying a fine piece of roast beef—or at least beef for roasting—which I had begged of the captain of a vessel who came from Alexandria, and intended for Lord Raglan. But I must here observe that it would have been dangerous to cross the camp with such a precious treasure unguarded, as some of those marauding Jack Sheppards of Zouaves would have thought nothing of taking possession of it. They always went in strong bodies, and were ever on the lookout for prey. I said to myself, "If, in the middle of the road, and under my own eyes, they will steal a horse, nothing is more certain than they will try to borrow this"—the word "steal" was not allowed to be mentioned in the French camp, the word "borrow" sounding more genteel.

The loss of the beef, added to the rumoured loss of the four horses, would indeed have afforded abundant materials for fun; so I sent my avant-guard by the road on foot, instead of across country, and followed him on horseback. This plan gave me an opportunity of seeing Mrs. Seacole, to thank her for her kind exertions, although the missing pony had not been found. On reaching her place, I found several mounted officers taking refreshment; when Miss Sally Seacole (her daughter), whose name I have not yet introduced, called out—"Mother, mother! here is Monsieur Soyer!" This announcement brought her out immediately, and she exclaimed, "Good luck to you, my son! we have found your pony: come down. Here are some officers who say they have had a grey pony like yours in the stables of their regiment these last few days. Didn't you say so, gentlemen?"

"Yes, Monsieur Soyer!" said one, "but you must look sharp, for they are going to sell it tomorrow, if no one claims it."

"Many thanks for the warning. I will ride over directly. Pray, what is the number of the regiment?"

"The 93rd—fourth division—near the Woronzoff road. I am almost sure it is yours."

"Well, my son," said Mrs. Seacole, "didn't I tell you that it would be found?"

"Really, Mrs. Seacole, I don't know what I shall give you for the trouble you have taken in this affair. At all events, here is something on account,"—saluting her upon her deeply-shaded forehead, at which every one present laughed and joked.

"Gentlemen," said I, "I knew you would be surprised; though it is very natural for a son to kiss his mother. At any rate, you cannot say that, upon this occasion, I have shown my love and taste for the fair sex." A hearty laugh concluded this innocent bit of fun.

My guardsman, Thomas, who had continued his journey, had by this time nearly reached his destination. After a sharp gallop I caught him, and just in time to rescue the piece of beef he had carried safely so far. I found him drinking brandy with several of the French Imperial Guard, at their canteen; and he was exhibiting the choice piece, which I had wrapped up so carefully in a cloth and packed in a basket. It was the admiration of all who formed the merry group. They said to him, "Anglais roast beef—bono Johnny." This was all their conversation upon the subject previous to its capture, which I have no doubt would have been the case had I not made my appearance. Seeing the imminent danger in which the choice morsel was placed, and aware that nothing but a *ruse de guerre* could rescue it from the hands of the enemy—

"Thomas," said I, in French, "how dare you stop drinking in this way, when you know that General Canrobert must have that beef roasted for his dinner; and it is already past three o'clock. ('By Jupiter!' said one of them, "it's no go . . . 'it's for the Commander-in-Chief.') Go along with you! (He began to inquire what I said.) Don't answer me, sir, or you shall have a night in the guardhouse. Pray, my fine fellow, which is the nearest way to the French headquarters? I had better carry it myself—I shall be there first. Give it me," said I, taking the basket, and ordering Thomas to follow.

Bidding the astonished soldiers adieu, I galloped off with my prize. Upon arriving at headquarters, I rated Thomas for his stupidity, and went to the kitchen to ask for a large dish to put the beef on. It quite astonished Monsieur Armand, as he had seen none of that quality before. Indeed, it contrasted strangely with some beef he had upon the table.

"You are more comfortable now," I said, "since those few additions have been made to your kitchen?"

"Very much so; and I am extremely obliged to you for what you have done."

"You have a very good roasting fireplace. Will you be kind enough to have that piece of beef roasted to a turn for Lord Raglan's dinner tomorrow, as it is Sunday?"

"Yes," said he; "it comes quite *à propos*; and I will roast it as well as I can, but must suspend it by a cord, as I have no spit."

"Do so—that will be more camp fashion; but pray don't bake it, for that would spoil it, and you don't know the trouble I had to get it as far as this in safety."

I then told him about Thomas and the French soldiers, at which he could not help laughing, saying, "It has had a narrow escape, for those devils of Zouaves will steal the coat from your back. A few days ago they stole a whole sheep from that bit of a larder I have here in the yard."

"You had better give it to the steward to keep in his pantry till tomorrow—it will then be safe."

"I will do so."

As Thomas was carrying it into the house, we met several officers, who inquired whence it came. I went and showed it to Colonel Steele, begging that he would be kind enough to offer it to Lord Raglan, with my respects. While I was in Colonel Steele's room, in walked Sir George Brown and his aide-de-camp.

"Bravo," said the latter, looking at it; "you have indeed improved the ration meat, if this is a specimen."

"It is," I replied; "but I am sorry to add that it is both specimen and stock."

"It is certain," said the general, "I have seen no such meat since I left England. Where does it come from?"

"Alexandria, general."

"Oh, that's a long way to bring it in large quantities."

"Truly, general; but this is only an out-of-the-way piece. I think we may shortly have plenty, and at a moderate price, and from a nearer place. No time is lost; but, as the proverb says, 'the world was not created in a day.'"

At this moment Lord Raglan came in, quite by chance. "Hallo, Monsieur Soyer," said he, "what have you got there?"

"A piece of ration beef, my lord, with a certain addition of fat; and I beg your acceptance of it for tomorrow's dinner. I have seen Armand about it, and he has promised to do it to a turn."

"That's very kind of you," said his lordship, giving his orders to the colonel, and inquiring, at the same time, about a very important telegraphic despatch.

"But I must again tell you, as I mentioned once before, you will not find my cook a first-rate *cordon bleu*."

"Well, my lord, no doubt he does his best, according to the quality of the provisions, which, your lordship must be aware, are not first-rate. At all events, I shall trust this marvel to his skill; and if he does it to a turn, as he has promised, he will prove the correctness of my countryman's words—Brillat Savarin—who says, in his *Physiologie du Goût*, 'On devient cuisinier, mais on est nait rôtisseur.'"

"That is a charming work of Savarin's," said his lordship. "Well, Soyer," continued he, "this certainly looks like English beef. Where does it come from?"

"From Alexandria, my lord. I dined the other day on board the *Etna*, and we had a splendid piece of roast beef for dinner. I at once claimed a portion for your lordship's table; and the captain ordered the best piece to be put by—and here it is."

"Very kind of him, very kind—and of you too, Monsieur Soyer." As Lord Raglan said this, he turned and gave his orders to Colonel Steele.

"Have you found your pony?"

"I believe so. I hear it is in the stables of the 93rd Regiment, and I am going to look for it directly."

"You are lucky," said he; "for some fellows have actually stolen thirty live sheep and several mules from here."

"Have they indeed?"

"Yes, I assure you it is too true. Is it not, Steele?"

"So I was told."

"Oh, I hear Miss Nightingale is soon going back."

"Yes, as soon as she is sufficiently strong to bear the voyage."

Lord Raglan then left the room. Never was there a man at all times more composed and collected than he was; and he always had a kind word and smile for those around him, even at the most critical times.

Several days had by this time elapsed since the departure of the expedition for Kertch, and no news of its movements had been received. The harbour looked very dull. Not knowing how to spend my evening, I went with a friend to Kadikoi, and dined there. Whilst at table, an officer who knew me, and who was reading the last number of the *Illustrated London News*, addressed me with a "Hallo, Monsieur Soyer, they have got you in the *Illustrated* this week."

"Have they?" said I. "Oh, I see—it is the last letter I sent from Scutari."

"Yes, it is," he replied.

"About the opening of my kitchen? Yes, and here is the sketch. I did not notice that before."

He then passed the paper to me. On perusing the letter, I perceived that the printer had made a slight mistake, and one of vital importance to me, as it operated to the detriment of the purveyor-in-chief at Scutari, as well as to the authorities. The blunder was as follows. In one passage of my letter I made special remarks upon the inferior quality of the provisions to be *obtained* at Constantinople. They had inserted the inferior quality of provisions *purchased* at Constantinople. I hardly knew how to rectify such a serious mistake, so I at once resolved to go and explain the matter to Lord Raglan, before he could hear from any other quarter, of what he might suppose to be my ill-feeling towards a party from whom I had previously informed his lordship I had received the greatest assistance and kindness. I immediately returned to the *Baraguay d'Hilliers*, and found Peter Morrison on board. I showed him the paper; and he at once approved of my resolve, and offered to accompany me to headquarters.

Though rather late—it was dusk—I borrowed a pony from the Commandant and a mule from Colonel Dennis. By way of a change I rode the mule, and off we went in true campaigning style. We were overtaken by night before we could reach headquarters. It was at all times imprudent to be out after dark, as violence and robbery were of daily occurrence. At length, after a detour of about a mile, we saw the gleam of several lights, and riding towards them, found ourselves safe at headquarters, having fortunately hit upon the place. The party were at dinner. After waiting a short time, the steward came and told me that dinner was over, and the gentlemen were taking their wine. I then begged him to inform Colonel Steele of my arrival, and say I should feel obliged if he would step into his room for a few minutes, as I had something important to communicate. Upon receiving my message, Colonel Steele immediately came out.

"Good evening, colonel. Very sorry to disturb you."

"Never mind that, Monsieur Soyer. But what brings you here so late at night? Are you staying here?"

"No, my dear colonel; I am still at Balaklava, but on the *Baraguay d'Hilliers* instead of the *London*."

"Indeed. Well, she's a much better vessel. But what can I do for you?"

"I will tell you. I am much annoyed at a mistake which has occurred in the printing of a letter of mine which has appeared in this number of the *Illustrated London News*. There are only two words misplaced, but they entirely alter my meaning. Pray read those few lines, colonel," I continued, giving him the paper, and pointing them out; the letter being to the following effect:—

That in the description they gave of the opening of my kitchen at Scutari, in the number of the 14th inst., an error crept in, occasioned by the omission of a word, which entirely alters my sentiment, and if not contradicted would reflect much discredit upon the authorities at Scutari, [and thereby inflict a serious injustice. The sentence to which I referred appears in the paper thus—] "That I prepared my bill of fare according to the provisions allowed, which are at all times of an inferior quality;" whilst the passage should run as follows:— *"That I prepared my bill of fare according to the provisions allowed, which at all times are of an inferior quality at* CONSTANTINOPLE *in comparison to English provisions."*

"I suppose you meant to say, the provisions to be obtained."

"Exactly, colonel."

"What do you wish me to do?"

"Merely to be kind enough to explain the error to Lord Raglan tomorrow, as it would appear very ungrateful on my part to the authorities at Scutari; more especially as I informed his lordship that those gentlemen had done everything in their power to assist me."

"I had better do it at once. His lordship has just done dinner. I will go and show it to him; you can walk in with me."

"No, I thank you; I had rather wait here."

In a few minutes he returned with the paper, saying, "I have shown it to Lord Raglan, and he will make a note of it."

He had scarcely uttered the words, when I heard his lordship inquiring in the corridor, "Where is Monsieur Soyer? where is he?" and in he walked, followed by his Staff, seven or eight in number, among whom was Dr. Pennefather. The commander-in-chief was dressed in plain clothes, and looked very well, full of health and vigour. His fine open countenance, so characteristic of the man, was more brilliant than ever, and his conversation quite jocular. After alluding to the step I had just taken, and which, he observed, was very thoughtful on my part, he promised to have the parties informed of the mistake, and of my explanation.

"Monsieur Soyer," (Lord Raglan, as he said this, was standing in the doorway, leaning on his right shoulder, with his legs crossed, and surrounded by several gentlemen, forming a group which I shall not forget as long as I live,) "you must have known my old friend Ude?"

"I did, my lord."

"How many years were you at the Reform Club?"

"Above twelve. It was old Mr. Ude who gave the late Madame Soyer away when we were married; so we often visited him."

"Lord Alvanley, who had apartments at Mr. Ude's, lived there for years, and I frequently visited him," said Lord Raglan.

"If so, no doubt your lordship will recollect a very interesting picture of a country girl going to market, with a basket of poultry under her arm?"

"I do, very well indeed, and I know it was painted by your wife. It was very cleverly done. But you had all her best pictures at the Reform Club. You showed them to me yourself."

"I recollect doing so perfectly well."

"She was a very talented woman indeed!" observed several of the gentlemen present, who had seen her pictures.

"She was an Englishwoman, was she not, Monsieur Soyer?" said his lordship.

"Yes, my lord; her maiden name was Emma Jones."

"Of course," rejoined one of the group, "her paintings were well known by that name."

"So they were, captain, and fetched high prices too. I do not sell any now; on the contrary, I still have my gallery complete, and have bought in several since her death. I offered old Ude fifty guineas for the painting in his possession called 'La Jeune Fermière;' but he would not part with it, as it was presented to him by her. Previous to my departure from England for the East, I was advised by the chaplain of the cemetery to insert on the monument the country of her birth, as many believed her to be a foreigner. The inscription was simply 'TO HER.' I then composed the following laconic epitaph:—

> 'TO THE MEMORY OF MADAME SOYER.
> England gave her birth,
> Genius immortality.'"

"Very good indeed," said his lordship. "I myself have seen the monument, which is considered one of the finest in Kensal Green Cemetery.

"I was saying, Soyer, that I frequently visited Alvanley; and we always knew when Ude and his wife were at home, for they never ceased quarrelling. They kept five or six dogs, and what with their barking and the quarrelling of master and mistress, I never heard such a noise in my life. I often wondered how Lord Alvanley could put up with it; but he said he was used to it, and could hardly feel comfortable anywhere else."

"Talk of quarrelling, I believe they could not exist without it—not even on birthdays; and if you will allow me, I will relate a singular birthday anecdote."

"Pray do, Soyer."

"You must know that the old gentleman, though very avaricious, now and then came out in first-rate style with his gastronomic parties; but the great day of all was the 15th of August in each year—being the fête and birthday of the illustrious and far-famed Louis Eustache Ude. Upon these occasions, about four-and-twenty of his most devoted and illustrious disciples were invited, with their wives, to a most sumptuous dinner at his house. The grandeur of the gold and silver ornaments was actually cast into the shade by the elegance and succulence of the *mets* they contained. The choicest articles in season—viz., fish, flesh, poultry, vegetables, and fruit—seemed to have been waiting to come to perfection for this high priest of the gastronomic art, and many culinary inventions which still delight the scientific palates of the epicures of the day had their origin at the Lucullusian anniversary.

"Upon one of these great occasions, Madame Soyer and myself were invited. As it was the first to which I had been invited, I was very anxious to go. About a week previous, so strong was my wish to be present at this feast, I asked the committee to grant me leave of absence from duty for one evening, and they kindly acceded to my request. To the minute, *heure militaire*, we were there, and were saluted upon our arrival by the usual dogmatic chorus, which for a few minutes prevented our hearing a word that was spoken. At length we were all seated, Mr. Ude at the top of the table, and Mrs. Ude facing him.

"It was, I must repeat, a most superb and elegantly laid out board. The best part of the dessert, which is always refreshing to the sight, 'particularly in the middle of

August,' had been made a perfect study. Soup was duly served, and highly praised by the culinary *convives* and judges. It was a *bisque d'écrevisses*. The Madeira was circulating cheerfully round the table, to the trinquing* of glasses, after the old French fashion, when an unfortunate guest, having probably too far to reach a beloved friend, put his foot forward, and unfortunately deposited it upon the paw of one of the *enfants chéris de la maison*. Vermilion—that was the name of the plaintiff—being an *enfant gâté*, seized upon the leg, which happened to be bootless, as the unlucky guest wore thin shoes. The dog made a slight indenture with his teeth, causing him involuntarily to reply to the attack of Vermilion; three or four more of the four-legged tribe joined the battle-cry, and the noise was intolerable. The compliments which passed between the host and hostess were pithy and violent, though scarcely heard through the din, excepting by those who happened to be seated close to them. We were fortunately about the centre of the table, and all we could catch was—

"'Oh, you stupid old man! why did you not lock the dogs upstairs, as I told you to do?'

"'Be quiet, madam!' replied Mr. Ude. 'This is my birthday, and I will have no quarrelling.'

"'No more will I; but why did you not lock up your dogs?'

"'Well, madam, I am sure they were quiet enough till that stupid young man trod upon poor Vermilion's paw.'

"'Stupid young man, did you say? Mr. Ude, pray how dare you insult my relation? If any one is stupid here, it is you, Mr. Ude!'

"'Will you be quiet, madam?'—'No, I shall not!'

"'What, not on my birthday! There, take that.'

"As he said this, he threw some almonds across the table, and his wife replied with some projectiles snatched up at random from other portions of the dessert. The dogs joined in the fray, and entirely upset the party. All the ladies left the table. The young man who had been bitten attempted to apologize; in return for which concession on his part, the great Louis Eustache and his amiable spouse returned a volley of abuse. An hour elapsed before anything like order could be established, when several ladies returned to the table, while a few remained to console the victimized spouse. The great Mr. Ude had bravely retained his important position, and, still violently excited, commenced helping the fish—a magnificent crimped Gloucester salmon, procured at Groves's in Bond Street—which was by this time as cold as ice.

"'Only fancy,' ejaculated the enraged Amphitryon, 'even on my birthday! Upon my word, she is a wretch! She never will—' Then, by way of parenthesis, to the waiter, 'Go round with the sauce, you stupid! don't stand there staring like a fool.'—'Prosper! no, I'm sure she never, never will prosper!'

"At length something like harmony was restored; but only six ladies out of eleven returned; the others remained with Mrs. Ude, and, I believe, dined upstairs. Much to our sorrow and disappointment, one of the finest dinners of the season was served up cold, and entirely spoiled, through the pugnacity of Louis Eustache Ude's favourite pup."

All laughed heartily at the anecdote, particularly Lord Raglan, who then told us that Ude had called upon him several mornings respecting a cook he had applied

---

* Clinking, Soyer's mixture of French and English.—AB

for to Mr. Ude, for his brother, the Duke.

"Ude," said Lord Raglan, "called several mornings, first with two dogs, then three, next four. At last I said to him, 'I am very much obliged to you, Mr. Ude, for your kind visits respecting my brother's cook, and shall be happy to see you at any time—but in future without your four-legged companions.'

"'Why?' asked the great *chef*, rather put out.

"'My dear sir, if you want an explanation, inquire of the housemaid!' He rushed out, and never called again; but he sent the cook all the same. Ude was an excellent manager, and a good cook, but had a very odd temper; he died very rich." '

"Very rich indeed."

"To whom did he leave his fortune?"

"Oh, to his favourite pet, Madame Ude. She is still alive, and lives in the same house in Albemarle Street."

"Really, I did not know that!"

"My lord, and gentlemen, I wish you good evening, and thank you for your kindness."

"You must take some refreshment, Soyer, before you go. Order what you want. Steward, wait upon Monsieur Soyer."

They then all went out, and sat upon the doorsteps, smoking their cigars. Lord Raglan was that night in a very jovial mood: Colonel Steele observed to me, "Did you ever know or see a finer man for his age? Is he not still full of life and vigour, and the picture of an English nobleman?"

"He is, indeed; and I always notice that he has plenty of fun and jokes."

"That is true; but more so with you, as you are not a military man. He is very strict on duty."

As I was taking some refreshment, Lord Raglan came to me, and said, "Monsieur Soyer, I wish you would give my cook, Armand, the receipt to make that excellent French *pot-au-feu* you gave me when I saw you at the Reform Club."

"I will; and those vegetables-chollet I have submitted to your lordship will be the very thing for it. They are made of common vegetables, exactly suitable for that soup. It is by far the best, most wholesome, and nutritious for the troops."

"I am confident of that," said his lordship, going back to his seat.

I then went out through the side door to fetch my mule, which P. Morrison had been walking about the courtyard along with his pony. Jumping upon it, I rode up to the group, to say goodnight to Lord Raglan and all present.

"Hallo," Lord Raglan exclaimed, "where is the charger you had the other day? What is that you are mounted upon?"

"A mule, my lord, belonging to Colonel Dennis of the Dragoons."

"Ah, you are much safer upon that."

"I feel so, I assure you, my lord. The charger to which you allude belonged to Colonel Hardinge."

"So I heard."

"It was a good joke on the part of the Commandant. I asked him to do me the favour of lending me his light pony, and he sent me his large charger, which ran away with me, but fortunately not towards Sebastopol." At this they all laughed heartily; and I and P. Morrison departed.

When we were about half a mile from headquarters, we heard a sharp fusillade in the direction of Sebastopol, and there was a lull in the cannonade and shelling, which had not ceased during my stay at headquarters. We proceeded to the Turkish camp, situated on the heights to the right, from whence we could plainly see the firing. The Turkish soldiers were in high glee, singing, dancing, smoking, drinking coffee, and playing no end of Oriental instruments, which, however well tuned, were by no means in harmony. They were bivouacked all over the camp; some of the officers who were smoking offered us chibouques and coffee, which we declined, as it was then so late. We left, thanking them for their civility.

As we rode along, I could not help remarking to P. Morrison the extraordinary contrast of the two scenes, witnessed nearly on the same spot and within a short interval—the present one all fun and glee, the other a scene of death and carnage, where hundreds of human beings were being launched into eternity. Such are the chances and the variation of war. It was after twelve when we arrived at Balaklava, and were safe on board. My heroic companion related the terrible fright he had been in all the way back, having seen most dreadful things, in the shape of ghosts, brigands, and murderers. It is true that on one occasion we were arrested; but it was by a wide ditch, which we could not easily jump over without risking a bath with the frogs, it being one of the resorts of those aquatic quadrupeds. We had lost our way, the road being invisible, and no landmarks, as the camps were being daily changed from one spot to another. These were the tribulations caused by the printer or my illustrious secretary. The next morning the captain of the vessel came to my cabin, and informed me that Kertch and other places in the Sea of Azoff were taken.

The news of such a victory was most welcome, and the harbour was gaily decorated with hundreds of coloured flags of the Allied nations. Everything seemed to revive, and all felt anxious to visit the newly-conquered land of Kamara, which had been taken a few days before. In company with a few others, I started at four a.m. to visit these *champs fleuris*. Nothing could be more refreshing than the sight of that gorgeous harvest, which seemed to have suddenly sprung up amidst deserted and arid rocks, sand, and gravel, where all had before been condemned to exile. Nothing in my whole existence appeared more grateful and refreshing to the mind, as well as the eye, than the odour from those perfumed valleys of myriads of wild flowers, shaded from the burning heat of the sun by a tall verandah of long green grass, the top of which softly caressed the chests of our horses as they trotted through these thickly-populated floral prairies. Myriads of *étoiles des champs*, daisies, buttercups, bluebells, cornflowers, poppies, birdseyes, &c., and many others unknown in this country, were seen on every side. Clouds of butterflies were seen gaily sporting from flower to flower, taking from each a kiss perfumed by the zephyr of the morn. Even our horses seemed to enjoy the scene so fully, that we let them graze for about an hour. We then arrived near the charming rivulet and valley, the Tchernaya, which, though far from being as beautiful as many in France or England, possesses numerous charms to an uninitiated eye.

We mounted our horses, and went through the Kamara Mountains, the scenery of which resembles that of Devonshire, Wales, or the Highlands of Scotland. We returned home by the edge of the beautiful cliffs which border the Bay of Balaklava. Such a day is not to be easily forgotten, rendered still more agreeable by the cordial reception we met with from the officers in the French and Sardinian camps, and the presence of a most charming *compagnon de voyage* (Mr. Stowe), a very promising young man in high literature. The various notes he took on the spot are worthy of Thomson's *Seasons*.

I heard from Mr. Bracebridge that Miss Nightingale was greatly improving, of which I was of course well aware, as I went every day to the Sanatorium to prepare a few light things for her lunch or dinner. He also informed me that her intention was to leave Balaklava shortly for Scutari; to which I replied, that having done all I could in the camp for the present, I was quite ready to go. As I had also heard that my field stoves had arrived, and had been landed by mistake at that place, I decided upon going to fetch them myself. Mr. Bracebridge having found some round stoves which were sent out for winter use, proposed having the tops cut off and some pans introduced, which would make them similar to mine (as he thought). "At all events," said he, "I shall make a trial, and show it at headquarters."

I very reluctantly consented to this. It took five or six days to make a strong tin pan, which, when done and fixed in the stove, we took to headquarters, and showed to Lord Raglan and a number of generals present. I made some coffee in it (that being the quickest thing), which was approved of. But having brought my small model stove with me, I pointed out to Lord Raglan that each pan would cost thirty shillings, and the stoves would not be worth five shillings soon afterwards, as they would be burnt through, thus proving the superiority of my plan. Lord Raglan advised me to wait till my own arrived. Mr. Bracebridge and myself afterwards went to the General Hospital, and there saw Dr. Mouatt, who had not succeeded in getting the bricks for the kitchen oven.

Having completed our camp rounds, Mr. Bracebridge said he was compelled to leave me upon some private business. I afterwards learnt that he went to the trenches, and, being both very imprudent and curious, was as nearly as possible taken prisoner or shot. He had appointed to meet me by five o'clock at headquarters, but did not come. I paid Dr. Hall and a few friends round headquarters a short visit, as I feared I might not have another opportunity previous to my departure from the Crimea. It was quite dark when I got back. Mr. Bracebridge had not returned, and we were beginning to fear that something had happened to him. The next morning he was on board early, and active as ever, recounting his adventures. I that morning went on board Lord Ward's yacht, but its owner was on shore—so I left word that I would call again. The next day I had the honour of receiving the following invitation from Lord Ward, to go on an excursion in his yacht as far as Lukas, the palace of Prince Woronzoff.

Steamship "London," Balaklava Harbour, Wednesday.

Sir,—You were kind enough to promise to visit me on board my ship, the *London*. To-morrow we propose visiting Yalta and Aloupka, calling on the way at the pretty country seat belonging to Prince Woronzoff. If not engaged, will you go with us? You will perhaps at the same time be kind enough to give a few hints to my cook in the mysteries of the art of which you are so great a master.

I have the honour to remain, yours,
WARD.

About eighty persons were invited, and it was with regret that I was obliged to decline; but a day was indeed a day to me.

Miss Nightingale got better and stronger every day, and she seemed inclined to remain in the Crimea, observing that, owing to her illness, she had not done half she had intended to do. Everyone, and especially the doctors, tried to persuade her that the change of air would do her an immense deal of good.

It was at last settled that a berth in the first convenient ship leaving the harbour for Scutari should be placed at Miss Nightingale's disposal. The *Jura* was fixed upon, as she was then hourly expected, and had only to discharge cargo and return immediately. She had four hundred horses on board, and several hundred troops. The day before her departure Miss Nightingale was brought from the Sanatorium upon a stretcher, carried by eight soldiers, and accompanied by Dr. Hadley, the Reverend Mr. Parker, Mr. Bracebridge, myself, and several Sisters of Charity. When we reached the *Jura*, tackles were attached to the four corners of the stretcher, and Miss Nightingale was slung on deck by means of pulleys. We found a very disagreeable smell, caused by the great number of horses, which had only been landed that morning. Miss Nightingale was carefully carried to the chief cabin, a very comfortable one; yet even there the smell was very offensive. This I mentioned to the captain, who agreed with me, but said, "We shall no sooner get to sea than it will disappear."

The invalid was therefore made as comfortable as possible, and the doctors and everyone left. No sooner were they gone than Miss Nightingale fainted. I and the boy Thomas ran in every direction for a doctor. Dr. Hadley, who had just arrived at his residence on the Genoese Heights, came at once, and immediately ordered her to be removed to another vessel. Not being able to find either Captain Heath or Admiral Boxer, I thought of the *Baraguay d'Hilliers*, to which Miss Nightingale was at once safely removed, and where I hoped she would be very comfortable till we could get an order from the admiral for another ship. The same evening Admiral Boxer came on board to say that he would at once look out for one. The next afternoon Mr. Bracebridge and myself went to headquarters, to apprise Lord Raglan of the cause of Miss Nightingale's non-departure. His lordship was out, and Mr. Bracebridge left a message to the effect that he hoped Lord Raglan would not trouble himself about the matter, as Admiral Boxer would attend to it, and that Miss Nightingale was quite comfortable on board the *Baraguay d'Hilliers*. We then made a few farewell calls at the First and Third Divisions, and also at the Guards' camp, near Balaklava.

It was nearly midnight when we were shouting, pianoly, [*sic*] "*Baraguay d'Hilliers* ahoy!" No reply was made to either the first or second hail, so I raised the dismal melody a few notes higher, which at last brought, to our astonishment, a beautiful boat manned by six smart oarsmen. The craft was handsomely painted, having a small red and white burgee at the stern. At first I thought it was an optical delusion, or a fairy scene raised by the magic power of Ondine, the queen of the waters. In less than two minutes they neared the shore, and one of the fairies addressed us thus: "Pray, are you the gentlemen who are accompanying Miss Nightingale?"

"We are," said I.

"I and my men have been waiting for you, sir, these three hours."

"How is that?" asked Mr. Bracebridge.

"I cannot tell you further, than that we were sent to fetch Miss Nightingale, and referred to you. I believe you are Mr. Bracebridge?"

"Yes; and I am at a loss to understand what you mean."

"I've brought a letter from our master, Lord Ward, which will explain all."

"Where is it?"

"I have delivered it on board; but the last orders from his lordship were, that if I had to wait all night, I was to bring you to him."

"Why? Don't you know?"

"Not exactly. But I am sure his lordship is still waiting for you; so you had better come as far as the *London*—it won't take you ten minutes."

We then jumped in. Mr. Bracebridge said, "I tell you how it is: no doubt Lord Ward has heard of what has happened, and probably intends to offer to take Miss Nightingale in his yacht to Scutari."

"Very likely; but it would not do to accept the invitation without first obtaining the permission of Admiral Boxer."

"We shall see, Mr. Bracebridge. Perhaps Lord Ward will lend it to the invalid; for he has only just arrived, and it is doing nothing."

On getting on board the *New London*, we found that Lord Ward, tired of waiting, had retired to rest, having left special orders to be called the instant we arrived, no matter at what hour. As it was nearly one o'clock, we made all kinds of objections to his being disturbed, but in vain. The lamps were lit in the saloon, and we were invited to walk in. We found Lord Ward *en robe de chambre*, quite ready to receive us.

"Welcome, gentlemen," said he.

We were about to apologize for being so late, when Lord Ward proceeded to say that he had heard of the non-departure of Miss Nightingale, and the cause, and that if she would accept his yacht, he should be happy to place it at her disposal to convey her to Scutari. He added, that she might take her own time, as he intended to remain a fortnight in the Crimea, and that no one should be on board excepting those whom she chose to take with her, and his medical attendant.

Mr. Bracebridge thanked Lord Ward in his own and Miss Nightingale's name, and said that he would inform the lady of his lordship's kind offer in the morning, and communicate her decision. We then left, thus terminating a most unexpected midnight conversation, on the 7th of June, 1855. Nothing was heard in the now peaceable harbour but the splashing of the oars of our fashionable oarsmen, who seemed at every pull to be smashing the Koh-i-noor diamond into hundreds of pieces while disturbing the transparent liquid. The flashes from the guns at Sebastopol were distinctly seen reflected, but not a sound was heard save our good-night to the fairy rowers, as we ascended the rope ladder of the bulky *Baraguay d'Hilliers*.

The following morning Mr. Bracebridge consulted with Miss Nightingale. The lady expressed her thanks for Lord Ward's kind offer, but at the same time justly observed that the matter was in the hands of the admiral, as he might by this time have arranged with another vessel. Inquiries having been made, the admiral recommended Miss Nightingale to accept Lord Ward's offer, remarking the advantage of having the vessel to herself, while it would be morally impossible for him to give her a passage with the same facilities. It was then decided that the offer should be accepted. Lord Ward soon after called for an answer, and was highly gratified by that lady's acceptance. He returned on board his vessel, to have every preparation made for her reception. Miss Nightingale was to go on board at four in the afternoon, and sail at eight or nine the next morning. Mr. Bracebridge, Lord Ward's medical attendant, the Honourable Mr. Wellesley, and myself, were the only persons to accompany her. For the last time I went my hospital and camp rounds; and in the latter part of that day I thought of going once more to headquarters, to acquaint Colonel Steele of the final arrangements for our departure. I met the Rev. Mr. Wright, the clergyman, in front of the General's house, and asked him where Omer Pacha's tent was situated, being anxious to leave my card with his excellency before leaving. Mr. Wright kindly pointed out the spot. As I was entering the house, I met Lord Raglan coming out.

"Oh, here you are, Monsieur Soyer! I heard you were gone, or going, with Miss Nightingale. When do you start?"

"Early tomorrow, in Lord Ward's yacht."

"So I hear. I am very glad of it. She will be much more comfortable."

"Doubtless, my lord."

"Let me see (looking at his watch); where are you going?"

"Back to Balaklava direct, my lord, having only to make a call for a minute in the Turkish camp."

"If I thought I should not be too late, I would go with you, to say farewell to her."

"Pray don't give yourself so much trouble. It is getting very late, and must be near your dinner-time. I will inform Miss Nightingale of your kind intentions—that will be quite sufficient."

"Wait a few minutes."—"I will."

It was getting dusk, and having waited nearly twenty minutes, I made inquiries as to whether it was likely that Lord Raglan was going to Balaklava.

"No," was the answer from one of the Staff, "for he is very busily engaged."

I started for the Turkish camp. On my arrival there, I found that Omer Pacha was dining out; so I left my card and respectful compliments, and took the road through the artillery camp. This gave me an opportunity of visiting Colonel St. George, who resided near the small village of Carrara, about two miles from Balaklava. The kind reception I met with from the Colonel, whom I had not seen since I left Scutari, caused some little delay, and I did not get on board till nearly nine o'clock. To my surprise, I learned that Lord Raglan had just left the *London*, after paying a farewell visit to Miss Nightingale. This I could hardly believe to be true—the space of time was so short. I much regretted not having waited longer, though certain that his lordship could not be offended, as I had left a message with the man on duty in the entrance hall to the effect that I was informed that he was not coming.

XXIII

OUR STEAM VOYAGE IN THE LONDON

WE slept that night on board the *Baraguay d'Hilliers*, though all our baggage had been removed to the *London*, and at seven next morning we went on board. Miss Nightingale had passed a most excellent night, and the weather was very fine. Lord Ward, who had slept at the Commandant's, came on board at half-past seven. After inquiring of Mrs. Roberts, the nurse, whether Miss Nightingale had been comfortable, he gave the captain orders for departure, which he had fixed for twelve o'clock, instead of nine. As the weather was so fine, he proposed that a sofa-bed should be placed upon deck, and that the captain should take us as far as the Bay of Sebastopol, where we might have a fine view of the besieged city, without incurring the slightest danger.

One of the mates told the captain that a vessel full of powder had taken fire in the night, and that Admiral Boxer had been there since two in the morning, working like a negro with the men, and therefore that he could not see him. I believe Lord Ward knew this, but did not speak of it for fear of causing alarm, and this was no doubt the cause of the delay in our departure. The deck was crowded the whole morning with visitors, particularly officials, who wished to pay their respects to Miss Nightingale; but the doctors had given positive orders for her to see no one. Balaklava was in a great state of excitement, on account of the fire on board the powder-ship. Some called it the Gunpowder Plot at Balaklava, and an attempt to destroy the British fleet. This was the opinion in the French camp and at Kamiesch. The fleet, by the bye, was at that time at least twenty miles from the supposed scene of explosion.

As there were several matters which I wished to settle before my departure, I asked the captain whether I could land for an hour.

"Certainly you can. I don't think we shall sail before three o'clock; but be on board by twelve, if possible, or half past at the latest."

"I shall be sure to return in time."

I called at the Commissariat respecting the preserved vegetables, the samples of which were daily expected; next, upon Mr. Fitzgerald, the purveyor; and then went to the *Abundance*. On my way to the steamer, I met Mr. Bracebridge going to Colonel Dennis; and although I had already had the pleasure of saying goodbye to the colonel and his lady, I went back with him. The colonel, who had been seriously ill for several months, was to sail the next day for England, or Malta (I don't exactly recollect which), and was saying how much he regretted being obliged to leave his regiment—that he feared the voyage would not do him much good, as the steamer he was going by was so full of sick. He had scarcely spoken the words, when in walked Admiral Boxer.

"Well, Dennis, my friend! I bring you good news."

"What's that, admiral?" said the colonel.

"Why, I have another vessel going tomorrow, with very few sick on board, and I have secured a good large cabin for yourself and lady."

"Many, many thanks! my dear admiral," said Colonel Dennis, in which his lady also joined.

"Ah! Monsieur Soyer, are you here? How are you today?"

"Quite well, admiral. I hope you are the same!"

"No; I am very tired."

"Will you take a glass of wine, admiral," said Colonel Dennis, "and sit down a minute?"

"No, I thank you; my nephew is waiting lunch for me, and I have been up since three o'clock this morning helping to put out the fire on board that ship in the harbour."

"Well, how did you leave it, admiral?" inquired the colonel.

"The powder is safe, but the vessel is much damaged. Goodbye, Mr. Bracebridge; goodbye, Monsieur Soyer. I shall see you again—I am coming on board in an hour. You will not sail till three o'clock. Indeed," said he, going out, "I must take some lunch first, for I feel very faint."

"You're right, admiral," said I; "you work so hard, that if you don't take care of number one, you will kill yourself."

"No fear of that, Monsieur Soyer; nothing can hurt an old fellow like me."

He then almost ran, instead of walking. Bidding the colonel and his lady adieu, Mr. Bracebridge and myself immediately went on board, fearing we might get late. Many visitors were still there, and the captain and Lord Ward begged of them to retire. A few minutes after, we were *en route*. The admiral was expected, but did not come; he sent some of his officials instead. As soon as we were under way, the couch was brought on deck—Miss Nightingale lying upon it. Mrs. Roberts held a white umbrella over her face to screen her from the extreme heat of the sun, fanning her at the same time. In the saloon, Lord Ward and myself were busily engaged in a most extraordinary sport, hunting the Crimean Zouave flies, which, no matter how you repulsed them, always came back to the charge. We had by this time entered the bay, but were still on half steam. Lord Ward bade Miss Nightingale farewell, as well as all on board, and went off in a small boat. We then shaped our course for Constantinople direct, it being too late to go and see Sebastopol. It was striking eight bells as we cleared the Bay of Balaklava.

We were at sea; and our heroine was where I had recommended her to be, viz., between heaven and the ocean.

Miss Nightingale remained on deck till nearly dusk. The sea was calm, and the burning sky was so strongly reflected upon its surface that we seemed to be rapidly traversing a lake of fire. The radiant face of the sun itself had for some time been concealed by the majestic rock upon which stands the monastery. The turbulent noise of the harbour was succeeded by a dead calm; even the zephyrs seemed to have deserted the collapsed sails, and nothing was heard but the rapid action of the paddles. Of all on board, only Miss Nightingale, her nurse, and myself seemed to enjoy this new scene of enchantment. The rest of the passengers were slumbering in the saloon. Even the turbulent voice of the cannon in and before Sebastopol was mute to our astonished and still-confused ears. Time, it is truly said, tries all! We were at the seat of war, looking at my watch, only eighty-seven minutes before.

Owing to the noise of a busy seaport, as well as the succession of importunate visitors who, though not admitted, were announced and politely answered, Miss Nightingale must have been, I was well aware, much fatigued. I therefore did not touch upon any important subject of conversation, but begged of her to be prudent and return to her cabin before the evening dew began to fall. She could not help expressing her gratification at the sublimity of the sudden change. Her countenance appeared to have imbibed the balm of health, and to have extended it to her feeble frame.

"Did I not tell you true, mademoiselle," said I, "when I begged of you to leave, were it only for a short time, 'ces soucieux rochers, et cette terre d'esclaves?'"

She smiled, and requested the captain to have her removed to her cabin, which was immediately done.

Mr. and Mrs. Bracebridge, and myself, cheerfully obeyed the invitation of an intelligent silver bell which summoned us to dinner at his lordship's table. I trusted a genuine appetite without the slightest reserve to a well-provided and well-conceived dinner, regretting only having lost the use of my substantial appetite. The wine was on a par with the dinner—excellent.

Early morn found me shaking hands with my illustrious *confrère* the *chef*, in his turret-like kitchen. I thanked him much for his capital dinner. "Pray what have we for today?" was the last political question I put to him. I am unwilling to append the bill of fare, as it might give an unexpected appetite to my readers, and thus induce them to drop this light reading for something more substantial. That would not answer my purpose, as I wish them to go on with the book without depreciating the cook. The night had been rather rough, and everyone on board was ill. The day passed as it generally does when persons have been so roughly nursed by the mother sea. The dinner was probably excellent, but no one could tell—not even myself. Towards night, the rolling waves grew a little more sociable; so we entered into conversation, and the wine and grog circulated freely. The captain, like all captains who have never been sick or drowned, laughed at us, saying we were bad sailors.

"The title of 'good sailor' I am not ambitious to merit, captain," said I.

Next morning, I was on deck walking to and fro with the captain; the night had been a little calmer than the previous one, but very foggy.

"Bless my soul!" said he, "what a bother it is we left Balaklava so late. It is just like his lordship—we never know when we are going to start. I would not give a fig for a voyage of pleasure at sea: business men, sir! business men for navigation. All is calculated and goes right; but for the present I don't know where we are, it is so foggy. We are not far from the coast; but we can't for the life of us get in, even if we were abreast of the entrance of the Bosphorus. We ought to have got under way, as I proposed, at nine o'clock. Have you good sight, sir?"

"Yes, I have."

"Well, look with this glass to the right; I fancy I see the land about seven or eight miles off."

"Yes," said I; "the fog is clearing off on that side, and I believe it is the land."

"In that case," said the captain, "we are nearly thirty miles out of our way. Though it is very provoking, we may thank our stars the weather was more favourable than the night before."

It was now nearly five a.m., and the dew was falling very fast. Feeling chilly, I went below, and reposed for a short time upon the sofa. Being thirty miles out of our course gave me time for a good rest before entering the Bosphorus; upon making which I was, at my request, called up. As the sun rose, the fog cleared off, though slowly; the captain made out a landmark, and found that we were, as he had before said, about thirty miles out of our course. The *London* was fitted up in a princely style; she had two funnels, and was very long. She rolled very much during the voyage, though the sea was not very rough; her being short of ballast was probably the cause. At all events, it made Miss Nightingale very ill.

However, our troubles were now at an end; we were slowly entering the mouth of the Bosphorus, amidst a shower of pearls, which gathered in millions upon the rigging and the deck. This was a great relief to us, after the grey fog and thick fine rain—besides being unaware of our exact position, and floating at hazard on the sea; though, thanks to the caution and watchfulness of the captain, we had been in no danger. It was like the opening of a fairy scene; the clouds were slowly disappearing, disclosing to our fatigued and overstrained eyesight the unique panorama of the Bosphorus. Its strong current appeared to overpower the steam, and we seemed to have come to a stand-still. The thousands who have returned from the arid and devastated soil of the Crimea, under its burning sun, must have enjoyed the refreshing sight I have here attempted to describe. Even Miss Nightingale had enjoyed it from her cabin. She had been removed to the beautiful saloon upon deck, where she had a good view of the enchanting panorama, and appeared almost recovered from her fatiguing voyage; which proves how near pain is allied to pleasure, and *vice versa*, particularly as refers to sea-sickness. Miss Nightingale requested to see me. I went and inquired after her health, which, she said, had improved since we entered the river. She then referred to various things she wished to have in her extra-diet kitchen, and to numerous other matters of importance connected with the hospitals. I requested her to keep her mind quiet, and to depend upon me.

"No doubt, mademoiselle," said I, "I shall not have the pleasure of seeing you for some time, and I would certainly advise you not to go out till you are quite restored to health: I will, therefore, send you a journal of my daily proceedings by Mr. or Mrs. Bracebridge, whom I, of course, shall see every day."

"Exactly, Monsieur Soyer; but I hope I shall soon be able to go about."

"So do I, mademoiselle, but do not attempt it before you are quite well; and I can assure you, if I were your doctor, I should be very strict with you, as I hear you are more inclined to devote your kind attention to patients than to yourself."

She smiled, and replied, "Well, Monsieur Soyer, one is much more gratifying to my feelings than the other."

I then spoke about Lord Raglan's visit, and expressed my regret at not having waited longer for him.

"I certainly did not expect to see him," said Miss Nightingale.

"Ah, you may expect anything from his lordship, he is such an amiable and gallant man."

"So he is, Monsieur Soyer; and he has always enjoyed that reputation."

We were at last before the Great Barrack Hospital; the anchor was let down, breakfast was served, and highly relished by the assembled guests. The *chef* had distinguished himself upon a dish of semi-grilled and devilled fowl, an omelette aux fines herbes, &c. &c.; and thus ended our voyage on board the *London*. We returned our hearty thanks to the captain, doctor, and all on board, for their kind attention to us, and for the extreme kindness shown to Miss Nightingale; saw our luggage landed, and went on shore. Miss Nightingale would not land till the afternoon, the heat of the sun being so powerful.

Having apprised Lord W. Paulet of our arrival, I went my way, and Mr. Bracebridge his. At five o'clock we again met at the landing-place, and went for Miss Nightingale. One of the large barges used to remove the sick, manned by twelve Turks, was brought alongside. As the roof nearly reached the steamer's bulwarks, Miss Nightingale was easily lowered upon it. Mrs. Roberts was kneeling at her side, and holding a white umbrella over her head. We went below; the sailors gave three cheers; and our dismal gondola soon reached the shore. Upon landing, the invalid was carried upon a stretcher by four soldiers, accompanied by Lord W. Paulet and Staff, Dr. Cumming (who had visited her on board), followed by an immense procession, to her private house—at which place all dispersed.

I do not recollect any circumstance during the campaign so gratifying to the feelings as that simple, though grand, procession. Every soldier seemed anxious to show his regard, and acknowledge his debt of gratitude to one who had so nobly devoted her soul and comfort to their welfare, even at the risk of her own life.

MISS NIGHTINGALE ON CATHCART'S HILL.

XXIV

THREE WEEKS AT SCUTARI

MR. and MRS. BRACEBRIDGE remained with Miss Nightingale. I went and paid my first visit to Lord William Paulet, having only had the pleasure of catching sight of his lordship at the wharf, owing to the immense crowd. I sent in my card; and the General no sooner received it, than he kindly walked towards the kiosque drawing-room door to meet me, and gave me a most cordial reception.

"Ah, Monsieur Soyer," said he, "I am glad to see you again! How are you? I have very frequently heard of you! I hope your services have been as useful in the Crimea as they were here. I am happy to say that, during your absence, I have not heard any complaints, and your system works admirably. Dr. Cumming and I have often spoken on the subject since you have been away."

"It is extremely gratifying to my feelings to hear you speak so favourably of my humble services; and I have returned for a short time to give a look round, according to promise, as it is very important that no change should take place in the management—which might occur, inasmuch as my head man Julien seems determined to leave. I must find someone capable of replacing him, or must take to cooking again myself till I can find a proper person."

"I hope, Soyer, you will be fortunate enough to meet with a proper person, as, no doubt, you will be obliged to return to the Crimea."

"I am pleased to hear that Serjeant Thompson, whom we placed as superintendent over the soldier-cooks, and the men under him, have behaved so well. He says the men have learned to cook; but what he and my man Julien complain of is, that as soon as anybody is well acquainted with his duty, he is recalled to his regiment. I really believe that is the reason why Julien is leaving. He says, as soon as he gets a good man, he is taken away, and his successor requires to be taught. This will always be the case, my lord, until a medical corps is formed, in which all the different members are subject to the discipline of the army, without being subject to frequent changes. Till such steps are taken, the duties of military hospitals will never be properly performed. I assure you, when I heard Julien was about to leave, I was much annoyed, and would have given anything to have been able to return forthwith to Scutari. One day's neglect would have upset all my former success, and corroborated the remark made by your friend Colonel Dennis—'that it was all very well so long as I was present; but as soon as I went away, it would be as bad as ever.' His words would have proved true enough, had I not introduced my simplified system of cookery, and my printed receipts, by following which it is impossible for them to err. At all events, I have now been absent two months; all has gone on right, nor do I see why it should not continue to do so; but I must repeat, the importance of having the duties of the military hospital properly performed is such, that all the persons employed ought to be subject to military discipline. I cannot depend upon civilians for cooks, although they are so well paid."

"Very true, Monsieur Soyer; I am quite of your opinion, and will take a note of it."

"The most important thing at present would be for your lordship to secure a few men, about ten, whom I will instruct in the method of cooking with my new field stoves."

"I cannot do that, Monsieur Soyer; I have no power away from this; but Lord Raglan, who I hear is very partial to you, will soon see the importance of so doing, and will grant your request."

"Your lordship is quite right, for Lord Raglan, as well as yourself, has shown me the greatest kindness; so have all the officials—Colonel Steele in particular, with whom I have had more to do than with anyone else."

"I have received a letter from my friend Colonel Douglas, of the 11th Hussars, who tells me they had the pleasure of your company to dinner, and that you kept them quite alive with your funny songs. You were the real cock of the walk, and kept them in a roar of laughter from the beginning to the end."

"We did spend a very pleasant evening. There were above twenty guests."

"Ah, I know! they sent me a list of names. You are aware that was my regiment before I came here."

"Of course I am. Your lordship was in the glorious charge at Balaklava. I hear that the charger your lordship rides is the one you rode on that memorable day."

"Yes, it is; and we were both very fortunate, as you see."

"Very, my lord. In these times everybody is subject to the chances of war, as I observed that evening to Major Peel and Colonel Douglas, upon taking my leave of them: 'a few hours such mirth as this—c'est autant de pris sur l'ennemi'—the French soldier's proverb."

"You are right. How did you find Admiral Boxer?"

"Rough and good-hearted—working very hard."

"I heard several anecdotes of you and the admiral with the Sardinians."

"Did you? Then you must have heard of my losing four horses."

"No! I heard of your having lost one, while paying your addresses to the fair Mrs. Seacole."

"That was it. We had a good laugh over it, at all events. Mrs. Seacole took a deal of trouble in the matter, and found the pony again. She is an excellent woman, kind to everybody, I can assure you."

"Ah, yes, I know her well; she paid me a visit on her way to the Crimea."

"She told me she had spent a few days with Miss Nightingale."

"Talking of Miss Nightingale—she is very much altered?"

"Very much indeed. She has looked much worse, but is now improving fast. Her life was in the greatest danger."

"So I heard. I hope Lord and Lady Stratford de Redcliffe are well."

"Yes. I had the pleasure of dining with them at Therapia last Sunday: they inquired after you."

"I am very happy to hear it, and shall soon pay my respects to them. I much regretted not being in the Crimea during their visit. The *Caradoc* left Balaklava the day the *Robert Lowe* left Constantinople; we therefore passed at sea."

"So I heard."

"The young ladies were very much pleased with their trip; but Lady Paget remained there. I suppose you saw her?"

"Yes, I did. Her ladyship was staying on board the *Star of the South*. I called several times, but at last met her ladyship in the camp, driving out in a species of vehicle, and accompanied by Lord Paget on horseback, to whom I had the honour of being introduced by her ladyship. She really looked so pretty, and her equipage was so bad, that a Canova would have sculptured her as a Venus in a wheelbarrow, instead of in a shell."

"Well, I must say, that would be a new, and, no doubt, an interesting subject. By the bye, we shall shortly have a visit from the Duke of Newcastle. I hope you will be here."—"Indeed!"

"Yes, I expect him in seven or eight days."

"I hope his grace will do me the honour of visiting my sanctorum."

"Of course he will, you may depend upon that; but I will let you know all about it."

"As it is near your dinner-time, I wish you good afternoon."

"Where are you going to dine, Monsieur Soyer? I believe I have but meagre fare to offer you—a little soup and a leg of mutton. Will you dine with me?"

"Many thanks—not today: we had a late lunch on board; and I have not been to Soyer's Castle yet, nor seen any of my people."

"I suppose Lord Ward has a first-rate cook on board his steamer?"

"A very good one, and excellent provisions and wine. The only thing we required was missing—that was appetite. Though fine at starting, we had a rather rough passage for the time of year."

The conversation terminated, and I took my departure. It was now too late to make any more calls, so I went straight to the noble mansion called Soyer's House—a real kiosque, built of wood, very much like a cage. The proprietor was a Turkish carriage-builder, a kind of a duck of a fellow, who always retired to rest at dusk, and rose before daybreak to work. He and four bulky Turkish boys accompanied their incessant hammering by an Oriental chorus, which lasted from four till seven in the morning—their breakfast-time. We not only had the satisfaction of hearing them, but from my bed I could see them at work, through my sieve-like bedroom floor, the boards of which did not meet by about half an inch—no doubt to facilitate the ventilation of this Moslem edifice. The weather being hot, this was bearable; but the harmony of such inharmonious birds was not tolerable; so for several days, and while they were in full chorus, various accidents, in the shape of upsetting large buckets of water, occurred. The refreshing liquid at once found its way to the back of our illustrious landlord, and he changed his tone and air, to invoke the blessing of Mahomet upon our devoted heads: upon which I gave them to understand, through an Armenian groom, that if they dared kick up such a row, the general would turn them out of their house. After that we had less singing, but the same quantum of hammering. At all events, we were better than under canvas.

The house was very spacious: it contained nine rooms of a good size. I had left it tenanted by good company—viz., three civilian doctors—Burn, Ellis, and Howard—but found it deserted upon my return, by all but the rats and other vermin. I and my people preferred that to living and sleeping at the hospital, and, after a few days' sport, and stopping about three hundred holes, it became habitable. The landlord fortunately had the toothache, and the fat boy, to whom I gave a few piastres to hold his noise, was silent. The ablution of the other now and then with a jug of hot water kept this extraordinary establishment quiet.

If the interior of this wooden crib was not all comfort, its outside was very cheerful, and rather elegant. It had the appearance of a large Swiss chalet. Vines grew round it; and if the windows were left open, branches of cherry and mulberry trees, loaded with ripe fruit, hung above one's head as one lay in bed. The strong morning sea-breeze made the house rock like a cradle, and in shaking the trees which were planted close to the house, forced the branches in. Such was, in a few words, Soyer's House, in Cambridge Street, Scutari, so much envied by almost all, except the man himself. Five of my people had kept possession in spite of several attempts to take it by storm during my absence. It appeared that lodgings were so scarce, they wanted to take it from them.

One evening after supper, my man Julien, who possessed a first-rate tenor voice, was delighting us with the modulations of it, when suddenly the house began to shake most awfully, and the branches of the trees outside the windows entered very abruptly, and much farther than usual, sweeping off all the goblets and bottles from the table, to our great astonishment, nearly upsetting us; when our friend P. M. exclaimed, "Who is shaking the house?" Julien, who had travelled much, replied, "Don't be alarmed—it is only an earthquake."

"Only an earthquake, eh!" said P. M., bolting.

In rushing to the street he upset my Greek servant, who was entering with a bowl of blazing punch, which gave both house and man the appearance of being on fire. We saw no more of P. M. till the next day, as he said he preferred being gulped up by mother earth at one nibble to being smothered beneath the ponderous timbers of my castle. The same day the Barrack Hospital shook so much, that the patients were actually seen in a state of nudity in the barrack-yard. Several jumped through the windows; one man was killed, and the others all more or less severely injured.

Each day I devoted to various hospitals; all went well, excepting the Palace Hospital, where there were not less than forty or fifty sick officers, who were much annoyed by the indifference and neglect of their steward. When I called there, they complained to me, and invited me to try if I could not remedy it, as well as remain and dine with them. I accepted their kind invitation, and soon found where the evil lay. I informed Lord W. Paulet, Drs. Cumming and MacIlray, and Mr. Robertson, the purveyor-in-chief; and a new kitchen was built, larger than the former. A civilian cook was placed there, and, to their delight, a new steward. Everything then gave more satisfaction to the illustrious patients, who always received me with the greatest kindness—so much so, that if nature had endowed me with several appetites daily, I could have dined three or four times per diem.

Without mentioning names, I may summon as witnesses the unfortunate heroes who were at that time gathered around the invalids' table. So happy was I in their company—and I believe they were equally so in mine—that I felt perfectly ashamed at being quite well; for even the Doctor was sick, in consequence of the harassing nature of his duties; he had so much to do—which is ever the case in time of war. With reference to their former steward, whom we had christened "la prima donna Antonio," as a set-off to his trickery in supplying the invalid officers with dessert in the shape of bad ices, unripe fruit, &c.,—things not fit for weak stomachs,—he used, at the request of a few, to bring his guitar, and delight with his voice à la Veluti the ears of those whose palates he had so cruelly displeased. By the aid of a most amiable and kind lady—Mrs. Moore, who some time after died of fever, much regretted by all—I had already their comforts, and, having previously established a better system of cookery, thought I had done some good for those to whom I was so much indebted for their kind and polite attention. Though I did not remain more than three weeks at Scutari on this occasion, never, perhaps, during the whole of my martial career, was my heart so severely tried and tortured. The following letters, addressed to the metropolitan press, speak volumes:—

SCUTARI, *27th June*, 1855.

MR. EDITOR,—Three weeks have hardly elapsed since my departure from the Crimean shores, and Death, that implacable deity of the dark abode, has had to engrave upon his mournful tablet a column of names of some of the most distinguished heroes of the present day—viz., Admiral Boxer, Adjutant-General Estcourt, Sir John Campbell, Colonel Yea, Captain Lyons, General della Marmora, &c.—and W. H. Stowe, a young civilian and bright ornament of the literary world. Everyone has heard or will hear of their fame. History will relate facts, but time, as usual, will partly efface from the memory of man the cause of their martyrdom or sudden ill fate; while I—yes, I can relate, though with a sorrowful heart, the circumstances of their social position, having still on the ear a vibratory sound of their pure and candid voices, for it is only a few days since that I was amongst them, cheerfully shaking hands with them, transacting important business with some of them, partaking of the rural hospitality of others, they of mine, and overwhelmed by the kindness of all. Life then seemed proud of them; the bloom of nature was radiant upon their brows. Their eyes spoke volumes. Their hearts were as great in the devotion of the national cause, and the glory of their country, as the pure soul which has since departed from them for a better world. Every drop of their blood no longer belonged to them, but to their Queen, their country, their children—their names to posterity, their fame the beacon to future generations of immortality.

They breathe no more! Such are the chances of war, of life's uncertainty. Man proposes, and the Supreme Being disposes. Instead of cheerful anecdotes, which a few weeks ago I could have related of those noble departed, I must here, for the present, cast a tenebrous veil over such earthly frivolity, and implore Providence to bestow a better fate upon the still great and noble and brave army.

With the most profound respect, I have the honour to remain,

Your most obedient servant,

A. SOYER.

P.S. By the next steamer I shall return to the Camp to join the staff I have just sent there, and terminate, I trust with success, my culinary mission, and then return to the shores of Albion.

H.M.S.V. "Caradoc," CONSTANTINOPLE, *5th July*, 1855.

Mr. Editor,—Scarcely has the seal of my late painful communication had time to set, when the rocky shores of the Black Sea are moaning and re-echoing the solemn report of the minute-gun, while the foaming current of the Bosphorus is rapidly carrying to the snowy white cliffs of Albion the remains of a really great man, Field Marshal the Lord Raglan. To him, above all, I cannot but feel most grateful for the success of my undertaking in the Crimea. The last kind word and smile I received while at the seat of war were from that noble martyr to his country's cause.

With the highest consideration, I have the honour to be,

Your most obedient servant,

A. SOYER.

P.S. The great desire of paying the last tribute of respect to the remains of that noble and brave warrior has delayed for a few days my departure for the Crimea.

One morning I had a serious discussion with one of my workmen, who declined to cook any more for the hospitals unless I gave him the same wages as my head man, Julien, in whom I placed all my confidence, having known him for years as an honest, industrious, and well-educated man. He was much respected by all in the hospital: Lord William Paulet made much of him, as also did Dr. Cumming, Mr. Robertson, purveyor-in-chief, and, above all, Miss Nightingale and Mr. Bracebridge, for his attention to business and polite manners.

I had left a hundred pounds in his care till next morning, having that day to go to Pera about the printing of my hospital receipts. Upon my return, I learnt that he had disappeared, taking the money with him, except twenty pounds, which he gave to one of the boys: the remainder he afterwards returned. No one knew where he was gone. My first thought was to return to the hospital, and superintend the kitchen department in person. Everything must, I knew, be in great confusion, producing upon the people employed under him much the same effect as the similar defection of a general would on the eve of a battle; and such a battle, too—one that must be fought daily, with the greatest resolution.

It is indeed a question of life and death, that brave dinner-time. So long as we get it regularly, we think nothing about it; but let one day pass without satisfying those imperious natural wants—what do I say?—one day! Even an hour's delay causes us to make several inquiries—half-an-hour, ten minutes—ay, and even less. Now, suppose I had not, by the merest chance in the world, been apprised of his departure, or had I been ill, and incapable of replacing him and his subordinates, who thought to frighten me by requiring the same wages—which, had they behaved themselves well, I might have granted;—had anything gone wrong, which could not fail in either of those events to be the case, my name and reputation would have been perilled. Thanks, however, to my lucky star, although I have experienced an immense deal of trouble in my various undertakings, I have invariably succeeded in the end. This is one of the hundreds of tribulations and disappointments I met with during my Eastern mission.

A few days after my arrival at Scutari, I had the pleasure of being introduced to the Pacha, who was also Governor of Asia Minor. At a dinner given to him by the colonel and officers of the 11th Hussars, to which I was invited, we had for dragoman or interpreter her Majesty's messenger, the worthy Mr. Webster. The banquet was given at the humble, dilapidated, and almost decapitated restaurant of Sir Demetri, it being partly unroofed. Demetri, a Greek by birth and name, was a most obliging man. He spoke French, Russian, and English remarkably well, and was much esteemed by all the gentlemen who knew him. I am sorry to say that his followers did not merit the same commendation. British Scutarians, I humbly appeal to your grateful conscience for the former.

To be brief, the Pacha was received in the same room where, a few days previous, we had vainly attempted to sleep. Our most excellent friend and ally, the son of the Prophet, having quaffed with delight and common sense the limpid liquid which takes its birth in France or any other country, but which, for all that, is called champagne, became very witty and cheerful—in fact, good company,—we all felt much interested in the description he gave of his stormy career, which put me very much in mind of that of Ali Baba or the Forty Thieves. His glory seemed to centre in those serious, though childish tales. But, in spite of all eccentricities, the Pacha was amiable and very good company. His health was proposed, with twice the number of his tales, to which he very fervently and cleverly replied, according to our learned interpreter's report. The evening closed very merrily. We parted, and our illustrious guest left, followed by his numerous suite. The farewell having taken place, the guests evaporated like a light cloud in the atmosphere.

We heard next day that some of the party belonging to the Light Infantry were found herborizing in most profound silence upon the greensward which surrounds the Sultan's mosque before the Barrack Hospital. No doubt, they had changed their mind on their way home, and preferred staying out to trying unsuccessfully to find their home—the weather being so very hot.

A few days after, all the guests paid their respectful duty to the Pacha. I was one of the last, and having my dragoman with me, was very kindly received by his pachaship, who informed me of his intention to return the compliment of the dinner given to him by Colonel Peel and party upon their return, as they had left the next morning for the Crimea. According to Turkish politeness, I had no sooner entered than all rose from their seats. There were about seven officers with the Pacha, and I was offered the seat next to him. A richly-ornamented chibouque was presented, and of course accepted; various sherbets, lemonade, sweetmeats, and snow-water were handed round in vermeil vases, and gracefully poured into glittering cups.

The conversation was specially directed to me by the Pacha himself. My dragoman carefully translated what was said, and informed me of all that was going on, and what I was to do. It happened to be the time of the Ramadan, and all the minarets were illuminated. I was remarking to the Pacha what an extraordinary and beautiful effect Constantinople and its mosques illuminated produced upon a European, when suddenly the following cry was heard from the street: "Ingan var Scutari!" A regular panic seized upon all present; and they immediately started to their feet. The Pacha took me by the hand; and while he was giving his orders, my dragoman quickly informed me it was the cry of fire, but I was on no account to take my hand from that of the Pacha. I inquired where the fire was? "I don't know," he replied; "somewhere in the town. You had better say goodnight, as the Pacha must be present."

The Pacha was now giving his orders fiercely, which I could find, not only by the perpetual motion of his tongue, but by the nervous and strong feeling of agitation of his hand, as he made me walk up and down the large saloon five or six times without even looking at me.

The horses were ready, when a fireman, wet through, arrived, and requested the Pacha not to disturb himself, as the fire was already nearly extinguished. All immediately re-entered in order, except myself, as I wanted to be off.

"No," said the Pacha; "sit down; we must have a second chibouque, and a round of coffee."

Though I did not taste it, I must say I never in my life so much appreciated the offer of a cup of coffee as I did this, which procured the release of my hand, so long a prisoner in that of the Turkish magistrate. Smoking a second chibouque made me feel rather sick, so I requested my dragoman to thank the Pacha for his kind reception, and say that as I was going to the Crimea in a few days, I would do myself the pleasure of paying him a visit before my departure for England. These words being interpreted to him, the first thing he did was to arrest me again, but luckily not by the same hand. He then spoke very fast to my dragoman, who informed me that the Pacha wished me to go with him as far as lower Scutari. It was one of their great Ramadan nights; he was obliged to go, and would esteem it a favour if I could accompany him.

"With all my heart!" was my reply, as I really wished to witness the religious ceremony of the Ramadan.

Ten horses were waiting for the Pacha, and my dragoman informed me that his highness was anxious to do me the Turkish honours, and would walk hand in hand with me through the town. Bowing respectfully to his highness, I begged Mr. Mason (a Greek and my dragoman) to say that I should be delighted with the honour—that I much appreciated the extreme politeness and kind intention of his highness.

We then started, the Pacha taking my hand, preceded by six men, bearing five large lanterns, and a glass one with three bougies in it. Behind came his suite, composed of about ten gentlemen; next, the chiboukshis and the horses. Mason, my man, was of course close to me to interpret what the Pacha said, which, however, was of no great importance. Our brilliant *cortège* slowly wended its way through the dense crowd at lower Scutari. Everyone stopped and bowed respectfully to the Pacha. Still holding my hand, he presented me to the assembled crowd. My dragoman here observed, "By seeing the Pacha on foot, and holding you by the hand, all are aware you must be a high personage, and a respected friend of his excellency." Hearing this, and seeing the soldiers at the various stations go through their military evolutions as we stopped before them, I really began to fancy I was a great man. Thanks to my common sense, I recollected the humble part I had to play on life's great stage, and could I at the time have obtained possession of my left hand (which my illustrious friend had retained in his own from his door to the spot where we were then standing, a distance of more than two miles), I should have shaken hands with myself, exclaiming, in the words of Shakespeare,* "Richard's— no! Soyer's himself again!"

This was indeed a splendid soirée, and could I spare space, the extraordinary scenes I witnessed while going the rounds of magisterial duty with the Pacha would of themselves make a very interesting chapter. Our progress came to an end at a confectioner's shop, the largest and principal one in Scutari. Here sherbet, coffee and chibouques, iced lemonade, sweets, and all kinds of fruit in season, were handed to us, as we sat upon the divans in open view to the public, a great crowd having been attracted to the spot.

Numbers entered and saluted the Pacha, and retired. His pachaship having inquired if I would take anything else, Mr. Mason replied in the negative. He then said that he was obliged to remain out all night on his magisterial duty, and that he wished me the repose of the dead till morning.

In return for this lively desire, I wished him the night of the living, and we parted. Two lantern-chibougies preceded us, by his order; our horses followed; and about an hour after, we dismissed our Jack-o'-lanterns with rather a comfortable baksheesh.

It was striking three, and the sentry refused to let Mason enter the Barrack

* Soyer is mistaken, this comes from Cibber's Richard III, not Shakespeare's—AB

Hospital, where he was quartered. I offered him a lodging at my house, which he accepted. Though very late, we arrived in time to scare two thieves away over the garden wall; and in stumbling over a basket, we perceived their booty consisted of only a few cherries and mulberries, nothing being deranged or stolen from the house.

Having frequently visited the General Hospital and Kululee, and as the time for my second voyage to the Crimea was approaching, I requested Lord W. Paulet, who was always very desirous of seeing everything himself, to pay one more official visit to the various hospitals, which he agreed to do, and fixed a day for that purpose. He also informed me that the Duke of Newcastle was expected daily. Miss Nightingale had almost recovered, and had recommenced her assiduous exertions.

My long-expected field stoves had arrived. I made a trial with them before the military and medical authorities, which succeeded admirably, even surpassing my expectations in all respects. I was more anxious than ever to return to the Crimea, and make my grand experiment before General Simpson; and, if approved of by the authorities, to have the proper number ordered by Government for the supply of the whole army, reform the old system, and introduce my new one. The stoves would of course require an outlay at first, which would soon be saved in the great economy of fuel and transport, and the small number of men required, independently of the immense improvement in cookery, which was at first the only object I had in view.

Lord W. Paulet's visit took place, as agreed upon, about three days previous to the arrival of the Duke of Newcastle. He found everything in good order, and I was much pleased. A few days after, I was, owing to the sudden departure of my head man, Julien, busily engaged at my forges, surrounded by my soldiers, like a modern Vulcan, dressed in my culinary attire, and in the act of manupulating some hundreds of *mock rice puddings* (made without eggs or milk—see receipt in Addenda) for my numerous convalescent guests, the brave British, when suddenly my kitchen was filled with military gentlemen of all ranks, amongst whom was no less a personage than the late Minister-at-war, the Duke of Newcastle, Lord W. Paulet, and numerous other high officials—military, medical, and civil. His Grace, setting all etiquette aside, advanced towards me, his hat in one hand, and kindly offered me the other, saying, "How are you, Monsieur Soyer? it is a long time since we had the pleasure of meeting."

"True," I replied; "not since I had the pleasure of seeing your Grace, then Lord Lincoln, at the Reform Club."

"You are right, Monsieur Soyer; you have an excellent memory."

Though my present occupation was one of the humblest in the category of my art,—viz., making puddings for the soldiers, still the kind condescension of his Grace, and the complimentary remarks he made upon my services, caused me to feel more proud of my humble occupation than I did when I was dressing the great Ibrahim Pacha fête at the Reform Club, in the year 1846, or preparing my hundred-guinea dish at the York banquet, in the year 1850.

The Duke of Newcastle was not the first nobleman of his high rank who had honoured me with that degree of favour; but the others had a certain interest in so doing. For instance, while at the Reform Club, a number of epicures used to pay me visits, shake me heartily by the hand, and most cordially inquire about my health. These had, I always considered, a twofold object in view: first, to induce me to give them the best of dinners; secondly, to ascertain whether I was feverish or in good health. In the former case they would postpone their dinner-party for a few days, or else try to persuade me to follow the plan of the celebrated Marquis de Coucy, one of the greatest French epicures of the nineteenth century, who never engaged a cook without having a written agreement, giving him power to compel him to take medicine a couple of days before he gave any of his grand dinners, which never exceeded twelve in the Paris season. Extra pay was allowed for this pleasant concession on the part of the *chef de cuisine*, who no doubt turned the funds to *tisane*—most probably, *tisane de champagne*.

In the present case, his Grace had no such object in view, as I had nothing to offer him but soldiers' hospital rations, diets, &c., composed of beef-tea, mutton-broth, rice puddings, &c., and my new biscuit-bread, which had been made three months, having the date of baking stamped upon it. I drew the Duke's attention to this, and then broke a little into some mutton-broth; and in five minutes it had all the appearance of a piece of fresh bread soaked in broth. In its dry state, it was much more agreeable to eat than the usual biscuit. His Grace was highly pleased with it, and advised me to recommend its adoption to the War Office upon my return to London.

The kitchen was by this time full of officers and medical men, come to pay their respects to the Duke, forming a numerous escort as he went round the hospital. I gave a short account of my proceedings since my arrival at Scutari, where I had closed all the kitchens but this one, minutely explaining all its details, as well as the plan I had adopted to keep it so clean and so cool; at which the Duke was much struck. Cooking was done daily in it for more than one thousand men, the weather being then intensely hot. After honouring me with most flattering compliments, the Duke and party retired. Lord William kindly informed me that the Duke would visit the other hospitals in a day or two, and that he would give me due notice of his visit. Accordingly, two days afterwards, we showed the Duke over the General, Hyder Pacha, and the Palace Hospitals, with the arrangements of which he expressed himself satisfied.

A few days after, the Duke of Newcastle left for the Crimea, but, prior to his departure, honoured me with the following letter:—

MESSERIE'S HOTEL, 23rd July, 1855.

DEAR M. SOYER,—Accept my best thanks for the copy of your book.

Your philanthropic labours in this country deserve the thanks of every Englishman, and for one I am grateful for what I have seen of your good work at Scutari.

I am, yours very truly,

NEWCASTLE.

At length I found two tolerably good cooks, and re-established everything in the culinary department to my satisfaction. My presence being no longer required, I prepared for my departure. I had taught about a dozen soldiers my system of camp-cooking and the use of my new field stoves. I also engaged a French Zouave, named Bornet, belonging to the 3rd Regiment, whose term of service was just out. He was to act as my aide-de-camp, écuyer, master of the horse, and shield, in case of blows. He knew the savate,* single-stick, sword, foil, and could box well; was a

---

* A kind of boxing using feet as well as fists—AB

capital shot and extraordinary good horseman; he could sing hundreds of songs, and very well too; had a good voice, danced excellently, and was altogether of a very happy disposition.

Among his other then unknown qualities, he was very quarrelsome; a great marauder *à la* Zouave; remarkably fond of the fair sex, in his martial way, running all over the camp after the heroic *cantinières*; and, though never drunk, seldom sober, always ready to fight anyone who he thought wished to injure or speak ill of me. In fact, he was, much against my will, my bulldog, and kept barking from morning till night. He was allowed to wear his costume for twelve months longer. In fact, my Zouave was a model of perfection and imperfection. The doctor of his regiment, who admired him for his bravery and cheerful abilities, impressed upon me that he was the man I required. "Very scarce they are," said he; "there are not more than one hundred left out of the whole regiment who began the campaign; and he is sound, although wounded at Inkermann."

Upon this strong recommendation, and having to run so much risk about the camp, as well as for the curiosity of the thing, I engaged Bornet, the Zouave; had a new costume made for him; introduced him to Lord W. Paulet, Miss Nightingale, &c. &c. Everybody found him extremely polite, good-looking, and intelligent. We bought four horses, and he had the sole command of the cavalry department. All admired his extraordinary good style of horsemanship, particularly Lord W. Paulet. Thus, the illustrious François Patifal Bornet, late of the 3rd Zouaves, was recognised as belonging to the British army. He and twelve soldiers composed the brigade of Captain Cook—a title I had assumed in the camp.

We were now ready to enter upon our campaign. I had paid my respects to Lord and Lady de Redcliffe at Therapia, and to General Vivian at Buyukderé: he was then at the Palais de Russie. In this town I and my Zouave created quite a sensation. I had adopted an indescribable costume. It seemed to have attracted John Bull's particular attention on his supposed visit to the camp. Such, at least, was the case according to the *Times* correspondent, who, in a dialogue with John Bull, says, "I beg your pardon, but who is that foreign officer in a white bournous and attended by a brilliant staff of generals—him with the blue and silver stripe down his trousers I mean, and gold braid on his waistcoat, and a red and white cap? It must be Pelissier?"

"That! why, that's Monsieur Soyer, *chef de nos batteries de cuisine*; and if you go and ask him, you'll find he'll talk to you for several hours about the way your meat is wasted. And so I wish you good morning, sir."

XXV

FESTIVITIES AT SCUTARI AND VISITS TO FRENCH HOSPITALS

PREVIOUS to entering upon this second campaign, in which my life was daily likely to be more or less in danger, my gastronomic star was, unawares to me, shining brightly. An unexpected invitation arrived from the Pacha of Scutari to a grand Oriental summer banquet, to which not less than eighty guests were invited. Lord W. Paulet was to be the chairman. The day arrived, we all met at headquarters, and the principal authorities were present. Lord W. Paulet soon joined us; we started, forming a very formidable and brilliant cavalcade, everybody being in full costume. The Pacha had sent a mounted escort to accompany us, consisting of six cavaliers. Our first halt was at Ismail Pacha's, who received us cordially at his pretty kiosque. He spoke excellent French, and invited us to be seated in his large and elegantly-furnished drawing-room, where a chibouque was presented to each guest, with the indispensable Turkish thimble-cup of coffee. We had a very interesting conversation with the Pacha about the war, and his opinion upon it; also a short review of Paris and London, as he had visited both.

We then walked under very delightful foliage, where fountains were playing, Asiatic and aquatic flowers growing—plants of rare beauty—orange and lemon trees, &c. We all fancied we had arrived at our destination, when the Pacha's horse was brought into the yard where ours had been left. The signal was given: we all mounted, and started afresh. A very coquettish square kiosque erected in the garden, and well latticed round, seemed to be very animated within. It was the Pacha's harem, from whence no doubt the imprisoned odalisques were enjoying the lively scene passing in the yard, by peeping, not exactly à la Peeping Tom, but from behind the railings, or, more properly speaking, lattice.

Headed by the Pacha and suite, with Lord W. Paulet, Major Sillery, &c., we again started. In ten minutes we reached another kiosque, not by any means so luxurious as the first. We alighted, and were received in the garden by Hiera Bey, to whom the place belonged. In the drawing-room the same ceremony of chibouques and coffee was performed. The Bey and his suite joined our party, and we went to the residence of another pacha, where the same ceremony was about to be renewed, but to which we unanimously objected. His pachaship and suite, altogether about twelve persons, also joined us, thus doubling the number of our cavalcade, which, as we passed along the narrow lane bordered on either side by thick and high hedges, had the appearance of an immense serpent stealing through the grass about to swallow its prey: the head being represented by the Oriental corps and costume, admirably suited the effect I have described. Prey was indeed in store for the imaginary serpent. Of the truth of this my reader will be able to judge by the bill of fare, which I carefully preserved, as one of my first Oriental culinary reminiscences.

The sound of strange instruments informed us that we were near our destination. A military band of about fifty were playing Oriental airs, half wild, half melodious. We were conducted through a garden towards an elegant *maison de plaisance*, leaving the horses at the entrance; some of them, not being partial to music, began fighting and kicking. It took nearly an hour to pacify them and make them behave themselves. They were horses of different nations, and this was probably the reason why they could not agree.

Several were lost, which gave a little extra occupation to the Asiatic palfreniers.* By this time we had all been received by the Governor of Asia Minor and his numerous friends, who were sitting upon divans in the open air, smoking chibouques. We were invited to do the same, which we did, forming a circle of considerable circumference. A regular forest of long chibouques was brought towards us, and one was presented to each guest. We were thus, for the third time, obliged to enjoy this everlasting Oriental splendour; but in lieu of coffee, raki was introduced, a liquor somewhat similar to perfumed gin, or the French absinthe. It more particularly resembles the latter, as it turns white when mixed with water. It is much drunk in Turkey—usually before dinner. Many prefer it neat, but it is very intoxicating. The usual salutations having been exchanged, we all drank, and the glasses were taken away by slaves.

After smoking another half-hour, I went to Mr. Dixon, Lord W. Paulet's dragoman, and asked him to request permission of the Pacha for me to see the kitchen. As I knew that two whole sheep and two lambs were to be roasted, I felt anxious to see the process. He had no sooner mentioned my wish than the Pacha rose, and, offering me his hand, conducted me towards the place where the sacrifice was being consummated. We were thus again, as at Scutari, hand-in-hand, if not hand and glove. About forty cooks were at work preparing the dinner. I felt much interested in their primitive way of roasting large pieces, which can only be equalled by gas. With the intestines they make a kind of black pudding, sausages, and rolls of tripe, with which they surround the neck of the animal: they have also skewers of tripe and liver, heart, &c., tied on each side of the haunch. The Pacha ordered some to be cut off for me to taste, which I did with great gusto, and really much approved of their sound judgment in turning everything to advantage, and making additional dishes of what we civilized people so cleverly throw away. It was so good, that I begged the Pacha to send a small dish up for Lord W. Paulet and a few others to taste, as it was best while very hot. It had a peculiar aromatic taste which imparts a delicate flavour, and was very palatable.

The liver, which we of course use, was cut into small portions, and mixed with the intestines. The lambs were dressed in the same way, and were still more delicate; they were so perfectly roasted, that every part of the animals was the colour of a lump of gold.

ORIENTAL WAY OF ROASTING SHEEP AND LAMBS WHOLE, À LA TURQUE.

Though a primitive method, it is far from being a bad one. About a hundredweight of wood is set on fire in an open place, yard, kitchen, or elsewhere, and when burnt the ashes are piled up pyramidically to about the length of the lamb. Four stones, about a foot high, are then

* Grooms—AB

placed two at each end, and about eighteen inches from the fire; the lambs are spitted, head and all, upon a long piece of wood, with a rough handle similar to that of a barrel-organ. They are then put down; each one being turned by one man, who now and then moves the ashes to revive the fire, at the same time basting the lambs with a bunch of feathers dipped in oil. A pan should be placed underneath to receive the fat. This was on this occasion omitted. Each lamb took about three hours doing by that slow process; but I must repeat, they were done to perfection, and worthy of the attention of the greatest epicure.

The productions of the other culinary dainties are duly noticed in the following gigantic bill of fare.

Cavvat alle sis ka-babby
Yeade ra-dash yor nesee
Terbelee partsha

Vegetables.

Dolmah asmae a back
Ahgem ka back yah ne see
Arabertan ham yersee
Ser kresheur kap a massee
Patlezan dol massee
Cavarta yah prai il ha doline
Bag silk massee
Guvetts tu lur soo
Eskaille keftee
Pelaffee
Puff borree
Adgec ah med borro
Bad am lee charsa

Confiture.

Baclava
Ecmeck card aikae
Yur mur tarla lock moh
Kavanne
Hi varta cleasee
Touh cleuksu
Evgbet pupered by Jorept Zetala
Parson fruture
Peti parta ougrah
Cutalette
Pura patat assause espariol
Crab miones
Puopon mohoness
Cram alla vanneil
Cram ah coffee
Vn espeak derubea
Eurotee despadree
Glass oh citrone
Glass alla cream
Turk cook mahamet
Prissole

Sarmagoll
Cheverma cugickabby
Surmah pelich ka-babby
Capammah ordack parlazee
Coccorrets ka-babby
Fassula illa tuge ka-babby
Cavoticla ahmet ka-babby
Kahoat he la sahe slam ka-babby
Kultug dol massy
Tuga yaha ne see
Sham keflasee
Rahat lokoum

Amidst a clump of trees, situated on a plot of grass, and though so close at hand, quite out of sight, a large marquee had been erected, under which an elegant banqueting-table was covered with choice fruits, flowers, pastry, valuable ornaments, and sweets of all kinds. Each guest had his place numbered. I was fortunately near the centre, facing the chairman, and only two from the worthy host. The *tout ensemble* was charming: the various costumes, profusion of light, and the Turkish music, gave such a novel feature to this liberal entertainment, that, for the first time, I began to understand the reality of the Oriental luxury so much vaunted by poets.

Wine, though abominated by the Moslem, flowed in profusion. Excellent Bordeaux, Champagne, Madeira, &c., was freely passed round and quaffed with gusto, to the number, I should say, of several gross of bottles. The children of the Crescent drank as freely as ourselves. The sheep and lambs, dressed up whole, were placed upon the table, and every guest helped himself *à la Turque*. The meat was pulled from the animal by the Hadji Bachi, with his fingers, in presence of the company, placed in a large dish, and handed round to the gourmets, who also helped themselves with their fingers. The lamb was admirable; an Apicius would have gone to Turkey to dine, had he known such delicacies were to be obtained there. That worthy left Rome in a vessel, specially chartered by him, to go to Greece, in order to obtain some crayfish rumoured to be larger than any Rome could produce. On arriving, he found they were only the same. He asked the fisherman, who had been some time expecting him, "Have you never caught larger crayfish than that?"

"No, signor, never!" was the reply.

Rubbing his hands with delight, he ordered the captain to sail back at once, saying, "I have left some at home larger than these, and they will be spoiled if the wind is not in our favour."*

* This is the ancient who, after partaking of the best dinner ever prepared, unfortunately inquired of his private secretary how his cash account stood, and finding that he had only a few millions of dollars remaining, for fear of being in future obliged to dine badly, or at least compelled to curtail his incalculable expenditure, one day dined magnificently by himself, and ordering the most luxurious banquet that Rome could boast of. On that solemn occasion, though there were enough culinary *chefs-d'œuvre* to delight an immense number of epicures, he only invited himself! "Sublime idea!" he ejaculated; "after dining like two Vitelliuses, or several Luculluses, to die in the midst of plenty!" Thereupon he swallowed poison, and was found dead at the head of his table.

The other dishes were eaten in the European fashion, with knives and forks. The fête was under the management of a gentleman I had the pleasure of knowing well, Mr. Ralli, a large proprietor at Kadikoi and a Greek merchant, who, to oblige the Pacha, took upon himself all the responsibility of carrying out his excellency's liberal ideas.

London, or even Paris, could not have produced more effect or given more *éclat* to the entertainment, though, of course, in a different style. Healths were proposed, and toasts given. The speeches were short, but to the purpose. The music was very original; the fireworks were extremely bad, and the illuminations very tenebrous.

Names of Guests at the Dinner given by the Pacha of Scutari.—Brigadier-General Lord William Paulet; Hon. Captain Macdonald; Captain Seager; Major Sillery; Major Morris; Dr. Rowdon, civil surgeon, late professor of anatomy at Middlesex Hospital; W. Heaton, Esq., medical staff; Richard Ambler, Esq.; J. S. Robertson, Esq., purveyor-general to the forces; Rev. George Lawless, senior chaplain; Rev. Hugh Drennan, chaplain; Rev. W. Fergusson, chaplain;—Hawkes, Esq., barrister-at-law; Eustatio S. Ralli, Esq., sen., Greek merchant; Etienne Eustatio Ralli, jun., Esq.; —Dixon, Esq., first-class interpreter to Lord William Paulet; Monsieur Soyer, &c. &c. Indisposition prevented the attendance of his Excellency Omer Pacha.*

After five hours of eating and drinking, we returned thanks to our illustrious host, and rose to retire. He accompanied us as far as his Scutari residence. The evening was very dark, and the horses were mixed together, so that we had some trouble in finding our own. At length we started. I was the last to quit his pachaship. As I lived in Cambridge Street, I was a near neighbour of his, and he kindly escorted me to my door, followed by his men bearing lanterns. He would not leave me till the door was opened, and I had entered the house. We then parted, and I shall never forget the generous reception I received from our worthy Mussulman ally, the governor of Asia Minor.

Before my departure, I took Lord W. Paulet, Dr. Cumming, Mr. Robertson, and Miss Nightingale's orders, which were numerous; said farewell to all, and left everything in a most satisfactory state. I requested Sergeant Thompson to send me a weekly report of the proceedings in the kitchens at the various hospitals. Mr. Robertson, the purveyor-in-chief, also promised to keep a sharp look-out himself, and acquaint me with anything important which might occur. I spent a few days with Dr. Humphrey at Kululee Hospital, then under the admirable management of Miss E. Hutton and the Sisters of Charity. Mr. and Mrs. Bracebridge, after exerting themselves to the utmost, during the hardest time of all, in the Scutari hospitals, had left for England: important family affairs, I believe, required their presence at home. Miss Nightingale had quite recovered; and she proposed to visit the Crimea again in less than a month, and had requested me to attend to various matters before she arrived. Of these, as they were numerous, I made a list, saying, "I shall be happy to attend to your commissions even if you tripled the number." As my twelve field stoves had been sent to the Crimea, I knew that my time would be principally taken up by field-cookery, and that I should only be able to give a casual look through the various hospitals.

---

* Ahmet Pacha, who speaks French, has his country residence at the *greater* Chamlija; and that of Selim Pacha, where we dined, is in the *lesser* Chamlija.

I was anxious to obtain an insight into the culinary arrangements and system of management in the French hospitals. This I effected by the aid of Dr. Pincoff, who had frequently brought French doctors to visit my kitchens, and taste my new diets—of which they seemed to approve. Some of them would say, "They are too good and expensive for our hospital;" others, "Your diets are excellent; but our soldiers would not like them, not being used to that kind of food." This, probably, might at the commencement have been the case; but a man soon gets accustomed to a good thing. I had tried this upon several hundred English soldiers, who never refused it, but, on the contrary, did not like to return to the old system of diets. I had not the slightest doubt they would like the change, but it could not be effected. At all events, this increased my curiosity. Dr. Pincoff, a friend, and myself, determined to go at six o'clock in the morning (the time of their first rounds) to visit the Great Hospital of Pera.

This early hour of visiting patients I cannot but give my disapproval of, as it is the time they are likely to repose, or at all events feel more languid than any other part of the night; which disturbance reminds me of the anxious servant, who being requested by his master to awake him at an early hour, knocked at his room-door four or five times during the night to apprise him of the number of hours he had left for sleep. Indeed, even more than this, they actually ask the patients, at that early hour, what they would like for dinner?—the patient, instead of the doctor, prescribing. We arrived at half-past five a.m., through a burning sun, which I consider, at that hour and that time of year, more oppressive in the East than at ten, eleven, or even twelve in the day, when the sea-breeze refreshes the Oriental atmosphere. We were immediately introduced to the medical gentleman on duty, who had just commenced his rounds. He was attended by two orderlies and a Sister of Charity; one of the former carried a tray, upon which the Sister seemed to have placed articles of food belonging to her department: she was also noting down on a tablet the orders of the doctor as to a few articles of extra-diet. We watched the proceedings closely, which lasted nearly an hour: each doctor had two wards to attend, and each ward contained about sixty patients.

Having made several remarks on the various subjects to the doctor, and thanked him for his attention, I promised to forward him a book of the new dietaries I had so successfully introduced in the hospital at Scutari. Though far from anticipating that any eminent member of the French faculty would change his system, and adopt mine in preference to the French medical *régime*, still, as I have learnt a great deal from the system pursued in the French hospitals, I should feel very proud if any of my receipts proved acceptable. In fact, I should be delighted to show my gratitude for the generous reception afforded me when I applied for leave to visit the French hospitals upon my passage through France on my way to the Crimea.

The order with which all was carried on was admirable. Without the slightest intention of making myself officious in this matter, I cannot help remarking, that the broths and tisanes given to the patients were rather of a thinnish nature, and given in much larger quantities than by the English doctors to patients affected with similar diseases;—my opinion on the subject being, that for the man who has lived too well, a close and light diet is most beneficial, his blood being too rich; while the debilitated soldier's blood requires regenerating: which caused me to submit succulent diets for dysentery and diarrhœa, and cooling ones for fever.

XXVI

MY SECOND TRIP TO THE CRIMEA

Two days later, I and my people started on board the *Ottawa*. The day of our departure was magnificently fine; the Bosphorus and Black Sea looked like a sheet of glass. I remarked to the captain, "One might cross the Black Sea in a caique."

"Yes," he replied, "in its present state; but who knows how soon we may have it dancing mountains high? I have seen it so before; and where would you be with your caique then, Monsieur Soyer?"

"Of course, you are right, captain; but I suppose it is not often thus at this time of the year."

"Even at this time of year, I should be sorry to be one of the caidjees."

Captain Bone was a very agreeable man—high-bred—educated at Oxford—well stored with *bons mots* and good anecdotes—always laughing at other people's jokes as well as his own—very severe on deck and very funny with his friends. He kept a good cook, and therefore a good table, looking sharply after it himself—spending, probably, no more money than other captains, but faring better—very anxious to please passengers—and at all times very liberal. The proverb says, "Speak of a man as you find him;" and in this manner I speak of the worthy captain.

The ship was very full, especially of recovered invalids from Scutari. Numbers of doctors from Rankioi and Smyrna were on board, on their way to the Crimea, where their services were required. I had engaged a young Sardinian named Antonio, a good-looking youth with a very good voice. As the evening was fine, he and my Zouave began singing, which they did admirably, everyone joining in chorus. Thus we spent a delightful soirée on the bosom of the Black Sea.

P. M., who by this time was becoming quite a brave man, still formed part of my suite. That gentleman's intrepidity was such, that no one could prevent him from facing at all times the most animated fire—I mean the fire of a short pipe or a long cigar. My Zouave was everywhere about the vessel, which did not seem large enough for him and his four horses. I at last quieted him, by requesting he would think of nothing while on board but eating and drinking moderately, as well as singing a song at night when I required it. He promised faithfully not to throw my Armenian groom overboard, nor to smash the brains of my Italian servant Antonio, but to live like a Christian, in good fellowship with all, and sing when I pleased. One of my cooks, named Jean, an Albanian, while quarrelling, had threatened to cut another, named Victor, into four pieces, and throw them into a pickle tub. He also gave up this professional job. They all shook hands, and the greatest harmony appeared to reign in my culinary troop.

My secretary, T. G., a gentleman of colour, now accompanied me for the second time to the Crimea; and the contrast presented by us, myself being equipped in an Oriental costume, T. G. clothed in white, and my Zouave rigged in full feather, was very great; and my suite always created a sensation throughout the camp, more especially when accompanied by the invincible P. M., who was attired in nankeen, a very peculiar style, he being an extensive patronizer of the eminent firm of Messrs. Nicoll.

All on board the *Ottawa* had for some time retired to their berths. I can seldom sleep at sea; so I was sitting on deck, smoking my cigar, now and then addressing a word to the man at the wheel and the second mate. We praised the fineness of the weather: the upper deck was as steady as a drawing-room floor, and the ocean seemed to belong to us alone.

It was nearly one o'clock, and Morpheus, who generally deserts me on such occasions, stole upon me softly like a zephyr. I felt inclined to submit, and went below to lie down. Wrapped in deep repose, I seemed to quit this world of realities, and to wander in the regions of dream-land. This continued till seven in the morning, when a tremendous crash awoke me suddenly, and I perceived that we were dancing mountains high.

The crash was caused by two glasses and a bottle of soda-water, belonging to my companion P. M. in the upper berth. They had been left upon the wash-hand stand; both glasses were smashed, and the bottle broken, with a tremendous report, making me fear that in the night we had, by mistake, approached too near to Sebastopol, and were being fired into by the batteries. Turning round, I perceived the supposed enemy on the cabin floor in a fearful state of dilapidation—the bottom of the soda-water bottle rolling to and fro, according to the will of the waves, which, it appeared, had risen to that pitch in an incredibly short space of time—a thing common enough in the Euxine, or Black Sea.

"Good heavens!" exclaimed P. M., "where are we?"

"Don't be alarmed," said I. "We are under fire; every man to his gun; so let us go up on deck and fight like Britons."

"The devil we are! Oh dear, I can't fight, I am so sick."

"Then you must swim or sink."

In less than a minute he rushed from the cabin, and concealed himself under the large dinner-table.

As I was dressed, I went upon deck.

"At half-past five," said the mate on duty, "it began to rain, and the wind suddenly changed. At seven o'clock, a gust of wind actually bent the sails across the yards, taking us dead aback; and in less than an hour, the sea rose to the state you see it in now."

The captain, who was giving his orders from the cross-bridge, called out to me, laughing, "Well, Monsieur Soyer, where is your caique now? Are you ready for your breakfast?"

Of course I was, though I could not boast of having much appetite. The remaining part of the passage was very rough. The *Ottawa* rolled very much, having, if I recollect right, shot and shell for ballast. The contrast afforded by the sudden change from the calm of the previous day, no doubt caused us to feel its effects the more. At all events, we arrived in due time quite safe. An unexpected bad passage at all times makes everybody feel uneasy and low-spirited. The nearer I approached Balaklava, the more uneasy I felt. A kind of melancholy had come over me, and my feelings were so indescribable, that while we were entering the harbour of Balaklava, I was surprised to see the sun shining over that picturesque spot, and traffic going on as usual. Instead of a lugubrious veil hanging over the whole fleet, all was going on pretty much in the same manner as when I had left. Even nature seemed to have smiled upon the hills, valleys, and mountains, which were gayer than before.

Such a scene caused me to breathe more freely. I felt that the noble departed, who but a few days before were in enjoyment of health, honour, power, and rank, had been removed by their gracious Creator, and therefore, though Lord Raglan, Admiral Boxer, Sir J. Campbell, General Estcourt, and numbers of other great men, had been called away during my short absence, they were only summoned from this world—so, at least, we are bound to believe—to fulfil their mission in another and a better sphere.

On the day of our arrival, I paid my respects to several great personages, who, on account of the sad events before mentioned, were mostly newcomers, although they knew me either personally or by name. It was like beginning my mission afresh, making it not only very painful as far as feelings went, but also difficult. It was something like being compelled to build an edifice which had fallen to the ground when near its completion.

Such were my feelings upon my arrival on my second visit to the Crimea. As I could only remain a couple of days on board the *Ottawa*, as she was to return immediately to Constantinople, I employed my time in settling my plan of campaign.

First of all, I paid my respects to Admiral Freemantle, on board the *Leander*, and I was very kindly received. Next I went to Sir George Maclean, the new Commissary-General; and a more amiable gentleman I did not meet during my mission in the Crimea. He informed me that the dry vegetables from Messrs. Chollet had arrived, and that some had already been issued to the troops, and were highly approved of. I requested an order to go and inspect them in the stores, with which I was immediately favoured.

Having executed all Miss Nightingale's commissions, as well as others, the next morning I started early for headquarters, and arrived there about nine. Much important business was going on at the time. A number of horses, foaming with perspiration, were in the yard, the despatch-riders having no doubt quite forgotten that the success which attended their mission was owing to their poor quadrupeds. I was at once received by Colonel Steele, who was much pleased to see me. After expressing our regret at the lamentable events which had occurred since our last meeting, we entered upon business.

"Well, Monsieur Soyer," said the colonel, "if you like to wait, you can see General Simpson; but, as tomorrow is Sunday, he will be able to grant you a longer interview. Today he could not spare ten minutes."

"Much obliged, colonel," I replied; "and I will not fail to be here tomorrow at ten, as you advise."

"Very well, Monsieur Soyer; I shall be here, and happy to see you."

My Zouave, whom I had brought with me, had disappeared, leaving word with the man at the entrance-hall that he would return in ten minutes, but that he could not resist paying a visit to his old comrades, who were encamped that day at the French headquarters. He was *en petit costume*, as I did not wish him to attract too much attention. I expected, when I learnt he had gone, that the ten minutes would be doubled and tripled, and probably extend to hours: I therefore made up my mind to go about my business in the different hospitals and regiments. First of all, I visited Dr. Hall, the authorities, and my friends round headquarters.

In the afternoon I returned, but no Zouave had been seen. A note was handed to me by the canteen-man, worded thus:—

MY DEAR GOVERNOR,—Your humble servant, Bornet the Zouave, is half drunk, and will feel much obliged if you will allow him to get quite so. He has met with a few old comrades, who very likely will not last much longer than the others who have died for their country.

Upon receipt of this, having nothing better to do, I started for the French head-quarters. I soon found the regiment. This was not enough—I wanted my man. My next inquiry was for the canteen, quite sure that the cantinière, whether blonde or brunette, no matter which, would have heard of him. It turned out as I had antici-pated, and, not giving me time to ask twice, she said, "Yes, Monsieur, he is here—the dear fellow!" And so he was, fast asleep. He no sooner awoke and saw me, than he came and apologized, seemingly almost sober. I say seemingly, for all at once he began to sing and dance like a madman, harmoniously introducing me to his friends, whom I had the pleasure of shaking cordially by the hand.

Some of these recollected my former visit, so I begged of them to sit down. At the same time I offered them something to drink. The liquid material—viz., two quarts of wine and one of rum—with tin cups, was brought, and the French and Jamaica nectar was poured out, with a certain elegance and graceful smile, by the Crimean Bacchante, to these reckless children of Mars. In a short time many of them had fallen in the dreadful struggle. They were *enfants perdus*, and were all singing different tunes and dancing different steps.

The cantinière was elegantly dressed in her Zouave uniform, ready for starting to the trenches: she wore a red gown, and trousers of the same material, a jacket like that worn by the men, and a red fez cap with a long tassel. She carried a stoup full of spirits, a large basket of provisions, and followed her companions like a trooper.

The Zouaves gave me a pressing invitation to go and see them perform, which I promised to do that day week. They were perfectly satisfied, though I was not at all, with my Zouave, Bornet. As he was not fit to follow me, I gave him up, and, after seeing his horse right and him wrong, I left him, and started alone for Balaklava, returning in solemn solitude to my nautical home—the *Ottawa*.

At six the next morning he was on board, busily engaged preparing for our departure, so soon as a spot could be selected in the camp for us to pitch our tents. The horses were landed, and my military pupils sent to different quarters, and set to work cooking. I retained three with me for the opening of my field-kitchens. As I approached my deserter, the Zouave, in order to reprimand him for his conduct the preceding day, he remarked, by way of apology, "I know, mon cher governor, what you are going to say—that is, if I play you any more such tricks, you will not keep me, as we agreed when you engaged me."

"Certainly not," said I.

"We will begin fresh today; but yesterday, you see, governor, the temptation was too strong for me. When I saw my old comrades Riflard and France Chatbeau, Panaudet, et la cantinière—Beni Zoug Zoug—des vieuz amis de la tente, with whom I had braved all dangers, and so few of us left—not more than fourteen or fifteen of our company—why, voyez-vous, it carried me away, and I could not help standing the picton (which means something to drink), like a Frenchman and a man. And what a fine lass la petite Mère Jouvin is! Don't she look well in her Zouave dress?"

"Certainly, but did she go to the trenches?"

"Of course she did. She was on duty last night. Her husband goes one night, and she the other."

"Did you see her this morning?"

"I did. The darling had just returned for more liquor. She told me they had a kind of sortie, and for twenty minutes were peppering one another like fun, and no mistake. Rabbit-shooting, governor—rabbit-shooting! We lost about seventeen men, besides the wounded. But that's nothing. Last year I saw three times as many knocked over in a sort of skirmish which only lasted ten minutes. We were half frozen and partly starved; and hundreds were found dead or nearly frozen, lying under shelter of those who had been shot, endeavouring to warm themselves before the bodies got cool."

"Pray, Bornet, don't recall those things to my mind: they are too painful; but, after all, are only the chances of war, and must be endured."

"Well, governor," said he, while cording a large box, "you have gained the esteem of the 3rd Zouaves; and should you require the services of the whole regiment, could it be spared, you would have them, including la petite Mère Jouvin."

In uttering the last word he gave an extra pull at the rope, which caused it to break, and bang went my Zouave flat upon his back. A general laugh was heard upon deck. He picked himself up quickly, and, rubbing his back, said, "By the explosion of a thousand shells, here is a stunning piece of straw."

A gentleman present asked him if he had hurt himself. "Very well" he replied, being all the English he knew, except "yes" and "no."

Seeing everybody laugh, he went on working at the box, and singing his favourite refrain—

> J'aime le vin, l'amour et la gaîté,
> Les plaisirs, la gloire,
> Et je suis, sans vanité,
> L'enfant de la gaîté.

I perceived some spots of blood on his shirt-sleeve, and pointed them out to him. "Oh," said he, "that's no novelty. I've seen a sample of my blood before this, many times."

On pulling up his sleeve, we found a deep scratch in his arm, from which the blood flowed pretty freely.

"You had better have it attended to," said I.

"Bah! bah! nonsense! We Zouaves never trouble anyone, particularly the doctor, about such trifles. Be kind enough to tie my pocket-handkerchief round it."

This done, he kept at his work. Thus I discovered the determined character of these wild soldiers. They made up their minds to care for nothing—were ready either to fight or sing—be out all night without sleep, or comfortable under their tents—were content with much to eat and drink, or little—but so long as they had sufficient to sustain life, be gay, or at least appear so—never making a direct complaint, whatever might happen to them. In fact, though French soldiers like the rest of the army, they had created themselves a body of invincibles, and a company of very odd fellows, who would at all times much prefer robbing a man to wronging him; this being one of their mottoes:—"Nous aimons mieux voler que faire du tort."

All on board the *Ottawa* was bustle and confusion. Although not half unloaded, they were receiving the sick, expecting to sail the same evening. We were busy removing to the *Baraguay d'Hilliers*. She was a transport, and full of hospital provisions. Captain Heath advised me to select her, as she was the vessel likely to remain the longest in harbour, and I should require a *pied à terre* in Balaklava. Under the direction of my Zouave, all our luggage was soon put on board; and about ten o'clock he was in full dress, it being Sunday. The horses were ready, and we started for headquarters.

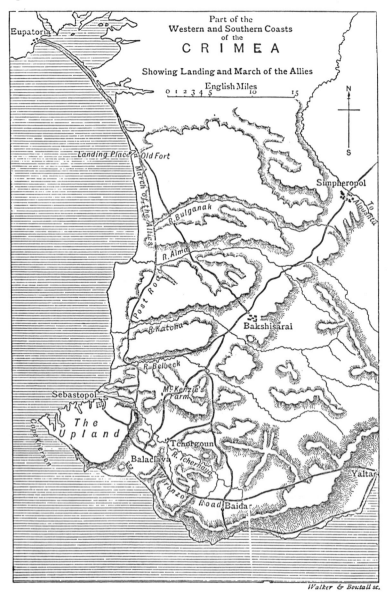

Part of the
Western and Southern Coasts
of the
CRIMEA

Showing Landing and March of the Allies

Walker & Boutall sc.

XXVII

CAMP LIFE AT HEAD-QUARTERS

As Bornet was a dashing cavalier and a very good horseman, he created quite a sensation in Kadikoi, and upon our arrival before the Sardinian headquarters, General della Marmora and staff came upon the balcony to look at him. He saluted the general, who appeared much surprised to see a Zouave on horseback in my suite, and not wearing the exact costume of that corps, as I had made some stylish improvement in it, in order to distinguish him from the common soldiers.

As I had to see General Simpson about eleven o'clock, off we went at full gallop, being rather short of time. Mrs. Seacole, who was at her door with her daughter Sarah, had only time to call out, "Go it, my sons!" as we rattled past the house. We arrived in due time, and I saw Colonel Steele, who told me that General Simpson would be happy to receive me directly, and at once conducted me to his audience-chamber. The new Commander-in-chief rose politely as I entered, shook me by the hand, and invited me to be seated. I had previously left a letter for him from Lord William Paulet respecting my mission, and I showed two I had received from the War Office, in which the Minister-at-War expressed in flattering terms his approbation of them.

After the usual compliments of a first interview, General Simpson told me that he had read the letter with great interest, and would give me all the assistance in his power to enable me to carry out my project, which was, first, to make a trial before the commander-in-chief, the generals and officers of the army, Dr. Hall, &c. &c. If on that occasion my new system was approved of, it was my intention to introduce the same for the benefit of the army at large. To this General Simpson gave his assent, saying, "You have only, Monsieur Soyer, to tell me what you require."

"First of all, general, that you should select a spot where the trial can take place, and name a regiment with which I can begin."

"You will require a building for your kitchen."

"Not at all, general—no masons, carpenters, nor engineers. My stoves are adapted for the open air, to cook in all weathers, and to follow the army."

"I am aware of that, as I saw the model when you were here last."

"Exactly. All I shall require will be three bell-tents for myself and assistants, as I must reside in the camp."

"Very well; I will give orders to that effect."

"I would also recommend you to select a regiment near headquarters for your own convenience in visiting and watching the progress of the kitchens."

"I think the Guards in the First Division will suit our purpose best. Do you know where they are?"

"I do; but perhaps you will be kind enough to send some official with me to select the spot."

"We will ride over this afternoon. You had better dine with us this evening. You know the greater part of the gentlemen of my Staff; and those you do not, know you."

"Many thanks, general, for your kind invitation, which I accept with the greatest pleasure."

"Have you anything in that parcel to show me?"

"Yes; one of my new bread-biscuits, which I wish you to taste."

On opening the parcel, he took it out, saying, "Lord bless you! this will be too hard for my teeth."

"Not so hard as you think. It is much softer than the ordinary biscuit which it is intended to replace. At any rate, it may be issued in turn, and will afford an excellent change for the troops. I have kept some above three months, and they are quite good. The Duke of Newcastle tasted one of them, and was much pleased with it."

Having broken a piece off and tasted it, the general partook of some and found it very good, though not nearly so hard as he anticipated. He declared that it was much more palatable than the common biscuit, and that he quite enjoyed it. General Simpson was at that time very unwell, and he seldom ate anything but arrowroot and biscuit soaked in boiling water. I tasted some of his fare, and found it tolerably good, but not nutritive enough for a man who worked hard. He informed me that he was often occupied eight or ten hours a day writing. As his complaint was diarrhœa, I proposed boiling some plain rice after the receipt given in Addenda, which was at all times so much approved of by the doctors. This I did the next day. The general took a great deal of bodily exercise in the camp and in the trenches.

On quitting General Simpson, I paid my respects to General Eyre, with whom I had some business to transact. He was then at the head of the Ordnance Office, and General Simpson had referred me to him for all I might require from that department. The general gave me a very kind reception, and granted all that I required. Having two hours to spare, I made up my mind to go to the French camp or headquarters. I had not had the pleasure of seeing General Pelissier since he received the appointment of commander-in-chief. As I was going out, I met General Jones, the engineer.

"Do you recollect, Monsieur Soyer, where we met last?"

Aware that the General—now Sir John Jones—was the siege and trench engineer, I thought that he referred to my wild expedition when I lost my way in the blood-stained labyrinth. I was, however, quite mistaken. He informed me that it was in Ireland, when I opened my kitchens in the year 1847. I then recollected the circumstance, as I had myself shown him round the kitchens, and explained the method and the process of cooking by steam for ten thousand people, if required, with only one furnace, and by means of steam-pipes connected with a double boiler—a plan, I believe, still in use in many large governmental and civil institutions.*

I gave Sir John to understand what great pleasure it afforded me to hear of such

---

* That kitchen was put up at the South Union Workhouse, where no doubt it still remains. In some institutions steam tubes have since been introduced into the boiler amongst the food. This, I beg to say, forms no part of my plan, as has been publicly reported. I disapprove of the system altogether, for many reasons, which it would be out of place to discuss in this work.

reminiscences, and inquired if he intended to go for a ride as far as the First Division.

"No, Monsieur Soyer," said he, "I don't think I can. In fact, I have to be in the trenches, where I shall be happy to see you when you have fixed upon the spot for your field-kitchens."

"I thank you, general for your kind invitation, but would rather see you out of them, and a good distance off, particularly as a person is more exposed to the fire of the enemy on entering or leaving than when inside."

Finding that I had hardly time to go as far as the French headquarters, I went to the kitchen and inquired what there was for dinner. The *chef* was named Nicolo, and had lived with Sir George Brown.

The horses were at the door in readiness for the general. All the Staff were in attendance before the house, some sitting on the steps, others standing. Among them were Generals Barnard and Airey, Colonels Steele and Blane, Captains Colville, Lindsay, &c., with whom I conversed upon various matters, especially upon my long stay at the Reform Club. General Barnard, as usual, was very talkative and witty.

When Colonel Steele saw General Simpson coming, he called to me to mount, and a few minutes after we set off to the First Division. On our way, we conversed upon various topics, particularly respecting a poor fellow named Harvey, who had been shot in his tent during the night. A ball from one of the enemy's long-rangers had fractured both his legs, and he died a few hours after receiving the wound. The most remarkable part of the occurrence, as I told the General, was this:—The person who usually occupied the spot got drunk the night before, and was put in the guardhouse: this saved his life. The ball made a hole about two feet deep at the very spot where he generally slept, every inch of room being turned to account in the tents. He must have been smashed to atoms, had he been there. The man who was killed had his legs close to this spot, and the shot falling in a slanting direction, cut them both off. The general said he had heard that a man had been killed during the night, but that he was not aware of the circumstances.

"On my way to the General Hospital," I continued, "in the morning, I saw the tent and the place where the cannon-ball fell. I have the piece of canvas the shot passed through; it was given me by Dr. Taylor of the Third Division, who took me to see it. It bears the name of the man killed and the date of the accident. The doctor, after cutting out the piece which was hanging to the tent, wrote the particulars upon it himself. I will show it to you this evening, general. My man has the relic with him."

Some officers came and conversed with the general for a short time while we were before the Guards' camp. On the esplanade the men were parading for the trenches; there might have been four companies. The general spoke to the commanding officers, and they all started. A detachment of the Scots Fusiliers, headed by a band of music playing a lively tune, were returning from the funeral of one of their officers. This scene made a singular impression upon me. I was, in the first place, struck at seeing those fine fellows going, some probably to their doom—for who could tell how many would get back safely?—and in the second place, at the sight of the return of the funeral, playing such a joyous strain. This I learned, upon inquiry, was always the case after interring the corpse and leaving the cemetery.

One company had not started for the trenches. It was commanded by Colonel Seymour of the Guards, now aide-de-camp to H. R. H. Prince Albert. General Simpson, who had been some time talking with that officer, said to me, "Monsieur Soyer, here is Colonel Seymour, who will render you any assistance you may require."

"Much obliged, general."

"Oh," said the colonel, "Monsieur Soyer and myself are old acquaintances. I often paid you a visit at the Reform Club."

"Indeed, colonel!"

"Certainly—very often."

Though the face was well known to me, I could not for the life of me recognise the colonel, he had such a large beard and mustachios. General Simpson then left us together, and I observed that I should give him as little trouble as possible, but for a short time should require all his kind assistance for the opening of my kitchen.

"You may depend upon me, Monsieur Soyer," he said,—"that is, if I return safe from the trenches."

"I sincerely hope you may."

"No one can tell. Thank God, I have been very fortunate so far."

"I hope that you will continue to be so."

We made an appointment. He started on horseback at the head of his men. I was introduced to numerous other officers by the general, and afterwards by the colonel, with many of whom I had the honour of being previously acquainted. Having selected a spot on the esplanade facing the centre avenue which divided the Coldstreams from the Scots Fusiliers, I returned alone to headquarters, it being then nearly dinner-time. My Zouave had got back from Balaklava, whither I had sent him to fetch my evening dress, in which I immediately attired myself, as dinner was upon the table. We sat down about twelve in number. As I was nearly opposite General Simpson, I had the opportunity of conversing with him upon various subjects. For a Crimean dinner, it was a very good one indeed. Colonel Steele and Captain Colville, who were sitting next me, attributed it to my presence, and said that the cook—Nicolo—had certainly distinguished himself upon the occasion.

"I am much pleased," I replied, "to be the cause of so great an improvement in the culinary department, and hope for the future the commander-in-chief will avail himself of my influence by often inviting me to dine at headquarters."

After dinner, the evening passed very merrily, and the general cordially joined in the fun, though he seemed full of business, leaving the table several times to write despatches in his cabinet. We were smoking on the balcony at the back of the house, facing the vineyard, when the general returned from one of his short excursions, and I showed him the piece of canvas which I had obtained from my Zouave.

"Had the ball," I said, "fallen upon a stone, or anything offering resistance, it might have killed twenty men, as it fell in the thickest part of the Third Division. The deep hole it made in the tent was as polished and hard as the interior of a marble mortar. This was no doubt caused by the rapid revolutions of the ball in burying itself before its force was spent. I noticed this whilst looking at the cavity; and the men who were lying in the tent were of my opinion, and assured me that it kept making a tremendous noise for some time after its fall."

While we were engaged in conversation I believe that another despatch arrived, for the general and some of his Staff were called out. Observe, reader, that for a full hour the cannon and mortars had not ceased roaring throughout the camps, continually vomiting forth death and destruction on every side; yet everyone present, I as well as the rest, appeared quite indifferent to that mournful noise. We were, however, soon awakened by the fierce rattling of the fusillade. All listened attentively, but without moving from their seats. A message from the general and fresh orders caused us to break up the party. I was leaving the house, intending to return to Balaklava, when I met Major Lindsey, one of the aides-de-camp of General Simpson, entering with, I believe, another despatch. He asked me where I was going to sleep: I answered, at Balaklava.

"Oh, nonsense! don't go away. We are all ordered for half-past three in the morning. A great battle is expected, as the Russians are going to attack us upon a fresh point. I will give you a plank and a blanket in my room to lie upon for an hour or so."

I accepted his kind offer, and he left me. When I informed my Zouave of the anticipated battle,

"By Jove!" said he, "I hope they will give me a gun and sword to go and fight. I shall make a busy day of it. I smell powder. Pray, governor, do beg of the general to let me go with them."

The fellow had taken a drop too much, and he went on like a madman—no one could check him. We retired to our hospitable abode, and I went to sleep; but the mad Zouave was anywhere and everywhere. At three o'clock I awoke. The general and his Staff started—the cannonade was going on fiercely, but no fusillade was heard. At seven the general and all returned; and it was, as he said, a false alarm.

My Zouave returned at eight, loaded with provisions, which he told me he had borrowed of some fellows he had found fast asleep. We arrived on board the *Baraguay d'Hilliers* about ten, faint with fatigue and hunger, having had no breakfast.

Such was camp-life at headquarters. It was like swimming between life and death. No one seemed to apprehend the least danger, while a successful sortie on the part of the enemy would have placed everyone's life in the greatest peril. So much for the unprofitable business of war!

Having fixed upon a spot for my kitchen, I immediately sent the stoves to the camp. As they happened to be close to the railway, they arrived early the next morning. In the course of the day I reached my field of battle, and to my great surprise found—what? Why, all my battery firing for the support of the Highland Brigade. The stoves had arrived early enough for the men to use them in cooking their dinners. Though I had given special orders that no one should meddle with them until I arrived, it gave me great pleasure to find that the men were using them to the best advantage and without instruction. In the first place, they could not possibly burn more than twenty pounds of wood in cooking for a hundred men, instead of several hundred-weight, which was the daily consumption. Although I had not given them my receipts, they found they could cook their rations with more ease, and hoped they should soon have them for everyday use, instead of the small tin camp-kettles, and their open-air system of cooking. The process was very unsatisfactory, being dependent upon good, bad, or indifferent weather, and the fuel was often wet and difficult to ignite. Colonel Seymour, whom I invited to see the men using the stoves without tuition from me or anybody else, can testify to the accuracy of this fact, having witnessed the process and interrogated them upon the subject.

My reason, reader, for relating this circumstance, is because it afforded me an assurance that I could render service to the army, and that my exertions were of some use. I saw even further than that; for I inferred that if a soldier, who is not a cooking animal, being paid for other purposes—and that talent a peculiar gift conferred in a greater or less degree upon humanity—could without trouble or instruction cook well in the open air and in all weathers, the stoves would certainly be useful in all establishments, from a cottage to a college. I do not say anything of their use in hospitals, because they had been tried in those establishments with full success, as far as military cooking was concerned. The idea of connecting baking, roasting, boiling, and steaming crossed my mind; and this, I felt with confidence, would render them beneficial and useful to the public at large. This idea I at once communicated to the makers, and they have already acted upon my suggestion. I resolved upon my return to England to bring them out at as cheap a rate as possible for the use of small or large families. A really useful and economical cooking stove is as much wanted in England as sunshine on a November day—a stove by which all the usual domestic cooking can be carried on, without having recourse to bricks and mortar, and chimney-sweeps. Smoky chimneys, as well as other minor nuisances too numerous to mention, would be thus avoided. Twelve pounds of coal, or fifteen pounds of coke, will cook for one hundred men.

"War," said I to myself, "is the evil genius of a time; but good food for all is a daily and a paramount necessity." These reflections led to a further communication with Messrs. Smith and Phillips, of Snow Hill. I took out a patent for the stoves. This I did not like to do before I had introduced them to the Government, as every one would have supposed that I wished to make money by the patent. The object of a patent, after such a decided success, was to secure the solidity and perfection of the article. As it was difficult to make, and certain to be badly imitated, my reputation must have suffered. Instead of being expensive, they will be sold at a reasonable price, sufficient to repay the manufacturers, and to leave a fair profit; thus placing them within the reach of all—the million as well as the millionaire.

As the Highlanders had already used the stove, I changed my plan, and instead of placing them between the Guards' camp, thought it would be better to have them in the centre of the Highland Brigade, as near as possible to Sir Colin Campbell's headquarters, which would enable him to watch the proceedings without trouble. For this purpose, I went to his quarters, and was told that the best time to see him was from eight till nine in the morning at the latest. Next morning I was on my way to the Scotch camp by seven o'clock. I saw Colonel Stirling, Sir Colin's private secretary, who informed me that Sir Colin would be happy to receive me. My reception by that brave and illustrious general was highly gratifying to my feelings.

"Welcome, Monsieur Soyer!" exclaimed the general, as I entered his tent. He shook me by the hand, with a smile on his face which one could see came from the heart. The fine long beard which then adorned his visage could only be portrayed by a Rembrandt or a Titian. The amiable and fine qualities of that noble-hearted general, so well known to every Englishman, made me feel proud of being so cordially received by one the pride of his country.

"How are you, Monsieur Soyer?"

"Never better, general," was my answer. "I am happy to see you are enjoying good health."

"Thank God, I am. Be seated, and tell me what I can do for you."

"I shall esteem it a great favour, general, if you will allow me to place my new field stoves in your brigade, instead of on the esplanade. Your men have, unknown to me, commenced cooking with them; and as they already know how to use them, I should prefer leaving them in their hands."

"Very well, Monsieur Soyer; select the spot, and Colonel Stirling will give you all the assistance you may require."

"Thank you, general; but I must observe that this is only a trial, and they will be removed as soon as the commander-in-chief has seen them in use, and decided upon their merits."

After taking some refreshment, kindly offered by the general, I went to Colonel Stirling, and informed him of the general's decision. He promised to have everything ready to commence operations the next morning.

The following day I was out very early at the Inkermann heights, with a numerous party, looking towards the Tchernaya Bridge. It was the 16th of August, the day of that memorable battle, which does not require a description on my part. From four till eight that morning I looked on, and saw the retreat of the Russians and the triumph of the French and Sardinians.

On my return, I had the pleasure of riding with Lord Rokeby, who was on his way to his quarters to give some important orders. I had a very interesting conversation with his lordship, who explained the plan of the battle—how it commenced and ended, with the probable loss on both sides. He had been up all night: reinforcements were pouring in from all directions of the Allied camps, with the cavalry, then commanded by General Scarlett, as another attack was expected. Near Lord Rokeby's quarters we met Colonel Seymour, who gave him a despatch, whereupon the former immediately left us. The colonel rode with me some distance, giving me more details respecting the engagement. He then remarked that I had not called the day before, according to promise. I told him that I had been detained later than I anticipated: I also mentioned my interview with Sir Colin Campbell. He said—

"You have done well, Monsieur Soyer; but of course I shall not be able to do so much for you, as I am in another brigade: however, I will do my utmost." He then observed, "I believe, though I was introduced to you the other day by General Simpson, you do not recollect me."

"To be frank with you, colonel, I must acknowledge that your face is very familiar, but I cannot recall where I had the pleasure of seeing you before."

"You will remember me, when I tell you I have been many times in your kitchen at the Reform Club. Do you recollect me now?"

This explanation not having enlightened me, he continued—

"It was I—then Captain Seymour—who accompanied the Prince of Prussia, the Duke of Saxe-Coburg, the Grand Duke Michael, the Princess Clementia of France, and his Royal Highness Prince Albert, whose aide-de-camp I was for several years."

It was not until he said this that I recalled the colonel's face, as he had been completely metamorphosed from the drawing-room dandy to a fierce and war-worn warrior. I was now much delighted to find so firm a supporter of my undertaking. I could not, however, account for the sudden change in his appearance since I had seen him at the Reform Club.

I went to see Colonel Stirling, though not expecting to find him or Sir Colin in the camp, when, by chance, he returned, having important business to transact. Upon seeing me, he said—

"Ah, Monsieur Soyer, you have selected a very glorious day for the commencement of your hostilities; but I regret I shall not be able to assist you, as we do not know how this affair will be decided."

"You do not for a moment suppose, colonel, that I would intrude upon your valuable time on such an occasion? Having slept in camp, I only called *en passant*. Goodmorning, colonel."

"Goodday, Soyer. I would advise you to call tomorrow."

Having given a look at my Highlanders' cooking, and tasted some coffee which they had prepared for breakfast according to my receipt, I retired, much pleased with their success.

I remained at the camp till nearly three in the afternoon. About one, a long train of mules made their appearance, bearing wounded French and Russian soldiers— the latter prisoners. About twenty were wounded; the rest followed the mournful procession. Assisted by a few of my men, I gave them some wine, brandy, porter, &c.—in fact, whatever we could get at the canteen—which seemed to afford them much relief. I of course treated the wounded Russians in the same manner as the French; though two refused to take anything, fearing poison.

Not doubting that many more would pass, as I had some provisions in a tent for the opening of my kitchens, I made some sago jelly, with wine, calfs'-foot jelly, &c., which unfortunately was not used, as the other prisoners went by a different road, though taken to the General Hospital at the French headquarters. Upon leaving, I ordered my men to be on the look out, and if any wounded or prisoners came by, to offer them some refreshment.

Just as I was going, I perceived a few mules approaching the Guards' camp. As they advanced, I and one of my men went towards some of the wounded with a basin of sago in hand, saying, this was a sort of half-way ambulance, where they might obtain all they might require. I was aware that some of the Russian prisoners in the first convoy would not accept any refreshment, for fear of being poisoned, of course not knowing better. The case of two poor French soldiers I cannot pass in silence. One had been severely wounded in the head, and was almost in a state of insensibility; the other had had his leg amputated on the field of battle. The first, after taking a few spoonfuls of the hot sago, asked for a drop of brandy, saying he felt faint. The conductor at first objected to this, but upon my asking him to take a glass with me and the patient, he agreed that it would do him no harm if it did him no good—adding, that very likely he would not survive the day. Having mixed it with water, he drank it, and thanked me warmly. The other was an officer. After giving him some wine-jelly, I conversed with him.

"How good this jelly is!" said he, in French; "pray give me another spoonful or two, if you have it to spare."

Having done this, he said that he suddenly felt very thirsty. This was, no doubt, owing to the loss of blood. I gave him some lemonade. He drank above a pint, and felt more composed, and proceeded to the hospital, near the English headquarters. I accompanied him, and he told me that his leg had just been amputated; and, with tears in his eyes, added, in a low voice, "All I regret is, that my military career should have ended so soon. I am but thirty years of age, and have only been two months in the Crimea."

"My dear friend," I replied, to cheer him, "many thousands have done less, and died; but you will survive, and be rewarded for your gallant service—you belong to a nation which can appreciate noble devotion."

"Ah!" said he, "you have done me a deal of good, no matter who you are; if my life is spared, I beg you will let me see or hear from you."

Though he gave me his name, not having my pocketbook with me, I could not make a note of it. Some time after, I visited the hospital, in company with Dr. Wyatt of the Coldstream Guards. We learnt that the man who had been wounded in the head had died, but that the officer whose leg had been amputated had been sent home to France.

About six in the evening, I and my Zouave visited the field of battle. The sight was indeed a melancholy one. The French and Sardinians were busily engaged burying their dead, as well as those of the enemy, but were compelled to desist several times in consequence of the Russian cannonade from the heights.

Bornet, my Zouave, perceiving that the Russians were firing upon the Allies while burying their dead, got in such a towering passion, that I thought he would have gone alone and taken the Russian batteries. I had great difficulty in getting him home, for, as I have before said, the smell of gunpowder was to him like the scent of a rat to a terrier.

On arriving on board the *Baraguay d'Hilliers*, we learnt from the captain that he was to take his departure in a few days, at which I was very sorry, not having opened my kitchen, nor being as yet installed in the camp. I applied to the harbour-master, who advised me to choose the *Edward*; as she was a transport and laden with hospital stores, she was likely to remain longest in harbour.

I was at this time busily engaged pitching my tents in the camp. The opening of my kitchen was delayed in consequence of the troops being on duty at the Tchernaya. This lasted for about ten days, when it was rumoured that Sir Colin Campbell wished to remove his camp to Kamara, in order to be nearer the spot at which it was supposed the expected attack would take place. I therefore pitched my tent on the spot I had at first selected. The day for my opening ceremony was fixed upon by General Simpson; and my friend Colonel Seymour very kindly assisted me in many ways, and even wrote letters of invitation to the colonels and officers of the different regiments. I was anxious for them to give their approval or non-approval of the method. Two days before, Colonel Seymour and myself had settled everything to our satisfaction, and wishing to make a kind of *fête champêtre* of the opening day, we applied at proper quarters for a band of music, which was granted.

My opening day was the one fixed upon for the distribution of the Order of the Bath. In parting from the colonel, he observed, "Well, Monsieur Soyer, I think we shall make a good thing of this, unless something happens to me in the trenches to-night. I am just going there."

These words were said in as light-hearted a manner as though he was going to a ball, and passed from my mind as quickly. The gallant colonel was then going perhaps for the hundredth time to his dangerous and uncertain duty.

I returned to Balaklava for the last time previous to taking up my permanent residence at the camp. I had settled all to my entire satisfaction. With Sir George Maclean, the Commissary-General, I had arranged respecting the quantity of rations required for a certain number of men; with Mr. Fitzgerald, the Deputy Purveyor-in-chief, for the fresh meat; and with the butcher for a supply of four ox-heads and six ox-feet, out of the number he daily buried. I placed all my people in their different stations according to merit and qualification. I obtained from Major Mackenzie, through the kindness of Sir Thomas Eyre, the Ordnance Master, some wood and four carpenters to put up some tables and a few benches, and ordered from Messrs. Crockford, at Donnybrook, a certain quantity of wines and refreshments worthy of the illustrious guests I was about to receive.

OPENING OF SOYER'S FIELD KITCHEN BEFORE SEBASTOPOL.

XXVIII

MY GREAT FIELD DAY

MY gallant master of the ceremonies, Colonel Seymour, had kindly taken the most important part of my duty off my hands, by inviting all the heads of the military and medical authorities, with a great number of whom, in consequence of my short stay in the Crimea, I was not yet, or, at least, only partially acquainted. I had now removed to the *Edward*, and also left her, but still kept, if not a *pied à terre* (as we say in French), at least a *pied sur mer*, for myself and people, in case I should require to go to Balaklava and stay there for the night.

This was on the 26th of August, 1855—the 27th was to be the opening day. All my people had left for the camp, with arms and baggage. I was certain of success and without the slightest anxiety. On arriving at my field of operations, I learnt, to my deep sorrow, that my right hand, Colonel Seymour, had, during the night, been dangerously wounded in the trenches. I immediately went to his quarters to ascertain the nature of his wound. His servant told me, that for the present no one could tell; he had been struck by the splinter of a shell at the back of the neck, the wound was not so bad as had been at first anticipated. His servant announced me, and although very weak, the colonel begged I would enter his tent. He was lying upon the ground upon a blanket, covered with another, and his military cloak over that. His head was bandaged with a turban of white linen stained with blood. His first words were, "Monsieur Soyer, you see what has happened at last. I much regret it, as I shall not be able to perform my promise to you respecting your opening."

"Never mind, colonel; don't let us talk about that subject now, but about yourself."

"Well," he replied, "the doctor has just been, and says that the wound is not mortal, nor even so dangerous as he at first anticipated."

"Colonel, you want repose, so I will retire."

"There is no occasion for that, Monsieur Soyer; I feel strong again. When I was struck, I did not feel the wound, and fell immediately, remaining for some time insensible, the wound, as the doctor says, having acted upon the brain."

"Don't exert yourself, my dear colonel, by talking. Thank God it is no worse. I will go and send you some lemonade. I have asked the doctor what was best for you, and am happy to say I have some ice."

"Many thanks for your kind attention, Monsieur Soyer."

I then retired. Upon reaching my kitchen, I found that no one had yet arrived. The four carpenters had left me in the lurch, having run away in the night, and abandoned their work, after stealing all they could from the tents. Mr. Doyne, the chief of the Army Works Corps, kindly supplied me with workmen, and offered to lend me, for a few days, as many tents as I required. As the weather was then intensely hot, I accepted his offer, and requested the loan of a large marquee, under which a couple of hundred people could stand. Captain Gordon lent me two smaller ones, and by the evening they were pitched, and my provisions had all arrived, and my people were at their posts.

I much regretted that many persons of distinction were not invited, in consequence of the unfortunate accident to Colonel Seymour, which happened before he had sent out all the invitations. At all events, the day, though fixed at hazard, turned out extremely well adapted for the reception of a large party.

Early in the morning the camp seemed full of life and gaiety. Mounted officers in full uniform might be seen rushing about in all directions; bands were playing, regiments filing past, and everything bearing the appearance of a great festival. I set cheerfully to work, and, in spite of difficulties which can only be understood by those who have been in the Crimea, I succeeded in getting all in tolerably good order for my great martial banquet *al fresco*. I made several messes with the soldiers' rations, and at the same expense, though I had introduced sauce and ingredients which could easily be added to the army stores without increasing the cost, thus making a nice variation in the meals, so important to the health of a large body of men like the army or navy, to the latter of which it is as easily applicable as the former.

The bill of fare consisted of plain boiled salt beef; ditto, with dumplings; plain boiled salt pork; ditto, with peas-pudding; stewed salt pork and beef, with rice; French pot-au-feu; stewed fresh beef, with potatoes; mutton, ditto, with haricot beans; ox-cheek and ox-feet soups; Scotch mutton-broth; common curry, made with fresh and salt beef. (See receipts in Addenda.)

By three o'clock my guests began to arrive. The stoves were in the open air, placed in a semicircle, and, though in a state of ebullition, no one could perceive that any cooking was going on, except on raising the lids. A material point I had in view was that no fire should be seen when used in the trenches. A common table, made of a few boards, and garnished with soldiers' tin plates, iron forks and spoons, composed my open-air dining-room.

About four o'clock my reception commenced. Lord Rokeby, accompanied by several French officers in full dress, was the first to honour me with a visit. This gave me an opportunity of fully explaining to him and his friends the plan and construction of the apparatus, as well as its simplicity, cleanliness, and great economy in the consumption of fuel. At the same time, I showed with what ease and certainty the men could regulate the heat and prepare the new receipts—which will be found at the end of this work.

I must also observe, for the information of those who only saw them upon that occasion, that the stoves, having been made for the General Hospital, were too large and heavy for campaigning. That I might lose no time in making my trial before the authorities, I used them upon that occasion, as the process was the same as regards cooking in those as in the smaller ones. The sole difference was in the size, as it was understood that two would cook for a company of one hundred and twenty men, and might be carried by one mule while on march, with sufficient dry wood inside for the next day's cooking. This was of the utmost importance, in order to ensure the regularity of the soldier's meal, which ought always to be ready at the minute fixed by the rules of the service.

Thus I had surmounted every difficulty by the invention of this apparatus. In addition to its simplicity and economy, it had the merit of making cooks of soldiers, of which they had previously neither the inclination nor the chance. Smaller stoves on the same principle were also to be provided for picket and outpost duty, as first suggested to me by Lord Raglan. After giving the foregoing information to my illustrious visitors, we passed to the grand process of tasting the various messes. They all gave perfect satisfaction.

By this time several hundred visitors had made their appearance, and gay and animated was the scene. All present were in the same costume as that in which they appeared at the grand chivalric ceremony which had taken place at headquarters—the installation of the Order of the Bath. I was also highly favoured, I may say, by the presence of a charming group of the fair sex, about ten in number, escorted by their cavaliers. After taking some refreshment under the monster tent, they came to add their charms to the martial banquet, and taste with gusto the rough food of the brave. I had nothing out of doors to offer their delicate palates but the soldiers' rations, transmogrified in various ways. My task now became extremely difficult. The crowd was so great, that my batteries were quite taken by storm (*de cuisine*, of course). Refreshments of all kinds were distributed pretty freely throughout the day. The band in attendance was ordered to play, and struck up "Partant pour la Syrie." All were immediately on the *qui vive*, when Captain Colville galloped up to me, and said—

"General Simpson has sent me to inform you that General Pelissier and himself will be here in a few minutes."

A gorgeous cavalcade was soon seen in the distance. It consisted of the Allied Generals and staff, and a numerous suite. General Pelissier alighted from his carriage, and joined General Simpson. I went and met the distinguished visitors, who had come from headquarters after the ceremony of the distribution of the Order of the Bath by Lord Stratford de Redcliffe.

Upon the arrival of the generals, the band continued playing "Partant pour la Syrie." The cannon of Sebastopol appeared to redouble its roar—so much so, that General Pelissier, with a smile, called General Simpson's attention to the fact: added to which, the hundreds of uniforms, cocked hats and feathers—French, English, and Sardinian—gave full effect to the lively scene.

In course of conversation, General Simpson said, "Monsieur Soyer,—Lord Stratford de Redcliffe, in reply to your letter, sends his compliments, and regrets he shall not be able to attend your opening, as he must be on board the *Caradoc*, now lying in Kamiesch Bay, by five o'clock, on his way to Constantinople."

I thanked General Simpson for his kindness in troubling himself about the message, and the review of my culinary camp, which upon this occasion was rather extensive, commenced. It comprised four bell-tents, one marquee, and a large square tent, capable of holding more than two hundred persons. A luncheon *al fresco* was served in the camp, and four of my cooks attended upon the guests. The tops of the tents were surmounted with flags and garlands of evergreens composed of vine-leaves; the same were also attached to the posts which supported the rope forming the limits of the enclosure, giving to the whole a martial and lively appearance. The weather was so fine that everyone preferred remaining in the open air.

Generals Pelissier and Simpson proceeded to taste the various articles of food. The *pot-au-feu*, or beef-soup, was prepared partly from ox-heads, which were usually buried, instead of being used as food for the soldiers, no doubt in consequence of the difficulty of cleaning them.

General Pelissier tasted several samples of the pot-au-feu, and, addressing General Barnard, declared that he felt as interested in this unexpected exhibition as in the ceremony of the morning. The witty General Barnard replied, "Your excellency must agree with me that this day has been remarkably well spent: we devoted the morning to the *cordon rouge*, and the afternoon to the *cordon bleu*." General Pelissier much enjoyed the *bon mot*, and repeated it to the officers of his staff, thus creating great hilarity amongst them.

I requested many of my visitors to taste the different preparations, and, much to my satisfaction, I believe almost all of them did so, and expressed their approbation of them. After pointing out the merits of the stoves to the commanders-in-chief, I conducted them to the spot where the Scotch Division formerly cooked their rations in the old tin camp-kettles. On our way, I observed to General Pelissier that I had visited the French camp-kitchens, and found their marmites superior to the English. The soup made by the French soldiers, I said, was very good. At this the General seemed much pleased.

The space required for three or four regiments extended about three hundred and fifty feet in length. A rough wall of loose stones had been erected by the men to form a screen, which when the regiment moved was, of course, left behind. The furnaces were also constructed of loose stones, held together by iron hoops; upon these the tin cans were placed and the rations cooked. By this plan an immense quantity of wood was inevitably wasted, and the fires were sometimes extinguished by the heavy rains. My stoves completely obviated all those previously insurmountable difficulties.

Having listened to this explanation, the commanders-in-chief admitted the beneficial results and advantages of the stoves. However, General Simpson observed that I, of course, applied the contrast to my advantage; but also said, it was nothing but fair, and I was perfectly justified in so doing. In the first place, my stoves occupied but little room, and cooked much better than those formerly in use.

The Allied Generals remained with me above an hour. This gave me an excellent opportunity of conversing with General Pelissier, who minutely described camp life in Algeria, after which the General and Staff retired. As it was then nearly seven o'clock, a great number of officers followed. No less than eight hundred or a thousand persons of distinction visited the kitchens during the day: many were not invited, in consequence of the unfortunate accident to Colonel Seymour. About nine all was over, and the band played "God save the Queen."

Nothing could have succeeded better than this opening, a drawing of which appeared in the *Illustrated News* of September 22nd, 1855.

General Pelissier's Letter

J'ai eu le plasir, le vingt-sept Août, 1855, de visiter l'établissement culinaire de Monsieur Soyer, et j'ai été bien satisfait de ce que j'y ai vu; j'ai été frappé surtout de l'économie de temps et de chauffage apporté dans l'alimentation des troupes. Les chaudières paraissent bien entendues; j'ai tout goûté, et à tout, je le reconnais, j'ai trouvé un goût excellent et très-appétissant.*

GENERAL A. PELISSIER.

* On the 27th of August, 1855, I had the pleasure of visiting Mr Soyer's culinary establishment and I was well satisfied with what I saw there. I was particularly struck with the saving of time and fuel which has been made in catering for the troops. The stores appear well arranged. I tasted everything and found it all most appetising.

General Simpson's Letter.

CAMP BEFORE SEBASTOPOL, *31st August*, 1855.

I had much pleasure in visiting Monsieur Soyer's field-kitchen last Monday, the 27th instant. I there saw several excellent soups made from ration meat, compressed vegetables, and other things within reach of the soldier's means, and cooked with very little fuel. I consider Monsieur Soyer is taking great pains in devoting his time and great talents to the good of our military service, especially in the field, and I wish him every possible success and honourable reward.

JAMES SIMPSON,
General Commanding.

WAR OFFICE, *6th August*, 1855.

SIR,—I am directed to acknowledge the receipt, on the 2nd ultimo, of your report upon the culinary department of the hospitals in the East; and, in returning the thanks of the Secretary-at-War, to acquaint you, that he recognises, with the greatest satisfaction, the exertions you have made and are still making for the benefit of the army in the field, and also of the sick and wounded in the several hospitals.

I am, Sir, your obedient servant,

M. Soyer, Scutari.   FRED. J. PRESCOTT.

About the 5th of September, I was at headquarters, when who should walk in but Sir Edmund Lyons! I had not the pleasure of seeing him before, and I took this opportunity of introducing myself, and informing the Commander of the British Fleet in the Black Sea that I was very anxious to pay my respectful compliments to him.

Upon this, Sir Edmund Lyons, with the kindest feeling, at once offered me his hand, saying, "Monsieur Soyer, I assure you I am delighted to make your acquaintance. You are doing much good for our brave soldiers; but you must not forget our worthy sailors. Come and see us on board the *Albert*; you will be well received and quite welcome. I have heard much about your field-kitchens, and it was only the other day I was reading a very important complimentary letter which General Pelissier had written in their favour."

"He did me that honour, admiral, and he seemed highly gratified."

"I can assure you he was, Monsieur Soyer, for I heard him say so."

A few days after the grand opening ceremony, a meeting took place, by order of the Minister-at-War and General Simpson, to consider the possibility of supplying a pint of hot soup to the men in the trenches during the winter. The meeting was held at Lord Rokeby's headquarters, on the 3rd or 4th of September. I was ordered to be present. On my way there I had the pleasure of meeting General Barnard, who in his humorous manner addressed me thus:—

"Hallo, General Soyer! I'm not so much behind as I thought; for you are only just going to the general meeting, or the meeting of generals."

"You are right, general," I replied. "Thank you for the noble title you have bestowed upon me, and at the seat of war too."

"The fact is, I understood the meeting was to be held at headquarters, and went half-way there, when I met some officers who told me it was to be at Lord Rokeby's. But they cannot proceed without you, general. Never mind, Soyer, we are only a few minutes behind time."

When we arrived, the Board was sitting. Sir Colin Campbell had sent a message, stating that some important duties would prevent his attendance. The proceedings then commenced, and the order was read by General Bentinck; which, as far as I can recollect, was worded thus:—

Lord Panmure, the Minister-at-War, anxious for the comfort of the troops in the Crimea, is desirous that, if possible, every man in the trenches should be supplied with a basin of hot soup during the winter nights; the allowance of rum to be, in consequence, either diminished or entirely withheld. His lordship believing Monsieur Soyer to be still in the Crimea, requests the Board to inquire of him if such would be practicable.

I at once replied that it could be done, and without difficulty, for any number of men, by the application of my field stoves. This answer met with the general approbation of the assembled Board. I next remarked that the stoves might be placed in the trenches, even in front of the enemy, as not a spark of fire could be seen either by day or night while they were in use. This point having been satisfactorily settled, the question of taking away or reducing the quantity of rum was seriously debated. General Eyre was of opinion that the men would not like to part with any portion of their rum. Generals Bentinck, Rokeby, &c., were in favour of giving the soup as an addition, and allowing the rum to be issued as usual. It struck me that by giving only half a gill of rum the other half would almost entirely cover the expense of the soup, if economically managed. I also proposed another plan, which was to give less rum and less than a pint of soup, which was discussed.

When the inquiry was over, I said—"Gentlemen, I shall feel obliged if you will favour me with a visit to my field kitchen. I have made several experiments in diets for you to taste, and if you approve of them, have no doubt when you know the cost, you will be able to settle the question of supplying soup in the trenches with more certainty."

All present agreed, excepting General Eyre, who was of opinion that what he as a soldier had for so many years found answer for the men, would answer now; nor did he see why the soldiers should live better than himself. "I should be very happy," said he, "to improve the daily food of the troops, but do not like anything to be overdone. I like judicious discipline in all things."

Though I must frankly admit I was anything but enchanted with the general's way of thinking at first, I could not but admire the latter part of his argument, which was as sincere as it was severe.

Several debates took place upon the subject, and, after a little persuasion, I induced them all to come, and taste the samples I had prepared for their inspection. I proudly led my very select cavalcade towards my batteries, which upon that occasion were in charge of the troops. I had only given the written receipts for them to act upon, and charged a serjeant to watch over them, and see that the proportions in the receipts were properly attended to. An infallible plan of ensuring success at all times is to appoint a man of superior grade as overlooker. One to each regiment would be sufficient.

Upon our arrival we found everything in perfect order: the stoves were clean, the contents properly cooked, and the consumption of fuel four hundred per cent. less than in the usual way. Only five different messes were prepared upon this occasion—viz., ox-head soup, stewed fresh beef, Scotch hodge-podge of mutton, salt pork and beef with dumplings. Everything was done to perfection. After carefully explaining the process to Generals Eyre and Bentinck, who were not present on the great opening day, we sat down to test the quality of the articles. A sumptuous lunch was displayed from the soldiers' rations—always excepting the ox-heads, which I had obtained from the butcher, as usual, on the eve of their funeral. With these I made an excellent *pot-au-feu*, enough for fifty men. Lord Rokeby was so highly delighted with it, that he recommended it to all, and requested me to give this receipt, as well as that for stewed beef, to his cook—for which see Addenda.

A goblet of Marsala wine, with a lump of ice, terminated this martial collation under a burning sun, and amid the everlasting roar of the bombardment of the besieged city. The guests retired, quite satisfied. Even General Eyre, though still adhering to his opinion that it was too good for soldiers, and would make them lazy, said, "Soldiers do not require such good messes as those while campaigning." At which remark the gentlemen present could not refrain from laughing.

"Well, general," said I, "your plan has been tried, and, as you perceive, has not answered. I was therefore obliged to introduce a simpler style, by which soldiers might cook with pleasure and less difficulty, and, having once learnt, always will cook properly, and with less trouble. You must also observe, general, that it is with the same rations as before. And is it not better to make a few good cooks out of an army than to have an army of bad cooks?"

By this time the general was on his charger. He said, "We are both right. For my part, I mean what I say: you will improve the cook, but spoil the soldier."

I then thanked them for their gracious condescension, and they started for their several divisions, promising to let me know their final decision.

Amongst the military authorities who visited me that day were General Scarlett and staff, Colonel St. George, Colonel Handcock and lady, a very charming person, and extremely merry. She observed, when I presented her with some champagne and ice in a large tin goblet, as she sat upon her horse, "Upon my word, Monsieur Soyer, champagne is better in tin cups in the Crimea than in crystal goblets in England."

"I am glad you like it, madam. Shall I offer you another?"

"No, I thank you."

"Madam would like to taste some of the men's rations," said Colonel Handcock. "Would you, madam?"

"Many thanks, Monsieur Soyer. I think not, after the champagne."

After paying a visit to my abode, my guests departed.

A few days afterwards, I heard that that poor creature was plunged in the deepest sorrow. Upon making a chance visit, I could not believe her to be the same person; the bloom of life appeared to have suddenly deserted her laughing cheeks, which wore a cadaverous hue. Such was the effect sorrow soon produced on the appearance of one usually so animated and full of mirth. (See page 226.)

As I noticed that the men daily threw the fat away from their salt beef and pork, the last of which is of first-rate quality, I proposed to Colonel Daniell, of the Coldstream Guards, to make his men cook for his regiment, which was agreed upon. He always took great interest in the welfare of his soldiers and in my culinary proceedings, and I had the honour of being acquainted with him for some years as a subscriber to benevolent institutions, and in particular to soup-kitchens for the poor. The next day the rations were brought in; the salt beef and pork were cooked, and a few dumplings added, as an innovation. The wood was weighed, and twenty-seven pounds were sufficient to cook the rations for the whole regiment. The meat was done to perfection, and without trouble. I begged that the sixteen cooks daily employed for the regiment might be present. Two would have done, or even one, as the water and provisions were brought by a fatigue party, therefore fifteen men might have been spared; and only forty-seven pounds of wood were used, instead of one thousand seven hundred and sixty. When the meat was cooked, we skimmed off forty-two pounds of fat as white as snow, and not black, as was the case when cooked in the small canteen-pans with little water. This spoilt the fat, which might be used in lieu of butter on bread or biscuit. To do this properly, soak the biscuits in water for about ten minutes; take them out, let them dry a little; put some fat in the pan; when hot, fry them as you would a piece of bacon: a few minutes will do them. When crisp, season with salt and pepper, if handy. They make an excellent article of food.

For this saving and improvement, Colonel Daniell, whom I will back for discipline and straightforwardness of opinion against anyone in the army, gave me the following letter:—

COLDSTREAM GUARDS' CAMP, BEFORE SEBASTOPOL, *Sept.*, 1855.

I have this day attended Monsieur Soyer's course of instruction to the cooks of my battalion, and have tasted the messes cooked and served to the men, consisting of salt pork and beef. The mode in which the salt is extracted and the meat rendered comparatively tender by the apparatus used, the facility with which the grease is taken off and rendered serviceable for other purposes, is admirable; and I consider the arrangements relative to the small consumption of wood, and the simplicity with which the cooking is conducted, will, if adopted, tend much to the health, comfort, and well-being of the soldier.

The present size of the "chaudrières" being objectionable, I am glad to hear from Monsieur Soyer that he is about to procure some of a less size. The fuel consumed today for cooking the messes of eight companies was hardly more than on ordinary occasions is consumed by one company; and from four hundred and twenty rations of salt pork and beef forty-eight pounds of excellent lard was procured, which usually is wasted. These facts alone render Monsieur Soyer's plan at once economical and desirable, and I have great pleasure in testifying my appreciation of the manner with which he conveys instruction to the men, in saying how highly I approve of his recipes and arrangements for carrying out his scheme of camp cookery.

(Signed)   H. J. DANIELL,
*Col. and Capt. in Command, First Battalion
Coldstream Guards.*

The regiments being at that time greatly reduced, were only 428 strong, therefore the weight of meat, at one pound per man, was 428 pounds, from which 42 pounds of excellent fat were obtained, much preferable for cooking purposes to the rancid butter sold in the canteens at a very high price. As I was anxious to form a perfect regimental kitchen, I proposed to Colonel Daniell to fit up one for his regiment. His men were already well acquainted with the use of the field stoves; and it would serve as a model for all. Colonel Daniell agreed, and in less than an hour the stoves were removed to the camp, where they remained by sanction of the General-in-Chief till the end of the war.

At this time I went to headquarters, and urged the necessity of telegraphing an order for four hundred small field stoves, which order had been agreed upon in case my plan succeeded and was adopted by the authorities. I also had several interviews with General Airey upon the subject. This number was sufficient for the supply of the whole of the army then in the Crimea. As there was so much business at head-quarters in consequence of the anticipated attack upon Sebastopol, the order was postponed for a few days.

SOYER'S FIELD STOVE

XXIX

THE EIGHTH OF SEPTEMBER

EARLY on the 3rd of September we started for Kamiesch; but, as usual, Bornet could not forget his old trade, and love for his fellow-soldiers. "Governor," said he, "the 3rd Zouaves who were on duty in the trenches last night are on their return to camp. It is eight o'clock, and if we take this ravine we shall meet some of them, and learn what is going on."

Having the whole day before us, I consented to go; we took the road called the French Ravine, which led from the French headquarters to the trenches before Sebastopol. The returning Zouaves we met, but the cannon balls also met us. Being in the ravine, we were not in great danger, as they passed over our heads and fell on our left side. The principal danger was when they struck a large stone, causing it to roll down the side of the ravine, sometimes at a terrific rate.

The shells were far more objectionable; but, thanks to Providence, none hit us. While retreating, Bornet said, "By a thousand bombs, governor, it must be a fresh battery they are firing from: we always used to go this way to the trenches."

"Well," said I, "new or old, let us get out of it."

Putting our horses to a gallop, we were soon out of danger, and on the road to Kamiesch. Near the French headquarters we met two Zouaves. They told us the French trenches were now within twenty yards of the Malakhoff tower. "The cannon," they said, "project about twenty feet over our heads, and cannot touch us; but the grenades, which the Russians throw among us by hundreds, cause the loss of many men, though we extinguish a great number when they fall."

Bornet now proposed the *vin blanc*, but to his regret and my delight, they refused, or we should probably not have seen Kamiesch that day. In many instances I have known French soldiers refuse.

At length we arrived at Kamiesch, which I had so long seen from my quarters, but could not reach before, owing to the engrossing nature of my occupations. This French town of pasteboard, or light wood, was so different from Balaklava, that I cannot give my readers a better idea of it than by stating that it bears the same resemblance to Balaklava that Ramsgate does to Boulogne in the height of the season. The traffic, business, markets, restaurants, cafés, billiard-rooms, theatre, &c., display the difference of character between the French and English, as forcibly as Balaklava does the English from the French.

It was really remarkable to see the type of two great nations, such near neighbours, on the same foreign soil, so far from their native homes, so distinctly preserved, while the people agreed so well together. Some of the restaurants were pretty good, very expensive, not very clean, but always full. Money seemed of no consequence, as everyone tried to get it out of you if you were rash enough to eat, drink, or purchase anything.

The sea-port was very fine; Kamiesch, flat, sandy, and unpicturesque. Balaklava was a perfect garden; Kamiesch a well populated desert.

The evening of the 7th of September was a memorable one. Each mind was animated; men of the most pacific disposition were transformed into lions or tigers, furiously seeking to devour their prey.

Amidst the most terrible discharges of cannon, the order for the general attack was announced to the troops for the following day. The news acted like an electric spark, and inspired all hearts. Each soldier appeared to breathe more freely; hope, the enchantress, filled the hearts of the brave with enthusiasm; fear was unknown; all faces were radiant with lust of glory and vengeance.

Having heard that the attack was to take place, at midday I visited the French camp with my Zouave, where we found the same animation and excitement. One of the soldiers said to my Zouave,—

"By all the camels in Arabia, Bornet, are you coming to join in the dance? If you are, I invite you for the first quadrille; but you must play the clarionet (slang term for gun). Here's a chance of having your portrait spoiled—it just suits me."

"What do you think of it, governor—shall I go?"

"It is impossible, my dear fellow, for me to oblige you upon this occasion, as your services will be more useful tomorrow, when no doubt, whichever way the victory may turn, the hospitals will be full. Therefore I hope you will forgive me for saving your life against your will. I am sure, if you had a chance, you would be the first to mount the breach, and consequently the first to be knocked over."

His late comrades in arms did not see the force of this. They knew he had some money, and did not like to part with him. The idea struck me to order a few bottles of wine at the canteen near their tents, in return for their hospitality in offering us their ration rum and brandy. About five-and-twenty more joined us when I gave the invitation. I knew that Bornet had only a few shillings in his pocket, which shillings, by the bye, were very liberally taken by the vivandière as a great favour, at the value of a French franc. After several farewells we parted.

The morning of the 8th of September, 1855, arrived. Aurora smiled gaily upon the far-famed city, the sentinels on all sides were at their posts, and in the Russian camp no doubt the watchword circulated as usual. It was thus in the allied camps, but pronounced quicker; the step of the relief guard was that of quick march, every nerve was in action, and strained to the utmost. The scene at the race for the Derby alone could give the reader an idea of the sudden energy which filled every bosom, on hearing that the attack was to take place, with this difference, that life seemed of less consequence to everyone in the Crimea than the loss of money on that terrible day of chance. All had a share in the lottery. Glory was to turn the wheel of fortune, and everyone seemed sure of winning. All hoped to gather laurels from the arid soil so long moistened with blood.

At four o'clock we were all up; about five the Guards were on their march towards the besieged city; troops from all quarters were silently marching in the same direction; every heart was beating high; the day had at last arrived which was to decide a great question. At seven all were at their post. Bornet and myself started on horseback directly, after seeing the Scots Fusiliers pass through the Guards' camp, close to our tents. On catching sight of them, my Zouave exclaimed, "What a splendid regiment, gouverneur, que ces Montagnards Ecossais! I have a great mind to follow them: I shall, too!"

"I am sure you shan't," said I, clutching him by the coat collar.

After making a long detour, a sentinel let us pass. As we were nearer the Woronzoff Road than the Cathcart Hill Cemetery, we went in that direction, and took up our position to witness the grand spectacle. For some time a profound silence reigned amongst the troops, who seemed as though they were buried in the trenches. The weather, which had been fine the preceding days, and even till sunrise on that eventful morning, suddenly changed. In a short time the elements assumed a threatening aspect, and a furious tempest raged in every direction. A clouded sky had replaced the azure blue, the fierce gusts of wind raised thick clouds of dust, which rolled majestically towards us like a moving castle, blinding everyone for a time. The cold air chilled everybody, and was so violent that one could scarcely keep one's saddle, or see twenty yards in advance. Showers of hail burst here and there over the now excited and infuriated camp and Sebastopol; the scene of action was almost invisible. It appeared as though the evil genius of the storm had on that glorious day attached his seal of destruction to that desecrated spot. Even the sun (*l'ami Soleil*), the world's friend, seemed to fear to face this scene of horror and desolation, and while smiling upon the remainder of the mighty globe, had, in appearance, withdrawn from the harrowed city of Sebastopol.

Suddenly the batteries opened fire in every direction, shaking the very soil on which we stood. Clouds of smoke enveloped the besieged city. Not a thing could be seen or heard but a continuous rolling noise similar to that of an earthquake. All at once the noise ceased, and the rattle of musketry was heard, with, at intervals, cannon and mortar shot. By degrees, thanks to the heavy gale, the atmosphere got clearer, and by the aid of a telescope one could distinctly see the French flag floating from the Malakhoff, and the troops mounting to the assault. An hour had scarcely elapsed when the news was brought of the capture of the Malakhoff by the French, and of the Redan by the English. Aides-de-camp were flying in every direction; and numbers of wounded were on their way to the hospitals. We quitted our post to go to the General Hospital, in order to see whether our services were required. As we were crossing the English camp, a corpse was borne past us, carried by four soldiers. Upon inquiry I learned, with sorrow that it was the body of Colonel H. R. Handcock, whom, a few days before, I had had the pleasure of entertaining at my kitchens, with his young and very interesting wife.

The latter had been an eye-witness of the assault, and I was informed that, by the greatest imprudence, the mutilated body of her husband had just been uncovered before her. She fainted at the sight, and was borne to her residence, where she lay for some time dangerously ill. This will account for the sudden alteration in her appearance before mentioned.

The fight still raged, the weather was a little calmer, and we left the field of battle, intending to gallop at once to the hospital. On reaching the line of sentries, we met two naval officers who were trying to pass, in order to obtain a view of the action from Cathcart's Hill. They were having a rather warm discussion, the sentry doing his duty by stopping them. I pulled up my horse, and told them that unless they had an order from headquarters they could not pass. Though much vexed, they thanked me, and submitted to the disappointment. I was about leaving them, when I heard one say to the other—

"What shall we do? I would give any money for a glass of wine or a cup of coffee."

"So would I," said the other. "Where is there a canteen, sentry?"

"It would be of no use my telling you," the sentry replied, "as they are all closed during the siege, or at least for today, in order to prevent men left in the camp from quitting their post. Several robberies were perpetrated in camp upon former occasions."

I overheard their conversation, in which they stated that they had started without breakfast, and been a long way round—nearly seven miles among the hills—and had seen nothing after all, as the pickets would not let them pass the line of Balaklava.

"Gentlemen," said I, "if you will come with me to my tent, I think I can keep you from starving, and have no doubt you will fare there as well, if not better, than in a canteen. I can also give you a description of the siege, having been an eyewitness of the same."

They thanked me, and accepted my offer. On our way to quarters, I recounted the melancholy death of Colonel Handcock. My Zouave had by this time arrived—no one but the groom was at home, and he could speak neither French nor English, being a Greek—so I set my Zouave to lay the table; and with my magic stove I cooked some ration-mutton, made an omelette, brought out a piece of cold beef, bread, &c., and gave them a bottle of ale and a glass of sherry. In twenty minutes their hunger was appeased, and I told them they were welcome to stay, but that I must proceed to my duty. At the same time I informed them, that at six o'clock dinner would be ready, and they were welcome to partake of it if they happened to be about the camp; but that they were on no account to wait for me in case I did not return, as I did not know what I might have to do in the hospitals. They thanked me for my hospitality, and said they would try and see something of the battle, and if anywhere about my quarters, would be too happy to return to dinner.

We then parted; they proceeding towards Sebastopol, and I to the hospital. On my arrival I found, to my surprise, that not one wounded man had been brought in. After waiting some time I saw Dr. Mouatt, and inquired if anything extra was wanted; his reply was, "We have all that is needed for their reception."

I then went to the purveyor, and to the kitchen; but fearing, as the battle was raging fiercely, the number of wounded might exceed the means at their disposal, I remained about the hospitals. I did this in case my services might be required, as I was well aware of the importance of speedy relief to the sufferers.

Towards evening the wounded began to arrive, though not in great numbers. I left my Zouave there and returned to the camp, telling him if anything was required, to ride home at once and inform me, as the doctors would be so much engaged—and in particular Dr. Mouatt, who would most probably not be able to devote his time to the culinary department. As I rode towards Sebastopol to have another look at the battle, I met only a few wounded. Upon inquiring of the orderlies in charge whether there were many more, they replied that they could not say, but they believed that they were a great number. I then returned to my tent, and a few minutes afterwards my naval friends arrived. The dinner was served up, and they told me that they had had a good view of the besieged city from the French lines. In the course of conversation, they informed me that Colonel (now General) Wyndham had invited them to dinner that day. I replied, "I am very anxious about him, as he led the storming party in the Redan, and I have heard the attack has been very severe, and many were killed and wounded on both sides." I also heard that it had been retaken by the Russians, and feared he might have been taken prisoner, if not wounded or killed.

When dinner was over, I proposed to pass them through the lines and make inquiry about him. We proceeded to Cathcart's Hill—it was then nearly dusk—I on horseback, they on foot. The camp around us was as still and deserted as in the morning; scarcely anyone was to be seen till we reached the lines. Very few shots were heard, but everyone was at his post. Upon reaching Cathcart's Hill, I alighted to speak with his Grace the Duke of Newcastle, who had been in the trenches all day and had just returned. He was kind enough to give me the details of the attacks on both sides, and said that he was waiting for General Bentinck, who had not yet been seen, and that he hoped nothing had happened to him. I observed, "This is a most anxious hour for all who have friends engaged in so serious and dangerous an encounter."

While conversing with the Duke, I missed my two companions. Thinking they knew the position of Colonel Wyndham's quarters, I went there expecting to find them. My first and most anxious inquiry of the servant, who knew me well, was, "What news of the Colonel?"

"Oh, all right, Monsieur Soyer," he replied with great satisfaction. "If you wish to see him, he is gone to Colonel Wood's tent—you know where it is."

"No I don't."

"Then I'll show you—he will be glad to see you."

"I will not trouble you, as I would not disturb him on such a day for the world. I am glad to hear he is safe; but have you seen two gentlemen?"

"No one excepting yourself, sir. You must come with me; my master is alone, waiting for the Colonel, and I'm sure they will both be happy to see you."

Colonel Wyndham had just changed his clothes before going to the Colonel's to dine. His servant showed them to me; they were covered with blood and dust. I followed him to Colonel Wood's hut, and found Colonel Wyndham walking quickly to and fro in the hut, apparently much preoccupied and excited. His eyes emitted flashes of fire, his open countenance had assumed its usual majestic calm and dignity, his lips were parched, his proud brow betokened much restlessness, and though his forehead was covered with glory, you could perceive through the wreath of laurel which had only a few hours before been deposited there by Mars, a deep shadow of thoughtfulness and care. His physiognomy told a tale. Victory had of him made a great hero, without having had time to put her final seal to his martial and petulant ardour. Another battle was yet to be fought.

Seeing me, he came forward and shook me by the hand, inviting me to enter. We were together about half-an-hour, and he related to me the great events of the attack upon the Redan, now so well known to the public. Colonel Wood came in, also free from wounds, to the delight of all, and invited me to dine with them. I told him that I had already dined, but could not refuse the honour upon so memorable an occasion.

We then sat down to dinner. François,* the Colonel's French cook, with whose culinary capacities I was well acquainted, having dined several times with the Colonel, told me he never felt less interest, or prepared a dinner with so much reluctance, fearing no one would return to eat it after such a sanguinary battle. Highly delighted was he when Colonel Wyndham came in, and more so when he found that his excellent governor (as he called him) had returned safe and sound. Every officer in the camp knew François, and the Colonel's table got quite in repute through the exertions of this culinary disciple of Vatel.** He used to go to the trenches, leaving his own batteries to brave those of the enemy, and all this for the comfort of his excellent governor. He was much liked by all, and always had a budget of anecdotes, some of them very interesting. He had lived as cook and major domo for several years with Madame Grisi. The last time I saw him he was in daily expectation of the Sebastopol medal.

The dinner was served, but I must say it was not so *recherché* as on former occasions; it seemed to have been prepared for sick epicures, or at least those who hovered between life and death. The conversation upon the events of the day was so animated that no one but myself perceived the difference. The Colonel's excellent wine was highly relished, and in drinking the health of Colonels Wyndham and Wood, I requested the former to make a note of the fact that I had the honour of dining with him and Colonel Wood a few hours after the battle, as probably no one would credit it. This the Colonel immediately did, and Colonel Wood added his autograph, of which the following is a copy:—

8th September, 1855, 9 p.m.

I had the pleasure, after my return from leading the storming party of the 2nd Division to the Redan, of dining with Colonel D. Wood, and meeting at dinner Monsieur Soyer.

D. WOOD,	C. A. WYNDHAM,
Lieut.-Col. Commanding,	*Col. Commanding,*
R. A. 4th Division.	*2nd Battalion.*

* He related the following anecdote of something that had passed between him and Sir John Campbell, on the eve of the attack of the 18th of June. Sir John had for some time inquired after him, and at last meeting him going to his master's quarters, called out and said, "François, how much am I in your debt?"

"Why, Colonel, it is only the middle of the month; I will give you your small bill at the end."

"No, no," said Sir John, "I want it now, François."

"Have I offended you, Colonel?"

"Offended me, no! on the contrary, I am much obliged to you for your kind services; but the end of this month may be tomorrow for me, as we shall have a terrible attack upon the Redan; so I want to settle all my little affairs today."

"Oh, I'm sure, General, it will be all right."

"Indeed I must have it—how much does it amount to?"

"Well, General, if I must, I must—it is one pound seventeen, or somewhere thereabouts."

The General wished him good night, and with a smile upon his countenance returned to his cave, and François to his duty. That noble-hearted man seemed to have a presentiment that he should not survive the attack. The tears stood in his eyes while he was relating this to me, and I found my own in much the same state in listening to the recital.

** Celebrated maître d'hôtel to the Prince de Condé. He killed himself in 1671 fish for a banquet failed to arrive—AB

They had hardly signed this when a loud knock was heard at the door, and an orderly entered with a dispatch from General Simpson, who wished to see Colonel Wyndham directly. The Colonel lost no time in attending to his commander's orders, and we mounted our horses and started for headquarters. "An immediate attack on the Redan is what I shall recommend to the general-in-chief" were the last words uttered by the Colonel before leaving the hut. The firing had ceased; the night was very dark, but the weather calm. It was with great difficulty we found our way through the camps, which appeared very silent after such a stormy day and day of storm. In about a quarter of an hour Colonel Wyndham observed, "Monsieur Soyer, I believe you are close to your quarters," pointing to several lights. "There," said he, "is the Guards' camp." I wished him good evening, and we separated.

My Zouave had not returned from the hospital, but shortly after made his appearance rather intoxicated. He related all that he had seen, and said that a few wounded Russians had been brought to the hospitals. "They have all they require," said he; "and, in case of need, I told a man to call us up." When he had put everything in order, he said, "I'll keep watch," and commenced singing his favourite songs. He made so much noise that we could not sleep if we had wished to do so, especially as the soldier-cooks and servants joined him in chorus.

XXX

FALL OF THE DOOMED CITY

Two days before I had been invited to dine with Colonel de Bathe, in order to partake of a Crimean fat goose. Though disappointed of my dinner, I was anxious to know if anything had happened to him and his brave companions in arms, and I therefore went round the camp and visited the Coldstream and Fusilier Guards. Many had not returned. Those off duty had retired to rest, which can be easily understood after the fatigues of such a day. I therefore returned, and laid down for a few hours. About four in the morning I went to the hospital, and found that every ward would soon be encumbered with sick and wounded. The cooks were over-fatigued, having been up all night at work. I at once proposed to furnish Dr. Mouatt with what he required, provided the purveyor would send the provisions to the Guard's camp. The doctor thanked me for the offer, and gave an immediate order to that effect. My Zouave had brought me a cross, which had been worn by a Russian officer who was killed. I presented it to one of the prisoners, who kissed it fervently and passed it to his comrades. There were about fifteen of them. No difference was made in the attendance or care bestowed upon them and that shown to our own troops, though not less than four or five hundred were in the hospital at the time, and more were coming in. Such a scene of suffering can never be effaced from memory, and is not to be described.

While waiting for the provisions, I galloped as far as Cathcart's Hill, and was much surprised to find that hostilities had entirely ceased. I met Colonel Steele just returning from the Redan.

"It's all over, Monsieur Soyer," said he.

"What do you mean, Colonel?" I replied.

"The Russians have retreated and abandoned Sebastopol! I have just been in the Redan, which exhibits a fearful scene. The loss has been great on all sides."

He then left in a great hurry, saying he must return to headquarters and telegraph the news to the War Office. A few houses were burning, and thick smoke was issuing from various parts of the city. Some of the Russian ships were burning in the bay. The weather was as calm as it had been boisterous the day before. Amongst the group upon the hill were the Duke of Newcastle, Mr. Russell, and a few others, not above twenty in all. Our attention was attracted by the arrival of a soldier with the first spoils of the conquered city. These consisted of two chairs, a dressing table and a looking-glass. He also carried a hare in one hand. On being asked where he got these various articles, he answered, "From the city. The French troops are plundering, and not a Russian is to be found. Yet the place is very dangerous, as explosions are continually taking place."

Shortly after, a long train of wounded, carried on mules, was seen going towards the General Hospital, amongst whom were a number of Russians. The *cortège* was followed by about twenty Russian prisoners; and I could not help remarking the youthful appearance of the latter, their age not exceeding from eighteen to twenty-five. This, I concluded, was owing to the immense number the enemy must have lost during the campaign.

My Zouave had, unknown to me, left on an expedition to the city. Although much against my will, it was impossible to stop him. My endeavours to impress upon his mind the importance of remaining with me upon that occasion were of no avail.

On returning to the camp I prepared a quantity of lemonade, arrowroot, beef-tea, arrowroot-water, barley-water, rice-water and pudding, boiled rice, &c., and through the kindness of Colonel Daniell and Major Fielden, twelve men were sent to carry them to the hospitals. I spent the remainder of the day in the hospitals, which were situated about a mile from the Guards' camp, where I witnessed the most painful scenes and numerous amputations. Amongst those operated upon were several Russians. I could not help remarking what a blessing to the sufferer chloroform proved. Wonderful was the kindness and celerity with which the doctors performed the operations. These were so numerous that before night several buckets were filled with the limbs, and the greater part of those operated upon were doing well. The hospitals, although they contained nearly forty wards, were full. Some of our wounded, as well as the Russians, were placed under marquees and other tents. The wounds received by some of the Russians were fearful, and the groans of those who were mortally wounded awful. Having done all that was required at the hospital I returned to the camp, where an invitation awaited me to dine at the Carlton Club. This I was much pleased to accept. The painful scenes I had witnessed weighed heavily upon the heart and mind, and a little relaxation became necessary. At about eight o'clock I repaired to the appointed place, and eight or nine guests sat down.

The dinner was very good; and though the bill of fare was rather extensive, every dish was cleared. Was this due to the skill of the *chef de cuisine*, or to the sixteen hours of hard work in the trenches? If the latter was really the cause of this, I should recommend a blasé epicure, who has lost his appetite, to try this simple and effective process. It will not fail to succeed—that is, should he escape with life after sixteen hours of shooting or being shot at, like pigeons at the Red House. The conversation became very animated, and so interesting that a small pamphlet might be written upon it. All had seen something and had something to relate.

My description of the hospitals was the great feature of the evening, as none present had seen them, having other occupation at their posts with the various regiments. The Queen's health, that of the Emperor of the French, and of the Sultan, were toasted with three times three and one more cheer. In the midst of this, Buckingham!! the renowned Buckingham!!! (who had displayed all his *savoir faire* in the *service de table*, acting upon that occasion as *maître d'hôtel en chef*, with a few utensils made a display worthy of a first-rate à la mode beef house, nothing to be laughed at in a Crimean popote) rushed into the tent, crying "Colonel! Colonel! the whole of Sebastopol is in flames." It was true. In less than ten minutes streets had taken fire with the rapidity of a firework, and every minute the conflagration seemed to be upon the increase. Nothing but fire and smoke could be seen from the Guard's camp. I proposed that we should order our horses and go to Cathcart's Hill to see what was going on. To my surprise, no one seemed inclined to move.

They all said that they had had enough of Sebastopol, and were tired to death. On urging the matter, the only answer I got from some of my gallant friends was, "Not tonight, Monsieur Soyer, not tonight."

"Surely," said I, "gentlemen! you don't expect the Russians will set a Sebastopol on fire every day at a few hours' notice to please you."

"That is not likely," said Major Fielden; "but for all that I feel convinced that no one will go."

As the fire seemed to extend and the sky became one lurid mass, I determined to go and get a sight of it. I bade my companions adieu, went back to my tent, ordered my horse, and tried to awake my Zouave in order to take him with me. He was so intoxicated I could not succeed. He had spent the day with some of his comrades, and had completely lost his senses. As I could not find either groom or any of my men, I went to Mr. Mesnil's tent. My major domo, being an old campaigner, had as usual turned in all dressed to be ready for any contingency. Rousing him, I requested him to accompany me. The eternal reply of "Not tonight" was again heard.

"Oh, hang the place, let it burn," said he.

As this was my last resource, I would not leave him. At last, in no very kindly mood, he turned out and agreed to go. The night was pitch dark, so we preferred going on foot. My friend was armed with a Russian sword and a night glass; I with a poignard-revolver and a lanthorn. Our intention was to get as near the city as possible, and we were prepared for any unpleasant encounter by firelight instead of moonlight. The purlieus of the camp were at this period anything but safe. With much difficulty, we reached Cathcart's Hill, having lost our way in trying what we thought would be a short cut. The camp was silent, and apparently deserted. Although only eleven o'clock, we did not meet a soul, with the exception of sentries, on our way.

So sublime was the scene witnessed by us from the summit of Cathcart's Hill, that it induced me, in my business correspondence with my publishers, Messrs. Routledge and Co., to forward them the following descriptive letter of the extraordinary effects this monstrous scene produced upon my senses. It has already appeared, I believe, in the public prints.

Flagstaff, Cathcart's Hill, near Sebastopol,
9th September, 1855.

GENTLEMEN,—Sebastopol has fallen, and almost every part of its superstructure is in flames. From the very spot I write, I can distinctly enumerate at least fourteen different conflagrations. The sight is at once sublime and terrific. A Martin or a Danby alone could trace on canvas, with their vigorous tints and their wild genius, the stupendous scene which my eyes are now beholding. The incessant roaring of the cannon, the explosion of shells, the blowing of the trumpet, the beating of drums, mingled with the groaning of the wounded and the anxious bustling of myriads of souls—adding to this the most tempestuous hurricane, the coldness of the weather, falling of hailstones, and the previously forest-like clouds of dust springing out from the harrowed Crimean soil, which raged during the whole of yesterday over the Allies' camps, have suddenly given place to the most profound calm and glowing breeze. The semi-defunct city and all the camps are as silent as the graves by which I am now surrounded. Ten yards from here lie the remains of the immortal Cathcart, encircled by several of his noble companions in arms. From half-past eleven to this present time, two a.m., not a living creature, save myself and a friend, besides the picket-sentinel, has been here to witness, from this remarkable spot, the downfall of the venerated Russian city.

With the highest consideration, I have the honour to be,

Your most obedient servant,

A. SOYER.

By the aid of the night-glass we obtained so good a view that we did not deem it advisable to proceed further. The heat of the fire was felt even at that distance, and explosions were frequent. The cause of the solitude in the camp at that hour can only be attributed to the excessive fatigue consequent upon the tremendous exertions of the previous day; the curtain had fallen on this grand drama—all was repose. We then returned to quarters through the same mournful solitude, not having met a soul either going or returning. This dreariness impressed me with the idea of chaos, after the destruction of a world and its empires.

Early the following morning, attended by my Zouave, who had recovered his sober senses, I started for the General Hospital.

We saw about thirty dead bodies laid out in a row, and stitched up in their blankets, with their name and nation marked upon each. I believe there was not a single case of amputation amongst them; they had all been mortally wounded. This speaks volumes in favour of the use of chloroform, the efficacy and safety of which, for a time, was much doubted, even by eminent medical men. Amputations were still being performed with skill and celerity worthy of a Guthrie or an Astley Cooper. The principal medical men were Drs. Mouatt, Lyons, &c. &c., who appeared to vie with each other in their kind attention to the sufferers.

Perceiving that nothing further was required for the present, and that all was going on well, I went to visit Sebastopol. My Zouave knew the road, as he had been there the day before. Our first visit was to the Redan, where we were refused admission. My intrepid Zouave, not contented with this rebuff, took me round another way, and, leaving our horses outside, we scaled the works and got in. The scene of death and destruction here was awful, and has been described too often for me to dwell upon it. Nothing but the effects of a devastating earthquake can give anyone an idea of the *débris* of the interior, or of the destruction caused by the fire of the Allies, and the explosions that had ensued. We proceeded to the city by the Arsenal, on the British side. The town was still burning. On reaching the large barracks, we visited the kitchens and bakeries. In the former, some of the boilers contained cabbage-soup; others, a kind of porridge made with black flour. In the bakeries, loaves of bread were still in the ovens, and dough in the troughs. We removed a loaf from the oven and tasted it. As we had brought no provision with us, and there was none to be obtained in the burning city, we ate about half a pound of bread each, and finished our frugal repast with a good draught of water: the latter was retailed at the small charge of sixpence a pint. A quarter of an hour after, I looked my Zouave hard in the face, saying, as I placed my hand upon my stomach, with a rueful face and in a piteous tone of voice—

"Bless me, Bornet! do you feel anything wrong?—because, if you don't, I do!" Looking still more pitiful, I continued—"I *am* confident the bread has been poisoned!"

"The deuce it has!" he replied, turning pale, and putting his fingers in his throat in order to throw off the dreadful meal, but without success.

I laughed at him, and called him a coward.

"Coward!" said he; "no, no, governor, I am no coward. I should not mind a round-shot, sword, or bayonet wound, in the field of battle; but, by Jupiter! to be poisoned ingloriously like a dog, would be base in the extreme."

"You're right," said I. "Come, don't fear, let's go and taste the soupe-aux-choux."

To this invitation he most decidedly objected, saying, "No more of their relishes for me, if you please."

In my culinary ardour I tasted it, and found it extremely bad and entirely deprived of nutritious qualities, but no doubt in it was to be added some black bread which would improve it.

Among the culinary trophies we brought away were a long iron fork, a ladle, some of the dough, biscuits, and a large piece of the black bread taken from the oven. I intended to test its merits upon my return to the camp. After visiting the docks, in which the vessels were still burning, as well as some in the harbour, we went to the Malakhoff, at the foot of which lay a number of dead bodies and horses. I met several acquaintances, and, on obtaining permission, visited the tower and its interior. The scene here was the same as at the Redan—one of destruction and desolation, though this place was not so much knocked about—but none could fail to appreciate the talent and skill displayed by the Russians in their style of forti-fication. The electric wires connected with the mines had been discovered and cut, rendering our visit comparatively safe. The men were busy burying the dead in all directions. My Zouave drew me towards the Black Battery, by which the division Bosquet had so severely suffered in valiantly defending their position. On arriving there, he recognised the dead body of one of his late comrades, and he implored me to allow him to remain till it was buried. As it was getting dark, and it was not probable that they would bury him that evening, I promised to allow him to return in the morning. Looking pitifully at the corpse, he said—

"Poor Adrien, what fun we had in Algeria! and now you are dead." Stooping down over the body and kissing it on both cheeks, he continued—"Tomorrow I will return and perform the last sad duty of a friend. Look, governor, would you not think he smiles? He was such a fine fellow—I am sure his soul has gone straight to headquarters."

It was almost dark, and we galloped home. The next morning my Zouave attended the funeral of his friend, and it took so long that I did not see him again for forty-eight hours. When he returned, he brought two Zouaves with him, and they were all laden with trophies; among them was an entirely new tent, which, from its very superior quality, was supposed to have belonged to some general offi-cer. The Zouaves had pitched upon Prince Orloff as the owner, no doubt to increase its value. It really was worthy of a commander-in-chief. I purchased it, and have it still in my possession. The rest of the booty consisted of guns, swords, church relics, &c.—in fact, all they could lay hands upon which was likely to be converted into money. The only thing which surprised me was, that he had returned sober. While I was reprimanding him for his long absence, he coolly replied,

"You are right, governor; but you see, after paying the last duties to poor Adrien, in order to drown the melancholy feeling of human existence, I got boozy enough to make all the wine sellers, and even old Father Bacchus himself, turn pale. When I began to find that I could no longer see, I said to myself, 'Bornet, my friend, you must not disgrace the governor's quarters. Go to bed upon the straw like a pig as you are.' In ten hours my drunken fit had passed away like a vaporous cloud; and here, governor, is your Zouave, in a fit state, ready to dance upon a rope without a balance-pole."

The original and comic nature of the excuse caused me to laugh at him, instead of scolding him.

He then proposed to go in the evening and find the remaining part of Count Orloff's tent, spend the night in Sebastopol, and meet me the next morning at the Greek church in the town.

All was going on well at the General Hospital. It was crammed full, and amputations were being performed night and day. I called there daily with some of my men, and sent the others in various directions. The next day I visited Sebastopol, and went to the French side. I could not find Bornet, but saw one of his friends, who told me that he had slept in the French camp. I therefore gave him up, and determined to get rid of him as soon as possible. After visiting the town in company with a few friends whom I happened to meet there, we went to the Russian hospital, which we had been told was full of dead, sick, and wounded. During the few days that had elapsed since the capture of the city I had witnessed many awful scenes, but this was the most harrowing of all.

Perhaps one of the most awful and sickening sights possible for humanity to conjure up was witnessed by myself and many others in the Russian hospital in the interior of Sebastopol. Piled up one on the other, or lying singly on the bare flooring, were strew hundreds of Russians, dead and dying. The view would have struck terror into the heart of the greatest stoic. These men seemed to have been placed here out of the way to suffer and die, uncared for, unattended. On one side might be seen a poor creature writhing in the last throes of dissolution; on the other, a fine fellow with almost divine resignation, who had just rendered himself up to his Maker, having died in dreadful agony. Men without legs or arms, and some with frightful body wounds or bayonet thrusts, lay huddled in helpless confusion. Desolation and death grimly met us at each step. Then the effluvia arising from the bodies was horrible beyond description.

XXXI

ILLNESS AND CHANGE OF SCENE

For a few days all business seemed suspended in the camp, and the rage with everyone was to visit the ruins of the far-famed city. The hospitals in the camp and at Balaklava were quite full, though most of the patients were going on very satisfactorily. Much bustle was observed at both the French and English headquarters. As the soup was no longer required for the soldiers in the trenches, the order for the field-stoves remained some time in abeyance, and all appeared like holiday time. In fact, people kept flocking, with and without permission, into Sebastopol. Deeming this a favourable opportunity, I proposed giving a déjeuner in the Malakhoff two days after its capture, and cooking it with my magic bivouac-stove. Among the guests invited were Colonels Daniell, De Bathe; Brigadier Drummond; Majors Fielden, Armitage; Captain Tower, &c. &c. We were to muster about twelve; the great dish was to be the *poulets sautés à la Malakhoff*, cooked on my pocket bivouac-stove in the open air. All was prepared, and we were about to start, when I learnt that we should not be allowed to enter the tower. Colonel Daniell, who had some business at headquarters, promised to try and obtain permission. I at once went to General Pelissier for the order, which could not be granted in his absence. I saw General Rose, who said any other day he should be happy to make the request. The appetites of my invited guests were sharpened and the stomachs waiting, and they would have grumbled had they not been satisfied. We therefore agreed that in lieu of having it in the Malakhoff, we should make ourselves satisfied with the Mamelon Vert *à la Carleton*; and a very jovial reunion we made of it. Alas! it was the last I was destined to enjoy for some time.

Seven or eight days after, I was laid up with a very severe attack of Crimean fever. Not being aware of the nature of my illness, I thought rest was all I required, after the fatigue I had undergone: I therefore went to bed—but what kind of bed?—under damp canvas, with a muddy floor, as it had rained heavily for some days. I felt so ill, that I could neither lie, sit, nor stand, without great suffering. Imagining that I could conquer the disease, I did not send for the doctor. Fortunately for me, a short time after my attack, as I lay in bed, Dr. Linton, who often visited me, chanced to call at my tent. I told him of my indisposition, and he at once sent me some medicine, more blankets, and kindly offered his services; at the same time informing me that I had a serious attack of fever. I was in the Coldstreams' camp; and Dr. Wyatt claimed me as his patient, and paid me a visit. He immediately ordered me to keep my bed. For some days he watched my case most diligently, and under his skilful care I soon got better. During my illness I received visits and kind inquiries from almost all the heads of the forces, for which I shall ever feel grateful; their attention was most gratifying to my feelings, and I am proud of the consideration evinced for me by that noble band, the British army.

Directly I recovered and was allowed to go about, I felt anxious to have a decided answer respecting the stoves—for the matter was at that time in abeyance. I also wished to visit the various regimental hospitals in which my men were engaged teaching the soldiers. In my eagerness to attend to these things, I overfatigued myself, and brought on a second attack, much worse than the former. Dr. Wyatt was almost in despair, and privately informed Mr. Mesnil that I was in great danger. However, owing entirely to his great care and kind attention, in three weeks I had partly recovered, but was so much altered that scarcely anybody could recognise me. I one day visited Lord William Paulet, who had left Scutari, and was on board the *Leander* in Balaklava Bay. I was so much changed, that neither Admiral Freemantle nor his lordship knew me. Miss Nightingale had returned, and was much in want of my services. Not being aware of my illness, she sent for me; and as soon as I recovered, I waited upon and accompanied that lady to the Monastery Hospital. The fatigue consequent upon my exertions brought me so low, that Dr. Wyatt insisted upon my leaving the Crimea, saying he would not be responsible for my safety any longer in that climate.

A few days before my departure the following laughable circumstance occurred, which has already been related in the columns of the *Illustrated News* by an amateur correspondent:—

AN UNEXPECTED VISITOR AND A CONVERSATION

I had an amusing adventure the other evening. A stranger visited me, and I entertained a late distinguished *attaché* of the Reform Club unawares. It was getting dusk, and I was very tired, having been engaged in the hospital marquees all day—for we had a very sudden and violent outbreak of cholera. Phillipo, my Maltese servant, was down on his hands and knees, blowing the lighted charcoal in my fireplace, with the intention of expediting dinner. My fireplace, I must tell you, consists of a hole dug in the earth, with three pieces of iron hooping stretched across by way of grate; and a very admirable kitchen-range it is. Phillipo had just afforded me the agreeable information that dinner would not be ready for nearly an hour, and I was in the act of lighting my pipe, when I heard an unaccustomed step climbing up the rock side, close to my tent, and a musical and hilarious voice exclaimed, "Is Guy Earl of Warwick at home?" I laid down my pipe utterly astounded; and in another moment a hand drew aside the canvas, a head appeared at the entrance of my tent, and the portly figure of a man speedily completed the apparition. For a moment my visitor surveyed me, evidently as much astonished as I was. "Ah! I see, I have made one grand mistake!" (he spoke tolerable English, but with a decided French accent). "You will think me strange. I was looking for my old friend Warwick, and made sure this was his tent. We call him Guy Earl of Warwick. Ah! ah! badinage. It may be you know him?"

By this time I had fully surveyed my visitor. He was a tall, stout, rather handsome-looking man, aged about fifty years. He wore a drab-coloured "wide-awake" wrapped round with a red scarf, and a white blouse, heavily braided about the sleeves. His hair had been black, now rapidly changing into grey; and his whiskers, moustache, and beard (the latter primly cut), were of the same "Oxford mixture." Observing that the walk up the hill had slightly affected his breathing, I invited him to take a seat on one of my bullock-trunks, the only "ottoman" of which my Turkish tent could boast. (It is no slight exertion to get up to my tent, as I have pitched it almost at the top of a hill, in order, if possible, to evade the rats, which swarm in the Crimea; indeed, I scarcely know whether rats, flies, or fleas are the greatest nuisance.) In a few moments we got into conversation.

"I am going to Balaklava shortly," said the stranger; "I am going on board ship. I have been out here some few months; my health has been gone ever since I came. They tell me I am older ten years this last five months. I am going to England."

"And I am only waiting till this Crimean drama is over to follow your example," said I. "I must see the Russians finally driven out, and then I go home too. As to campaigning, the curiosity which brought me here is gratified; as to the moving accidents of war, I have supped full of horrors!—But here comes Phillipo with the dinner."

The Maltese entered, and placed upon the table a piece of beef baked in an iron pot, also some boiled potatoes. I observed that my visitor eyed the dinner curiously, and I was almost angry to observe the instantaneous elevation of his eyebrows, when with great difficulty I succeeded in whittling off with a sharp carving-knife a slice of the outside.

"Nice beef, but not done quite enough," said my visitor.

He might well say so; it was almost raw. I stuck a fork into the potatoes; they were as hard as pebbles. I was in despair. The stranger laughed aloud. I was rapidly getting sulky.

"I see you have a good fire outside," said my visitor; "that charcoal gives a beautiful heat. Now, if you will take my advice, I should say, cut a slice or two——"

"Excuse me," I replied, "but if there is one thing more than another that I pride myself on, it is my cooking. I can cook with any fellow in the Crimea, perhaps excepting Soyer; and some people say that he is a great humbug."

"Do they indeed?" said he. "Well, he must be rather a clever humbug to sell 40,000 of his books."

"I must confess," I said, "that his shilling Cookery Book is a great invention. I have made many capital dishes by its direction. The fact is, I generally superintend the cooking myself."

"And your politeness to me has spoiled your dinner. Now look here."

And, almost before I could interpose a word, my potatoes were in slices, a large onion was dissected piecemeal, my beef was submitted to the knife, a pinch or two of ration salt and pepper completed the preparations, and my little canteen-pan was on the fire. I looked on, regarding these proceedings with much astonishment, and not a little jealousy. After a few minutes the stranger gave the pan a graceful wave or two over the fire, and then replaced it on the table. There was a dinner fit for Sardanapalus! Never shall I forget the elegant curl of that steam, or the exquisite odour which soon pervaded the atmosphere of my tent. I could not help thinking of and half excusing a certain hairy man who lived in the first ages, and who for just such a mess of potage disposed of his estates.

"How do you like it?" said the stranger.

"Don't talk at present," I answered; "I consider dinner one of the most serious duties of life."

"Ah! ah! then you would not call Soyer a humbug to make this?"

"Soyer!" I said in disdain—"Soyer never made or invented a dish half as good in his life! Talk about French slops in comparison with prime English beef and onions! Bah!"

I was carried away by my enthusiasm, and quite forgot that I was at that moment eating part of the carcase of a wretched Armenian beast, that would not have fetched 50s. in an English market. At last dinner was over.

"One more glass of sherry," said the stranger, "and then I go. I am very glad to have made your acquaintance, and I hope you will come and see me when you come down to Balaklava. I shall be on board the ship *Edward* in the bay. I am going to stop there a little time for my health. Come on board and ask for me."

"With very great pleasure—and your name?"

"Oh! my name—*Soyer*," said he; and he sat down and laughed still the tears stood in his eyes.   W.C.

Soon after I left Balaklava for Scutari on board the *Imperador*, Captain Brown. His humorous countenance would alone have sufficed to restore the gaiety of the most shattered constitution, setting aside his good-nature and continual kindness to his numerous passengers, particularly the invalids. What visitor to the Crimea has not known or heard of Captain Brown of the *Imperador?* His heart was as large as his ship, and his mind as brilliant as his gorgeous saloon: moreover, his table was worthy of any yachting epicure. He was in every way a credit to that noble class of men, the pet children of the ocean, the captain's kingly race. At the time of my trip he was an invalid, having broken two of his ribs; but he did not consider the case a serious one, and consoled himself by saying this accident was nothing compared with the one he had met with a few months before. "Then," said he, laughing, "I actually fell into the coal-hole, and broke my collar bone; and (showing his lame arm) I shall be lame for life through it. However, these broken ribs are nearly set again, and I shall soon be well. But pray do not make me laugh—come, let us have another glass of port," closed his argument. (This was cheese-time dialogue.)

We had a fine passage, as well as agreeable companions in the passengers, amongst whom were three American gentlemen just returning from Russia. They were in Sebastopol during the storming on the 8th of September, and had been sent by their Government upon important duty. Owing to my weakness at the time, I have forgotten the purport of their mission. They had been introduced to the Emperor Alexander, and spoke in high terms of his Majesty's courtesy. They had come from America in their own ship, which was at that time in the Bosphorus undergoing repairs. I was invited to dine with them some day, which I promised to do, but was not able to keep my promise, in consequence of my continued illness. "The dinner," said one of them, shall be cooked *à la* Soyer, for we have your book on board—the one called the *Modern Housewife*."

I felt much flattered when they afterwards told me that my book was very extensively used in America. "Your Cookery Book, Monsieur Soyer, is the national book, or 'household words.' Every respectable family has it. Indeed, you are as well known by reputation in America as in England. Take this for a standing invitation. Should you ever come as far as our American land of freedom, we invite you to be our guest."

At this I was highly gratified, and almost promised, if I recovered, to accept their invitation. At all events, in case I should not go, I take this opportunity of thanking them heartily for their kind invitation, in hopes that this book, like its predecessors, will cross the Atlantic, and come under their notice.

To me everything on board the magnificent ship *Imperador* wore a smiling aspect, and I began to feel myself again. I no sooner arrived at Scutari, than I went and visited Brigadier-General Storks, with whom I had not the pleasure of being acquainted. He had succeeded Lord William Paulet. I was kindly received by the general. He congratulated me in flattering terms upon the good system I had introduced into the kitchen department of the hospitals, of which he was at that time the governor. I felt myself quite at home with the general, who, though an Englishman, could have taught me my own language. He certainly spoke it more fluently than I did myself: I had been so long in England, and had, moreover, employed so many people of different nations—Greeks, Armenians, Turks, French, Italians; and I must not omit two Maltese, who, to render them justice, were worth all my other cooks put together for intelligence and activity—that I began to forget my native tongue. My readers can easily suppose that, amidst such a miscellany of languages, one might easily murder one's own. General Storks is not only a good French scholar, but has all the tournure and appearance of the French *beau idéal*.

After about half-an-hour's chat upon business and other matters, I left the general, and promised to have the pleasure of visiting him frequently during my stay in Scutari, which was to be about a week—it being then my intention to return to England to regain my health.

I visited my first Crimean doctor, Dr. Linton, who had left the Crimea to replace Dr. Cumming. He would hardly condescend to know me, so much had I altered; and I found this to be the case with everyone I met. I frightened my cooks when I entered the kitchen. They had heard that I was dead, which I afterwards personally denied; but they did not think it was possible I could look so bad. Purveyors, comptrollers, civilian and military doctors, Sisters of Mercy, all consoled me by saying, "I fear you will never get over it, Monsieur Soyer."

"Well," I replied to some of them, "that's my business; at all events, I will do my best to deceive you."

Nothing is less likely to restore a man when he is half dead than trying to persuade him that he must succumb. Thanks to my lucky star, I have deceived them all; and some richly deserve it, as they had laid bets upon my chance, particularly my Zouave and another of my men. The former answered all inquiries respecting the state of my health by, "The governor, you see, is in a very bad way. His hash is settled; it is all over with him. It is a pity, for he is a good man, and he had promised to take me with him to London, a place I very much wish to visit."

A few days after my arrival in Constantinople my health again failed me, and having no further need for the services of my Zouave, to his great regret we parted, but on such friendly terms, that he afterwards often observed, "Look ye, governor, you have been a good master to me, and if you ever recover from your serious illness, which is not very probable, send for me—I am still your man, and will follow you anywhere and everywhere, even to England; and if any fellow annoys you, here is the arm (showing it to the shoulder) which will make them bleed to death and bury them after."

I took up my residence at Soyer House, where I enjoyed the gay and interesting prospect for an invalid of the monster lugubrious cemetery, or Grand Champ des Morts, on one side, and the hospital on the other. The weather was wet and wretched—the house, as usual, splendidly ventilated, and had been robbed of its furniture by a Greek servant I had left there. It was, moreover, populated by rats and other vermin. Before I could set it in order, I fell ill for the third time, and had, in addition to my former malady, a severe attack of dysentery. I left my dismal abode, now become unbearable, crossed the Bosphorus to Pera, and took up my lodgings at an hotel for a few days, as I then anticipated, having determined upon my departure for England. However, instead of improving in health, I grew worse and worse, and was laid up for three months; in fact, I began to fear my Zouave would win his wager. During this time, I received notice that the order had been given for four hundred stoves, which were to be forwarded as fast as they could be made. I therefore decided upon remaining at Constantinople, in the hope of being able, in the event of getting better, of returning to the Crimea, and distributing them to the different regiments.

One day I had crossed over to Scutari in order to visit Miss Nightingale, who had just arrived from Balaklava, when I met the celebrated Dr. Sutherland, who, like the rest, gave me a very encouraging view of his scientific opinion upon the state of my health. "For God's sake, Soyer," said he, "do leave this country, and go immediately to Malta—not England—or you are a dead man."

"Not so, doctor," I replied; "I am much better these last few days. In fact, I am going back to the Crimea; my stoves are expected daily, and I must go and distribute them."

"In that case, don't forget to take your tombstone with you."

"A very interesting thing to do, doctor; but I shall chance the voyage for all that, if I improve; and as to the tombstone, I shall leave that to friendly hands in case it is required."

I thanked him for the valuable medical advice he had given me, as well as the suggestion of a visit to Malta. I left my German doctor, Mr. Morris, a very eminent man I believe, but his German style of treatment did not seem to agree with my John Bull constitution. I had no sooner left him and adopted the English style of treatment (and here I cannot refrain from expressing my thanks to a young medical gentleman named Ambler, who was most assiduous in his kind attentions to me, and through following his prescriptions, which were very strengthening, I ultimately recovered) and was able to cook nice things for myself, instead of starving *à l'Allemande* upon a rigorous diet, than I regained strength enough to go about and look to business, and even to ride from hospital to hospital—go to the Isles des Princes, Therapia, Buyukderé, &c., for change of air, and was at last strong enough to accept the following invitation to the grand ball at the English Embassy:—

La Vicomtesse Stratford de Redcliffe prie Monsieur Soyer de venir passer chez elle la soirée de Jeudi, 31 Janvier, à 10 heures.
Bal Costumé.

This grand annual festival, so eagerly looked for by the fashionables of Pera and Constantinople, presented this year quite a new phase. In addition to the usual diplomatic corps of the various nations represented by their ambassadors and their noble families, there were the *élite* of the Allied armies. The full-dress costumes of the diplomatic corps, as well as those of the military men, intermixed with hundreds of exquisite fancy costumes, formed a ravishing *tout ensemble*.

Such an assemblage of members of all nations probably never met beneath the same roof, and very likely never will again—the advent of the war being the cause. The greatest attraction of the ball was the assemblage of ladies in their brilliant costumes. Independent of those from the various embassies, were French, English, German, Greek, Armenian, Italian, and Circassian ladies—in fact, all nations except the one the ball was given to, viz., Turkish ladies, the only lady in that Oriental costume turning out to be a colonel of cavalry. At an early hour, the magnificent ballroom, which is lit from the roof by thousands of wax lights, was full. At nine precisely the cannon was heard announcing the arrival of the Sultan at the Palais d'Angleterre. The *coup d'œil* was really fairylike upon the entrance of his Majesty and suite, the latter attired in full uniforms, which could not fail to astonish the most initiated eye by the gorgeous display of gold, jewels, and diamonds, coupled with the idea that such a scene had never before been witnessed except on high Turkish festivals, which are even more solemn than our grand ceremonies. Upon this occasion were assembled all the grandees and chief Turkish officers, attired in their sacred festival uniforms, with a smile upon their countenances, instead of the usual stolid and serious cast of features so peculiar to the Moslems during their grand ceremonies. His Sublime Majesty was nobly though plainly attired, and shone above his suite by his magnificent simplicity.

Lord Stratford de Redcliffe met the Sultan at the foot of the great marble staircase, that architectural *chef-d'œuvre* of the Palais d'Angleterre; and her ladyship and family, surrounded by her noble circle, received him at the summit. His Majesty, with great affability, expressed through Lord de Redcliffe the gratification he felt at being presented to her ladyship and her numerous visitors. He was shown through the various saloons, which were brilliantly illuminated and profusely decorated with choice flowers: they were all crowded. The expression of his Majesty's countenance showed that he took the most vivid interest in the novel scene witnessed by him for the first time. The ladies' fancy dresses were in exquisite taste, particularly the "Elizabethan Quadrilles," led by Lady de Redcliffe and the young ladies, forming a perfect representation in *tableau vivant* of the Elizabethan period, brilliantly executed. The costumes most to be admired in that assemblage of aristocratic beauty were, the Pompadour, Ninon de l'Enclos, ancient Greek, Circassian, Roman peasant, Albanaise, Catalanaise, and Pierrettes.

All the gentlemen, except the diplomatic and high military corps, were in fancy character, which gave a cheerful appearance and *ensemble* to the ball; and the Sultan, prior to his departure, expressed to Lord and Lady de Redcliffe the gratification he felt at witnessing such a lively scene.*

Towards five in the morning, its dazzling grandeur had disappeared, and very forcibly presented to some of us the reverse of the medal. To a mild evening succeeded a most tempestuous and cold morning: snow fell heavily in the Oriental city. The change of temperature was so sudden and violent, that one might have fancied oneself transferred by enchantment from summer to winter, or from Paradise to Pandemonium. The sudden change of scene and temperature presented a sad contrast to the mind. A few friends accompanied me who were, like myself, very lightly clad, being in character, and we had to go home in that storm of snow on foot. On reflection, I felt that I had acted very imprudently in going at all, in the state I was then in, and that it might prove fatal to me. "After all," said I to my friends, who, like myself, were floundering about in the snow, by that time six inches deep in some places, "I should very much regret not having been, no matter what may be the consequences. To be present at an entertainment which the Padischah for the first time had honoured with his presence, viz., a Christian ball, is far from being a common thing."

We reached our hotel door as wet as frogs, the movements of which reptile we had been for some time imitating by jumping from tombstone to tombstone in the Petit Champ des Morts, that being our nearest road home. The door was opened, after we had knocked about twenty times. Nevertheless, we had no reason to be dull or impatient, as there was defiling before us the everlasting caravan of donkeys

---

* A few days after, his Majesty honoured with his presence the grand anniversary ball given at the French Embassy by Monsieur Thouvenel, the French ambassador. It was also very splendid, but not being a fancy one, did not offer the same points of interest. The English ball had the advantage of being the first ever attended by a Moslem monarch: nevertheless, his Sublime Majesty remained longer at the latter than at the former, having, doubtless, taken a fancy to our European social customs.

laden with coffins for the daily consumption of the French hospital at Pera. Never, perhaps, upon any stage was there such a sudden change from the sublime to the gloomy. The door at last opened, and we were saluted with a "Very sorry, gentlemen, to keep you waiting, but we did not expect you so early." It was only half-past six a.m.

I made sure that I should be ill after such a series of events, and, wishing to be quiet, I gave special orders that no one should be permitted to disturb me, excepting the doctor, who was in the habit of calling occasionally. I had scarcely fallen asleep, when I was aroused by a knock at the door, and a letter put into my hands apprising me that part of my stoves had arrived. I was, therefore, obliged to rise immediately and to go in person to the Admiralty, as my head man had left for Scutari the night before. The steamer was on its way to Balaklava, and the captain did not know what he was to do with them. I immediately wrote to Colonel Blane at headquarters upon the subject, and received the following letter in reply:—

HEADQUARTERS, CRIMEA, 19th March, 1856.

SIR,—In reply to your letter of the 13th inst., I am directed to acquaint you that the new field-stoves will not be issued by Captain Gordon until he receives instructions to that effect from the Quartermaster-General. Lieut.-Colonel Halliwell, Assistant Quartermaster-General of the Fourth Division, will give you, on your arrival in the Crimea, every information as to the hut which was directed to be built for your use in the camp of the Fourth Division.

I have the honour to be, Sir,
Your most obedient servant,

Monsieur A. Soyer,   ROBERT BLANE, Lieut.-Col.,
Barrack Hospital, Scutari.   *Military Secretary*

The exertion I had undergone for nearly twenty-four hours, I fully expected would have laid me up for as many days. On the contrary, however, I felt as strong again as the day before the ball, and to this event alone I attribute my cure. This proves that a sudden change may often be beneficial in cases of violent disease. In a few days I once more embarked on board the *Ottawa*, and was again *en route* to the Crimean shore, but received the following letter from Lord de Redcliffe before leaving:—

BRITISH EMBASSY, *February* 20th, 1856.

DEAR MONSIEUR SOYER,—I cannot let you go back to the Crimea, which I understand you think of doing, without receiving my written thanks, in addition to those which I have already expressed by word of mouth.

It must be a great satisfaction to you to have found so excellent a field for the application of your skill and humanity; and I sincerely hope that your name will be never dissociated from the great and memorable events of the present war.

Believe me, very sincerely yours,

Monsieur A. Soyer.   STRATFORD DE REDCLIFFE.

Prior to my departure, to my great satisfaction, the Medical Staff Corps were well established in the Barrack and General Hospitals, these being the only ones remaining. All the responsibility of the culinary department in those establishments was thus taken off my hands, as the Medical Staff were well acquainted with my system, which was followed to the last.

The following letters which I wrote to the Government and General Storks will prove the necessity that exists for the establishment of such a corps for military hospitals; and it ought to be established by every nation.

To General Storks, Commanding Officer

BARRACK HOSPITAL, SCUTARI, *March* 11*th*, 1856.

MONS. LE GENERAL,—My field stoves for the army, so long expected, having just arrived; in a few days I shall proceed to the Crimea to distribute them to the different regiments, as per special orders from the War Office.

Prior to my departure hence, I am happy to inform you that the Medical Staff Corps is now instructed by Victor, the civilian cook, in the management of the kitchen department of the hospital under the new system introduced by me and approved of by the medical authorities, which up to this time (a period of twelve months) has perfectly succeeded.

As I shall require Victor with me in the Crimea, I shall leave the future management in the hands of the said corps: I would recommend its introduction in all the military hospitals, it being of the utmost importance for the regularity of the diet for the sick, that the *employés*, when once initiated, should not be removed, as was the case with the soldier cooks, and which removal was much commented upon by myself and Dr. Cumming on my arrival at Scutari, and induced me to introduce civilian cooks. The introduction of the new corps will also tend to the regularity and economy of the extra-diet system, which is a matter of great importance in so large an establishment, and has till now been attended with difficulty, as the civilian cooks could not be subjected to the rigid discipline of the new corps.

I feel myself in duty bound to say that Mr. Robertson, the purveyor-in-chief, has assisted me in every way to bring the system to the state of perfection in which it now is; which system I am confident will, by the introduction of my printed receipts, be adopted at home in the civil as well as military hospitals—it leaving been submitted to both military and civilian medical officers, who have approved the same, and also assisted me with their valuable knowledge and suggestions in its formation.

With the highest consideration, I have the honour to be,

Your most obedient servant,

A. SOYER.

———

To the Right Hon. Lord Panmure, Secretary-at-War

BARRACK HOSPITAL, SCUTARI, *March* 11*th*, 1856.

MY LORD,—The ship *Cape of Good Hope*, with the first consignment of my stoves on board, has just passed through the Bosphorus to Balaklava, and, to my great disappointment, without stopping here; as I was in daily expectation of her arrival in order to proceed in her to the Crimea, and distribute them to the different regiments, having with that view requested from the Admiralty Office, and the wharf-master at Scutari, notice of her arrival. I have just been apprised that the ship was ordered direct for Balaklava, and I shall follow her as early as possible. I have written to headquarters to that effect, and beg to enclose the copy of a letter to General Storks, in which your lordship will perceive how highly I approve of the introduction of the new Medical Staff Corps.

I have the honour to be,

Your most obedient servant,

A. SOYER.

XXXII

CAMP OF THE FOURTH DIVISION

I THUS had the opportunity of taking my civilian cooks away with me, as I wanted their services in the Crimea. Upon my arrival at Balaklava, I paid my respects to General Codrington. My stoves had arrived just before, and the fact of their having been adopted was mentioned in the orders of the day.

Mr. Phillips, the engineer I had requested the Government to send out to superintend or repair the stoves if required, arrived on board the *Argo*. I am happy to say that, as far as repairs were concerned, this gentleman's services were not needed. Although the stoves were frequently moved from camp to camp, and from one regiment to another—were in continual use in the open air, exposed to all weathers, and some of them for above twelve months, they did not stand in need of any repairs. This fact speaks volumes for their fitness for campaigning.

Mr. Phillips was the son of one of the partners of the firm of Smith and Phillips. He had nothing to do professionally as regards the repairing of the stoves, but I must acknowledge that he made himself very useful as well as agreeable. He rose very early, and accompanied me in my camp cruises, racing from stove to stove. He woke at daybreak, but always felt rather drowsy till he had taken a strong cup of tea, with a stronger drop of rum in it, which set him, as he said, upon his mettle. He then mounted his horse, which had gloriously served his country for nearly fourteen years in the French cavalry under a heavy cuirassier. The only inconvenience with this warrior quadruped was that my cockney Zouave was never sure which regiment he should visit first, as he was no sooner on the back of this old pensioner, than he began to fidget, and off he went in any direction, but always stopped at some regimental stable. This did not so much matter, as I had stoves in almost every regiment. The only plan was to make no positive appointment.

On two or three occasions he was less successful, for *Ventre-à-terre*—such was the French name of that Pegasus—took him full gallop through the French camp. The first inconvenience was my having no stove there; the second, the French had arrested him for galloping through the camp, and were about to put his horse in the pound and himself in prison. I arrived quite by chance, and he was liberated. As he spoke no French, he was endeavouring to assure them in English that he was not the culprit, but his horse. I explained the case to the French serjeant, and recommended, as a point of justice, as it was the animal's fault, that he should be put in the stable and the horse in prison. This amused the group of Imperial Guards, who surrounded us by scores, and a few bottles of very, very acid wine, procured at Madame Fleur des Bois', the mistress of the canteen, terminated in full glee the adventure of my cockney Zouave of Snow Hill in the French camp of the Crimea.

Mr. Phillips was an excellent vocalist, and his collection, unlike that of my Zouave Bornet, with his "En avant les Bataillons d'Afrique," "Storm of Constantine," "Bravest of the Brave," "Cannon Ball," "Shell Polka," &c., was of a softer nature, including "Sally in our Alley," who, he pretended, was the love of his heart. Another of his favourite pieces intimated that the soft part of that organ was bursting for the love of Alice Gray, whom he very much wished to meet by moonlight alone, or in company with the "Ratcatcher's Daughter," while walking round the garden with "Villikins and his Dinah." I am induced thus minutely to depict the merits of my Snow Hill Zouave, because he will be so well recognised by those who were in the camp. He was short, fair, fat, and full of London jokes, which he had the fault of laughing at more himself than those did who listened to him. He is a good son, good husband, good father, a good fellow, but a bad punster.

The chief evil in the old canteen cooking apparatus was, that it so easily got out of repair. There was no possibility either of mending them or of obtaining new ones, as they were only issued at certain periods. I saw some that had been mended in a most extraordinary style. When the hole was too small, the soldiers would poke a rusty nail into it; if large, a nail with a piece of leather attached. Other operators would cut a piece off the cover in order to mend the bottom or side; and as after that scientific repair leakage was unavoidable, they were obliged to keep putting in fresh water, or to let the canteen burn.

After our interview, General Codrington promised me his assistance. The Congress was then sitting, and rumours of peace were flying about. I asked the general whether it would not be better to prevent more stoves being sent out. He replied—

"Perhaps it would."

"I am glad to hear you say so, your excellency, it being a sign of peace, as war I consider at all times unprofitable."

"On the contrary, Monsieur Soyer; we are making greater preparations than ever for war."

It was decided that, for the time being, one stove should be delivered to each regiment, and be removed from company to company, in order to give all the men an insight into the method of using them, and of my system of cooking. This was immediately done; and on the receipt of the following from Colonel Blane, I went to Colonel Halliwell:—

HEADQUARTERS, CRIMEA.

MY DEAR SIR,—By applying to Colonel Halliwell of the Fourth Division, he will give you possession of the hut which has been built for yourself and suite, and will assist you in every manner possible.

I am, yours ever,
S. J. BLANE, Col.,
Mil. Sec. to Gen. Sir W. Codrington, Commanding.

To Monsieur Soyer.

In a very short space of time my tents were pitched, and myself and my people were installed, on that celebrated spot called after that great and deeply-regretted man, General Cathcart—viz., Cathcart's Hill.

This was now my castle, and proud was I of the noble site granted to me, as well as of my neighbours, from whom I received a most kind and friendly reception. Indeed, it was with the highest gratification that I found in the Fourth Division the same welcome and urbanity I had received in the First. I shall ever be grateful to Colonel Halliwell, who, by the bye, is a very distinguished artist and a discriminating epicure. Excuse the remark, dear reader, but a man, as I have already remarked in my *Regenerator*, may be either a gourmet or a gourmand, but never both: "car le gourmand n'est jamais gourmet; l'un mange sans déguster, l'autre déguste en mangeant." The gourmet is the Epicurean dilettante, who eats scientifically and with all his organs—ears, of course, included. The gourmand's stomach alone acts; he swallows all that is put before him, never praises the culinary artist, and seldom complains of the quality of the food, but frequently of the want of quantity.

Therefore, gourmets, epicures, high-livers, and wealthy merchants, who are gifted with a fine intellect, never allow yourselves to be called a gourmand if you are really deserving of the title of gourmet—and this title I confidently bestow upon my honourable friend Colonel Halliwell, who was not only a gourmet, but also a very good amateur cook. I defy anyone to make a better mayonnaise, not even excepting professionals.

The plan I had adopted for the introduction of my stoves was as follows:—I first had an interview with the colonel of the regiment, who introduced me to the quartermaster—the latter to the storekeeper. Then I went to the commissariat in each division, where I looked over the stores, in order to regulate the distribution of the provisions and condiments with judgment and according to common sense.*

To remedy this evil in a private family would only require a few minutes' conversation with the cook; while in an army it would take years, as military rules would have to be changed and fresh ones introduced. Simple as the change may appear, it is still very difficult to carry out, particularly in a camp extending over such a large space of ground. Fortunately, I was invested with the power of doing so without

---

* When I say "according to common sense," I am speaking within bounds. Salt and pepper, fresh and preserved vegetables (the latter either in tins or in cakes), were distributed from the regimental quartermaster's stores to the cooks of each company for three days' consumption at a time. The consequence was that, in a couple of days, and sometimes in one, the three days' rations had either been consumed or were wasted. The first day, the soup or other food was badly prepared, on account of the excess of these ingredients; and it was still worse on the following days, on account of their being short of all with the exception of the meat, which was therefore boiled in plain water with rice, but often without either salt or vegetables. The food was thus rendered insipid and unwholesome. Such was the system I found in general use, and it was a great pity, seeing the Government had so liberally provided all that was required. Proper regulation was all that was needed in order to increase the comforts of the men. The meals of the whole army constitute a very important matter. Any improvement was certain to be felt daily; for can anything be more unpalatable than a piece of fresh beef boiled in plain water, without seasoning? There was no salt to eat with it, although plenty was allowed for each man. This is what I call want of attention and lack of common sense. I do not mean to say this was always the case, as some quartermasters, who noticed the evil, distributed the vegetables daily, instead of for three days at once. Many of the men were intelligent enough to divide the allowance, but the greater number were very careless; it therefore became of the utmost importance to establish a rule which would not leave them the chance of doing wrong. The great evil is, that after being thus deprived of salt for a day or two, they then receive salt rations, which they boil in small tin camp-kettles, and without soaking, in merely a few pints of water, which becomes like so much brine. Thus various diseases, which are seldom attributed to the real cause, are engendered, and all medicinal equilibrium is completely upset. The rectifying of this was one of the numerous difficulties I had to encounter during my mission.

troubling the authorities: nevertheless, it was only by the following plan that I succeeded. To effect this very important object, as well as to introduce my new system, I devoted an hour to attend in person and give the first lesson myself to the soldier-cooks. As the colonel, quartermaster, and a serjeant were present, besides many officers as lookers-on, a great impression was thus created upon the men, who immediately saw the importance of following my instructions. I supplied the cooks with receipts printed at headquarters, which gave them quite an official appearance. The annexed specimen will give an idea of their simplicity, and of the facility with which they might be adopted:—

SOYER'S SIMPLIFIED RECEIPT TO COOK SALT MEAT FOR FIFTY MEN.

HEADQUARTERS, CRIMEA, 12th May, 1856.

1. Put 50 lbs. of meat in the boiler.
2. Fill with water, and let it soak all night.
3. Next morning wash the meat well.
4. Fill with fresh water, and boil gently three hours.

P.S.—Skim off fat, which, when cold, is an excellent substitute for butter.

SOYER'S ARMY SOUP FOR FIFTY MEN.

1. Put in the boiler 30 quarts, 7½ gallons, or 5½ camp-kettles of water.
2. Add to it 50 lbs. of meat, either beef or mutton.
3. The rations of preserved or fresh vegetables.
4. Ten small tablespoonfuls of salt.
5. Simmer three hours, and serve.

P.S.—When rice is issued, put it in when boiling. Three pounds will be sufficient. About 8 lbs. of fresh vegetables, or 4 squares from a cake of preserved ditto. A tablespoonful of pepper, if handy.

Skim off the fat, which, when cold, is an excellent substitute for butter.* (For other variations of receipts, see Addenda.)

Thanks to the kindness of the colonels and of the authorities of each regiment, every man did his best, and not one found fault with either the stoves or the receipts: on the contrary, they all took pride in their task, and only regretted being compelled to return to the use of the camp-kettles, as sufficient of my stoves had not then arrived to enable me to supply them all. The cooking out of doors was also very agreeable to them, besides the saving of labour, in not having to cut, split, or saw several hundredweight of wood for each company, as they now only required a few pounds.

Having proved the utility of the stoves, the military authorities and doctors tasted the different soups and messes, with which they were also well pleased. The following letters, will fully corroborate my statement on both these points:—

---

* For a regiment of one thousand men, increase the number of stoves in proportion. If one hundred regiments are to be cooked for, repeat the same in each regiment, when you will have cooked enough food to perfection without much trouble for an army of one hundred thousand men, at the same time effecting a saving of above 400 per cent. in fuel.

WAR OFFICE, *June 8th*, 1855.

SIR,—I am directed to acknowledge the receipt of your letter of the 11th ultimo, reporting your arrival at Balaklava, and the steps taken by you for improving the condition of the kitchens and cooking arrangements of the hospitals there; and to acquaint you, that your account of your proceedings and progress is very satisfactory.

I am, Sir, your obedient servant,

Monsieur Soyer,
The *Robert Lowe*,
Balaklava Harbour, Crimea.

FREDERICK J. PRESCOTT.

WAR OFFICE, *19th September*, 1855.

SIR,—I am directed to acknowledge the receipt of your letter of the 6th ultimo, enclosing a copy of your arrangements at Scutari prior to your leaving for the Crimea, and to convey to you the thanks of the Secretary-at-War for that very satisfactory communication.

I am, Sir, your obedient servant,

Monsieur A. Soyer,
Scutari.

FRED. J. PRESCOTT.

WAR DEPARTMENT, *20th October*, 1855.

SIR,—I am directed to convey to you his lordship's thanks for your communications of the 8th and 22nd September, and 2nd instant; and, in reply, to inform you, that on your recommendation his lordship has sanctioned an order for 400 stoves to be manufactured by Messrs. Smith and Phillips, of Snow Hill, London; and has given direction that every exertion be used to despatch them at as early a period as possible.

I am, Sir, your obedient servant,

Monsieur Soyer,
Crimea.

JOHN CROOMES.

WAR DEPARTMENT, *7th December*, 1855.

SIR,—With reference to your letters of the 10th and 14th November, I am directed to acquaint you that Lord Panmure has pleasure in affording you the facilities you desire in making another visit to the Crimea for the purpose of seeing that a proper use is made of the cooking stoves which have been ordered to be sent out.

His lordship has written to Sir W. Codrington, instructing him to allow you the use of a hut, and to extend to you the same advantages which you were afforded under Sir James Simpson's command; but I am to add, that up to the present time, none of the stoves have been actually dispatched, although it is expected that a portion of them will be ready very shortly.

You must exercise your own discretion, therefore, as to the time for your proceeding to the Crimea.

I am, Sir, your obedient servant,

Monsieur Soyer,
Scutari.

E. CHUMLEY.

WAR DEPARTMENT, *25th April*, 1856.

SIR,—I am directed by Lord Panmure to acknowledge the receipt of your letter dated 31st March, and to express his lordship's pleasure in learning that the cooking arrangements which you have introduced in the hospitals at Scutari have answered so perfectly.

Lord Panmure approves of your presenting one of the stoves to Marshal Pelissier, provided you previously obtain the concurrence of Sir W. Codrington.

I am, Sir, your obedient servant,

Monsieur Alexis Soyer,
Crimea.

JOHN CROOMES.

WAR DEPARTMENT, *6th June*, 1856.

SIR,—I am directed to acknowledge the receipt of your letter of the 6th ultimo, reporting the success of your field stoves in the Crimea, and enclosing two receipts for the preparation of food for the army, and to express Lord Panmure's satisfaction thereon.

I am, Sir, your obedient servant,

Monsieur Soyer, &c.,   J. BACON.
Crimea.

After having started them in person, I sent my cooks every morning on their rounds to see if the men followed my instructions, and I visited each regiment daily. The hospitals, thank God, were at this time almost empty. When a division had made use of the stoves about a week, I requested the general commanding that division to inquire of the colonel, officers, and men, their opinion of the results of my labours; and in that manner I acquired the above-mentioned numerous letters of commendation, having in my possession many others, but space will not allow of their insertion.

One of the days on which salt rations were issued, I requested General Garrett to go round his division and ask the men what they did with the fat. This he very kindly did, accompanied by his aide-de-camp, Major Dallas. The first cook we visited, in the 18th Regiment, had rations for 94 men (the whole of his company). They were being cooked in one stove: the two stoves for the same quantity would have been much better, as the more water the meat is boiled in, the more salt is extracted from it. The boiler was filled to the brim, the contents simmering gently: the meat was beautifully cooked. There were about four inches of clear fat, as sweet as butter, floating on the top. The stove was in the open air, and the cook only burnt from ten to fifteen pounds of wood (or hardly so much) to cook for that number—viz., the whole of his company. The allowance of wood had been reduced from 4½lbs. to 3½lbs. per man daily. The advent of peace gave me a full opportunity of thoroughly instructing the men, and thus I was enabled firmly to establish my new system. The saving in wood alone, supposing each company to consist of one hundred men, would, at the former rate of allowance, amount to 450lbs. per company per diem, allowing 25lbs. for cooking, which is ample. This in a regiment of eight companies would make a daily saving of 3600lbs. of wood, independent of the economy of transport, mules, labour, &c. In an army of forty thousand men, it would amount to the immense figure of 180,000lbs., or 90 tons, per day saved to the Government, or 32,850 tons per annum.

General Garrett asked the man what he was going to do with the fat.

"Throw it away, general," was the answer.

"Throw it away!—why?" said the General.

"I don't know, sir, but we always do."

"Why not use it?"—"The men don't like it, sir."

I observed that when the salt meat was cooked in the small canteen pans, the fat was lost for want of the necessary quantity of water to allow it to rise to the surface, as well as to purify it of the salt. Asking the man for a leaden spoon and a tin can, I removed the fat as I had before done in the Guards' camp. On weighing it the next day, I found upwards of 14lbs. of beautiful clean and sweet dripping, fit for use as described in the receipts. Thus about 800lbs. of this were wasted weekly by each regiment—salt rations being issued four days a week.

General Garrett expressed a decided opinion that my apparatus was much superior to the old canteen pan, and gave me a letter.

The signature of the treaty of peace changed all the proceedings in the camp, except mine; for in anticipation of the distribution of the remainder of the stoves among the various regiments in the camps at Aldershot barracks, &c., as well as to those on foreign stations, I continued my daily course of instruction, in order that the men, upon arrival at home or elsewhere, might be well acquainted with their use, and be able to impart their knowledge to others. I have since hit upon a plan by which I shall introduce an oven and steamer, and thus do all that is required to vary the cooking of the daily meals in barracks—a subject of great importance.

War having ceased, the camp bore the appearance of a monster banqueting-hall. "We have done fighting," said everyone, "so let us terminate the campaign by feasting, lay down our victorious but murderous weapons, and pick up those more useful and restorative arms—the knife and fork."

All appeared to have caught a giving-parties mania. You could scarcely meet a friend or even a slight acquaintance without being apostrophized by, "When will you dine with me?" as regularly as though it had been inserted in the order of the day. The first invitation I received was from the witty General Barnard, who so generously entertained his friends, under the superintendence of his major-domo, Captain Barnard (the gallant general's son). A good table, good wine, and plenty of everything, or at least the best that could be obtained, were provided; and no less than five times had I the honour of being invited to enjoy the noble general's good cheer. Next came invitations from my noble friend and neighbour, General Garrett, Lord W. Paulet, Colonel de Bathe, Colonel Peel, Major Fielden, Lord Vane, Lord Dunkellin, and the great epicure of epicures, Colonel Haly, of the 47th, &c. &c.; to each and all of whom I cannot but feel grateful—not alone for their liberal welcome, but also for the honour of having been admitted to their friendship.

I could do no less than return the compliment, which was of course expected from me, the Gastronomic Regenerator. The first dinner I gave was honoured by the presence of the following gentlemen—viz., Lord William Paulet, Gen. Garrett, Gen. Wyndham,. Gen. Barnard, Col. Halliwell, Col. R. Campbell (90th), Col. Haley (47th), Major Earle, Major Dallas, Captain Barnard, &c.

The bill of fare was as follows:—

> Potage à la Codrington.
> Filet de turbot clouté à la Balaklava.
> ———
> Quartier de mouton à la bretonne.
> Poulets à la tartarine.
> ———
> Queues de bœuf à la ravigote.
> Côtelettes de mouton à la vivandière.
> Rissolettes de volaille à la Pelissier.
> Filet de bœuf piqué mariné, sauce poivrade.
> ———
> La mayonnaise à la russe, garnis de caviar.
> ———
> Les plum-puddings à la Cosaque.
> Les haricots verts à la poulette.
> Les gelées de citron garni.

Les croûtes à l'abricot.
———
La bombe glacé à la Sebastopol.
———
Hors-d'œuvres.
Les anchoix—sardines—lamproies à l'huile—mortadelle de Vérone
—olives farcies—thon—cornichons à l'estragon—salade—légumes—
dessert—café—liqueurs.

Though there was nothing very *recherché* in the dinner, it met with the approval of all the guests. The appearance of my humble but originally-decorated hut, profusely lit up with wax lights, and a rather nicely laid-out table, surrounded by military men of high standing, in their various uniforms, was exceedingly novel. The occasion formed quite an epoch in my life, and I shall probably never again have the honour of entertaining such a distinguished circle under similar circumstances. Encouraged by this my first success, I felt in duty bound to continue the series of these *petites fêtes Anacréontiques*, at which were assembled wit, mirth, good appetite, and delightful harmony. Amateur artistes of no little note, who had emerged triumphant from the murky atmosphere produced by the incessant bombardment of Sebastopol, were there. By their exertions the barriers of freedom and civilization were opened to all, and the autocrat Czar was compelled to submit. Those who but a few days before had been enemies were now friends. In fact, the war had ceased, and peace, that mother of sociability, offered her delights freely to all. Care seemed banished from every brow, excepting the sincere regret devoted to the memory of those brave men who had so nobly died for the glory of their country. In addition to the theatres, which had amused the camp throughout the winter, madrigal and glee clubs were instituted. At one of my *petits dîners* (at which the filet de bœuf piqué, mariné was duly discussed and highly praised by my Epicurean guests) the leader of the madrigal club, Colonel de Bathe, proposed that, as I had the largest and most convenient hut for the purpose, besides being well provided with culinary as well as table utensils, as a finale, and to crush the last vestige of sorrow in everyone's heart on account of this memorable war, I should give a dinner-party, after which the whole of the members of the Crimean Madrigal Club would harmoniously close the evening with a concert. The proposition was unanimously agreed to. I promised my guests to do my best to close the season of war by producing an excellent gastronomic popote. A general invitation was given, and the day fixed.

When General Lüders courteously invited the French and English generals to honour him with their presence at his famed camp on the well-known Mackenzie Heights, the invitation was accepted for the following day. Everybody was anxious to go, and the invitation being a general one, lucky were they who had heard of it. The next day a stream of general officers of the Allied armies poured towards the Tchernaya Bridge. This was our first friendly meeting with those who had so bravely defended themselves and sacrificed their blood in defence of the national cause: General Lüders himself had lost two of his sons in the battlefield. The reception was grand and interesting, the review imposing, the lunch excellent, the bizarrerie of some very eccentric performance by the Cossacks highly amusing, the weather very fine, and the welcome joyous and hearty. It showed what marvels could be produced by a few strokes from a pen guided by a powerful and prudent hand. Only a few days before, the soil upon which we were treading peacefully was trodden by these same human beings with hearts full of revenge, thirst of blood, and destruction. In place of these, good understanding, as if by magic, restored to each heart the feelings of humanity and religion. Thousands of enemies were in a few minutes changed to hospitable friends. The hostile line of demarcation was now removed, and the camp of our late enemies free to all; and, instead of gaining inch by inch of ground by the sweat of the brow and waste of blood and life, there was welcome for all. Such was the effect produced upon my mind by the advent of peace, after that memorable and sanguinary Eastern war, through which I thank God for sparing my life during my humble mission, in the prosecution of which I had the honour of witnessing the finale of that great European question, in which the honour and glory of mighty nations were deeply involved.

After this solemn day of reception, the fusion of the armies took place. Our camp was invaded by Russians, as theirs was by our men. The works and fortifications, as well as Bakschiserai, Simpheropol, Perekop, &c. &c., were immediately taken without bloodshed. The popping of the well-corked champagne had replaced the monstrous and unsociable voice of the cannon. The sparkling liquid, poured in tin pots or cups—anything but crystal champagne-glasses—seemed to unite all hearts. All the taverns, hotels, inns, huts, marquees, bell tents, &c., had their visitors; and no people more than the Russians proved their immediate attachment to us, by making it a rule not to disoblige anyone who asked the favour of their company. Rather than do this, they preferred staying a week, a fortnight, or even a month. This I, as well as some of my friends, had the felicity of experiencing, as often the whole family—father, mother, sons and daughters, horse, cart, and dogs included—would take up their residence with one. Most of us made a pilgrimage to Bakschiserai, Simpheropol, Yalta, and other places, after the proclamation of peace; and, to the honour and credit of the inhabitants, all were received with a cordial welcome, after being first introduced to the governor of the city. Freely indeed was their hospitality bestowed, and it was our duty to return the compliment by an invitation to our camp, which seldom failed to be accepted, and shortly after put in execution, after the style above mentioned.

Justice must also be done to the Tartar families whom we visited, for their liberality and friendship. I never saw a man more put out than one near Bakschiserai on an occasion when a friend and myself had entered a house in order to obtain some refreshment. We there found a very numerous family, among which were three small children, from three to ten years of age. The father, who was an old man, made us understand by telegraphic signs, _à la Tartare_, that he, and he alone, was the father, which we had not the slightest objection to believe. Two rather good-looking girls, also daughters, waited attentively upon us, and in less than ten minutes a frugal repast was offered. The old man and his rather young wife gave us to understand that they had laid before us the best they had, for which we, by telegraphic signs, made them comprehend that we were quite pleased and very grateful. When we had satisfied our appetites, we made ready to start, and offered to pay for the accommodation we had received: but scarcely had the English sovereign fallen upon the stone slab before the old father, who was nursing the two youngest scions of his race upon his knees, than he rose up with a spring, dropped the children on the floor, and stroking his long white hair with one hand, made a sign for the sovereign to be immediately returned to the pocket with the other, as if he feared that the heaven towards which his eyes were directed would punish him for violating the laws of hospitality if he accepted the money. We did as he desired, and peace and friendship were at once restored. It was a scene worthy of the *Dame Blanche* of Boieldieu, taken from Sir Walter Scott's *Monastery*, where the Highland farmer says to travellers like ourselves, "The Scotch mountaineers dispense their hospitality, but never sell it."

Soon after this charming incident had occurred, we left our generous host and his fine family in their peaceable dwelling. This love of hospitality did not prevail amongst the retail dealers, who, on the contrary, endeavoured to fleece visitors in every possible way, as if anxious to get one's skin in order to sell it for what it would fetch. As curiosity had allured us thus far into the bowels of the land, and as we were not particular about trifles, even in money matters, on this auspicious occasion, these human vultures were permitted to gorge themselves at our expense and that of our pockets. Champagne was sold at a pound and more the bottle, stout at ten shillings, and everything else at the same exorbitant rate, but by way of compensation all was of an inferior quality.

MISS NIGHTINGALE'S CARRIAGE

XXXIII

HOSTILITIES AT TABLE

As two or three months had still to elapse before the final evacuation of the Crimea took place, I employed the interval in completing the culinary education of my soldier-pupils, anxious that they might be able to confer the benefit of my instructions upon others, when the remainder of the stoves should be issued either at home or abroad. By the aid of my receipts, which were to be printed upon parchment framed, and hung up in every barrack kitchen, the cooks could not fail in the proper performance of their duties. I very much regret that, owing to some misunderstanding, one or two regiments did not receive my personal attendance, though I believe they had the stoves. To the colonels of those regiments I beg to offer this as an apology for the apparent neglect, which I assure those gentlemen I can only attribute to some oversight on the part of those I employed to see the stoves shifted from one regiment to the other. It was no easy matter to traverse such an immense space of ground, upon which above forty regiments were encamped; and the difficulty was increased by my having to deal with different persons in each Although I had several of my own men to go about and assist me, I was the responsible person; and all I have to say is, that from six or seven in the morning till night, their humble servant was on horseback, reviewing his various regiments which, for a bad cavalier, was a great exertion, especially after so severe an illness Yet to that exertion I believe I owe my recovery, as it enabled me gradually to get the better of a most violent attack of dysentery, which had at one time reduced me so low, that the following civilian doctors, who were my neighbours at Scutari— viz., Messrs. Burn, Howard, and Fraser—were almost inclined to give me up.

Upon my arrival at Balaklava I met Miss Nightingale, who had left Scutari a few days previous to my departure from that place, in order to take the management of two new hospitals, under the superintendence of Dr. Taylor, my Scutari culinary friend. He told me that, to his sorrow, he had completely failed in the construction of the kitchen in those Crimean hospitals, on account of not being able to obtain the necessary utensils, &c. I immediately proposed to set this to rights for him, as I had to build two new extra-diet kitchens at Miss Nightingale's request. Dr. Taylor accepted my offer, and in less than a week both kitchens were satisfactorily completed, and they were also in full activity. In the extra-diet kitchens Miss Nightingale's new stoves were adopted. The establishment called the Left Wing Hospital was in charge of the Sisters of Charity; the other, called the Right Wing in that of Miss Stuart, a most excellent lady, and although of high family, subordinate to Miss Nightingale. During a period of six months, she rendered the greatest service, by ably assisting that lady in her exertions.

I substituted my caldrons for the old ones in the large hospital kitchens. Slight wooden sheds were built to shelter them; and the establishments, at last complete formed two of the most elegant, cleanly, and useful hospital kitchens in the camp—

burning but little wood, instead of always running short, as was the case when the common caldrons, placed upon two stones in a dark stone building which could never be kept clean, were in use. They met with the approval of both Drs. Hall and Taylor. I explained to these gentlemen, that with those stoves and a few planks, an excellent hospital or camp-kitchen could easily be made, instead of the very inferior ones before in use; and that for an army of a hundred thousand men or more, it would only be necessary to increase the number, as the stoves would never get out of repair, and might easily be carried with the army, either on mules, or by any other conveyance which the Land Transport Corps might adopt.

The two following letters confirm the truth of my assertions. The one is from Miss Nightingale, and the other from Dr. Taylor:—

SCUTARI BARRACK HOSPITAL, *July 28th*, 1856.

I have great pleasure in bearing my testimony to the very essential usefulness of Monsieur Soyer, who, first in the General Hospitals of Scutari, and afterwards in the Camp Hospitals of the Crimea, both general and regimental, restored order where all was unavoidable confusion, as far as he was individually able,—took the soldiers' rations and patients' diets as they were, and converted them into wholesome and agreeable food.

I have tried his stoves in the Crimean hospitals where I have been employed, and found them answer every purpose of economy and efficiency.

FLORENCE NIGHTINGALE.

———

Monsieur Soyer's cooking-stoves have been solely used in the Right and Left Wing Hospitals, Light Infantry Corps, during the last three months for the regimental hospital diets, for which they are admirably adapted as regards despatch, cleanliness, and economy.

G. TAYLOR, M. D.,

Crimea, 5th July, 1856.   *S. Surgeon, 1st Class.*

It was on the way to these hospitals that the vehicle conveying Miss Nightingale and her nurses was upset, and they all had a most miraculous escape. It was drawn by a mule, and no doubt driven by a donkey, who drove over a large stone, and thus caused the accident.

One of the nurses was severely wounded. After this accident, Colonel Macmurdo gave Miss Nightingale the carriage, a sketch of which appeared in the *Illustrated London News* of the 30th August, 1856. Upon leaving the Crimea, after a long search, I succeeded in rescuing it from the hands of some Tartar Jews, as I considered it a precious relic for present and future generations. The Jews were going to purchase it the next day among a lot of common carts, harness, horses, &c. I called upon Colonel Evans, of the Light Infantry Corps, and spoke to him upon the subject, when he kindly allowed me to purchase it. I sent it to England by the *Argo*, and the sketch was taken on board that ship by Landells, the artist of that journal. It arrived and was safely landed at Southampton; and Mr. Andrews, the mayor of that city, very kindly allowed the carriage to remain in his warehouse till my return to England.

The extraordinary exertions Miss Nightingale imposed upon herself after receiving this carriage would have been perfectly incredible, if not witnessed by many and well ascertained. I can vouch for the fact, having frequently accompanied her to the hospitals as well as to the monastery. The return from these places at night was a very dangerous experiment, as the road led across a very uneven country. It was still more perilous when snow was upon the ground. I have seen that lady stand for hours at the top of a bleak rocky mountain near the hospitals, giving her instructions, while the snow was falling heavily. I observed this to the Rev. Mr. Holt, who accompanied her almost daily as her clerical orderly, as he called himself, and he admitted that it was very imprudent on her part. All one could say to her on the subject was so kindly received, that you concluded you had persuaded her to take more care of herself. Yet she always went on in the same way, having probably forgotten good advice in her anxiety for the comfort of the sick.

I often warned her of the danger she incurred in returning so late at night, with no other escort than the driver. She answered by a smile, which seemed to say, "You may be right, but I have faith." So impressed was I with a sense of the magnitude of the danger she was daily incurring, that I addressed a letter to a noble duchess, who, I knew, had much influence with her.

It was reported that the Russian general, Lüders, intended to pay Marshal Pelissier a visit at the French headquarters, and that the general and his staff were to be received at the Tchernaya Bridge at seven in the morning. As I had that day to go to the Highland Brigade at Kamara, accompanied by one of my cooks, we started at five; and after receiving the popotes at the various regiments, I left my artiste and galloped to the bridge.

I found about thirty thousand troops drawn up in line, extending from the bridge to General Pelissier's headquarters. After the salvo of artillery, a most warm reception was given by General MacMahon to General Lüders, both commanders-in-chief remaining at the French headquarters to receive him. The cavalcade, consisting of French and Russians, set off at a hard gallop along the line of French troops, which extended about four miles. The discharges of cannon and the firing of musketry never ceased. The day was a brilliant one, and the sun's rays glittered upon the helmets, swords, cuirasses, and bayonets, reflecting myriads of diamonds in the air. The various uniforms of the staff which accompanied General Lüders, and in particular that of the Cosaques du Don, gave to this martial and animated scene an *éclat* hardly ever witnessed even at the grandest review, which is generally held on a flat surface, this being cheerfully accidented by hillock and dale. On such occasions, the army is generally formed in square, instead of being in a long line eight files deep on one side only, as on the occasion to which I now refer. The reception by General Pelissier was brilliant, and worthy of that offered to him on the Mackenzie Heights a few days previous.

Amongst the excursions we had projected was one which had been some time pending. It was to be a trip to Yalta by water, where we intended to spend a couple of days. A vessel had been provided, the provisions were ordered, and guests in abundance were invited. A series of fine days had followed, and the whole management was placed in the hands of the person with whom the idea of the excursion originated, the Rev. Mr. Parker. What man amongst the numbers in the Crimea did not know that distinguished, enterprising, and worthy man? His fame extended far and wide, and he was equally celebrated for his benevolence and intelligence; and he never saw a difficulty in anything he undertook, from the building of a church to an hospital, a hut, kitchen, or an ice-house. Workmen and materials were found by him, people hardly knew how or where. Under his clerical wand, wooden palaces were erected, not without difficulty, but still the work was accomplished. If any good provisions arrived in the harbour, the worthy minister was the first to hear of it, and, to oblige his friends, made all inquiries and obtained every information respecting price and quality. Like all clever men, he was fond of good living, and was not at all a bad judge of the good things of this life. It was during the time that he officiated at Balaklava that the church, which once had the appearance of a barn, was changed into a handsome religious edifice. Sebastopol had fallen, and, as a trophy, one of the bells of the Greek church ornamented his building, and called the faithful to their duty as regularly as the peal of any parish church. He was, in fact, the perfection of the *aumônier du régiment*; but, as in the case of all great geniuses, now and then, success was followed by failure, and victory by defeat—which the following will prove.

The day for the excursion had been fixed, postponed, and was again decided upon. For this change of plan I cannot account; no doubt it was owing to some unavoidable cause. At length the day was finally settled; there was to be no more postponing—off we must go. Our vessel was called the *Alar*, and she belonged to Mr. Crockford. As she was very small and short of accommodation, she was soon filled above and below. The evening before we were to start, the news of a great event for the following day was published in General Orders. It was to the effect that General Lüders would honour General Codrington with his presence at a grand review. This favour was not so highly appreciated by the nautical tourists as by their gallant Commander-in-chief, as at that time it materially interfered with their anticipated excursion. At all events, a serious discussion took place as to whether the excursion would or would not be postponed on that account. The answer "would not!" resounded in the camp from regiment to regiment, like a *mot d'ordre*, and the final order to all was, not to be on board a minute after eight o'clock; but the *Alar*, by way of punctuality, started at half-past seven. I sent two of my cooks to the vessel, but they never saw anything of the boat. A few minutes before eight o'clock, the Rev. Mr. Parker, myself, and others, got into a Maltese boat to join the steamer; instead of which, the steamer joined us. Not thanking either the *Alar* nor her captain for their trouble in coming to us instead of allowing us to go to them, the reverend gentleman and three more bravely boarded her, and in so doing kicked our bark away, and left us, in consequence of the swell caused by the motion of the paddle-wheels, very unsafely dancing an entirely new hornpipe in the harbour of Balaklava. At last, by the assistance of a large wave which nearly capsized us all, I managed to get hold of the man-rope by one hand; this happened to be the left one, so I could not raise myself on board, and there I was left hanging over the infuriated waves, the vessel all the while increasing her speed. As a precaution in walking through the wet fields, I had put on my India-rubber boots, which dipping in the water, soon became as slippery as a second-hand leech which will not take or bite at anything. The confusion on board the vessel, already a wreck, having been just dismasted in a serious collision with a larger steamer, prevented the people on board from perceiving my perilous position. My strength was rapidly becoming exhausted, and I must in a second or two have fallen into the water, when a reverend gentleman, whose name I regret to say I cannot recall, saw the imminent danger in which I was placed, and rescued me. Thanks to his assistance, I managed to lay hold of another rope with my right hand. I fancied I could travel miles in that position, it appeared to be so safe. Other assistance arrived, and a few minutes after I was hauled upon deck, scrambling amongst the wreck and loose ropes. A friendly voice addressed me with, "Hallo, Soyer! you are behind time."

I replied, "I should have preferred being later still, and not have come at all."

When the incident was known on board, it caused much merriment among our fellow-adventurers. As we were going on pleasure, all were allowed to laugh at the various adventures, as well as misadventures, of the party; so I laughed, and all laughed, soon afterwards, and very heartily. We were no sooner out of the harbour, than the good ship *Alar*, which had not received her proper quantum of breakfast or ballast in her wooden or iron stomach, began her hanky-panky rolling tricks, which never ceased from the time we started till our return. Breakfast was ready and upon the table; but, for some unaccountable reason, no one appeared ready for breakfast. As we were out upon a pleasure excursion, each person was at liberty to enjoy himself in his own way. Some did this by remaining upon deck, others by looking overboard, &c., till at length the generous sun, taking pity upon us, threw out his beams and guided us round the beautiful rocky coast of the Balaklava and Lukan shores. A few glasses of champagne were circulated, healths were pledged, and everything got cheerful and lively; and the joy had even extended to some of the ladies on board.

Indeed, reader, I have not yet had time to introduce our fair companions to your notice; but I will do so shortly. Some of them actually went so far as to ask me what I thought was good for dinner. "Upon my word," said I to my fair interlocutor, "I do not know what will be good, madam, but I'll tell you what will be bad. Look behind you at that black cloud which seems to follow us so closely: I have no doubt that is a squall coming, which will soon spoil our bill of fare as well as our appetites."

In about half-an-hour we came in sight of the beautiful Palace of Lukan, belonging to Prince Woronzoff. A short time before, we had anticipated landing and being able to dine in the gardens. This was rendered impossible, as the weather had assumed a very tempestuous aspect, and bore every appearance of a violent storm. Many began to think of a second wreck, and quite lost the idea of dining. The steamer was put about in a very unsociable gale of wind, which, thank God, dropped shortly after, and allowed us, after several attempts, to return safely to our harbour. This, considering the state the *Alar* was in after the accident she had met with, she ought not to have left, especially upon a pleasure-trip.

My friend, Mr. Frederick Crockford, who so kindly lent his boat, assisted me, and we set to work during our stormy return to prepare the dinner, which we had decided should be got ready, although almost everyone on board was ill. So we began our fantastic and gymnastic culinary exertions by looking up the stores; and by dint of a wonderful amount of animal and physical perseverance, we managed to dish up two turkeys, a number of fowls, hams, roast lamb, tongues, roast beef, plum-puddings, salad, dessert, &c. &c., and cut bread enough for more than *à discrétion*. The reader will please to observe that it was by this time late in the afternoon, and that the *Alar* sylph was rolling quite sufficiently to prevent any willing turkey from remaining upon the dish, when a tremendous wave came to its aid, and sent three parts of our luxuries rolling about the cabin-floor, breaking no end of plates, dishes, bottles, glasses, &c. Fortunately, our dinner was not lost, as we knew where it was—rolling to and fro on the wet cabin-floor, playing at the don't-you-wish-you-may-get-me game. Mr. Crockford and myself had succeeded in making a semi-monster lobster salad, which for safety he had held on to all the time, almost at the peril of his valuable life, he being knocked about fearfully against the cabin-boards and bulkheads. At last we made the harbour. It was nearly dusk; and not being expected back so soon, nor even the next day, we were kept dancing for above an hour at the entrance. No doubt, this was done to sharpen our appetites.

A rumour was circulated that we should not be allowed to enter at all, the *Alar* being a merchant vessel. This was our fate till about six o'clock, when signals were made for her to enter. We availed ourselves of this permission, and in twenty minutes the two large tables were set out *à la marinière*. Everybody was glad to partake of the most welcome repast ever bestowed upon a party after the enjoyment of so charming a day of pleasure. The *salade mayonnaise* was voted excellent. Champagne was gaily flowing in bowls, basins, teacups, goblets, &c. Healths were proposed; her Majesty's first—next that of the Allied armies—then that of the Emperor of the French, Mr. Crockford's and mine, in honour of the *salade mayonnaise*; and a vote of thanks was returned to the Rev. Mr. Parker, for the extremely pleasant day he had been the cause of our enjoying, especially the dinner in the harbour he had so well provided, which soon made us forget our nautical tribulations.

I have almost forgotten the members of the fair sex, whose health was proposed in the first place. They had been very ill all day. About eleven, all, expect myself, had left the *Alar* in the full conviction of having enjoyed themselves very much indeed. Among the party, which would have been far too numerous, had not circumstances prevented many of those invited from making their appearance, were Commissary Drake, lady and daughter; Mr. and Mrs. Burnett. Lady Seymour and friend, who were to accompany the party, did not come. This is the sum total of the ladies present, which for the Crimea was a very fair array of the *beau sexe*. As it was impossible for me to return to camp that evening, the captain and Mr. Crockford offered me a bed on board. I of course jumped at the offer. About one o'clock we were drinking a parting glass, when a boat was heard approaching the vessel, and a voice called out—

"*Alar* ahoy! Is Monsieur Soyer still on board?"

"Yes," was the answer.

In a few seconds, a gentleman, whom I recognised as my friend Captain Brown of the *Ottowa*, stepped on board.

"Hallo, captain!" I exclaimed, "what ever has brought you on board at this time of night?"

"I will tell you. They have sent for you from headquarters, and you have been sought in all directions. Captain Ponsonby has been looking everywhere for you. A grand déjeuner is to be given tomorrow in honour of General Lüders' visit. I happened to hear of it where I dined and knowing the *Alar* had returned with you on board, I have come to inform you that your aid is required. By the bye, you were suspended a long time this morning between wind and water: I made so sure you could not hold on much longer, that I had one of my sailors ready to jump over and pick you up."

"Thanks, captain, for two eminent services in one day. I cannot, however, go to headquarters till morning, as I have no pony at Balaklava."

"All right," said he. "Call upon Major Ross in the morning; he will let you have all you require."

"At daybreak I will be there."

"Mind, the lunch is to be ready at two o'clock."

"I shall not be able to assist much, as there will hardly be time to turn round. However, goodnight, captain, and a thousand thanks."

"I'm off in a few hours for Constantinople," he called out from his boat, "and shall be back in a week. Goodbye."

The sentinels, as usual, cried—"All's well." I must say, I did not think it was well with me. "What can I do," said I to myself, "for an event of historical importance?" Neither Mr. Crockford nor the captain could assist me, when an idea struck me:— "If you can't give me an idea," said I to my friends, "at any rate lend me a dish."

"That I will," said the captain.

"Recollect, I want a large one."

"You had the largest for your salad yesterday."

"That one will do; it will hold enough for twenty-five persons."

"Then here goes," said I, writing. "Today I shall dress in it the *Macédoine Lüdersienne à l'Alexandre II.*"

"A very good name in honour of the event," said Mr. Crockford. "But pray, of what is it to be composed?"

"Oh! for that," said I, "if I were to implore the Genius of Gastronomy, from Lucullus to Apicius and Vitellius, or Vatel to Ude and Carême, I could get nothing from them but inspiration; while what I require is something substantial, and not artificial. It strikes me that a word from you to your head man at Kadikoi (as you will not be there tomorrow) would do more for me in a few minutes than the whole of those defunct celebrities, whom I am not now inclined to trouble upon so material a subject. Pray give me *carte blanche* to get anything you may have and I require for the composition of this modern Babylon, which must be constructed upon a base sufficiently strong to resist the joint attack of the heads of three of the most powerful armies in the world, and only be destroyed after having conquered the conqueror's *place d'armes*, the stomach, so called in military parlance."

The order was readily given by my friend Mr. Crockford, and we then lay down to sleep, being both completely exhausted with the fatigues of what was called a day of pleasure. We had hardly closed our eyelids, when morning caused them to be reopened; so up we got. My friend started for Constantinople, and I for headquarters. On my way I called upon Major Ross, who kindly lent me a pony, and told me of the message left with him. I started immediately—bought a few things in Balaklava market—called at Crockford's store at Donnybrook, which I ransacked and despoiled of condiments of every description. Instead of going direct to headquarters, I changed my mind and went home to prepare, having decided, as the time was so short, to produce one good dish only, instead of several small and insignificant ones. This was, however, to be worthy of the occasion. I was well aware that General Codrington's cook, under the liberal management and command of Captain Ponsonby, would turn out something worthy of the event. Upon arriving at my hut, I sent two of my cooks to assist him, despatched my groom on horseback to Kamiesch for various things, and then began the construction of my *Lüdersienne* upon the lid of my new field stoves, the dish I had brought from the *Alar* being too small.

My novel dish was completed, and carried to headquarters by two soldiers; and at a quarter to two I personally placed my culinary wonder upon the table. It was called—

SOYER'S CULINARY EMBLEM OF PEACE,

The Macédoine Lüdersienne à l'Alexandre II.

This monster dish was composed of—

12	boxes of preserved lobsters
2	cases of preserved lampreys
2	cases of preserved sardines
2	bottles of preserved anchovies
1	case of preserved caviar
1	case of preserved sturgeon
1	case of preserved tunny
2	cases of preserved oysters
1	pound of fresh prawns
4	pounds turbot clouté
12	Russian pickled cucumbers
4	bottles pickled olives
1	bottle mixed pickles
1	bottle Indian ditto
1	bottle pickled French beans
2	bottles pickled mushrooms
½	bottle pickled mangoes
2	bottles of pickled French truffles
2	cases of preserved peas
2	cases of preserved mixed vegetables
4	dozen cabbage lettuces
100	eggs
2	bottles of preserved cockscombs.

The sauce was composed of six bottles of salad oil, one of Tarragon vinegar, half a bottle of chilli vinegar, two boxes of preserved cream (whipped), four ounces of sugar, six eschalots, salt, cayenne pepper, mustard, and a quarter of an ounce of Oriental herbs which are quite unknown in England.

The dining-room, decorated under the artistic superintendence of Captain Ponsonby, presented a ravishing *ensemble* well adapted to the occasion. It was hung, ceiling and all, with the Allied flags, to which the Russian standard, so long absent, had been happily reinstated in the bond of friendship and civilization. Those few pieces of printed cloth spoke volumes to my mind. These adopted colours of different nations had not waved together for a long while, and their playful movements, caused by a fresh breeze, which seemed to have purified itself in passing swiftly over the cheerful vineyard attached to headquarters, pleased me very much.* The god of war had put his seal and autograph upon them, just in the same manner as we see a name upon a bank-note, which only acquires value from national convenience and conventionality. Still these rags, which the will of mighty

---

* A few hundred yards further, where the French review had taken place, on an ill-selected spot, the dust was blinding both to men and horses, the wind being very high.

empires had favoured with their high regard, were so proud of their post, that they appeared to float and flutter in the air with more grandeur than a common piece of stuff just brought from the loom, as was the case with them before their glorious national christening, would have done. They appeared as proud and superior to their brothers and sisters as a race-horse is to one of his less fortunate fellows—a cart-horse.

I was left almost alone in that ever-memorable spot (everyone having gone to the review), giving the last *coup d'œil*, with Captain Ponsonby and the maître d'hôtel, to the well-provided table. The illustrious guests were momentarily expected. Volumes, indeed, could I read in those printed sheets—symbols and emblems of glory. Upon them seemed engraved, in letters of gold, "L'union fait la force," and "Regeneration instead of destruction!" Such were my sentiments on that memorable occasion. The world at large was interested in this mighty fusion; the end of this grand drama I could plainly read, though merely printed upon pieces of common calico.

Professionally, I was doubly proud of the honour of contributing my mite of industry to this California of grandeur and great events. My monster Macédoine was placed in the centre of the table, and, though only a few persons were present, was much admired. "In a few minutes," said I to myself, "those great men whose names are echoed and re-echoed throughout the world by the trumpet-blast of fame will be here, not only gazing upon my impromptu *chef-d'œuvre*, but, I hope, also freely partaking of it—and, while enjoying the pleasures of the table, cementing the sentiments of peace and of friendship."

So much was my mind absorbed by the superficial, that I had almost forgotten the material. The words, "the review is over, and the generals are coming," recalled my wandering senses. A gorgeous cavalcade was seen approaching, headed by four generals-in-chief in full uniform, and their respective Staffs, wearing their decorations, followed by above thirty generals. A few minutes after, I was attending upon General Pelissier, Lüders, and Sir W. Codrington, who were sitting together—General Pelissier on the left and General Lüders on the right of Sir William. The following persons were sitting at the same table:—General della Marmora and Sir Colin Campbell were facing; and at the same table sat Admiral Freemantle; Generals MacMahon, Martinprey, Wyndham, Garrett, Barnard, Lord Rokeby, Lord W. Paulet, Cameron; Colonels Scariatini and M. Amazzoff, aides-de-camp to General Lüders; and the aides of the other generals.

My anticipations were realized; for no sooner had the guests taken their seats than the conversation became more animated. I had placed at the apex of my pyramidal Macédoine a small card, with the dedication written upon it. Sir W. Codrington handed it to General Lüders, who, after showing it to several of his suite, requested permission to keep it as a reminiscence of the day. This request was granted by Sir William with a smile.

The entrées, roasts, and the entremets had been handed round, and a serious attack upon my Lüdersienne commenced, almost every guest partaking of it twice. Captain Ponsonby requested me to remove it, as several gentlemen at the other table wished to taste it. General Pelissier, with whom I had the honour of conversing longer than with anyone else, was in an excellent humour, and full of that vivacity and wit so characteristic. He bantered me several times for not having stoned the olives which formed part of the Macédoine. I told him that time would not permit of this, as I had received such short notice of the banquet, and that I went the evening before on an excursion by water to Lukan. At the same time, I expressed my regret to Sir William at not being at home when sent for.

"Never mind, Monsieur Soyer," replied Sir William. "I am, at all events, very happy to see you here, and thank you kindly for your exertions."

General Pelissier again addressed me: "You may say what you like, Monsieur Soyer, but you might as well have stoned the olives."

"Very true, general, if time had allowed. It is all very well for you to take the Malakhoff in a few minutes, but it took me four hours to make that dish." At which reply he could not help laughing.

"Your friend General Barnard," said he, pointing to that officer, who was sitting at the bottom of the table, "would like to taste it. Go and offer him some."

I did so; but the general had been served. I then made a tour round the table, asking each guest, above thirty in number, whether he had been attended to.

The time was getting short, and another review—that of the English army—had to come off. The iced champagne had performed a grand *rôle* during the repast; all seemed highly gratified and full of animation. What a burst of enthusiasm was elicited when General Lüders rose, and proposed the health of her Majesty the Queen of England and that of the French Emperor! which enthusiasm was renewed when Sir William Codrington responded by proposing that of the Emperor Alexander.

The *mot d'ordre* was given, and all were soon mounted, and proceeded to the review, at which, having terminated my culinary duties, I assisted as a spectator, arriving just time enough to have a glance at the spectacle, which to my mind was superior in point of effect to that of the magnificent French army in the morning. It was in a splendid square; while the French army, though more numerous, being in a line, covered more ground, but produced less effect. I remarked this to General della Marmora, with whom I was conversing. He seemed to be of my opinion. The Scotch, with their bagpipes merrily playing, were then filing past the Etat-Major, and the vibrating sounds of their wild mountain music impressed itself for ever on my ear. It was their last song on the Crimean shore. A few minutes more, and all was over. General Lüders entered his carriage, and started full gallop, followed by his staff. General Codrington and suite lined the fields on either side the road along which the carriage passed. On reaching the Balaklava road, which crosses the high mountain leading to the Guards' camp, the Russian general made a full stop; so did Sir W. Codrington and suite. They bade each other adieu; and after General Lüders had returned thanks for the excellent reception he had received, Sir William said, "I hope, general, you are not over-tired?"

"No, not at all, thank you. I only felt rather cold standing still during the last review."

This was spoken in French.

The Russian cavalcade galloped away towards the Tchernaya, whilst the English returned to headquarters.

It was getting quite dark; the weather, which had been so warm in the morning, turned very cold—the sky looked grey, and not a soul was to be seen. I ascended the rocky and steep mountain on horseback. A few minutes after, I was in lonely solitude on the top of the plateau. Not a sign of life was to be seen or heard; grave-yards alone ornamented this desolate spot.

"What a curious life mine is!" said I, musing. "Compare the last forty-eight hours with the time when I was hanging by one hand, suspended between life and death, from the man-rope of the *Alar*, in the harbour of Balaklava." It reminded me of a rocket, which, while soaring brightly in its flight towards the sky, shines radiant for a few seconds only, and then vanishes in space.

XXXIV

CRIMEAN FESTIVITIES

On reaching home, I found Cathcart's Hill as quiet and deserted as I did on the 8th of September, but under less solemn circumstances, for Sebastopol had then fallen—whereas now it was likely to rise again like a phœnix from its ashes. The headquarters of the Fourth Division were wrapped in deep repose. I could not even wake my groom to put my small charger into the stable; but this had often occurred before, and gave me the chance of learning how to attend to my own horse. It is true, it was nearly twelve o'clock; for in passing the Guards' camp I had paid several visits, and the kind reception accorded would not have failed to detain the greatest misanthropist till a late hour. I had in particular called upon Colonel de Bathe and the members of the Madrigal Club, being anxious to ascertain from that body of artists when our great festival was to take place.

"Tomorrow you are invited," said Colonel de Bathe, "to dine with us at General Barnard's, and we will settle that matter there."

Having to meet Miss Nightingale the next day at the Land Transport Corps Hospital in order to accompany her for the last time through the camp, I managed to be there about ten o'clock. Miss Nightingale had not arrived; so I made an inventory of the various kitchen utensils which were to be sent back to England or Malta.

While I was waiting for the Sister of the Brave, I made it my duty to pay my respects to the illustrious Mrs. Seacole; and, like a good son or a ship in full sail, I was immediately received in the arms of the *mère noire*. On perceiving me, she exclaimed—

"Hallo, my son! I saw you at headquarters yesterday!"

"Did you really? I didn't see you, Mrs. Seacole."

"I dare say you did not, my son. I was amongst the great dons in the vineyard, and had a very fine view of the proceedings. I met all my friends there."

"No doubt you did, Mrs. Seacole."

"Very kind they were, I assure you; they all shook me by the hand enough to last me for life. What do you think of the Russian general, Monsieur Soyer?" Before I could reply, she said, "He is a fine man, and no mistake; is he not, my son?"

She was in the act of dressing the wound of an Army Works Corps man, who had been thrown, and was cut severely in the forehead.

"What's the matter with the poor fellow?" said I.

"He is getting better now. What will you take to drink, Monsieur Soyer?"

"Nothing at present; it is too early, my dear madam."

"Don't forget, before you go, to come and take a parting glass with an old friend. Mr. Day and myself will be very glad to see you, depend upon it. By the way, how is Miss Nightingale?"

"I thank you, she was quite well the last time I had the pleasure of seeing her. I have to meet her at the Land Transport Hospital this morning, by appointment."

"What nice kitchens those are of yours at the Land Transport Hospital! I saw them several times; and the doctors and Mrs. Stuart are highly pleased with them, I assure you. How nice and clean the Sisters of Charity keep everything! You may say that of both hospitals." Mrs. Seacole then said, "What nice things they prepare in the extra-diet kitchens for the patients! I tasted everything.—Pray give my respects to Miss Nightingale, and say, if I were not so busy I should run as far as the hospital, to pay my duty to her. You must know, Monsieur Soyer, that Miss Nightingale is very fond of me. When I passed through Scutari, she very kindly gave me board and lodging."

This was about the twentieth time the old lady had told me the same tale. Shaking her by the hand—

"Goodbye, my son," said she; "I wish you had let me taste some of that fine dish you made yesterday."

"How could I, my dear mother? I did not know you were there."

At this point of the conversation, the Egyptian beauty, her daughter Sarah, entered.

"My dear Sally, how are you?" said I. "I never see you in our alley now."

"Go along with you!" said smiling Sally; "you are always making fun of me."

"Fun of you, my dear?—never. I swear by your blue eyes and black hair, that I never do. Do I, mother?"

"If you did, it would not matter; a little innocent mirth now and then does one good. For my part, my son, I could not live without laughing."

"Yes; but you told a certain colonel that it was I who was dressed as a Scotchman at the French ball given the other day in honour of the young Emperor," said the daughter.

"What harm is there in that? All the great people were invited, and why should you not have been there?"

"Indeed, do you think mother or myself would go to such a place, where the women wear soldiers' clothes? Not likely. And what soldiers?—the Scotch Brigade!"

We all laughed; and I then parted, quite pleased with Sally's modesty. Sally richly deserves the title of the Dark, instead of Fair, Maid of the Eastern War.

On my return to the hospital, I found Miss Nightingale had arrived, accompanied by the chaplain, Mr. Hone, who informed me that she could not possibly go through the camp that day. As I was thus disengaged, I called upon Mrs. Stuart, in order to inquire whether she required anything in my department. To my astonishment, she informed me that a field stove, of which she was greatly in want to heat water for the baths, had not arrived. As I had sent it with the others, which had reached their destination, I promised to inquire about it at once, and sent my engineer, Mr. Phillips, to see after it. It was, however, three days before it was found. I relate this fact out of hundreds which occurred during the campaign, to show the mishaps of so difficult an undertaking. This I must repeat, that I was well supported by the authorities, and my demands were always granted. To Colonel Macmurdo, and Captains Evans and Power, I am greatly indebted for their never-ceasing courtesy.

In conversation with Miss Nightingale, I did not forget to mention Mrs. Seacole's kind inquiries. She said with a smile—

"I should like to see her before she leaves, as I hear she has done a deal of good for the poor soldiers."

"She has indeed, I assure you, and with the greatest disinterestedness. While I was there this morning, she was dressing a poor Land Transport Corps man, who had received a severe contusion on the head. In order to strengthen his courage for the process, as she said, she made him half a glass of strong brandy and water, not charging him anything for it; and I hear she has done this repeatedly."

"I am sure she has done much good."

I told Miss Nightingale that I had despatched Mr. Phillips in search of the missing stove; and, as our visit was postponed, I bade her adieu, requesting her to drop me a line in the Fourth Division at any time she might require my services.

That day I had the pleasure of meeting Dr. Hall, who apprised me that the troops would shortly leave the Crimea, and the Sanatorium be closed. The Monastery was so already; and, as I had anticipated, the Land Transport Corps remained the last in the field. Passing to headquarters, I found everything at a standstill. The commander-in-chief was out, the precise order of the previous day seemed in abeyance, and General Wyndham was sitting to a celebrated Sardinian artist for his portrait. It was taken in his Redan dress, which was freed from the blood and dust of that day, as I think very injudiciously, which caused me to ask if it was the same; the general replied that it was. I believe the picture was for the King of Sardinia, to be added to his Majesty's collection of the heroes of the Crimea.

Captain Ponsonby was occupied in his open-air photographic studio, taking portraits of everybody who came in his way, amongst them myself. Captain Hall was herborizing in his *petite chambre* upon some salad cress and cheroots. Colonel Blane was very busy writing and giving orders. Major Curzon and others of the staff were very seriously occupied lunching. In the kitchen, the stoves were cooling, and all the cooks out. At the Post Office and Telegraph all seemed still. The printing press alone was slowly going.

Upon returning to the dining-room, I found only a few at lunch; several were smoking at the doorsteps—in fact, compared with the day previous, the contrast was so great, that it appeared like a holiday after a week's hard labour. The conversation turned upon the grandeur of the review, and the success of the entertainment, which seemed to have given great satisfaction to all.

In the evening a most charming entertainment was prepared for us at General Barnard's. The company included General Rose; the French general, Bombaki; Colonel de Bathe, &c.

After an excellent dinner, at which a very fine turkey was the *pièce de résistance,*—(it had been reared under the farming care of Captain Barnard; this is a valuable quality in the Crimea: the turkey was accompanied by a delicious piece of boiled ration pork, and in addition two made dishes, two sweets, vegetables, &c.; the whole washed down by delicate claret cup *à la Barnaby*)—the topic of conversation turned upon the great events of the previous day. Perfect harmony prevailed, when suddenly a warlike sound was heard round the general's wooden dwelling. A friend entered, crying aloud, "The Russians—the Russians are coming!" and three Russian officers immediately entered, saying they had lost their way, and requesting a guide. The general's first impulse was to give them hospitality, and then put them in their right way. Captain Barnard got up to usher them in, and soon returned with the newcomers, who, we perceived, had not only lost their way, but also their senses. Having seated themselves, the general asked them what they would take. "Tout ce que vous avez" ("Everything you have," instead of "Anything you please"), one of them answered. To this the gallant general demurred, not being at all desirous of having his place pillaged, particularly in time of peace, after having escaped that sad tribute during the war. One of them was quite unmanageable: he spoke French, but was not such a good scholar as the Russian nobles generally are; he made sad havoc with that fashionable language, and used rude expressions, which were very unpleasant to the party. The Russians were anxious to explain what they had been doing at Kamiesch, the recital of which was much too droll to be pleasant. The noisiest of the party poured out a large tumbler of brandy, and, before anyone could stop him, swallowed half of it, drinking the health of every mortal thing, including the French, English, Russians, and the Turkish Emperor's. One who was more rational tried to appease him, but in vain. At all events, after an hour's desultory conversation, owing to the great coolness of the general, we got rid of them, and they mounted their waggon, which was anything but a fashionable one. They were going to the Mackenzie Heights, and the French general, Bombaki, who was going that road, kindly undertook to point out the way. They said that they had finished twelve bottles of champagne at Kamiesch. Nice company this to drop in after an excellent *petit dîner*, just as we were about commencing the harmony of the evening! This strange incident completely broke up our party. We fixed the great madrigal soirée at my hut for the 27th of May, hoping on that occasion to be more fortunate. We afterwards heard that the Russian officers were stopped at the Traktir Bridge, and locked up for a few days—no doubt to give them time to get sober.

We began to hope that in case we should be visited by any Czarewitchian company at our semi-grand concerto—and there were plenty daily in the camp—that they would call before, and not after, their visit to the then reckless town of Kamiesch, at which place a friend and myself had, a few days previous, witnessed several very comical scenes. This was owing to the influx of visitors from the different armies. It was more particularly the case at the theatre, where the funniest part of the performance was acted in the pit, stalls, boxes, and gallery, instead of upon the stage. On one occasion, General Pelissier was compelled to have a few of the new spectators boxed for the night in the guard-house, in order to be allowed to enjoy the privilege of his own private box.

In return for their visits to us, both French and English officers daily returned the compliment, and the Russians did all they could to make themselves agreeable. General Garrett met with a very cordial reception from Major-General Vassileffsky, who commanded after the departure of General Lüders. General Garrett, in return, invited him to the headquarters of the Fourth Division, which invitation was graciously accepted by the Russian general. I was spending the evening with General Garrett, when he observed that he wished to give General Vassileffsky a lunch, but that it would be a difficult matter, as he had no convenience for that purpose.

"Never mind that, general," said I; "send out your invitations, and leave the rest to me. A lunch for twenty or thirty shall be upon your table in due time."

"They are coming tomorrow morning."

"Rather short notice, general; but never mind, it will be all right in spite of time:

difficulties are common enough in time of war. Pray leave the matter to Major Dallas and myself—we will turn out a lunch worthy of yourself and your guests."

I immediately set to work, and in a few hours extra provisions and rations had taken various shapes and forms; some were being stewed, others baked, and some boiled. Everything was going on so smoothly, that I almost wished the lunch had been for that day. My men had returned from their daily regimental rounds, and were all at work. In the midst of this, the worthy general begged of me to give him a call, when he informed me that he was sorry to say that the Russian general's visit was postponed, General Sir W. Codrington having invited him to headquarters for that day.

"No matter," said I; "if your lunch is not postponed too long, the provisions will improve, instead of deteriorating."

"You think so?"

"I am sure of it, general. All the animal food we get in the camp is too fresh: the beast is no sooner slaughtered than it is either in the pot, oven, or on the gridiron."

"We shall be about twenty."

"So I perceive, and that my name figures amongst your illustrious guests. You must, however, general, leave me entirely free on that occasion; I will sit down to table when I think proper."

"Do as you like, but you must sit down with us."

"On that day, general, I claim precedence, and even command, over the head of your division."

He laughed heartily, saying, "It shall be so. Tomorrow there is to be a review of two divisions in honour of General Vassileffsky, and no doubt the lunch will come off the day after."

"Very well, general; only give me due notice, I will answer for the rest. After such success at headquarters, the Fourth Division must not fail."

As there was nothing more to be done, I gave my people a holiday to see the ruins of Sebastopol, which they had not been able to do owing to the press of business. I thought I might as well go myself, as my engineer, Mr. Phillips, had not seen them. The horses were ordered—Mesnil and Phillips accompanied me. We mounted and galloped towards the dilapidated city, which, although from the hill it seems close at hand, afterwards appears to recede further and further. We arrived at the Ravin des Boulets—so called from the extraordinary crop of that article which lay there after the ploughing of that piece of land by the hand of Mars, the god of iron vegetables made of solid materials. Our gallant cockney Zouave, who had never smelt any other powder than gunpowder tea, was quite intrepid, and he mounted to the Redan as though he intended to take it by assault. He was always ahead; and no sooner had a view from that far-famed historical spot, of which he had so successfully taken possession, than the rage of valour seized upon him; no one could arrest his progress—he bounded off upon his steed several hundred yards in advance, shouting in frantic enthusiasm, "To Sebastopol! to Sebastopol!" My friend and myself were rather cooler upon the subject, and trotted slowly along the ravine direct to the Mast Battery. I called my invincible engineer back, telling him that he was going the wrong way, as we wanted to visit that battery before going into the city. He therefore returned.

"I tell you what," said I, "young boiling-hot warrior from Snow Hill, if you had been here this time last year, you would not have charged like that; the Russians would have smashed your crown for you."

"No doubt they would, had I given them a chance; but I should have said with the coward, Peter Morrison, 'The time to show courage has arrived, my brave fellow; let us hide ourselves.' He had scarcely perpetrated this old joke, when a tremendous explosion was heard, shaking the earth under our horses' feet and almost upsetting them. I made sure it was a mine that had been sprung; and a few seconds after, a thick short piece of wood, partially ignited, fell at about ten paces from my horse's head. The animal began to kick, and we were enveloped in a dense cloud of smoke smelling of powder, and so thick that for a few seconds we positively could not see anything. I expected that my two friends had been blown into the air, and they thought that I had met with the same fate. We soon perceived there was no harm done. Our horses advanced a few paces; and upon turning the corner of the ravine, about ten yards in advance, we perceived three sailors lying dead, as we thought, and the ground about them covered with blood. Two of them were screaming; the other had one leg blown to atoms, and was badly wounded in the other. We lifted the man who was lying on his face, thinking that he was the worst of all, when to our surprise we found that he had not been touched, excepting by a few fragments of his friend's limbs, which had fallen upon his back. His companion was slightly wounded in four places: it was a most extraordinary circumstance that his trousers were torn to ribbons, and a piece of the bridge of his nose was taken clean off, from which wound he bled copiously. We perceived that it was not a mine, but a thirteen-inch shell, which had exploded, though not a vestige of it remained near the spot; nothing but a train of burnt powder about five feet long and three inches wide could be seen near the poor fellows who had so imprudently risked their lives. We did all we could to alleviate their sufferings. It was extremely awkward to meddle with the first, who remained perfectly motionless, and no hospital was near nor doctor to be obtained. I gave a French soldier five shillings to run to the French camp and fetch a doctor: he did not succeed, but returned with a stretcher. I also sent to Sebastopol, but without success. I had just tied the poor fellow's leg very tight above the knee, in order to stop the loss of blood, when General Dacres and a number of officers who had heard the report came to the spot. I told the general how the accident had occurred, as it had been explained to me by the man who set it going, as he called it. Although he was nearest to the deadly missile when it exploded, he was not even scratched.

The affair happened thus:—About half-way up the hill they found a live shell, and for amusement, as they said, rolled it about the ravine. In doing this some of the powder escaped, of which one of the party made a devil: this he placed on a stone. In the meantime the shell had rolled some distance, leaving in its course a train of powder. Not perceiving this, he set the devil on fire; it communicated with the train, and ignited the shell.

"How imprudent those foolish sailors are!" said General Dacres; "they are all alike."

As no doctor made his appearance, the general observed the best plan would be to convey the wounded man on board the *Gladiator* steam-frigate: she was the first foreign ship of war that had entered the harbour. On our way we met two doctors who had been visiting the ruins. They examined the sailor's wound, and having attended to it, followed him to the *Gladiator's* boat, which was waiting at the floating bridge from the Karabelnaia to the French side. I saw him on board, and the surgeon of the ship, Dr. Thompson, immediately amputated his leg. The other two went their way, one of them patched up in four places, but able to walk. I afterwards heard from the doctor that his patient was doing well, and that he was a deserter, for which he would be punished. "A double gratification, doctor," said I: "that's what a sailor calls a day's spree."

The most remarkable part of the affair was the escape of the man who had set the shell a-going; he was not even scratched. The reason of this he explained thus:—"When I had set the devil on fire, to my surprise I saw the flame running towards the shell; I expected it would explode, and threw myself flat upon my face. My eyes! wasn't it a rum 'un!—it gave me such a blow on the pate—the report, I mean—I can hardly hear now."

That man was not four feet from the shell when it exploded. I consider that we had a most miraculous escape, as our brave cockney observed, looking as pale as though he hadn't a drop of blood left, though generally possessing a regular rubicund face, the vermilion colour of which nothing but a good coat of whitewash could have affected. He was, in fact, quite stupefied, and asked me if it was likely that another would burst. "Very likely," said I, "if anybody sets it on fire."

"You in particular, my young fellow," said I, "have had a narrow escape. If I had not called you back, you would have been blown to atoms, as a large branch was sent clean off a poplar tree near which you were standing."

The wooden fusee, a piece of the other fellow's trousers, and a regular fright, were some of the trophies I gathered of this sad event.

On our way home, our Snow Hill friend, who could not get rid of the bombshell feeling, and felt rather shaky, related the following clever move on the part of himself and Mr. Mesnil. It occurred a few days before in one of the ravines, and he almost trembled in relating the anecdote.

"Ah," said he, "you blame those poor fellows for setting fire to that shell. I'll tell you what Mr. Mesnil and myself did the other day. As we were walking, we found a live shell, and being anxious to ascertain whether it contained those bundles of fused nails we had been shown by Joseph at Stuart's canteen in the morning, we actually took up a sixty-four pound shot which was at hand, and pounded the shell four or five times, in order to split it, that we might inspect the contents. This did not succeed, so at length we gave it up in despair."

"Never!" exclaimed I.

"We did, I assure you. Ask Mesnil."

Calling him as he was riding on before, I asked him if it was true.

"Don't mention it—it's true enough. I have been thinking seriously about it; indeed, I feel quite nervous. What fools we were! and what luck to have escaped!"

"I never heard of such a senseless trick in all my life," said I. "Hardly anyone would believe it."

"The danger and imprudence of the act would never have struck me, had I not witnessed this day's accident. Let us change the conversation."

After all, I must say it was very imprudent to leave them about in that manner. The soldiers were rightly enough ordered not to pick them up with the cannonballs; but a hole should have been dug, and each shell buried separately: then no danger could possibly have occurred.

This plan I had *en passant* suggested to some of the authorities.

The next day another accident happened with a shell. A fatigue party were engaged picking up round shot, and one of the men had a shell upon his shoulder. His comrade perceiving it, said, "You have a live shell upon your shoulder, and we are not allowed to pick them up." The man that was carrying it threw it down. It fell upon a stone, and immediately burst, wounding three or four of the party, as well as a poor rifleman who was sitting upon a rock at some distance eating his dinner. He was struck on the head by a splinter, which cut away part of his skull, exposing the brain. He was trepanned the next day; and although he at first did very well, he died a few days afterwards. Such accidents were of almost daily occurrence.

On reaching home I found a note from Major Dallas, General Garrett's aide-decamp, apprising me that the lunch would take place in two days. This delay gave us plenty of time to distinguish ourselves in the culinary department. Colonel Halliwell, our excellent neighbour, had left for good, as he was appointed to do duty at Balaklava. He was replaced by Captain Brooks, his secretary, who was superseded by Colonel Hugh Smith, and the latter by Major Willis. This department was of great importance and assistance to me in removing the stoves from one regiment to another. I here take the opportunity of thanking those gentlemen, whose kindness almost made me forget, as far as business was concerned, the worthy Colonel Halliwell, who had removed his headquarters to Balaklava, and pitched his tent upon the top of the hill facing the Genoese Tower, called the Marine Heights. The ordnance-house was his place of business and mess-room; but now and then the warrior gourmet elevated the gastronomic art to the highest pitch by giving small parties on the summit or pinnacle of the rocky mountain. This was the case one day when I called. The gallant colonel was very busy embarking troops, but found twenty minutes' spare time, in which he concocted the most delicious *Mayonnaise de Homard* I ever tasted, and which was partaken of by two Russian lady visitors. They were mother and daughter, of high birth, and accompanied by a Russian officer. The party had accepted the colonel's invitation when he visited Bakschiserai. The elder lady was one of the maids of honour to the Dowager Empress of Russia. The lunch, though soon over, was exquisite, the colonel's servant being every bit as good a judge of good things as his master. The champagne was as good as the mayonnaise. As the colonel had to attend to business after lunch, the Russian officer, Colonel Halliwell's aide-de-camp, two friends, and myself, had the pleasure of accompanying the ladies for a walk. Nothing proved more interesting to them than a visit to the Sanatorium Hospital, in hopes of seeing Miss Nightingale, of whom they had heard much. The former they saw, and were much pleased with it; but the good lady, to their chagrin, was absent at the Monastery. They consoled themselves by looking round her hut; but there was nothing to distinguish it from the others: it was, indeed, worse built, having been put up in a hurry. Their enthusiasm was the pure effect of imagination; and had we pointed out any other as the residence of that lady, it would have produced the same result.

The decline of the sun apprised our Russian visitors that time was flying; and they had far to go. We parted from them near the top of the Crow's Nest, one of the finest spots in the world to get a view of a good sunset.

Early the next morning all the people in authority were astir. Generals, colonels, officers, and men in light marching order, might be seen quickly crossing and re-crossing the plateau in every direction. I had, with my brigade of cooks, been busy since daybreak, and a white stream of communication had established itself between the general's palazzo, built of fine white stone,* and the villarette of your humble servant, so conspicuously erected in almost the centre of the plateau. This was no other than my cooks in their white culinary attire, running like mad to and fro, fetching and carrying the portions of the collation which I had prepared in my kitchen. At ten, to the minute, the party were to sit down; at five minutes to ten the collation was on the table, and in military order. The bill of fare was as follows:—

DÉJEUNER POUR VINGT-QUATRE PERSONNES,

Offert au Général Vassileffsky par le Général Garrett.

Filets de turbot clouté à la Dame Blanche.
Côtelettes de mouton à la vivandière.

———

Relevées chaudes.
Les hanchettes de mouton à la Brétonne.

———

Pièces froides.

Le dindonneau farci à l'anglaise.   Les poulets demi-rôtis.
Le gros jambon de Westmoreland glacé.   Le gannet garni d'ortolans à la Victoria.

———

La Macédoine Lüdersienne à l'Alexandre II.

———

Petits hors-d'œuvres.

Les escalopes de mortadelle de Verone.   Le thon italien mariné.
Les olives de Provence farcies.   Les lamproies et sardines
Les anchois.   marinées.
Les cornichons à l'estragon.   Indian pickles.

———

Entremets de douceur.

Gelées d'oranges.   Idem au marasquin.
Plum-pudding à la Exeter.   Un turban Savarin au Madère.

———

The Crimean cup à la Marmora.

———

Dessert assorti.

Salades d'oranges.   Compotes de poires.
Figues, raisins, amandes, &c.

———

* It was commenced by General Bentinck, continued by General Wyndham and Lord W. Paulet, and finished by General Garrett. It was situated on the spot once inhabited by Sir John Campbell. The Duke of Newcastle also had his tent pitched there during his stay in the Crimea, not fifty yards from the place where General Cathcart and other great heroes are interred. The reader's humble and respectful servant is not a little proud to have had the honour of having his last culinary encampment, called Soyer's Villarette, on that celebrated and glorious locality.

My engineer, Tom Shell-proof, as we afterwards called him, undertook to gallop round to the various regimental kitchens, and see that all was in order.* This brought to my recollection the applicable and pithy remark made by my friend Mr. Charles Pierce, who, in the preface of his valuable work entitled *The Household Manager*,† says that "The warrior general who looks forward to the successful termination of his coming engagement, first, with careful study and practised thought, views in prescience each possible exigency, and provides a means to meet it, strategically considering the country in which his scene of action is laid, and the appliances in all respects necessary to his victory." The school from which the author of the above-quoted work emanates is Chirk Castle, where, upwards of twenty years ago, I first made his acquaintance. His then young master, Colonel Myddleton Biddulph, is the present Master of the Household to her Majesty. Mr. Pierce was himself afterwards attached to the household of the reigning Duke of Lucca, and was fellow-servant and a most intimate friend of Baron Ward, who ultimately became not only Master of the Household, but Prime Minister, to the Duke of Parma. Mr. Pierce himself, as is well known, is *maître d'hôtel* to the Russian Embassy.

At ten to the minute, the Russians arrived. After the introduction, the guests sat down, and every jaw was soon doing its best; for in less than twenty minutes there were only the names of the various dishes to be seen, and they were upon the bill of fare—which was not eaten. The Russian general, who has only one arm, ate as much as two men with the use of both. A servant waited upon him, and carved his meat. Better-looking men I have seen, but not more military. He seemed as hard and as round as a cannon-ball. Between three and five was the general's hour of rising in time of peace. When he told me this, I said, "Then I suppose in war-time you don't lie down at all, general?"

"Very little indeed," was the reply.

"That I can conceive. But in time of peace you must admit four or five to be rather an early hour to call upon a friend, as you proposed doing to General Garrett."

The general was a man of very agreeable manners—spoke French rather fluently—had a very quick eye—was no sooner seated than he took a survey of the company. The lunch was much relished—the speeches were short and to the point, and all went on to everybody's satisfaction. The Russian general was particularly pleased, and highly complimented his host upon the dainty repast, which he could not conceive was to be had in the Crimea. His aide-de-camp informed me that he was a bit of an epicure, and always kept a good table when at home. Both the aides-de-camp were much taken with the engravings from the *Illustrated News* pasted round the walls of the general's dining-room. They could not make out how it was that General Pelissier wore a Russian uniform, and Prince Menschikoff the French

---

* Upon my asking General Garrett the reason why the lunch was fixed so early, "So early, say you!" answered the general, laughing. "What do you think? When I asked Major-General Vassileffsky what was the most convenient time for him to pay me a visit, his reply was—from four to five in the morning."

"Which, no doubt, general, you thought too late, or too early."

"True enough," said the general.

† Lately published by George Routledge & Co.

military order—that General Canrobert was dressed like the Emperor Alexander II. while his Majesty was dressed in the French general's costume. Count Orloff wore the French imperial uniform; and above all, their general-in-chief, Prince Gortschikoff, appeared attired as a Highlander, while the Grand Duke Constantine was rigged out as a Zouave. They remained some time after the general had left the table, puzzling over these strange contradictions.

"This," said I, "was done during the cut-throat time; but now we are at peace, and in future everyone will carry his own head upon his shoulders, and each military man wear his own uniform and orders. War," I continued, "is a mischievous evil, which turns everything topsy-turvy, while peace will restore every head to its proper owner."

This explanation appeared to puzzle them more than the thing itself; so I showed them that the heads had been cut off with scissors and placed upon other bodies. This amused them so much, that the general had to wait some time for them. They were entirely engrossed by those illustrated pasquinades, which appeared to be quite a novelty to them.

The review followed. Lord Alexander Russell commanded. The very next morning, Colonel Lockhart of the 92nd Highlanders called at my hut, to consult me about a grand banquet which was to be given at Kamara to Sir Colin Campbell (only six miles off) before his departure for England. Though it was impossible for me to undertake it myself, being still fatigued from the effects of the exertions of the previous day, I could not refuse my assistance. After a great deal of trouble and persuasion, I prevailed upon Mr. F. Crockford to undertake it, and we made out the bill of fare.

The banquet took place on the 9th of May, 1856, to the entire satisfaction of all present; and a great day it was. The gallant general had reviewed his troops that morning, and he bade them adieu, as they were leaving the seat of war, where they had so nobly done their duty both in and out of the trenches. The air re-echoed with shouts at each sentence the worthy general uttered, till he was at last so moved by their enthusiasm that he—Sir Colin Campbell—shed tears. Such was the interesting scene which took place the morning before Sir Colin Campbell left his proud Scotch Zouaves in the mountains and vales of Kamara.

A few hours after that touching martial ceremony I had the honour of an interview with Sir Colin. He thanked me kindly for the trouble I was taking in getting up the banquet. I availed myself of this opportunity to request the general to favour me with his autograph. He smiled and consented. The document forms one of the most interesting relics in my Crimean archives, as the general addressed it to me, with the date, &c. (It was also countersigned by General Cameron.)

The banquet at night went off admirably, and the coup d'oeil, for a battle field, was brilliant. About a hundred sat down to dinner. Sir Colin Campbell made a very touching speech; so did General Cameron, who succeeded to the command, and Colonel Stirling, Sir Colin's aide-de-camp. The evening closed merrily. After the generals and the Staff had retired, the bagpipes continued playing, and all that remained in the banqueting-hall commenced dancing—people, plates, dishes, bottles, and glasses included. The next day, Sir Colin, after paying a friendly farewell visit to all, embarked at Kamiesch on board the French mail.

A few days before Sir Colin Campbell's departure, a grand dinner was given to

General della Marmora at headquarters, and Captain Ponsonby called upon me to ask whether I could not prepare something new in honour of the Sardinian general. I promised to turn my attention to the matter. As the dinner was fixed for the following day, I had but a short time to produce any novelty. The idea struck me that a new and well-iced beverage would be very acceptable during the hot weather. This led to the invention of the Crimean cup *à la Marmora*, which met with high approbation, and was quaffed with great gusto at the grand Marmora dinner at headquarters. The receipt is as follows:—

RECEIPT FOR CRIMEAN CUP À LA MARMORA, OR POTAGE À LA MER BLANCHE.

Proportions.—Syrup of orgeat, one quart; cognac brandy, one pint; maraschino, half-a-pint; Jamaica rum, half-a-pint; champagne, two bottles; soda-water, two bottles; sugar, six ounces; and four middling-sized lemons.

Thinly peal the lemons, and place the rind in a bowl with the sugar; macerate them well for a minute or two, in order to extract the flavour from the lemon. Next squeeze the juice of the lemons upon this, add two bottles of soda-water, and stir well till the sugar is dissolved; pour in the syrup of orgeat, and whip the mixture well with an egg-whisk in order to whiten the composition. Then add the brandy, rum, and maraschino; strain the whole into the punch-bowl, and just before serving add the champagne, which should be well-iced. While adding the champagne, stir well with the ladle: this will render the cup creamy and mellow.

Half the quantity given here, or even less, may be made; this receipt being for a party of thirty.

I perceived that my anticipation had been fully realized, and that after the proclamation of peace the whole camp was converted into an immense banqueting-hall. The continued demand for my assistance in reference to dinner-parties, and invitations to the same, almost made me regret the war-time, during which I used to live in comparative peace, at least as far as high cookery went, having only to attend to my duties, which of course I did not neglect. In addition to all this, I felt compelled, in return for all these polite invitations, to tender hospitalities at home, and thus kept my camp establishment a regular *petit* Lucullusian temple.

The day fixed for the grand festival was at this period drawing near; the number invited increased daily, while the temple only occupied the same space of ground. The places were measured to an inch, and it was found that it would just hold fifty-four with ease, or sixty if they were packed like sardines in a tin box. The number was therefore limited to fifty. To do the thing well for such a party in the Crimea, required both judgment and perseverance. In the intervals between the hours of duty, I laid out my plans, how I should not only please, but also astonish my illustrious guests. A number of regiments were daily leaving; and this caused fresh invitations to be made and issued, in order to fill up the vacancies. At last the day arrived. The morning was very wet, and the sky clouded; two of my men were ill, as was usually the case when anything of importance was about to take place; and consequently the commencement was inauspicious. Owing to the rain, to my great annoyance, the muddy soil of the Crimea accumulated in the hut, caused by the ingress and egress of half-a-dozen soldiers, who had been kindly granted for a few hours to fetch some green plants from a distant ravine to ornament my *fête champêtre* and harmonical soirée. It was nevertheless very refreshing to see for the first time on the rocky summit of Cathcart's Hill the green branches of the valley and the wild flowers of the fields. In less than two hours, the entrance of the villarette, which before only presented the appearance of a comfortable lucifer match box, or fifth-rate kiosque *à la Turque*, assumed quite a rural aspect. My six brave fellows had mounted, not to the assault, but on ladders and cross-beams, those indispensable ornaments in such a villarette, and, as if by enchantment, had transformed it into a perfumed bosquet, or retreat worthy of the goddess Flora. Bunches of flowers, wild lilac, green branches, and evergreens were profusely spread all over both the interior and the exterior of my villarette. These were interspersed with small flags—red, blue, green, and yellow paper lanterns. These decorations gave it quite a fairy appearance. Wax lights were profusely distributed all round; and in the centre hung a chandelier of original shape, constructed by the celebrated Tom Shell-proof, of Snow Hill, London. The entrance was ornamented by a bold bunch of evergreens and many-coloured flowers. Twelve glass lamps, procured at an immense expense for this occasion only, were carefully cleaned, trimmed, and hung along the front and roof of the hut. They had been painted in blue stripes with ultramarine, by the celebrated theatrical artist, Corporal Stainer. By twelve o'clock the interior was finished—tables, benches, sideboards and all. The only thing to be done was to clear out about half a ton of mud, as that sadly interfered with the general appearance of the now enchanting spot.

All was progressing satisfactorily in the cooking department; the weather began to clear up, and at length everything seemed to smile upon my final and most difficult undertaking. Had this festival proved a failure, my guests, who would, no doubt, have been polite enough not to say anything on the point before me, must have formed a very unfavourable opinion of my gastronomic knowledge, which I should not have had another chance of retrieving. It was therefore of the utmost importance that a failure should not occur, or even be thought of. To my sorrow, I suddenly perceived that the turf which had been freshly put down a few days previous in my grand green grass-plot and avenue had turned quite yellow, from the effects of a burning sun. My outside illumination—viz., lamps made out of ration fat, which then could only be obtained by purchase (the soldiers knowing the value of it)—would not consequently produce the effect I intended—the reflection of light upon the green turf. Ambitious as I was of producing quite a novel impression upon the minds of my guests, I felt much vexed at this failure. While deeply pondering over the affair, in walked Colonel de Bathe, with a most extraordinary long face. He said, "You see me quite in despair: we have lost Major Neville and his brother, two of our best madrigal singers, and I really do not think we can sing at all. You have spoken so highly of our singing club, and the company you have invited will all be disappointed."

"Do come, colonel," I replied, "and, if necessary, I will sing myself."

"I will come; but we shall be very imperfect.

"Never mind: we will make up for that by wit, *bonmots*, and frolic."

I succeeded in reassuring the worthy colonel, and he left, promising to come early. A few minutes afterwards, a man entered, and informed me that I could not have the knives, forks, crockery, glasses, &c., which Mr. Crockford had promised, as they had not been returned from Kamara. He added that they would probably be back in the evening or early the next morning. The French rolls I had ordered at Little Kamiesch the day before could not be made in time, and the baker sent to know if common bread would not do as well. "I should think it would," said I, in no pleasant mood. No more American ice was to be had at Kamiesch; and this was indispensable for the crowning triumph of the affair, upon which I relied so much—viz., my new cup *à la Marmora*. There were, in addition, innumerable culinary vexations. It was by no means certain that the promised band from the Rifles would favour me by attending, as Lord Alexander Russell was absent, and General Garrett did not like to grant the necessary permission in his absence, and no one knew when his lordship would return.

Let me observe, the way I first saw the grass turn was not under the influence of my friend, merry champagne. Not at all; but it had playfully acted upon my mind, and given me an entirely new and original idea. No matter how ridiculous it may appear to my reader, it was original. This was to go to the theatre and get a pot of opal green colour, and set some military artists to paint the grass, which was quickly done to perfection. In fact, it was so well executed, that the horses picketed near were actually taken in, and played all manner of capers to get loose and have a feed. My guests were astonished, and could not account for the sudden change, having noticed how brown it looked in the morning. Well, reader, what think you followed this sudden bright green inspiration? Why, the arrival of the crockery, &c., bread, and the American ice, two fresh waiters, and Mr. Crockford's cook, who rendered great assistance.

Twilight was conquered by ration fat, lampion-shells were profusely and artistically placed on the then green grass, tables sumptuously laid out, the chandelier and wax lights ingnited, the globe lamps in front of the villarette blazing in volcanic splendour, the band of the Rifles playing, and the noble company as nobly arriving. O Vatel! you felt gloriously, for your banquet had succeeded; and while your wealthy patron, the Prince de Condé, was receiving from Louis XIV the praise due to your genius, you were no more. All honour to your names! I, like you, immortal Vatel, had all the horrors of an unexpected failure before my eyes. The idea of suicide did not come into my mind, as it did to yours, noble defunct and incomparable *chef!* probably because I had not the honour of wearing the sword of the courtier. Though I had a stock of guns, swords, bayonets, &c., the idea of suicide never struck me, inasmuch as all these weapons were taken as trophies from the Russians, who were now friends and brothers, and those emblems of carnage would have been disgraced if soiled with the blood of so humble an individual as myself. On the contrary, though inclined to despair, I lost no time, but opened a bottle of champagne for a friend who had just popped in. At the second glass—*mirabile dictu!*—the thick curtain which shaded my brow vanished; the unsightly brown grass turned green, and everything appeared *couleur de rose;* and though no material amelioration had yet taken place, I felt that success was certain. *Nil desperandum!* How many men who have ceased to live through an anticipated failure would now be living had they struggled against adverse fate, and not been led away by the dread of an imaginary evil!

The soirée was indeed in jeopardy; but in revenge I had the gratification of receiving from every guest invited a polite note, worded thus: "General, Colonel, or Captain So-and-so, will be very happy to spend the evening at Monsieur Soyer's villarette." General Wyndham, who was at one time uncertain whether he could come or not, sent his aide-de-camp to inform me that he should be able to attend, and to know the hour. Everything, in fact, tended to render my position more unpleasant; and the proverb, "Plus on est de fous, plus on rit," was anything but clear to my mind. It would be clear enough if a good supper and good entertainment were provided; but if the contrary, I should say, "Plus on est de fous, moins on rit." It was three o'clock, p.m., and nine was the hour on the invitation cards. There remained but six hours for success or failure.

O Vatel! my noble master in the science of *curée*, I then for the first time understood the true extent of your devotion to your art. Humiliation and dishonour awaited you; and Death—yes, Death! god of Starvation, with his frail, bony limbs—was grinning at you. Fortunately you lived in an era of gastronomic grandeur, when a *chef de cuisine* bore a high rank, and had your own aristocratic weapon wherewith to do the noble deed which gilds your name.

The gallant Colonel de Bathe was the first to arrive, with plenty of musical support. The programme was settled. Each noble general, as he arrived, was received *à la militaire*, not, as the song says, "sans tambour ni trompette," but *sans cérémonie*. Everyone being acquainted, introductions were not necessary.

At half-past nine the band, which had performed all the while, ceased playing, and the grand madrigal concert commenced, followed by glees, &c., and at intervals the band played lively quadrilles, polkas, &c., till eleven o'clock, when the supper took place. The band melodiously accompanied the knife-and-fork chorus, the champagne gallop, and pop, pop of the confined corks. Shortly after, the amiable Lord Rokeby, who had kindly undertaken the office of chairman, made a most affable and, to me, interesting speech, dilating in high and flattering terms upon my mission to the East.

After supper, the band again ceased, and, while they enjoyed their nocturnal repast, madrigals, glees, duets, solos, &c., followed in rapid succession. All of a sudden (I happened at the time to be in the back room) an alarm was given by General Wyndham, who called out, "Soyer, Soyer, your hut is on fire!" The general was getting up, when a young officer sprang from beam to beam till he reached the top of the hut, where a large paper lantern had taken fire and ignited the roof. My principal fear was for my picture, painted by the late Madame Soyer, called the "Young Bavarian;" which was the admiration of all my Crimean visitors, and well known in London amongst the connoisseurs, having repurchased it at the sale of the great Salt-marsh collection, at Messrs. Christie and Mason's, in the year 1846—(subsequently, when travelling in the South of France, I met on my route the illustrious Horace Vernet, and in Paris, had the honour of showing him this painting in his study at the Institute, when he expressed his opinion in the following words:— "That no female artist had ever painted in such *a bold* style, nor with such a truthfulness of colour and design." He added that it was worthy of the pencil of Murillo). It hung directly under the conflagration. But, thanks to the gymnastic agility of our unknown fireman, calm was soon restored; the band recommenced playing, and the punch *à la Marmora* circulated freely, for everything was abandoned for that exciting mixture, even grogs and champagne. At about two o'clock Lord Rokeby and General Craufurd left. I then introduced a comic song, in which all joined, including between two or three hundred spectators who had collected round the hut. As the hour advanced, the company diminished; but at five in the morning there were still a few guests inquiring for their horses. And thus ended the last party on Cathcart's Hill previous to the breaking up of the Fourth Division and its return to England.

The following is an account, from the *Times*, of the banquet, and of the names of some of my noble visitors:—

This evening, a number of distinguished guests honoured M. Soyer with their presence at supper at his villarette near Cathcart's Hill. The exterior of the hut was illuminated with lamps fed with ration fat; the interior was embellished with numerous wreaths and festoons of the beautiful natural plants and flowers now so abundant over the less-trodden parts of the plateau. Some glees of Kücken, Mendelssohn, Fleming, &c., very well executed by Mr. Clarke Dalby, Major Colville, R. B., Colonel de Bathe, Scots Fusilier Guards, and others, formed an agreeable introduction to an excellent supper—a triumph of culinary art over Crimean resources, which was, however, soon subjugated in its turn by the ferocity and unconquerable steadiness of the British appetite. Lord Rokeby proposed M. Soyer's health, and passed a high eulogium on the services he had rendered to the army by his exertions to promote good cooking and the use of palatable food; and M. Soyer returned thanks with propriety and feeling, acknowledging the aid and support he had received from generals, officers, and privates in the introduction of his improvements.

Among the guests were General Wyndham, Chief of the Staff; General Lord Rokeby, General Lord W. Paulet, Colonel Lord Alexander Russell, Lord Sefton, Sir Henry Barnard, General Garrett, General Craufurd, Colonel Blane, Colonel Hardinge, Colonel P. Fielding, Colonel Drummond, Colonel Ponsonby, Major Dallas, Lieutenant-Colonel Hugh Smith, and about thirty other officers. About this time twelve months the long rangers, of which we wisely held our tongues for fear the Russians would find out how unpleasant they were, and redouble their attentions, might have interrupted the proceedings very abruptly.

XXXV

LAST DAYS OF BRITISH OCCUPATION
OF THE CRIMEA

THE following day I begged Sir William Codrington to fix a day for my final trial, when I intended to place twelve stoves in the 56th Regiment, then quartered at the back of the vineyard facing headquarters, and thus cook for the whole regiment. This would afford Sir W. Codrington an opportunity of judging of their efficacy, and enable him to give his opinion upon the subject. Lord Gough had arrived to distribute the Order of the Bath; and, as his lordship was to remain a couple of days longer in the Crimea, I was anxious that he should be present at the inspection. The following Sunday was fixed for the purpose, and the inspection was to take place after divine service. Accordingly, Lord Gough, Sir W. Codrington, General Wyndham, General Barnard, General Garrett, Colonel de Bathe, Colonel Blane, Colonel Walker, Captain Ponsonby, with their respective staffs, were present, and tasted the various kinds of food I had caused to be prepared by two soldiers only for the whole regiment, about six hundred strong. About thirty gentlemen had assembled; and they all expressed in high terms their satisfaction and approval, not only of the quality of the food produced from the soldiers' rations with so little trouble, but also of the small quantity of fuel consumed in its preparation. In corroboration of this, I the next day received the following letter from Lord Gough:—

LORD GOUGH begs, with his compliments, to inform Monsieur Soyer that he had much pleasure in seeing his new cooking-stoves for the army. Any measures which Monsieur Soyer may have in view to simplify the cooking arrangements of the soldier will always meet with Lord Gough's hearty approval.
Sebastopol, 10th June, 1856.

The French as well as the English camps diminished daily. Each evening was ushered in by large bonfires, indicative of the early departure of either French or English troops. This style of farewell to the battlefield was generally adopted in both armies; but some of the French, not satisfied with burning their lumber and loose wood, which was very properly allowed by the authorities for those joyful volcanoes, commenced setting fire to their huts, kitchens, &c.; for which they were very severely reprimanded by their general, who, instead of allowing them to start the following day, as intended, kept them in camp to the last—compelling them to bivouac upon the spot, and thus fully enjoy the consequences of their folly, having no kitchens to cook in, nor huts to lie under. This was a good lesson for the remainder of the army.

The Fourth Division, under the command of Lord William Paulet, received orders to depart. Every regiment distinguished itself more or less by its peculiar style of bonfire. They were to be fired simultaneously on the eve of their departure.

Some were raised to the height of thirty feet; one even exceeded that, with a base of at least sixty feet in circumference, being composed of not less than ten or twelve tons of wood and rubbish, brought together by the men of the 57th Regiment, who worked very hard for some days in getting it ready. The night arrived, all the bonfires, with the exception of the large one, which was kept for the last, were fired; and when the smaller ones were about half consumed, this monster was ignited in four places. The *coup d'œil* was indeed grand. The burning of Sebastopol had not offered such a column of fire in one spot; added to which, all the regiments composing the division had joined, and were dancing round that mountain of flame—shouting, singing, playing on marrow-bones and cleavers, and upon hundreds of tin camp-kettles as a substitute for drums. The camp was richly illuminated for miles around till about ten o'clock, when, as usual, all mustered in military order. The burning sky had recovered its former azure splendour; the stars were twinkling and shooting; and the next day nothing remained to tell the tale to the newcomers but a kind of large black seal, about eighty feet in circumference.

That evening I had the pleasure of joining a farewell party, given by Lord W. Paulet to a number of friends at his headquarters. The time passed very merrily and agreeably, leaving a most delightful impression upon the minds of all.

The next morning, at daybreak, the whole of the division were on their way to Balaklava. A long red line was seen marching in the distance; the sound of the bands playing "Cheer, boys, cheer," was faintly heard, gradually receding from both sight and hearing. Those brave fellows were then off for good. The Guards had left their camp some days before; but they went in detachments—the Coldstreams first, the Grenadier Guards next, and the Fusiliers last. I paid my respectful farewell visits to Lord Rokeby, General Craufurd, Colonels Drummond, Foley, &c. &c.

Upon this occasion, Colonel Foley invited me to lunch at their grand mess-room, which invitation I accepted with great pleasure. Everyone being on the move, invitations to dinner entirely disappeared from the order of the day. The rations were the only provisions which graced the last day's bill of fare. Still, the salt pork, beef, and the fresh meat were very good, and highly relished by a Crimean appetite: added to which, the remains of a good English cheese, a salad *à la Zouave*, and good English draught ale, completed the sumptuous gala. While freely partaking of the gallant colonel's hospitality, a number of officers joined us; amongst whom I recognised the scion of a celebrated epicure, who sat next me, and commenced manipulating in his plate a most relishing sauce. Upon tasting this, I could not resist exclaiming—

"Oh! Sefton, Sefton! may your noble ashes repose in peace in your tomb! The glory of your name has not faded: your grandson, the youthful Lord Sefton, is an epicure!"*

Some of my stoves remained in use in the Crimea till the day of the departure of the First Division. I was in duty bound to watch over and rescue them from the hands of the marauding Tartars, who seemed to claim as their own everything left behind by each regiment, even previous to the surrender of the Crimea by the Allied Governments.

---

* The best known recipe associated with the epicure Lord Sefton is *Sefton, or Veal Custard*—AB

All that remained of the British army consisted of the 20th with two Scotch regiments at Kamara, and a body of the Land Transport Corps at Cathcart's Hill, (the Land Transport Corps were even at that time raising their bonfires); and the 56th Regiment at headquarters, as Sir William Codrington's bodyguard. So few troops being left upon such a vast space, made it not only very dull, but also very unsafe, compelling us to keep loaded guns and revolvers at the head of our beds. The precaution was most necessary, for, with all our care, we were daily and nightly robbed by the Tartar Jews who infested the camp. Tents actually disappeared, and several huts were fired in the English camp; and no one could detect the authors of these outrages.

The Fourth Division retained its name and the ground, but that was all. The chief of that colossal body alone remained—General Garrett having to the last maintained his headquarters upon the memorable spot. The loss most felt upon Cathcart's Hill was the departure of Lord Alexander Russell's brigade of Rifles, who were in the habit of parading and exercising daily upon the plateau. A parting dinner given to his lordship by General Garrett, and to which I was invited, closed merrily enough; but the day after their departure the camp was as desolate as a desert; only one regiment, the 20th, remained. General Garrett and myself were the only proprietors on that far-famed spot, Cathcart's Hill, though no end of new tenants were arriving in shoals; I mean the rats from deserted camps, who boldly took possession of our headquarters. All around had in a few days assumed such an aspect of desolation, that it appeared to me like a sudden exile from a lively and brilliant capital to a deserted rock: the beating of drums, sounding of trumpets, and the harmony of the bands; as well as the eternal morning parade catechism of the drill-serjeant, shouting with all his might, "Fall in! eyes fifteen paces to the front!"—or occassionally, as the French would say, "Les yeux fixes et la tête à quinze pas!" "Shoulder arms! slope arms!" Now and then, an awkward fellow would be thus apostrophized by the witty serjeant: "Now, my man, has not your country been generous enough to present you with a musket? Then, do your country justice by learning the use of it."

The profound silence which succeeded the tumult of camp life would have depressed the greatest philosopher. Stuart's celebrated canteen, attached to the theatre, and which appeared in the series of engravings already published, was on the move; and Stuart's head man, Joe, was at his last score of bottle-breaking, when I called and ordered half-a-dozen of pale ale.

"You may boast," he exclaimed, "of being the last served here, for we are going off to Kadikoi immediately." I then walked into the theatre. The stage offered a singular *coup d'œil*: the figure of a child, as well as a black doll, were hanging by the neck from a cross beam at the top of the stage; the elaborately-painted curtain was torn into ribbons, the scenery partly whitewashed over, and the furniture of the apartment of Serjeant Blowhard was thrust into Miss Greenfinch's bedroom; while Slasher and Crasher had left the theatre in a most dilapidated state. Female attire, including wings, ringlets, caps, bonnets, bunches of flowers, crinolines, and toilets of all fashions, bedaubed with chalk, bismuth, vermilion, and red brickdust, instead of carmine, were scattered about the stage in such a state that a French *chiffonnier* would not have disgraced his hamper by including them amongst its contents. The painting-room floor was like a rainbow; all the powdered colours had been kicked in every direction, forming a mulligatawny of shades enough to puzzle an Owen

Jones and his disciples. The benches in the stalls and pit were piled up into a formidable barricade. Nothing had been respected but her Majesty's royal arms, which ornamented the centre of the proscenium. These had been painted by Major Dallas, General Garrett's aide-de-camp.

By the aid of a ladder, I carefully removed them, with the intention of placing them amongst my Sebastopol trophies, as a memento of the dramatic art in the Crimea. Upon leaving this desolated skeleton temple of Melpomene, I inquired of Mr. Stuart's bottle-breaker the cause of this awful disorder. He told me, frankly enough, that so far as the wardrobe was concerned, the rats had taken possession, but that for the remainder, himself and a few friends had done the work of devastation by way of closing the season. Thus terminated the dramatic performances in the Theatre Royal of the Fourth Division; and it was, no doubt, a fair specimen of what happened in other divisions, if left in the hands of similar good managers.

Indeed, I could not but feel hurt at this sudden devastation, for it was only a few evenings before that this tumble-down temple of Momus was gloriously shining through the resplendent glare of a dozen brown candles, and that the celebrated band of the Rifles (by permission of Lord A. Russell) was delighting a crowded audience numbering upwards of five hundred soldiers, when, at the end of the first piece, to the astonishment of all, and myself in particular, a distinguished artist and "non-*commissioned*" poet came forward, who, though not in the style of Victor Hugo or Moore, but rather in the poet-*less "or you-go-not style,"* poured forth the following song, to the amusement of the audience, who at its conclusion encored it most lustily. The *"poetry"* (?) ran as follows:—

SOYER'S NEW INVENTION.

A trifling thing, gentlemen, I am going to mention;
Oh tell me, pray, have you seen this great and new invention.
To cook in camp I believe it is their intention;
For Soyer's patent, I confess, it is a perfect creation.
Steam! Steam!

For in it you can burn coal, wood, or patent fuel,
Put in your meat, and then you'll find it will soon be doing;
And when lighted, away it goes, and everything in motion;
For Soyer's patent, I confess, it is a perfect creation.
Steam! Steam!

They gather round for to see the wonderful man who made it,
And stand in amaze and have a gaze, and then begin to inspect it.
All the cocked hats, I believe, say it's a stunning notion;
For Soyer's patent, I confess, it is a perfect creation.
Steam! Steam!

It's greatly approved of, I believe, by all the nation,
And they are about to contract for this great new invention.
I sincerely hope that there's no harm in anything I mention;
For Soyer's patent, I confess, it is a perfect creation.
Steam! Steam!

Composed by A. THOS. PRICE,
Lance Corporal 20th Regiment.

My presence being discovered, the whole of the troops rose *en masse*, and favoured me with three cheers, when, mounting a bench, I addressed them as follows:—

"My worthy friends and brave fellows, allow me to express to you my most profound gratitude for the honour you have conferred upon me thus unexpectedly. My humble services have often been approved of by your superior officers, but believe me, nothing can be more gratifying to me than your genuine and spontaneous approval of my endeavours to improve the cooking of the soldiers' rations; and now that peace has re-established order amongst us all, I shall only be too happy to devote my time in instructing you in the plain art of cookery; for, believe me, it is the desire of her Most Gracious Majesty the Queen, and your superiors, that you should live well, long, grow fat, and die happy."

Shouts of laughter and rounds of cheers terminated this unexpected dramatic impromptu. The performance in consequence terminated twenty minutes later than usual.

On leaving this heap of ruins, I felt as though haunted by a day-mare instead of one worthy of Young's Night; but I persisted in conquering the feeling, and in continuing my sorrowful pilgrimage. As if to add to the gloomy appearance of the deserted camp, the sun, which long threw his burning rays upon the dry soil, disappeared behind vaporous clouds, and rain fell fast. Nevertheless, nothing could prevent me carrying out my first idea, which was to visit in all their loneliness the various camps. I reasoned thus with myself:—"I am probably the only person who has the chance of doing this, and, therefore, the only person who will be able to tell the tale." In spite of the great desire I had to continue my journey, as evening was approaching, I was compelled, though reluctantly, to put an end to my camp review until the day prior to my evacuating the Crimea; therefore I returned to Balaklava, which place, together with Kamiesch, alone showed signs of martial movement, the latter less so than the former. The French troops got away before our own, and at last there were as many Russians as French at Kamiesch. I had scarcely anything to do, which was not amusing after having had so much business continually upon my hands. Mr. Crockford asked me whether I should like to take a trip to Odessa. I jumped at the proposal with delight. That gentleman kindly allowed me to invite a few friends, and assured me that the trip would only occupy five or six days, going and returning. In less than four hours the list was filled, and two days afterwards we were on board the *Belle Alar*, but under more prosperous circumstances than on our former pleasure expedition. The weather was fine, the vessel properly ballasted, and furnished with provisions of all sorts, besides a cargo of goods. Our appetites were first-rate; and after thirty-eight hours of fair steaming, we came in sight of the far-famed city of palaces—Odessa, into the harbour of which we were at once admitted.

Thanks to General Lüders, who obtained of the governor a suspension of quarantine, and Brigadier-General Staunton, whose arrival had been telegraphed, we were allowed to enter even without passports. Among the fortunate tourists were General Staunton, Colonel Smith, Major Earle, Mr. William Russell, Mr. Angel, Mr. Crockford, and myself.

During the trip, our party was as turbulent as the ocean was calm. Each day commenced and ended with shouts of laughter, contrasting singularly with the former melancholy days in the camp. I need not relate that which is so well known to everyone—that the most successful parties are those which are got up *à l'impromptu*. This was the case with this delightful trip; so much so, indeed, that some who came on board at five o'clock were not aware of it till two or three.

I do not think I can give a better idea of this delightful trip than by republishing the following descriptive letter, which appeared in the *Times*:—

SOYER AT ODESSA.

To the Editor of the Times.

SIR,—From the arid and partly-deserted soil of the Crimea, and the everlasting view from Cathcart's Hill of the now silent ruins of Sebastopol, nothing can be more refreshing to the mind than the aspect of a civilized and inhabited town.

I and a few friends agreed to make a trip by water to the famed city of Odessa, where we are now enjoying the favours of peace, and it is with great pleasure that I return our sincere thanks to the authorities and inhabitants of that city of palaces for the most cordial and charming reception which could have been conferred upon strangers after such a destructive war.

Being anxious to visit the public buildings, military hospitals, and the various institutions, I expressed my wishes to General Lüders, which his Excellency not only acceded to, but deputed his aide-de-camp, Colonel Scariatine, to accompany us in our visitorial pilgrimage.

The party consisted of Brigadier-General Staunton, 4th Division, Adjutant-General Colonel Smith, Major Earle, and myself.

This noble man, who spoke excellent French and English, was indeed a valuable *cicerone*. The most important of the institutions we visited are the Military and Civil Hospitals, the Foundling Institution, the Salles d'Asile, and the Hospital of the Sisters of Charity. We were received at, and shown over, the Hospital by the chief medical officer, Dr. Grime, and staff; at the Foundling, by the director, Mr. Fourman; at the Salles d'Asile, by the inspectress, Madame Pera Ergard; and by the Superior of the Sisters of Charity, Madame Marie Retchakoff—one of the latter had just arrived from Bakschiserai; she had been all through the campaign, and was slightly wounded in the trenches. She related that several sisters were killed in Sebastopol, and many wounded during the siege; the latter are now recalled to St. Petersburg, and enjoy the favour and patronage of the Empress. These ladies were most anxious to hear of Miss Nightingale's doings, and spoke of her with the greatest veneration. They listened with much interest to my account of that excellent lady's efforts in the cause of humanity.

All these institutions, though based upon similar principles to those in England and France, possess a type of their own, both as regards the expense and management. Cleanliness, simplicity, and judicious economy seem to be closely studied in all the establishments.

The culinary department, which, of course, was of vital interest to me, I found extremely clean and well constructed, though rather complicated. The boilers are made of wrought iron, which I at first sight feared was copper, but the lids only were made of that showy but dangerous metal in such vast establishments, where the apparatus is in continual use and tinning difficult to be often repeated.

We were at the Orphans' School in time to taste their food, which consists of a basin of soup, one pound of meat, one ounce of oatmeal, and one pound and a half of white bread. The soup is of a thinnish nature, and strongly flavoured with pleasant aromatic herbs, the whole forming, no doubt, a very wholesome and nutritious food, and well adapted to the climate. Their beverage, which is the one of the soldiers', is called Quielyë and Chtschy in Russian, and Quataee in the Polish language. It is made with rye, mead, and a small portion of hops, requiring only a few hours to prepare it.

I must say that to an uninitiated palate it is anything but a pleasant drink, but, no doubt, very refreshing and agreeable when used to it; for after drinking one goblet of it my thirst was allayed for several hours during one of the hottest days I had experienced for some time.

Now, a few words for the epicures. The sturgeon, which is here abundant, and in England despised and valueless, forms a principal and an exquisite article of food, which is partly owing to the method they have of dressing it. On my return I intend to try and reinstate this queenly fish in its pristine fame.

Fresh caviar, which is made from the roe of the fish, is daily eaten by the Russian population as an introduction to the dinner. Crawfish of an extraordinary size are caught in the small rivulets close to the town; they are cheap and very plentiful. The tail and claws are generally the only parts eaten, and tons weight of the part which makes the exquisite bisque d'écrevisses are monthly thrown away.

The receipt of this excellent soup I have promised to send to the worthy host of the Europa Restaurant, he having promised to give it a trial, and thereby enrich his already luxurious bill of fare.

With the highest consideration, I have the honour to remain, your very obedient,

A. SOYER.

Europa Hotel, Odessa, June 23.

We left the far-famed city of Odessa, and thus joyfully terminated our trip to that land of new friends.

Upon our return to Cathcart's Hill, we found that General Garrett and suite had removed to the commandant's house at Balaklava, the general having succeeded to that important post at the departure of Colonel Hardinge, which post he retained till the final close of this great political and military drama. My major domo, my engineer, and followers, were not able, with all their bravery, to resist the nightly attacks of the Tartar camp-rovers. Robbery it was impossible to prevent; for they in one night, as I heard, cleared off everything out of doors, as well as an old bell tent and a box with the servant's clothes. The matter at last grew so critical, that my people were obliged to fire upon them in the night at random. Such Arabian marauders are worthy of the finest type of Zouaves for pillaging.

I found also, on my return, that my people had, immediately after I set off on my trip, left the hill, at the recommendation of General Garrett. He kindly sent word that he did not consider it safe for them to remain there any longer. They were quartered in one of the wards close to the General Hospital, where some of the Sardinian sick remained. They had all daring, adventurous, and extraordinary anecdotes of what had occurred during my absence to relate. Shell-proof, in particular, pretended to have wounded several in the nocturnal engagements.

On his departure for Odessa, Mr. Wm. Russell had left his iron castle, with his farmhouse, stables, garden, and dependencies, in a most flourishing condition; but upon his return that gentleman found the castle pulled down, folded up, and packed ready for removal by land pirates. He thus describes his feelings on the occasion:—

MY DEAR MONSIEUR SOYER,—What do you think? I am now a houseless, homeless wanderer: they have pulled down my house, so it is really time for me to evacuate the Crimea. The shell of the house only stands; and as I am not a lobster or an oyster, that will scarcely give me a shelter; so I must hang out on Cathcart's Hill, in the old cave where Sir John Campbell lived long ago.

W. H. RUSSELL.

Upon returning to Balaklava, we found it but a dismal place. Everybody you met—and the number was not great—quietly asked, "What, not gone yet!—when are you going?"

"In a few days," was the general reply, or perhaps "today" or "tomorrow."

For my part, I told everyone who inquired that I had gone, and what they saw going about dressed like me was only my shadow. Joking apart, I may state, for the information of those whom I respect and who deserve to know the truth, my reason for remaining so long was this: I was in duty bound to see the remainder of my field-stoves, which were in use till the last moment of the campaign, shipped for England. Not only was I responsible for them, but I had to give my official report to Sir William Codrington, and close the mission entrusted to me by the British Government.

Glad was I to be once more at liberty, as my health, though partially restored, was anything but satisfactory. The commander-in-chief had gone to Odessa only for a few days, it is true; but during his absence there was nothing doing. Balaklava was deserted, the camp lifeless; Kadikoi still more so—not a hut, tent, shed, store, canteen, shop, or stable, was inhabited. Brick and stone houses, as well as hospitals, were to let at the very moderate price of nothing at all, and glad to get tenants at that rather reduced rate. It was not at all extraordinary for one to rise a poor man in the morning, and at night find oneself a large proprietor. Every person, upon leaving, presented you with rows of houses, shops, &c., which they could not sell or take away. Nevertheless, all was stale, flat, and unprofitable, as a day or two after coming into possession you yourself had to give them up. Riding through the camp, even at midday, was a dangerous experiment, as it was invaded by hundreds of people of all kinds and tribes, who prowled about, pillaging everything they could put hands upon. Therefore Balaklava was the only safe quarter, and dull enough into the bargain. The heat was great, and amusement scanty. Like the song of the Manchester operatives, "we had no work to do-oo-oo." Eating little, drinking much, and sleeping all day, was our principal occupation. I removed from the General Hospital to a very comfortable hut, then recently occupied by an officer of the Commissariat, comprising three rooms, a stable, and yard.

About noon one day, while in deep slumber, I was suddenly aroused by a joyful voice. It came from Captain Hall, General Codrington's aide-de-camp. "Hallo!" said he, "I fear I am disturbing you."

"Not at all, captain; pray walk in—I have nothing to do. I was taking an Oriental nap, which calms one's senses, to that extent that I had in imagination travelled as far as England and back again to my duty in the East in less than half an hour."

"I have done more extraordinary things than that," said he. "By the same conveyance I have been as far as the East Indies and back to headquarters in the Crimea in twenty minutes."

"You have certainly beaten me; and I think the human mind can at any time beat the electric telegraph for speed."

"What do you intend doing tomorrow?"

"The same as today, captain—nothing."

"Captain Leyland and family have just arrived in the harbour in the beautiful yacht, the *Sylphide*. I have spoken to him about you, and he will be glad to make your acquaintance. They called upon you at Cathcart's Hill, but you were at Odessa. If you like to see that gentleman at once, I will introduce you."

"Most happy, captain." In a short time we were climbing up the side of the bulky *Sylphide*, an immense yacht. From her deck, her beauty was seen to the best advantage. The real Sylphide was, however, just perceptible, surrounded by a group of gentlemen and ladies, beneath a large union-jack which formed an awning upon deck. This was no other than Miss Leydell, a beautiful lady eighteen years of age, with blue eyes, fair hair, rows of pearls for teeth—in fact, a real Sylphide, a sight of whom would have driven Taglioni to despair. After I had had the honour of an introduction to her sylphideship and the surrounding group, the conversation became animated. The topic was upon a monster gipsy party which was to take place the following day in the valley of Baidar, and to which I received an invitation, no sooner made than accepted by your humble servant. The captain then offered to show us over his yacht, which might be compared to a nobleman's floating house for elegance, perfection, and comfort.

The Land Transport Corps and Commissariat had all left, and only the General-in-chief and staff remained, forming the last link of the chain which still bound them to the Crimean soil. They were at the time preparing for an excursion to Odessa, on a visit to General Lüders. The excellent account of the courteous reception we had received at his hands, as well as from the inhabitants of that beautiful city, rendered them more anxious to go. Miss Nightingale was preparing for her departure. I was waiting the closing of the Land Transport and General Hospitals, to see my field stoves embarked; and after delivering them in person to Captain Gordon, I was anxious to follow. Balaklava church, now deprived of its sacerdotal character, was being prepared for the reception of the commander-in-chief upon his return from Odessa, as headquarters had been given up to the original proprietors. General Wyndham, accompanied by his aide-de-camp, had left for England.

The *Algiers* had arrived in port to conduct Sir William Codrington to England, via Constantinople and Malta. A few days afterwards, Miss Nightingale and nurses left for Scutari. All the hospitals in the Crimea were then closed.

A few days after the departure of Miss Nightingale, a marble monument of immense size arrived, and was erected, by an order left by that lady, between the Sanatorium heights and the Sardinian graveyard and monument, situated on the peak of a mountain. It is perceptible from a great distance at sea. The Nightingale Monument is a monster marble cross, twenty feet high, of beautiful Marmora marble. I believe it was ordered and paid for by that benevolent lady, and dedicated by her to the memory of the brave, and the deceased Sisters of Charity. Nothing was written upon it when we left; but the following line was, as I was informed, to be inscribed:—

> Lord have mercy upon us.
> Gospodi pomilore nass.

Shortly after the return of Sir W. Codrington, Sir John Hall, the chief doctor, and Dr. Mouat departed. The only acting parties now left upon the Crimean shores after the awful struggle were General Sir William Codrington, Admiral Freemantle, Rear-Admiral Stewart, General Garrett, Colonel Halliwell, Major Dallas, Captains Hollis and Barnard, Colonels Hugh Smith and Ross, and Captain Gordon; Mr. Osborn, the Commissariat officer, and Mr. Fitzgerald, the purveyor.

The last day, so anxiously waited for and so sweetly anticipated, had arrived. It was ushered in by nightly burnings of huts and canteens.

The day before our departure, and the one prior to the surrender of Balaklava to the Russians, being fixed for my grand review, after in vain endeavouring to induce several individuals to accompany me, I had to go alone, as nobody else took any interest in my solitary pilgrimage.

Even my Snow Hill Zouave at the same time pretended that he had too much to do to waste his valuable time, as he called it—valuable indeed was the word; for at that instant my Cockney Zouave, the brave, was busily engaged making a family drawing. A Stanfield would have been at a standstill at the ingenuity of this modern Joseph Vernet, as a marine painter. Miss Nightingale's carriage had the night previous arrived at my domicile from a store in the Land Transport Corps camp, where I rescued it from a heap of vulgar wagons; it was now standing before the door of my hut, which faced the General Hospital, and had attracted the attention of Mr. Landells, the corresponding artist of the *Illustrated London News*, who was first struck at the many peculiarities of this vehicle, and afterwards more so with the production of my artist, when he broke out into a genuine shout of laughter, after gazing for an instant on my Zouave's picture. Nothing for originality could have matched it, but a late Turner, in its *demi-chef d'œuvre*, from which the halo of glory had departed, and age had left genius alone galavanting from his palette to its now immortal canvas. Turner did I say—yes, and without disgracing the name of that great man; for in the presence of Mr. Landells, my modern Stanfield, who was anxious to gather as much as he could for the edification of his large family on a small sheet of foolscap, and being compelled from the great heat of the morning sun to keep indoors, would occasionally get up and peep round the corner. On being asked by Mr. Landells how he could see from where he was sitting the entire range of the harbour, and more particularly the Genoese Tower, which was situated directly opposite the back of my hut, my clever Zouave, disgusted with Mr. Landells' ignorance of the rudiments of sketching, and vexed at being disturbed, quietly replied, "D——n it! did you not see me turn round the corner?"

"Pray don't, my dear sir," I exclaimed, "interrupt my artist; as you may perceive he is a regular Turner—round the corner, I mean."

With the courage of Don Quixote, but without a Sancho Panza, I undertook my grand military review. I could not but regret the absence of my brave travelling gent, Peter Morrison, who, through an assumed illness, had three months previous abandoned the field of glory, thus terminating his brave and brilliant military career; for had he been still with me, I might have depended upon his formal refusal to follow me.

It was six in the morning: the sun was shining feebly through watery clouds; the breeze blew freshly; the road was moist, my pony in good order, sandwich-case full, leather bottle filled with brandy-and-water, and my revolver loaded. My mind was full of anxiety and wild reverie, for I was about to pass a review of, to me, a defunct army, with the fortunes of which I had been so intimately connected during the war. I knew that upon my return to England I should only meet a few fragments of this splendid force, and not the entire mass, as I had done in the Crimea. I had twelve hours before me.

I commenced at the Sanatorium Hospital, which had been to me such a scene of animation and vivid interest. A mournful silence reigned in this small wooden city, My kitchens had suffered the least in the terrible ordeal; all the framework and brick stoves were still standing, and looked just as if waiting to be again put in action. The grand row of huts forming the various wards, without being much disturbed, were rather in a state of dilapidation. Lastly, I visited Miss Nightingale's sanatorium residence, situated on the peak of a rock at the end of the row of huts. This wooden palace, with its rough verandah, was divided into three separate apartments, giving it a more cheerful appearance than the rest. The iron stove, and its rusty pipe, beds, &c., had been removed, but the remainder of the furniture was intact. Tables, benches, wooden stools, empty pots and bottles which had contained medical comforts, a few rags, a piece of an apron, no end of waste paper, a pair of wooden shoes, and a live cat that appeared to have lived upon the remnants of the kitchen-diets, or more likely the rats, met my inquiring gaze. I caught Miss Puss and closeted her in Miss Nightingale's store-room, with the wooden stool in daily use, intending to send for both at night. The latter I proposed to keep as a relic, and to restore the former to society by either taking him on board ship or letting him loose in the town. I sent my servant; but the pillage had commenced—the cat was gone, and I only got the stool.

Anxious to continue my tour of inspection, I ascended the mountain towards the old Sardinian camp, lately occupied by a few English regiments shortly before embarkation. In the space of a few hundred yards I passed not less than six cemeteries—viz., the one for the Sisters of Mercy and doctors, Sailors' Hospital, Sanatorium, a large Turkish one, and two belonging to the Sardinian troops. Leaving the Marmora Monument on the left and the Nightingale Cross on the right, I merely cast a *coup d'œil* to the tumbledown Sardinian hospital and fragment of camp, and took the road to Kamara. Not a soul did I meet for three miles while crossing the rustic road, cutting immediately through the peak of these lofty mountains, with their base in the Euxine on one side, and on the other, through deep ravines, solemnly reposing on Balaklava's glorious plain. No, nothing but a poor horse, who had been ineffectually shot, was grazing near a pool of blood. Life, the mother of all, seemed to have rescued him from the grasp of Death—the animal was no longer bleeding, the perforation made by the bullet appeared to be healing up. I gathered him a heap of grass, gave him some water from an adjacent rocky rivulet, washed his wound, and to my regret abandoned him.

Shortly after, I crossed through the late camp of the Highland Division, through the vales, dales, and rocky mountains of Kamara. Russian officers and soldiers had taken possession of Sir Colin Campbell's and General Cameron's headquarters, with its green turret. Although no sentries were posted, any quantity of Tartars were wandering about laden with spoils of the deserted camp. What a contrast! Only a few days ago this picturesque spot was all life and animation; indeed the cloth was hardly removed from the festive board, the echo of the shrill pibroch was still vibrating through the adjacent mountains. It was there, only a short time since, that I bade farewell to the brave generals, Sir Colin Campbell and Cameron. Space will not allow me further to descant on the past beauties of this scene; a volume could be filled with its splendours. Not a mile from there stand the fortifications and mud-built huts of the Sardinians, looking more like a deserted rabbit-warren than the abode of an army; it was on this spot they bravely withstood the attack of the enemy at the battle of the Tchernaya on the 16th of August, 1855. Gipsy families had taken possession of a farm and small church on the left, which is so well known.

I looked with amazement at the once blooming gardens of the French camp, and the myriads of wild flowers. Death and desolation seemed then to be the only attendants on this once fascinating scene. Crossing the plain of Balaklava at full gallop, over the celebrated ground where the grand charge of cavalry took place, a distance of several miles, I perceived a white speck: it was the remains of the grand ballroom built by the French in honour of the birth of the Imperial Prince. Heaps of ruins were perceptible at a great distance; this was the once over-populated, but now deserted, Kadikoi. A few minutes after I reached the plateau of Inkermann, arriving near the celebrated windmill where, at the time of this battle, his Royal Highness the Duke of Cambridge and staff were encamped (see Addenda). I next proceeded through the park of artillery, and went direct to the Light Division's headquarters, carefully inspecting the late abode of Lord William Paulet, where once more I met with a most cheering reception, this time from a Tartar family who had taken possession, and they supplied myself and horse with refreshment. The only gloomy reminiscence from this spot was the sight of the numerous graveyards, where mother earth had wrapped in her bosom all that was mortal of many hundreds of her brave sons. At the bottom of the ravine the watering-place for the horses still remained. The water, as usual, was gurgling on its way from tub to tub; an abandoned mule was alone slaking his thirst where once hundreds of horses were to be seen drinking. From here it took me only a few seconds to reach the Second Division and General Barnard's headquarters. The Russians by this time had indeed taken possession of all he had left there, though still I must say that all things were here kept in good order; labouring men were making a garden close to the hut. Soon after this, roaming to the top of Cathcart's Hill, I found the theatre and canteen in perfect keeping, both having been burnt to the ground. Soyer's villarette, though very dilapidated, still remained. The green plot of grass was in great disorder, no doubt the work of the loose horses, who, anticipating a feed, had found to their disgust that art, for once, had been triumphant over nature, and they accordingly vented their spite upon the painted grass. The clergyman's hut had been respected. General Garrett's palazzo had been invaded by an indescribable *miscellanea* of animals. The rocky grotto, which had been severally tenanted by General Sir John Campbell, General Wyndham, General Paulet, General Bentinck, and his Grace the Duke of Newcastle, was left to the mercy of the rats, who here vegetated by hundreds; the floor was strewn with rags, paper, and other rubbish, which had been gathered by these industrious and destructive vermin.

Immediately after ascending and descending three steps, hat in hand, I paid my last solemn duty and respects to the resting-place of the dead brave. A picture indeed it was to see the respect paid to those who had so gloriously died for their country's cause—Père la Chaise or Kensal Green could not look in better condition than this solitary cemetery. With my heart full of emotion I bade adieu to this consecrated spot, and retired. Once more, and for the last time, I gazed on the ruins of Sebastopol. Life seemed to have deserted this once mightly city; one solitary chimney alone emitted smoke; the sun was still shining on this defunct place, which a few days previous I had visited in detail, and found still in the deserted state so often described.

Crossing Lord A. Russell's Rifles' quarters, I soon arrived in the Third Division. General Adams's villarette had been turned into a farmhouse; sheep and other cattle grazed in the ravine.

From this spot I visited the General Hospital located in this division; which I found in a similar state as the Sanatorium. Not a sign of life was perceptible in this mournful spot, where so lately I had witnessed so many painful scenes. From here I journeyed to the Brigade of Guards, the theatre of my semi-martial *début*, having previously inspected the intermediate camp. All was as silent as the grave. A line of obstruction lay on the ground where once the busy railway passed. The Rokeby Castle and its vicinity had the appearance of a travelling caravan of gipsies reposing; children in rags escaped from the group to solicit alms; a few halfpence contented them. In the camp, the kitchen and a number of huts had been bequeathed to me by the gallant colonel before his leaving. Colonels Walker, De Bathe, and the late Colonel Drummond's habitations were selected as a home by the wandering tribe of gipsies.

General Craufurd's headquarters were uninhabited; a few loose horses were grazing near, on the celebrated cricket-ground. The close of my visit was to the English and French headquarters; in the former I was informed the proprietor had reinstated himself on his domains. The turmoil and traffic of war had here given place to the quietude and repose of peace. The post office, telegraph, and printing machines had ceased their movements; the vineyards alone appeared refreshing to the eye. Dr. Hall's snuff-box hut was left open, and partly unroofed; General Wyndham's quarters were quite deserted. The rope curtains taken from the Redan, and laid on the ground before the hut door, was all that remained which I could recognise, as they had upon my demand, been presented to me by the general's aide-de-camp, whose name, to my regret, has escaped my memory.

The French headquarters presented a similar aspect, but was more animated by crowds of adventurers.

Having on my way home taken a glimpse at the ruins of the Seacole Tavern, Land Transport Corps, Army Works Corps, and hospital, I arrived at Bleak House (the headquarters of Mr. Doyne the engineer), which was drearier than ever, and, like a lost balloon in mid air, entirely deserted; all that remained was the almost indescribable view which, at one glance, stamped the scene as something more than beautiful. From the rock where I stood I could pass in review the remainder of the camp, as yet unexplored by me. On my left once lay Colonel Wood's park of artillery, and towards it were a few mules clambering, led by Tartars. At the foot of the hill were Captain Gordon's late quarters of the Land Transport Corps, in the occupation of Colonel M'Murdo and Captain Evans; but the most striking object in view was the combined Railway Station and Engine House, once the focus of noise, but now the abode of repose. In abandoning this rural spot, and running my eye a few hundred yards below me, lay a most charmingly built villarette, most suitably called Prospect House, which was the private residence of Mr. Doyne. Science had here conquered what was wanting in material; the goddess Flora had, like the owner, abandoned this pretty landscape; the dry soil and the sun's rays had "dishabilled" each root from its flower. The cavalry camp and its numerous rows of stables were the last I visited. Dusk gently stole over the horizon when I re-entered the Col of Balaklava. The stars were brightly shining; it was nine o'clock; every bell in the harbour was tolling. Before retiring to rest no less than thirty-seven cemeteries did I count on my daily tablet, which I had passed during my solitary wandering.

The night before the surrender of Balaklava, a large fire broke out in the village of Kadikoi, which, had the wind been high, would have destroyed more than a thousand huts. As usual, the miscreant who had done the mischief escaped detection. General Sir W. Codrington was much vexed at this, as some huts had been sold to the Russian officers. I was, in consequence, deputed by Mr. Bennett, of the Army Works Corps, who was just leaving in another vessel, (at that time I was on board the *Argo*, and ready to sail the following day) to accompany the Russian officer to Sir W. Codrington, to inform him of the fact that the money had been received, and to request that it might be returned. Sir William, though overwhelmed with business, it being the eve of his departure, kindly attended to the Russian officer's request; and the next morning, as I was going on board the *Argo*, I had the pleasure of meeting the commander-in-chief on his way to the spot where the fire had taken place, in order to assure himself that the huts burnt were those which had been paid for. I had a short walk and conversation with Sir William upon various subjects, and took the opportunity of thanking him for the following letter, with which he had kindly favoured me, containing his opinion of my culinary services during the war:—

BALAKLAVA, *July 9th*, 1856.

I believe Monsieur Soyer to have given great assistance in showing the soldier how to get the best meal from the food that is given to him; and I have no doubt Monsieur Soyer's stoves accomplish this purpose in a standing camp or barracks with but little expenditure of fuel. It gives me great pleasure to say that Monsieur Soyer has always been ready to advise and personally superintend the carrying out of improvements in the system of cooking: his knowledge and attention have therefore been of service to the army in the Crimea.

W. CODRINGTON, *General*.

We then parted, the general going to Kadikoi; and I, to select my berth, and see Miss Nightingale's carriage shipped.

The day turned out fine, though rather gloomy in the early part, and very windy. As the last day of such a series of fine weather, it was anything but a promising farewell. At twelve precisely, the keys of Balaklava were to be given up. A picket of the Land Transport Corps were placed on the small bridge at the Col of Balaklava.

A few minutes after, three or four gentlemen sailors, accompanied by some parties whom we at first took for heroic Kadikoi tradesmen, arrived at full gallop, crying out—"The Russians are coming!" which report spread alarm through the camp, and in less than two minutes caused all the troops, twenty-five in number, to be under arms, and rush full speed upon the assailants, by whom they were entirely defeated—as in a few minutes Balaklava was retaken, and has ever since remained in the hands of the Russians. Thus ended that friendly battle of which I was so anxious to be an eye-witness, where champagne flowed freely in lieu of blood.

The grand reception and ceremony was to take place at the commandant's headquarters. A few minutes after twelve, Captain Stamaki, the new governor of Balaklava, made his appearance, accompanied by only one aide-de-camp. Being met by the English authorities, he made a full stop, and the password was exchanged, I believe, in the Greek language. The governor of Balaklava then galloped into his new kingdom. In about twenty minutes a bodyguard of about seventy men, some on foot and some mounted, made their appearance. The horsemen, upon nearer approach, we found to be a picket of Cossacks. When about one hundred yards from the bridge, the British picket went towards them—the Russians having halted. This conventional performance lasted but a few minutes; and then the British posts were relieved by the Russians as they passed on their way to the commandant's, where they were received by Sir W. Codrington, General Garrett, Admirals Freemantle, Stewart, Captain Codrington, &c. &c. A squadron of the 56th, the last regiment remaining in the Crimea, were in attendance with their band. On one side were the English, and the Russians opposite, for the first time on duty facing each other in friendly feeling. The centre was occupied by the authorities. Amongst the group of lookers-on was the illustrious Mrs. Seacole, dressed in a riding-habit; and for the last time this excellent mother was bidding farewell to all her sons, thus ending her benevolent exertions in the Crimea. Having given her my parting salute, I left the *mère noire* for the Black Sea. The sun shone brightly upon the animated group, now performing the last scene of the great drama enacted upon those shores.

A few minutes after the curtain had fallen, spectators and performers had separated, and all were entering upon their new duties. The last remnant of the British army was that day ordered to sail for home.

The weather, which had been rather boisterous, increased in violence; and in consequence, the captain of the *Argo*, with whom I had been in company since the morning to witness the grand closing scene, made sure that we should not sail till the next day. He therefore proposed inviting several of the Russian officers to dine on board. This I immediately communicated to them in French, and they politely accepted the invitation. The party was six in number: among those invited was Monsieur le Conte de Maison, a French nobleman who had lived many years in Russia, and was a large proprietor in the Crimea. After replying to several of his questions, I told him my name. He appeared doubly interested, having heard, as he said, so much about me in the Crimea. In Russia this gentleman was looked upon as an epicure, and probably the interest he felt in my acquaintance had something to do with the good dinner he anticipated. Dinner was to have been upon the table at six, and at half-past five the boat of the *Argo* was to fetch them on board. All was settled, and a pleasant evening with our new friends expected. A violent shower of rain scattered us in all directions, and, much to our sorrow, we never met again.

We had hardly regained the ship, when Admiral Stewart came on board and ordered the captain to sail immediately. I went home through the rain to inform my people of the sudden change of orders, and found they had already heard the news and had started. I arrived just in time to prevent a Tartar stealing one of my horses, of which I had made a present to Mr. Smith, a wine-merchant, as there was no possibility of selling him. Horse-dealing with the Russians about that time was pretty much after this fashion: a rather decent horse would fetch from three to five roubles—which latter sum makes a pound sterling. Under these circumstances, to place them in good hands was not only a charity, but a duty.

Everybody had got on board, and the newcomers were under shelter. The rain fell heavily, and not a soul did I meet in my way from the General Hospital to the *Argo*, which was lying at the other side of the harbour. Nobody was out but myself, my horse, and my umbrella, which I had much difficulty in holding up in the gale I was then braving. The thousands who had witnessed and mingled with the noisy crowd which for so many months had encumbered the place, can form but a faint idea of the gloomy appearance of the desolate Balaklava.

XXXVI

LAST SCENE OF THIS EVENTFUL HISTORY

ON board ship all was bustle and confusion. As the vessel steamed slowly out, we passed the few remaining steamers, including the bold *Algiers*, Captain Codrington, which was smoking with might and main. We went ahead, digging our way through the mountainous waves, which appeared to have accumulated in the harbour purposely to say farewell, or dash our brains out against the bulwarks or the perpendicular rocks of the bay. Black, sulphurous and reddish clouds were rolling from mountain to mountain, burying the peaks of each in their course, and giving the aspect of a universal deluge, by the union of earth to heaven. We could perceive nothing excepting now and then a glimpse of two white spots: one was the Sardinian funeral monument, dedicated to their defunct heroes; the other, the white marble Nightingale Cross, which, as I have before mentioned, had just been erected by that lady to the memory of departed heroes, and the deceased Sisters of Charity and Mercy. So rough a day had not visited us since that eventful one on which Sebastopol had fallen. It was getting dark, and a misty rain kept falling, which made any but joyful reminiscences of our final departure from the theatre of war and the arid soil of the Crimea. The sable veil of night soon fell over our colossal steamer, the *Argo*, as she pitched and rolled in the hollow of the sea, having on board three hundred horses—a rather awkward cargo,—besides having been only recently patched up from some serious damage she had received in consequence of a collision with a French man-of-war. It had made a large hole in her, and carried away her figurehead. She had been for some time in the greatest danger in consequence of this, and though not materially so on the night of our departure, the remembrance of the accident was disagreeable enough to make all uncomfortable and spoil our appetites. A few extras had been added to the bill of fare in anticipation of the visit of our Russian friends; but I beg to inform my readers that I and a few of my *compagnons de voyage* saw no more of the banquet than did our much-disappointed guests on shore, who may probably think the invitation was a joke played off upon them by the captain, and that he was aware of the time of his departure.*

At about eleven, most of the passengers retired to their fully-inhabited cabin. The captain passed the night upon deck; so did I partly, as Morpheus often refuses to visit me when I am upon the mighty ocean, in either rough or smooth weather. Three times was the deck submerged by the heavy seas, washing the passengers from larboard to starboard, and *vice versa*—a sort of gymnastic exercise neither

---

* I take this opportunity of informing Monsieur le Comte de Maison, to whom I shall do myself the pleasure of sending a copy of this work, that the disappointment was on our side, and that—the captain in particular—all regretted the impossibility of acquainting those gentlemen with our sudden departure.

pleasant to man nor beast. Several horses broke their lashings and fell during those heavy shocks. The next morning was not more pleasant, but the afternoon turned out fine. At about three everybody was on deck, cheerfully conversing, walking, reading, smoking, &c. Nothing, I believe, is so soon forgotten as rough weather at sea, especially when the sun favours one with a few brilliant smiles. The dinner-table was well attended, and everybody very chatty. I sat near the captain and General Garrett. The former (whose anxiety seemed to have entirely disappeared) said to me, "I am going to relate a curious incident respecting yourself, Monsieur, of which you are perhaps not aware, but you will call it to mind when I tell you."

"What is it? I hope it is nothing likely to bring me into discredit, or to shock my modesty?"

"On the contrary, it is all in your favour."

"Such being the case, pray proceed. What think you, General Garrett?" said I.

"By all means," he replied.

"Do you remember," the captain began, "on the morning of the 8th September, as you were coming back to your camp, meeting with two naval officers who were endeavouring to pass the lines in order to get to Cathcart's Hill and have a sight of the storming of Sebastopol?"

"That I do; and what's more extraordinary, I do not know their names: in fact, I could not make out who they were, nor where they came from."

"These are the very points on which I am about to enlighten you. You rendered them an important service on that occasion by your hospitality, for which I can assure you they are even to this day very grateful."

"They were very welcome; but who were they?"

"At the time the adventure occurred, they both belonged to this ship: one was our doctor, and the other the son of a member of the company, who intends, upon your arrival in England, to give you an invitation to spend a few days at his seat near Southampton."

"I am much obliged; but pray, when you see them, say I am already highly repaid for anything I did, as it was entirely through them I had the high honour of dining with General Wyndham upon the day on which he immortalized himself as the hero of the Redan."

"You don't say so!" exclaimed the captain.

Perceiving his astonishment, I related the circumstances mentioned in a former chapter. Of course these were well known to General Garrett.

It was with regret I was leaving the Crimea without knowing the heroes of this simple, though to me singular, adventure. How strange it is that at last, and upon my way home, I should ascertain that which I had so often inquired about!

A few rounds of champagne to their health and prosperity terminated this singular affair.

The invalided *Argo* had regained her perpendicular upon the smooth surface of the ocean, and stood as firm as St. Paul's upon its foundations. In fact, the good vessel appeared quite motionless, and made our ocean saloon as lively as any upon *terra firma*. The night seemed to be jealous of the fineness of the day, and not a breath of wind disturbed its serenity. The unwieldy ship glided over the sea, which flashed as though it had been a lake of diamonds. The breeze was just strong enough to fill the few sails spread to catch it. Everyone was upon deck, as busy as bees upon a hot summer's day. The order was given to muster the soldiers and lower deck passengers, and in a few minutes they were all upon the main deck. Amongst them appeared a lad all in rags, barefooted, and with a black and a blue eye. His dirty, ragged jacket was covered with blood and mud. He stood cross-legged and leaning upon his elbow against the coping of the bulwarks, his right hand thrust in the hole where a pocket had no doubt once existed. The lad, in spite of his attire, looked as brisk and independent as a modern Diogenes or a Robert Macaire.* To the questions put to him by the captain, he replied somewhat in the style of the Grecian philosopher to Alexander the Great. There was, however, this difference—those great men understood each other, while the captain's English was entirely lost upon the ragged hero. After several attempts and failures on the part of the captain, a gentleman, Mr. Souter, who spoke the Russian language, interrogated him, and asked him how he got on board. His reply was, "With the baggage, to be sure." He then, boldly and in a fine tone of voice, suiting the action to the word, told the following tale:—"I am an orphan and a Russian serf belonging to Prince Meshersky. My name is Daniel Maximovitch Chimachenka; and since my owner, the prince, went to the war, the serfs have been much ill-treated by the agent in charge. This was particularly the case with myself, as I was attached to the agent's personal service. He beat me daily, and gave me scarcely anything to eat. One day two English officers passed through the village, and I held their horses for them while they took some refreshment. When they came out, they gave me a shilling. Though it was nearly dark, I watched the road they went, and followed them at a distance. After walking some time, I lost sight of them, and slept in the wood till daybreak. Two days after, having travelled through forests and over mountains in order to avoid detection, I found myself at Balaklava. This was only just before the departure of the fleet. I was determined to follow those kind people the English, who had given me so much money for so little work. Being aware that you were all going away, I bethought myself of hiding on board one of your ships, thinking that when discovered you could not treat me worse than the prince's agent had done. I made the attempt in two different vessels, but was discovered and put on shore again. This vessel being one of the last, I went on board assisting some Maltese sailors with the luggage, and amidst the bustle managed to hide away amongst the horses." In this manner the youth got to Constantinople.

The following letter, published in the journal of that city, will inform my readers of the rest:—

Monsieur Soyer, now so well known in the East, has taken under his protection a Russian boy who was in the greatest destitution, having stowed himself away on board the steam-ship *Argo* at Balaklava. He was only discovered when the muster of soldiers and deck-passengers was called. The poor lad was in rags and barefooted. He had received a terrible contusion on the head, and his black swollen eyes and blood-stained face rendered his appearance anything but prepossessing. Being cross-questioned by a passenger who understood Russian, he stated that he got on board under pretence of assisting the sailors with some luggage, and contrived to hide himself amongst the horses till the ship was at sea, fearing that he should be put on shore, as had already happened to him twice before. During the night, he came upon deck and fell asleep. About three in the morning, a violent hurricane came on, and a heavy sea broke over the bows, nearly washing the soldiers and himself overboard. It was at this juncture that he received the contusion, and became for some time senseless. He asked for nothing to eat during the passage, fearing discovery, but satisfied the

* A typical villain in French Comedy—AB

cravings of hunger with orange-peel and pieces of broken biscuit, which the soldiers had thrown about the deck. He said that he was an orphan, twelve years old, and left his native village through the ill-treatment of his owner's agent. Some English gentlemen, in passing through the village, gave him a piece of money for holding their horses; so he decided upon following such kind people, in the hope of obtaining employment and living amongst them.* He appears very intelligent, and is quite indignant at being taken for a Tartar. He is, he says, a true Russian. Instead of allowing him to be turned adrift in Constantinople, Monsieur Soyer claimed and took him under his protection, taking a certificate from the captain to that effect, in presence of General Garrett and his staff, who were passengers on board the *Argo*. As he is now free, no doubt a prosperous future is in store for the poor Russian lad, through the kindness of Monsieur Soyer.—*Journal de Constantinople et Echo de l'Orient*, Thursday, 21st July, 1856.

While on shore at Constantinople, I sent this unsightly and dirty-looking urchin to a Turkish bath, and by this simple, "gentle," and delightful Oriental process removed two or three coats of dirt from his skin. I had a suit of livery *à la russe* made for him, which greatly improved his appearance. When quite recovered from the effects of his bruises and black eye, he turned out to be a very smart, clean, and extremely intelligent lad. So grateful was he for my kindness, that he came every morning at six o'clock to fetch my clothes to brush, kissing my hands at the same time, whether awake or asleep, as a mark of his gratitude. I have him with me in London, and intend to educate him, and hope he will turn out a good man of business and useful to society. It is most probable that had he been left to himself in Constantinople, he would have become a great rascal or a thief; for he possesses enough intelligence to be either a clever, honest man, or an arrant rogue.

THE BOY AS FOUND.

THE BOY AS HE IS.

* Yalta, the place from whence he started, was a distance of forty miles by road from Balaklava; the journey, however, took the lad six days, as he did not know the direct road. He also informed me that at night he used to climb and sleep in a tree, fearing the wild animals, feeding on wild fruit and beech-nuts.

We were anchored in the Bosphorus, opposite the Barrack Hospital. It was about ten in the morning. Everybody had an extra wash upon the occasion, and all were dressed in their best. The weather was very warm and fine, and all appeared gay and merry. General Garrett being anxious to see the wonders of the Mahomedan city, I offered, as I was now pretty well acquainted with its *chefs-d'œuvre*, to be his *cicerone*, which offer he immediately accepted. We started, accompanied by Colonel Hughes and Major Dallas. After paying our respects to Admiral Grey at the Admiralty, we hired two caiques and repaired to the ancient quarter of Stamboul. There we took horses, and for six hours ascended and descended the intolerable muddy and badly-paved streets of the real Constantinople, where are to be seen so many Mussulman works of art—viz.: St. Sophia, the Bazaar, Seraglio Palace, and Hippodrome, &c. &c. &c., with which the general and suite were much delighted. Our intention was to dine at Messerie's Hotel, and we had just arrived there, when we were informed that the Sultan that day intended to give a grand dinner in honour of Generals Pelissier and Codrington. Captain Hall, who brought the news, requested General Garrett to pay an immediate visit to Lord Redcliffe, adding, that no doubt the ambassador would wish him to be present. General Garrett replied— "It would be utterly impossible for me to be present at the ceremony, inasmuch as I cannot get my uniform, which is at the bottom of the hold of the *Argo*. I will, however, pay my respects to Lord Stratford."

We immediately started for that purpose. The general remained some time with our ambassador, and upon coming out informed us of the kind reception and invitation he had received to be present at the grand Dolma Batchi Palace banquet, saying he must manage to go somehow. The only difficulty was to get his own uniform, or any other that would fit him, for the occasion. I merely left my card at the Embassy, intending to pay my respects to Lord Stratford some other day.

This banquet had been postponed for several days, on account of the non-arrival of Sir W. Codrington from Balaklava. The dinner was at last decided to take place on the 18th of July, 1856, at seven o'clock. The English general had not arrived, but was hourly expected. About three p.m. his ship appeared in sight, and at five entered the Bosphorus. All on board who were invited were ready dressed; so they only had to disembark at the splendid marble terrace which forms the landing-place of the Sultan's new palace of Dolma Batchi, where numerous attendants were waiting to receive them. But, as usual, "Man proposes, and God disposes." The severe gale we encountered on leaving Balaklava, far from sparing the great *Algiers*, had delayed her more than it did our good ship. While passing in front of Therapia, her progress was again arrested by one of the most furious hurricanes ever known in the Bosphorus.

The illustrious guests had arrived minus the commander-in-chief, who was expected every minute. They were sitting in the grand reception-room. The dinner-hour arrived, and the doors of the magnificent Mahomedan hall were thrown open to the assembled guests. They were amazed at the splendour and richness of the architecture of that cathedral-like throne-room, which is a perfect copy of St. Sophia on a very splendid scale, the dome being only fourteen feet less in height than that of St. Sophia. The appearance of the table, placed in the centre, though very large and well garnished with elegant table ornaments, fruits, flowers, and a most *recherché* dessert, left, as far as the dinner goes, much to be desired. The mixture of French and Turkish cookery, of which I much approve, would have been preferable to all French, so difficult of perfect execution, particularly at Constantinople. As a whole, the *coup d'œil* was perfectly pyramidal and magical. The guests were seated according to rank and precedence, and each had his name and number on his plate, which plan prevented any confusion. The soup, as well as several *hors-d'œuvres* and other dishes, had been handed round, when a tremendous hurricane shook the frame of the stupendous edifice, extinguished the lights in the orchestra, and made the colossal chandelier (perhaps the largest in the world) swing to and fro until fears were entertained of its falling. For a short time we were uncertain whether it was a hurricane or an earthquake; and though the festive board was encircled by old invincibles whom the cannon of Sebastopol had never unnerved for a minute, it must be confessed that the fear of an earthquake produced an ominous silence.

In a short time the music recommenced, and everyone was himself again. The busy traffic of a large banquet had resumed its regular course; the guests had forgotten this vexatious event, and were conversing cheerfully. When the dinner had been removed, and the dessert was placed upon the table, the band played the "Sultan's Grand March," and his Sublime Majesty entered in all his Oriental pomp, followed by the dignitaries of the empire. This pageant was indeed worthy of the antique style of Oriental grandeur. Still, it is to be regretted that it had lost much of its magnificence from having been simplified and modernized. After this gracious mark of cordial union between the Mahomedan monarch and his Allied guests, which has been so well and elegantly described by the public press, the Sultan retired; and thus ended this sumptuous entertainment, which will ever hold a distinguished place in the gastronomic annals of nations. It was at least the first, and probably will prove the last, at which the magnates of three great nations met together beneath the roof of the great Pacha's palace to partake of Mahomedan hospitality *à la française*, which in my opinion ought to have been Anglo-Franko, but at all events half Turko.

The only thing to be regretted was the untoward absence of Sir W. Codrington, which happened as follows:—The *Algiers* started a few hours after the *Argo*; but being considerably heavier than that vessel—being a man of war—and owing to the bad weather and foul winds, she arrived ten hours after us, instead of four or six, as had been expected. In spite of this delay, she would have arrived in time, but for the extraordinary hurricane which came on as she entered the Bosphorus. Every gentleman invited was dressed and ready to land upon arriving at Dolma Batchi Stairs. It was all to no purpose; for on coming before Therapia, the safety of the ship compelled the captain to order the anchors to be let go; and as no caiques could venture out, it was impossible to land. My chief reason for mentioning this fact is because it was reported in Constantinople and Pera that the French and English commanders of the Allied armies disagreed politically, and would not meet. Through my friendly influence with important persons in Constantinople and Pera, I caused this report to be contradicted by the press, as it might have left an evil impression upon the public mind.

The *Argo* was to sail about four p.m. the next day. At two I went on board to claim my Russian *protégé*, and found the boy, who was aware of my being in Constantinople, and as the steamer was about to sail, had lost all hope of being rescued by me. In expectation of being landed at Constantinople and left to the mercy of the world, he was seated on the poop of the ship, anxiously looking out with the same anxiety as Sister Anne from the top of the tower, in the tale of *Bluebeard*, to see if anyone was coming. At length he perceived a caique with two caidjees approaching the ship *Argo*; in it was seated a rather stout gentleman, dressed in the Oriental style, as he afterwards related, with a large white round hat, encircled with a turban of white and red gauze, and wearing a bournous. "It can only be my new master," exclaimed the boy to those around—or at all events he made them comprehend as much. Nothing could exceed the boy's joy when I set foot upon deck; but, as I was not aware of his anxiety, I took but little notice of him, as I had many persons to see in a short space of time. Observing this, the poor lad began to cry. Had he been retaken, he would have been sent to the mines for fifteen years, and afterwards as a soldier for life. I requested the captain to draw up a statement to the effect that the boy had run away of his own accord, and begged of General Garrett to be present as a witness; and he was accordingly transmitted to me as a free boy from the time of his destitution.

The following is a copy of the statement:—

Steam-ship "Argo," Constantinople, 16th July, 1856.

I hereby certify that a Russian boy, about twelve or fifteen years of age, was found on board this ship after leaving the Crimea. He states that he came on board for the purpose of getting employment. His name, he says, is Daniel, and that he was a serf of Prince Meshersky's. Monsieur Soyer, a passenger on board, now takes him into his service, to prevent his starving.

H. B. BENSON, *Commander.*

N.B.—The boy's name is Daniel Maximovitch Chimachenka. He says he is an orphan— has been very badly treated by his master's steward—and begged of Monsieur Soyer to grant him protection, and is very willing to go with him wheresoever he pleases rather than return to his former master. As he was quite destitute on arriving at Constantinople, Monsieur Soyer is kind enough to take him under his protection.

I hereby certify that the above is quite correct, having interrogated the boy in his own language (Russian).

P. POUTEAU, *Kt. S. A.*

I then bade a cordial farewell to all my *compagnons de voyage*, who were very anxious to have my company to London; but I had made up my mind to take six months' holiday, and travel wherever my fancy might lead me, especially to my native city of Meaux, which I had not seen for twenty-six long years. I also wished to write this work in peace, having lost my notes. I informed them that I could not have the pleasure of accompanying them, as I meant to take a Continental tour, but hoped to meet them in London upon my return, which would probably be in the beginning of the then ensuing spring.

Wishing to visit at my leisure the civil and military institutions of this interesting city of Constantine, and, above all, to become well acquainted with the system of cookery, in which I had already recognised a deal of merit and originality, I determined to remain some weeks at Constantinople, as well as to offer to his Sublime Majesty the Sultan, through the kind intercession of Lord Stratford de Redcliffe, to whom I had paid my humble duty, a complete set of my various culinary works, as well as my magic and model stoves. I established myself at the hotel, and, accompanied by a friend, and my Russian boy dressed *à la cosaque*, proceeded to visit on horseback all the curiosities of the Mahomedan city.

As I have already observed, though I frequently wished to inspect minutely the great metropolis of Constantine, my incessant duties never allowed me time for this: I therefore now devoted my leisure time to seeing Constantinople. I had fixed three weeks as the space requisite to visit in detail the wonders of that city. To do this, I engaged a dragoman of some intelligence, and requested him to conduct me to every place worthy of being seen, at the same time acquainting him that three weeks would be the utmost stay I should make in Constantinople.

Having obtained a firman, or *passe-partout*, we were to be seen flying from palace to palace, mosque to mosque, bazaar to bazaar, kiosque to kiosque, hospital to hospital, cemetery to cemetery, prison to prison; from turning to howling dervishes, and from the Sweet Waters of Europe to those of Asia, and last, not least, to the Sultan's kitchen, which to me was the only object of paramount interest.

Almost everyone attached to the army had left the banks of the Bosphorus and returned to England. Only now and then did one meet a British uniform in Pera. These were the officers of the Commissariat or the Turkish Contingent. Amongst the former were Commissaries Smith, Adams, Osborn, &c.

The post office and hospitals were given up: Therapia and Buyukderé alone could boast of possessing the tail of the British army and navy. General Storks was still on a visit to Lord Stratford de Redcliffe; Sir Edmund Lyons was on board his splendid man-of-war, the *Royal Albert*, in the Bosphorus; Admiral Grey had left, and only a few acting naval men remained at the Admiralty.

I afterwards addressed the following letter which appeared in the *Times*:—

M. SOYER AT CONSTANTINOPLE.

To the Editor of the Times.

SIR,—In reply to no end of inquiries from persons meeting me in the streets of Pera, Buyukderé, Therapia, the Isles des Princes, &c., as to what I am doing in Turkey now the whole of the army has gone, and as everyone here seems so anxious, probably others may feel interested, it has struck me, sir, to inform you personally why I remain here. In the first place, Constantinople and its vicinity are far from being destitute of vital interest, and those who have only seen its beauty from the Bosphorus, and then at first sight condemned the interior of this gigantic city of Constantine, have seen nothing, and are utterly incompetent to speak of it, much less to write upon the curiosities, manners, customs, and way of living, of this singular and almost unknown people, though lodged nearly in the centre of Europe. Thanks now to my last visit to Constantinople, which time nor duty did not admit of before, I now know it and its neighbourhood as well as London, and much better than Paris. I am pretty well acquainted with Turkish institutions, as well as manners and habits, which indeed deviate so much from our fashions that they cannot prove uninteresting to relate, if not to follow. Though so many authors have written upon Turkey, they have yet left me several virgin pages, and those pages are upon the national cookery of the Moslem people.

They have many dishes which are indeed worthy of the table of the greatest epicure, and I shall not consider my Oriental mission terminated to my satisfaction till I see in the bills of fare of France and England their purée de volaille au ris, tomates, et concombres, and purée de Bahmia aromatisée à la crème, by the side of our potages à la Reine, Tortue, Jullienne, and Mulligatawny; near our whitebait, red mullets, turbot, and salmon, their fried sardines, bar fish, gurnet, sturgeon, red mullets aux herbes, oyster pilaff, mackerel, salad, &c.; and with our roast beef, saddle-back of mutton, and haunch of venison, their sheep, lamb, or kid roasted whole, and the monster and delicious kebab; by our entrées of suprême de volaille, salmis, and vol-aux-vents, their doulmas kioftee, shish kebabs, haharram bouton, pilaff au cailles, &c.; with our vegetables, their Bahmia, fried leeks and celery, Partligan bastici, and sakath kabac bastici; with our macédoines, jellies, charlottes, &c., their lokounds, moukahalibi, Baclava gyneristi, ekmekataive. Their coffee, iced milk, and sherbet—in fact, all their principal dishes might, with the best advantage, be adopted and Frenchified and Anglicised. Not so their method of serving, in which they mix sweet and savoury dishes throughout the repast; and less likely still their method of eating with their fingers, though, after several trials, I must admit that it has some peculiar advantages; their sauces being of a thinnish nature, require to be absorbed with a piece of bread in order to partake of them, which could not be performed equally well with a knife or fork. Their custom of serving only one hot dish at a time is not new to us, we having borrowed it from the Russians, who probably took it from the Turks. No nation as yet has been able to boast of having introduced a single innovation in the way of living to this singularly incommunicative race, the cause of which I can only attribute to the immense distance placed between the relative social position of the two sexes: for while in Europe the "*beau sexe*" forms the soul of society and sociability, in Turkey they are kept in entire seclusion, and almost without any kind of education. My stay here has not only produced me the high honour of an interview with the Sultan, but also the advantage of becoming acquainted with one of the most useful and principal officers of his Sublime Majesty's household, called the Hachji Bachji, or general-in-chief of the culinary department of his Sublime Majesty the Padischah, and he speaks with pride of having held that office five years with the late Sultan and Padischah Mahmoud, and has now retained it seventeen years with his present Sublime Majesty. Independent of the private kitchen of the Sultan, he has under his command in the various palaces about six hundred men cooks, and had in the time of Sultan Mahmoud upwards of one thousand. Having expressed a wish to become acquainted with some of the principal Turkish dishes, and the way in which the dinner was served, he not only gave me the required information, but invited me to a dinner, "*à la turc*," at the new palace of Dolma Batchi. We were only four guests, including himself; above seventy small dishes formed a luxurious bill of fare, which, after the Turkish fashion, were partaken of quickly, as the Moslems only taste a mouthful of each dish which may take their fancy. He then informed me that the repast we had partaken of was the *facsimile* of the dinner daily served up to his Majesty the Padischah, who always takes his meals alone, and as no bill of fare is made, every dish in the Turkish cookery code must be prepared daily throughout the year, and only varies in quantity according to the abundance or scarcity of the provisions to be obtained in the various seasons, so that his Sublime Majesty may find everything he may desire within his Imperial call. Further details upon this subject I shall give when I publish my other work, which will be entitled "The Culinary Wonder of all Nations."*

The Armenian cookery turns very much upon the Turkish style, while the Greek has a type of its own, which, I regret to say, is far from meeting with my approbation, though in high Greek families I have partaken of most excellent dinners; but the Turkish dishes were always the most satisfactory, the common cookery of the Greeks being sloppy and greasy, while, *per contra*, the Turk has studied the art of preserving the essence of all the provisions employed, which method will at all times produce a palatable as well as a nutritive food. Prior to my departure, which will be in a few days, I shall pay a visit to Scutari, to contrast the earlier state of that busy spot with its now, as I hear, totally deserted aspect. My remarks upon this subject I shall do myself the pleasure of sending in a future letter, in hopes that they may prove interesting to the thousands who have visited that celebrated place on the Asiatic side of the Bosphorus.

With the highest consideration, I have the honour to remain,

Sir, your obedient servant,

Pera, Constantinople, Hotel d'Angleterre, Sept. 8, 1856.   A. SOYER.

---

* Never completed by Soyer. He died in August 1858—AB

This visit was more laborious than most persons may imagine, but the idea of beginning a new and agreeable campaign, after having terminated a long, dreary, and perilous one, was very pleasing. I was free as regarded my actions, and my health was partly restored. Shortly after my arrival at Scutari, my governmental mission as well as hospital duties ceased, these establishments being closed. I therefore settled everything with the purveyor-in-chief, Mr. J. S. Robertson, General Storks, Miss Nightingale, and Lord Stratford de Redcliffe, who all honoured me with documents expressive of their high approbation of my services. Prior to my final departure, I sent the full report of my proceedings and labours at Scutari, as well as in the camp, to Lord Stratford de Redcliffe.

The following is his Excellency's reply:—

THERAPIA, *August 2nd*, 1856.

DEAR MONSIEUR SOYER,—I return you the papers you were good enough to send for my perusal. The honourable testimonials you have obtained have been well earned.

I shall have much pleasure in asking the Sultan's permission as to your sending him the articles you mention.

A Monsieur   Sincerely yours,

     Monsieur Soyer.   STRATFORD DE REDCLIFFE.

The day after the receipt of the above letter from his Excellency I was summoned by Mr. Etienne Pizanni, the first dragoman of the Embassy, who left a message at the Hôtel d'Angleterre to the effect that the following morning I was to be at Topané Cannon Foundry landing-place, with the various articles I intended to offer for the acceptance of his Sublime Majesty. At ten o'clock precisely I arrived. The caique of the Embassy was already waiting. A few minutes after we had crossed the short and chopping waves, *aux collerettes d'argent*, or bright silver hue, which, with the morning breeze, take birth in that fairy lake, the cradle of romance and beauty as night approaches. Shortly after we were safely landed on the monster marble quay, the private landing-place of the Sultan, which proudly unites the Bosphorus with the gigantic palace of Dolma Batchi; from here we were inducted to the Grand Chamberlain's kiosque, where coffee-cups and chibouques of great value, being ornamented with gold, pearls, emeralds, and diamonds, were filled by slaves and handed to us, and partaken of with great gusto.

In a few minutes Prince Galamaki was shown into the apartment. He had come for the purpose of taking leave of his Sublime master prior to leaving Turkey for his post as ambassador to the Court of Vienna; and having myself had the honour of knowing this distinguished diplomatist when he was ambassador to the Court of St. James, he at once recognised me, and the conversation being opened by Mr. Pizanni, we had a most interesting dialogue on semi-diplomatic matters, embracing a period of fifteen years.

Two hours had now elapsed. Chibouques and coffee had been handed round many times, when the Prince remarked that his Majesty was later than usual. Shortly after, an officer of the palace entered, and desired Mr. Pizanni and myself to accompany him to the Sultan's private palace, a distance of several hundred yards. Crossing a floral carpet of sweet perfume, interwoven with plots of choice exotic plants and flowers, marble fountains, vases, baths, &c., we ascended a staircase, and were introduced to a simply but costly-furnished apartment, when Mr. Pizanni remarked that we had already made a near approach to the person of his Majesty. Hardly had he uttered the remark, when a eunuch entered, and requested us to follow him. We passed through several long dark corridors, richly tapestried, and here and there interposed with coloured glass, which threw a golden-yellow light, reflecting a peculiar hue on the eunuchs who were here and there stationed, keeping guard. Silence reigned supreme. We soon reached a very spacious area. A screen was suddenly removed, when, standing on the summit of a grand crystal staircase, most brilliantly illuminated with resplendent vermilion glass shades, stood erect a figure, which, at first sight, I took for an idol or statue belonging to this enchanting place. Mr. Pizanni advanced, with great veneration, towards it, bidding me follow, over a highly-polished glassy-looking floor, which I did not without fear of slipping—when, to my astonishment, I found myself standing before Abdul Medjid Khan, the Padischah, who, though simply attired in a rich robe de chambre and a plain fez,—which I believe is the oriental dress of reception,—the sublimity of the monarch's countenance will never be effaced from my memory. Mr. Pizanni, addressing his Majesty in the Turkish language, introduced me, when, through that gentleman, I ascertained that his Majesty wished me well, and that his heart was well disposed towards me (meaning a great deal in a few words). His Majesty was then informed of the purport of my mission, commencing at the hospitals of the Bosphorus, then in the Crimea. His approbation was expressed by the slow movement of the head from left to right, the body remaining motionless. Then took place the offering of my various productions, culinary and literary, eight in number, which lay on a large, richly-ornamented piece of furniture, in the centre of this large cupola. The simplicity of the field stove obtained his Majesty's high approbation. "I well understand them," said he, talking all the time to Mr. Pizanni, who translated word for word to me. After having complimented me very highly on the services of my undertaking, "I am much pleased," were the last words his Majesty uttered. We then retreated backwards. Though the conversation had been varied and animated, not a movement on the part of his Majesty did I perceive all the twenty minutes we were conversing. We left the idol as we found it.[*]

The time fixed for my stay in the far-famed city of Constantinople was fast drawing to a close; a short visit to the Isles des Princes, that focus of nightly revels, was to put a final seal to my Mohammedan review. I went there on a Sunday, and had the pleasure of meeting, amongst thousands, with Admiral Lyons and his maritime staff. Here monks, caidjees, donkeys, green fruit, cakes, fireworks, and gambling-tables thrive in a most flourishing manner. As the night approached, the Admiral left to join his ship, escorted down the silvery Bosphorus by hundreds of lighted torches, and shouts from thousands of visitors. The next day I was on board the *Albert*, anchored before Buyukdéré, and bade adieu to the gallant admiral. I then paid my farewell respects to his Excellency Lord de Redcliffe and his family; the day was now fixed for my departure, everything was packed up, and my Russian boy, Daniel Maximovitch Chimachenka, had, with the greatest intelligence and delight, corded my last box, and seemed as if he was already breathing the air of

[*] For a description of the interior of the Palace, see Addenda.

freedom. For some time previous, a monster gipsy party had been in embryo; illness had prevented this rural festivity coming off, but on my return to Pera, it was luckily fixed for the following day—the illustrious Mr. Messerie being the giver of this monster picnic. At five the next morning everyone was attired in their best summer array, and streams of people were pouring from all directions to the Galata Pier. A steamer, gaily trimmed, was waiting for the guests. When all were on board, the paddles commenced their revolutions; and, as we floated along the limpid bay of the Golden Horn, Greek music kept time with our race. Soon we arrived at Therapia, and landed on the pier of the Hôtel d'Angleterre, where light refreshments were provided for the innumerable guests. About forty caiques with double caidjees were waiting near the shore, while two caiques of large dimensions were filled with instrumental musicians. We then all started, crossing the Bosphorus towards Ibraham Pasha's marble palace, and to the melodious sound of the music, we landed in one of the many pretty valleys of which the Bosphorus alone can boast; it was called the Sultana, near the Sultan's valley. Such a culinary encampment I never before beheld; four men-cooks were busily engaged in dishing up sixteen hot *entrées*, fowls were being grilled, quails and dottrels were being roasted, kebabs frizzling, and all kinds of fish were submitted to the science of cookery; four sheep and two lambs were roasted whole in the adjacent forest, while a table for about a hundred and fifty people was laid out under the shadowy folds of a huge tree, luxuriously situated at the base of a delightful Turkish fountain; sherbet, ices, jam, and cakes were also freely partaken of. At twelve, to the minute, the open-air banquet was placed upon the table, and soon the warning note of the tum-tum assembled all around it. Oriental fruit and flowers profusely ornamented the festive board, while Smyrna melons of large dimensions perfumed the air. The banquet lasted two hours, after which dancing and oriental games were in full swing in all directions, including the Greek, Armenian, and Albany dances, accompanied by the twang of music, to the great delight of the participators, as well as the admiration of several hundred Turkish spectators, both men and women, dressed in their best, this being their Sabbath. It gave this scene a purely oriental aspect, which cannot be beheld anywhere but under the heavenly paradise of Mahomet. As the evening approached, more animated became the party, and no finale could have wound up the day's fun better than the dance of all creeds, each dancer holding a lighted torch, which flickered about the forest like so many will-o'-the-wisps. Turkish fireworks terminated this day of romance, which ended to the sorrow of all. Iron pots elevated on poles, along the shore, filled with wood and vitriol, were then fired, throwing a blaze of light on the caidjees, who were gaily fluttering round the shore on the agitated ripples of the Bosphorus; each caique, headed by its pot of fire—blue, green, or yellow—bands of music, hurrahs of twelve times three to Mr. Messerie, the donor of this magnificent fête, and at midnight, landing at Therapia terminated this ever to be remembered day.

My last day was devoted to my grand review of the Asiatic shore, Barrack Hospital, &c., and I devoted the morning hour to my final call on numerous oriental friends from whom I had received so much kindness and friendship during my long sojourn in the East.

Arriving early the next morning at Smyrna, where forests of fig-trees abound, caravans of camels and noted brigands thrive—while at the Hôtel des deux

Augustes, I wrote my Scutari journal, of which the following is a copy, being the continuation of that which appears at page 30.

HÔTEL DES DEUX AUGUSTES, SMYRNA,
September 14*th*, 1856.

Having devoted my last day in Constantinople to visit the Asiatic side of the Bosphorus, I and a few friends went accordingly to Scutari. Our first visit was to the Selinie Quicklaci, so well known by the English as the Barrack Hospital, in anticipation of gathering the latest details relating to that once so celebrated spot. We found it occupied by four thousand Turkish soldiers of the Imperial Guard, lately arrived from Erzeroum. Ten or twelve thousand is the number it will hold; but at a pinch, as we were informed by one of the officers, "and no one acquainted with the place can doubt it," fifteen thousand may be quartered in this monster barracks, which, in consequence of the events of the last three years, will be long remembered in the history of England.

After some formalities, we obtained permission from the govenor, Selim Pacha, to enter the precincts of the late British Hospital; and the scene, I need not say, was entirely changed, everything having put on an Oriental aspect, and nothing remains as evidence of its late occupation by the British army but a few shelves and numbers of the beds in the various wards and corridors; and on the staircase, the partitions of the dispensaries and extra-diet kitchens, which in a few weeks longer will have passed into oblivion. The various offices which were from morning to night crowded, as well as the residence of General Storks, are now occupied by the commanding officers of the Turkish army, by whom business seems to be transacted quietly by signs, salutations, and kissing of hands, such being the Turkish fashion, scarely a word being spoken by these living automatons. We were very politely shown through the building, accompanied by several officers. The large kitchen in the yard, which I had the fitting of, still remains, the partition which formerly divided it to form an extra-diet kitchen only being removed, making it now one vast cook-house. The twenty-four large boilers, set in marble, were in use for making the daily meal for the troops, which that day was the meat Pilaff, a dish suitable for the million of any nation, it being composed principally of rice, and the addition of a little spice or curry-powder will make it highly palatable to the English soldier. The kitchen-floor, after the Turkish fashion, was anything but cleanly; but in their cooking apparatus the contrary exists, the copper boilers being well tinned and very clean. The meat-house, store-rooms, &c., present but a meagre appearance contrasted with that, when filled with meat and provisions of all kinds, during their occupation by the English. Returning thence, we were attracted to the building by a band of music rehearsing in the Malakoff ward, the brassy sounds of which in former days would have proved anything but harmonious to the ears of the patients: several airs arranged by the late Donizetti, the Sultan's bandmaster, and brother of the celebrated maestro, were performed for us with great precision, especially "God save the Queen" and the "Sultan's March," though still with the Oriental twang, which at first is anything but agreeable or pleasing to a European ear. We then walked round the barracks, through those I recollect once encumbered but now empty corridors, the immensity of which is almost indescribable: the centre of the pavement alone, which in some parts is nearly worn out by the daily traffic between the rows of beds placed on either side, brought to my mind those days of sorrow and anguish in which so many brave men had nobly expired in the service of their country. Before leaving, I was very anxious to visit another department, viz., the one so lately occupied by Miss Nightingale, when, to my astonishment, our *cicerone*, without being asked, conducted us to it. But what an extraordinary change was there!—no longer were hangings of black cloth curtains before the doors; neither was seen within the pleasing appearance of the well though simply furnished apartment, erst filled on all sides with religious books, &c., relics of departed soldiers bequeathed to their friends and relations, and numerous samples of diet comforts, many of which I had experimented upon before that benevolent lady in her sanctorum. The walls were also devoid of a fine portrait of her Majesty, and numerous scripture drawings; added to that, the loss of the gentle voice of that excellent lady mingled with that of her devoted satellites. No article of furniture is now to be seen there, with the exception of a common Turkish divan, "which is far from breaking the monotony of the bare whitewashed walls," round which were seated a dozen of dark-coloured warlike looking officers, who very politely rose when we entered. Hardly had we seated ourselves, at their request, than an army of Chiboukchi Bachis entered and presented us with long Chibouques; which while we were smoking, the same formidable army re-appeared, each bearing a cup of coffee and sherbert, which we partook of; and a few minutes after, we retired, though thick clouds of smoke and smell of coffee, and no end of salutations from our illustrious hosts, among whom were Osman Pacha, whose politeness will for ever be engraved upon my memory. My mind was so struck with the sudden *changement à vue* at the time, that I could almost have attributed it to an effect of the magic wand of Harlequin.

Thanking them for their kind entertainment, we retired, they politely conducting us to the grand entrance. We then took a stroll through the town, which we found comparatively deserted: the names of the streets remain, as well as the designations of Clarendon House, Russell House, Chaplain House, Victoria House, &c. We next visited Hyder Pacha, called the General Hospital, where there were about three hundred and forty sick, and amongst them were about ten sick Polish soldiers: there were no cases of cholera, and but few of fever, dysentery, &c. Nothing there seemed changed, except the introduction of Turkish utensils in lieu of English ones. The numbers of the beds were engraved upon copper crescents, and each man had a round tinned copper tray, tankard, and spitting-vase; and here and there were copper water-jugs of an elegant form, and basins of elaborate workmanship for the doctors to wash their hands. Cleanliness seemed to be closely attended to. The kitchen there remains exactly as I had planned it; and the extra diets, though very limited, were prepared on charcoal stoves.

We then went to the Cemetery, which we found in very good order, with the exception of two tombstones not yet fixed; one in memory of Capt. W.R.N. Campbell, of the 5th Dragoon Guards, who died at Scutari the 23rd of December, 1854; and the other to the memory of Lieut. J.M. Holford, 25th Regiment, who died November 29th, 1854. And though there was a Turkish guard or labourer in the Cemetery, he could not inform our dragoman when or where they were to be placed; and as there are no English remaining in Scutari, it would be prudent of the friends of the deceased to inquire as to their placement, for if left to the Turkish authorities a mistake might occur, and we could find no indication of the spot where the remains were interred. The grave of Major Sorrell, with whom I had the pleasure of being acquainted, and whose death (by fever) was so lamented, he being only ill one day, is marked by a plain piece of board bearing his name. There is also the grave of the Russian General Chekachoff, who was wounded at the Alma and taken prisoner: he died a few days after his arrival at Scutari, in his last moments expressing his gratitude for the kindness he had received from the medical officers who attended him. This fact was related to me by Signor Marco Vido of the British Embassy, who was present at his decease. His grave bears no more permanent memento.

The spot selected for the Scutari Monument about to be erected, though not in the centre of the Cemetery, will be a lasting national testimonial to the memory of the brave, as it will form a landmark which cannot fail to be seen from the sea of Marmora, Pera, Stamboul, the Isles des Princes, Kadikoi, &c. &c. The tombstones, though not numerous, are well executed and in good preservation: amongst them may be mentioned those of the Honourable Grey Neville, 5th Dragoon Guards, and Henry Neville, Grenadier Guards, sons of Lord Braybrooke, surviving each other only six days—both wounded at Inkermann. There is also a memento to William Frederic Viscount Chewton, son of the Earl of Waldegrave, killed at Alma, September 20th, 1854.

The wooden cavalry barracks present a most desolate heap of ruins and destruction, and are about to be removed.

We were now obliged to return through the grand Champ des Morts, the vast and mournful spot where millions of souls have rested for centuries in the dark shade of the cypress forest; and I can assure you, Mr. editor, that the day was anything but one of gaiety, but, on the contrary, very solemn though interesting.

With the highest consideration, I have the honour to remain, &c.

Our next stay was at Malta, where I received a most gratifying reception from the governor, military and civil authorities, as well as from the gentlemen of the press. A stay of ten days in that city of ancient chivalry will in my memory form an historical page of most agreeable reminiscences, and could I have accepted all the dinners offered me by the Crimea, three months would hardly have sufficed in fulfilling the invitations. To Colonel Haley of the 47th, I cannot but feel grateful for the magnificent banquet he gave on the occasion, when about fifty of the heads of the army there stationed sat around the festive board, and at which our epicurean soldier distinguished himself by concocting a most excellent potage aux crevettes, and two dressed fish, peculiar to Malta.*

Our next stay was at Marseilles, and being accompanied by Mr. Robertson, the celebrated photographist of Constantinople, we once more degustated the celebrated bouillabaisse. We afterwards took a stroll through the part of France so lately inundated, where we met the celebrated Horace Vernet; after a few hours at Lyons, we reached Paris the same evening, which to our astonished eyes displayed quite a new aspect, with her Rivoli rods of fire, magnificent palaces, and stupendous streets. Above two years had elapsed since my last visit, and had created, under the guidance of the imperial wand of Napoleon III, these wonders. After gazing with amazement over that far-famed city, I retired to my native place, Meaux-en-Brie, the birthplace of Bossuet,** which I had not visited for upwards of twenty-six years, having only a local interest in the place, I being the last of my family left. During the progress of this work, when returning to Paris, I had, after an application, the honour of an interview with his Imperial Majesty the Emperor, who took a most vivid interest in the descriptive narrative I gave him of my Eastern mission, and entered into the most minute details on hospital and camp cookery, &c. Our interview took place at the Chateau des Tuileries, and lasted about half an hour; and after submitting and explaining to his Imperial Majesty a model of my field-stove, he desired to have an ordinary one forwarded from London, to serve as a model for his army. His Majesty also took a vivid interest in the perusal of my simple hospital dietary and army receipts. The affability of his Majesty towards me in alluding to his high appreciation of my services in the East, more than repays me for my very humble duties.†

In accordance with my aforementioned promise, having already gathered so much matter for this narrative work, I find myself compelled to reserve what I have so carefully collected for another work, already mentioned in a note at the foot of

---

* The Maltese culinary productions, and well-provided markets, I must defer commenting upon till my work entitled "The Culinary Wonders of all Nations" is produced.

** He was born at Dijon and did not go to Meaux until he was about 50.—AB

† A few days after, I was deputed, by order of the Emperor, to visit and report on the public kitchen for the working classes in Paris, called the Fourneaux de l'Impératrice; for description of which see Addenda.

the preceding page, in which I shall insert only the dishes most renowned in each country, and thus render them practical everywhere. I have, during my six months' travels since leaving the Crimea, personally visited and become acquainted with the cookery of Russia, Turkey, Germany, Greece, Malta, Italy, and France, also that of its great provincial towns—of the latter till now unknown to me. They all enjoy a high reputation for peculiar dishes so much esteemed by the real gourmet. With Strasbourg, my culinary peregrinations closed. I addressed to the local paper of that antique and interesting city the following letter respecting the production of its delicious *foies gras* and erroneous Inquisitional Romance:—

ARTICLE PUBLISHED IN THE "COURIER DU BAS RHIN."

It has been said and generally credited in England and in France, that the enormous development of the fat livers is obtained by a system of torture inflicted by the Strasburghers upon the unfortunate goose, the protecting bird of the Capitol. A certain English publication states, "they are confined in dark cellars, nailed to the floor by the feet before a slow fire which is kept constantly burning, and they are then crammed to repletion, so much so that the first cramming keeps the digestive organs in action for weeks. This system of torture, worthy of the mysteries of the Spanish Inquisition, dries up the frame of the poor bird to a skeleton, and thus the liver acquires its enormous development under the combined influence of cramming, want of exercise, and the constant slow heat."

"I am happy," says Monsieur Soyer, "to show there is no truth in this statement, and, from personal observation while at Strasbourg, to be able to contradict those absurd fables so long credited in England. I can certify that the geese intended for fattening are allowed to roam about the farms and grass-fields in Alsace till they are seven or eight months old, kept in flocks, and well watched and tended.

"Having reached their requisite degree of maturity, they are brought to the city market by the country farmers and sold to persons who make the fattening a special business. They are now crammed three times a day with dry and ripe Indian meal, kept in clean wooden cages, and allowed to drink as much water as they like; others, in greater numbers, roam about in large barns, very light and well ventilated: these are also kept extremely clean. Each bird consumes about a bushel of Indian meal before attaining the requisite fatness, and but few die from disease during the process. I have been assured that the quality of the water in Strasbourg contributes greatly to the development of the livers, but cannot vouch for the authenticity of this statement."

Here is the whole of the mystery of the cruel process so long commented upon in England; and, far from being Torquemadas, the parties who follow this business, on the contrary, treat the victims destined for the celebrated *pâtés de foies* with great care and humanity. Every Englishman may henceforth eat his *pâté* with a clear conscience, as does the French *gourmet*, without contravening the law of Grammont.

The livers are usually sold at five, six, ten, and even twelve and fifteen francs each, according to the size and quality.

There is no special market for them, but the fatteners carry them round for sale to the pastry-cooks and private establishments.

Independently of the liver, the dealer reaps a further profit upon the goose (which is in general very plump and fat), besides the down and the goose-grease.

I purpose adding to this *recherché* and universal bill of fare, a few receipts from Spain, Portugal, America, India, and China; closing this small but well-filled volume with the roast-beef and plum-pudding of Old England, which they are at present totally incapable of cooking properly in Paris, but which I intend compelling them to do, inasmuch as they now have in that city of gourmets and cradle of gastronomy nearly as good meat as any to be found in the English metropolis.

The work will be published at a moderate price, and printed in different languages, and will, I hope, prove acceptable to the public, as well as beneficial, in a culinary point of view, to all nations.

———

A few weeks after my visit to his Majesty the Emperor Napoleon III, and having delivered my report upon the kitchens for the working classes, to my joy the time had arrived to sail for England's happy land, which two years previous I had so unexpectedly left. Double pleasure was attached to my return, for I felt assured that within its sea-girt shore thousands of true British hearts were wishing me well, to use his Majesty the Sultan's term. And indeed I was not disappointed, for in less than forty-eight hours after my arrival in its mighty metropolis, I had been so fervently shaken by the hand, that I could not but help exclaiming for a short time, "Save me from my friends." Added to this, my kind reception by the home authorities was to me more than gratifying: then the last, though not least, reminiscence of my late campaign which occurred in Hyde Park, on the occasion of the distribution of the Order of Valour by her Most Gracious Majesty, when, being recognised amongst the thousands assembled in the stand by the valiant general, Sir Colin Campbell, the elevation of my hat was not sufficient for the impetuosity of the major domo of this grand and imposing ceremony—the last link of the late memorable Crimean Campaign. On my going towards Sir Colin I was greeted with a hearty shake of the hand, and the usual kind and affable inquiries so peculiar to the amiable General having passed between us, I could not help expressing to the gallant warrior how highly gratified I had been by the admirable and perfect manœuvring of the troops. Shortly after he bade me adieu, and, accompanied by his staff, left the ground. At this time I much regretted not having had the opportunity of paying my duty to one of the generals in command, as it would have closed, in a most *apropos* manner, the last page of this work, my "Culinary Campaign;" but, thanks to my star, an hour after the termination of the proceedings, while walking along Piccadilly towards my residence, a friend's voice behind me exclaimed— "Halloo, Monsieur Soyer!" On turning round, who, to my astonishment, should I perceive, mounted on his Balaklava charger, and followed by his aide-de-camp, but the very gallant general whose absence I had just been regretting. It was no other than Lord William Paulet, who was turning the corner to enter his chambers in the Albany. "I have," exclaimed his lordship, "been looking out everywhere for you, having learned from Sir Colin Campbell that you were upon the ground."

"So have I been looking for you, my lord, and with great anxiety, but unfortunately I was deprived of the pleasure of meeting you."

"By-the-bye, Soyer, I saw your portrait in the historical Scutari painting, by Barrett, this morning at Buckingham Palace, and I consider it an excellent likeness."

"I am glad you think so, my lord, and for my part I consider the whole of the picture remarkably well executed. At the same time allow me to inform your lordship, that as you are so near home, I should have been very sorry to have had the pleasure of meeting you in the Park."

"Why so, Soyer?" remarked his lordship, leaning over his charger, and still retaining my hand in his.

"Well, my lord, the reason is simple. Having so prosperously commenced my culinary campaign under your command and very kind assistance, while your lordship was Brigadier-General of Scutari, nothing could be more in accordance with my wishes than that the last page of a work which I am now about completing, in anticipation of perpetuating the style of cookery introduced by me both at Scutari and in the camp before Sebastopol, should terminate at the very threshold of your door, and while you were returning from the last national ceremony relating to the great Crimean campaign."

"Well, upon my word, it is very remarkable; and I am happy to think, Soyer, that you have written a work upon so important and interesting a subject."

We then parted. A few minutes had thrown a curtain over this grand military display, which will ever be remembered in history, as well as graven on the memory of man.

The Author, after his laborious campaign, in bidding adieu to his readers, does not intend to remain *Soyer tranquille*, as he is most anxious, after having chronicled his culinary reminiscences of the late war, to put his views into action by simple practice; and as he had no other object in writing this book, he sincerely hopes it may be the means of causing a lasting amelioration in the cooking for both army and navy, and all public institutions. Such a result to his labours, after his long culinary experience, would make the author happy indeed, and he would for the future be found as traced below.

SOYER TRÈS HEUREUX.

ADDENDA

SOYER'S HOSPITAL DIETS,

AS INTRODUCED BY HIM WITH THE CONCURRENCE OF THE LEADING MEDICAL GENTLEMEN OF THE BRITISH MILITARY HOSPITALS IN THE EAST.

The importance attaching to weights and measures in the accompanying receipts is fully recognised; it is therefore necessary that regimental as well as civil hospitals should be supplied with scales, and with measures for liquids.

No. 1—Semi-Stewed Mutton and Barley. Soup for 100 Men.*

Put in a convenient-sized caldron 130 pints of cold water, 70lbs. of meat, or about that quantity, 12lbs. of plain mixed vegetables (the best that can be obtained), 9lbs. of barley, 1lb. 7oz. of salt, 1lb. 4oz. of flour, 1lb. 4oz. of sugar, 1oz. of pepper. Put all the ingredients into the pan at once, except the flour; set it on the fire, and when beginning to boil, diminish the heat, and simmer gently for two hours and a half; take the joints of meat out, and keep them warm in the orderly's pan; add to the soup your flour, which you have mixed with enough water to form a light batter; stir well together with a large spoon; boil another half-hour, skim off the fat, and serve the soup and meat separate. The meat may be put back into the soup for a few minutes to warm again prior to serving. The soup should be stirred now and then while making, to prevent burning or sticking to the bottom of the caldron.

The joints are cooked whole, and afterwards cut up in different messes; being cooked this way, in a rather thick stock, the meat becomes more nutritous.

Note.—The word "about" is applied to the half and full diet, which varies the weight of the meat; but ½lb. of mutton will always make a pint of good soup: 3lbs. of mixed preserved vegetables must be used when fresh are not to be obtained, and put in one hour and a half prior to serving, instead of at first; they will then show better in the soup, and still be well done.

All the following receipts may be increased to large quantities, but by all means closely follow the weight and measure.

No. 2—Beef Soup.

Proceed the same as for mutton, only leave the meat in till serving, as it will take longer than mutton. The pieces are not to be above 4 or 5lbs. weight; and for a change, half rice may be introduced; the addition of 2lbs. more will make it thicker and more nutritive; ¼lb. of curry power will make an excellent change also. To vary the same, half a pint of burnt sugar water may be added—it will give the soup a very rich brown colour. (Vide Receipt No. 32.)

No. 3—Beef Tea. Receipt for six Pints.

Cut 3lbs. of beef into pieces the size of walnuts, and chop up the bones, if any; put it into a convenient-sized kettle, with ½lb. of mixed vegetables, such as onions, leeks, celery,

---

* This receipt, so much approved of by the medical authorities, was in daily use for more than fifteen months from the date of its introduction by me.

turnips, carrots (or one or two of these, if all are not to be obtained), 1oz. of salt, a little pepper, 1 teaspoonful of sugar, 2oz. of butter, half a pint of water. Set it on a sharp fire for ten minutes or a quarter of an hour, stirring now and then with a spoon, till it forms a rather thick gravy at bottom, but not brown: then add 7 pints of hot or cold water, but hot is preferable; when boiling, let it simmer gently for an hour; skim off all the fat, strain it through a sieve, and serve.

No. 3a—Essence of Beef Tea.

For camp hospitals.—"Quarter pound tin case of essence."
If in winter set it near the fire to melt; pour the contents in a stewpan and twelve times the case full of water over it, hot or cold; add to it two or three slices of onion, a sprig or two of parsley, a leaf or two of celery, if handy, two teaspoonfuls of salt, one of sugar; pass through a colander and serve. If required stronger, eight cases of water will suffice, decreasing the seasoning in proportion. In case you have no vegetables, sugar, or pepper, salt alone will do, but the broth will not be so succulent.

No. 4—Thick Beef Tea.

Dissolve a good teaspoonful of arrowroot in a gill of water, and pour it into the beef tea twenty minutes before passing through the sieve—it is then ready.

No. 5—Strengthening Beef Tea, with Calf's-foot Jelly or Isinglass.

Add ¼oz. calf's-foot gelatine to the above quantity of beef tea previous to serving, when cooking.

No. 6—Mutton and Veal Tea.

Mutton and veal will make good tea by proceeding precisely the same as above. The addition of a little aromatic herbs is always desirable. If no fresh vegetables are at hand, use 2oz. of mixed preserved vegetables to any of the above receipts.

No. 7—Chicken Broth.

Put in a stewpan a fowl, 3 pints of water, 2 teaspoonfuls of rice, 1 teaspoonful of salt, a middle-sized onion, or 2oz. of mixed vegetables; boil the whole gently for three quarters of an hour: if an old fowl, simmer from one hour and a half to two hours, adding 1 pint more water; skim off the fat, and serve. A small fowl will do.

Note.—A light mutton broth may be made precisely the same, by using a pound and a half of scrag of mutton instead of fowl.
For thick mutton broth proceed as for thick beef-tea, omitting the rice; a tablespoonful of burnt sugar water will give a rich colour to the broth.

No. 8—Plain boiled Rice.

Put 2 quarts of water in a stewpan, with a teaspoonful of salt; when boiling, add to it ½lb. of rice, well washed; boil for ten minutes, or till each grain becomes rather soft; drain it into a colander, slightly grease the pot with butter, and put the rice back into it; let it swell slowly for about twenty minutes near the fire, or in a slow oven; each grain will then swell up, and be well separated; it is then ready for use.

No. 9—Sweet Rice.

Add to the plain boiled rice 1 oz. of butter, 2 tablespoonfuls of sugar, a little cinnamon, a quarter of a pint of milk; stir it with a fork, and serve; a little currant jelly or jam may be added to the rice.

No. 10—Rice with Gravy.

Add to the rice 4 tablespoonfuls of the essence of beef, a little butter, if fresh, half a tea-spoonful of salt; stir together with a fork, and serve.

A teaspoonful of Soyer's Sultana Sauce, or relish, will make it very wholesome and palat-able, as well as invigorating to a fatigued stomach.*

No. 11—Plain Oatmeal.

Put in a pan ¼lb. of oatmeal, 1½oz. of sugar, half a teaspoonful of salt, and 3 pints of water; boil slowly for twenty minutes, "stirring continually," and serve. A quarter of a pint of boiled milk, an ounce of butter, and a little pounded cinnamon or spice added previous to serving is a good variation.

This receipt has been found most useful at the commencement of dysentery by the med-ical authorities.

No. 12—Calf's-foot Jelly.

Put in a proper sized stewpan 2¼oz. of calf's-foot gelatine, 4oz. of white sugar, 4 whites of eggs and shells, the peel of a lemon, the juice of three middle-sized lemons, half a pint of Marsala wine; beat all well together with the egg beater for a few minutes, then add 4½ pints of cold water; set it on a slow fire, and keep whipping it till boiling. Set it on the corner of the stove, partly covered with the lid, upon which you place a few few pieces of burning char-coal; let it simmer gently for ten minutes, and strain it through a jelly-bag. It is then ready to put in the ice or some cool place. Sherry will do if Marsala is not at hand.

For orange jelly use only 1 lemon and 2 oranges. Any delicate flavour may be introduced.

Note.—I find that the preparation now manufactured by Messrs. Crosse and Blackwell, of Soho Square, London, is preferable to any other, being also cheaper than boiling calfs' feet on purpose, which takes a very long time, and is more difficult to make. This preparation will keep as long as isinglass, to prove which I am induced at the same time to give the fol-lowing receipt, when the other cannot be procured. Ox-feet or cow-heel may be used instead of calfs'-feet, only requiring an hour more simmering. In summer ice must be used to set the jelly.

Jelly Stock.

Made from calf's-feet, requires to be made the day previous to being used, requiring to be very hard to extract the fat. Take two calf's-feet, cut them up, and boil in three quarts of water; as soon as it boils remove it to the corner of the fire, and simmer for five hours, keep-ing it skimmed, pass through a hair sieve into a basin, and let it remain until quite hard, then remove the oil and fat, and wipe the top dry. Place in a stew-pan half a pint of water, one of sherry, half a pound of lump sugar, the juice of four lemons, the rinds of two, and the whites and shells of five eggs; whisk until the sugar is melted; then add the jelly, place it on the fire, and whisk until boiling, pass it through a jelly-bag, pouring that back again which comes through first until quite clear; it is then ready for use, by putting it in moulds or glasses. Vary the flavour according to fancy.

No. 13—Sago Jelly.

Put into a pan 3oz. of sago, 1½oz. of sugar, half a lemon-peel cut very thin, ¼ teaspoonful of ground cinnamon, or a small stick of the same; put to it 3 pints of water and a little salt;

---

* The following is made from the *Lancet* of August the 22nd, 1857:—"*Dyspeptic.*—We recommend our correspondent to try some of M. Soyer's new sauce, called the Sultana Sauce. It is made after the Turkish receipt, its flavour is excellent, and it affords considerable aid in cases of slow and weak digestion."

boil ten minutes, or rather longer, stirring continually, until rather thick, then add a little port, sherry, or Marsala wine; mix well, and serve hot or cold.

No. 14—Arrowroot Milk.

Put into a pan 4oz. of arrowroot, 3oz. of sugar, the peel of half a lemon, ¼ teaspoonful of salt, 2½ pints of milk; set it on the fire, stir round gently, boil for ten minutes, and serve. If no lemons at hand, a little essence of any kind will do.

When short of milk, use half water; half an ounce of fresh butter is an improvement before serving. If required thicker, put a little milk.

No. 15—Thick Arrowroot Panada.

Put in a pan 5oz. of arrowroot, 2½oz. of white sugar, the peel of half a lemon, a quarter of a teaspoonful of salt, 4 pints of water; mix all well, set on the fire, boil for ten minutes; it is then ready. The juice of a lemon is an improvement; a gill of wine may also be introduced, and ½oz. of calf's-foot gelatine previously dissolved in water will be strengthening. Milk, however, is preferable, if at hand.

No. 16—Arrowroot Water.

Put into a pan 3oz. of arrowroot, 2oz. of white sugar, the peel of a lemon, ¼ teaspoonful of salt, 4 pints of water; mix well, set it on the fire, boil for ten minutes. It is then ready to serve either hot or cold.

No. 17—Rice Water

Put 7 pints of water to boil, add to it 2 ounces of rice washed, 2oz. of sugar, the peel of two-thirds of a lemon; boil gently for three-quarters of an hour; it will reduce to 5 pints; strain through a colander; it is then ready.

The rice may be left in the beverage or made into a pudding, or by the addition of a little sugar or jam, will be found very good for either children or invalids.

No. 18—Barley Water

Put in a saucepan 7 pints of water, 2oz. of barley, which stir now and then while boiling; add 2oz. of white sugar, the rind of half a lemon, thinly peeled; let it boil gently for about two hours, without covering it; pass it through a sieve or colander; it is then ready. The barley and lemon may be left in it.

No. 19—Soyer's Plain Lemonade

Thinly peel the third part of a lemon, which put into a basin with 2 tablespoonfuls of sugar; roll the lemon with your hand upon the table to soften it; cut it into two, lengthwise, squeeze the juice over the peel, &c., stir round for a minute with a spoon to form a sort of syrup; pour over a pint of water, mix well, and remove the pips; it is then ready for use. If a very large lemon, and full of juice, and very fresh, you may make a pint and a half to a quart, adding sugar and peel in proportion to the increase of water. The juice only of the lemon and sugar will make lemonade, but will then be deprived of the aroma which the rind contains, the said rind being generally thrown away.

No. 20—Semi-citric Lemonade.   Receipt for Fifty Pints

Put 1oz. of citric acid to dissolve in a pint of water; peel 20 lemons thinly, and put the peel in a large vessel, with 3lbs. 2oz. of white sugar well broken; roll each lemon on the table to soften it, which will facilitate the extraction of the juice; cut them into two, and press out the juice into a colander or sieve, over the peel and sugar, then pour half a pint of water through the colander, so as to leave no juice remaining; triturate the sugar, juice and peel together for a minute or two with a spoon, so as to form a sort of syrup, and extract the aroma from the peel and the dissolved citric acid; mix all well together, pour on 50 pints of cold water, stir well together; it is then ready. A little ice in summer is a great addition.

Observation.—The two following Lemonades, which have been submitted to eminent Doctors at Scutari, have been approved of, and can be made for either the Hospitals or the Camp, and will be found to answer equally for domestic consumption, if lemons are not to be obtained.

NO. 21—SOYER'S CHEAP CRIMEAN LEMONADE

Put into a basin 2 tablespoonfuls of white or brown sugar, ½ a tablespoonful of lime juice, mix well together for one minute, add 1 pint of water, and the beverage is ready. A drop of rum will make a good variation, as lime juice and rum are daily issued to the soldiers.

NO. 22—TARTARIC LEMONADE

Dissolve 1oz. of crystallized tartaric acid in a pint of cold water, which put in a large vessel; when dissolved, add 1lb. 9oz. of white or brown sugar—the former is preferable; mix well to form a thick syrup; add to it 24 pints of cold water, slowly mixing well; it is then ready.

It may be strained through either a colander or a jelly-bag; if required very light, add 5 pints more water, and sugar in proportion; if citric acid be used, put only 20 pints of water to each ounce.

NO. 23—CHEAP PLAIN RICE PUDDING, FOR CAMPAIGNING,

In which no eggs or milk are required: important in the Crimea or the field.

Put on the fire, in a moderate-sized saucepan, 12 pints of water; when boiling, add to it 1lb. of rice or 16 tablespoonfuls, 4oz. of brown sugar or 4 tablespoonfuls, 1 large teaspoonful of salt, and the rind of a lemon thinly peeled; boil gently for half an hour, then strain all the water from the rice, keeping it as dry as possible.

The rice-water is then ready for drinking, either warm or cold. The juice of a lemon may be introduced, which will make it more palatable and refreshing.

THE PUDDING

Add to the rice 3oz. of sugar, 4 tablespoonfuls of flour, half a teaspoonful of pounded cinnamon; stir it on the fire carefully for five or ten minutes; put it in a tin or a pie-dish, and bake. By boiling the rice a quarter of an hour longer, it will be very good to eat without baking. Cinnamon may be omitted.

NO. 23A—BATTER PUDDING

Break two fresh eggs in a basin, beat them well, add one tablespoonful and a half of flour, which beat up with your eggs with a fork until no lumps remain; add a gill of milk, a teaspoonful of salt, butter a teacup or a basin, pour in your mixture, put some water in a stewpan, enough to immerge half way up the cup or basin in water; when boiling put in your cup or basin and boil twenty minutes, or till your pudding is well set; pass a knife to loosen it, turn out on a plate, pour pounded sugar and a pat of fresh butter over, and serve. A little lemon, cinnamon, or a drop of any essence may be introduced. A little light melted butter, sherry, and sugar, may be poured over. If required more delicate, add a little less flour. It may be served plain.

No. 24—Bread and Butter Pudding.

Butter a tart-dish well, and sprinkle some currants all round it, then lay in a few slices of bread and butter; boil one pint of milk, pour it on two eggs well whipped, and then on the bread and butter; bake it in a hot oven for half an hour. Currants may be omitted.

No. 25—Bread Pudding.

Boil one pint of milk, with a piece of cinnamon and lemon peel; pour it on two ounces of bread-crumbs; then add two eggs, half an ounce of currants, and a little sugar: steam it in a buttered mould for one hour.

No. 26—Custard Pudding.

Boil one pint of milk, with a small piece of lemon peel and half a bay leaf, for three minutes; then pour these on to three eggs, mix it with one ounce of sugar well together, and pour it into a buttered mould: steam it twenty-five minutes in a stewpan with some water, turn out on a plate and serve.

No. 27—Rich Rice Pudding.

Put in ½lb. of rice in a stew-pan, washed, 3 pints of milk, 1 pint of water, 3oz. of sugar, 1 lemon peel, 1oz. of fresh butter; boil gently half an hour, or until the rice is tender; add 4 eggs, well beaten, mix well, and bake quickly for half an hour, and serve: it may be steamed if preferred.

No. 28—Stewed Macaroni.

Put in a stewpan 2 quarts of water, half a tablespoonful of salt, 2oz. of butter; set on the fire; when boiling, add 1lb. of macaroni, broken up rather small; when boiled very soft, throw off the water; mix well into the macaroni a tablespoonful of flour, add enough milk to make it of the consistency of thin melted butter; boil gently twenty minutes; add in a tablespoonful of either brown or white sugar, or honey, and serve.

A little cinnamon, nutmeg, lemon peel, or orange-flower water may be introduced to impart a flavour; stir quick. A gill of milk or cream may now be thrown in three minutes before serving. Nothing can be more light and nutritious than macaroni done this way. If no milk, use water.

No. 29—Macaroni Pudding.

Put 2 pints of water to boil, add to it 2oz. of macaroni, broken in small pieces; boil till tender, drain off the water and add half a tablespoonful of flour, 2oz. of white sugar, a quarter of a pint of milk, and boil together for ten minutes; beat an egg up, pour it to the other ingredients, a nut of butter; mix well and bake, or steam. It can be served plain, and may be flavoured with either cinnamon, lemon, or other essences, as orange-flower water, vanilla, &c.

No. 30—Sago Pudding.

Put in a pan 4oz. of sago, 2oz. of sugar, half a lemon peel or a little cinnamon, a small pat of fresh butter, if handy, half a pint of milk; boil for a few minutes, or until rather thick, stirring all the while; beat up 2 eggs and mix quickly with the same; it is then ready for either baking or steaming, or may be served plain.

No. 31—Tapioca Pudding.

Put in a pan 2oz. of tapioca, 1½ pints of milk, 1oz. of white or brown sugar, a little salt, set on the fire, boil gently for fifteen minutes, or until the tapioca is tender, stirring now and then to prevent its sticking to the bottom, or burning; then add two eggs well beaten; steam or bake, and serve. It will take about twenty minutes steaming, or a quarter of an hour baking slightly. Flavour with either lemon, cinnamon, or any other essence.

NO. 32—BOILED RICE SEMI-CURRIED, FOR THE PREMONITORY SYMPTOMS OF DIARRHŒA.

Put 1 quart of water in a pot or saucepan; when boiling, wash ½lb. of rice and throw it into the water; boil fast for ten minutes; drain your rice in a colander, put it back in the saucepan, which you have slightly greased with butter; let it swell slowly near the fire, or in a slow oven till tender; each grain will then be light and well separated.

Add to the above a small tablespoonful of aromatic sauce, called "Soyer's Relish or Sultana Sauce," with a quarter of a teaspoonful of curry powder; mix together with a fork lightly, and serve. This quantity will be sufficient for two or three people, according to the prescriptions of the attending physician.

NO. 33—FIGS AND APPLE BEVERAGE.

Have 2 quarts of water boiling, into which throw 6 dry figs previously opened, and 2 apples, cut into six or eight slices each; let the whole boil together twenty minutes, then pour them into a basin to cool; pass through a sieve; drain the figs, which will be good to eat with a little sugar or jam.

NO. 34—STEWED FRENCH PLUMS.

Put 12 large or 18 small-size French plums, soak them for half an hour, put in a stewpan with a spoonful of brown sugar, a gill of water, a little cinnamon, and some thin rind of lemon; let them stew gently twenty minutes, then put them in a basin till cold with a little of the juice. A small glass of either port, sherry, or claret is a very good addition. The syrup is excellent.

NO. 35—FRENCH HERB BROTH.

This is a very favourite beverage in France, as well with people in health as with invalids, especially in spring, when the herbs are young and green.

Put a quart of water to boil, having previously prepared about 40 leaves of sorrel, a cabbage lettuce, and 10 sprigs of chervil, the whole well washed; when the water is boiling, throw in the herbs, with the addition of a teaspoonful of salt, and ½oz. of fresh butter; cover the saucepan close, and let simmer a few minutes, then strain it through a sieve or colander.

This is to be drunk cold, especially in the spring of the year, after the change from winter. I generally drink about a quart per day for a week at that time; but if for sick people it must be made less strong of herbs, and taken a little warm.

To prove that it is wholesome, we have only to refer to the instinct which teaches dogs to eat grass at that season of the year. I do not pretend to say that it would suit persons in every malady, because the doctors are to decide upon the food and beverage of their patients, and study its changes as well as change their medicines; but I repeat that this is most useful and refreshing for the blood.

NO. 36—BROWNING FOR SOUPS, ETC.

Put ½lb. of moist sugar into an iron pan and melt it over a moderate fire till quite black, stirring it continually, which will take about twenty-five minutes: it must colour by degrees, as too sudden a heat will make it bitter; then add 2 quarts of water, and in ten minutes the sugar will be dissolved. You may then bottle it for use. It will keep good for a month, and will always be found very useful.

No. 37—Toast-and-Water.

Cut a piece of crusty bread, about a ¼lb. in weight, place it upon a toasting-fork, and hold it about six inches from the fire; turn it often, and keep moving it gently until of a light yellow colour, then place it nearer the fire, and when of a good brown chocolate colour, put it in a jug and pour over 3 pints of boiling water; cover the jug until cold, then strain it into a clean jug, and it is ready for use. Never leave the toast in it, for in summer it would cause fermentation in a short time. I would almost venture to say that such toast-and-water as I have described, though so very simple, is the only way toast-water should be made, and that it would keep good a considerable time in bottles.

Baked Apple Toast-and Water.—A piece of apple, slowly toasted till it gets quite black, and added to the above, makes a very nice and refreshing drink for invalids.

Apple Rice Water.—Half a pound of rice, boiled in the above until in pulp, passed through a colander, and drunk when cold.

All kinds of fruit may be done the same way.

Figs and French plums are excellent; also raisins.

A little ginger, if approved of, may be used.

Apple Barley Water.—A quarter of a pound of pearl barley instead of toast added to the above, and boiled for one hour, is also a very nice drink.

Citronade.—Put a gallon of water on to boil, cut up one pound of apples, each one into quarters, two lemons in thin slices, put them in the water, and boil them until they can be pulped, pass the liquor through a colander, boil it up again with half a pound of brown sugar, skim, and bottle for use, taking care not to cork the bottle, and keep it in a cool place.

For Spring Drink.—Rhubarb, in the same quantities, and done in the same way as apples, adding more sugar, is very cooling.

Also green gooseberries.

For Summer Drink.—One pound of red currants, bruised with some raspberry, half a pound of sugar added to a gallon of cold water, well stirred, and allowed to settle. The juice of a lemon.

Mulberry.—The same, adding a little lemon-peel.

A little cream of tartar or citric acid added to these renders them more cooling in summer and spring.

Plain Lemonade.—Cut in very thin slices three lemons, put them in a basin, add half a pound of sugar, either white or brown; bruise all together, add a gallon of water, and stir well. It is then ready.

French Plum Water.—Boil 3 pints of water; add in 6 or 8 dried plums previously split, 2 or 3 slices of lemon, a spoonful of honey or sugar; boil half an hour, and serve.

For *Fig, Date, and Raisin Water*, proceed as above, adding the juice of half a lemon to any of the above. If for fig water, use 6 figs.

Any quantity of the above fruits may be used with advantage in rice, barley, or arrowroot water.

Effervescent Beverages.

Raspberry Water.—Put 2 tablespoonfuls of vinegar into a large glass, pour in half a pint of water; mix well.

Pineapple Syrup.—Three tablespoonfuls to a pint.

Currant Syrup.—Proceed the same.

Syrup of Orgeat.—The same.

Orange-Flower Water.—The same, adding an ounce of lump sugar, is a most soothing drink, and is to be procured at Verrey's, in Regent Street, or Kuntz's, opposite Verrey's. Put two tablespoonfuls to a glass of water. It is also extremely good with either Soda, Seltzer, or Vichy Water, the last of which is to be obtained at the depot, Margaret Street, Cavendish Square.

ARMY RECEIPTS

SOYER'S FIELD AND BARRACK COOKERY
FOR THE ARMY

N.B.—These receipts are also applicable for barracks, in camp, or while on the march, by the use of Soyer's New Field Stove, now adopted by the military authorities. These receipts answer equally as well for the navy.

Each stove will consume not more than from 12 to 15lbs. of fuel, and allowing 20 stoves to a regiment, the consumption would be 300lbs. per thousand men.

The allowance per man is, I believe, 3½lbs. each, which gives a total of 3500lbs. per thousand men.

The economy of fuel would consequently be 3200lbs. per regiment daily. Coal will burn with the same advantage.

Salt beef, pork, Irish stew, stewed beef, tea, coffee, cocoa, &c., can be prepared in these stoves, and with the same economy.

They can also be fitted with an apparatus for baking, roasting, and steaming.

No. 1—Soyer's Receipt to Cook Salt Meat for Fifty Men.

Headquarters, Crimea, 12th May, 1856.

1. Put 50lbs. of meat in the boiler.
2. Fill with water, and let soak all night.
3. Next morning wash the meat well.
4. Fill with fresh water, and boil gently three hours, and serve.

Skim off the fat, which, when cold, is an excellent substitute for butter.

For salt pork proceed as above, or boil half beef and half pork—the pieces of beef may be smaller than the pork, requiring a little longer time doing.

Dumplings, No. 21, may be added to either pork or beef in proportion; and when pork is properly soaked, the liquor will make a very good soup. The large yellow peas as used by the navy, may be introduced; it is important to have them, as they are a great improvement. When properly soaked, French haricot beans and lentils may also be used to advantage. By the addition of 5 pounds of split peas, half a pound of brown sugar, 2 tablespoonfuls of pepper, 10 onions; simmer gently till in pulp, remove the fat and serve; broken biscuit may be introduced. This will make an excellent mess.

No. 1a—How to soak and plain-boil the Rations of Salt Beef and Pork, on Land or at Sea.

To each pound of meat allow about a pint of water. Do not have the pieces above 3 or 4lbs. in weight. Let it soak for 7 or 8 hours, or all night if possible. Wash each piece well with your hand in order to extract as much salt as possible. It is then ready for cooking. If less time be allowed, cut the pieces smaller and proceed the same, or parboil the meat for 20 minutes in the above quantity of water, which throw off and add fresh. Meat may be soaked in sea water, but by all means boiled in fresh when possible.

I should advise, at sea, to have a perforated iron box made, large enough to contain half a ton or more of meat, which box will ascend and descend by pulleys; have also a frame made on which the box might rest when lowered overboard, the meat being placed outside the ship on a level with the water, the night before using; the water beating against the meat through the perforations will extract all the salt. Meat may be soaked in sea water, but by all means washed.

No. 2—Soyer's Army Soup for Fifty Men.

Headquarters, 12th May, 1856.

1. Put in the boiler 60 pints, 7½ gallons, or 5½ camp kettles of water.
2. Add to it 50lbs. of meat, either beef or mutton.
3. The rations of preserved or fresh vegetables.
4. Ten small tablespoonfuls of salt.
5. Simmer three hours, and serve.

P.S.—When rice is issued put it in when boiling. Three pounds will be sufficient. About eight pounds of fresh vegetables. Or four squares from a cake of preserved ditto. A tablespoonful of pepper, if handy. Skim off the fat, which, when cold, is an excellent substitute for butter.

No. 2a—Salt Pork with Mashed Peas, for One Hundred Men

Put in two stoves 50lbs. of pork each, divide 24lbs. in four pudding-cloths, rather loosely tied; putting to boil at the same time as your pork, let all boil gently till done, say about two hours; take out the pudding and peas, put all meat in one caldron, remove the liquor from the other pan, turning back the peas in it, add two teaspoonfuls of pepper, a pound of the fat, and with the wooden spatula smash the peas, and serve both. The addition of about half a pound of flour and two quarts of liquor, boiled ten minutes, makes a great improvement. Six sliced onions, fried and added to it, makes it very delicate.

NO. 3—STEWED SALT BEEF AND PORK.

For a Company of One Hundred Men, or a Regiment of One Thousand Men.
Headquarters, 12th June, 1855.

Put in a boiler, of well-soaked beef 30lbs., cut in pieces of a quarter of a pound each.

    20lbs. of pork.
    1½lb. of sugar.
    8lbs. of onions, sliced,
    25 quarts of water.
    4lbs. of rice.

Simmer gently for three hours, skim the fat off the top, and serve.

Note.—How to soak the meat for the above mess.—Put 50lbs. of meat in each boiler, having filled them with water, and let soak all night; and prior to using it, wash it and squeeze with your hands, to extract the salt.

In case the meat is still too salt, boil it for twenty minutes, throw away the water, and put fresh to your stew.

By closely following the above receipt you will have an excellent dish.

NO. 4—SOYER'S FOOD FOR ONE HUNDRED MEN, USING TWO STOVES.

Headquarters, Crimea

Cut or chop 50lbs. of fresh beef in pieces of about a ¼lb. each; put in the boiler, with 10 tablespoonfuls of salt, two ditto of pepper, four ditto of sugar, onions 7lbs. cut in slices: light the fire now, and then stir the meat with a spatula, let it stew from 20 to 30 minutes, or till it forms a thick gravy, then add a pound and a half of flour; mix well together, put in the boiler 18 quarts of water, stir well for a minute or two, regulate the stove to a moderate heat, and let simmer for about two hours. Mutton, pork, or veal, can be stewed in a similar manner, but will take half an hour less cooking.

Note.—A pound of rice may be added with great advantage, ditto plain dumplings, ditto potatoes, as well as mixed vegetables.

For a regiment of 1000 men use 20 stoves.

NO. 5—PLAIN IRISH STEW FOR FIFTY MEN.

Cut 50lbs. of mutton into pieces of a quarter of a pound each, put them in the pan, add 8lbs. of large onions, 12lbs. of whole potatoes, 8 tablespoonfuls of salt, 3 tablespoonfuls of pepper; cover all with water, giving about half a pint to each pound; then light the fire; one hour and a half of gentle ebullition will make a most excellent stew; mash some of the potatoes to thicken the gravy, and serve. Fresh beef, veal, or pork, will also make a good stew. Beef takes two hours doing. Dumplings may be added half an hour before done.

NO. 6—TO COOK FOR A REGIMENT OF A THOUSAND MEN.

Headquarters, Crimea, 20th June, 1855.

Place twenty stoves in a row, in the open air or under cover.

Put 30 quarts of water in each boiler, 50lbs. of ration meat, 4 squares from a cake of dried vegetables—or, if fresh mixed vegetables are issued, 12lbs. weight—10 small tablespoonfuls of salt, 1 ditto of pepper, light the fire, simmer gently from two hours to two hours and a half, skim the fat from the top, and serve.

It will require only four cooks per regiment, the provision and water being carried to the kitchen by fatigue-parties; the kitchen being central, instead of the kitchen going to each company, each company sends two men to the kitchen with a pole to carry the meat.

No. 7—Salt Pork and Puddings with Cabbage and Potatoes.

Put 25lbs. of salt pork in each boiler, with the other 50lbs. from which you have extracted the large bones, cut in dice, and made into puddings; when on the boil, put five puddings in each, boil rather fast for two hours. You have peeled 12lbs. of potatoes and put in a net in each caldron; put also 2 winter cabbages in nets, three-quarters of an hour before your pudding is done; divide the pork, pudding, and cabbage in proportion, or let fifty of the men have pudding that day and meat the other; remove the fat, and serve. The liquor will make very good soup by adding peas or rice, as No. 1A.

For the pudding-paste put one quarter of a pound of dripping, or beef or mutton suet, to every pound of flour you use; roll your paste for each half an inch thick, put a pudding-cloth in a basin, flour round, lay in your paste, add your meat in proportion; season with pepper and a minced onion; close your pudding in a cloth, and boil.

This receipt is more applicable to barrack and public institutions than a camp. Fresh meat of any kind may be done the same, and boiled with either salt pork or beef.

No. 8—Turkish Pilaff for One Hundred Men.

Put in the caldron 2lbs. of fat, which you have saved from salt pork, add to it 4lbs. of peeled and sliced onions; let them fry in the fat for about ten minutes; add in then 12lbs. of rice, cover the rice over with water, the rice being submerged two inches, add to it 7 tablespoonfuls of salt, and 1 of pepper; let simmer gently for about an hour, stirring it with a spatula occasionally to prevent it burning, but when commencing to boil, a very little fire ought to be kept under. Each grain ought to be swollen to the full size of rice, and separate. In the other stove put fat and onions the same quantity with the same seasoning; cut the flesh of the mutton, veal, pork, or beef from the bone, cut in dice of about 2oz. each, put in the pan with the fat and onions, set it going with a very sharp fire, having put in 2 quarts of water: steam gently, stirring occasionally for about half an hour, till forming rather a rich thick gravy. When both the rice and meat are done, take half the rice and mix with the meat, and then the remainder of the meat and rice, and serve. Save the bones for soup for the following day. Salt pork or beef, well soaked, may be used—omitting the salt. Any kind of vegetables may be frizzled with the onions.

No. 9—Baking and Roasting with the Field Stove.

By the removal of the caldron, and the application of a false bottom put over the fire, bread bakes extremely well in the oven, as well as meat, potatoes, puddings, &c. Bread might be baked in oven at every available opportunity, at a trifling cost of fuel. The last experiment I made with one was a piece of beef weighing about 25lbs., a large Yorkshire pudding, and about 10lbs. of potatoes, the whole doing at considerably under one pennyworth of fuel, being a mixture of coal and coke; the whole was done to perfection, and of a nice brown colour. Any kind of meat would, of course, roast the same.

Baking in fixed Oven.—In barracks, or large institutions, where an oven is handy, I would recommend that a long iron trough be made, four feet in length, with a two-storey movable grating in it, the meat on the top of the upper one giving a nice elevation to get the heat from the roof, and the potatoes on the grating under, and a Yorkshire pudding, at the bottom. Four or five pieces of meat may be done on one trough. If no pudding is made, add a quart more water.

No. 10—French Beef Soup, or Pot-au-feu, Camp Fashion, For the ordinary Canteen-Pan.

Put in the canteen saucepan 6lbs. of beef, cut in two or three pieces, bones included,

¾lb. of plain mixed vegetables, as onions, carrots, turnips, celery, leeks, or such of these as can be obtained, or 3oz. of preserved, in cakes, as now given to the troops; 3 teaspoonfuls of salt, 1 ditto of pepper, 1 ditto of sugar, if handy; 8 pints of water, let it boil gently three hours, remove some of the fat, and serve.

The addition of 1½lb. of bread cut into slices or 1lb. of broken biscuits, well soaked, in the broth, will make a very nutritious soup; skimming is not required.

No. 11—Semi-Frying, Camp Fashion, Chops, Steaks, and all Kinds of Meat.

It is difficult to broil to perfection, it is considerably more so to cook meat of any kind in a frying-pan. Place your pan on the fire for a minute or so, wipe it very clean; when the pan is very hot, add in it either fat or butter, but the fat from salt and ration meat is preferable; the fat will immediately get very hot; then add the meat you are going to cook, turn it several times to have it equally done; season to each pound a small teaspoonful of salt, quarter that of pepper, and serve. Any sauce or maître d'hôtel butter may be added. A few fried onions in the remaining fat, with the addition of a little flour to the onion, a quarter of a pint of water, two tablespoonfuls of vinegar, a few chopped pickles or piccalilli, will be very relishing.

No. 11a—Tea for Eighty Men.

Which often constitutes a whole Company.

One boiler will, with ease, make tea for eighty men, allowing a pint each man. Put forty quarts of water to boil, place the rations of tea in a fine net, very loose, or in a large perforated ball; give one minute to boil, take out the fire, if too much, shut down the cover; in ten minutes it is ready to serve.

No. 12—Coffee a la Zouave for a Mess of Ten Soldiers.

As I have taught many how to make it in the camp, the canteen saucepan holding 10 pints.

Put 9 pints of water into a canteen saucepan on the fire; when boiling add 7½oz. of coffee, which forms the ration, mix them well together with a spoon or a piece of wood, leave on the fire for a few minutes longer, or until just beginning to boil. Take it off and pour in 1 pint of cold water, let the whole remain for ten minutes or a little longer. The dregs of the coffee will fall to the bottom, and your coffee will be clear.

Pour it from one vessel to the other, leaving the dregs at the bottom, add your ration sugar or 2 teaspoonfuls to the pint; if any milk is to be had make 2 pints of coffee less; add that quantity of milk to your coffee, the former may be boiled previously, and serve.

This is a very good way for making coffee even in any family, especially a numerous one, using 1oz. to the quart if required stronger. For a company of eighty men use the field stove and four times the quantity of ingredients.

No. 13—Coffee, Turkish Fashion.

When the water is just on the boil add the coffee and sugar, mix well as above, give just a boil and serve. The grouts of coffee will in a few seconds fall to the bottom of the cups. The Turks wisely leave it there, I would advise every one in camp to do the same.

No. 14—Cocoa for Eighty Men.

Break eighty portions of ration cocoa in rather small pieces, put them in the boiler, with five or six pints of water, light the fire, stir the cocoa round till melted, and forming a pulp not too thick, preventing any lumps forming, add to it the remaining water, hot or cold; add the ration sugar, and when just boiling, it is ready for serving. If short of cocoa in campaigning, put about sixty rations, and when in pulp, add half a pound of flour or arrowroot.

Easy and excellent way of Cooking in Earthen Pans.

A very favourite and plain dish amongst the convalescent and orderlies at Scutari was the following:—

Soyer's Baking Stewing Pan, the drawing of which I extract from my "Shilling Cookery." The simplicity of the process, and the economical system of cooking which may be produced in it, induced me to introduce it here.

Each pan is capable of cooking for fifteen men, and no matter how hard may be the meat, or small the cutting, or poor the quality,—while fresh it would always make an excellent dish. Proceed as follows:—Cut any part of either beef (cheek or tail), veal, mutton, or pork, in fact any hard part of the animal, in 4oz. slices; have ready for each 4 or 5 onions and 4 or 5 pounds of potatoes cut in slices; put a layer of potatoes at the bottom of the pan, then a layer of meat, season to each pound I teaspoonful of salt, quarter teaspoonful of pepper, and some onion you have already minced; then lay in layers of meat and potatoes alternately till full; put in 2 pints of water, lay on the lid, close the bar, lock the pot, bake two hours, and serve.

Remove some of the fat from the top, if too much; a few dumplings, as No. 21 in it, will also be found excellent. By adding over each layer a little flour it makes a thick rich sauce.

SOYER'S BAKING STEWING PAN

Half fresh meat and salt ditto will also be found excellent. The price of these pans is moderate, and they last a long time—manufacturers, Messrs. Deane and Dray.*

SERIES OF SMALL RECEIPTS FOR A SQUAD, OUTPOST, OR PICKET OF MEN,

Which may be increased in proportion of companies.

CAMP RECEIPTS FOR THE ARMY IN THE EAST.

(From the Times of the 22nd January, 1855.)†

No. 15. Camp Soup—Put half a pound of salt pork in a saucepan, two ounces of rice, two pints and a half of cold water, and, when boiling, let simmer another hour, stirring once or twice; break in six ounces of biscuit, let soak ten minutes; it is then ready, adding one teaspoonful of sugar, and a quarter one of pepper, if handy.

---

* If no oven, put the pan in water three-parts up, and give half an hour longer. For public institutions, fish, meat, and game may be cooked in a similar manner, for which receipts refer to my "Shilling Cookery."
† The following receipts were written by me in reply to a request inserted in the *Times* in January, 1855. Each receipt is for two men, but may be increased by adding to the proportions.

No. 16. Beef Soup.—Proceed as above, boil an hour longer, adding a pint more water.

Note.—Those who can obtain any of the following vegetables will find them a great improvement to the above soups:—Add four ounces of either onions, carrots, celery, turnips, leeks, greens, cabbage, or potatoes, previously well washed or peeled, or any of these mixed to make up four ounces, putting them in the pot with the meat.

I have used the green tops of leeks and the leaf of celery as well as the stem, and found that for stewing they are preferable to the white part for flavour. The meat being generally salted with rock salt, it ought to be well scraped and washed, or even soaked in water a few hours if convenient; but if the last cannot be done, and the meat is therefore too salt, which would spoil the broth, parboil it for twenty minutes in water, before using for soup, taking care to throw this water away.

No. 17.—For fresh beef proceed, as far as the cooking goes, as for salt beef, adding a teaspoonful of salt to the water.

No. 18. Pea Soup.—Put in your pot half a pound of salt pork, half a pint of peas, three pints of water, one teaspoonful of sugar, half one of pepper, four ounces of vegetables cut in slices, if to be had; boil gently two hours, or until the peas are tender, as some require boiling longer than others—and serve.

No. 19. Stewed Fresh Beef and Rice.—Put an ounce of fat in a pot, cut half a pound of meat in large dice, add a teaspoonful of salt, half one of sugar, an onion sliced; put on the fire to stew for fifteen minutes, stirring occasionally, then add two ounces of rice, a pint of water; stew gently till done, and serve. Any savoury herb will improve the flavour. Fresh pork, veal, or mutton, may be done the same way, and half a pound of potatoes used instead of the rice, and as rations are served out for three days, the whole of the provisions may be cooked at once, as it will keep for some days this time of the year, and is easily warmed up again.

N.B. For a regular canteen pan triple the quantity.

No. 20—Receipts for the Frying-pan.

Those who are fortunate enough to possess a frying-pan will find the following receipts very useful:—Cut in small dice half a pound of the solid meat, keeping the bones for soup; put your pan, which should be quite clean, on the fire; when hot through, add an ounce of fat, melt it and put in the meat, season with half a teaspoonful of salt; fry for ten minutes, stirring now and then; add a teaspoonful of flour, mix all well, put in half a pint of water, let simmer for fifteen minutes, pour over a biscuit previously soaked, and serve.

The addition of a little pepper and sugar, if handy, is an improvement, as is also a pinch of cayenne, curry-powder, or spice; sauces and pickles used in small quantities would be very relishing; these are articles which will keep for any length of time. As fresh meat is not easily obtained, any of the cold salt meat may be dressed as above, omitting the salt, and only requires warming; or, for a change, boil the meat plainly, or with greens, or cabbage, or dumplings, as for beef; then the next day cut what is left in small dice—say four ounces—put in a pan an ounce of fat; when very hot, pour in the following:—Mix in a basin a tablespoonful of flour, moisten with water to form the consistency of thick melted butter, then pour it in the pan, letting it remain for one or two minutes, or until set; put in the meat, shake the pan to loosen it, turn it over, let it remain a few minutes longer, and serve.

To cook bacon, chops, steaks, slices of any kind of meat, salt or fresh sausages, black puddings, &c. Make the pan very hot, having wiped it clean, add in fat, dripping, butter, or oil, about an ounce of either; put in the meat, turn three or four times, and season with salt and pepper. A few minutes will do it. If the meat is salt, it must be well soaked previously.

No. 21—Suet Dumplings.

Take half a pound of flour, half a teaspoonful of salt, a quarter teaspoonful of pepper, a quarter of a pound of chopped fat pork or beef suet, eight tablespoonfuls of water, mixed well together. It will form a thick paste, and when formed, divide it into six or eight pieces, which roll in flour, and boil with the meat for twenty minutes to half an hour. A little chopped onion or aromatic herbs will give it a flavour.

A plainer way, when Fat is not to be obtained.—Put the same quantity of flour and seasoning in a little more water, and make it softer, and divide it into sixteen pieces; boil about ten minutes. Serve round the meat.

One plain pudding may be made of the above, also peas and rice pudding thus:—One pound of peas well tied in a cloth, or rice ditto with the beef. It will form a good pudding. The following ingredients may be added: a little salt, sugar, pepper, chopped onions, aromatic herbs, and two ounces of chopped fat will make these puddings palatable and delicate.

SOYER'S SCUTARI TEAPOT.

This teapot, which is registered, is manufactured by Messrs. Deane and Dray, London Bridge, and sold by all ironmongers in the kingdom.

The top of the minaret forms the lid, and the tube which holds the tea, being moveable, allows every facility for cleaning, and amongst its many advantages the most prominent are its cheapness, elegance, and simplicity. It can be made any size.

BILL OF FARE FOR LONDON SUPPERS.

IN introducing the subjoined Bill of Fare, applicable to the London suppers, I must here repeat that which I have previously mentioned, that my idea is far from replacing the dishes now so much in vogue both at the "Albion," Simpson's in the Strand, Evans' Cider Cellars, and such-like places; but now and then a couple of dishes taken from these receipts cannot fail to prove agreeable to the partakers, without much interfering with the regular routine of the nightly business of such establishments.

NO. 1—PLAIN MUTTON CHOPS AND RUMP STEAKS.

Though almost anybody can boast of being able to cook a plain steak or a chop, very few can say they can do them to perfection. First of all, to obtain this important point, either the mutton or beef ought to be kept till properly set, according to season; secondly, the chop especially is more preferable when cut and beat, some time before cooking, so as to set the meat and prevent its shrinking; it at all times requires a sharp fire (the broiling City fires may be taken as an example, and the continual red heat of the gridiron); lay your gridiron over a sharp fire, two minutes after lay on your chop or steak, turn three or four times; when half done, season highly with salt and pepper, and when done, serve *immediately*, on a very hot dish. Ten minutes will do a steak of 1½lb., and about six minutes a chop.

NO. 2—RUMPSTEAK AND POTATOES.

Of all steaks, rumpsteaks are far more preferable than any other, not excepting the fillet of beef, as the meat in England is so rich, while in France they eat only the fillet of beef—that being the only eatable steak of a French ox. Have your steak cut as even as possible, nearly an inch thick, and weighing from about 1½lbs. to 2lbs.; broil it sharply as described above, season when properly done, lay it on a very hot dish, put on 2oz. or more of maître d'hôtel butter (No. 2), turn it three or four times on the dish quickly, when a most delicious gravy will be formed, then place about a pound of fried potatoes round it, and serve. For smaller steaks, for cooking be guided by size.

Ditto with Anchovy Butter, of which use 2oz. in lieu of the maître d'hôtel butter, and omit the potatoes.

Same with Pimento Butter.

Same with Shallot Butter, well rubbing the dish prior to putting the steak on it.

NO. 3—MUTTON AND LAMB CUTLETS A LA BOUCHERE.

The word à la bouchère, in English, means the butcher's wife's plain fashion, and at one time had only the merit of economy; but a real gourmet, the illustrious Cambacérès, who lived in the time of the first Empire, being served with this dish at a little country inn, while travelling, discovered the correctness of the proverb that "the nearer the bone the sweeter the meat," and on returning to Paris introduced it to the fashionable circle, and for a long period this exquisite côtelettes d'agneaux de maison, or house-lamb cutlet, and the dainty and justly celebrated cutlets de pre-salé, were figuring on all the banqueting tables of the Paris gourmets in perfect *négligé*, being dressed in the following unceremonious manner:— Take either a neck of lamb or mutton, neither too fat nor too lean, chop the cutlets about six inches in length, cutting them as usual, leaving a bone in each; flatten them with the chopper, not trimming them at all, season them highly with salt and pepper, broil them very quick, and serve hot. Lamb, mutton, and veal cutlets may be done the same.

For plain cutlets with fried potatoes, cut them either à la bouchère *or trim them*, and proceed as for rumpsteak.

Ditto for Cutlets à la maître d'hôtel.

For relishing sauce, see List of Sauces.

No. 4—Lamb and Mutton Cutlets, semi-Bouchere.

Cut your cutlets from the neck, one inch thick; beat them flat with a chopper without trimming them, roll them in flour, butter over; season with salt, pepper, a little chopped shallot; broil on a sharp fire, turn three or four times, and serve.

No. 5—Relishing Steak.

(Mutton, Veal, Pork, Chops and Cutlets, Fowls, Pigeons, Grilled Bones, Kidneys, &c.)

Chop fine a tablespoonful of green pickled chillies: mix with two pats of butter, a little mustard, a spoonful of grated horseradish; have a nice thick steak, spread the steak on both sides with the above, season with half a teaspoonful of salt, put on a gridiron on a sharp fire, turn three or four times; put on a hot dish with the juice of half a lemon and two teaspoonfuls of walnut ketchup, and serve. If glaze is handy, spread a little over the steak.

Mutton, lamb, veal, pork, chops and cutlets may be done the same; as well as kidneys; also grilled fowls, pigeons—the latter may be egged and bread-crumbed. Proceed the same for cooking according to size. Any of the above may be half done before rubbing in the chili butter.

No. 6—Fillet de Bœuf, Parisian Fashion.

Cut a piece of the fillet of beef crosswise, including some fat, the thickness of an inch; beat it slightly flat with a chopper, set on a gridiron, put it on a very sharp fire, turn it two or three times; when half done, season with a quarter of a teaspoonful of salt, quarter that of pepper, put on a hot plate, rub over with an ounce of maître d'hôtel butter (as No. 2); serve up with fried potatoes.

Mutton chops, veal chops, and lamb chops may be dressed similar.

No. 7—Fillet of Beef, semi-Chateaubriant.

Cut it double the thickness of the above, butter lightly over, set on the gridiron on a slowish fire, turn several times; when half done, place it nearer the fire; season with half a teaspoonful of salt, quarter one of pepper, a little cayenne, and serve with sauce à la Mussulman (as No. 17). Maître d'hôtel butter or anchovy butter may be used instead; serve fried chipped potatoes round.

No. 8—Chops, semi-Provençal, or Marseilles Fashion.

When the chop is half broiled, scrape half a clove of garlic and rub over on both sides of the chop; serve with the juice of a lemon. For semi-Provençal, the clove of garlic is cut in two, and the flat part is placed at the end of a fork and rubbed on the chop.

No. 9—Chop or Steak a la Sultana.

Add a tablespoonful of Sultana sauce in a dish to each pound of meat; place in a dish and serve; when the steak is done, turn it in it three or four times, and it will make a most delicious gravy.

No. 10—Mushroom Kidney Sandwich.

Broil 3 plain kidneys à la Brochette to keep them flat. Broil also 6 large mushroom heads; well season with salt and pepper (cayenne if approved of). A few minutes will do them; then rub a little fresh butter inside the mushrooms; dish up each kidney between two mushrooms while very hot, and serve.

If a large quantity is required, proceed thus—well butter a sauté pan, lay in 20 or more heads of large mushrooms just washed, season well with salt and pepper; let stew for twenty minutes gently in an oven, or till done; make your kidney sandwich as above, add a table-spoonful of the gravy over, and serve. The same may be served on thin toast; a tablespoonful of the Sultana Sauce to every half-dozen kidneys, makes a dish worthy of an Epicurean. The stems of the mushrooms may be stewed and served with the dish.

No. 11—Minced Sandwiches.

Cut in small thin slices some dressed ham, ox tongue, game, or poultry, with a few pickled gherkins and olives, the whole in equal portions; mix well together; butter the bread and spread some mustard over, place the cut meat over the butter, cover over with the other slice, cut small, and serve.

No. 12—Kidneys Saute, with Sherry, Port, or Champagne.

Cut three kidneys each in five pieces, put an ounce of butter in the pan; when very hot, and beginning to smoke, add the kidneys; stir round for two or three minutes with a spoon till set; add a teaspoonful of flour, quarter ditto of salt, the third part of that of pepper; mix well; add half a gill of broth, a small wineglass of either of the above wines; if no broth, use water, adding a little glaze. A tablespoonful of colouring (No. 15) is a great improvement to the appearance of the sauce. Ox, calf, or pig's kidneys may be dressed the same, following the proportions according to the quantity made. All the above are extremely good on toast, which would require a little more liquor. A few mushrooms are an improvement. If brown sauce can be obtained, omit the flour and broth. Do not let them boil; a few minutes will do them.

No. 13—Semi-Curried Kidneys.

Take three kidneys, which forms a portion, make a small incision in the fleshy part, so as to enable you to remove the outer skin; cut each in five pieces crosswise, put some butter in a stewpan, salt, pepper, a little chopped onion, give it a fry, add the kidneys, stir them for a few minutes till set, put four tablespoonfuls of curry sauce (No. 9), and serve. If no curry sauce, add a quarter of a teaspoonful of curry powder, one of flour, and one gill of broth; serve with rice.

No. 14—Kidney Toast.

Split the kidney in two, remove the sinews and outer skin, mince it up, and then chop fine; place in a stewpan some chopped eschalot and parsley, with a small piece of butter, and fry the same lightly; when done, add a small spoonful of Sultana Sauce, a little flour, and boil again; while boiling, mix in the chopped kidneys; add salt, pepper, and nutmeg to taste.

Spread the composition upon slices of toast slightly buttered; mask them up with bread-crumbs mixed with Parmesan cheese, place in a sharp oven for ten minutes, brown them with the salamander,* and serve quite hot.

No. 15—Mutton, Lamb, or Veal Cutlets en Papillote, or wrapped in Paper. Ditto, quarter of Fowls and half Pigeons, Devilled.

Cut two or three veal or mutton cutlets half an inch thick, then put in a sauté, or frying-pan, four tablespoonfuls of oil, season your chops thoroughly with salt and pepper, cook them gently in the pan, turning them several times; before they are quite done, take them off, add in; mix with oil remaining in the pan two tablespoonfuls of fine chopped onions, one tablespoonful of chopped parsley, fry these gently on the fire for a few minutes, stirring continually; when they become a little yellowish, add a tablespoonful of flour, mix quick,

---

* A method of browning by placing a long handled iron disk, hot from the fire, over the dish. A modern grill takes its place—AB

then put in a pint of broth, boil till forming a thick sauce, add salt and pepper in proportion; put back the chops into the pan, simmer a few minutes, turning them; cut some paper in the shape of a heart, large enough to envelope one chop, oil it well, put a tablespoonful of the sauce on the paper, then place on it a chop, then more sauce, and plait the paper round the edge of the cutlet to inclose it; then place in the pan in a hot oven, or broil slowly. These cutlets might be prepared the day before using, and placed more conveniently in paper when cold.

No. 16—Pork Chops a la Tartare.

Which has one great charm—simplicity. It is seldom to be obtained, even in Crim Tartary, and when it is, the animal is in no very nice condition. When procurable in a first-class Tartar family, they are dipped in vinegar for about an hour prior to being fried or broiled. Thin slices of raw onions are eaten with the above, and a kind of cucumber peculiar to Russia, and most delicious when properly pickled; they are cut in slices with the onions very thinly, the chop is then placed over a layer while very hot, and another layer placed over the chop, until it forms a vegetable sandwich. Such is the dish so much relished by our hospitable Tartar families.

No. 17—Lamb Chops a l'Africaine.

Cut a lamb chop as usual, broil it very sharply, turning it continually; when nearly done, season highly with salt and pepper, rub over with chutney (about a teaspoonful to each chop) on both sides, then broil another minute and serve. Light melted butter with a chopped gherkin makes a good variation for such as veal, pork, and broiled fowls, pigeons, and also for devilled poultry.

I must also observe that chutney is excellent with all kinds of broiled devils; a little curry-powder may be introduced.

Lamb Chops a la Printaniere.

Add to the maître d'hôtel butter (as No. 2) chopped tarragon and chervil instead of parsley.

Pork Chops with Pimento Butter.

Plain broil, and rub over, in proportion, half an ounce to each chop. Add two tablespoonfuls of mushroom ketchup on the dish.

No. 18—Lamb Chops a la Boulangere.

This lady, the boulangère, or baker's wife, was invented by a lady of the French Court, in opposition to the masculine manners of the butcher's wife.

Cut and trim neatly, eight, ten, or twelve small lamb cutlets, enough for a small entrée; season lightly with salt, pepper, and a little cayenne; dip them gently in olive oil, then in the flour box, and broil very gently on a slow fire; while doing put a gill of cream in a stewpan, set it on the fire, and when boiling add in two ounces of fresh butter, a tablespoonful of chopped chervil, the juice of half a lemon, a little salt and pepper; stir quick till the butter is melted and it forms a nice smooth sauce, then pour it over your cutlets and serve quick.

No. 19—Stewed Tripe.

Select two pounds of double tripe, cut in strips of a quarter pound each, put in a clean stew pan, add a pint of water, ditto of milk, two teaspoonfuls of salt, half that of pepper, eight middling-sized onions carefully peeled, which put in; set to boil rather fast, then simmer till done, which will be half an hour or rather more; turn out into a deep dish or tureen, and serve.

No. 20—Curried Tripe.

Make about a pint of curry sauce, as No. 9; cut each half-pound in four pieces; warm gently in it for half an hour, and serve with rice.

No. 21—Gratin Tripe in Shell.

Add to the above 2 yolks of eggs; mix quick; having taken the stewpan off the fire, stir quick; put in the scolloped shells, throw breadcrumbs over a little butter, put in an oven, salamander the top, and serve.

No. 22—Tripe Lyonnaise Fashion.

When any cold tripe remains, cut in thin slices about the thickness of an inch square, mince 2 onions, put some butter, in proportion, in a frying-pan, add in the onions, fry till they are partly done, add the tripe, let fry for about 10 minutes, tossing them; season with salt and pepper, three teaspoonfuls of vinegar to each 1lb., and serve. This is a very favourite dish in Lyons and Paris, both amongst the gourmet and the gourmand. Well dry the tripe on a cloth before frying; it will take 3 ounces of butter to the pound.

No. 23—Grilled Chicken with Sharp Sauce.

Prepare your chicken as for grill, oil it over slightly, season with salt and pepper in proportion to size, then place it on a gridiron, on a rather fierce fire. When ready done, put by degrees two tablespoonfuls of Sultana Sauce over it, losing none of it. When done, have on a dish an ounce of butter; pour over the butter another tablespoonful of sauce; mix well, and after turning the chicken two or three times, serve it up.

For Relishing Sauce proceed the same, pouring half a pint of that sauce over it, No. 12.

No. 24—Broiling or Universal Devil.

Any kind of bones which are to undergo the process of broiling ought not to exceed a quarter of a pound each in weight, a deep incision being made in the fleshy part. The same for game and poultry. Rub each piece with the Mixture No. 70, the quantity according to palate, and broil very sharply, turning the bones often.

Strong plain gravy may be served under all.

No. 25—Sandwiches for Evening Parties.

Chop fine some cold dressed ham—say about a quarter of a pound, put it in a basin with a tablespoonful of chopped gherkins and a teaspoonful of mustard, a little pepper or cayenne; put about 6oz. of butter in a basin, and with a spoon stir quickly till it forms a kind of cream; add the ham and seasoning, mix all well; have the sandwich bread cut in thin slices. Have already cut, thinly intermixed with fat, either cold roast beef, veal, lamb, mutton, poultry, fowl, pheasant, grouse, partridge, &c., either of which lay evenly, and not too thick, on your bread; season with a little salt and pepper, cover over with another piece of bread; when your sandwich is ready, cut them in any shape you like, but rather small and tastily, and serve. You may keep them in a cold place, if not wanted, as they will keep good under cover for twelve hours. Chopped tongue may be introduced instead of ham, in thin slices.

No. 26—Lamb's Fry.

Cut in middling-sized pieces about 1lb. of lamb's fry, fairly mixed; put one quart of water in a stew-pan; when boiling, add in the fry, boil fast for ten minutes, lay the fry on a cloth, dry it well, have some fine bread-crumbs ready made, to which you add a teaspoonful of salt, two of chopped parsley, a little grated nutmeg, break and beat one or two eggs well, dip the fry in by pieces, roll them in the bread-crumbs, and slightly beat with a knife, to make the bread-crumbs adhere to the fry; have some fat or lard very hot, though not burning, ready in a frying-pan, in which place your fry for three or four minutes, when nicely coloured take off, and dish very hot on a napkin; serve with either fried parsley or chervil, free from water, which have ready in a wire colander; dip the colander in the fat, which will fry the parsley in less than a minute. For lambs fry devilled, rub over with mixture prior to using. See receipt No. 70. This I consider a light dish for supper.

No. 27—Mutton or Lamb Chops a la Turc.

Cut either thin, put on a dish, season with salt and pepper, mince an onion; pick out 20 leaves of parsley, add over a little oil, rub the chop in it well, let them soak in it two hours; plain broil sharply, and serve. This is an imitation of the Turkish kebab.

No. 28—Lobster Curry.

Make about a pint of curry sauce, No. 9, take the flesh of a middle-sized lobster, which cut in neat slices, let them simmer for ten minutes in the sauce; serve on a dish, on toast, or in the shell, or bordered by rice. Boiled as No. 8 in Hospital Receipts.

No. 29—Lobster Curry in the Shell.

Add one or two raw yolks of eggs to the above receipt while boiling hot, mix quickly; when the eggs are set, put the meat back in the shells, cover the surface with bread-crumbs, a few small pieces of butter on each; put in the oven; when nicely browned, serve. By extracting the meat from the body, tail, and claws, without breaking the shells, they can be filled again with the preparation, and put together as a whole lobster; or split the lobster lengthways and serve in two halves.

Scalloped Lobster

Put in scallop in lieu of shell. Proceed the same.

No. 30—Lobster au Gratin for those who do not like Curry.

Chop a middling-sized onion, and put it in a stewpan with 2oz. of butter; fry of a light brown, add a small tablespoonful of flour, stir together, pour over half a pint of milk, season with half a teaspoonful of salt, a quarter of pepper, and an eighth of cayenne, a little sugar, nutmeg, and chopped parsley; boil a few minutes, till rather thick, add the lobster meat, give a boil, add the yolk of an egg, mix quick, fill the shells—egg and bread-crumb, put in an oven for ten minutes, brown on the top with a hot salamander or shovel, and serve.

No. 31—Lobster Cutlets.

Cut a lobster in dice, letting the flesh weigh about half a pound; when done, put in a pan 2oz. of butter, 2 teaspoonfuls of chopped onions; put all on the fire, fry for a minute or two, add 1 teaspoonful of flour; mix well, stir in for a minute; add half a pint of milk; season with salt, pepper, and one saltspoonful of cayenne, two teaspoonfuls of chopped parsley; let all boil for a minute or two, stirring all the time; add your lobster, give it a boil; add two yolks of eggs; mix quick, put on a dish to cool. When quite cool and firm, divide in six parts, giving each the shape of a small cutlet; egg and bread-crumb twice. Put a piece of the very small claw to the end of each cutlet, so as to form a bone; fry for a few minutes, like you would a sole, in plenty of fat; lay on a cloth, and serve on a napkin, with plenty of fried parsley; you may adopt any shape you choose, if cutlets are too troublesome, as you would a croquette. No sauce is requisite.

The lobsters for the two preceding receipts may be prepared, shaped, and bread-crumbed hours before wanted.

No. 32—Crabs au Gratin in the Shell.

Have the crab prepared as for plain, lay in the empty shell a layer of the soft part, then a layer of American crackers or biscuit, grated, then add the fleshy part of the crab over, on which pour a tablespoonful of mushroom ketchup, cover it with slices of cold, hard eggs, cut crosswise; season with a little salt, pepper, and cayenne; cover all with the remainder of the soft part of the crab, make it even with a knife; egg, and bread-crumb over, or more grated biscuit; put a few nuts of butter on the top, set in an oven for twenty minutes or half an hour, and serve very hot.

No. 33—Stewed Oysters on Toast.

Open a dozen of oysters, put them in a small stewpan, add to them two grains of black pepper, a little salt, butter, cayenne, and sugar; set on the stove for a few minutes until set— say three or four minutes; having only given them a slight boil, put in a piece of butter as big as a walnut, which you have mixed with half a teaspoonful of flour, shake the stewpan round by the handle, to melt the contents, put it back on the fire just to simmer, and serve on toast. A drop of cream is an improvement. If not enough liquor add a drop of milk.

Over-stewed oysters are as bad as over-cooked kidneys. For a large quantity, proceed the same. The only thing to be observed is, that the oysters are properly set before serving, they being neither raw nor overdone.

No. 34—Oysters stewed American Fashion.

Take a dozen large oysters in their liquor, bring them to a boil, add salt, pepper, and a piece of butter about the size of a nutmeg, and half a teaspoonful of chopped chervil, and serve with cracker biscuits.

No. 35—Fried Oysters, New York Way.

Take 12 large raw oysters, dip them in Indian meal, throw them into the hot fat immediately, like you would fried fish, and serve as soon as browned.

No. 36—Oyster Soup, New York Way, for a Party of Five Persons.

Take 50 oysters and the liquor, place them in a pan with salt, cayenne pepper, and a teaspoonful of chopped chervil; when boiling, add a *liaison* (or thickening) of 5 yolks of eggs, with a piece of butter the size of an egg, and serve.

Should the oysters not give liquor sufficient, add water and salt, if necessary. One-fourth of this quantity may, of course, be made.

No. 37—Game for Supper.

In spite of the petits soupers de la Régence, in the early part of the reign of Louis XV., when the gastronomic art was nightly unfolding its luxurious delicacies before the illustrious guests of the Court of France, game, dressed in numerous shapes, forming the most succulent dishes, used to adorn the bills of fare of those nocturnal bacchanalian repasts which had almost triumphed over the daily festive board, the dinners then at Court being only a secondary consideration when compared with the suppers. For my part, I much prefer the former, which, as I have already mentioned, forms the focus of sociability; but when you are compelled to sup late, why not partake of game, which is much lighter food than solid meat, overdone kidneys, or oysters; for what can be more relishing and palatable for supper than the remains of either pheasant, grouse, partridge, &c., devilled or plain broiled, while plain roast game is also highly recommendable for such meals.

No. 38—Soyer's Grouse and Black Game Salad.

This dish is also very commendable and relishing. Roast a young grouse, not overdone; when cold, cut in eight pieces; put in a salad bowl enough salad for two persons, lay the pieces of grouse over with 2 or 4 hard eggs cut lengthwise; make the sauce thin, put in a basin a tablespoonful of finely-chopped shallot, 1 ditto of parsley, ditto of pounded white sugar, the yolks of 2 raw eggs, a teaspoonful of salt, quarter one of pepper, 2 tablespoonfuls of chili vinegar, 4 of oil; mix all together with a spoon, whip half a pint of cream, which add carefully to your mixture; it will then constitute a delicious salad sauce; pour over your salad, and mix carefully. Pheasants and partridges, when properly kept, are also very good.

No. 39—Lobster Salad, for two Persons.

Take a middle-sized lobster, break the claw carefully, extract the tail without splitting it, cut your lobster in fine, though large, slices, crosswise, put some salad in a bowl in proportion for two, either cos or cabbage lettuce, or endive, or mixed salad, have boiled 3 or 4 hard eggs, cut crosswise when cold, then form a crown on your salad by intermixing alternate layers of egg and lobster, placing the soft part of the interior of the fish in the centre. Cucumber and beetroot may be used instead of eggs. Then put into a basin a small teaspoonful of salt, quarter ditto of pepper, 2 tablespoonfuls of vinegar, 4 of oil, a little sugar, stir well together, pour over your salad, which mix gently with a spoon and fork, and serve; the addition of chopped parsley, tarragon, and chervil, or chopped shallot, is an improvement.

No. 40—Crab Salad, with Eggs.

Place the soft part of the crab in a bowl, having made it into a pulp; add to it the quantum of oil, vinegar, salt, pepper; mix all well together, as above. If too thick, add half a gill of milk, to form a thinnish sauce; put your salad in a bowl according to proportion, over which put lightly the meat of the crab; pour your sauce over, having cut four eggs lengthwise in quarters; toss it well, stir round, and serve as above.

No. 41—New Salad, Tartar Fashion.

Prepare your salad, well washed and dried; (cabbage or cos lettuce are preferable); boil 4 onions; when cold cut in thick slices; cut also 4 pickled cucumbers, Israelite fashion, put a layer of the salad at the bottom, then a bed of cucumber and onion, and another of salad, at the top; have 2 mild salt herrings, ready broiled, with all the bones extracted; cut it in small square pieces, season with salt, pepper, vinegar, and oil, in proportion, tossing all well together, as this plan is preferable to using a spoon and fork.

No. 42—Plain Salad, with Anchovies.

Put your salad in a bowl, wash and shake as above; wash and scrape a dozen of anchovies; bone them by splitting them up; have 2 hard eggs, chopped fine; put them over the salad; chop about 2oz. of either piccalilli, pickle, or plain gherkin. The above is for four persons; then add salad enough for that number; season with a teaspoonful of salt, a quarter that of pepper, 4 tablespoons of oil, 2 of vinegar; stir well, but lightly, and serve. Cos and cabbage lettuce are preferable. Anyone who does not object to oil, 5 tablespoonfuls may be used to 2 of the best French vinegar. For mixed salads proceed the same. Anchovies, eggs, and gherkins may be omitted, and yet will make an excellent salad.

No. 43—Endive Salad.

Highly appreciated by French gourmets.

Wash quickly four heads of very white endive. The French is much preferable to the

English, and is imported in abundance to the London markets. Why they should be washed quickly is, that if they remain in the water any length of time they become as bitter as gall. Take off the green leaves, if any; cut the stem off and the leaf in two when too long, shake well in a cloth to dry, and put in your salad bowl, which you have previously rubbed with a piece of garlic; add in your salad, a teaspoonful of salt, quarter one of pepper, 5 tablespoonfuls of oil, 2 of vinegar; rub a piece of garlic on two crusts of bread, each about the size of a walnut; add them to your salad, which you stir well for a few minutes with a spoon and fork, and serve. The garlic in this salad, far from being objectionable, gives only a slight flavour, to which no one can object, but which, on the contrary, is highly appreciated by the gourmet. Garlic may be either increased or diminished according to taste.

No. 44—Omelettes with Fine Herbs.

Six eggs will make a nice omelette for two persons for supper; add a teaspoonful of salt, quarter ditto of pepper, break them carefully in a basin, as a tainted egg will spoil all the rest; add three-quarters of a tablespoonful of salt, a quarter one of pepper, two of chopped parsley, half a one of fine chopped onions; beat them well; add 2oz. of butter in a nice clean and dry frying-pan, place it then on the fire, and when the butter is very hot then pour in your eggs, which keep mixing quick with a spoon until all is delicately set, then let it slip to the edge of the pan, *en masse*, laying hold of the handle, raising it slantwise, which will give an elongated form to the omelette; turning the edges, let it set a minute, turn on a dish, and serve.

No. 45—Omelettes with Mushrooms.

Add in a couple of middling-sized mushrooms, cut very thin, and proceed as above.

No. 46—For Bacon and Ham Omelettes

Cut 2oz. of either in small dice, not too salt, fry two or three minutes in the butter before putting in the eggs,—and proceed as above.

No. 47—Omelettes with Sprue Grass.*

Cut the sprue half an inch in length, plain boil them in salt and water till done, add two tablespoonfuls to your eggs,—and proceed as above.

No. 48—Omelettes with Parmesan.

For Parmesan omelettes, put into your eggs two tablespoonfuls of grated Parmesan cheese—Gruyère or any good dry English cheese will do as well.

No. 49—Poached Eggs with Cream.

Put in a small pan a pint of water, a teaspoonful of salt, four of vinegar; when boiling break carefully in the pan two, three, or four nice fresh eggs, simmer for four or five minutes, or till properly set firm, but not hard; serve either on toast or on a plain dish. Put in a small stewpan half a gill of cream, a little salt, pepper, and sugar; when the cream is on the boil add an ounce of fresh butter, take off the stewpan, toss it round till the butter is melted, pour over and serve. Fried ham and bacon may be laid on toast, poached eggs placed over, and served plain. None other but fresh eggs will poach; the quality may be ascertained by holding them up to the candle; if the shell is spotted, they are useless for poaching, though of use for other purposes.

* Asparagus—AB

No. 50—Poached Eggs with Maître d'Hotel Butter.

Put two ounces of maître d'hôtel butter in a hot stewpan, and stir round till melted; pour over your eggs which you have placed on toast.

No. 51—Poached Eggs, Semi-curried, with Ham or Bacon.

Proceed as No. 56, pouring a gill of curry sauce over.

No. 52—Battered Eggs with Mushrooms.

Put in a stewpan 2oz. of butter, break over four fresh eggs, add a tablespoonful of chopped mushrooms, half a teaspoonful of salt, quarter that of pepper. Set on the fire, and stir continually with a wooden spoon till it forms a thickish consistency; have buttered toast on a plate, pour your eggs over, and serve.

No. 53—Battered Eggs with Sprue Grass.

Add 2 tablespoonfuls of boiled sprue grass (as No. 47), and proceed as above.

No. 54—Ham with Shallots, Parsley, and Chervil.

Cut in small dice 1 oz. of clean cooked ham, put in your eggs, and cook as above. A spoonful of either shallot, parsley, or chervil will vary this dish.

No. 55—Mirrored Eggs.

Put 1 oz. of butter into a small tin pan, spreading it all over; in it crack 4 eggs without breaking the yolk if possible, season over with salt and pepper, and small nuts of butter here and there; put in an oven before the fire till set, and serve.

No. 56—Eggs au Miroir, with Ham or Bacon.

Cut the ham or bacon in thin slices, fry a few minutes in a pan, put on your plate, break your eggs over, set in oven till set, and serve, and proceed as above. The ham may be cut in thicker slices if preferred, but will take rather longer cooking.

No. 57—Eggs with Chopped Ham or Tongue.

Cut 2oz. of dressed ham in small dice, butter the bottom of the plate or dish, and place the ham upon it; break the eggs over, season, and proceed as before.

No. 58—Eggs and Mushrooms.

Wash, peel, and slice a few mushrooms, butter the dish thickly, spread the mushrooms over, season with salt and pepper, and set the dish in the oven till the mushrooms are done; break the eggs over and proceed as before.

No. 59—Eggs and Truffles.

Wash, peel, and cut in very thin slices, a fresh truffle, butter the dish, add a tablespoonful of sherry; salt and pepper; lay the slices of truffles flat over the bottom of the dish, and put it in the oven a few minutes; when boiled a minute or two, break the eggs over and cook as usual. English truffles are excellent for this purpose.

No. 60—Eggs with Sprue Grass.

Boil about a quarter of a pint of sprue grass; butter the dish as usual, spread the grass over, season with a little powdered sugar, salt, and pepper; break the eggs over, place in the oven, and proceed as before.

No. 61—Eggs a la Bonne Femme.

Cut a middle-sized onion in dice, put it in a stewpan with a pat of butter, and fry of a light brown; when done add a teaspoonful of vinegar; butter the dish lightly, spread the onions over, season with pepper and salt, and break the eggs over; put in the oven; when done mask the eggs with fried bread-crumbs, and serve.

No. 62—Curried Eggs.

Boil three eggs for ten minutes, put them in cold water; when cold, shell, cut them in two lengthwise, and throw them into a curry sauce, give them a boil, dish them on the flat side in the form of a star; this will make a very good and pretty dish. Eggs boiled too hard are very unwholesome, especially for supper; done this way they will be perfect; they may be put entire in the sauce, and cut when dished up; they will take the flavour of the curry just the same.

No. 63—Eggs a la Tripe, or Onion Sauce.

Boil 3 eggs as above, cut them in slices, and put in a sauce you have prepared thus:—
Cut 2 middle-sized onions in slices, put them in a stewpan with an ounce of butter, and fry them till done without taking colour; add a small tablespoonful of flour, and moisten with a teacupful of milk: season with salt, pepper, and nutmeg, give a boil, toss the eggs up in the sauce, and serve. The same may be served with tomato sauce.

No. 64—Eggs with Tomato Sauce.

Proceed as for curried eggs, using tomato sauce instead of curry.

No. 65—Rarebit a la Soyer, with Sherry or Champagne.

Cut half a pound of rich cheese in small dice; put in a stewpan 2 pats of butter with a teaspoonful of mixed Durham mustard, a little salt, half a teaspoonful of pepper, one wineglass of sherry or champagne; put on a slow fire, stir gently with a wooden spoon till properly melted, though not stringy, which might occur if turned too quickly; have a nice toast half an inch thick done at the last minute, pour your cheese over and serve. Leaving in a few minutes in an oven is an improvement.

No. 66—Fried Potatoes.

Fried potatoes being much lighter for supper than baked ones, would be an excellent introduction to the London supper bill of fare. I shall also observe that a potato when well fried does not retain a particle of grease, and therefore is not rich, or likely to be so, when properly done. Where a quantity are required, put in a wide stewpan three or four pounds of either lard, beef, or mutton fat;—see receipt No. 20, page 347, how to clarify the two last. Set it upon the fire, and while heating, peel a pound of potatoes about the size of a large egg, cut them in thin slices crosswise upon a clean cloth, to absorb the moisture, taking care they are well separated; when the fat is hot, "but not burning," which you will ascertain by its giving out a light smoke, or else dip your finger in cold water and let a drop fall in the fat—if it hisses it is then at a proper heat; throw in the potatoes, and keep moving them with a skimmer to prevent them sticking together; in about three or four minutes they will be cooked and well fried, of a pale gold colour; take them out upon a cloth, sieve, or colander; sprinkle scientifically with salt, and serve plain, or upon a napkin, or round a steak, fillet of beef, &c.

No. 67—Fried Potatoes with Maitre d'Hotel Butter.

While in the colander, and just having been fried, add to a portion of potatoes about half an ounce of maître d'hôtel butter, toast till melted, and serve either plain or round steak.

No. 68—Fried Potatoes with Cayenne Pepper.

When just done throw half a saltspoonful of cayenne over them, toast them, and serve.

No. 69—Chipped or Ribboned Potatoes.

Cut some potatoes crosswise about the thickness of an inch, then peel them thinly in ribbons, fry as above—they will require a little longer doing; when they are crisp take them out, place them on a clean cloth, and sprinkle them over with salt, cayenne, and black pepper to fancy, and serve.

No. 70—Soyer's Universal Devil Mixture,
Which will be found applicable to all devilled food.

To devil the same, rub each piece over with the following mixture, having made a deep incision in any article of food that may be subjected to this Mephisthophelean process. Put in a bowl a good tablespoonful of Durham mustard, which mix with four tablespoonfuls of chilli vinegar; add to it a tablespoonful of grated horseradish, two bruised shallots, a teaspoonful of salt, half ditto of cayenne, ditto of black pepper, and one of pounded sugar, two teaspoonfuls of chopped chillies, if handy; add the yolks of two raw eggs; take a pastebrush, and after having slightly seasoned each piece with salt, rub over each piece with the same, probing some in the incisions. First broil slowly, and then the last few minutes as near as possible to the Pandemonium fire. The yolks may be omitted.

No. 71—A Plainer Way for the Million.

Mix the mustard with plain vinegar; add one half more cayenne; use the same quantity of salt, pepper, and sugar; use onions instead of shallots. The liquor of pickles is even preferable to vinegar.

Proceed as above for grilling; remains of meat, game, and poultry are very relishing when done as above, especially for an early luncheon or a late supper.

No. 72—Chicken, American Fashion.

Have a small fowl ready for grilling, season with salt, pepper, and a little cayenne; beat an egg well, rub it over; mix some American grated crackers with maize, roll it in and beat it with a knife to make it adhere to the chicken; put it on a gridiron, and when hot through put small nuts of butter here and there; broil to a very nice colour and serve 2 doz. stewed oysters, as No. 33, on toast, which place under the fowl. Any sharp sauce instead of oysters will do for this dish.

No. 73—Herring a la Rob Roy.

Well wash and clean a red herring, wipe it dry and place it in a pie-dish, having cut off the head, and split it in two up the back; put a gill or two of whiskey over the herring, according to size, hold it on one side of the dish, so that it is covered with the spirit, set it alight, and when the flame goes out the fish is done.

No. 74—Cold Asparagus Salad, While in Season.
A very refreshing and delicious dish for supper.

When this vegetable is in season, put in a soup plate a tablespoonful of vinegar, two of oil, quarter teaspoonful of salt, half that of pepper, mix together, a little chopped parsley may be introduced, and dip each head of cold grass as you eat them in the mixture.

No. 75—New Potato Salad, German Fashion.

Boil some rather waxy potatoes, peel when just done, cut in slices, put them in a bowl, add to every pound one tablespoonful of vinegar, two of oil, half a teaspoonful of salt, quarter that of pepper, toss up well, and eat it cold. Add a little chopped parsley.

No. 76—New Potato Salad, French Haricot, and Haricot Beans.

Have your vegetables properly cooked, and when cold put a pound of French or the other beans in a bowl, season with salt, pepper, oil, vinegar, as above, and a teaspoonful of chopped parsley; toss well, and serve. The French beans only require to be boiled in a plain way. The French haricots—put a pint in two quarts of cold water, add one ounce of butter, and boil very gently for two hours, or till tender, let it get cold and make your salad. For lentils proceed the same as haricots.

No. 77—Bouillabaisse Anglicised

The fish I would recommend in England for that far-famed dish would be red mullet, whiting, and barble, or a small turbot, all cut up crosswise, in pieces of about two ounces to a quarter of a pound each; slice up two large onions, place them in a good-sized stewpan, large enough to contain your fish all at the bottom—a flat wide pan is preferable. Add to this two tablespoonfuls of olive oil, and fry the onions of a pale brown colour; next place the pieces of fish in the pan, cover them with warm water, only just to the depth of the contents. To each pound of fish, sprinkle about half a teaspoonful of salt, or a little more, a quarter that quantity of pepper, half a bay leaf, the flesh of half a lemon, without pips or rind, cut in dice; cut also two tomatoes in dice, having extracted the seed, add a glass or two of sherry or light wine, a few peppercorns, and half a clove of garlic, instead of four, as done at Marseilles, as mentioned at page 37; set on a fierce fire, and boil very fast from ten to twelve minutes. By this time the liquor should be reduced to a third of its original quantity; add a small portion of saffron, according to taste, a tablespoonful of fresh chopped parsley; allow all to boil one minute longer, and remove from the fire, for it is then ready for dishing up. (For which process see page 37.)

Second-class Bouillabaisse.—Use gurnet, plaice, soles, &c. Bouillabaisse may be made also of fresh-water fish, such as perch, tench, trout, and pike, proceeding precisely as above; if the broth is required for an invalid, omit the wine and some of the seasoning, according to the order of the doctor.

No. 78—Soyer's Crimean Cup a la Wyndham

Thinly peel the rind of half an orange, put it into a bowl with a tablespoonful of crushed sugar, and macerate with the ladle for a minute; then add one large wine-glass of Maraschino, half one of Cognac, half one of Curaçao. Mix well together, pour in two bottles of soda-water, and one of champagne, during which time work it up and down with the punch ladle, and it is ready.

Half a pound of Wenham Lake ice, if to be procured, is a great improvement.

No. 79—Soyer's Balaklava Nectar

Thinly peel the rind of half a lemon, shred it fine, and put it in a punch-bowl; add 2 tablespoonfuls of crushed sugar and the juice of 2 lemons, the half of a small cucumber sliced thin with the peel on; toss it up several times, then add 2 bottles of soda-water, 2 of claret, 1 of champagne, stir well together and serve.

No. 80—Pierce's Claret and Champagne Cup a la Brunow

This gentleman, whose excellent and useful book I have quoted in the body of this work, has favoured me with the following claret and champagne cup, which ought, from its excellency, to be called the nectar of the Czar, as it is so highly appreciated in Russia, where for many years it has enjoyed a high reputation amongst the aristocracy of the Muscovite empire.

To three bottles of claret, take two-thirds of a pint of Curaçao, one pint of sherry, half ditto of brandy, two wine-glasses of ratafia, three oranges, and one lemon, cut in slices; some sprigs of green balm, ditto of borage, a small piece of rind of cucumber, two bottles of German seltzer-water, three ditto of soda-water; stir this together, and sweeten with capillaire or pounded sugar until it ferments, let it stand one hour, strain it, and ice it well; it is then fit for use.

The same for Champagne Cup—Champagne instead of claret; noyau instead of ratafia.

This quantity is for an evening party of forty persons. For a smaller number reduce the proportions.

SAUCES

1—MELTED BUTTER.

Put 2oz. of butter in a stewpan holding about a quart, and 2oz. of flour, half a teaspoonful of salt, a quarter one of pepper; mix together with a spoon till forming a thick paste, add a pint of cold water, place all on a fire, stir continually; take the pan off the fire when it simmers; add another of fresh butter in it, stir till melted; it is then ready for use. A little grated nutmeg and a drop of vinegar is an improvement. This sauce being the base of so many others, requires attention in making, and as flour will sometimes be stronger than at others, and likely to make it too thin or too thick, take for a rule that the proper thickness when done ought to form a transparent coating over the back of the spoon.

2—BEURRE A LA MAITRE D'HOTEL, OR HOTEL KEEPER'S BUTTER.

Put on a plate a quarter of a pound of fresh butter, a quarter of a spoonful of salt, ditto of pepper, two of chopped parsley, the juice of a middle-sized lemon (if no lemon, use vinegar), and a little grated nutmeg; mix well together, and keep in a cool place till required. This is excellent with kidneys and all broiled meats. Nutmeg may be omitted.

3—ANCHOVY BUTTER, OR BEURRE D'ANCHOIX.

Take 6 anchovies from a bottle, scrape and wash them, pound and pulp them, or bruise them on a board; mix 6oz of fresh butter, pass through a sieve, and use when required. Keep the sauce in a cold place.

4—CHERVIL AND TARRAGON BUTTER.

To 2oz. of butter add a teaspoonful of chopped chervil and tarragon; add salt, pepper, a little cayenne, 1 tablespoonful of tarragon vinegar, or the juice of half a lemon.

5—PIMENTO, OR CHILLI BUTTER.

For 2oz. of butter put a teaspoonful of chillies chopped fine, 1 of parsley, a scrape of garlic as large as a pea; add to it half a teaspoonful of salt, a little pepper, and the juice of half a lemon; mix well.

6—SHALLOT BUTTER.

Put a quarter of a pound of butter and a teaspoonful of chopped shallot in a dish, a little cayenne, salt, pepper, half a teaspoonful of mustard, the juice of a lemon; mix together.

7—BLACK BUTTER, OR BEURRE NOIR.

Put 2oz. of butter in a stewpan, set it on the fire till it acquires a brownish colour, throw in about 20 parsley leaves, 2 tablespoonfuls of vinegar, half a teaspoonful of salt, a quarter of pepper; boil together one minute. It is also excellent with boiled mackerel and skate.

8—Onion Sauce, or Sauce a la Tripe.

Peel and cut 6 onions in slices, put them in a stewpan with 2oz. of butter, a teaspoonful of salt, one of sugar, half one of pepper; place on a slow fire to simmer till in pulp, stirring now and then, to prevent getting brown; add a tablespoonful of flour, a pint of milk, and boil till of a proper thickness. This sauce should be a little thicker than melted butter.

9—Curry sauce.

Peel and cut 2 middling-sized onions in slices, 1 apple, cut in dice, and an ounce of bacon; put them in a stewpan with two ounces of butter; put it on the fire and fry gently for five or six minutes; add 3 teaspoonfuls of flour, 1 of curry powder, moisten with a pint and a half of milk, add half a teaspoonful of salt, and 1 of sugar; boil till rather thick; pass through a sieve, and serve with any article requiring curry sauce.

10—Bread Sauce.

Put in a stewpan 4 tablespoonfuls of bread-crumbs, a quarter of one of salt, an eighth of pepper, 6 pepper corns; peel a small onion, cut it in four, add it to the crumbs, with half a pint of milk and half an ounce of butter. Boil for ten minutes, and you will have an excellent sauce. Add more milk if requisite.

11—Maitre d'hotel Sauce.

Mix 2oz. of maître d'hôtel butter to half a pint of hot melted butter sauce, and shake, and when the butter is melted it is ready.

12—Relishing Sauce.

For broiled bones, fowls, meat, fish, &c. &c.

Put a tablespoonful of chopped onions into a stewpan, with 1 of Chili vinegar, 1 of common vinegar, 3 of water, 2 of mushroom ketchup, 2 of Harvey's sauce, 1 of anchovies; add to it a pint of melted butter, as receipt No. 1; let it simmer until it adheres to the back of the spoon; add half a teaspoonful of sugar; it is then ready for use. The many ingredients found in this are always to be obtained in every tavern.

13—Tomato Sauce.

Cut in dice 2oz. of lean ham or bacon, put either in a stewpan, with 2oz. of butter, a sliced onion, a few sprigs of parsley, 4 peppercorns, and 1 bay leaf; fry on the fire till getting slightly brown; add in then about 2lb. of fresh tomatoes, cut across, lightly extract the seed; let them stew about fifteen minutes, or till in pulp; add to it 2 tablespoonfuls of flour; mix well; then about a pint of broth or milk, a teaspoonful of salt, quarter that of pepper, one of sugar, a sprinkle of cayenne, boil all ten minutes; pass through a sieve or colander; put them back again in the stewpan; give another boil, it is then ready for use when required. A tablespoonful of ketchup may be added; also a piece of glaze, if handy.

14—Semi-Sultana.

Add 3 tablespoonfuls to 1 pint of thin melted butter; boil a few minutes; it is then ready.

15—Piccalilli Sauce.

Cut in slices, or in small dice, 2oz. of mixed pickles, called piccalilli, add it to half a pint melted butter, with 2 tablespoonfuls of liqueur, and use when required.

16—Browning for Sauces.

Put half a pound of brown sugar into an iron saucepan, and melt it over a moderate fire for about twenty-five minutes, stirring it continually, until quite black, but it must become so by degrees, or too sudden a heat will make it bitter, then add two quarts of water, and in ten minutes the sugar will be dissolved. Bottle for use.

17—New Mayonnaise Sauce.

Put a quarter of a pint of melted aspic or savoury jelly upon ice in a stewpan, which keep whisking until becoming a white froth, then add half a pint of salad oil and six spoonfuls of tarragon vinegar, by degrees—first oil and then vinegar, continually whisking until it forms a white smooth sauce, to all appearance like a cream; season with half a teaspoonful of salt, a quarter ditto of pepper, and a little sugar; whisk it a little more, and it is ready to serve; it is usually dressed pyramidically over the article it is served with. The advantage of this sauce (which is more delicate than any other) is, that you may dress it to any height you like, and it will remain so for a long time; if the temperature is not too hot, it will remain hours without melting or appearing greasy.

No. 18—Mussulman Sauce.

Put in a pint stewpan two yolks of eggs, a quarter of a pound of butter, a quarter teaspoonful of salt, half that of pepper, the juice of a middling-sized lemon; put on a slow fire, and stir round quickly till the whole forms a thick rich sauce; it is then ready for using. This must be done extremely quick, else it will turn to oil; two minutes will do it. If too thick, add a drop of milk.

No. 19—Tomatoes, American Way.

Cut the tomatoes in two, leaving the seeds and juice in; cut a middling-sized onion in dice, pass it in butter till slightly browned; add the tomatoes, salt, pepper, a teaspoonful of vinegar, and sufficient bread-crumbs to thicken them; stew gently for twenty minutes, and serve with roast meat or poultry.

Bread-crumbs.—Take a piece of the crumb of a stale loaf, not too hard, put it in a cloth, bruise it with your hand well, till it falls in crumbs; pass it through either a wire sieve or colander, and use when required.

No. 20—How to melt Fat.

Take 3 or 4lbs. of either beef or mutton suet, cut in small dice; put in a stewpan, with half a pint of water; place on the fire to melt, stirring now and then; when the suet turns to a light yellow colour, pour it through a colander, which you have already placed in a basin, press the suet with the back of a spoon to extract the oil of the fat; it is then ready for use, and will keep a long time without spoiling; you may fry many times with the same.

21—Chopping of Herbs, Parsley, Chervil, &c.

This may appear a very simple thing to do well, yet it is often done badly, by which the flavour is lost. The herbs should be well washed and dried, and then the leaves taken in the left hand, pressing upon them with your fingers, and chop as fine as possible, not by placing the point of the knife on the board, and raising it and letting it fall, but with a good sharp cut, so that they are cut, not pressed. Onions should be peeled, and cut in halves lengthwise, and then with a thin knife cut each half in slices, leaving them joined at the root; again cut into slices contrariwise, and then from top to bottom; thus having cut into very small squares, chop it with both hands with the knife. You may also wash them. When half-chopped, press them in a cloth, and chop them still finer, and use when required. Proceed the same for shallots.

ANECDOTES, ETC.

THE DUKE OF CAMBRIDGE'S HEAD-QUARTERS PRIOR TO THE BATTLE OF INKERMANN.

His Royal Highness's quarters were situated about one hundred and thirty yards to the left of the windmill on the Woronzoff Road. Five parallel bell-tents were occupied—one by the duke, the others by Colonel Macdonald, Colonel Tyrwhitt, Major Clifton, and Dr. Gibson, his staff. M. Comte, *chef de cuisine* to the duke, and to whose devotion to all who came in his way and needed help while in the Crimea I before have had in this work occasion to allude, has since related to me that on the morning of the Battle of Inkermann he got up at three o'clock, the weather being chilly and damp and a thick heavy fog surrounding the camp, and having lit his fire he made himself some tea, when, about five, as he was quietly smoking his pipe *à la bivouacaire*, within range of the fire (of his open-air battery) the duke came up to him, exclaiming, "Halloo! M. Comte, you are about early this morning."

"Yes, your Highness," he replied; "the fact is, the weather is so cold and damp, that for the life of me I could not sleep, therefore I turned out and made myself a cup of tea."

"You are right," said the duke, warming his feet by the fire; "the weather is truly wretched."

Hardly had the duke said these words, than several volleys of musketry and loud shouts reverberated through the camp, something like the growls of thousands of wild animals. Leaving no doubt that it was an attack of the enemy, the duke immediately left me and ran

THE DAWN OF INKERMANN.

for his horse, and was soon mounted, and started alone towards the scene of action; a few minutes after, his staff followed in the wake of their gallant leader. So sudden was his departure, that, having made a bowl of tea which I had intended for him, though I ran after him with it in my hand, his Highness started without partaking of it. Not till five o'clock in the evening did the duke return, his horse wounded, and a bullet having passed through his coat-sleeve without injuring him. Major Clifton had been wounded in the cheek during the battle, and came back to quarters during the day to have his wound dressed by Dr. Gibson. On returning once more to the field of battle, he had his horse shot under him. When he again returned he was seen carrying the saddle of his defunct animal on his back. At the return of the staff in the evening, the outside of the duke's headquarters had the appearance of a field hospital, M. Comte having taken on himself to supply refreshment to all the wounded who were brought to his nursing care. I have heard that no less than six or seven hundred had been supplied with succour in the course of two or three days by his Highness's faithful *chef de cuisine*.

On the 11th of the same month, and while the duke was staying on board the *Resolution*, in the harbour of Balaklava, our heroic *chef de cuisine* was ordered to remain in possession of the commandant's house in Balaklava, awaiting the return of his royal master, and also having under his charge no less than fifteen female prisoners of war, whom he was charged by the authorities to watch over with the aid of sentries, as it was thought that these female Amazons might fire Balaklava. Amongst them was the Governor's wife and children. All the men being ordered out of the establishment, the Governor's lady, with a smile on her lips, in very good French, inquired of M. Comte if two gentlemen present would be allowed to remain, which favour, after serious consideration on the part of the new Governor *pro tem.*, was granted, these gentlemen being of the advanced ages respectively of three and five years. "Never did I feel a greater relief," said M. Comte, "than when these lady prisoners were taken out of my charge, as each day discovered some fresh attempts at conspiracy." It was during the governorship of this semi-warrior that the dreadful storm took place in the Bay of Balaklava, and uprooted the beautiful avenue of poplar trees which ornamented his capital, and which, to his sorrow, much disfigured the prettiest part of his dominions.

On a previous occasion, just after landing, before the battle of the Alma, this indefatigable

A STORM IN A FRYING-PAN.

THE CULINARY SENTRY

culinary artist, who by the bye is an old traveller, was seen, under a heavy shower of rain, cooking beneath the wings of an open umbrella, preparing a dish of fried croquettes, at a time when the duke himself did not anticipate such a delicacy. The umbrella was used to stop the rain falling in the pan, which would have prevented the completion of this dainty dish, water and fat being irreconcilable foes.

Early the following morning an alarm took place, when our warrior-cook deserted his umbrella, and shouldered his gun in his right as commander-in-chief of his own battery (*de cuisine*). The moon was faintly shining, and with its rays appeared the duke, who indistinctly seeing someone, exclaimed, "*Who's there?*" when M. Comte replied, "It is me, your Highness. Having heard the alarm, I considered your tent and my battery could not be too well guarded, so I have just taken up this musket to be on the defensive." The duke replied, "Really, Comte, vous êtes impayable;" and immediately started with his staff to the supposed scene of action. After a few hours everything was restored to order, when Comte grounded arms, inspected his battery, and had breakfast ready to the minute as usual.

A VISIT TO THE SULTAN'S NEW PALACE OF DOLMA BATCHI

In the month of March, 1856, I was fortunate enough to obtain an order, which I procured by great favour, to visit this huge pile of marble, prior to its final completion and occupation by his Majesty the Sultan and his harem; and although many parts of it were open to the public by ticket, yet very few visitors could boast of having seen so much of the interior as myself of this stupendous and most elegant area, where the modern houri of Mahomet were shortly to be located, they at this time still remaining in the old palace on the Bosphorous. The large room preparing for the reception of the Sultan's favourites had but very little moveable furniture, but at the same time was most elegantly decorated. Nothing but couches were placed round the room, while the flooring was of highly-polished wood of a most tasty design; the whole of the hangings and coverings were of a rich satin of a lavender colour, with a large flowery pattern; twenty chandeliers, of immense dimensions—about seven feet in height—sprang from the ground, proudly bearing each more than one hundred wax-lights. The wall was after the Oriental fashion, which I do not much admire, here and there painted *al fresco*, representing various views of either landscape, colonnades, palaces, &c. In spite of this defect, the effect was so peculiar at the first glance, that it produced on me a most extraordinary sensation. To my surprise I found the ceiling remarkably low, but which I found, on consideration, would not appear so to its future innumerable tenants, from their habit of squatting on the floor. The effect of the light on this apartment had been tried two nights before, and the ends of the wax-lights still remained in the sockets of the chandeliers, and which, when lit, must have had a most extraordinary effect. Here for the first time I had an uninterrupted view from the interior of a harem, through the latticed windows, which are now made on an improved principle to the old Turkish style, which give you more than ever an opportunity to see from the inside without being seen, the exterior of which is also painted with views of landscapes, which are visible from the Bosphorus. At the further end of this stupendous kind of drawing-room were several apartments for the favourites, most gorgeously decorated by valuable Oriental tapestry, hanging curtains, ottomans, &c. Next I was shown a narrow corridor with three doors; I learned that these were the penitential cells for any of the naughty beauties who might need correction; however, the dungeons did not bear a very dreadful aspect. From here we went to the Sultan's bedroom, which was gorgeously decorated with deep golden fringe and crimson velvet hangings of the richest description; the decorations of this room are almost indescribable. We then visited another room, called the Sultan's Cabinet de Travail, where I was much struck to see it entirely fitted up in the European style, quite *à la française*, after the style of Louis XV. Upon inquiring of my ciceroni, I learned that the whole of the furniture of the apartment had been presented to the Sultan by the Emperor of the French, Napoleon III., and I must say that the quiet, though superb, manner in which it was fitted was a most pleasant relief to me after wandering through so many gaudy and superfluously grand apartments. The Sultan had already occupied himself in this room. The carpet and table were covered with the finest red French cloth, while the ceiling was of a good elevation; in fact, the Tuileries (which I have lately visited) cannot boast a more tasty or better fitted-up apartment. The staircase leading to the harem was very striking, the lantern at the summit being covered with paintings, representing windows with pots of flowers, vases, birds, &c.; yet the whole of these, though well painted, presented quite a theatrical aspect to the really charming appearance of the marble staircase. My guide had observed to me while in the Cabinet de Travail, that he never recollected any stranger entering it before; he then showed me the *chef-d'œuvres* of the palace, which were the ladies' baths—the most expensive and luxurious part of this costly palace, the bath being the greatest luxury of the Turks, the whole of them being inlaid with sapphire stone boldly carved. We then passed through the Throne Room, which I have already described in this work: it is a regular *facsimile* of St. Sophia, but more gaudy. We then walked through the Reception Room for the ambassadors, which is simply decorated with gold and white, in the European style. On turning to the left, we came to the grand crystal staircase with its thousand jets of red light. I then begged to be shown the kitchen, which request at first I perceived was objected to by my guide, who expressed himself that it was impossible; but being armed with formidable letters, and making use of M. Roco Vido's name, who is well known to the Sultan's grand hatchi batchi, or chief cook, I at length prevailed on him to induct me to this pandemonium of scientific handicraft, where between three and four hundred cooks were busily engaged manipulating the most *recherché* dishes *à la* Turk, many of which I had the pleasure of tasting. The appearance and bustle of the kitchen, which was quite new to me, put me more in mind of a public market than what it really was; every man-cook was dressed in the Oriental fashion, all looking very clean. The copper vessels which they use are daily tinned—which fact I learnt from the *Chef*,—and shone like so much silver. The process of the Turkish cookery, though slow, I much approve of, as the succulence and aroma of every kind of food are retained, and it is far superior to our system, everything being cooked or stewed on the top of red-hot ashes laid on slabs of stone or marble. The floor of the kitchen was rather ill-paved, and the attendants were in the habit of strewing everything on the ground not wanted for use—an untidy trick. I could trace from the interior of this monster establishment no less than twenty huge shaft chimneys sprouting out from the roof of this gastronomic temple. It was now near twelve o'clock, when a shower of tray-bearers made their appearance in the kitchen, and with the greatest celerity were loaded with heaps of dishes belonging to the first, second, and third course. I ascertained on inquiry that these were for the dinners of the ladies of the harem. White snowy-looking cloths were thrown over each tray, and they were carried, to my astonishment, to the old palace on the Bosphorus, a distance of nearly half a mile, on the bearers' heads,—the large kitchen at the latter place having been destroyed by fire, and the Sultan's meals only being prepared there in a private kitchen, his Majesty always dining alone; which order was instituted by Mahomed II, the story being, that that monarch had so little confidence in those around him, that he always feared they would rob him of his food while carrying it from plate to mouth. Delighted with my visit, I deposited in my cicerone's hands the golden key, in the shape of baksheesh, with which I had so successfully opened the palace door of the Sublime Porte.

THE PARISIAN KITCHEN FOR THE WORKING-CLASSES,

Or Fourneau de L'imperatrice.

The kitchens for the working-classes are sixty-eight in number, each capable of supplying from one thousand to twelve hundred mechanics with good food, for which each one pays about two-thirds of the value received, although nothing is given gratuitously. They are attended by Sisters of Charity, and kept extremely clean, while the deficit is, I believe, made up by her Majesty the Empress and the municipality of Paris, from whom these institutions derive their name of Fourneau de l'Impér5ace. The provisions are supplied from the central market of Paris, the Halle au Blé, which is under the superintendence of the Comptroller-General, M. Durand, by whom I was treated with the greatest courtesy while drawing up the report I made to his Majesty by imperial command; and I much regret that want of space prevents my giving it at full length here, although the report had chiefly a local importance. Wagons take the different articles of food early in the morning to all the establishments. These are most useful institutions, and in case of a scarcity of food, provisions could always, at a trifling expense, be dressed here for the needy. Indeed, every metropolis, and all large mercantile towns, ought to follow this excellent example, which, I believe, owes its origin to England.

THE TRAVELLING GENTLEMEN OF THE CRIMEA.

I cannot pass without notice the following little anecdote, related to me by Colonel Carleton of the Coldstreams—the principal personage connected with it. The day after the battle of Inkermann (said the gallant colonel) the field was visited by many T. G.'s, some of them contorting their optics with eye-glasses, and taking a survey of the many dead on the field, near to the spot where he was busily engaged in paying the last duty to the remains of the defunct brave; whereupon he made inquiry of one of his men if the gentlemen were known who seemingly took such an interest in the awful spectacle. He then desired them to come to him, which request, with a kind smile, they soon obeyed; but much were they disappointed when, instead of addressing them in a friendly manner, the Colonel ordered them to take their coats off and shoulder a pick and dig graves, which disagreeable task they could not avoid, as discipline was the order of the day, though very disgusting the task to our curious and no doubt wealthy pleasure-hunters. They were, the Colonel afterwards ascertained, merchants from one of our great commercial cities. When trapped, it was morning; when they finished their task, it was night. Thus our amateur gravediggers had not only a hard day's work, but a very unpleasant one in the bargain.

THE CONSUMPTION HOSPITAL, BROMPTON.

A Visit to the Kitchen, by Request.

While at the Reform Club, Captain Lyons, R.M., requested me to visit the kitchen of the above hospital, in the anticipation that I might be able to make some improvements in that department, if any should be requisite. The day following I went and found the place in the most perfect order, while all at once a stove of a very showy structure caught my eye, in which were placed eight or ten copper caldrons, well fixed in either iron or brick frames, each being labelled beef-tea, coffee, tea, &c. I could not but approve of the elegant appearance these utensils presented, but at the same time give my disapprobation of their having copper in use, while screwed down so tightly that but a small chance remained of their being properly tinned. In removing the lid, I remarked to the Captain that not the slightest particle of tin remained, and that therefore the cooking could not be done in any other but a highly dangerous manner. I then explained to the woman cook where the danger lay; when she quietly answered that there could be no danger, as she had each boiler cleansed two or three times a day; which of course was the root of the evil, having no doubt been the cause of the entire disappearance of the tin. In asking her how long it was since they were tinned, she replied,—"Not since she had been engaged there, nor, probably, since they had been fixed up;" when I explained to her the sad mistake in not having well tinned all such boilers, in large establishments such as this, where the utensils are in daily use, as they ought to be tinned at least once in every three months. I then made about a gallon of beef-tea with the hospital rations, in less than an hour, to which quick process she much objected, saying that she was certain the patients would not like it, as in that time it could not be thoroughly done, as she always stewed it for at least six or seven hours, by which time the meat was done to ribbons. I begged the Captain to allow several basins of my broth to be sent to the different wards to various patients, which was done, whom we afterwards visited. When the Captain inquired of one how he felt, he answered that he felt a great deal better that day, his taste having returned to him, which was a proof of the superiority of my plan over that of their cook's—a system, I regret to say, practised in many large establishments. (For Beef-tea, see Hospital Diets.)

Index to Addenda

HOSPITAL DIETS

ARMY RECEIPTS

BILL OF FARE FOR LONDON SUPPERS

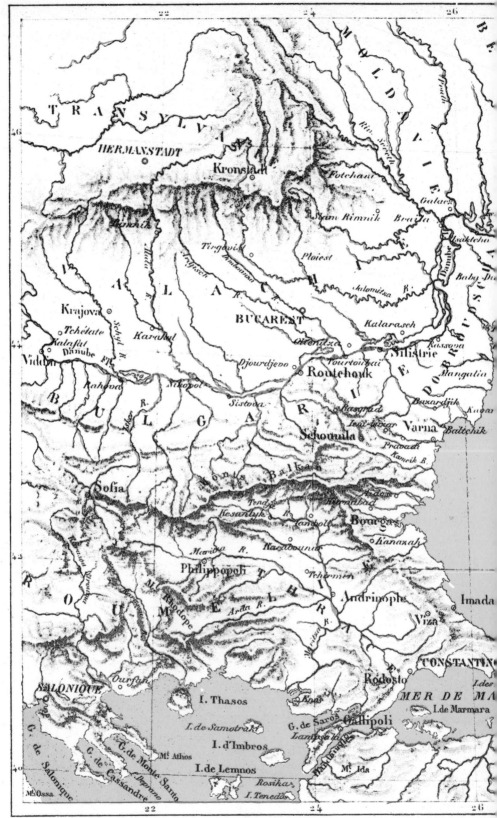